Nissan
Sunny
Owners
Workshop
Manual

I M Coomber

Models covered
All Nissan Sunny models with petrol engines;
Hatchback and Saloon/Pulsar (N13), Coupé and
Estate (B12), including ZX models and
special/limited editions
1270 cc, 1392 cc, 1597 cc, 1598 cc and 1809 cc

Does not cover Diesel engine models

(378-9T4)

ABCDE
FGHIJ
KLMN

Haynes Publishing Group
Sparkford Nr Yeovil
Somerset BA22 7JJ England

Haynes Publications, Inc
861 Lawrence Drive
Newbury Park
California 91320 USA

Acknowledgements

Thanks are due to the Champion Sparking Plug Company Limited, who supplied the illustrations showing spark plug conditions, to Holt Lloyd Limited who supplied the illustrations showing bodywork repair, and to Duckhams Oils, who provided lubrication data. Certain other illustrations are the copyright of the Nissan Motor Company Limited of Japan and are used with their permission. Thanks are also due to Sykes-Pickavant, who provided some of the workshop tools. Finally, thanks are due to all the staff at Sparkford who helped in the production of this manual.

© **Haynes Publishing Group 1991**

A book in the **Haynes Owners Workshop Manual Series**

Printed by J. H. Haynes & Co. Ltd., Sparkford, Nr Yeovil, Somerset BA22 7JJ, England

ISBN 1 85010 843 9

British Library Cataloguing in Publication Data

A catalogue record for this book is available from the British Library

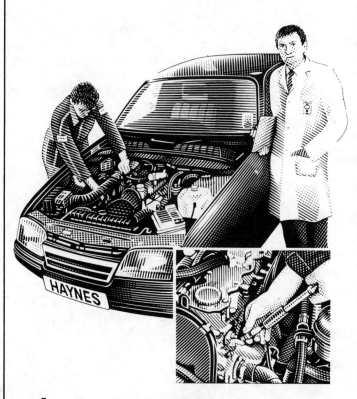

Contents

	Page
Acknowledgements	2
About this manual	5
Introduction to the Nissan Sunny	5
General dimensions, weights and capacities	7
Jacking, wheel changing and towing	8
Buying spare parts and vehicle identification numbers	10
General repair procedures	12
Tools and working facilities	13
Routine maintenance *(also see Chapter 13, page 276)*	15
Conversion factors	19
Safety first!	20
Recommended lubricants and fluids	21
Fault diagnosis	22
Chapter 1 Engine *(also see Chapter 13, page 276)*	26
Chapter 2 Cooling and heating systems *(also see Chapter 13, page 276)*	57
Chapter 3 Fuel, exhaust and emission control systems *(also see Chapter 13, page 276)*	68
Chapter 4 Ignition system *(also see Chapter 13, page 276)*	87
Chapter 5 Clutch *(also see Chapter 13, page 276)*	95
Chapter 6 Manual transmission *(also see Chapter 13, page 276)*	101
Chapter 7 Automatic transmission *(also see Chapter 13, page 276)*	121
Chapter 8 Driveshafts *(also see Chapter 13, page 276)*	128
Chapter 9 Braking system *(also see Chapter 13, page 276)*	133
Chapter 10 Suspension and steering *(also see Chapter 13, page 276)*	148
Chapter 11 Bodywork and fittings *(also see Chapter 13, page 276)*	174
Chapter 12 Electrical system *(also see Chapter 13, page 276)*	201
Chapter 13 Supplement: Revisions and information on later models	276
Index	395

Nissan Sunny SGX Hatchback

About this manual

Its aim

The aim of this manual is to help you get the best value from your vehicle. It can do so in several ways. It can help you decide what work must be done (even should you choose to get it done by a garage), provide information on routine maintenance and servicing, and give a logical course of action and diagnosis when random faults occur. However, it is hoped that you will use the manual by tackling the work yourself. On simpler jobs it may even be quicker than booking the car into a garage and going there twice, to leave and collect it. Perhaps most important, a lot of money can be saved by avoiding the costs a garage must charge to cover its labour and overheads.

The manual has drawings and descriptions to show the function of the various components so that their layout can be understood. Then the tasks are described and photographed in a step-by-step sequence so that even a novice can do the work.

Its arrangement

The manual is divided into thirteen Chapters, each covering a logical sub-division of the vehicle. The Chapters are each divided into Sections, numbered with single figures, eg 5; and the Sections into paragraphs (or sub-sections), with decimal numbers following on from the Section they are in, eg 5.1, 5.2, 5.3 etc.

It is freely illustrated, especially in those parts where there is a detailed sequence of operations to be carried out. There are two forms of illustration: figures and photographs. The figures are numbered in sequence with decimal numbers, according to their position in the Chapter – eg Fig. 6.4 is the fourth drawing/illustration in Chapter 6. Photographs carry the same number (either individually or in related groups) as the Section or sub-section to which they relate.

There is an alphabetical index at the back of the manual as well as a contents list at the front. Each Chapter is also preceded by its own individual contents list.

References to the 'left' or 'right' of the vehicle are in the sense of a person in the driver's seat facing forwards.

Unless otherwise stated, nuts and bolts are removed by turning anti-clockwise, and tightened by turning clockwise.

Vehicle manufacturers continually make changes to specifications and recommendations, and these, when notified, are incorporated into our manuals at the earliest opportunity.

Whilst every care is taken to ensure that the information in this manual is correct, no liability can be accepted by the authors or publishers for loss, damage or injury caused by any errors in, or omissions from, the information given.

Project vehicle

The vehicle used in the preparation of this manual, and appearing in many of the photographic sequences, was a Nissan Sunny SGX Hatchback.

Introduction to the Nissan Sunny

The new Nissan Sunny range was introduced in October 1986. Mechanically similar to the previous series of the Sunny, most of the changes made for the 'new' series are cosmetic. The engine and the transmission are of the same basic design of the earlier models. The engine is water-cooled, has an overhead camshaft, and the crankshaft runs in five main bearings. The manual or automatic transmission (as applicable), is attached to the rear end of the engine, the two being transversely mounted at the front of the car.

Drive is to the front roadwheels via driveshafts which are connected to the differential within the transmission at their inboard ends, and the wheel hubs at their outboard ends.

Four distinct body types are produced; the 2- or 4-door Saloon, the 3- or 5-door Hatchback, the 5-door Estate and the 3-door Coupe. The level of standard equipment is high, but a range of optional extras for each is available.

All models in the Sunny range are conventional in design and are therefore easy to maintain and repair.

Nissan Sunny LX Saloon

Nissan Sunny Coupe

General dimensions, weights and capacities

Dimensions
Overall length:
Hatchback	4061 mm (159.9 in)
Saloon	4215 mm (165.9 in)
Coupe	4230 mm (166.5 in)
Estate	4270 mm (168.1 in)

Overall width:
Hatchback	1640 mm (64.6 in)
Saloon	1640 mm (64.6 in)
Coupe	1665 mm (65.6 in)
Estate	1640 mm (64.6 in)

Overall height:
Hatchback	1379 mm (54.3 in)
Saloon	1379 mm (54.3 in)
Coupe	1323 mm (52.1 in)
Estate	1384 mm (54.5 in)

Weights
Kerb weight (typical – add 20 kg/44 lb for automatic transmission):
Hatchback	989 kg (2180 lb)
Saloon	991 kg (2185 lb)
Coupe	1019 kg (2246 lb)
Estate	1034 kg (2280 lb)

Maximum towing weight – with brakes:
Hatchback	999 kg (2202 lb)
Saloon	999 kg (2202 lb)
Coupe	899 kg (1982 lb)
Estate	999 kg (2202 lb)

Capacities
Fuel tank (all models)	50 litres (11 gallons)

Cooling system:
With aluminium radiator	4.9 litres (8.62 pints)
With copper radiator	5.5 litres (9.68 pints)
Engine oil (with filter change)	3.2 litres (5.63 pints)

Manual transmission:
4-speed up to January 1987	2.3 litres (4.05 pints)
4-speed from January 1987	2.4 litres (4.22 pints)
5-speed up to January 1987	2.7 litres (4.75 pints)
5-speed from January 1987	2.8 litres (4.93 pints)
Automatic transmission	6.3 litres (11.0 pints)
Power steering fluid	0.9 litre (1.6 pints)

Jacking, wheel changing and towing

Jacking

The jack supplied with the vehicle should only be used for emergency roadside wheel changing (photo).

Chock the roadwheels on the side opposite to that from which the wheel is being removed. Engage the jack in one of the two cut-outs at the base of the sill, either front or rear according to which wheel is being removed.

When carrying out overhaul or repair work use a trolley jack or a hydraulic bottle or screw jack. Locate the jack under the vehicle only at the positions indicated and **always** supplement the jack with axle stands placed under the side-members.

To avoid repetition, the procedure for raising the vehicle in order to carry out work under it is not included before each operation described in this Manual. It is to be preferred, and is certainly recommended, that the vehicle is positioned over an inspection pit or raised on a lift. Where these facilities are not available, use ramps or jack up the vehicle and supplement with axle stands, as described earlier.

Wheel changing

The removal and refitting of a roadwheel should be carried out in the following way.

Carefully prise off the centre trim (where fitted) from the roadwheel – the trim is easily broken, so do not use excessive force. Unscrew the roadwheel nuts just enough to release them, before raising the car. On roadwheels having a small plastic centre cap, twist it through a quarter-turn and remove it. Raise the roadwheel from the ground, remove the nuts completely, then lift the roadwheel from the studs (photo).

Refit the roadwheel, tighten the nuts as tightly as possible while the wheel is held against rotation with the foot. Lower the vehicle and tighten the nuts fully. Fit the cap/trim to the centre of the roadwheel.

Towing

The front and rear towing hooks may be used in an emergency. On vehicles with manual transmission, restrict the towing speed to below 50 mph (80 kph) and the distance towed to 50 miles (80 km). On vehicles with automatic transmission, restrict the speed to 20 mph (30 kph) and the distance towed to 20 miles (30 km).

If the transmission has a fault, then the front wheels of the vehicle must be raised and placed on a dolly.

Never tow a vehicle with automatic transmission by raising the rear wheels and leaving the front wheels in contact with the road.

Jack stowage location in luggage area (Hatchback)

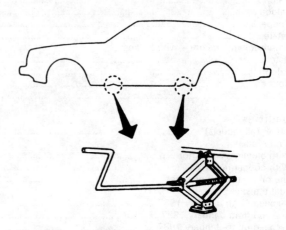

Standard (pantograph) type jack location points when raising the vehicle

Location for spare wheel and tools (Hatchback)

Loosen the roadwheel bolts ...

... then raise the vehicle

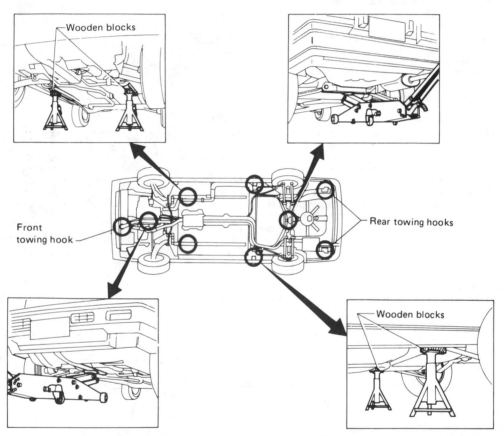

Location points under vehicle for axle (safety) stands. Also shown are the front and rear towing eye locations. Locate wooden blocks for protection when lifting at points indicated

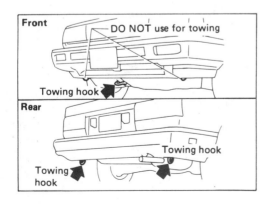

 Front and rear tow hook locations

Buying spare parts and vehicle identification numbers

Buying spare parts

Spare parts are available from many sources, for example: Nissan garages, other garages and accessory shops, and motor factors. Our advice regarding spare part sources is as follows:

Official appointed Nissan garages – This is the best source of parts which are peculiar to your vehicle and are otherwise not generally available (eg, complete cylinder heads, internal gearbox components, badges, interior trim etc). It is also the only place at which you should buy parts if your vehicle is still under warranty – non-standard components may invalidate the warranty. To be sure of obtaining the correct parts it will always be necessary to give the stores person your vehicle's engine and chassis number, and if possible, to take the 'old' parts along for positive identification. Remember that some parts are available on a factory exchange scheme – any parts returned should always be clean! It obviously makes good sense to go straight to the specialists on your vehicle for this type of part for they are best equipped to supply you.

Other garages and accessory shops – These are often very good places to buy materials and components needed for the maintenance of your vehicle (eg, spark plugs, bulbs, drivebelts, oils and greases, touch-up paint, filler paste, etc). They also sell general accessories, usually have convenient opening hours, charge lower prices and can often be found not far from home.

Motor factors – Good factors will stock all of the more important components which wear out relatively quickly (eg clutch components, pistons, valves, exhaust systems, brake cylinders/pipes/hoses/seals shoes and pads etc). Motor factors will often provide new or reconditioned components on a part exchange basis – this can save a considerable amount of money.

Vehicle identification numbers

The chassis number is located on a plate in the rear corner of the engine compartment. The number is repeated on the bulkhead upper panel in which it is stamped.

The engine number is stamped into a machined inclined surface on the crankcase just below the distributor mounting (photo).

The manual transmission serial number is located on the clutch release arm, and the automatic transmission serial number on the upper casing surface.

Engine number location

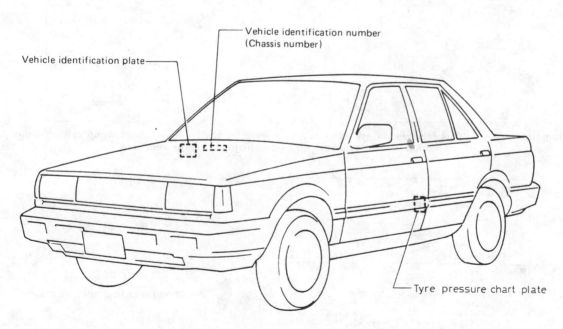

Vehicle identification number and tyre pressure chart locations
On RHD models, tyre pressure chart is on driver's pillar

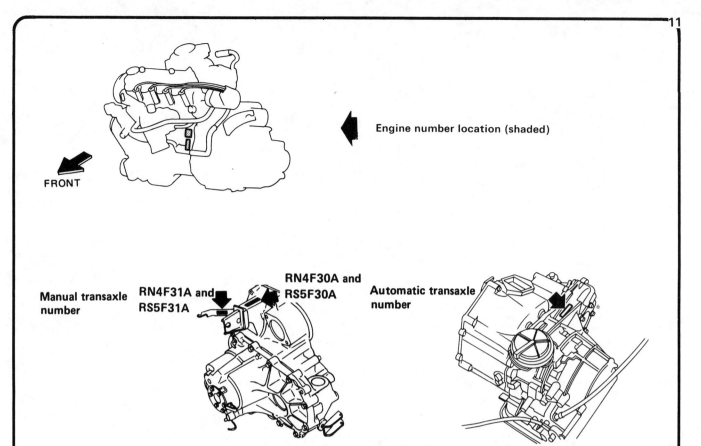

Engine number location (shaded)

FRONT

Manual transaxle number

RN4F31A and RS5F31A

RN4F30A and RS5F30A

Automatic transaxle number

Transmission number locations

General repair procedures

Whenever servicing, repair or overhaul work is carried out on the car or its components, it is necessary to observe the following procedures and instructions. This will assist in carrying out the operation efficiently and to a professional standard of workmanship.

Joint mating faces and gaskets

Where a gasket is used between the mating faces of two components, ensure that it is renewed on reassembly, and fit it dry unless otherwise stated in the repair procedure. Make sure that the mating faces are clean and dry with all traces of old gasket removed. When cleaning a joint face, use a tool which is not likely to score or damage the face, and remove any burrs or nicks with an oilstone or fine file.

Make sure that tapped holes are cleaned with a pipe cleaner, and keep them free of jointing compound if this is being used unless specifically instructed otherwise.

Ensure that all orifices, channels or pipes are clear and blow through them, preferably using compressed air.

Oil seals

Whenever an oil seal is removed from its working location, either individually or as part of an assembly, it should be renewed.

The very fine sealing lip of the seal is easily damaged and will not seal if the surface it contacts is not completely clean and free from scratches, nicks or grooves. If the original sealing surface of the component cannot be restored, the component should be renewed.

Protect the lips of the seal from any surface which may damage them in the course of fitting. Use tape or a conical sleeve where possible. Lubricate the seal lips with oil before fitting and, on dual lipped seals, fill the space between the lips with grease.

Unless otherwise stated, oil seals must be fitted with their sealing lips toward the lubricant to be sealed.

Use a tubular drift or block of wood of the appropriate size to install the seal and, if the seal housing is shouldered, drive the seal down to the shoulder. If the seal housing is unshouldered, the seal should be fitted with its face flush with the housing top face.

Screw threads and fastenings

Always ensure that a blind tapped hole is completely free from oil, grease, water or other fluid before installing the bolt or stud. Failure to do this could cause the housing to crack due to the hydraulic action of the bolt or stud as it is screwed in.

When tightening a castellated nut to accept a split pin, tighten the nut to the specified torque, where applicable, and then tighten further to the next split pin hole. Never slacken the nut to align a split pin hole unless stated in the repair procedure.

When checking or retightening a nut or bolt to a specified torque setting, slacken the nut or bolt by a quarter of a turn, and then retighten to the specified setting.

Locknuts, locktabs and washers

Any fastening which will rotate against a component or housing in the course of tightening should always have a washer between it and the relevant component or housing.

Spring or split washers should always be renewed when they are used to lock a critical component such as a big-end bearing retaining nut or bolt.

Locktabs which are folded over to retain a nut or bolt should always be renewed.

Self-locking nuts can be reused in non-critical areas, providing resistance can be felt when the locking portion passes over the bolt or stud thread.

Split pins must always be replaced with new ones of the correct size for the hole.

Special tools

Some repair procedures in this manual entail the use of special tools such as a press, two or three-legged pullers, spring compressors etc. Wherever possible, suitable readily available alternatives to the manufacturer's special tools are described, and are shown in use. In some instances, where no alternative is possible, it has been necessary to resort to the use of a manufacturer's tool and this has been done for reasons of safety as well as the efficient completion of the repair operation. Unless you are highly skilled and have a thorough understanding of the procedure described, never attempt to bypass the use of any special tool when the procedure described specifies its use. Not only is there a very great risk of personal injury, but expensive damage could be caused to the components involved.

Tools and working facilities

Introduction

A selection of good tools is a fundamental requirement for anyone contemplating the maintenance and repair of a motor vehicle. For the owner who does not possess any, their purchase will prove a considerable expense, offsetting some of the savings made by doing-it-yourself. However, provided that the tools purchased meet the relevant national safety standards and are of good quality, they will last for many years and prove an extremely worthwhile investment.

To help the average owner to decide which tools are needed to carry out the various tasks detailed in this manual, we have compiled three lists of tools under the following headings: *Maintenance and minor repair, Repair and overhaul,* and *Special*. The newcomer to practical mechanics should start off with the *Maintenance and minor repair* tool kit and confine himself to the simpler jobs around the vehicle. Then, as his confidence and experience grow, he can undertake more difficult tasks, buying extra tools as, and when, they are needed. In this way, a *Maintenance and minor repair* tool kit can be built-up into a *Repair and overhaul* tool kit over a considerable period of time without any major cash outlays. The experienced do-it-yourselfer will have a tool kit good enough for most repair and overhaul procedures and will add tools from the *Special* category when he feels the expense is justified by the amount of use to which these tools will be put.

It is obviously not possible to cover the subject of tools fully here. For those who wish to learn more about tools and their use there is a book entitled *How to Choose and Use Car Tools* available from the publishers of this manual.

Maintenance and minor repair tool kit

The tools given in this list should be considered as a minimum requirement if routine maintenance, servicing and minor repair operations are to be undertaken. We recommend the purchase of combination spanners (ring one end, open-ended the other); although more expensive than open-ended ones, they do give the advantages of both types of spanner.

> *Combination spanners - 10, 11, 12, 13, 14 & 17 mm*
> *Adjustable spanner - 9 inch*
> *Spark plug spanner (with rubber insert)*
> *Spark plug gap adjustment tool*
> *Set of feeler gauges*
> *Brake bleed nipple spanner*
> *Screwdriver - 4 in long x $^1/4$ in dia (flat blade)*
> *Screwdriver - 4 in long x $^1/4$ in dia (cross blade)*
> *Combination pliers - 6 inch*
> *Hacksaw (junior)*
> *Tyre pump*
> *Tyre pressure gauge*
> *Oil can*
> *Fine emery cloth (1 sheet)*
> *Wire brush (small)*
> *Funnel (medium size)*

Repair and overhaul tool kit

These tools are virtually essential for anyone undertaking any major repairs to a motor vehicle, and are additional to those given in the *Maintenance and minor repair* list. Included in this list is a comprehensive set of sockets. Although these are expensive they will be found invaluable as they are so versatile - particularly if various drives are included in the set. We recommend the ½ in square-drive type, as this can be used with most proprietary torque wrenches. If you cannot afford a socket set, even bought piecemeal, then inexpensive tubular box spanners are a useful alternative.

The tools in this list will occasionally need to be supplemented by tools from the *Special* list.

> *Sockets (or box spanners) to cover range in previous list*
> *Reversible ratchet drive (for use with sockets)*
> *Extension piece, 10 inch (for use with sockets)*
> *Universal joint (for use with sockets)*
> *Torque wrench (for use with sockets)*
> *'Mole' wrench - 8 inch*
> *Ball pein hammer*
> *Soft-faced hammer, plastic or rubber*
> *Screwdriver - 6 in long x $^5/16$ in dia (flat blade)*
> *Screwdriver - 2 in long x $^5/16$ in square (flat blade)*
> *Screwdriver - $1^1/2$ in long x $^1/4$ in dia (cross blade)*
> *Screwdriver - 3 in long x $^1/8$ in dia (electricians)*
> *Pliers - electricians side cutters*
> *Pliers - needle nosed*
> *Pliers - circlip (internal and external)*
> *Cold chisel - $^1/2$ inch*
> *Scriber*
> *Scraper*
> *Centre punch*
> *Pin punch*
> *Hacksaw*
> *Valve grinding tool*
> *Steel rule/straight-edge*
> *Allen keys (inc. Torx type)*
> *Selection of files*
> *Wire brush (large)*
> *Axle-stands*
> *Jack (strong trolley or hydraulic type)*

Special tools

The tools in this list are those which are not used regularly, are expensive to buy, or which need to be used in accordance with their manufacturers' instructions. Unless relatively difficult mechanical jobs are undertaken frequently, it will not be economic to buy many of these tools. Where this is the case, you could consider clubbing together with friends (or joining a motorists' club) to make a joint purchase, or borrowing the tools against a deposit from a local garage or tool hire specialist.

The following list contains only those tools and instruments freely available to the public, and not those special tools produced by the vehicle manufacturer specifically for its dealer network. You will find occasional references to these manufacturers' special tools in the text of this manual. Generally, an alternative method of doing the job without the vehicle manufacturers' special tool is given. However, sometimes, there is no alternative to using them. Where this is the case and the relevant tool cannot be bought or borrowed, you will have to entrust the work to a franchised garage.

Valve spring compressor
Piston ring compressor
Balljoint separator
Universal hub/bearing puller
Impact screwdriver
Micrometer and/or vernier gauge
Dial gauge
Stroboscopic timing light
Dwell angle meter/tachometer
Universal electrical multi-meter
Cylinder compression gauge
Lifting tackle
Trolley jack
Light with extension lead

Buying tools

For practically all tools, a tool factor is the best source since he will have a very comprehensive range compared with the average garage or accessory shop. Having said that, accessory shops often offer excellent quality tools at discount prices, so it pays to shop around.

Remember, you don't have to buy the most expensive items on the shelf, but it is always advisable to steer clear of the very cheap tools.

There are plenty of good tools around at reasonable prices, but always aim to purchase items which meet the relevant national safety standards. If in doubt, ask the proprietor or manager of the shop for advice before making a purchase.

Care and maintenance of tools

Having purchased a reasonable tool kit, it is necessary to keep the tools in a clean serviceable condition. After use, always wipe off any dirt, grease and metal particles using a clean, dry cloth, before putting the tools away. Never leave them lying around after they have been used. A simple tool rack on the garage or workshop wall, for items such as screwdrivers and pliers is a good idea. Store all normal wrenches and sockets in a metal box. Any measuring instruments, gauges, meters, etc, must be carefully stored where they cannot be damaged or become rusty.

Take a little care when tools are used. Hammer heads inevitably become marked and screwdrivers lose the keen edge on their blades from time to time. A little timely attention with emery cloth or a file will soon restore items like this to a good serviceable finish.

Working facilities

Not to be forgotten when discussing tools, is the workshop itself. If anything more than routine maintenance is to be carried out, some form of suitable working area becomes essential.

It is appreciated that many an owner mechanic is forced by circumstances to remove an engine or similar item, without the benefit of a garage or workshop. Having done this, any repairs should always be done under the cover of a roof.

Wherever possible, any dismantling should be done on a clean, flat workbench or table at a suitable working height.

Any workbench needs a vice: one with a jaw opening of 4 in (100 mm) is suitable for most jobs. As mentioned previously, some clean dry storage space is also required for tools, as well as for lubricants, cleaning fluids, touch-up paints and so on, which become necessary.

Another item which may be required, and which has a much more general usage, is an electric drill with a chuck capacity of at least 5/16 in (8 mm). This, together with a good range of twist drills, is virtually essential for fitting accessories such as mirrors and reversing lights.

Last, but not least, always keep a supply of old newspapers and clean, lint-free rags available, and try to keep any working area as clean as possible.

Spanner jaw gap comparison table

Jaw gap (in)	Spanner size
0.250	1/4 in AF
0.276	7 mm
0.313	5/16 in AF
0.315	8 mm
0.344	11/32 in AF; 1/8 in Whitworth
0.354	9 mm
0.375	3/8 in AF
0.394	10 mm
0.433	11 mm
0.438	7/16 in AF
0.445	3/16 in Whitworth; 1/4 in BSF
0.472	12 mm
0.500	1/2 in AF
0.512	13 mm
0.525	1/4 in Whitworth; 5/16 in BSF
0.551	14 mm
0.563	9/16 in AF
0.591	15 mm
0.600	5/16 in Whitworth; 3/8 in BSF
0.625	5/8 in AF
0.630	16 mm
0.669	17 mm
0.686	11/16 in AF
0.709	18 mm
0.710	3/8 in Whitworth; 7/16 in BSF
0.748	19 mm
0.750	3/4 in AF
0.813	13/16 in AF
0.820	7/16 in Whitworth; 1/2 in BSF
0.866	22 mm
0.875	7/8 in AF
0.920	1/2 in Whitworth; 9/16 in BSF
0.938	15/16 in AF
0.945	24 mm
1.000	1 in AF
1.010	9/16 in Whitworth; 5/8 in BSF
1.024	26 mm
1.063	1 1/16 in AF; 27 mm
1.100	5/8 in Whitworth; 11/16 in BSF
1.125	1 1/8 in AF
1.181	30 mm
1.200	11/16 in Whitworth; 3/4 in BSF
1.250	1 1/4 in AF
1.260	32 mm
1.300	3/4 in Whitworth; 7/8 in BSF
1.313	1 5/16 in AF
1.390	13/16 in Whitworth; 15/16 in BSF
1.417	36 mm
1.438	1 7/16 in AF
1.480	7/8 in Whitworth; 1 in BSF
1.500	1 1/2 in AF
1.575	40 mm; 15/16 in Whitworth
1.614	41 mm
1.625	1 5/8 in AF
1.670	1 in Whitworth; 1 1/8 in BSF
1.688	1 11/16 in AF
1.811	46 mm
1.813	1 13/16 in AF
1.860	1 1/8 in Whitworth; 1 1/4 in BSF
1.875	1 7/8 in AF
1.969	50 mm
2.000	2 in AF
2.050	1 1/4 in Whitworth; 1 3/8 in BSF
2.165	55 mm
2.362	60 mm

Routine maintenance

For information applicable to later models see Supplement at end of manual

The routine maintenance instructions listed are basically those recommended by the vehicle manufacturer. They are sometimes supplemented by additional maintenance tasks proven to be necessary.

The maintenance intervals recommended are those specified by the manufacturer. They are necessarily something of a compromise, since no two vehicles operate under identical conditions. The DIY mechanic, who does not have labour costs to consider, may wish to shorten the service intervals. Experience will show whether this is necessary.

Where the vehicle is used under severe operating conditions (extremes of heat or cold, dusty conditions, or mainly stop-start driving), more frequent oil changes may be desirable. If in doubt consult your dealer.

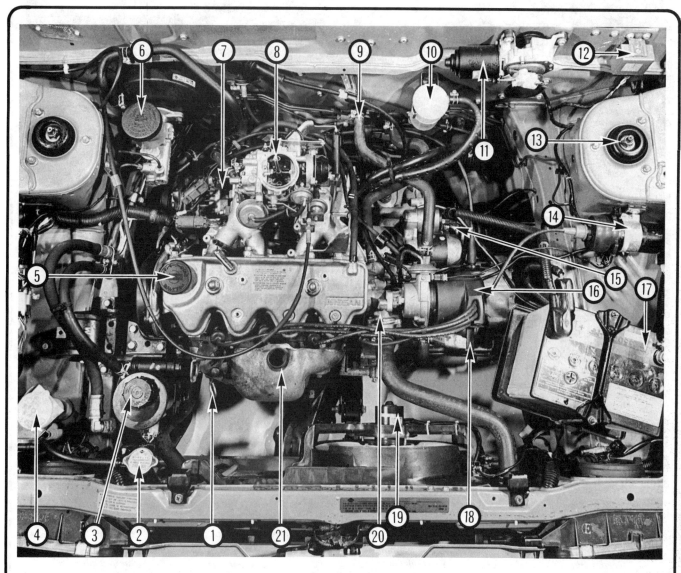

Under bonnet view – 1.6 engine

1 Engine oil dipstick	6 Brake master cylinder and	11 Windscreen wiper motor	16 Ignition distributor
2 Coolant filler cap	fluid reservoir	12 Headlight dim-dip switch	17 Battery
3 Power steering pump	7 Alternator	unit	18 Clutch release lever
reservoir	8 Carburettor (air cleaner	13 Front suspension strut upper	19 Cooling fan
4 Wiper/washer fluid	removed)	mounting	20 Coolant thermostat
filler/reservoir	9 Heater coolant hoses	14 Ignition coil	21 Exhaust manifold
5 Engine oil filler cap	10 Fuel filter	15 Starter motor	

View of front underside of vehicle – 1.6 engine with manual gearbox

1   Radiator drain plug
2   Gearbox drain plug and
    level/filler plug
3   Driveshaft and gaiter

4   Brake caliper unit
5   Transverse link arm
6   Gear selector control rod

7   Stabilizer (anti-roll) bar
8   Exhaust system – front
9   Steering tie-rod

10   Steering gear unit
11   Sump drain plug
12   Oil filter

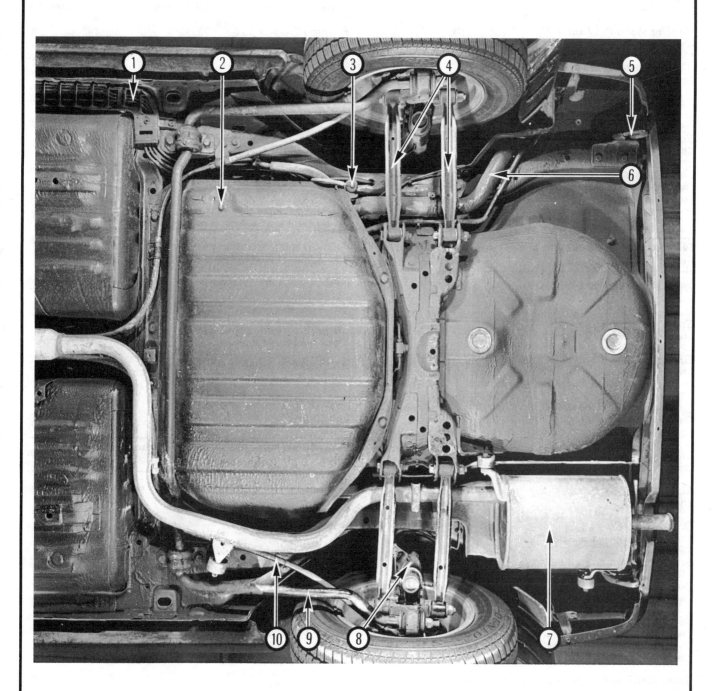

View of rear underside of vehicle – 1.6 Hatchback

1	Hydraulic brake lines and fuel lines	3	Fuel check valve	6	Fuel filler pipe	9	Radius rod
2	Fuel tank drain plug	4	Front and rear parallel links	7	Exhaust system – rear	10	Handbrake cable
		5	Rear towing eye	8	Rear strut		

Weekly, or before a long journey

Engine (Chapter 1)
Check oil level

Cooling system (Chapter 2)
Check coolant level

Automatic transmission (Chapter 7)
Check fluid level

Braking system (Chapter 9)
Check fluid level

Suspension and steering (Chapter 10)
Check tyre pressures (cold). Include spare

Electrical system (Chapter 12)
Check operation of all lights and horn, and add a screen wash such as Turtle Wax High Tech Screen Wash to the washer bottle reservoirs
Check battery test indicator colour (if applicable)

Every 9000 miles (15 000 km) or 6 months, whichever comes first

Engine (Chapter 1)
Renew oil and filter*

Cooling system (Chapter 2)
Check drivebelt(s) condition and tension

Fuel and exhaust systems (Chapter 3)
Check idle speed and mixture settings
Check exhaust system for condition and security

Ignition system (Chapter 4)
Clean and regap spark plugs
Check ignition timing

Clutch (Chapter 5)
Check adjustment

Manual gearbox (Chapter 6)
Check oil level

Driveshafts (Chapter 8)
Check for condition and security

Braking system (Chapter 9)
Check adjustment(s)
Check front pads for wear
Check system for leaks

Suspension and steering (Chapter 10)
Check for condition and security
Check power steering fluid level
Check tyres for wear

Bodywork and fittings (Chapter 11)
Lubricate hinges and locks
Check drain channels are clear

Nissan state that, if an oil filter which is not of Nissan Premium type is used, the oil and filter should be renewed every 6000 miles (10 000 km) or six months, whichever comes first

Every 18 000 miles (30 000 km) or 12 months, whichever comes first

In addition to the 9000 mile (15 000 km) maintenance requirements

Engine (Chapter 1)
Check valve clearances
Clean positive crankcase ventilation system hoses and check operation

Cooling system (Chapter 2)
Check hoses for condition and security

Fuel and exhaust systems (Chapter 3)
Renew fuel filter
Check vacuum hoses for condition and security
Check automatic temperature control operation

Ignition system (Chapter 4)
Renew spark plugs

Manual gearbox (Chapter 6)
Renew oil (if used in adverse conditions)

Automatic transmission (Chapter 7)
Renew fluid (if used in adverse conditions)

Braking system (Chapter 9)
Renew fluid
Check rear shoes for wear

Suspension and steering (Chapter 10)
Check front wheel alignment

Bodywork and fittings (Chapter 11)
Check seat belts for condition and security

Every 36 000 miles (60 000 km) or 2 years, whichever comes first

In addition to the 18 000 mile (30 000 km) maintenance requirements

Cooling system (Chapter 2)
Renew coolant

Fuel and exhaust systems (Chapter 3)
Check fuel lines for condition and security
Renew air cleaner element

Ignition system (Chapter 4)
Check wiring for condition and security

Braking system (Chapter 9)
Check servo and vacuum hoses for condition and security

Every 60 000 miles (100 000 km)

Engine (Chapter 1)
Renew timing belt

Conversion factors

Length (distance)

Inches (in)	X 25.4	= Millimetres (mm)	X 0.0394	= Inches (in)
Feet (ft)	X 0.305	= Metres (m)	X 3.281	= Feet (ft)
Miles	X 1.609	= Kilometres (km)	X 0.621	= Miles

Volume (capacity)

Cubic inches (cu in; in³)	X 16.387	= Cubic centimetres (cc; cm³)	X 0.061	= Cubic inches (cu in; in³)
Imperial pints (Imp pt)	X 0.568	= Litres (l)	X 1.76	= Imperial pints (Imp pt)
Imperial quarts (Imp qt)	X 1.137	= Litres (l)	X 0.88	= Imperial quarts (Imp qt)
Imperial quarts (Imp qt)	X 1.201	= US quarts (US qt)	X 0.833	= Imperial quarts (Imp qt)
US quarts (US qt)	X 0.946	= Litres (l)	X 1.057	= US quarts (US qt)
Imperial gallons (Imp gal)	X 4.546	= Litres (l)	X 0.22	= Imperial gallons (Imp gal)
Imperial gallons (Imp gal)	X 1.201	= US gallons (US gal)	X 0.833	= Imperial gallons (Imp gal)
US gallons (US gal)	X 3.785	= Litres (l)	X 0.264	= US gallons (US gal)

Mass (weight)

Ounces (oz)	X 28.35	= Grams (g)	X 0.035	= Ounces (oz)
Pounds (lb)	X 0.454	= Kilograms (kg)	X 2.205	= Pounds (lb)

Force

Ounces-force (ozf; oz)	X 0.278	= Newtons (N)	X 3.6	= Ounces-force (ozf; oz)
Pounds-force (lbf; lb)	X 4.448	= Newtons (N)	X 0.225	= Pounds-force (lbf; lb)
Newtons (N)	X 0.1	= Kilograms-force (kgf; kg)	X 9.81	= Newtons (N)

Pressure

Pounds-force per square inch (psi; lbf/in²; lb/in²)	X 0.070	= Kilograms-force per square centimetre (kgf/cm²; kg/cm²)	X 14.223	= Pounds-force per square inch (psi; lbf/in²; lb/in²)
Pounds-force per square inch (psi; lbf/in²; lb/in²)	X 0.068	= Atmospheres (atm)	X 14.696	= Pounds-force per square inch (psi; lbf/in²; lb/in²)
Pounds-force per square inch (psi; lbf/in²; lb/in²)	X 0.069	= Bars	X 14.5	= Pounds-force per square inch (psi; lbf/in²; lb/in²)
Pounds-force per square inch (psi; lbf/in²; lb/in²)	X 6.895	= Kilopascals (kPa)	X 0.145	= Pounds-force per square inch (psi; lbf/in²; lb/in²)
Kilopascals (kPa)	X 0.01	= Kilograms-force per square centimetre (kgf/cm²; kg/cm²)	X 98.1	= Kilopascals (kPa)
Millibar (mbar)	X 100	= Pascals (Pa)	X 0.01	= Millibar (mbar)
Millibar (mbar)	X 0.0145	= Pounds-force per square inch (psi; lbf/in²; lb/in²)	X 68.947	= Millibar (mbar)
Millibar (mbar)	X 0.75	= Millimetres of mercury (mmHg)	X 1.333	= Millibar (mbar)
Millibar (mbar)	X 0.401	= Inches of water (inH₂O)	X 2.491	= Millibar (mbar)
Millimetres of mercury (mmHg)	X 0.535	= Inches of water (inH₂O)	X 1.868	= Millimetres of mercury (mmHg)
Inches of water (inH₂O)	X 0.036	= Pounds-force per square inch (psi; lbf/in²; lb/in²)	X 27.68	= Inches of water (inH₂O)

Torque (moment of force)

Pounds-force inches (lbf in; lb in)	X 1.152	= Kilograms-force centimetre (kgf cm; kg cm)	X 0.868	= Pounds-force inches (lbf in; lb in)
Pounds-force inches (lbf in; lb in)	X 0.113	= Newton metres (Nm)	X 8.85	= Pounds-force inches (lbf in; lb in)
Pounds-force inches (lbf in; lb in)	X 0.083	= Pounds-force feet (lbf ft; lb ft)	X 12	= Pounds-force inches (lbf in; lb in)
Pounds-force feet (lbf ft; lb ft)	X 0.138	= Kilograms-force metres (kgf m; kg m)	X 7.233	= Pounds-force feet (lbf ft; lb ft)
Pounds-force feet (lbf ft; lb ft)	X 1.356	= Newton metres (Nm)	X 0.738	= Pounds-force feet (lbf ft; lb ft)
Newton metres (Nm)	X 0.102	= Kilograms-force metres (kgf m; kg m)	X 9.804	= Newton metres (Nm)

Power

Horsepower (hp)	X 745.7	= Watts (W)	X 0.0013	= Horsepower (hp)

Velocity (speed)

Miles per hour (miles/hr; mph)	X 1.609	= Kilometres per hour (km/hr; kph)	X 0.621	= Miles per hour (miles/hr; mph)

Fuel consumption*

Miles per gallon, Imperial (mpg)	X 0.354	= Kilometres per litre (km/l)	X 2.825	= Miles per gallon, Imperial (mpg)
Miles per gallon, US (mpg)	X 0.425	= Kilometres per litre (km/l)	X 2.352	= Miles per gallon, US (mpg)

Temperature

Degrees Fahrenheit = (°C x 1.8) + 32

Degrees Celsius (Degrees Centigrade; °C) = (°F - 32) x 0.56

It is common practice to convert from miles per gallon (mpg) to litres/100 kilometres (l/100km), where mpg (Imperial) x l/100 km = 282 and mpg (US) x l/100 km = 235

Safety first!

Professional motor mechanics are trained in safe working procedures. However enthusiastic you may be about getting on with the job in hand, do take the time to ensure that your safety is not put at risk. A moment's lack of attention can result in an accident, as can failure to observe certain elementary precautions.

There will always be new ways of having accidents, and the following points do not pretend to be a comprehensive list of all dangers; they are intended rather to make you aware of the risks and to encourage a safety-conscious approach to all work you carry out on your vehicle.

Essential DOs and DON'Ts

DON'T rely on a single jack when working underneath the vehicle. Always use reliable additional means of support, such as axle stands, securely placed under a part of the vehicle that you know will not give way.

DON'T attempt to loosen or tighten high-torque nuts (e.g. wheel hub nuts) while the vehicle is on a jack; it may be pulled off.

DON'T start the engine without first ascertaining that the transmission is in neutral (or 'Park' where applicable) and the parking brake applied.

DON'T suddenly remove the filler cap from a hot cooling system – cover it with a cloth and release the pressure gradually first, or you may get scalded by escaping coolant.

DON'T attempt to drain oil until you are sure it has cooled sufficiently to avoid scalding you.

DON'T grasp any part of the engine, exhaust or catalytic converter without first ascertaining that it is sufficiently cool to avoid burning you.

DON'T allow brake fluid or antifreeze to contact vehicle paintwork.

DON'T syphon toxic liquids such as fuel, brake fluid or antifreeze by mouth, or allow them to remain on your skin.

DON'T inhale dust – it may be injurious to health (see *Asbestos* below).

DON'T allow any spilt oil or grease to remain on the floor – wipe it up straight away, before someone slips on it.

DON'T use ill-fitting spanners or other tools which may slip and cause injury.

DON'T attempt to lift a heavy component which may be beyond your capability – get assistance.

DON'T rush to finish a job, or take unverified short cuts.

DON'T allow children or animals in or around an unattended vehicle.

DO wear eye protection when using power tools such as drill, sander, bench grinder etc, and when working under the vehicle.

DO use a barrier cream on your hands prior to undertaking dirty jobs – it will protect your skin from infection as well as making the dirt easier to remove afterwards; but make sure your hands aren't left slippery. Note that long-term contact with used engine oil can be a health hazard.

DO keep loose clothing (cuffs, tie etc) and long hair well out of the way of moving mechanical parts.

DO remove rings, wristwatch etc, before working on the vehicle – especially the electrical system.

DO ensure that any lifting tackle used has a safe working load rating adequate for the job.

DO keep your work area tidy – it is only too easy to fall over articles left lying around.

DO get someone to check periodically that all is well, when working alone on the vehicle.

DO carry out work in a logical sequence and check that everything is correctly assembled and tightened afterwards.

DO remember that your vehicle's safety affects that of yourself and others. If in doubt on any point, get specialist advice.

IF, in spite of following these precautions, you are unfortunate enough to injure yourself, seek medical attention as soon as possible.

Asbestos

Certain friction, insulating, sealing, and other products – such as brake linings, brake bands, clutch linings, torque converters, gaskets, etc – contain asbestos. *Extreme care must be taken to avoid inhalation of dust from such products since it is hazardous to health.* If in doubt, assume that they *do* contain asbestos.

Fire

Remember at all times that petrol (gasoline) is highly flammable. Never smoke, or have any kind of naked flame around, when working on the vehicle. But the risk does not end there – a spark caused by an electrical short-circuit, by two metal surfaces contacting each other, by careless use of tools, or even by static electricity built up in your body under certain conditions, can ignite petrol vapour, which in a confined space is highly explosive.

Always disconnect the battery earth (ground) terminal before working on any part of the fuel or electrical system, and never risk spilling fuel on to a hot engine or exhaust.

It is recommended that a fire extinguisher of a type suitable for fuel and electrical fires is kept handy in the garage or workplace at all times. Never try to extinguish a fuel or electrical fire with water.

Note: *Any reference to a 'torch' appearing in this manual should always be taken to mean a hand-held battery-operated electric lamp or flashlight. It does NOT mean a welding/gas torch or blowlamp.*

Fumes

Certain fumes are highly toxic and can quickly cause unconsciousness and even death if inhaled to any extent. Petrol (gasoline) vapour comes into this category, as do the vapours from certain solvents such as trichloroethylene. Any draining or pouring of such volatile fluids should be done in a well ventilated area.

When using cleaning fluids and solvents, read the instructions carefully. Never use materials from unmarked containers – they may give off poisonous vapours.

Never run the engine of a motor vehicle in an enclosed space such as a garage. Exhaust fumes contain carbon monoxide which is extremely poisonous; if you need to run the engine, always do so in the open air or at least have the rear of the vehicle outside the workplace.

If you are fortunate enough to have the use of an inspection pit, never drain or pour petrol, and never run the engine, while the vehicle is standing over it; the fumes, being heavier than air, will concentrate in the pit with possibly lethal results.

The battery

Never cause a spark, or allow a naked light, near the vehicle's battery. It will normally be giving off a certain amount of hydrogen gas, which is highly explosive.

Always disconnect the battery earth (ground) terminal before working on the fuel or electrical systems.

If possible, loosen the filler plugs or cover when charging the battery from an external source. Do not charge at an excessive rate or the battery may burst.

Take care when topping up and when carrying the battery. The acid electrolyte, even when diluted, is very corrosive and should not be allowed to contact the eyes or skin.

If you ever need to prepare electrolyte yourself, always add the acid slowly to the water, and never the other way round. Protect against splashes by wearing rubber gloves and goggles.

When jump starting a car using a booster battery, for negative earth (ground) vehicles, connect the jump leads in the following sequence: First connect one jump lead between the positive (+) terminals of the two batteries. Then connect the other jump lead first to the negative (–) terminal of the booster battery, and then to a good earthing (ground) point on the vehicle to be started, at least 18 in (45 cm) from the battery if possible. Ensure that hands and jump leads are clear of any moving parts, and that the two vehicles do not touch. Disconnect the leads in the reverse order.

Mains electricity and electrical equipment

When using an electric power tool, inspection light etc, always ensure that the appliance is correctly connected to its plug and that, where necessary, it is properly earthed (grounded). Do not use such appliances in damp conditions, and, again, beware of creating a spark or applying excessive heat in the vicinity of fuel or fuel vapour. Also ensure that the appliances meet the relevant national safety standards.

Ignition HT voltage

A severe electric shock can result from touching certain parts of the ignition system, such as the HT leads, when the engine is running or being cranked, particularly if components are damp or the insulation is defective. Where an electronic ignition system is fitted, the HT voltage is much higher and could prove fatal.

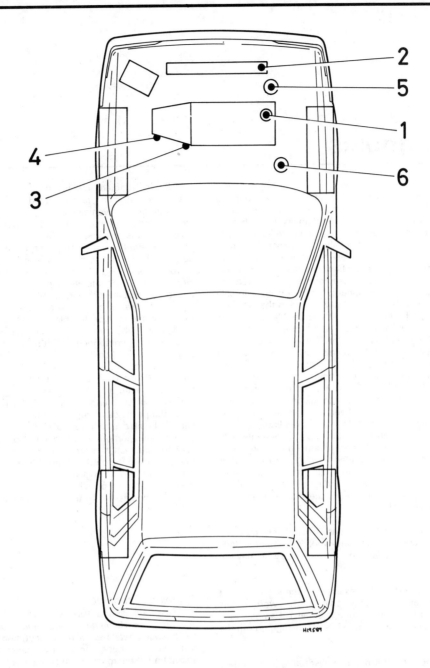

Recommended lubricants and fluids

Component or system	Lubricant type/specification	Duckhams recommendation
Engine (1)	Multigrade engine oil, viscosity range SAE 10W/30 to 15W/50, to API SE or SF	Duckhams QXR, Hypergrade, or 10W/40 Motor Oil
Cooling system (2)	Ethylene glycol based antifreeze, to BS 3151, 3152 or 6580, and soft water	Duckhams Universal Antifreeze and Summer Coolant
Manual gearbox (3)	Hypoid gear oil, viscosity SAE 80W/90, to API GL4	Duckhams Hypoid 80
Automatic transmission (4)	Dexron type ATF	Duckhams Uni-Matic or D-Matic
Power steering (5)	Dexron type ATF	Duckhams Uni-Matic or D-Matic
Braking system (6)	Hydraulic fluid to FMVSS 116 DOT 3	Duckhams Universal Brake and Clutch Fluid

Fault diagnosis

Introduction

The vehicle owner who does his or her own maintenance according to the recommended schedules should not have to use this section of the manual very often. Modern component reliability is such that, provided those items subject to wear or deterioration are inspected or renewed at the specified intervals, sudden failure is comparatively rare. Faults do not usually just happen as a result of sudden failure, but develop over a period of time. Major mechanical failures in particular are usually preceded by characteristic symptoms over hundreds or even thousands of miles. Those components which do occasionally fail without warning are often small and easily carried in the vehicle.

With any fault finding, the first step is to decide where to begin investigations. Sometimes this is obvious, but on other occasions a little detective work will be necessary. The owner who makes half a dozen haphazard adjustments or replacements may be successful in curing a fault (or its symptoms), but he will be none the wiser if the fault recurs and he may well have spent more time and money than was necessary. A calm and logical approach will be found to be more satisfactory in the long run. Always take into account any warning signs or abnormalities that may have been noticed in the period preceding the fault – power loss, high or low gauge readings, unusual noises or smells, etc – and remember that failure of components such as fuses or spark plugs may only be pointers to some underlying fault.

The pages which follow here are intended to help in cases of failure to start or breakdown on the road. There is also a Fault Diagnosis Section at the end of each Chapter which should be consulted if the preliminary checks prove unfruitful. Whatever the fault, certain basic principles apply. These are as follows:

Verify the fault. This is simply a matter of being sure that you know what the symptoms are before starting work. This is particularly important if you are investigating a fault for someone else who may not have described it very accurately.

Don't overlook the obvious. For example, if the vehicle won't start, is there petrol in the tank? (Don't take anyone else's word on this particular point, and don't trust the fuel gauge either!) If an electrical fault is indicated, look for loose or broken wires before digging out the test gear.

Cure the disease, not the symptom. Substituting a flat battery with a fully charged one will get you off the hard shoulder, but if the underlying cause is not attended to, the new battery will go the same way. Similarly, changing oil-fouled spark plugs for a new set will get you moving again, but remember that the reason for the fouling (if it wasn't simply an incorrect grade of plug) will have to be established and corrected.

Don't take anything for granted. Particularly, don't forget that a 'new' component may itself be defective (especially if it's been rattling round in the boot for months), and don't leave components out of a fault diagnosis sequence just because they are new or recently fitted. When you do finally diagnose a difficult fault, you'll probably realise that all the evidence was there from the start.

Electrical faults

Electrical faults can be more puzzling than straightforward mechanical failures, but they are no less susceptible to logical analysis if the basic principles of operation are understood. Vehicle electrical wiring exists in extremely unfavourable conditions – heat, vibration and chemical attack – and the first things to look for are loose or corroded connections and broken or chafed wires, especially where the wires pass through holes in the bodywork or are subject to vibration.

All metal-bodied vehicles in current production have one pole of the battery 'earthed', ie connected to the vehicle bodywork, and in nearly all modern vehicles it is the negative (–) terminal. The various electrical components – motors, bulb holders etc – are also connected to earth, either by means of a lead or directly by their mountings. Electric current flows through the component and then back to the battery via the bodywork. If the component mounting is loose or corroded, or if a good path back to the battery is not available, the circuit will be incomplete and malfunction will result. The engine and/or gearbox are also earthed by means of flexible metal straps to the body or subframe; if these straps are loose or missing, starter motor, generator and ignition trouble may result.

Assuming the earth return to be satisfactory, electrical faults will be due either to component malfunction or to defects in the current supply. Individual components are dealt with in Chapter 12. If supply wires are broken or cracked internally this results in an open-circuit, and the easiest way to check for this is to bypass the suspect wire temporarily with a length of wire having a crocodile clip or suitable connector at each end. Alternatively, a 12V test lamp can be used to verify the presence of supply voltage at various points along the wire and the break can be thus isolated.

If a bare portion of a live wire touches the bodywork or other earthed metal part, the electricity will take the low-resistance path thus formed back to the battery: this is known as a short-circuit. Hopefully a short-circuit will blow a fuse, but otherwise it may cause burning of the insulation (and possibly further short-circuits) or even a fire. This is why it is inadvisable to bypass persistently blowing fuses with silver foil or wire.

Spares and tool kit

Most vehicles are supplied only with sufficient tools for wheel changing; the *Maintenance and minor repair* tool kit detailed in *Tools and working facilities*, with the addition of a hammer, is probably sufficient for those repairs that most motorists would consider attempting at the roadside. In addition a few items which can be fitted without too much trouble in the event of a breakdown should be carried. Experience and available space will modify the list below, but the following may save having to call on professional assistance:

Spark plugs, clean and correctly gapped
HT lead and plug cap – long enough to reach the plug furthest from the distributor
Distributor rotor
Drivebelt(s) – emergency type may suffice
Spare fuses
Set of principal light bulbs
Tin of radiator sealer and hose bandage
Exhaust bandage
Roll of insulating tape
Length of soft iron wire
Length of electrical flex
Torch or inspection lamp (can double as test lamp)
Battery jump leads
Tow-rope
Ignition water dispersant aerosol
Litre of engine oil
Sealed can of hydraulic fluid
Emergency windscreen
Worm drive clips

Carrying a few spares may save a long walk!

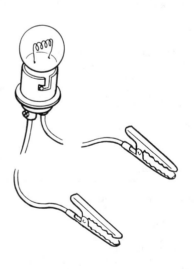

A simple test lamp is useful for tracing electrical faults

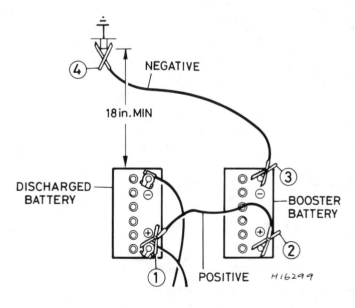

Jump start lead connections for negative earth vehicles –
connect leads in order shown

If spare fuel is carried, a can designed for the purpose should be used to minimise risks of leakage and collision damage. A first aid kit and a warning triangle, whilst not at present compulsory in the UK, are obviously sensible items to carry in addition to the above.

When touring abroad it may be advisable to carry additional spares which, even if you cannot fit them yourself, could save having to wait while parts are obtained. The items below may be worth considering:

Clutch and throttle cables
Cylinder head gasket
Alternator brushes
Tyre valve core

One of the motoring organisations will be able to advise on availability of fuel etc in foreign countries.

Engine will not start

Engine fails to turn when starter operated
Flat battery (recharge, use jump leads, or push start)
Battery terminals loose or corroded
Battery earth to body defective
Engine earth strap loose or broken
Starter motor (or solenoid) wiring loose or broken
Automatic transmission selector in wrong position, or inhibitor switch faulty
Ignition/starter switch faulty
Major mechanical failure (seizure)
Starter or solenoid internal fault (see Chapter 10)

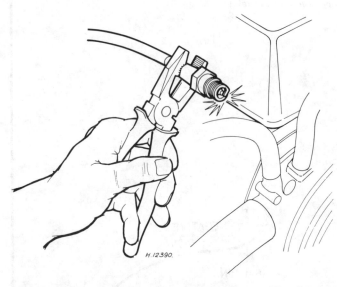

H.12390.

Crank engine and check for spark. Note use of insulated tool to hold plug lead

Starter motor turns engine slowly
Partially discharged battery (recharge, use jump leads, or push start)
Battery terminals loose or corroded
Battery earth to body defective
Engine earth strap loose
Starter motor (or solenoid) wiring loose
Starter motor internal fault (see Chapter 10)

Starter motor spins without turning engine
Flat battery
Starter motor pinion sticking on sleeve
Flywheel gear teeth damaged or worn
Starter motor mounting bolts loose

Engine turns normally but fails to start
Damp or dirty HT leads and distributor cap (crank engine and check for spark) - try moisture dispersant such as Holts Wet Start

No fuel in tank (check for delivery at carburettor)
Excessive choke (hot engine) or insufficient choke (cold engine)
Fouled or incorrectly gapped spark plugs (remove, clean and regap)
Other ignition system fault (see Chapter 4)
Other fuel system fault (see Chapter 3)
Poor compression (see Chapter 1, Section 18)
Major mechanical failure (eg camshaft drive)

Engine fires but will not run
Insufficient choke (cold engine)
Air leaks at carburettor or inlet manifold
Fuel starvation (see Chapter 3)
Ignition fault (see Chapter 4)

Engine cuts out and will not restart

Engine cuts out suddenly – ignition fault
Loose or disconnected LT wires
Wet HT leads or distributor cap (after traversing water splash)
Coil or condenser failure (check for spark)
Other ignition fault (see Chapter 4)

Engine misfires before cutting out – fuel fault
Fuel tank empty
Fuel pump defective or filter blocked (check for delivery)
Fuel tank filler vent blocked (suction will be evident on releasing cap)
Carburettor needle valve sticking
Carburettor jets blocked (fuel contaminated)
Other fuel system fault (see Chapter 3)

Engine cuts out – other causes
Serious overheating
Major mechanical failure (eg camshaft drive)

Engine overheats

Ignition (no-charge) warning light illuminated
Slack or broken drivebelt – retension or renew (Chapter 2)

Ignition warning light not illuminated
Coolant loss due to internal or external leakage (see Chapter 2)
Thermostat defective
Low oil level
Brakes binding
Radiator clogged externally or internally
Electric cooling fan not operating correctly
Engine waterways clogged
Ignition timing incorrect or automatic advance malfunctioning
Mixture too weak

Note: *Do not add cold water to an overheated engine or damage may result*

Low engine oil pressure

Gauge reads low or warning light illuminated with engine running
Oil level low or incorrect grade
Defective gauge or sender unit
Wire to sender unit earthed
Engine overheating
Oil filter clogged or bypass valve defective
Oil pressure relief valve defective
Oil pick-up strainer clogged
Oil pump worn or mountings loose
Worn main or big-end bearings

Note: *Low oil pressure in a high-mileage engine at tickover is not necessarily a cause for concern. Sudden pressure loss at speed is far more significant. In any event, check the gauge or warning light sender before condemning the engine.*

Engine noises

Pre-ignition (pinking) on acceleration
  Incorrect grade of fuel
  Ignition timing incorrect
  Distributor faulty or worn
  Worn or maladjusted carburettor
  Excessive carbon build-up in engine

Whistling or wheezing noises
  Leaking vacuum hose
  Leaking carburettor or manifold gasket
  Blowing head gasket

Tapping or rattling
  Incorrect valve clearances
  Worn valve gear
  Worn timing belt
  Broken piston ring (ticking noise)

Knocking or thumping
  Worn drivebelt
  Peripheral component fault (generator, water pump etc)
  Worn big-end bearings (regular heavy knocking, perhaps less under load)
  Worn main bearings (rumbling and knocking, perhaps worsening under load)
  Piston slap (most noticeable when cold)

Chapter 1 Engine

For modifications, and information applicable to later models, see Supplement at end of manual

Contents

Cylinder head – dismantling, overhaul and reassembly 17
Cylinder head – removal and refitting 6
Engine – complete dismantling 14
Engine – reassembly 20
Engine and automatic transmission – removal and separation 12
Engine and manual transmission – removal and separation 11
Engine/automatic transmission – reconnection and refitting 22
Engine components – examination and renovation 18
Engine dismantling – general 13
Engine/manual transmission – reconnection and refitting 21
Engine reassembly – general 19
Engine removal – method 10

Fault diagnosis – engine 24
General description 1
Initial start-up after major overhaul 23
Lubrication system – general 15
Major operations possible without removing the engine 3
Oil pump – removal and refitting 7
Piston and big-end bearing shells – renewal 9
Positive crankcase ventilation system (PCV) 16
Routine maintenance 2
Sump pan – removal and refitting 8
Timing belt – removal and refitting 5
Valve clearances – checking and adjustment 4

Specifications

General

Type	Four-cylinder, in-line, overhead camshaft, mounted transversely
Designation and capacity:	
E13	1270 cc (77.50 cu in)
E16	1597 cc (97.46 cu in)
Bore:	
E13 and E16	76.0 mm (2.99 in)
Stroke:	
E13	70.0 mm (2.76 in)
E16	88.0 mm (3.46 in)
Compression ratio:	
E13	9.0 to 1
E16	9.6 to 1
Compression pressure – bar (lbf/in²) at 350 rpm:	
E13 Normal	12.45 (181)
E13 Minimum	9.81 (142)
E16 Normal	13.44 (195)
E16 Minimum	10.79 (156)
Pressure limit difference between cylinders	0.98 (14)
Firing order	1–3–4–2 (No 1 at timing belt end)

Cylinder block

Material	Cast iron
Maximum bore out-of-round	0.015 mm (0.0006 in)
Maximum taper of bore	0.02 mm (0.0008 in)

Crankshaft
Number of main bearings 5
Main journal diameter .... 49.940 to 49.964 mm (1.9661 to 1.9671 in)
Crankpin diameter .... 39.961 to 39.974 mm (1.5733 to 1.5738 in)
Maximum journal and crankpin out-of-round .... 0.03 mm (0.0012 in)
Endfloat:
    Standard .... 0.05 to 0.165 mm (0.0020 to 0.0065 in)
    Wear limit .... 0.30 mm (0.0118 in)
Main bearing running clearance:
    Nos 1, 3 and 5 .... 0.031 to 0.056 mm (0.0012 to 0.0022 in)
    Nos 2 and 4 .... 0.031 to 0.092 mm (0.0012 to 0.0036 in)
    Wear limit .... 0.10 mm (0.0039 in)
Main bearing undersizes .... 0.25 mm (0.0098 in)

Connecting rods
Side play at big-ends .... 0.10 to 0.37 mm (0.0039 to 0.0146 in)
Wear limit .... 0.50 mm (0.020 in)
Big-end bearing running clearance:
    E13 .... 0.018 to 0.052 mm (0.0007 to 0.0020 in)
    E16 .... 0.010 to 0.044 mm (0.0004 to 0.0017 in)
Big-end bearing undersizes .... 0.25 mm (0.0098 in)

Gudgeon pin
Pin-to-piston clearance:
    E13 .... 0.008 to 0.010 mm (0.0003 to 0.0004 in)
    E16 .... 0.008 to 0.012 mm (0.0003 to 0.0005 in)
Interference fit in small end .... 0.017 to 0.038 mm (0.0007 to 0.0015 in)

Piston rings
Side clearance in piston groove:
    Top .... 0.040 to 0.073 mm (0.0016 to 0.0029 in)
    Second .... 0.030 to 0.063 mm (0.0012 to 0.0025 in)
    Oil scraper – type 1 .... 0.065 to 0.140 mm (0.0026 to 0.0055 in)
    Oil scraper – type 2 .... 0.006 to 0.175 mm (0.0002 to 0.0069 in)
    Wear limit (top and 2nd) .... 0.2 mm (0.008 in)
Ring gap:
    Top (type 1) .... 0.14 to 0.26 mm (0.0055 to 0.0102 in)
    Top (type 2) .... 0.20 to 0.30 mm (0.0079 to 0.0118 in)
    Second (type 1) .... 0.28 to 0.37 mm (0.0110 to 0.0146 in)
    Second (type 2) .... 0.15 to 0.25 mm (0.0059 to 0.0098 in)
    Oil scraper (rail) .... 0.20 to 0.60 mm (0.0079 to 0.0236 in)

Pistons
Standard diameter (at skirt) .... 75.967 to 76.017 mm (2.9908 to 2.9928 in)
Oversizes .... 0.02 mm (0.0008 in), 0.25 mm (0.0098 in) and 0.5 mm (0.020 in)
Clearance (to cylinder wall) .... 0.023 to 0.043 mm (0.0009 to 0.0017 in)

Jackshaft
Endfloat .... 0.045 to 0.105 mm (0.0018 to 0.0041 in)
Journal diameter:
    Front .... 31.987 to 32.000 mm (1.2593 to 1.2598 in)
    Rear .... 28.587 to 28.600 mm (1.1255 to 1.1260 in)
Journal-to-bush clearance:
    Front and rear .... 0.020 to 0.098 mm (0.0008 to 0.0039 in)
    Maximum allowable clearance .... 0.020 mm (0.0008 in)
Fuel pump cam height .... 27.7 to 27.8 mm (1.091 to 1.094 in)

Camshaft
Journal diameter:
    Nos 1, 3 and 5 .... 41.949 to 41.965 mm (1.6515 to 1.6522 in)
    Nos 2 and 4 .... 41.906 to 41.922 mm (1.6498 to 1.6505 in)
Bearing inside diameter .... 42.000 to 42.025 mm (1.6535 to 1.6545 in)
Camshaft running clearance:
    Nos 1, 3 and 5 .... 0.035 to 0.076 mm (0.0014 to 0.0030 in)
    Wear limit .... 0.15 mm (0.0059 in)
    Nos 2 and 4 .... 0.078 to 0.119 mm (0.0031 to 0.0047 in)
    Wear limit .... 0.20 mm (0.0079 in)
Camshaft sprocket run-out limit .... 0.10 mm (0.004 in)

Cylinder head
Material .... Aluminium alloy
Surface out-of-true (limit) .... 0.10 mm (0.004 in)

Valves

Clearance (hot), intake and exhaust	0.28 mm (0.011 in)
Clearance (cold), intake and exhaust	0.22 mm (0.009 in)
Valve seat angle:	
E13:	
Inlet and exhaust	45° 15′ to 45° 45′
E16:	
Inlet	60° 15′ to 60° 45′
Exhaust	45° 15′ to 45° 45′
Valve spring free length	46.70 mm (1.8386 in)

Valve guides

Outside diameter:	
Standard	12.033 to 12.044 mm (0.4737 to 0.4742 in)
Oversize	12.256 to 12.274 mm (0.4825 to 0.4832 in)
Inside diameter (reamed)	7.005 to 7.020 mm (0.2758 to 0.2764 in)
Guide hole in cylinder head:	
Diameter for standard guide	11.970 to 11.988 mm (0.4713 to 0.4720 in)
Diameter for oversize guide	12.200 to 12.211 mm (0.4803 to 0.4807 in)
Interference fit in cylinder head	0.045 to 0.074 mm (0.0018 to 0.0029 in)
Valve stem to guide clearance:	
Wear limit	0.10 mm (0.004 in)

Lubrication

Oil capacity:	
With filter change	3.2 litre (5.63 pints)
Without filter change	2.8 litre (4.93 pints)
Oil pressure (hot at 1050 rpm)	2.0 bar (29 lbf/in²)
Oil pump:	
Rotor tip clearance	0.12 mm (0.0047 in) – maximum
Outer rotor-to-body clearance	0.15 to 0.21 mm (0.0059 to 0.0083 in)
Side clearance (with gasket)	0.05 to 0.12 mm (0.0020 to 0.0047 in)
Oil type/specification	Multigrade engine oil, viscosity range SAE 10W/30 to 15W/50, to API SE or SF (Duckhams QXR, Hypergrade, or 10W/40 Motor Oil)
Oil filter	Champion C109

Torque wrench settings

	Nm	lbf ft
Crankshaft pulley bolt	108 to 127	80 to 94
Timing belt cover	5.1 to 6.5	3.8 to 4.8
Oil pump	13 to 16	10 to 12
Oil filter adaptor bolt	16 to 21	12 to 15
Flywheel	78 to 88	58 to 65
Driveplate (automatic transmission)	93 to 103	69 to 76
Jackshaft pulley	9 to 12	7 to 9
Belt tensioner locknut	16 to 21	12 to 15
Sump	6.3 to 8.3	4.6 to 6.1
Oil drain plug	29 to 39	21 to 29
Oil strainer	8.4 to 10.8	6.2 to 8.0
Connecting rod nuts	31 to 37	23 to 27
Main bearing cap	49 to 59	36 to 44
Rocker covers:		
1st	2.0 to 4.0	1.5 to 2.9
2nd	4.0 to 6.0	3.0 to 4.4
Rocker shaft bolt	18 to 21	13 to 15
Rocker arm locknut	16 to 21	12 to 15
Cylinder head front cover	5.1 to 6.5	3.8 to 4.8
Camshaft pulley	9 to 12	7 to 9
Cylinder head bolts (cold):		
Stage 1	29	21
Stage 2	69	51
Stage 3	Completely loosen all bolts	
Stage 4	29	21
Stage 5 (or angle tighten – see Section 6)	69 to 74	51 to 55
Spark plugs	20 to 29	15 to 21

Engine and transmission mountings – see Fig. 1.34
Engine-to-transmission bolts – see Fig. 6.4 (in Chapter 6)

1 General description

The engine is of four-cylinder, in-line overhead camshaft type.

The cylinder block is of cast iron construction while the cylinder head, which is of cross-flow design, is made of light alloy.

A five bearing crankshaft is used.

The camshaft runs in bearings which are machined directly into the cylinder head.

Valve clearances are adjusted in the conventional way by means of a screw and locknut on the rocker arms.

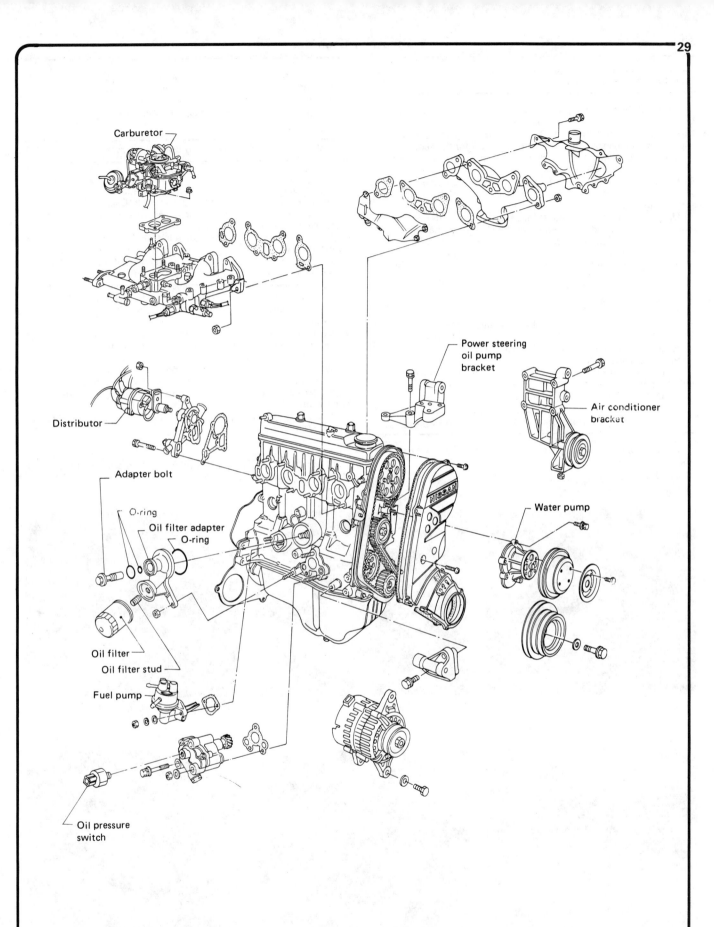

Fig. 1.1 General view of the engine and its associated components (Sec 1)

2 Routine maintenance

Carry out the following procedures at the intervals given in *Routine Maintenance* at the start of this manual.
1   Check the engine oil level. Do this by withdrawing the dipstick, wiping it clean, reinserting it and withdrawing it for the second time.
2   The oil level should be between the L and H marks. Top up if necessary.
3   Change the engine oil and filter at the intervals specified.
4   The oil should be drained when hot by removing the oil filler cap and the sump drain plug. Use a large bowl to catch the oil (photo).
5   Using a suitable filter removal tool, unscrew the cartridge type oil filter which is located on the cylinder block just to the rear of the alternator (photo). Be prepared for some spillage of oil.
6   Wipe the filter mating face on the cylinder block clean and smear the rubber sealing ring of the new filter with a little oil. Screw on the filter hand-tight only.
7   Refit the sump drain plug.
8   Refill with the correct quantity and type of engine oil. Refit the oil filler cap (photo).
9   Check and if necessary adjust the valve clearances as described in Section 4.
10   Renew the timing belt at 60 000 mile (100 000 km) intervals, or within this distance if the engine is having a major overhaul.
11   Periodically check the crankcase ventilation hoses for condition and security.

3 Major operations possible without removing engine

The following operations may be carried our with the engine in position in the vehicle.

Removal and refitting of the cylinder head
Adjustment of the valve clearances
Removal and refitting of the timing belt
Removal and refitting of the oil pump
Removal and refitting of the sump
Renewal of piston rings and big-end bearings

4 Valve clearances – checking and adjustment

1   When this adjustment is being carried out at a routine servicing, the engine should be at normal operating temperature.
2   Remove the air cleaner unit as described in Chapter 3.
3   Unbolt and remove the rocker cover. Unscrew and remove the spark plugs (photos).
4   Prise free the plug from the access hole in the side shield under the right-hand wing and then locate a socket wrench and extension on the crankshaft pulley bolt (photo). Turn the crankshaft until No 1 piston (at timing belt end of the engine) is at TDC. This can be ascertained if a finger is placed over No 1 cylinder spark plug hole and the compression felt as it is being generated as the piston rises. The notch on the crankshaft pulley should be opposite the O mark on the timing scale (photo).
5   Using a feeler blade of specified thickness check that it is a stiff sliding fit between the end of the valve stem and the ball end of the rocker arm adjuster screw on valves 1, 2, 3 and 6 (Fig. 1.2).
6   Where the clearance is not as specified, release the rocker arm adjuster screw locknut and turn the screw. Once the correct clearance is established, tighten the locknut without allowing the adjuster screw to turn (photo).
7   Now set No 4 piston at TDC on its compression stroke and repeat the operations on valves, 4, 5, 7 and 8.
8   The valve clearances are the same for both intake and exhaust valves.
9   Check that the rocker cover gasket is in good order, refit the rocker cover, air cleaner and spark plugs.

2.4 Engine oil drain plug

2.5 Oil filter location

2.8 Topping-up the engine oil

4.3 Rocker cover retaining bolt

4.4A Pass socket and extension through access hole to turn engine over

4.4B Crankshaft pulley timing mark at TDC (0) position

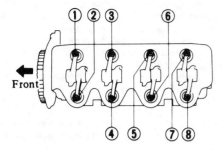

Fig. 1.2 Valve arrangement (Sec 4)

5 Timing belt – removal and refitting

The timing belt must be renewed at the intervals specified in Routine Maintenance. It is also advisable to renew it during an engine overhaul, irrespective of its age. If the drivebelt breaks during service the engine will be seriously damaged.

1 Disconnect the battery earth lead.

2 Detach the lower side and front dirt shields.

3 Loosen, but do not remove at this stage, the crankshaft pulley retaining bolt. Prevent the engine from turning by removing the starter motor and jamming the flywheel ring gear teeth or, on manual gearbox models, try putting the car in gear and get an assistant to apply the footbrake firmly (photo).

4 Remove the spark plugs, then turn the engine over and set it at TDC position with the No 1 cylinder on its firing stroke (see Section 4 for details). The engine can often be turned over using a 17 mm spanner on the alternator pulley bolt turned in the normal direction of engine rotation (clockwise when facing).

5 If fitted, remove the power steering pump drivebelt and, where applicable, the air conditioning system compressor drivebelt, as described in Chapter 2.

6 Remove the alternator drivebelt as described in Chapter 2.

7 Unclip the wiring harness from the alternator adjuster strap, then undo the strap retaining nut at the timing cover end, together with the two nuts shown (photo). Pivot the strap out of the way and remove the tandem washer and seals from the front of the timing case.

8 Unbolt and remove the water pump drive pulley (photo).

9 Position a jack under the engine and raise it to support the weight of the engine. Do not position the jack beneath the sump drain plug (Fig. 1.3). Protect the sump by interspacing a piece of flat wood between it and the jack.

10 Loosen the right-hand engine mounting bolts so that the mounting can be pivoted upwards to allow the upper timing cover to be removed.

11 Unscrew and remove the six bolts retaining the upper timing cover in position. All are Torx head type bolts and will therefore require a Torx socket (T30) to remove them. One of the bolts is longer than the rest so note its position when removing it. If a Torx socket is not readily available, an Allen key may suffice, but take care not to damage the bolt heads.

12 Remove the upper timing cover and the three hole spacer from the front of the cylinder head (photos).

13 Unscrew and remove the crankshaft pulley bolt and withdraw the pulley (photo).

14 Undo and remove the timing belt lower cover bolts then withdraw the cover (photo).

15 Release the nut on the timing belt tensioner pulley (photo). Using a screwdriver in the slot on the eccentric hub, turn the hub clockwise to release it from the belt, then tighten the nut again.

16 Note the rotational direction of the belt. Original belts are marked with an arrow. Unmarked belts should be marked. Remove the belt.

17 Do not turn the engine over when the timing belt is removed as the top of the pistons will hit the valves.

18 If required unbolt and remove the belt tensioner pulley and spring. Before refitting the timing belt, check that the timing positions of the crankshaft and camshaft have not been disturbed. They must be set as shown in Fig. 1.4. Note that there are two marks on the camshaft sprocket, and it is essential to ensure that the correct mark is used, depending on engine type. For E13 engines, the camshaft sprocket should be positioned with the locating dowel (knock pin) towards the

4.6 Adjusting a valve clearance

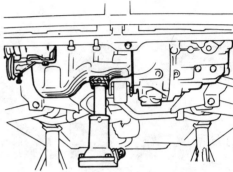

Fig. 1.3 Locate jack under engine at point shown (Sec 5)

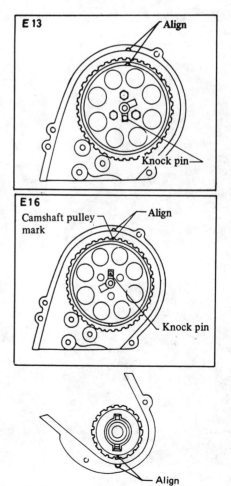

Fig. 1.4 Camshaft and crankshaft sprocket timing marks to align before refitting timing belt (Sec 5)

bottom of the sprocket. For E16 engines, the camshaft sprocket should be positioned with the locating dowel (knock pin) towards the top of the sprocket. Later models are fitted with a pressed camshaft sprocket, but the points mentioned above still apply. Ensure that the timing belt and the sprockets are clean and free of grease or oil.

19 If removed, fit the tensioner and its return spring. Turn the tensioner clockwise 70° to 80° and semi-tighten the locknut to temporarily secure the tensioner in position.

20 Locate the timing belt into position on the sprockets, but do not twist or bend it sharply when handling it. The rotation mark on the belt must face the direction of rotation. Keep the belt firmly in position on the camshaft and jackshaft sprockets (photos).

21 Loosen the tensioner locknut so that the tensioner can push against the timing belt, then turn the camshaft sprocket about 20° (2 teeth) clockwise.

22 Tighten the tensioner locknut to the specified torque wrench setting whilst preventing the tensioner from turning.

23 Relocate the outer crankshaft sprocket plate and bolt the upper and lower timing covers into position. Ensure that the three hole spacer is correctly located under the upper case (photo).

24 Refit the water pump pulley and the crankshaft pulley.

25 Lower and reconnect the right-hand engine mounting. Remove the jack from under the vehicle.

26 Refit the alternator adjuster strap, fit the three nuts and seals with tandem washer to the front face of the timing case.

27 Refit the alternator drivebelt and adjust its tension as described in Chapter 2.

28 Refit the power steering pump and air conditioning compressor drivebelts, and adjust the tensions (where applicable) as described in Chapter 2.

29 Refit the dirt shields.

30 Refit the spark plugs and reconnect their HT leads.

31 Check that all fastenings are secure. Reconnect the battery earth lead.

5.3 Crankshaft pulley and retaining bolt (shown with side shield removed)

5.7 Alternator strap and timing case retaining nuts

5.8 Remove the water pump drivebelt pulley

5.12A Remove the upper timing cover ...

5.12B ... and the three hole spacer

5.13 Crankshaft pulley removal

5.14 Lower timing cover retaining bolts removal

5.15 Releasing the timing belt tensioner

5.19 Timing belt tensioner and return spring

5.20A Timing belt rotation marks – E16 engine shown

5.20B Timing belt engaged on camshaft sprocket – keep timing marks (arrowed) in alignment (E16 engine shown)

5.20C Timing belt engaged on crankshaft sprocket – keep timing marks (arrowed) in alignment

5.23 Crankshaft sprocket outer plate washer location

6 Cylinder head – removal and refitting

1 Disconnect the battery earth lead.
2 Drain the engine coolant (Chapter 2).
3 Remove the air cleaner unit (Chapter 3).
4 Remove the rocker cover securing nuts and seal washers.
5 Remove the upper timing belt cover and disengage the drivebelt from the camshaft sprocket as described in Section 5.
6 Unbolt the camshaft sprocket, and remove the sprocket. The retaining bolt holes are asymmetric so there is no need to mark the sprocket fitted position.
7 Unbolt and remove the front cover from the front end of the cylinder head and camshaft. Note that the cover is secured by four bolts on the front face and one at the rear on the inlet side (photos).
8 Unbolt and detach the exhaust downpipe from the manifold. Disconnect the earth strap from the manifold/heat shield.
9 Unbolt and withdraw the combined distributor/thermostat housing from the rear end face of the cylinder head. The coolant hoses and ignition wires can be left attached to the housing. The housing may be stuck and prove difficult to remove, in which case lightly tap the

housing free using a soft-headed mallet, but take care not to damage the housing. If the thermostat and/or the distributor are to be removed separately from the housing, refer to Chapter 2 and/or 4 for their removal details.
10 Unbolt and withdraw the inlet manifold (complete with carburettor) from the cylinder head. A new cylinder head gasket will be needed when refitting, but by using this method the carburettor settings and connections remain unaltered. Alternatively, if preferred, the carburettor and inlet manifold can be removed with the cylinder head, in which case disconnect the throttle cable and wiring connections, the fuel supply and vacuum hoses (refer to Chapter 3 for details).
11 Remove the bolt from the intermediate bracket (located between the cylinder head and the block), and detach the bracket from the cylinder head.
12 The cylinder head retaining bolts can now be loosened and removed. Loosen them in three stages in the order shown in Fig. 1.5.
13 When all of the head bolts are loosened, check that the associated fittings are fully detached and are clear of the head, then carefully lift it clear. If the cylinder head is being removed with the inlet manifold attached, get an assistant to disconnect the wiring harness from the underside of the manifold as the head is lifted. The harness is secured

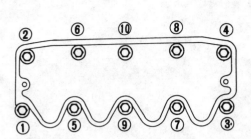

Fig. 1.5 Loosen cylinder head bolts in the numerical order shown (Sec 6)

to the manifold by metal clips which can be prised free.

14 Cleaning and servicing the cylinder head is described in Section 17.

15 Before refitting the cylinder head, make quite sure that the mating surfaces of the cylinder head are clean and free from carbon and old pieces of gasket.

16 Mop out the oil from the cylinder bolt holes in the block, clean the bolt hole threads and oil lightly.

17 If the rocker gear is fitted, release each rocker arm adjuster screw locknut and unscrew the screws a few turns.

18 Turn the crankshaft, by means of the pulley bolt until the timing mark on the crankshaft sprocket is at its lowest point, or the crankshaft pulley mark is aligned.

19 With reference to Section 5, paragraph 18, and Fig. 1.4, turn the camshaft sprocket until the timing marks are in alignment. This will eliminate the possibility of the valves hitting the pistons when the cylinder head is lowered onto the block.

20 Place a new gasket on top of the cylinder block (photo).

21 Lower the cylinder head carefully onto the block (photo).

22 Check that the flat washers are fitted on the cylinder head bolts (one per bolt). Three lengths of bolt are fitted and they must be located as indicated in Fig. 1.6 Tighten the bolts initially by hand so that they are finger tight.

23 Now tighten the bolts in the sequence shown in Fig. 1.7, in five stages to the specified torque wrench settings (see Specifications) (photo). Note that if an angle gauge wrench is available, the fifth tightening can be made as indicated in Fig. 1.8 (photo).

24 If they were removed from the cylinder head, reconnect the inlet and exhaust manifolds (using new gaskets) as described in Chapter 3.

25 Refit the camshaft, front cover and rocker gear to the cylinder head, but do not adjust the valves at this stage. Refer to Section 17, paragraphs 27 to 34 inclusive.

26 Refit the camshaft sprocket (if not already fitted).

27 Refit the timing belt and adjust its tension, then refit the timing belt covers. Refer to Section 5.

28 Adjust the valve clearances, as described in Section 4, then refit the rocker cover using new seals.

29 If removed, refit the distributor and thermostat housing to the rear face of the cylinder head. Ensure that the mating faces are clean and locate a new gasket (photo).

30 Refit the distributor (Chapter 4) and/or the thermostat (Chapter 2).

31 Refit the alternator adjuster link.

32 Refit the drivebelts, tensioning them as described in Chapter 2.

33 Refit the hot air collector to the exhaust manifold. This is held by two manifold bolts.

34 Refit the spark plugs and refit the ignition HT and LT leads (Chapter 4).

35 Refit the carburettor and/or the air cleaner unit and reconnect the throttle cable wiring, fuel lines and fuel supply hose with reference to Chapter 3.

36 Reconnect the battery (Chapter 12).

37 Refill the cooling system (Chapter 2).

38 Check and top up the engine oil level if necessary.

39 When the engine is restarted, run it at a fast idle speed to warm it up to its normal running temperature. The valve clearances must then be

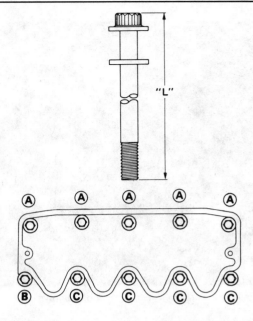

Fig. 1.6 Cylinder head bolt lengths and their locations (Sec 6)

A   L = 95 mm (3.74 in)
B   L = 110 mm (4.33 in)
C   L = 80 mm (3.15 in)

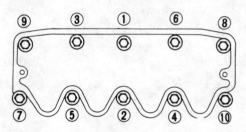

Fig. 1.7 Tighten cylinder head bolts in numerical order shown (Sec 6)

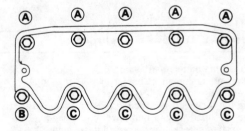

Fig. 1.8 Fifth stage angle tightening of bolts (Sec 6)

A   45 to 50°
B   55 to 60°
C   40 to 45°

rechecked and further adjustments made as necessary. Any adjustments to the carburettor and/or the ignition timing which may be required can then be made with reference to Chapters 3 and 4 respectively.

6.7A Undo the four retaining bolts at the front ...

6.7B ... and the bracket bolt at the rear ...

6.7C ... then remove the front cover

6.20 Locate the new cylinder head gasket

6.21 Lower the cylinder head into position

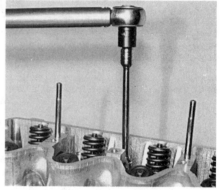

6.23A Tightening the cylinder head bolts to their specified torque settings

6.23B Tightening the cylinder head bolts to their Stage 5 tightening using an angle gauge

6.29 Refitting the distributor/thermostat housing

7.1 Oil pump and oil pressure switch

7 Oil pump – removal and refitting

1 The oil pump is located adjacent to the oil filter, beneath the alternator (photo). Removal of the alternator gives improved access.
2 Pull the lead from the oil pressure switch.
3 Unbolt and remove the oil pump.
4 If the pump is to be checked for wear, refer to Examination and Renovation (Section 18).
5 Refitting is a reversal of removal, use a new gasket and clean the mating faces.
6 If the alternator was removed, refit it and adjust the drivebelt as described in Chapter 2.

8 Sump pan – removal and refitting

1 Drain the engine oil into a suitable container for disposal.
2 Raise and support the vehicle on axle stands at the front end.
3 Unbolt and remove the central support member located under the sump and attached at each end to the underbody.
4 Unbolt the reinforcement strut from the rear corner of the sump and transmission (photos).
5 Disconnect the exhaust downpipe from the manifold and release the exhaust pipe front mounting.
6 Unscrew and remove the sump pan bolts and nuts (photo). The nut nearest the transmission is very inaccessible and will require the use of

a universally-jointed drive extension and socket to remove it.

7　To remove the sump pan, prise and tap it free from the cylinder block.

8　Use a suitable hand scraper to remove all traces of gasket sealant from the mating faces of sump and block (Fig. 1.9).

9　Before refitting the sump, apply an even bead of sealant (of the specified Nissan type: Fluid gasket 1207C) around the mating face of the sump as shown (Fig. 1.10 and photo). Run the bead of sealant in the groove and round the outside of the retaining bolt holes. The bead should be continuous and between 3.5 and 4.5 mm (0.138 and 0.177 in) wide.

10　Relocate the sump pan, insert the retaining bolts and nuts and tighten to the specified torque wrench setting in a progressive and even manner. Refit the drain plug.

11　Reconnect the reinforcement strut.

12　Reconnect the exhaust downpipe.

13　Refit the central support member.

14　A period of 30 minutes must have elapsed from when the sump was refitted before topping up the engine oil level and restarting the vehicle. This is to allow the sealant to set fully.

15　When the engine is restarted, run it up to its normal operating temperature and check around the sump for any signs of oil leakage.

9　Piston rings and big-end bearing shells – renewal

1　The renewal of piston rings or substitution with special proprietary rings may be decided upon as a means of reducing heavy oil consumption without incurring the heavy cost of reboring and new oversize pistons.

2　Remove the cylinder head and sump pan, as described in earlier Sections.

3　Note that the connecting rod big-end caps are numbered with matching numbers on adjacent machined surfaces on the connecting rod. Note to which side of the crankcase the numbers face; usually towards the jackshaft.

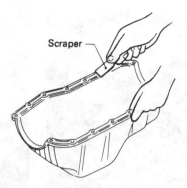

Fig. 1.9 Remove all traces of old sealant from the mating surfaces (Sec 8)

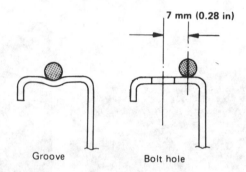

Fig. 1.10 Sump pan sealant bead location (Sec 8)

8.4A Reinforcement strut upper fixing

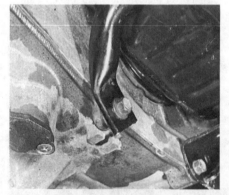

8.4B Reinforcement strut lower fixing

8.6 Sump pan bolt and nut at timing case end

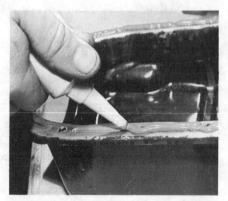

8.9 Applying the sealant bead to the sump pan mating face

9.9 Checking a piston ring groove clearance

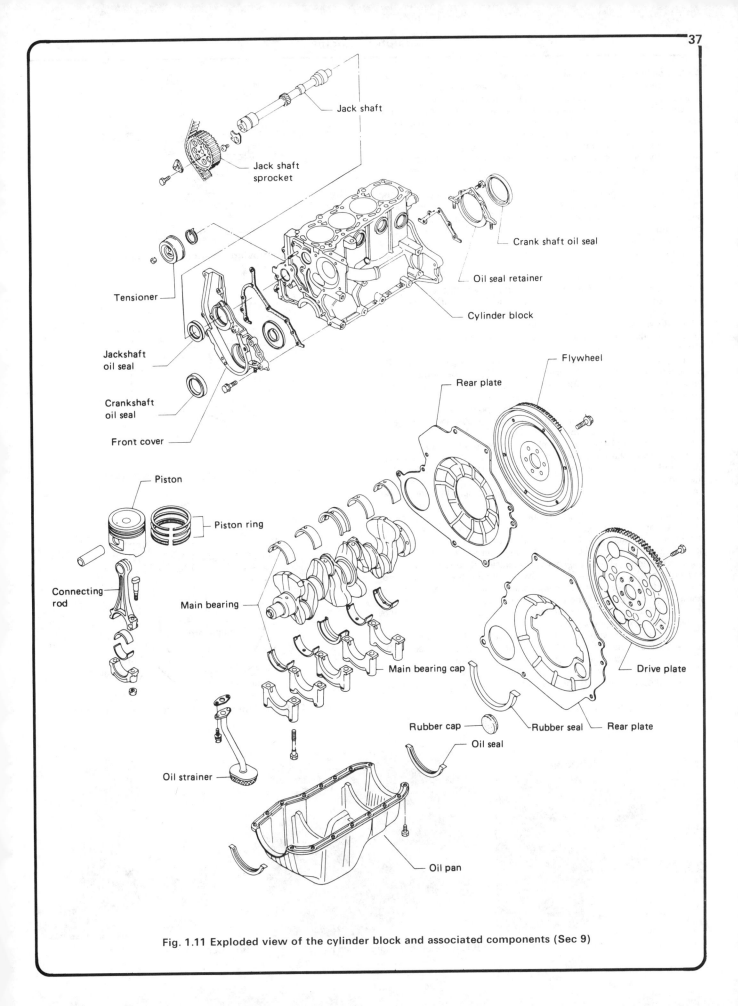

Fig. 1.11 Exploded view of the cylinder block and associated components (Sec 9)

4   Unbolt and remove the oil pick-up pipe from within the crankcase.

5   Unscrew the big-end cap bolts and remove the caps. If the cap shell bearings are to be used again, tape them to their caps.

6   Using the wooden handle of a hammer, applied to the big-end of each connecting rod push the piston/rod assemblies out of the top of the cylinder block. If the cylinder bores are severely worn, and a wear ring can be felt at the top of the bores, the wear rings may have to be reduced by careful scraping before the pistons rings will ride over it. Retain the bearing shells with their respective rods if they are to be used again (Fig. 1.12).

7   To remove the piston rings, slide three old feeler blades behind the top ring and position them at equidistant points. The ring can now be slid upwards off the piston using a twisting motion. Repeat on the remaining rings.

8   Clean the piston ring grooves completely free from carbon and other deposits. A piece of old piston ring makes an ideal tool for the purpose.

9   Check that the rings supplied have the correct groove clearance (photo) and end gap (see Specifications). Check the end gap by pushing the ring a little way down the cylinder bore, set it squarely and use a feeler blade to check the gap.

10 Fit the rings to the piston by reversing the removal operations. The rings are marked on their top surfaces. The top compression ring has a chamfer on both edges (Fig. 1.13).

11 If new rings are fitted then, to ensure rapid bedding in, the cylinder bores must have their hard glaze removed. This can be done using a rotary abrasive flap wheel. Alternatively, use fine glasspaper, rubbing it up and down at approximately 45° to the bore.

12 Stagger the piston ring gaps at equidistant points of a circle, oil the rings liberally and fit a piston ring compressor. These are available at most accessory stores. Oil the cylinder bores (Fig. 1.14).

13 Insert the first piston/rod assembly into its original bore so that the bottom edge of the compressor rests on the top face of the cylinder block and the mark on the piston crown is facing the timing belt end of the engine (photos).

14 Again applying the wooden handle of a hammer, this time to the piston crown, push the piston rod assembly into the cylinder bore. The ring compressor will be released. Repeat on the remaining pistons.

15 Draw the connecting rod of the first piston down to connect with the crankshaft crankpin. Make sure that the crankpins have been liberally oiled and the bearing shells are returned to their original positions (photo). Unless the shells are in excellent condition, without any signs of the copper underlay showing through the white bearing material, they should be renewed with ones of identical size. The size is stamped on the back of the shell. Standard shells are unmarked or stamped STD or 0-00. If not standard it will be stamped with the undersize, for example 0.25 mm.

16 Fit the big-end with its shell so that the matching numbers are adjacent (photo) and towards the jackshaft (or as noted on removal).

17 Insert and tighten the cap bolts to the specified torque (photo).

18 Repeat on the remaining three piston/rod assemblies.

19 Refit the cylinder head and the sump pan, as described in earlier Sections.

20 Refill the engine with oil and coolant.

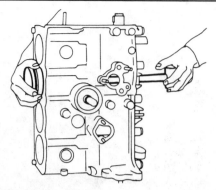

Fig. 1.12 Removing a piston/connecting rod (Sec 9)

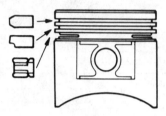

Fig. 1.13 Piston ring arrangement (Sec 9)

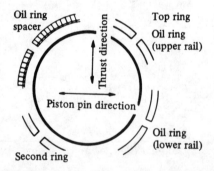

Fig. 1.14 Piston ring and gap setting diagram (Sec 9)

9.13A Piston ring clamp

9.13B Piston crown front marking (arrowed)

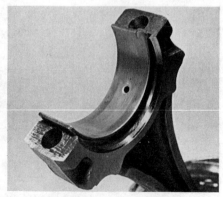

9.15 Connecting rod shell bearing

9.16 Connecting rod and cap markings

9.17 Tightening a big-end cap nut

10 Engine removal – method

The engine should be removed from the vehicle as a unit, complete with transmission. The help of an assistant will definitely be required.

A suitable lifting sling and hoist will be required, preferably one with a lock mechanism to hold the units in suspension if required when removing and refitting.

The engine and transmission units are removed upwards out of the engine compartment.

For vehicles with air conditioning

If components of the air conditioning system obstruct the overhaul of the engine and cannot be moved sufficiently within the limits of their flexible hoses to avoid such obstruction, the system should be discharged by your dealer or a competent refrigeration engineer.

As the system must be completely evacuated before recharging, the necessary vacuum equipment to do this is only likely to be held by your dealer.

The refrigerant fluid is Freon 12 and, although harmless under normal conditions, contact with eyes or skin must be avoided. If Freon comes into contact with a naked flame a poisonous gas is created which is injurious to health.

11 Engine and manual transmission – removal and separation

1   Disconnect the battery earth lead. Although not essential, it is advisable to remove the battery to avoid the possibility of damaging it during engine removal.
2   Drain the engine coolant (Chapter 2).
3   Unscrew the sump drain plug and drain the old oil into a suitable container for disposal.
4   Remove the air cleaner unit and disconnect the throttle cable from the carburettor. Also detach the wiring and hoses from the carburettor and inlet manifold. Refer to Chapter 3 for details.
5   Unbolt and remove the exhaust downpipe from the manifold. Disconnect the earth wire from the manifold.
6   If power steering is fitted, unbolt the pump, disengage and remove the drivebelt, then move the pump out of the way (Chapter 10).
7   If air conditioning is fitted, unbolt the compressor and the drivebelt idler pulley and move them to one side. **Do not disconnect the refrigerant pipelines**.
8   Undo the retaining clips and detach the coolant hoses from the radiator, and also the two heater hoses at the engine bulkhead (see Chapter 2).
9   Disconnect the ignition HT and LT leads from the ignition coil, or if preferred, remove the ignition distributor complete with leads from the rear of the cylinder head (Chapter 4).

10   Disconnect the oil pressure sender and temperature sensor wires from the engine. Note their colours and connections and move them out of the way.
11   Unbolt and disconnect the control and support rods at the transmission (photo).
12   Disconnect the speedometer at the transmission.
13   Loosen the front roadwheel bolts and then raise the car at the front end and support on axle stands. Remove the front roadwheels.
14   Detach and remove the undertray and sideshields, the latter being accessible under the right-hand wheel arch (photo).
15   Disconnect the starter motor leads.
16   Unbolt and remove the central support member (photos).
17   Disconnect the alternator leads.
18   Disconnect the earth strap from the gearbox.
19   Disconnect the reversing light lead at the in-line connector (above the gearbox).
20   Loosen the clutch cable adjuster and unhook the cable from the clutch lever.
21   Connect the lift hoist to the engine and raise it just enough to take the weight. Check that the lift height and angle are as required.
22   The driveshafts must now be detached from the transmission, but unless complete removal is required, they can be left attached to the wheel hubs. First detach the tie-rod end balljoint from the steering knuckle as described in Chapter 10.
23   Loosen the suspension arm-to-steering knuckle balljoint nut, then using a suitable metal bar, lever downwards between the suspension arm and the stabilizer bar, whilst simultaneously hitting the joint with a suitable mallet to separate it. When the joint separates, continue levering down on the suspension arm and unscrew the retaining nut. Separate the joint from the arm.
24   Using a suitable screwdriver as a lever, carefully prise the driveshaft inner end joint from the transmission. Get an assistant to pull the knuckle/strut unit outward as the driveshaft is levered free from the transmission. When the shaft is separated from the transmission, it can be lowered out of the way.
25   Repeat the procedure and remove the opposing driveshaft from the transmission.
26   Undo the mounting attachment bolts and release the engine and transmission at the points shown (photos).
27   Check that the engine and transmission are fully disconnected and that all components, wires and cables are out of the way.
28   Lift the engine/transmission up and out of the engine compartment (photo). Take care not to damage adjacent components of the wing surface.
29   With the unit removed, clean away external dirt using a water soluble solvent or paraffin, and a stiff brush.
30   To separate the engine from the transmission, unbolt and remove the starter motor and then withdraw the bolts which connect the clutch bellhousing to the engine. Note that some of these bolts retain the upper coolant tube, the sump pan-to-bellhousing reinforcement tube and the transmission mounting brackets. Mark their positions for

11.11 Detach the gear control and support rods

11.14 Unbolt and remove the undertrays (arrowed)

11.16A Unbolt the central support bolts at the front ...

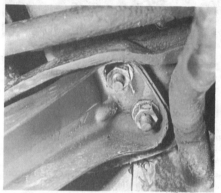

11.16B ... and nuts at the rear

11.26A Right-hand engine mounting

11.26B Left-hand mounting to transmission (manual gearbox shown)

11.26C Front engine mounting

11.26D Rear engine mounting

11.28 Engine and manual transmission removal

11.30 Upper engine-to-transmission fixing bolts also secure the coolant pipe

11.31 Transmission withdrawn from engine

ease of refitting (photo).

31 Support the weight of the transmission and then withdraw it in a straight line from the engine (photo).

12 Engine and automatic transmission – removal and separation

1 The operations for removal are very similar to those described for vehicles with manual transmission in the preceding Section but observe the following differences. Refer also to Chapter 7 and 8 as necessary.

2 Ignore any reference to the clutch cable.

3 Disconnect the speed selector cable from the transmission, also the inhibitor switch leads.

4 Disconnect and plug the oil cooler hoses.

5 When disengaging the driveshafts from the automatic transmission, the procedure is similar to that described for the manual transmission type, but remove the right-hand driveshaft first, then the left-hand shaft. The left-hand driveshaft is removed by driving it out of the transmission from the right-side using a suitable screwdriver or rod drift inserted through the right-hand driveshaft aperture (see Chapter 8). Take care not to damage the pinion mate shaft and side gear when driving out the shaft.

6 To separate the engine from the automatic transmission first unbolt and remove the starter motor. Also disconnect the kickdown cable.

7 Mark the relationship of the torque converter to the driveplate using a dab of quick-drying paint.

8 Unscrew the torque converter-to-driveplate connecting bolts. The crankshaft will have to be turned to bring each bolt into view in the cut-out in the torque converter housing before a spanner or socket wrench can be used. Remove the engine-to-transmission connecting bolts.

9 Withdraw the automatic transmission, at the same time have an assistant hold the torque converter in full engagement with the oil pump driveshaft to avoid loss of transmission fluid.

13 Engine dismantling – general

1 Before commencing a major engine overhaul, make sure that you have gathered together clean rags, brushes, freeing fluid and a good selection of tools – including a torque wrench.

2 A number of clean tins or other containers is useful to keep the various nuts and bolts safely. Mark the tins as a guide to where the fixings belong.

3 Have a pencil and paper handy to record sequences of assembly of small items, or to sketch an item which may present difficulty at reassembly or refitting.

4 Obtain all the necessary gaskets and oil seals in advance.

5 If it is known that only one component of the engine is worn or damaged the dismantling operations should only be pursued as far as is necessary to rectify the problem, the engine need not be completely dismantled.

14 Engine – complete dismantling

1 Place the engine in an upright position on the bench, or on a sheet of hardboard on the floor.

2 First remove any ancillary components such as the alternator (Chapter 12), distributor (Chapter 4), fuel pump (Chapter 3), manifolds (Chapter 3) and clutch assembly (Chapter 5).

3 Unscrew and remove the oil filter. Be prepared for some loss of oil.

4 Remove the alternator mounting bracket and also those for the power steering pump and air conditioning compressor (where these are fitted).

5 Unbolt and remove the oil pump.

6 Unbolt and remove the distributor thermostat housing.

7 Unbolt and remove the coolant pump pulley and then the coolant pump.

8 Carefully turn the engine onto its side and remove the sump pan (Section 8).

9 Using a piece of wood inserted between the crankcase and one of

the crankshaft counterweights to prevent the crankshaft rotating, unscrew and remove the crankshaft pulley bolt and the pulley.

10 As the flywheel bolt holes are not offset, mark the relationship of the flywheel to the crankshaft hub. Unscrew the bolts and remove the flywheel. Take out the temporary wooden chock. Pull the engine endplate from the dowels.

11 Working at the timing belt end of the engine, remove the belt upper and lower covers. The cover screws (Torx type) are tight and may require the use of an impact driver.

12 Unbolt and remove the belt tensioner pulley.

13 Remove the timing belt, marking its rotational direction if it is to be used again (not recommended).

14 Unbolt and remove the sprocket from the jackshaft. Unbolt the triangular mounting block used for attaching the alternator adjuster link.

15 Remove the crankshaft sprocket and the timing belt guide disc. If it is tight use a three-legged puller, taking care not to damage the teeth.

16 Remove the rocker cover.

17 Unscrew and remove the cylinder head bolts and remove the cylinder head and gasket, as described in Section 6. Unbolt the timing belt lower backplate. Take the oil slinger from the end of the crankshaft.

18 Extract the securing screw and remove the jackshaft retaining plate. Withdraw the jackshaft.

19 From within the crankcase unbolt and remove the oil pick-up pipe and strainer.

20 Remove the piston/connecting rod assemblies, as described in Section 9.

21 Unbolt and remove the crankshaft rear oil seal retainer.

22 Unscrew the main bearing cap bolts, working from the end ones towards the centre (Fig. 1.15). The caps are numbered 1 to 5, number 1 being at the timing belt end of the engine, but the numbers are legible from the flywheel end of the engine.

23 Lift the crankshaft from the crankcase. Refit the bearing shells with their respective caps. Note that the centre shell incorporates thrust flanges to control endfloat.

24 The engine is now completely dismantled and all parts should be cleaned and examined, as described in Section 18.

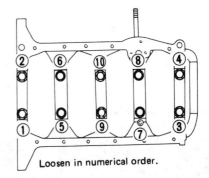

Loosen in numerical order.

Fig. 1.15 Remove the main bearing cap bolts in the sequence shown (Sec 14)

15 Lubrication system – general

1 The engine lubrication system depends upon oil contained in the sump pan being drawn into an externally mounted oil pump, which is driven from a gear on the jackshaft, and then pressurised to supply all the engine working parts.

2 Oil from the pump passes through an externally mounted full-flow disposable type oil filter.

3 An oil pressure regulator valve is incorporated in the oil pump and an oil pressure switch is located close to the filter which actuates a warning lamp if pressure loss occurs.

4 Intermittent flickering of the oil pressure warning lamp may occur when the engine is idling after a long high speed run. This should be ignored as long as the lamp goes out immediately the engine speed is increased.

5 A pressure relief valve is located in the oil filter mounting base

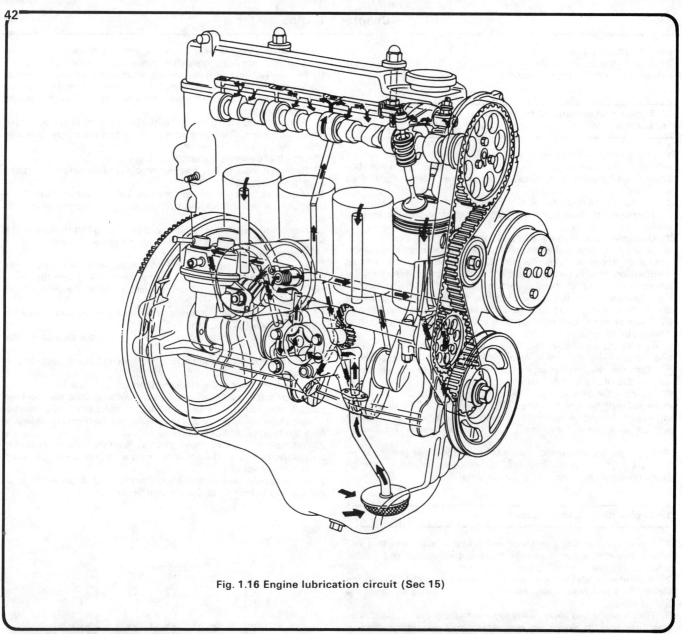

Fig. 1.16 Engine lubrication circuit (Sec 15)

15.5A Oil pressure relief valve location in the cylinder block ...

15.5B ... and the regulator valve and cap location in the filter housing (photos). Should it be seen to be cracked or broken when the oil filter is removed, the valve may be prised out with a screwdriver and a new one tapped into position. The purpose of this valve is to open and bypass the filter should the filter become clogged.

16 Positive crankcase ventilation system (PCV)

1 This is of positive, dual-line type which returns blow-by gas (which has passed the piston rings) from the crankcase to either the air cleaner or the intake manifold, according to manifold vacuum. According to engine load conditions a valve regulates the routing of the gas (Fig. 1.17).
2 Check the system connecting hoses regularly and clean them out.
3 To test the operation of the valve, have the engine idling and disconnect the hose from the side of the valve which is furthest from the intake manifold. Vacuum hiss should be heard coming from the open end of the valve and a strong suction felt if a finger is placed over it. If this is not so, renew the valve.

17 Cylinder head – dismantling, overhaul and reassembly

Cautionary note: *The cylinder head is of light alloy construction and special care must therefore be taken not to damage or mark it when working on it or its associated components.*
1 The manifolds and rocker cover should already have been removed as described in Section 6.
2 Progressively loosen the rocker pedestal bolts in two or three stages. Remove the bolts and lift the rocker assembly from the cylinder head. Identify which way round the assembly is located (also note the lockplates and caps fitted to 1, 3 and 5 bolts). Discard the caps after prising them off 1 and 5 bolts.
3 Unbolt and remove the camshaft pulley.
4 Unbolt and remove the cylinder head end cover (timing belt backplate). This retains the camshaft. Unscrew and remove the spark plugs.
5 Carefully withdraw the camshaft, taking care not to damage the bearings as the lobes pass through.
6 The valves and their associated components should now be removed. Owing to the depth of the cylinder head a valve spring compressor having a long reach will be required. If this is not available, temporarily refit the rocker shaft and then make up a lever with a fork at one end to compress the valve spring by using the underside of the rocker shaft as a fulcrum.
7 Compress the first valve spring, extract the split collets. If the valve spring refuses to compress, do not apply excessive force but remove the compressor and place a piece of tubing on the spring retainer and strike it a sharp blow to release the collets from the valve stem. Refit the compressor and resume operations.
8 Gently release the compressor, take off the spring retaining cap, the valve spring and the spring seat. Remove the valve. Keep the valve with its associated components together and in numbered sequence so that it can be refitted in its original position. A small box with divisions is useful for this purpose.
9 Remove the other valves in a similar way.
10 Use a blunt scraper or rotary wire brush to clean all traces of carbon deposits from the combustion spaces and the ports. The valve head stems and valve guides should also be freed from any carbon deposits. Wash the combustion spaces and ports down with a suitable solvent and scrape the cylinder head surface free of any foreign matter with the side of a steel rule, or a similar article.
11 If the engine is installed in the car, clean the pistons and the top of the cylinder bores. If the pistons are still in the block, then it is essential that great care is taken to ensure that no carbon gets into the cylinder bores as this could scratch the cylinder walls or cause damage to the piston and rings. To ensure this does not happen, first turn the crankshaft so that two of the pistons are at the top of their bores. Stuff rag into the other two bores or seal them off with paper and masking tape. The waterways should also be covered with small pieces of masking tape to prevent particles of carbon entering the cooling system and damaging the coolant pump.
12 Press a little grease into the gap between the cylinder walls and the two pistons which are to be worked on. With a blunt scraper carefully

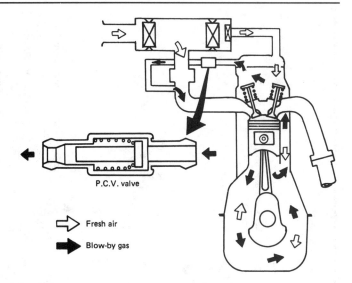

Fig. 1.17 Crankcase ventilation system (PCV) (Sec 16)

Fresh air

Blow-by gas

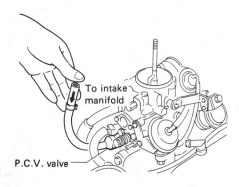

Fig. 1.18 Checking the PCV valve (Sec 16)

scrape away the carbon from the piston crown, taking great care not to scratch the aluminium. Also scrape away the carbon from the surrounding lip of the cylinder wall. When all carbon has been removed, scrape away the grease which will now be contaminated with carbon particles, taking care not to press any into the bores. To assist prevention of carbon build-up the piston crown can be polished with a metal polish. Remove the rags or masking tape from the other two cylinders and turn the crankshaft so that the two pistons which were at the bottom are now at the top. Place rag in the cylinders which have been decarbonised, and proceed as just described.
13 Examine the head of the valves for pitting and burning, especially the heads of the exhaust valves. The valve seatings should be examined at the same time. If the pitting on the valve and seat is very slight, the marks can be removed by grinding the seats and valves together with coarse, and then fine valve grinding paste.
14 Where bad pitting has occurred to the valve seats it will be necessary to recut them and fit new valves. This latter job should be entrusted to the local agent or engineering works. In practice it is very seldom that the seats are so badly worn. Normally it is the valve that is too badly worn for refitting, and the owner can easily purchase a new set of valves and match them to the seats by valve grinding.
15 Test the valves in their guides for side-to-side rock. If this is any more than almost imperceptible new guides must be fitted. This, as with valve seat renewal, is really a job for your dealer as the cylinder head must be warmed and the old guide driven out. New guides should be pressed in to protrude 15.0 mm (0.59 in) above the cylinder head and then reamed using a 7.005 to 7.020 mm (0.2758 to 0.2764 in) reamer (Figs. 1.20, 1.21 and 1.22).
16 The cylinder head can be checked for warping either by placing it on a piece of plate glass or using a straight-edge and feeler blades. If there is any doubt or if its block face is corroded, have it re-faced by your dealer or motor engineering works (Fig. 1.23).

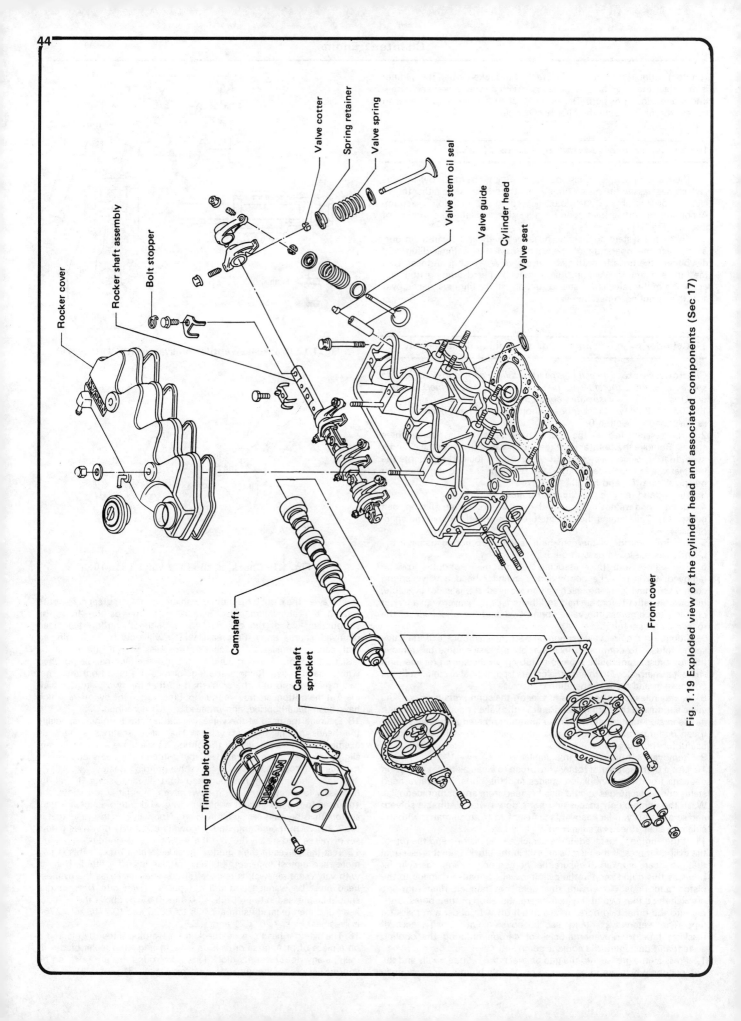

Valve cotter

Spring retainer

Valve spring

Valve stem oil seal

Valve guide

Cylinder head

Valve seat

Rocker cover

Rocker shaft assembly

Bolt stopper

Camshaft

Camshaft sprocket

Timing belt cover

Front cover

Fig. 1.19 Exploded view of the cylinder head and associated components (Sec 17)

Fig. 1.20 Checking the valves in their guides for excessive side play (Sec 17)

Fig. 1.21 Removing a valve guide (Sec 17)

Fig. 1.22 Valve guide projection from cylinder head (Sec 17)

14.7 - 15.3 mm (0.579 - 0.602 in)

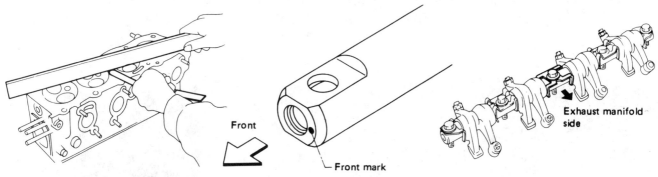

Fig. 1.23 Check the cylinder head surfaces for warping (Sec 17)

Front

Front mark

Fig. 1.24 Rocker shaft orientation punch mark (Sec 17)

Exhaust manifold side

Fig. 1.25 Cut-out in centre retainer must face towards the exhaust side (Sec 17)

17 Valve grinding is carried out as follows. Smear a trace of coarse carborundum paste on the seat face and apply a suction grinding tool to the valve head. With a semi-rotary motion, grind the valve head to its seat, lifting the valve occasionally to redistribute the grinding paste. When a dull matt even surface is produced on both the valve seat and the valve, wipe off the paste and repeat the process with fine carborundum paste, lifting and turning the valve to redistribute the paste as before. A light spring placed under the valve head will greatly ease this operation. When a smooth unbroken ring of light grey matt finish is produced on both valve and valve seat faces, the grinding operation is complete. Carefully clean away every trace of grinding compound, take great care to leave none in the ports or in the valve guides. Clean the valves and valve seats with a solvent-soaked rag, then with a clean rag, and finally, if an air line is available, blow the valves, valve guides and valve ports clean.

18 Check that all valve springs are intact. If any one is broken, all should be renewed. Check the free height of the springs against new ones. If some springs are not within specifications, replace them all. Springs suffer from fatigue and it is a good idea to renew them even if they look serviceable.

19 Check that the oil supply holes in the rocker arms are clear.

20 Renew the valve stem oil seals (photo).

21 Commence reassembly by oiling the stem of the first valve and pushing it into its guide (photo).

22 Fit the spring seat (photo), the valve spring (photo) and the spring cap (photo). The closer coils of the valve spring must be towards the cylinder head.

23 Compress the valve spring and locate the split collets in the valve stem cut-outs (photo).

24 Gently release the compressor, checking to see that the collets are not displaced.

25 Fit the remaining valves in the same way.

26 Tap the end of each valve stem with a plastic or copper-faced hammer to settle the components.

27 Lubricate the camshaft bearings and insert the camshaft into the cylinder head (photo).

28 Fit the cylinder head end cover to the timing belt end of the cylinder head, complete with new oil seal and new gasket (photo).

29 Bolt on the camshaft sprocket. The bolt holes are offset so it will only go on one way.

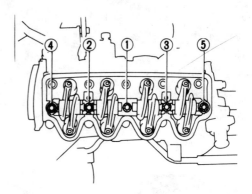

Fig. 1.26 Tightening sequence for rocker shaft bolts (Sec 17)

30 Before refitting the rocker gear, check the shaft for wear and the rocker arms for general condition (photo). Renew any worn components, but make sure when reassembling that they are kept in their original order.

31 Refit the rocker shaft, ensuring that it is correctly orientated. The punch mark in the end face of the shaft is towards the front of the engine and on its side as shown (Fig. 1.24), the oil holes in the shaft must face downwards and the cut-out in the centre retainer must be towards the exhaust manifold side (Fig. 1.25).

32 With the rocker arm adjuster screws fully released, bolt the rocker gear to the cylinder head.

33 The rocker shaft fixing bolts incorporate lockplates to eliminate the possibility of their working loose (photo). Always fit new lock caps to the end bolts (1 and 5) by tapping on using a suitable socket.

34 Tighten the rocker shaft assembly fixing bolts in a progressive sequence (two or three stages) to the specified torque wrench setting in the numerical sequence shown in Fig. 1.26.

35 Adjust the valve clearances as described in Section 4.

17.20 Valve oil seal on the guide

17.21 Fitting a valve into its guide

17.22A Valve spring seat

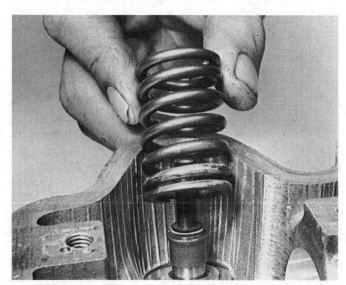

17.22B Valve spring

17.22C Valve spring cap

17.23 Compress valve spring and locate collets

17.27 Insert the camshaft into the cylinder head

17.28 Locate the new cylinder head front cover gasket

17.30 Rocker arms and shaft showing contact faces and oil holes

17.33 Tightening a rocker gear bolt

18 Engine components – examination and renovation

Cylinder block and crankcase

1 Examine the castings carefully for cracks, especially around the bolt holes and between cylinders.

2 The cylinder bores must be checked for taper, ovality, scoring and scratching. Start by examining the top of the cylinder bores. If they are at all worn, a ridge will be felt on the thrust side. This ridge marks the top of piston travel. The owner will have a good indication of bore wear prior to dismantling by the quantity of oil consumed and the emission of blue smoke from the exhaust, especially when the engine is cold.

3 An internal micrometer or dial gauge can be used to check bore wear and taper against Specifications, but this is a pointless operation if the engine is obviously in need of reboring – indicated by excessive oil consumption.

4 Your engine reconditioner will be able to rebore the block for you and supply the correct oversize pistons to give the correct running clearance.

5 If the engine has reached the limit for reboring, cylinder liners can be fitted, but here again this is a job for your engine reconditioner.

6 To rectify minor bore wear it is possible to fit proprietary oil control rings, as described in Section 9. A good way to test the condition of the

engine is to have it at normal operating temperature with the spark plugs removed. Screw a compression tester (available from most motor accessory stores) into the first plug hole. Hold the accelerator fully depressed and crank the engine on the starter motor for several revolutions. Record the reading. Zero the tester and check the remaining cylinders in the same way. All four compression figures should be approximately equal and within the tolerance given in Specifications. If they are all low, suspect piston ring or cylinder bore wear. If only one reading is down, suspect a valve not seating.

Crankshaft and bearings

7 Examine the surfaces of the crankpins and journals for signs of scoring or scratching, and check for ovality or taper. If a crankpin or journals are not within the dimensional tolerances given in the Specifications Section at the beginning of this Chapter the crankshaft will have to be reground.

8 Wear in a crankshaft can be detected while the engine is running. Big-end bearing and crankpin wear is indicated by distinct metallic knocking, particularly noticeable when the engine is pulling from low engine speeds. Low oil pressure will also occur.

9 Main bearing and journal wear is indicated by engine rumble increasing in severity as the engine speed increases. Low oil pressure will again be an associated condition.

10 Crankshaft grinding should be carried out by specialist engine reconditioners who will supply the matching undersize bearing shells to give the required running clearance.

11 Inspect the connecting rod big-end and main bearing shells for signs of general wear, scoring, pitting and scratching. The bearings should be matt grey in colour. If a copper colour is evident, then the bearings are badly worn and the surface material has worn away to expose the underlay. Renew the bearings as a complete set.

12 At the time of major overhaul it is worthwhile renewing the bearing shells as a matter of routine even if they appear to be in reasonably good condition.

13 Bearing shells can be identified by the marking on the back of the shell. Standard sized shells are usually marked STD or 0.00. Undersized shells are marked with the undersize, such as 0.25 mm.

Connecting rods

14 Check the alignment of the connecting rods. If you suspect distortion, have them checked by your dealer or engine reconditioner on the special jig which he will have.

15 The gudgeon pin is an interference fit in the connecting rod small-end and removal or refitting and changing a piston is a job best left to your dealer or engine reconditioner due to the need for a press and jig.

Pistons and piston rings

16 If the engine is rebored then new oversize pistons with rings and gudgeon pins will be supplied. Have the supplier fit the pistons to the rods so that the oil hole in the connecting rod is located as shown with reference to the front facing mark on the piston crown (Fig. 1.27).

17 Removal and refitting of piston rings is covered in Section 9.

Flywheel

18 Check the clutch mating surface of the flywheel. If it is deeply scored (due to failure to renew a worn driven plate) then it should be renewed. Slight roughness may be smoothed with fine emery cloth.

19 If lots of tiny cracks are visible on the surface of the flywheel this will be due to overheating caused by slipping the clutch or 'riding' the clutch pedal.

20 With a pre-engaged type of starter motor it is rare to find the teeth of the flywheel ring gear damaged or worn, but if they are the ring gear will have to be renewed.

21 To remove the ring gear, drill a hole between the roots of two teeth, taking care not to damage the flywheel, and then split the ring with a sharp cold chisel.

22 The new ring gear must be heated to between 180 and 220°C (356 and 428°F) which is very hot, so if you do not have facilities for obtaining these temperatures, leave the job to your dealer or engine reconditioner.

Driveplate (automatic transmission)

23 Should the starter ring gear on the driveplate require renewal, the driveplate should be renewed complete.

Camshaft

24 Examine the camshaft bearings for wear, scoring or pitting. If evident then the complete cylinder head will have to be renewed as the bearings are machined directly in it.

25 The camshaft itself should show no marks or scoring on the journal or cam lobe surfaces. Where marks are evident, renew the camshaft or have it reprofiled by a specialist reconditioner.

26 Check the teeth of the camshaft sprocket for wear, and the sprocket for excessive run-out. Renew the sprocket if necessary.

Timing belt tensioner

27 It is recommended that the belt is renewed at the specified intervals, or during any engine overhaul.

28 The tensioner should not be noisy or shaky when turned, and have good spring action. Where these conditions are not met with, renew the tensioner complete (photo).

Jackshaft

29 The jackshaft journals should be smooth – without scoring or scratches. Wear can be checked using a micrometer.

30 The bearings are renewable, but make sure that the lubrication

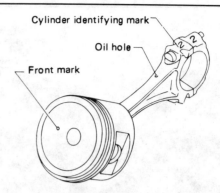

Fig. 1.27 Connecting rod/piston alignment (Sec 18)

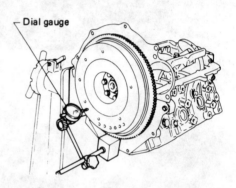

Fig. 1.28 Check the flywheel run-out (Sec 18)

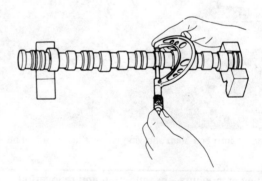

Fig. 1.29 Check the camshaft bearings for wear (Sec 18)

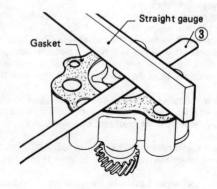

Fig. 1.30 Oil pump side clearance check with feeler gauge (3) (Sec 18)

holes line up with those in the crankcase as the new bearings are pressed in.

31 When refitting the jack shaft end plug (removed to extract the bearings) coat the edges with a suitable sealant.

Oil pump

32 To dismantle the oil pump, remove the cover screws and take off the cover.

33 Lift out the outer rotor (photo). The inner rotor with drivegear cannot be separated from the pump casing.

34 Clean and dry the pump components and refit the outer rotor. Using a feeler blade check the inner-to-outer rotor tip clearance (photo), the outer rotor-to-pump body clearance (photo), and the rotor side clearance (Fig. 1.30).

35 If, after these checks, the pump proves to be worn, renew it.

36 The pressure regulator components are seldom found to be faulty, but if they are to be inspected, unscrew the cap and extract the spring and valve plunger (photo). When refitting, remember to fit the sealing

washer and tighten the cap to the specified torque.

Oil seals and gaskets

37 It is recommended that all gaskets and oil seals are renewed at major engine overhaul (photos). Sockets are useful for removing or refitting oil seals. An arrow is moulded onto the seals to indicate the rotational direction of the component which it serves. Make sure that the seal is fitted the correct way round to comply with the arrow.

Cylinder head

38 This is covered in Section 17, during dismantling and decarbonising.

Cylinder block core plugs

39 Check the plugs for excessive corrosion and any signs of leakage.

40 To renew a plug, drill through the old plug, then lever it out of its housing. Clean the housing of old sealant.

41 Apply a suitable sealant to the plug surface in the housing then drive the new plug into position (photo).

18.28 Timing belt tensioner and spring

18.33 Oil pump rotors (note directional mark for correct fitting)

18.34A Checking oil pump rotor tip clearance with feeler gauge

18.34B Checking the outer rotor clearance

18.36 Oil pump pressure regulating valve components

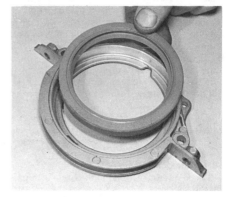

18.37A Oil seal renewal (crankshaft – rear)

18.37B Lower timing cover seal renewal

18.42 Cylinder block core plug

19 Engine reassembly – general

1   To ensure maximum life with minimum trouble from a rebuilt engine, not only must everything be correctly assembled, but everything must be spotlessly clean, all the oilways must be clear, locking washers and spring washers must always be fitted where indicated and all bearing and other working surfaces must be thoroughly lubricated during assembly.

2   Before assembly begins renew any bolts or studs, the threads of which are in any way damaged, and whenever possible use new spring washers.

3   Apart from your normal tools, a supply of clean rag, an oil can filled with engine oil (an empty plastic detergent bottle thoroughly cleaned and washed out, will do just as well), a new supply of assorted spring washers, a set of new gaskets, and a torque wrench, should be collected together.

20 Engine – reassembly

1   Stand the cylinder block in an inverted position on the bench.

2   Clean the shell bearing recesses in the crankcase free from all grit and dirt and fit the bearing shells. The centre shell is of thrust flange type (photo). Nos 1 and 5 are of grooved type (photo) and Nos 2 and 4 are plain.

3   Oil the shells and lower the crankshaft into position (photos).

4   Clean the recesses in the main bearing caps free from grit and dirt and fit the bearing shells to match those already fitted to the crankcase. Oil the shells.

5   Fit the main bearing caps in their numbered sequence so that the numbers can be read from the flywheel end. Cap No 1 is at the timing belt end. The caps will only seat one way round (photo).

6   Insert and tighten the cap bolts to the specified torque – working from the centre ones towards each end (photo) (Fig. 1.31).

7   Now check the crankshaft endfloat using either a dial gauge or feeler blades inserted between the flange of the centre bearing and the machined shoulder of the crankshaft (photo). Make sure that the crankshaft is pushed fully in one direction and then the other when measuring. If the endfloat is excessive (see Specifications) and new bearing shells have been fitted then it can only be due to an error at regrinding.

8   Bolt on the crankshaft oil seal retainer complete with a new oil seal and gasket (photos). Apply grease to the oil seal lips before pushing it over the flywheel mounting flange and check that the lip of the seal is not doubled under. Cut the protruding oil seal gasket flush (photo and Fig. 1.32).

9   Oil the cylinder bores and fit the piston/connecting rods (complete with bearing shells) into their respective cylinders, as described in Section 9. Make sure that the front mark on the piston crown is towards the timing belt of the engine.

10 Oil the crankpins.

11 Wipe out the recesses in the big-end caps and fit the bearing shells. Oil the shells.

12 Draw the connecting rods down onto the crankpins, fit the caps (numbers adjacent) and screw in and tighten the bolts to the specified torque (photo). Using a feeler gauge, check the respective connecting rod side clearances to ensure that they are within the limits specified (Fig. 1.33). If they are not within the specified limits, the connecting rods and/or the crankshaft will need renewal.

13 Oil the jackshaft journals, insert the jackshaft into its bearings and fit the retaining plate and screw, having applied locking fluid to the threads (photos).

14 Fit the cylinder head, as described in Section 6.

15 Fit the oil slinger to the front end of the crankshaft (photo).

16 Lubricate the oil seal lips, slide the collar into it, then fit the timing belt lower backplate using a new gasket and oil seals (photos). Note that the two longer bolts go into the lower holes.

17 Refit the timing belt guide disc to mate with the concave side of the crankshaft sprocket which should now be fitted (photos).

18 Bolt the sprocket to the jackshaft (photo).

19 Fit the three hole triangular mounting block for the alternator adjuster link.

20 The camshaft sprocket will normally have been fitted during reassembly of the cylinder head, if not fit it now.

21 Refit and retension the timing belt as described in Section 5.

22 Refit the oil pick-up pipe using a new gasket (photo), then refit the sump pan as described in Section 8.

23 Fit the timing belt upper and lower covers, using new seal strips. Also refit the reinforcement bracket.

24 Fit the engine end plate to its dowels at the flywheel end of the engine (photo).

25 Fit the flywheel, aligning the marks made before removal.

26 Apply thread locking fluid to the bolt threads and tighten them to the specified torque. Jam the flywheel starter ring teeth to prevent the flywheel from turning as the bolts are tightened (photo).

27 Fit the crankshaft pulley and tighten to the specified torque, again jamming the flywheel teeth.

28 Refit the coolant pump and pulley (Chapter 2).

29 Refit the distributor/thermostat housing to the rear end of the cylinder head, using a new gasket.

30 Locate a new gasket and bolt the oil pump into position.

31 Fit a new oil filter as described in Section 2.

32 Refit the alternator and mounting brackets, then locate and adjust the drivebelt as described in Chapter 2 (photo).

33 Where an air conditioner and/or power steering are fitted, bolt on the compressor and/or pump brackets (photos).

34 Refit the ancillary items such as the distributor and coolant thermostat, fuel pump, manifolds and the clutch unit with reference to the appropriate chapters for specific details.

35 Adjust the valve clearances and then fit a new seal to the rocker cover (photo) before fitting the cover into position. The cover is secured with domed nuts and special seal washers (photos).

36 Screw in the spark plugs, and then reconnect the ignition leads.

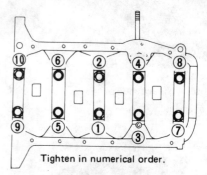

Tighten in numerical order.

Fig. 1.31 Crankshaft main bearing tightening sequence (Sec 20)

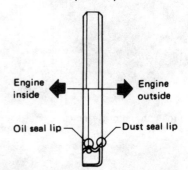

Engine inside   Engine outside

Oil seal lip   Dust seal lip

Fig. 1.32 Crankshaft oil seal orientation (Sec 20)

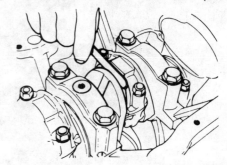

Fig. 1.33 Check the connecting rod side clearances (Sec 20)

20.2A Centre main bearing shell with thrust flanges

20.2B End main bearing shell

20.3A Oiling the crankcase main bearing shells

20.3B Lowering the crankshaft into position

20.5 Fitting the centre main bearing cap

20.6 Tightening a main bearing cap bolt

20.7 Checking the crankshaft endfloat

20.8A Crankshaft oil seal retainer gasket

20.8B Crankshaft oil seal and retainer

20.8C Cut oil seal retainer gasket flush

20.12 Main and big-end bearing caps

20.13A Inserting jackshaft into crankcase

20.13B Fit the jackshaft retaining plate and screw

20.15 Crankshaft oil slinger

20.16A Timing belt lower backplate gasket

20.16B Locate the oil seal collar ...

20.16C ... refit the timing belt lower backplate ...

20.16D ... engaging the collar groove over the crankshaft Woodruff key ...

20.16E ... and secure with bolts

20.17A Timing belt guide disc

20.17B Crankshaft sprocket

20.18 Securing the jackshaft sprocket

20.21 Bolt the oil pick-up pipe into position

20.24 Locate the engine endplate ...

20.26 ... and fit the flywheel

20.32 Alternator lower mounting bracket

20.33A Power steering pump lower mounting bracket

20.33B Power steering pump upper mounting bracket

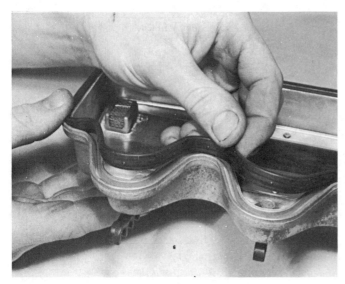

20.35A Fitting a new rocker cover seal

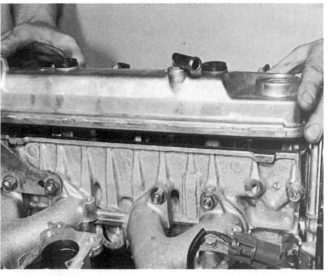

20.35B Fitting the rocker cover

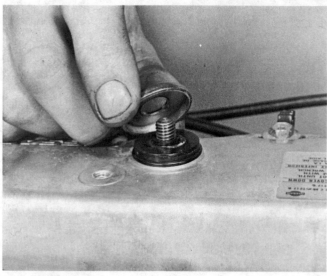

20.35C Rocker cover retaining nut washers

21 Engine/manual transmission – reconnection and refitting

Reconnection

Refer also to Chapter 6

1   Refer to Chapter 5 and make sure that the clutch driven plate has been centralised.

2   Apply a smear of molybdenum disulphide grease to the input shaft splines and then offer the transmission to the engine. As the input shaft splines pass into the hub of the driven plate, the transmission may require turning in either direction to align the splines.

3   Insert and tighten the flange connecting bolts, but remember to locate the coolant tube, the mounting brackets, and the sump-to-bellhousing reinforcement strut.

4   Bolt on the starter motor.

Refitting

5   Connect the hoist to the lifting lugs, then raise the engine/transmission and lower it carefully into the engine compartment, position the alternator under the brake master cylinder as the engine is lowered.

6   Engage the flexible mountings and fit the connecting bolts. The mountings and their associated components are shown in Fig. 1.34. Do not fully tighten the retaining bolts to their specified torque wrench settings until all of the mountings are located.

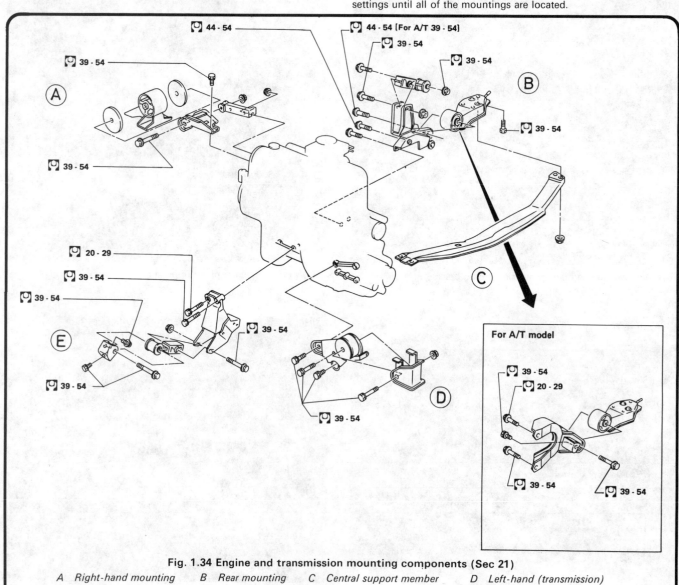

Fig. 1.34 Engine and transmission mounting components (Sec 21)

A Right-hand mounting	B Rear mounting	C Central support member	D Left-hand (transmission) mounting
E Front mounting			

Torque wrench settings are shown in Nm

7   Remove the hoist and sling.
8   Reconnect the alternator leads and the lead to the automatic choke.
9   Reconnect the ignition HT and LT leads, and the earth leads to the side of the cylinder head, the gearbox and the exhaust manifold. Note that the main wiring harness is located in a protective sleeve and is routed under the intake manifold. It is held in position by plastic straps on the underside of the manifold.
10 Reconnect the lead to the oil pressure switch.
11 Reconnect the leads to the coolant temperature switch and reverse lamp switch.
12 Reconnect the fuel hoses to the fuel pump. Also all vacuum and air hoses.
13 Reconnect the throttle cable, also the rocker cover vent hose (photo).
14 Reconnect the speedometer drive cable to the transmission.
15 Reconnect the clutch operating cable to the release lever. Adjust the clutch cable, as described in Chapter 5.
16 Reconnect the inboard end of each driveshaft to the transmission final drive, then reconnect the suspension arm to the steering knuckle and the tie-rod to the steering knuckle. Refer to Chapter 8 and 10 for full details.
17 Refit the side shield under the right-hand wheel arch then refit the right and left-hand front roadwheels.
18 Reconnect the gearchange rod and stabilizer rod (see Chapter 6).
19 Reconnect the exhaust downpipe to the manifold (Chapter 3).
20 Refit the central support member and tighten the retaining bolts and nuts to the specified torque wrench settings.
21 Reconnect the radiator coolant hoses and also the heater coolant hoses at the bulkhead.
22 Reconnect the cooling fan and thermal switch leads.
23 Refit the power steering and air conditioning compressor (if fitted), and adjust the drivebelt(s) as described in Chapter 2.
24 Raise the vehicle at the front end and remove the axle stands, then lower the vehicle.
25 Check that the drain plugs are securely fitted, then refill the engine and transmission oils to the required levels. Refer to Section 2 in this Chapter and Chapter 6.
26 Top up the cooling system as described in Chapter 2.
27 Refit the air cleaner unit (see Chapter 3).
28 Reconnect the battery (Chapter 12).
29 Refit the bonnet (Chapter 11).
30 Although the engine undertrays are still to be fitted, these are best left until the engine has been restarted and the final underside checks have been made for any signs of lubricant, coolant and exhaust system leaks.
31 The engine and transmission refitting should now be complete, but before attempting to restart the engine, make a thorough check to ensure that all fittings and connections are secure. Remove all tools from the engine compartment.

22 Engine/automatic transmission – reconnection and refitting

1   The operations are very similar to those described in the preceding Section, but the following special points should be noted.

Reconnection
Refer also to Chapter 7

21.13 Rocker vent hose connection

2   Before connecting the driveplate to the torque converter, check to see that the converter is pushed fully home by referring to Chapter 7.
3   Align the marks on the driveplate and torque converter (made before dismantling). Apply thread locking fluid to the clean threads of the connecting bolts and tighten them to the specified torque. Bolt on the starter motor, and reconnect the kickdown cable.

Refitting
4   Reconnect the speed selector control cable and adjust it, if necessary.
5   Reconnect the inhibitor switch leads.
6   Reconnect the oil cooler hoses.
7   Refit the front wing protective shield where fitted.
8   Top up the automatic transmission fluid (see Section 2 in Chapter 7).

23 Initial start-up after major overhaul

1   Set the idle speed screw to a higher setting than normal to offset the drag caused by new engine components.
2   Start the engine. This may take rather longer than usual as the fuel pump has to fill the carburettor with fuel.
3   Once the engine starts, allow it to warm without racing and then check for oil leaks.
4   There will be some odd smells caused by oil and grease burning off metal surfaces.
5   Treat the engine as a new unit for the first few hundred miles by restricting speed and load.
6   Once the engine is run-in after 600 miles (1000 km), check the idle speed, the valve clearances and the tightening torque of all engine nuts and bolts. Change the engine oil and filter at the same time.

24 Fault diagnosis – engine

Symptom	Reason(s)
Engine fails to turn when starter control operated	
No current at starter motor	Flat or defective battery
	Loose battery leads
	Defective starter solenoid or switch or broken wiring
	Engine earth strap disconnected
Current at starter motor	Jammed starter motor drive pinion
	Defective starter motor

Engine turns but will not start
No spark at spark plug

Ignition leads or distributor cap damp or wet
Ignition leads to spark plugs loose
Shorted or disconnected low tension leads
Defective ignition switch
Ignition leads connected wrong way round
Faulty coil

No fuel at engine

No petrol in petrol tank
Vapour lock in fuel line (in hot conditions or at high altitude)
Blocked float chamber needle valve
Fuel pump filter blocked
Choked or blocked carburettor jets
Faulty fuel pump

Engine stalls and will not restart
Excess of petrol in cylinder or carburettor flooding

Too much choke allowing too rich a mixture or wet plugs
Float damaged or leaking or needle not seating
Float lever incorrectly adjusted

No spark at spark plug

Ignition failure – sudden
Ignition failure – misfiring precedes total stoppage
Ignition failure – in severe rain or after traversing water splash

No fuel at jets

No petrol in petrol tank
Petrol tank breather choked
Sudden obstruction in carburettor
Water in fuel system

Engine misfires or idles unevenly
Intermittent spark at spark plug

Ignition leads loose
Battery leads loose on terminals
Battery earth strap loose on body attachment point
Engine earth lead loose
Low tension leads on coil loose
Low tension lead to distributor loose
Dirty or incorrectly gapped plugs
Tracking across inside of distributor cover
Ignition too retarded
Faulty coil
Slack timing belt

Fuel shortage at engine

Mixture too weak
Air leak in carburettor
Air leak at inlet manifold to cylinder head, or inlet manifold to carburettor

Lack of power and poor compression
Mechanical wear

Burnt out valves
Sticking or leaking valves
Weak or broken valve springs
Worn valve guides or stems
Worn pistons and piston rings

Chapter 2 Cooling and heating systems

For modifications, and information applicable to later models, see Supplement at end of manual

Contents

Coolant mixture – general	4	Heater/fresh air controls – adjustment	13
Coolant temperature switch and gauge – general	10	Heater – removal and refitting	12
Cooling system – draining, flushing and refilling	3	Radiator – removal, repair and refitting	6
Cooling system expansion tank – removal and refitting	11	Radiator cooling fan and switch – removal and refitting	7
Drivebelts – removal, refitting and adjustment	9	Routine maintenance	2
Fault diagnosis – cooling and heating systems	14	Thermostat – removal, testing and refitting	5
General description	1	Water pump – removal and refitting	8

Specifications

General

System type	Pressurised with belt driven coolant pump, radiator, thermostat and electric cooling fan
System test pressure	1.57 bar (23 lb/in²)
Radiator cap relief pressure	0.78 to 0.98 bar (11 to 14 lbf/in²)

Thermostat

Opening temperature	82°C (180°F)
Maximum valve lift	8 mm (0.31 in) at 95°C (203°F)

Drivebelt tension

Deflection is measured with moderate thumb pressure applied at the centre of the belt's longest run. The tension of a new drivebelt should be checked after the vehicle's first operating period.

Component:	Deflection (old belt)	Deflection (new belt)
Alternator	8.5 to 9.5 mm (0.33 to 0.37 in)	7.5 to 8.5 mm (0.30 to 0.33 in)
Power steering pump	7.0 to 9.0 mm (0.28 to 0.35 in)	6.5 to 8.5 mm (0.26 to 0.33 in)
Air conditioner compressor	9.0 to 10.0 mm (0.35 to 0.39 in)	6.0 to 8.0 mm (0.24 to 0.31 in)

System capacity (including heater and reservoir tank)

With aluminium radiator	4.9 litres (8.62 pints)
With copper radiator	5.5 litres (9.68 pints)

Coolant

Type/specification	Ethylene glycol based antifreeze, to BS 3151, 3152 or 6580, and soft water (Duckhams Universal Antifreeze and Summer Coolant)

Torque wrench settings

	Nm	lbf ft
Thermostat housing	5.1 to 6.5	3.8 to 4.8
Water temperature switch	9.3 to 10.3	6.9 to 7.6
Water pump	5.1 to 6.5	3.8 to 4.8
Water outlet housing	5.1 to 6.5	3.8 to 4.8
Oil cooler retaining nut (automatic transmission)	8.0 to 12.0	5.9 to 8.9

1 General description

The cooling system consists of a front-mounted radiator, a coolant pump, a thermostat and an electric radiator cooling fan.

Coolant from the engine cooling system also flows through the interior heater when the control valve is opened. The flow and return hoses are attached to the heater matrix at the engine compartment side of the bulkhead.

The coolant (water) pump is driven by the same belt that drives the alternator; the belt being driven by the crankshaft pulley. The fitted position of the alternator sets the drivebelt tension.

The coolant temperature is regulated by the thermostat, which is mounted at the rear end of the cylinder head. The electrically driven radiator fan cuts in to assist engine cooling when required in accordance with a thermal switch.

2 Routine maintenance

Carry out the following procedures at the intervals given in *Routine Maintenance* at the beginning of the manual.

1 With the engine cold, check the coolant level in the radiator or coolant expansion tank (as applicable). Do not remove the filler cap when the engine is hot as the system will be pressurized and steam or coolant will be suddenly released and scalding could result. If it is essential to remove the filler cap when the engine is hot, cover the cap with a cloth and slowly release the cap to its first position. Leave at this position until the pressure in the system is fully released before removing the cap, again covered with a cloth.

2 If necessary, top up the cooling system level as required then refit the filler cap. Note that cold coolant must not be added to a hot engine, and regular topping-up of the cooling system should not be necessary. If it is, check for signs of coolant leakage from the system components.

3 Check the cooling system hoses, the thermostat housing and the water pump for any signs of leakage, and if found, rectify as necessary.

4 Drain the coolant, flush the system and refill with fresh coolant as described in Section 3.

5 Check the adjustment and condition of the alternator/water pump drivebelt as described in Section 9. Renew and/or adjust as necessary.

3 Cooling system – draining, flushing and refilling

1 Preferably drain the cooling system when the engine is cold. Set the heater control to HOT, remove the radiator cap or expansion tank

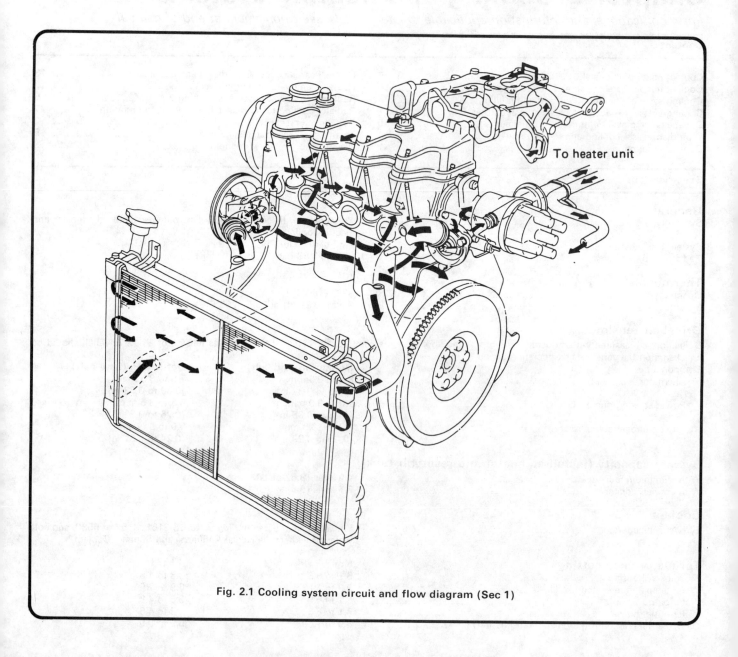

To heater unit

Fig. 2.1 Cooling system circuit and flow diagram (Sec 1)

cap and then unscrew the drain tap at the base of the radiator (photo).
2   If the system has been well maintained the coolant should run clear to the last drop, in which case, the radiator tap may be closed and the system refilled immediately with fresh antifreeze mixture (photo).
3   If the system has been neglected, and the coolant is badly contaminated with rust and sediment, flush it through by inserting a cold water hose in the radiator filler neck.
4   In severe cases of neglect it may be necessary to remove the radiator, invert it and reverse flush it. If after a reasonable period the water still does not run clear, the radiator may be flushed with a good proprietary cleaning agent such as Holts Radflush or Holts Speedflush. It is important that the manufacturer's instructions are followed carefully.
5   To refill the system on vehicles without an expansion tank, fill the radiator to 20 to 35 mm (0.8 to 1.3 in) below the base of the filler neck then run the engine for a few minutes with the radiator cap removed. Switch off and top up if necessary. Refit the radiator cap (Fig. 2.2).
6   To refill the system on vehicles with an expansion tank, fill the radiator brim full and fit the cap. Fill the expansion tank to the MAX mark. Run the engine for a few minutes and top up the expansion tank if necessary (Fig. 2.3).
7   A cylinder block drain plug is not fitted.

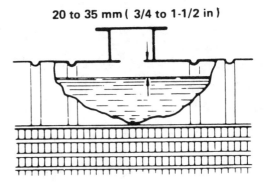

Without coolant reservoir

20 to 35 mm (3/4 to 1-1/2 in)

Fig. 2.2 Coolant level requirement in the radiator (Sec 3)

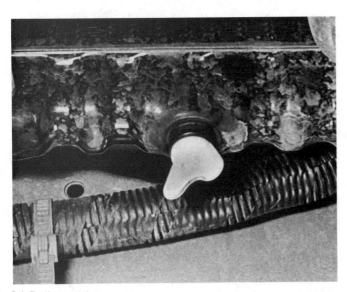

3.1 Radiator drain tap

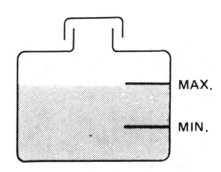

MAX.

MIN.

Fig. 2.3 Coolant level marks on the expansion tank (Sec 3)

3.2 Topping-up the coolant level

4   Coolant mixture – general

1   It is essential to keep the cooling system filled with antifreeze mixture instead of plain water. Apart from the obvious protection against damage caused by low temperatures, suitable antifreeze liquids contain an inhibitor against corrosion which, of course, works all year round.
2   Antifreeze should be mixed in accordance with the manufacturer's instructions on the container and the proportion of liquid to water should be chosen to meet the local weather conditions, although a 50/50 mixture will ensure maximum protection against freezing and corrosion.
3   Before filling the system with antifreeze mixture check that all the hoses are in sound condition and that all hose clips are tight. Antifreeze has a searching action and will leak more readily than plain water.
4   Renew the coolant mixture every 2 years, as the inhibitor in the solution will by then be of little value. When it is necessary to top up the cooling system, use a mixture of the same strength as that in the system.
5   Always buy a top quality antifreeze of glycol base. Other cheaper antifreeze products usually contain chemicals which evaporate during service and soon provide little protection.
6   If the car is operating in climatic conditions which do not require antifreeze, always use a corrosion inhibitor to prevent corrosion of the system, particularly its light alloy content.

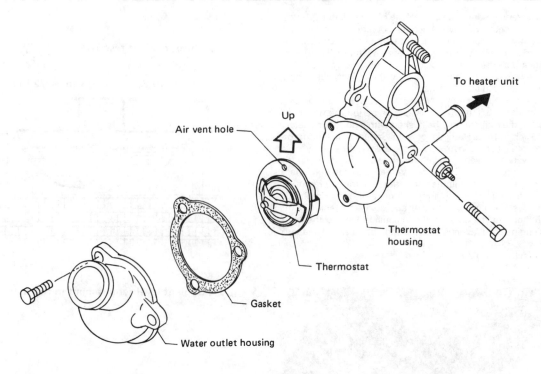

Fig. 2.4 Thermostat and housing components (Sec 5)

5 Thermostat – removal, testing and refitting

1   Drain sufficient coolant to bring the coolant level below the thermostat housing.
2   Disconnect the coolant hose from the thermostat housing (photo).
3   Unbolt and remove the thermostat housing cover, discard the gasket and withdraw the thermostat. If the thermostat is stuck tight, do not lever it out by inserting a screwdriver under its bridge piece, but cut around the edge of its rim using a sharp knife.
4   To check the thermostat, suspend it in water at a temperature near that of the opening temperature of the unit. Observe that it opens fully as the temperature of the water is increased. Allow the thermostat to cool, when it should be fully closed.
5   If a thermostat is seized in the closed position leave it out until a replacement can be obtained.
6   Refit the thermostat into a clean seat with its air bleed hole or jiggle pin uppermost. Use a new gasket, fit the cover and tighten the bolts securely, but do not overtighten them (photos).
7   Reconnect the hose and refill the cooling system.

6 Radiator – removal, repair and refitting

1   One of two radiator types will be fitted, being of copper or aluminium core construction (Fig. 2.5 or 2.6). Although the aluminium type can be dismantled, it is a task to be entrusted to a specialist as special tools are required.
2   Drain the cooling system, as described in Section 3. Retain the coolant if required for further use.
3   Where applicable unbolt the power steering pump and place it to one side without disconnecting the fluid lines.
4   As applicable, disconnect the radiator top, bottom and expansion tank hoses, and unbolt the bottom hose adaptor.
5   On automatic transmission models disconnect the fluid cooler lines from the bottom of the radiator and plug them.
6   Disconnect the wiring from the cooling fan motor and water temperature switch.
7   Unbolt the radiator top mounting (photo) and lift the radiator from the engine compartment, complete with cooling fan (photo).
8   If the radiator was removed because of a leak, it is best to leave

5.2 Thermostat housing and hose connection

5.6A Thermostat installed – note orientation markings

5.6B Refitting the thermostat housing cover

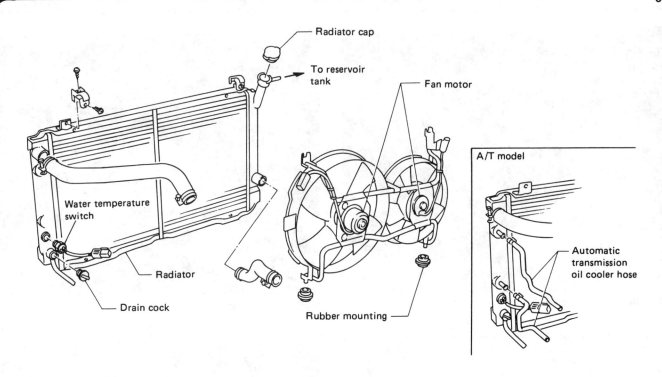

Fig. 2.5 Radiator and associated fittings – copper type (Sec 6)

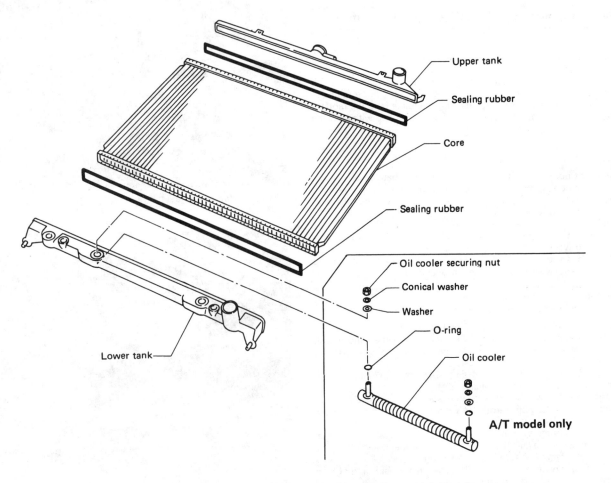

Fig. 2.6 Radiator unit – aluminium type (do not dismantle) (Sec 6)

6.7A Radiator top mounting

6.7B Radiator removal

its repair to a professional radiator repairer. In an emergency, minor leaks from the radiator can be cured by using a radiator sealant such as Holts Radweld with the assembly *in situ*. In some cases loss of coolant may sometimes be caused by a defective radiator pressure cap. Your Nissan dealer can test this for you.
9   Refitting is a reversal of removal, but fill the system as described in Section 3.

7   Radiator cooling fan and switch – removal and refitting

Fan
1   Open the bonnet and disconnect the battery negative lead.
2   Disconnect the leads from the fan motor.
3   Unbolt the fan mounting struts and lift the assembly from the engine compartment. If required, the fan motor unit can be removed from the mounting frame by first removing the frame from the radiator (three bolts) then undo the three fan-to-frame bolts and withdraw the fan unit (photo).
4   Refitting is a reversal of removal.

Switch
5   Open the bonnet and disconnect the battery negative lead.
6   Drain the cooling system as described in Section 3.
7   Disconnect the wiring from the switch located on the left-hand side of the radiator tank.
8   Unscrew the switch and remove the washer (photo).
9   The switch can be tested using a simple test bulb and battery if it is lowered into water and the temperature raised.
10 Refitting is a reversal of removal but use a new sealing washer and refill the cooling system as described in Section 3.

8   Water pump – removal and refitting

1   Drain the cooling system as described in Section 3.
2   Where applicable remove the power steering drivebelt and unbolt the power steering pump. Place the pump on one side without disconnecting the hoses.
3   Loosen the alternator mounting bolts, pivot the alternator toward the engine then remove the drivebelt.
4   Unbolt and remove the pulley from the water pump drive flange.
5   Unbolt the water pump from the cylinder block and remove the gasket.
6   The coolant pump cannot be overhauled, as new seals and internal components are not available. A new pump will therefore have to be obtained if the original one is worn or leaking.
7   Refitting is a reversal of removal, but use a new gasket and tighten the bolts to the specified torque (photo).
8   Tension the drivebelts (Section 9).
9   Refill the cooling system as described in Section 3.

7.3 Cooling fan motor retaining bolts

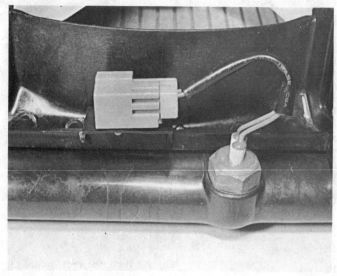

7.8 Radiator cooling fan switch

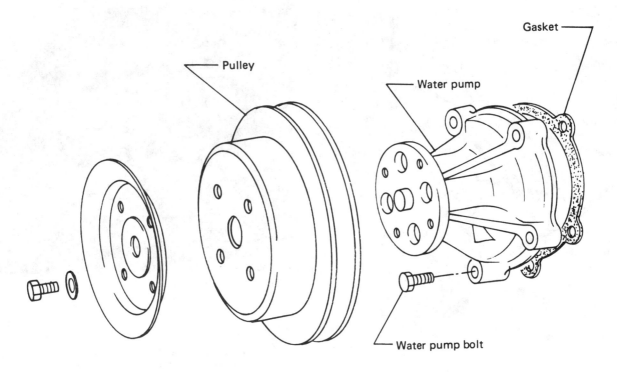

Fig. 2.7 Water pump components (Sec 8)

9 Drivebelts – removal, refitting and adjustment

1 The number of drivebelts fitted and their configuration will depend upon the units with which the particular vehicle is equipped.
2 An alternator is fitted to all models.
3 If the vehicle is equipped with air conditioning and power steering then the power steering pump drivebelt will have to be removed first, followed by the air conditioning compressor drivebelt (where applicable).

Power steering pump belt
4 Release the power steering pump bracket lockbolt. Turn the adjuster bolt to fully slacken the belt and then slip it off the pulley.
5 Fit the belt and tension in accordance with the table in Specifications.

Compressor belt
6 Release the idler pulley locknut and the adjuster nuts on the eye bolt.

7 Fully slacken the adjustment until the belt can be slipped off the pulley.
8 Fit the belt and tension in accordance with the table in Specifications.

Alternator belt
9 Release the alternator mounting and adjuster link bolts and push the alternator in towards the engine until the belt can be slipped off the pulleys.
10 Fit the belt and tension in accordance with the table in Specifications (photos).

General
11 Never overtension a drivebelt, or the coolant pump, alternator, power steering pump and/or compressor bearings may be damaged. When adjusted, the drivebelt must not touch the bottom of the drive pulley groove. The drivebelt tension must always be checked and adjusted when the engine is cold.

8.7 Refitting the water pump (note new gasket)

9.10A General view of the alternator/water pump drivebelt arrangement
Alternator adjuster strap arrowed

9.10B Checking the tension of the alternator/water pump drivebelt

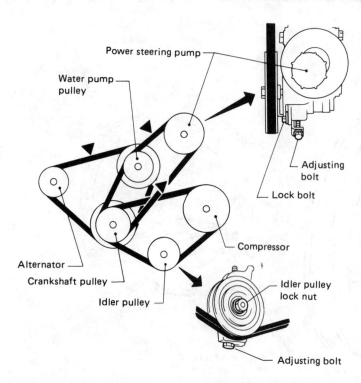

Fig. 2.8 Drivebelt arrangements showing tension check points (arrows) (Sec 9)

9.11 Power steering pump drivebelt adjuster (arrowed)

10 Coolant temperature switch and gauge – general

1   The coolant temperature switch can only be removed from its thermostat housing location after the cooling system has been partially drained (2.0 litres).

2   To test a coolant temperature switch requires the use of an ohmmeter, so this is a job best left to your dealer or auto-electrician.

3   Faulty indication of the temperature gauge may be caused by the switch-to-gauge lead earthing due to damaged insulation, check this first.

4   Immediate indication of maximum temperature when the ignition is switched on will be due to a fault in either the gauge or the switch.

11 Cooling system expansion tank – removal and refitting

1   Syphon out any coolant from the reservoir.

2   Disconnect the windscreen washer reservoir filler spout support bracket by undoing the retaining screw.

3   Unclip and detach the coolant hose at the expansion tank. If the manufacturer's hose clip is still fitted, cut it free and renew it with a suitable worm drive type clip during reassembly.

4   Undo the retaining screw from the inner wing panel and then remove the reservoir. The hose from the radiator can be plugged or clamped to prevent leakage if required. If the hose is in poor condition, it must be renewed.

5   Refit in the reverse order of removal, then top up the cooling system to complete.

12 Heater – removal and refitting

Blower motor

1   The blower motor unit is located under the front facia on the left-hand side. Before removing the unit, disconnect the battery earth lead (photo).

2   Disconnect the wiring at the blower motor.

3   Undo the three blower motor retaining bolts.

4   Lower the blower motor and disengage it from the side duct and the air control flap rod.

5   The heater motor can be removed from its housing by undoing the three retaining bolts and detaching the cable connector.

6   Refit in the reverse order of removal.

Heater control unit

7   Disconnect the battery earth lead.

8   Remove the central facia trim panel by undoing the retaining screws (Chapter 11, Section 25).

9   Pull free the heater control knobs and withdraw the facia control panel from the control unit (photos).

10   If required, the illumination bulb can now be removed from the control panel for inspection and if necessary renewal (photo).

11   To withdraw the control unit from the facia, undo the retaining screws from the ashtray holder plate and remove it. Now undo the screws securing the heater/fresh air control unit and withdraw it. For full removal, disconnect the control cables and the wiring connectors from the panel illumination bulb and fan switch.

12   Refit in reverse order of removal. Check for satisfactory operation of the heater/fresh air controls, and also the fan and control illumination. Adjustment of the control cables may be necessary in which case refer to Section 13.

Heater unit

13   Drain the cooling system as described in Section 3.

14   Disconnect the battery earth lead, then remove the instrument panel as described in Chapter 12. Disconnect and remove the main facia panels (Chapter 11).

15   Disconnect the heater/fresh air ducts from the heater unit, remove the duct between the heater and the blower motor.

16   Disconnect the control cables from the heater unit.

17   Disconnect the flow and return coolant hoses from the heater unit at the bulkhead connections on the engine compartment side. Allow for coolant spillage and plug the ports to prevent further spillage when the heater unit is withdrawn (photo).

18   Unbolt and remove the metal facia support frame, one screw each side at the top and two bolts each side to the central tunnel support bracket (photo).

19   Unscrew and remove the heater unit retaining bolts (photo), then carefully pull it rearwards from the bulkhead so that the flow and return pipes pass through the bulkhead, then manoeuvre the unit to the left and rearwards and remove the unit from within the car. Take care not to snag the unit on any wiring or control cables and also allow for further spillage of coolant from the matrix if it is defective or the flow and

12.1 Heater/fresh air control blower motor location

12.9A Pull free the heater control knobs and ...

12.9B ... remove the facia control panel

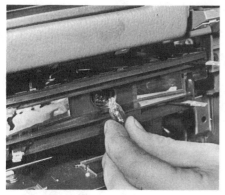

12.10 Heater control panel illumination bulb renewal

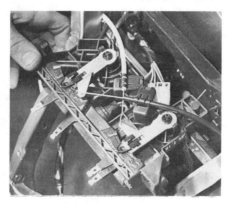

12.11 Heater/fresh air control unit removal

12.17 Heater coolant hose connection at the bulkhead (engine compartment side)

12.18 Metal support frame-to-floor bolts

12.19 Heater unit retaining bolt (lower right-hand side shown)

13.2 Heater control cable connection and outer cable retaining clip

return ports were not plugged as suggested earlier.

20 Once removed from the vehicle, the heater unit can be dismantled as necessary. The most likely item to need removal is the heater matrix (coolant core). Undo the retaining screws and withdraw the matrix from the front face of the heater unit. Renew as necessary.

21 Refit in the reverse order of removal. Arrange the routing of all wiring looms and control cables as required during reassembly. Ensure that all connections are securely made and check the various switches and controls for correct functioning on completion. Top up the cooling system with reference to Section 3.

22 When the engine is restarted check for any signs of coolant leaks and, if necessary, adjust the heater controls as described in Section 13.

13 Heater/fresh air controls – adjustment

1 Access to the heater controls can be made by removing the lower facia trim panels.

Control cable and rod

2 To remove the control cable from its clip, expand the clip by hand and extract the cable from it. If required the clip can be removed from the coolant base housing by compressing it by hand and withdrawing it. When fitting the clip, reverse the process but ensure that it contacts the bottom of the base housing (photo).

Ventilator door control rod
3   Detach the air control cable and door rod from the side link, pivot the link in the direction indicated in Fig. 2.9 then, with the top and bottom ventilator door levers held as indicated, connect the rods to the levers.

Defroster door control rod
4   Detach the air control cable and the door rod from the side link. Pivot the link in an anti-clockwise direction, simultaneously push the defroster door as shown and reconnect the door link rod (Fig. 2.10).

Air control cable
5   To reconnect the air control cable, push the outer cable and side link as shown, then clamp the outer cable in the retaining clip (Fig. 2.11).

Heater coolant valve control rod
6   Before making this adjustment, first detach the temperature control cable from the air mix door lever.
7   Move the air mix door as indicated (arrow), then pull the coolant valve control rod as indicated to provide the rod end to link lever clearance shown, then connect the rod to the door lever (Fig. 2.12). Reconnect and adjust the temperature control cable.

Temperature control cable
8   Disconnect the temperature control cable from the air mix door lever.
9   Push the cable outer case and the air mix door lever in the direction indicated (arrow), then connect the outer cable to its retaining clamp. Check that the heater control lever is in the maximum hot setting position (Fig. 2.13).

Intake door control cable
10 Unclip the outer cable, move the intake door lever in the direction indicated (arrow), then reconnect the outer cable to its retaining clip. The air control lever should be set at the position indicated (Fig. 2.14).

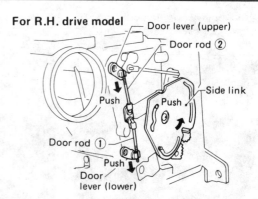

Fig. 2.9 Ventilator door control rod and associated components (Sec 13)

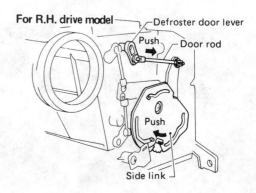

Fig. 2.10 Defroster door control adjustment (Sec 13)

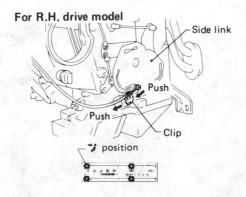

Fig. 2.11 Air control cable adjustment (Sec 13)

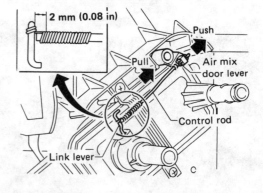

Fig. 2.12 Coolant valve control rod adjustment (Sec 13)

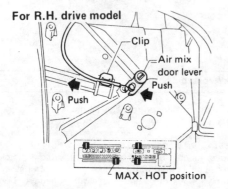

Fig. 2.13 Temperature control cable adjustment (Sec 13)

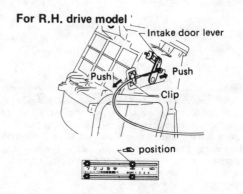

Fig. 2.14 Intake door control cable adjustment (Sec 13)

14 Fault diagnosis – cooling and heating systems

Symptom	Reason(s)
Overheating	Coolant loss due to leakage Faulty electric cooling fan or switch Water pump/alternator drivebelt slack or broken Faulty thermostat Radiator matrix clogged internally or externally
Overcooling	Faulty thermostat Faulty electric cooling fan switch
Coolant loss	External leakage (hose joints etc) Overheating (see above) Internal leakage (head gasket)
Blower fan failure	Fuse blown Blower motor defective Poor wiring connection
Heater too cool or too hot	Heater coolant control valve defective Heater controls broken or needing adjustment Fresh air controls broken or needing adjustment Heater matrix (core) leaking or blocked Cooling system thermostat faulty

Chapter 3
Fuel, exhaust and emission control systems

For modifications, and information applicable to later models, see Supplement at end of manual

Contents

Accelerator pedal and cable – removal, refitting and adjustment 15
Air cleaner – servicing, removal and refitting 3
Air temperature control (ATC) system – checking 4
Carburettor – checks and adjustments (general) 10
Carburettor – description 9
Carburettor – idle speed and mixture adjustment 11
Carburettor – overhaul 13
Carburettor – removal and refitting 12

Emission control system – general 14
Fault diagnosis – fuel, exhaust and emission control systems 17
Fuel filter – renewal 5
Fuel level transmitter and gauge – removal and refitting 7
Fuel pump – removal and refitting 8
Fuel tank – removal, repair and refitting 6
General description 1
Manifolds and exhaust system – general 16
Routine maintenance 2

Specifications

General

System type	Mechanical fuel pump, downdraught carburettor
Fuel tank capacity (all models)	50 litres (11 gallons)
Fuel ratings requirement (minimum):	
1.3	90 octane (RON)
1.6	97 octane (RON)
Fuel pump pressure	0.196 to 0.265 bar (2.8 to 3.8 lbf/in²)

Air cleaner element

1.3 and 1.6	Champion W108

Carburettor (basic adjustments)

Type	Dual barrel, downdraught, with automatic choke
Idle speed:	
Manual transmission	750 to 850 rpm
Automatic transmission (with manual steering)	800 to 900 rpm
Automatic transmission (with power steering)	900 to 1000 rpm
Fast idle speed:	
Manual transmission	2200 to 2600 rpm
Automatic transmission – 1.3	2400 to 2800 rpm
Automatic transmission – 1.6	2600 to 3000 rpm
CO content at idle	1.5 ± 0.5%

	R1	R2
Vacuum break clearance:		
1.3	1.17 to 1.45 mm (0.046 to 0.057 in)	1.52 to 2.16 mm (0.060 to 0.085 in)
1.6	1.09 to 1.29 mm ((0.043 to 0.051 in)	1.88 to 2.28 mm (0.074 to 0.090 in)

Dashpot touch speed:	
1.3	1700 to 2100 rpm
1.6	1800 to 2200 rpm
Dashpot gap:	
1.3	0.37 to 0.57 mm (0.0146 to 0.0224 in)
1.6	0.46 to 0.66 mm (0.0181 to 0.0260 in)

	H1	H2
Float height:		
1.3	14.5 to 15.5 mm (0.571 to 0.610 in)	44.5 to 45.5 mm (1.752 to 1.791 in)
1.6	16.5 to 17.5 mm (0.650 to 0.689 in)	46.5 to 47.5 mm (1.831 to 1.870 in)

Carburettor data

	Primary	Secondary
1.3 engine:		
Throttle chamber bore	26 mm	30 mm
Venturi diameter	19 mm	27 mm
Main jet (standard)	no 89	no 145
Main air bleed	no 70	no 60
Slow jet	no 40	no 80
Slow air bleed	no 80	no 80
Power jet	no 50	
1.6 engine:		
Throttle chamber bore	28 mm	32 mm
Venturi diameter	24 mm	27 mm
Main jet (standard)	no 98	no 135
Main air bleed	no 95	no 60
Slow jet	no 43	no 95
Slow air bleed	no 180	no 100
Power jet	no 45	

PTC heater

Operating range:	
Coolant temperature below 50°C (122°F)	System activated
Coolant temperature above 50°C (122°F)	System off

Torque wrench settings

	Nm	lbf ft
Fuel pump	13 to 16	10 to 12
Carburettor	6 to 7	4 to 5
Fuel tank	26 to 36	19 to 27
Fuel tank filler pipe to body	3.4 to 4.2	2.5 to 3.1
Exhaust downpipe to manifold	28 to 33	20 to 24

1 General description

The fuel system is the same on all models in the range, comprising a rear mounted fuel tank, a mechanical diaphragm fuel pump, and a dual barrel downdraught carburettor with an automatic choke.

The fuel pump is operated by a cam on the engine jackshaft.

The carburettor air cleaner has a dry paper element and the unit also contains an air temperature control in the intake. By regulating the air temperature in the unit, the carburettor is able to operate more efficiently, the warm-up period is reduced and there is an overall increase in efficiency to improve emission control.

When working on, or disconnecting any part of the system, particular care must be taken to guard against the risk of fire (see *Safety First* for general guidelines at the start of this manual).

Unleaded fuel

It is likely that Nissan Sunny models can be run on unleaded fuel following suitable modifications.

No adjustment information was available at the time of writing so refer to your dealer for guidance.

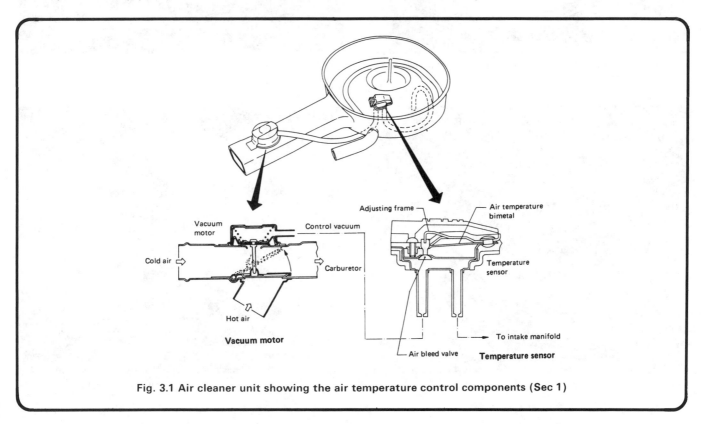

Fig. 3.1 Air cleaner unit showing the air temperature control components (Sec 1)

2   Routine maintenance

The following maintenance procedures must be made at the intervals given in *Routine Maintenance* at the start of this manual.

1   Check and if necessary adjust the engine idle speed and mixture settings (Section 11).

2   Check the condition and security of the fuel lines. Repair or renew as necessary.

3   Renew the air cleaner element at the specified intervals, or before if the vehicle is used in adverse conditions (city traffic or a dusty environment) (Section 3).

4   Renew the in-line fuel filter (Section 5).

5   Check the air temperature control valve for satisfactory operation (Section 4).

6   Inspect the exhaust system for any signs of leaks and/or damage and, if required, make the necessary repairs (Section 16).

3   Air cleaner – servicing, removal and refitting

1   The air cleaner fitted to all models in the range contains a dry paper type element which must be renewed at the specified intervals given at the start of this manual (see *Routine Maintenance*).

2   To renew the element, unscrew the wing nut and lift the air cleaner cover away. Lift out the air cleaner element (photos).

3   Wipe out the air cleaner casing so that it is clean and dry before fitting the new element into position, then refit the cover; aligning the arrows on the cover and case (see photo 3.2A).

4   To remove the air cleaner casing, remove the cover and element as previously described, then undo the casing and intake duct retaining bolts (photos).

5   Carefully lift the air cleaner away from the carburettor and detach the vacuum hoses and the flexible hot air hose from the manifold (photos). Also detach the throttle cable from its retaining clip on the top of the intake duct as the casing is removed.

6   Refitting is a reversal of the removal procedure.

3.2A Air cleaner cover wing nut. Note cover alignment arrows

3.2B Removing the air cleaner element

3.4A Air cleaner case retaining bolts to rocker cover

3.4B Air cleaner intake duct retaining bolts to front panel

3.5A Identify the hose connections ...

3.5B ... then lift the air cleaner from the carburettor ...

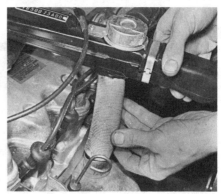

3.5C ... and the hot air hose from the exhaust manifold cowl

4 Air temperature control (ATC) system – checking

1 Check the condition and security of the vacuum hoses and repair or renew any which are perished or cracked.
2 Detach the extension duct from the air cleaner intake duct.
3 Detach the vacuum hose from the temperature sensor on the air cleaner duct. Start the engine from cold, allow it to idle and check that there is a strong vacuum through the hose. If not, check the hose for blockage or a leak, and repair as necessary. Reconnect the vacuum hose.
4 When the engine is cold, the valve in the intake duct will be in the closed position so that warm air is drawn from the hot air intake port on the underside of the air cleaner duct. As the engine warms up, the valve opens to allow cooler air through, and the hot air intake is closed off. This can be observed by holding a mirror at the end of the duct (Fig. 3.2).
5 If the valve operates in a satisfactory manner, reconnect the extension duct. If the valve is defective, the air cleaner unit complete will probably be in need of replacement, but first check the idle compensator.
6 The idle compensator device is fitted in the air cleaner body. The compensator is operated by a bi-metal strip in accordance with the intake air temperature. At temperatures below 55°C (131°F) the air valve is shut, but as the air temperature rises above 65°C (149°F), the valve should open fully. At intermediate temperatures, the valve can be open or closed (Fig. 3.3).
7 The operation of this device can be checked by warming it with hot air from a hair dryer whilst checking the temperature with a thermometer. The engine should be at its normal operating temperature for this test, the air cleaner cover removed and the warm air directed at the device whilst the compensator temperature is checked with the thermometer, held as close as possible to the compensator (Fig. 3.4).
8 If the compensator is in good condition, it should be open allowing air to pass through it and this will be obvious by the hissing sound. During this check take care not to damage the compensator bi-metal strip.
9 If defective, renew the air cleaner unit.
10 On completion, refit the air cleaner or its cover, as the case may be.

5 Fuel filter – renewal

1 An in-line type of fuel filter is used (photo).
2 Disconnect the hoses from the filter, and remove the unit from the clip.
3 Fit the new filter then start the engine and check for leaks.

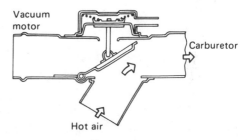

Fig. 3.2 Warm air flow circuit with the intake duct valve shut (Sec 4)

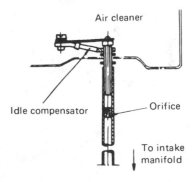

Fig. 3.3 Sectional view of the idle compensator (Sec 4)

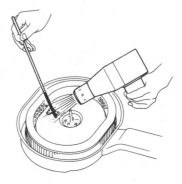

Fig. 3.4 Testing the idle compensator (Sec 4)

5.1 In-line fuel filter

6   Fuel tank – removal, repair and refitting

1   Disconnect the battery earth lead.
2   Position a suitable container under the fuel tank drain plug, undo the plug and drain the fuel from the tank. Store the fuel in a safe place.
3   Jack up the rear of the car and support it on axle stands.
4   Undo the retaining nut and remove the handbrake cable support bracket from the forward edge of the fuel tank.
5   Undo the retaining clips and detach the fuel filler hose and the vent hose (photo).
6   Disconnect the hoses and wiring from the fuel transmitter as described in the following Section.
7   Support the tank and then unscrew the mounting bolts from floor. Carefully lower the tank and manoeuvre it clear. It may be necessary to remove or partially disconnect the exhaust system and/or the rear radius rod to allow the tank to be removed.
8   Serious damage to the fuel tank will necessitate its renewal. Although minor damage or leaks may be repairable, such tasks must be entrusted to a specialist. Consult a Nissan dealer for advice if in doubt.
9   The removal of sediment or sludge can be carried out after first having removed the tank transmitter unit. Pour in some paraffin, or petrol, and shake the tank vigorously. Empty the tank and repeat the operations as many times as is necessary to clean it and then give a final rinse with clean fuel.
10   The fuel filter and vent hoses can be removed if required by

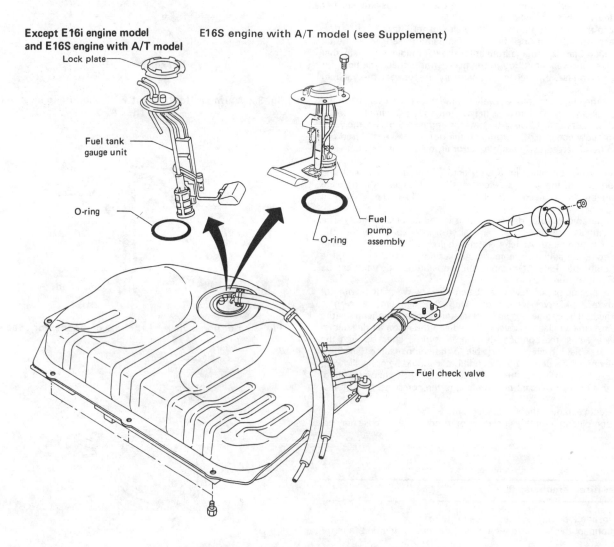

Fig. 3.5 Fuel tank and associated fittings (Sec 6)

6.5 Fuel filler and vent hoses

6.10 Fuel filler pipe flange nuts

6.11 Fuel check valve

undoing the four retaining nuts from the top flange, then lowering them from the car (photo).
11 If required, the fuel check valve hose can be removed by detaching the hose and withdrawing the unit from the bracket on the fuel tank. This valve must be renewed if it is suspected of malfunction (photo).
12 Refitting is a reversal of the removal procedure. Top up the fuel tank on completion and check for any signs of leakage from the tank and hose connections.

7 Fuel level transmitter and gauge – removal and refitting

1 Disconnect the battery earth lead.
2 Tilt the rear seat squab forward, then fold back the floor covering to gain access to the transmitter cover plate. Remove the cover plate, then disconnect the transmitter wires at their in-line connector.
3 Mark the hoses for identification, then loosen the retaining clips and detach the hoses from the transmitter (photo).
4 Untwist the transmitter unit by locating a screwdriver or a suitable flat piece of metal across the top of the unit between castellated sections and unscrew it. Withdraw the transmitter unit with care as it is easily damaged.
5 The fuel gauge can be removed after withdrawing the instrument panel, as described in Chapter 12.
6 Refitting is a reversal of the removal procedure. Renew the transmitter O-ring seal and ensure that all connections are securely made.

7.3 Fuel level transmitter and hose connections

8 Fuel pump – removal and refitting

1 The mechanically-operated fuel pump is of rocker arm type, actuated by an eccentric cam on the jackshaft (photo).
2 Disconnect the fuel hoses from the pump, and plug them to prevent loss of fuel.
3 Unscrew and remove the pump mounting nuts and washers and lift the pump from the crankcase. Discard the joint gaskets, but retain the insulator, if fitted (photo).
4 The fuel pump is of sealed type and, if clogged or faulty, will have to be renewed; cleaning and repair is not possible.
5 Clean the pump and crankcase mating faces, use new joint gaskets and bolt the pump into position.
6 Reconnect the fuel hoses, run the engine and test for leaks.

9 Carburettor – description

1 The carburettor fitted on all models is a dual barrel downdraught type with an automatic choke system. The calibration details of the carburettor are dependent on the engine and gearbox type used. The main components are as follows (photo).

Automatic choke
2 This is of bi-metal spring type, the heating being carried out

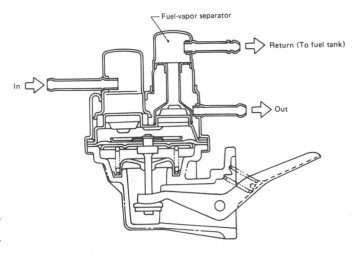

Fuel-vapor separator

Return (To fuel tank)

In

Out

Fig. 3.6 Fuel pump and connections (Sec 8)

8.1 Fuel pump location beneath the inlet manifold

8.3 Fuel pump removal

9.1 General view of the carburettor
A Automatic choke unit
B Choke unloader device
C Vacuum break diaphragm
D Secondary throttle vacuum diaphragm
E Fuel inlet union

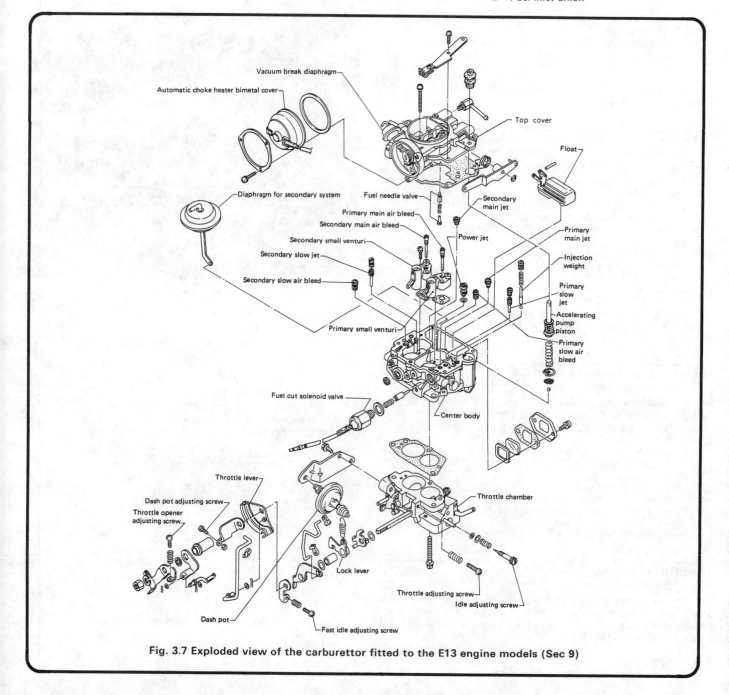

Fig. 3.7 Exploded view of the carburettor fitted to the E13 engine models (Sec 9)

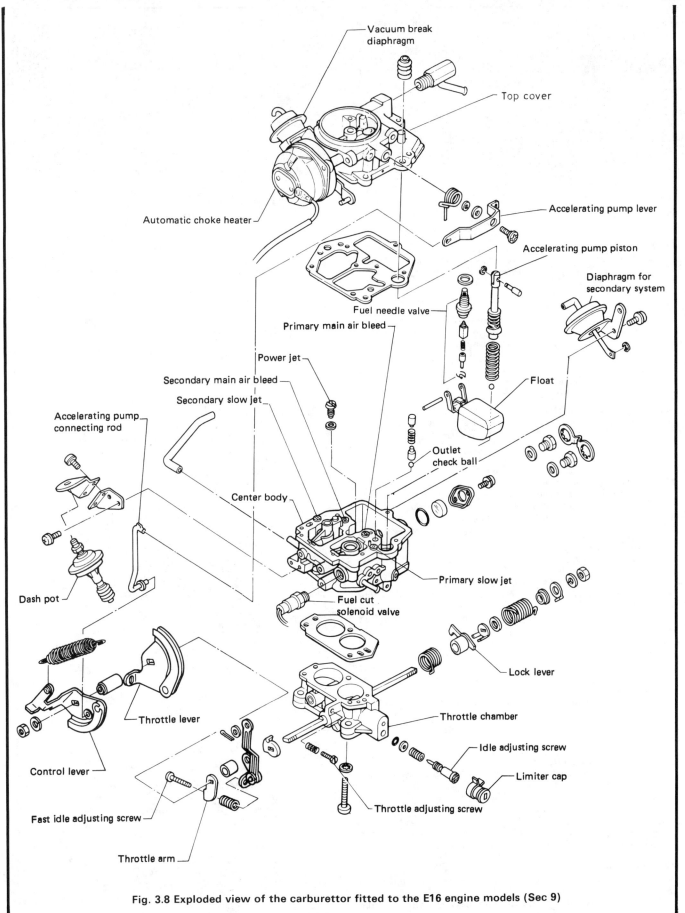

Fig. 3.8 Exploded view of the carburettor fitted to the E16 engine models (Sec 9)

electrically. A relay is located within the engine compartment for operating the automatic choke.

Fuel cut-off solenoid valve

3   The purpose of this valve is to prevent the engine running on when the ignition is switched off. This is done by cutting off the fuel supply to the idle circuit.

Secondary throttle vacuum diaphragm

4   This is actuated by vacuum conditions in the carburettor venturi. The diaphragm is linked to the secondary throttle in order to open it after the primary throttle valve plate has opened through an angle of 48°.

Dashpot

5   On certain models a dashpot is fitted to the carburettor to prevent the engine stalling during sudden braking or quick release of the accelerator pedal.

Choke unloader

6   This device opens the choke valve plate slightly when increasing the engine speed during the warm-up period to provide a suitable fuel/air mixture which would otherwise be too rich.

Vacuum break diaphragm

7   This is a double-acting type diaphragm which opens the choke valve plate immediately after cold starting to create a suitable fuel/air mixture in accordance with the prevailing engine vacuum conditions.

---

10 Carburettor – check and adjustments (general)

The following checks and adjustments should only be necessary if a malfunction or drop in performance and/or economy are noted.

Float level check

1   The float level can be easily checked with the carburettor *in situ* through the sight glass in the side wall of the float chamber. The vehicle must be standing level when making this check (Fig. 3.9).
2   The fuel level must be maintained at the level indicator index mark on the window. If adjustment is necessary, remove the top cover from the carburettor and adjust the float as described in Section 13.

Automatic choke

3   To make this check, the engine must be fully cold. Do not start the engine. Remove the air cleaner unit (Section 3).
4   Open the throttle valve to its full extent and check that the choke valve shuts properly. Operate the choke valve by pressing it with your finger and ensure that the valve has a smooth action.
5   Ensure that the index marks on the automatic choke cover and housing are in alignment (photo). Check that the automatic choke heater wires are securely connected, then start the engine and warm it up to its normal operating temperature, at which point check that the choke valve has fully opened. If it hasn't, then check the automatic choke heater wiring for continuity using an ohmmeter as shown (Figs. 3.10 and 3.11).
6   If the automatic choke wiring system is in order, the system relay is most probably at fault. Have the relay checked by a Nissan dealer and renew it, if necessary, ensuring that the replacement is of the correct type (Fig. 3.12).

Fast idle (automatic choke)

7   Bring the engine to normal operating temperature. Remove the choke housing cover.
8   Set the fast idle lever on the second step of the fast idle cam (photo).
9   Check that the fast idle engine speed is as given in the Specifications. If it is not, turn the fast idle screw as necessary, then refit the choke cover (photo).

Vacuum break

10 With the engine cold, remove the air cleaner and close the choke valve plate.
11 Using a vacuum pump as shown, apply vacuum to the vacuum break diaphragm and give a light push on the piston rod to shut the

Fuel level should be maintained in this mark.

Fig. 3.9 Carburettor float chamber sight glass and level mark (Sec 10)

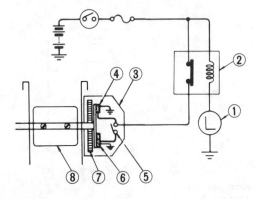

Fig. 3.10 Automatic choke unit electrical circuit (Sec 10)

1 Alternator "L" terminal	5 Bimetal switch
2 Automatic choke relay	6 PTC heater (B)
3 Automatic choke cover	7 Bi-metal strip
4 PTC heater (A)	8 Choke valve

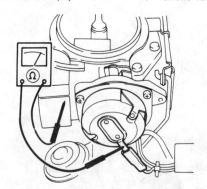

Fig. 3.11 Automatic choke heater wiring check method (Sec 10)

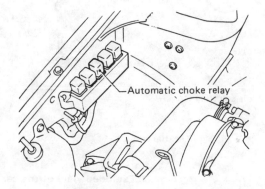

Automatic choke relay

Fig. 3.12 Automatic choke relay location (Sec 10)

10.5 Automatic choke housing/cover index marks at central setting

10.8 Choke cover removed to show fast idle arm (1) and cam (2), and operating lever (3)

10.9 View showing bi-metal strip in the choke housing cover. Engage strip tang with lever when refitting

choke valve. Now check that the clearance shown at R1 (Fig. 3.13) is as specified.

12 Now push the piston rod back towards the vacuum break diaphragm and check clearance at R1 again, but this time it should be as given for the R2 check. If required, bend the tongue to make any adjustments necessary.

Accelerator pump

13 For this check, the air filter must be removed and the engine switched off. Actuate the throttle lever and looking into the top of the carburettor venturi, ensure that petrol is injected smoothly from the injection nozzle into the primary port. If the injector fails to operate, first check that there is sufficient fuel in the float chamber, then check the pump linkage, piston and limiter assembly. The limiter is designed to provide a small injection of fuel directly after the movement of the throttle lever. Do not tamper or bend the pump stroke limiter.

Dashpot (automatic transmission)

14 Have the engine idling at normal operating temperature.

15 Turn the throttle lever on the carburettor by hand and have an assistant record the engine speed shown on the tachometer at the point where the dashpot just makes contact with the stop lever. If the speed is not as specified, release the locknut and turn the dashpot rod.

16 Tighten the locknut and make sure that the engine speed drops to 1000 rpm in three seconds (Fig. 3.14).

Fuel cut solenoid valve

17 If suspected of malfunction, detach the wiring to the solenoid and attach a live supply lead direct from the battery. When connected to direct live feed, the solenoid should be heard to click open, then when disconnected, to click close. Renew the solenoid valve if defective. Check for any signs of fuel leaks on completion when the engine is restarted (Fig. 3.15).

18 If the solenoid fuel cut-off valve was removed, screw it in, using a new sealing washer.

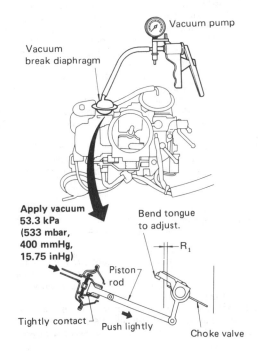

Apply vacuum 53.3 kPa (533 mbar, 400 mmHg, 15.75 inHg)

Vacuum pump

Vacuum break diaphragm

Bend tongue to adjust.

R_1

Piston rod

Tightly contact

Push lightly

Choke valve

Fig. 3.13 Carburettor vacuum break diaphragm check (Sec 10)

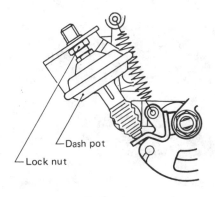

Dash pot

Lock nut

Fig. 3.14 Dashpot and adjustment locknut (Sec 10)

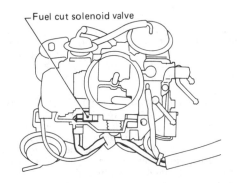

Fuel cut solenoid valve

Fig. 3.15 Fuel cut-off solenoid valve location (Sec 10)

11 Carburettor – idle speed and mixture adjustment

1   The mixture is preset during production and should not normally require altering. However, adjustment may be necessary if the carburettor has been overhauled or after a high mileage when the engine characteristics may have changed slightly due to the build-up of carbon or wear in the engine components.
2   On some models, the idle mixture screw is fitted with a limiter cap (photo). The screw can be turned if a screwdriver blade is ground to a shape similar to that shown in Fig. 3.16.
3   Have the engine at normal operating temperature with the ignition timing and valve clearances correctly set.
4   Note that on power steering models the front wheels should be in the straight-ahead position to ensure the pump does not affect the idle speed.
5   The headlamps (and, if fitted, the air conditioner) must be switched off during checks and adjustments.
6   Connect up a tachometer to the engine in accordance with the manufacturer's instructions. With the engine idling, turn the throttle speed screw (photo 11.2) as necessary to bring the speed within the range given in Specifications.
7   For accuracy, the idle mixture should be adjusted using a CO meter (exhaust gas analyser). Rev up the engine two or three times to clear it and then let it idle. Turn the idle mixture screw until the meter indicates a CO content within the specified tolerance. This adjustment should be carried out quickly. If it extends over more than two minutes, rev the engine again before resuming adjustment. The air cleaner must be fitted when checking the CO content.
8   If an exhaust gas analyser is not available, carry out the following alternative method of adjusting the idle mixture. Turn the idle mixture screw until the engine speed is at its highest level and does not increase any further. Make sure that the engine is idling smoothly and then readjust the throttle speed screw to bring the idle speed within the specified range.
9   If the idle mixture screw has been removed during carburettor overhaul, a starting point for mixture adjustment can be established if the screw is turned in very gently until it just seats and then unscrewed two full turns.

12 Carburettor – removal and refitting

1   Remove the air cleaner.
2   Disconnect the accelerator control cable from the carburettor.
3   Disconnect the electrical lead from the automatic choke unit.
4   Disconnect the lead from the fuel cut-off solenoid valve.
5   Disconnect and plug the fuel hoses (photo).
6   Unbolt and remove the carburettor from the intake manifold. Take care not to drop the mounting nuts into the carburettor intake (photo).
7   Refitting is a reversal of removal, but always use a new gasket at the manifold joint (photo).

13 Carburettor – overhaul

1   With the carburettor removed from the engine, clean away all external dirt and grease.
2   The need for complete dismantling of a carburettor seldom occurs. The usual reason is to clean the jets and fuel bowl and to check the adjustments described later in this Section. In fact, where the major components of the carburettor are worn, such as the throttle or choke valve plate spindles or bushes, and the unit has seen long service, it will almost certainly be more economical to purchase a new or factory-reconditioned carburettor.
3   Detach the accelerator pump lever connecting rod by extracting the split pin and removing the washer (photo).
4   Remove the split pin and washer from the automatic choke-to-throttle linkage connection and disconnect them (photo).
5   Remove the retaining screw securing the unloader stay bracket mounting plate stay arm to the side face of the top section (photo).
6   Detach the throttle return spring from the support bracket. Undo the single screw retaining the bracket to the side of the carburettor.
7   Undo the carburettor top section retaining screws, noting that one of the five also secures the throttle return spring support bracket to the

11.2 Throttle speed screw (A) and idle mixture screw (B)

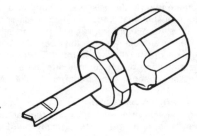

Fig. 3.16 Special screwdriver used to turn idle mixture screw (Sec 11)

12.5 Disconnect the fuel line from the carburettor

12.6 Removing the carburettor from the manifold

12.7 Always use a new carburettor gasket when refitting the carburettor

top of the carburettor, together with the idle cut-out solenoid lead retaining clip. Remove the bracket and lead clip, then carefully lift the top section away from the main body. Try not to break the gasket as it is separated in case a new gasket is not readily available, although this and any other gaskets in the carburettor which are disturbed should be renewed if possible.

8 The float and the fuel inlet needle valve can be removed once the float arm pivot pin is pushed out.

9 Clean out the float chamber and clean the jets and bleed holes by applying air pressure from a tyre pump. If the jets are badly clogged or are suspected of being the wrong ones they should be unscrewed. *Never probe a jet with wire,* but if air pressure fails to clear it use a nylon bristle. The jets can be checked for size by quoting the carburettor index number to your dealer's parts department.

10 To remove the main (centre) body from the throttle chamber, detach the lower flange insulator and gaskets.

11 Disconnect the secondary system diaphragm from the valve lever by extracting the split pin and removing the washer (photo).

12 Detach the vacuum tube from the choke unloader diaphragm.

13 Undo the retaining screws recessed in the lower mating flange and separate the throttle chamber from the main body and carefully remove the gaskets. The gaskets should be renewed if possible (photo).

14 Obtain a repair kit for your carburettor which will contain all the necessary gaskets, seals and other renewable items, including new split pins to secure the operating rods and levers.

15 Reassemble by reversing the dismantling operations, but as work commences check the float level setting as follows.

Float setting

16 Invert the carburettor cover so that the float arm rests on the fuel inlet needle valve under its own weight. Measure the distance $H1$ between the surface of the float and the face of the top cover (see Fig. 3.17).

17 If this is not as specified, carefully bend the float seat.

18 Now check the distance between the top cover face and the top of the float ($H2$), whilst raising the float so that its stopper is just in contact with the top cover. If not as specified, bend the float stopper to suit.

19 When the carburettor is refitted to the vehicle, recheck the fuel level through the sight glass on the side wall of the fuel bowl.

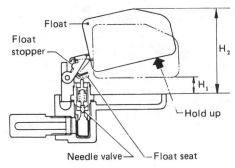

Fig. 3.17 Float setting diagram (Sec 13)
H1 and H2 see text

13.3 Accelerator pump lever-to-connecting rod joint (1). Detach lower end of rod from throttle barrel (2)

13.4 Automatic choke-to-throttle linkage (arrowed)

13.5 Unloader stay bracket screw (arrowed)

13.11 Secondary system diaphragm rod-to-valve connection (arrowed)

13.13 Underside view of carburettor showing throttle chamber-to-main body retaining screws and the primary and secondary throttle valves

14.3A PTC wiring connection

14 Emission control system – general

1   All models are equipped with basic emission control features, which comprise the following items:

   (a) Crankcase ventilation system (PCV), described in Chapter 1
   (b) Automatic temperature control (ATC), described in Section 4 of this Chapter
   (c) Positive temperature coefficient (PTC), described below

2   The PTC device comprises a heated grille, located between the carburettor and the inlet manifold. This heater is thermostatically controlled in accordance with the engine coolant temperature. A thermo-electric switch activates the heater element when the engine coolant is below 50°C (122°F), to warm the air/fuel mixture as it passes into the inlet manifold, through the primary venturi.

3   If the PTC unit is to be removed, disconnect the thermo-switch wiring (at the unit), remove the carburettor (Section 13) then lift the PTC unit from the manifold (photos).

4   Refitting is a reversal of the removal procedure, but the manifold gaskets must be renewed.

15 Accelerator pedal and cable – removal, refitting and adjustment

Pedal

1   Release the cable from the top of the pedal arm (photo).

2   Extract the E-clip from the pedal pivot shaft, disengage the return spring and remove the pedal. The pedal pivot bracket can be removed by undoing the two retaining bolts from the floor (photo).

3   Refitting is a reversal of the removal procedure but apply grease to the moving parts.

14.3B Removing the PTC unit

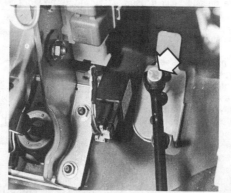

15.1 Accelerator pedal and cable connection (arrowed)

15.2 Accelerator pedal, pivot shaft and bracket

15.6 Detaching the accelerator cable from the throttle barrel

15.7 Accelerator cable location bracket and adjuster nuts

Cable
4   Disconnect the cable from the top of the pedal arm.
5   Loosen the cable adjuster nuts at the location bracket, then disconnect the cable from the bracket.
6   Disconnect the cable from the throttle barrel and then withdraw the cable from the engine compartment side (photo).
7   Fit the new cable by reversing the removal operations. Adjust it by

5   Always ensure that the gasket mating faces of the head and manifold are cleaned thoroughly before reassembling the manifold(s) (photos).
6   The exhaust system may have one or two downpipes (according to model) and all models incorporate an expansion box and silencer (photos).
7   The exhaust system is suspended on flexible mountings (photos).

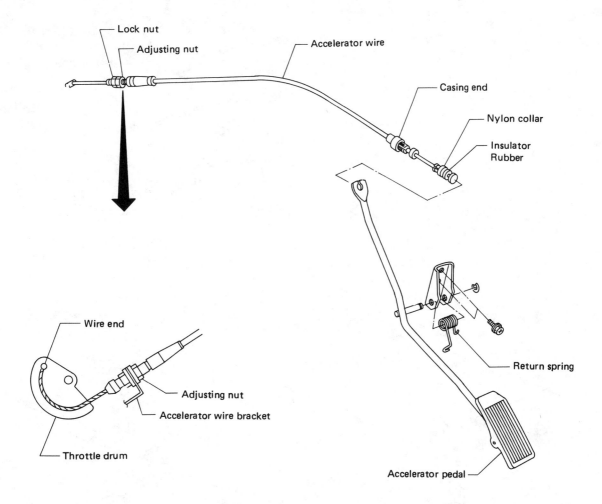

Fig. 3.18 Accelerator pedal and cable components (Sec 15)

tightening the adjustment nut to the point where the throttle drum just starts to move. At this point undo the adjuster nut 1$\frac{1}{2}$ to 2 turns, then secure by tightening the locknut (photo).
8   Check the accelerator pedal, cable and controls for satisfactory action, lubricate the moving parts (but not the inner cable) with multi-purpose grease.
9   On vehicles equipped with automatic transmission, check that the pedal can be depressed fully into the kickdown position (also refer to Chapter 7).

16 Manifolds and exhaust system – general

1   The manifolds are located on opposite sides of the engine. As the intake manifold is coolant heated, the cooling system must be drained before it can be removed.
2   The inlet manifold can be removed complete with the carburettor or separately. Removal of the carburettor gives improved access to the manifold nuts.
3   When removing the inlet manifold, the wiring harness must be unclipped from its underside as it is withdrawn.
4   New gaskets must be used when refitting the inlet and/or the exhaust manifolds, and the retaining nuts and bolts must be tightened securely.

8   When any one section of the exhaust system needs renewal it is possible that the remaining parts of the system are also in poor condition. In this situation it may be preferable to renew the complete system.
9   Where only one section of the exhaust system is leaking, this can often be repaired by using Holts Flexiwrap and Holts Gun Gum. Holts Flexiwrap is an MOT approved permanent exhaust repair.
10 It is most important when fitting exhaust systems that the bends and contours are carefully followed and that each connecting joint overlaps the correct distance. Any stresses or strain imparted in order to force the system to fit the hanger rubbers, will result in early fractures and failures.
11 When fitting a new part of a complete system it is well worth removing all the system from the car and cleaning up all the joints so that they fit together easily. The time spent struggling with obstinate joints whilst flat on your back under the car is eliminated and the likelihood of distorting or even breaking a section is greatly reduced. Do not waste a lot of time trying to undo rusted and corroded clamps and bolts. Cut them off. New ones will be required anyway if they are that bad.
12 Use an exhaust pipe joint sealant such as Holts Firegum when assembling pipe sections, to ensure that the respective joints are free from leaks.

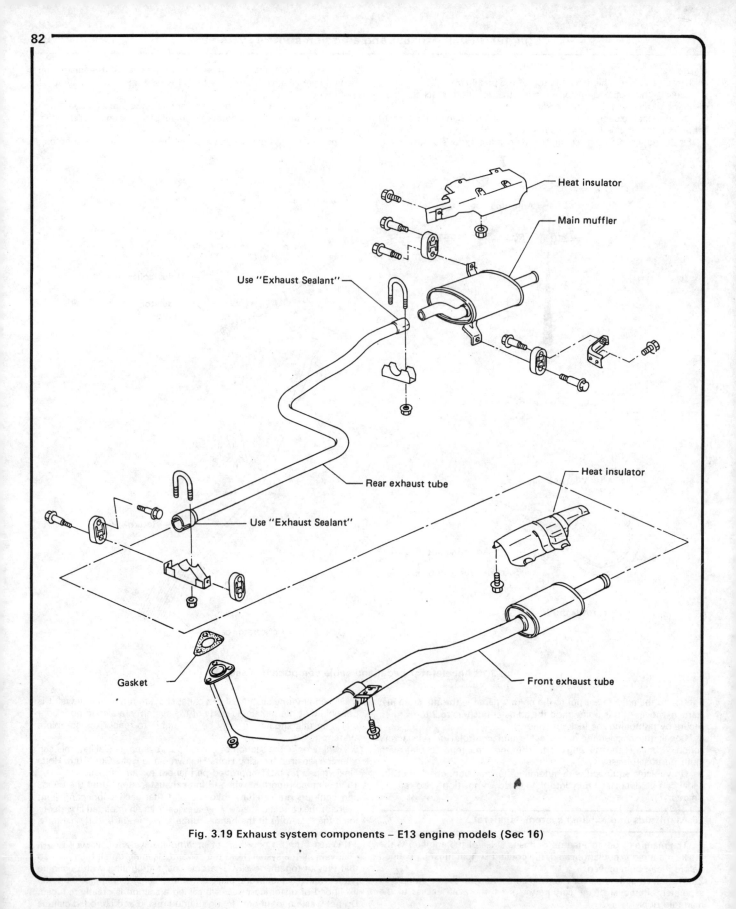

Heat insulator

Main muffler

Use "Exhaust Sealant"

Rear exhaust tube

Heat insulator

Use "Exhaust Sealant"

Front exhaust tube

Gasket

Fig. 3.19 Exhaust system components – E13 engine models (Sec 16)

Exhaust resonance – rectification

13 If exhaust resonance on acceleration from low speed is experienced, first ensure that all exhaust system mountings, brackets and heat shields are securely tightened. If it is suspected that a heat shield itself is the cause of the noise, any vibration in this area can be reduced by carefully introducing a crease or 'set' into the shield, using pliers. A modified main silencer (muffler) mounting bracket (part number 20742.50A15) fitted with a damper weight is also available from your Nissan dealer.

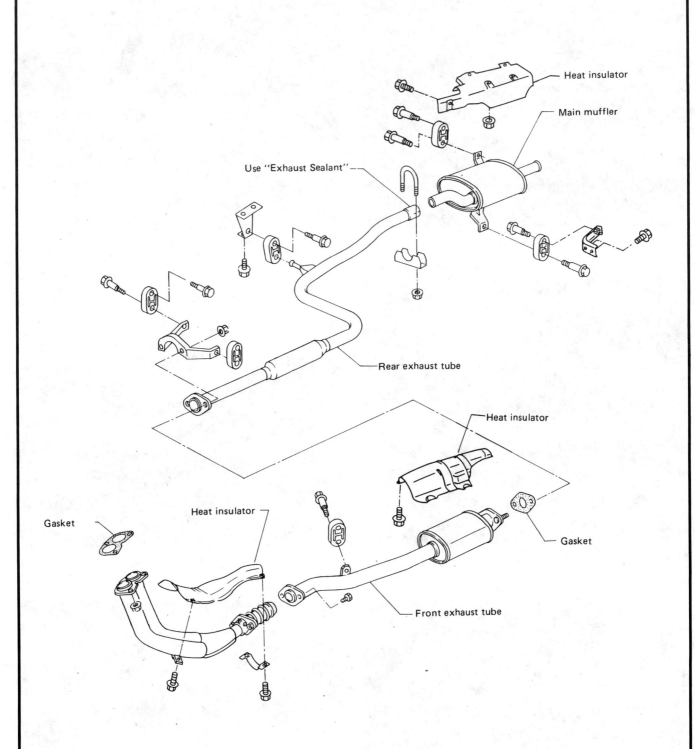

Heat insulator

Main muffler

Use "Exhaust Sealant"

Rear exhaust tube

Heat insulator

Gasket

Heat insulator

Gasket

Front exhaust tube

Fig. 3.20 Exhaust system components – E16 engine models (Sec 16)

16.5A Locate the new inlet manifold gaskets ...

16.5B ... fit the inlet manifold over the retaining studs ...

16.5C ... and tighten the nuts

16.5D Locate the new exhaust manifold gaskets ...

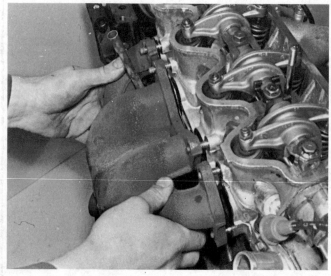

16.5E ... fit the exhaust manifold onto the studs ...

16.5F ... refit the manifold and heat shield. Note engine lift bracket is retained by upper two nuts at timing case end

16.6A Twin type downpipe-to-manifold flange joint and retaining nuts

16.6B Downpipe-to-exhaust pipe flange joint

16.7A Exhaust system suspension brackets and flexible mountings. Note earth strap and heat shield above exhaust

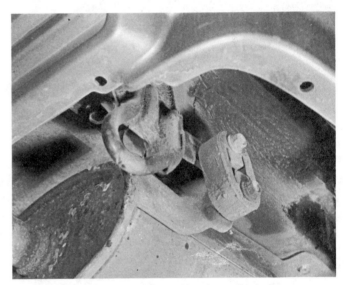

16.7B Exhaust flexible mounting and bracket at the rear

17 Fault diagnosis – fuel, exhaust and emission control systems

Unsatisfactory engine performance and excessive fuel consumption are not necessarily the fault of the fuel system or carburettor. In fact they more commonly occur as a result of ignition and timing faults. Before acting on the following it is necessary to check the ignition system first. Even though a fault may lie in the fuel system it will be difficult to trace unless the ignition is correct. The faults below, therefore, assume that this has been attended to first (where appropriate)

Symptom	Reason(s)
Smell of fuel when engine is stopped	Leaking fuel lines or unions Leaking fuel tank
Smell of fuel when engine is idling	Leaking fuel line unions between pump and carburettor injectors Overflow of fuel from float chamber due to wrong level setting, ineffective needle valve or punctured float
Excessive fuel consumption for reasons not covered by leaks or float chamber faults	Worn jets Over-rich setting Sticking mechanism Dirty air cleaner element Sticking air cleaner thermostatic mechanism

Difficult starting, uneven running, lack of power, cutting out	One or more jets blocked or restricted Float chamber fuel level too low or needle valve sticking Fuel pump not delivering sufficient fuel Faulty solenoid fuel shut-off valve (if fitted) Induction leak
Difficult starting when cold	Automtatic choke maladjusted Automatic choke not cocked before starting
Difficult starting when hot	Automatic choke malfunction Accelerator pedal pumped before starting Vapour lock (especially in hot weather or at high altitude)
Engine does not respond properly to throttle	Faulty accelerator pump Blocked jet(s) Slack in accelerator cable
Engine idle speed drops when hot	Defective temperature compensator Overheated fuel pump

Emission control system

Excessive HC or CO in exhaust gas	Air cleaner clogged Float level too high Faulty throttle opener control system Leaking intake manifold gasket
Excessive HC, CO and Nox in exhaust gas	Worn piston rings Incorrect valve clearances Faulty thermostat Blown cylinder head gasket Clogged PCV valve Incorrect idle mixture Clogged fuel filter Faulty idle compensator Choke not fully off Incorrect ignition settings Malfunction of emission control system component

HC   Hydrocarbons
CO   Carbon monoxide
NOx   Nitrogen oxide

Chapter 4 Ignition system

For modifications, and information applicable to later models, see Supplement at end of manual

Contents

Coil – description and testing	7	Fault diagnosis – ignition system	8
Distributor – overhaul	4	Ignition timing – checking and adjustment	5
Distributor – removal and refitting	3	Routine maintenance	2
General description	1	Spark plugs, HT leads and distributor cap – general	6

Specifications

General
System type	Electronic, with breakerless distributor
Firing order	1-3-4-2 (No 1 at timing belt end)

Spark plugs
1.3 and 1.6	Champion RN9YCC or RN9YC
Electrode gap	0.8 mm (0.032 in)

HT leads
1.3 and 1.6	Champion CLS 8, boxed set

Ignition timing
At idle with vacuum hose detached and plugged:
1.3	2° ± 2° BTDC
1.6	4° ± 2° BTDC

Distributor
Direction of rotation	Anticlockwise	
Air gap	0.3 to 0.5 mm (0.012 to 0.020 in)	
Carbon brush wear limit	10 mm (0.39 in) minimum	
Type number	**Manual transmission**	**Automatic transmission**
1.3	Hitachi D4R83-30	Hitachi D4R83-36
1.6	Hitachi D4R83-36	Hitachi D4R83-31

Coil
Type number	Hanshin STC-143
Primary resistance at 20°C (68°F)	1.0 to 1.3 ohm
Secondary resistance at 20°C (68°F)	8.4 to 12.6 ohm

Torque wrench setting
	Nm	lbf ft
Spark plugs	20 to 29	15 to 21

1 General description

1 A transistorised ignition system is fitted to all models. With this system the circuit is switched by an electronic unit (located in the distributor) incorporating a magnetic stator, reluctor and transistor control.

2 In order that the engine can run correctly, it is necessary for an electical spark to ignite the fuel/air mixture in the combustion chamber at exactly the right moment in relation to engine speed and load. The ignition system is based on feeding low tension voltage from the battery to the coil where it is converted to high tension voltage. The high tension voltage is powerful enough to jump the spark plug gap in the cylinders many times a second under high compression, providing that the system is in good condition and that all adjustments are correct.

3 The system is divided into two circuits: the low tension and high tension circuits. Low tension voltage is changed in the coil to high tension voltage by the alternate switching on and off of the primary circuit. The high tension voltage is fed to the relevant spark plug via the distributor cap and rotor arm. The ignition is advanced and retarded automatically to ensure that the spark occurs at the correct instant in relation to the engine speed and load.

4 Centrifugal weights in the distributor advance the ignition timing in relation to engine speed, and a vacuum unit on the side of the distributor controls the timing in relation to engine load.

5 To assist ignition timing control, and improve engine performance when the engine is cold, a vacuum delay valve and a thermal vacuum valve are incorporated into the vacuum line between the carburettor and distributor (Fig. 4.2 and photo).

6 *When working on electronic ignition systems remember that the high tension voltage can be considerably higher than a conventional system and in certain circumstances could prove fatal.*

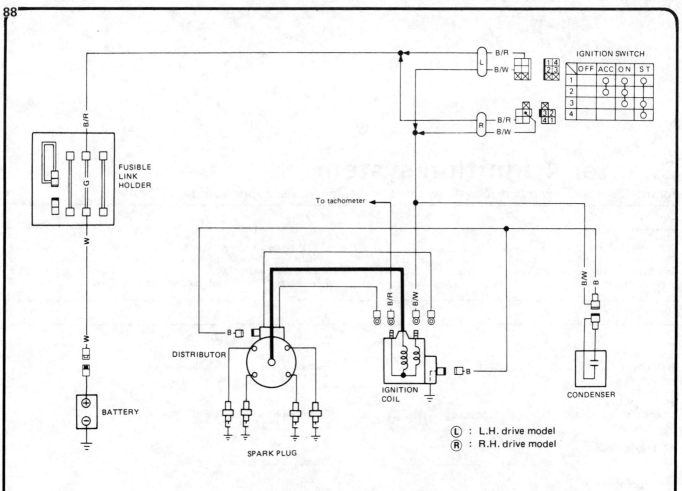

Fig. 4.1 Ignition system wiring diagram (Sec 1)

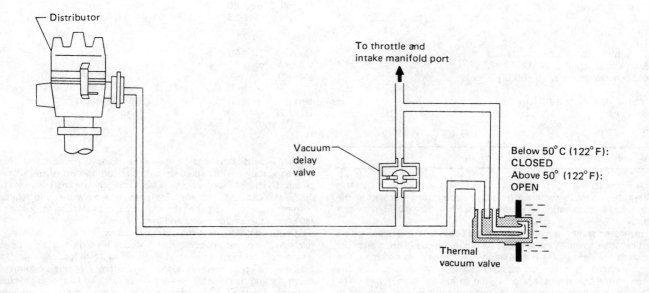

Fig. 4.2 Thermo-vacuum ignition timing control system (Sec 1)

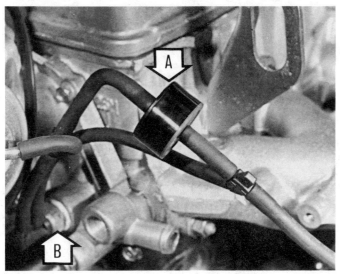

1.5 View showing vacuum delay valve (A) and thermal vacuum valve (B)

2 Routine maintenance

At the intervals given in *Routine Maintenance* at the start of this manual, carry out the following operations on the ignition system.

1   Remove the spark plugs as described in Section 6. Renew all four plugs if any are found to be in poor condition.

2   Renew the spark plugs at the specified intervals, even if they appear to be still in good condition.

3   Check the HT leads for condition and security. Renew if necessary.

Wipe clean the inside and outside of the distributor cap, also the top of the ignition coil.

4   Check the condition and security of all wiring and leads and their connections associated with the ignition sytem. Ensure that no chafing is occurring on any of the wires.

5   Check and if necessary adjust the ignition timing as described in Section 5.

3 Distributor – removal and refitting

1   The distributor is driven by the camshaft; the distributor drive dog engaging with a lug on the rear end face of the camshaft. The distributor is mounted in a combined distributor/thermostat housing which is bolted to the rear end of the cylinder head.

2   Each plug lead fitted during manufacture is numbered for identification (although later replacements may not be).

3   To remove the distributor, first unclip and remove the insulator cover from the distributor cap (photo).

4   Either undo the retaining screws and remove the distributor cap and then detach the LT leads (photos), or disconnect the LT leads and the HT lead at the ignition coil if the cap and leads are to be removed with the distributor.

5   Make a mark on the slotted flange of the distributor body in line with the mounting stud so that the ignition timing can be reset approximately when the distributor is refitted.

6   The distributor shaft incorporates an offset slot so there is no need to note the position of the rotor arm. Simply disconnect the vacuum hose, then unscrew the mounting nut and withdraw the distributor from the cylinder head (photos).

7   Refitting is a reversal of removal, but align the offset slot with the dog on the camshaft before inserting the distributor. Turn the rotor arm if necessary until the slot engages. If the ignition timing setting has been lost, it can be reset approximately by aligning the crankshaft timing marks (Section 5) with No 1 piston on compression, then turning the distributor within the adjustment slot until the reluctor peak is aligned with the stator post.

3.3 Distributor insulating cover and clips

3.4A Undoing the distributor cap retaining screws

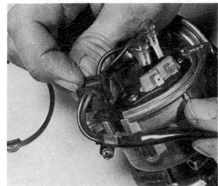

3.4B Disconnecting the LT leads from the distributor

3.6A Undo the distributor retaining nut

3.6B Distributor drive dog showing off-set slot

3.8 Refitting the rubber rim seal

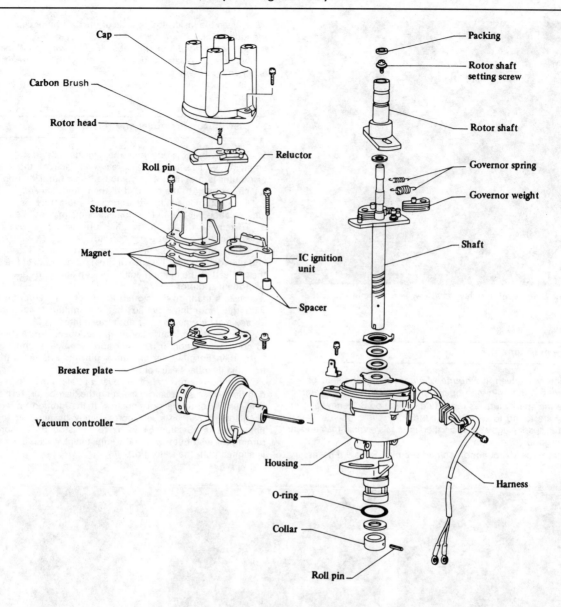

Fig. 4.3 Exploded view of the distributor (Sec 4)

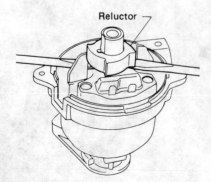

Fig. 4.4 Removing the reluctor (Sec 4)

8 When the LT leads are reconnected, refit the rubber rim seal (photo).
9 After refitting the distributor, check and adjust the ignition timing as described in Section 5.

4 Distributor – overhaul

1 With the distributor removed from the engine (Section 3), clean away the external dirt.
2 If not already removed, undo the retaining screws and remove the distributor cap, then disconnect the LT leads at the distributor (see photos in previous Section).
3 Pull the rotor head from the shaft.
4 Extract the fixing screws and remove the vacuum advance unit.
5 Using two screwdrivers as levers, prise free the reluctor from the shaft and recover the roll-pin. Take care when levering the reluctor not to damage its teeth (Fig. 4.4).
6 Extract the fixing screws and remove the breaker plate.
7 Undo the retaining screws and remove the IC ignition unit and spacers.
8 Remove the magnet, stator and spacers from the breaker plate.

Are your plugs trying to tell you something?

Normal.
Grey-brown deposits, lightly coated core nose. Plugs ideally suited to engine, and engine in good condition.

Heavy Deposits.
A build up of crusty deposits, light-grey sandy colour in appearance.
Fault: Often caused by worn valve guides, excessive use of upper cylinder lubricant, or idling for long periods.

Lead Glazing.
Plug insulator firing tip appears yellow or green/yellow and shiny in appearance.
Fault: Often caused by incorrect carburation, excessive idling followed by sharp acceleration. Also check ignition timing.

Carbon fouling.
Dry, black, sooty deposits.
Fault: over-rich fuel mixture.
Check: carburettor mixture settings, float level, choke operation, air filter.

Oil fouling.
Wet, oily deposits. Fault: worn bores/piston rings or valve guides; sometimes occurs (temporarily) during running-in period.

Overheating.
Electrodes have glazed appearance, core nose very white – few deposits. Fault: plug overheating. Check: plug value, ignition timing, fuel octane rating (too low) and fuel mixture (too weak).

Electrode damage.
Electrodes burned away; core nose has burned, glazed appearance. Fault: pre-ignition. Check: for correct heat range and as for 'overheating'.

Split core nose.
(May appear initially as a crack). Fault: detonation or wrong gap-setting technique. Check: ignition timing, cooling system, fuel mixture (too weak).

WHY DOUBLE COPPER IS BETTER FOR YOUR ENGINE.

Unique Trapezoidal Copper Cored Earth Electrode — 50% Larger Spark Area — Copper Cored Centre Electrode

Champion Double Copper plugs are the first in the world to have copper core in both centre <u>and</u> earth electrode. This innovative design means that they run cooler by up to 100°C – giving greater efficiency and longer life. These double copper cores transfer heat away from the tip of the plug faster and more efficiently. Therefore, Double Copper runs at cooler temperatures than conventional plugs giving improved acceleration response and high speed performance with no fear of pre-ignition.

TRAPEZOIDAL COPPER CORED EARTH ELECTRODE
NEW TRAPEZOIDAL COPPER CORED EARTH ELECTRODE   CONVENTIONAL SOLID NICKEL ALLOY EARTH ELECTRODE
50% INCREASE IN SPARK AREA

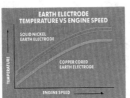

EARTH ELECTRODE TEMPERATURE VS ENGINE SPEED
SOLID NICKEL EARTH ELECTRODE
COPPER CORED EARTH ELECTRODE
TEMPERATURE
ENGINE SPEED

Champion Double Copper plugs also feature a unique trapezoidal earth electrode giving a 50% increase in spark area. This, together with the double copper cores, offers greatly reduced electrode wear, so the spark stays stronger for longer.

 FASTER COLD STARTING

 FOR UNLEADED OR LEADED FUEL

 ELECTRODES UP TO 100°C COOLER

 BETTER ACCELERATION RESPONSE

 LOWER EMISSIONS

 50% BIGGER SPARK AREA

 THE LONGER LIFE PLUG

Plug Tips/Hot and Cold.
Spark plugs must operate within well-defined temperature limits to avoid cold fouling at one extreme and overheating at the other.
Champion and the car manufacturers work out the best plugs for an engine to give optimum performance under all conditions, from freezing cold starts to sustained high speed motorway cruising.
Plugs are often referred to as hot or cold. With Champion, the higher the number on its body, the hotter the plug, and the lower the number the cooler the plug. For the correct plug for your car refer to the specifications at the beginning of this chapter.

Plug Cleaning
Modern plug design and materials mean that Champion no longer recommends periodic plug cleaning. Certainly don't clean your plugs with a wire brush as this can cause metal conductive paths across the nose of the insulator so impairing its performance and resulting in loss of acceleration and reduced m.p.g.
However, if plugs are removed, always carefully clean the area where the plug seats in the cylinder head as grit and dirt can sometimes cause gas leakage.
Also wipe any traces of oil or grease from plug leads as this may lead to arcing.

CHAMPION
DOUBLE COPPER

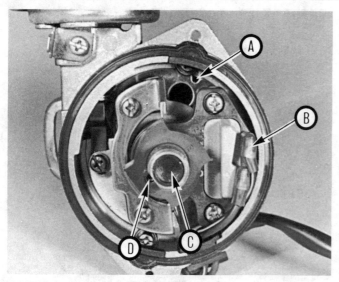

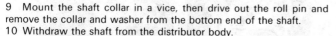

4.19 Top view of reassembled distributor
A *Breakerplate alignment notch mark*   C *Felt lubrication pad*
B *LT wire (black and white is positive)*   D *Reluctor roll pin*

4.22 Reluctor air gap check using feeler gauge blade of specified thickness. Stator setscrews are arrowed

9 Mount the shaft collar in a vice, then drive out the roll pin and remove the collar and washer from the bottom end of the shaft.

10 Withdraw the shaft from the distributor body.

11 Extract the felt lubrication pad from the recess in the top of the shaft and remove the screw now exposed. Separate the rotor shaft from the mainshaft.

12 If necessary, disconnect the springs and remove the counter-weights, but mark the location of the springs with a dab of quick-drying paint.

13 Clean and inspect all components. The reluctor and stator should be unscratched and not distorted, otherwise renew them. If the carbon brush is worn down to its specified minimum length, renew the cap.

14 Apply grease to all friction and bearing surfaces as work proceeds.

15 Reassembly is a reversal of dismantling, but observe the following points.

16 When reconnecting the counterweight springs, fit the smaller diameter spring first.

17 Set the relative position of the rotor shaft cut-out to the mainshaft offset groove as shown in Fig. 4.5.

18 Use a new roll pin to fix the drive collar to the shaft.

19 When fitting the breakerplate, make sure that its mark is in alignment with the one on the distributor body (photo).

20 Fit a new roll pin to the reluctor.

21 Make sure that the wiring harness spade terminals are correctly located.

22 Finally, set the reluctor air gap (reluctor peak to stator prong edge) to the specified dimension using a feeler blade (photo). Adjustment is made by loosening the screws and repositioning the stator.

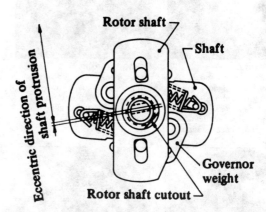

Fig. 4.5 Correct relation of the rotor shaft to the driveshaft (Sec 4)

5 Ignition timing – checking and adjustment

1 Run the engine to normal operating temperature then switch it off and connect a stroboscopic timing light in accordance with the manufacturer's instructions.

2 Disconnect and plug the vacuum advance hose at the distributor.

3 With the engine idling, point the timing light at the index above the crankshaft pulley. The notch in the pulley rim should be in alignment with the mark on the index which applies to your particular vehicle (see Specifications).

4 Any difficulty experienced in seeing the timing marks clearly can be overcome by applying a spot of white paint to the pulley notch and the specified timing mark on the index.

5 If the marks are not in alignment, release the distributor clamp nut and turn the distributor in either direction as necessary to align the marks.

6 Tighten the nut, switch off the engine, reconnect the vacuum hose, and remove the timing light.

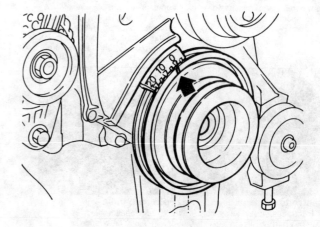

Fig. 4.6 Ignition timing marks and crankshaft pulley timing index mark (set at TDC) (Sec 5)

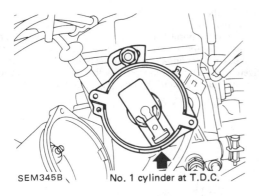

SEM345B   No. 1 cylinder at T.D.C.

Fig. 4.7 Distributor rotor arm at TDC (No 1 cylinder)
(Sec 5)

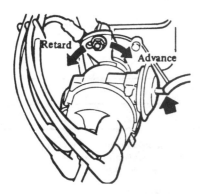

Fig. 4.8 Ignition timing adjustment (Sec 5)

6 Spark plugs, HT leads and distributor cap – general

1 The correct functioning of the spark plugs is vital for the correct running and efficiency of the engine. It is essential that the plugs fitted are appropriate for the engine, and the suitable type is specified at the beginning of this chapter. If this type is used and the engine is in good condition, the spark plugs should not need attention between scheduled replacement intervals. Spark plug cleaning is rarely necessary and should

not be attempted unless specialised equipment is available as damage can easily be caused to the firing ends.

2 To remove the plugs, first open the bonnet, and pull off the HT leads. Grip the rubber end fitting, not the lead, otherwise the lead connection may be fractured.

3 Brush out any accumulated dirt or grit from the spark plug recess in the cylinder head otherwise it may drop into the combustion chamber when the plug is removed.

4 Unscrew the spark plugs with a deep socket or a box spanner. Do not allow the tool to tilt, otherwise the ceramic insulator may be cracked or broken.

5 Examination of the spark plugs will give a good indication of the condition of the engine.

6 If the insulator nose of the spark plug is clean and white, with no deposits, this is indicative of a weak mixture, or too hot a plug (a hot plug transfers heat away from the electrode slowly, a cold plug transfers heat away quickly).

7 If the top and insulator nose are covered with hard black-looking deposits, then this is indicative that the mixture is too rich. Should the plug be black and oily, then it is likely that the engine is fairly worn, as well as the mixture being too rich.

8 If the insulator nose is covered with light tan to greyish brown deposits, then the mixture is correct and it is likely that the engine is in good condition.

9 The spark plug gap is of considerable importance, as, if it is too large or too small, the size of the spark and its efficiency will be seriously impaired. For the best results the spark plug gap should be set in accordance with the Specifications at the beginning of this Chapter.

10 To set it, measure the gap with a feeler gauge, and then bend open, or close, the outer electrode until the correct gap is achieved. The centre electrode should never be bent as this may crack the insulation and cause plug failure if nothing worse.

11 Special spark plug electrode gap adjusting tools are available from most motor accessory stores.

12 Screw each plug in by hand. This will make sure that there is no chance of cross-threading (photo).

13 Tighten to the specified torque. If a torque wrench is not available, just nip up each plug. **It is better to slightly undertighten rather than overdo it and strip the threads from the light alloy cylinder head.**

14 When reconnecting the spark plug leads, make sure that they are refitted in their correct order, 1-3-4-2, No 1 cylinder being at the timing belt end of the engine. The original leads are numerically marked for identification (photo).

15 The plug leads require no routine attention other than being kept clean and wiped over regularly. At intervals, however, pull each lead off the plug in turn and remove it from the distributor. Water can seep down into the joints giving rise to a white corrosive deposit which must be carefully removed from the end of each cable. A smear of petroleum jelly applied to the end fitting of the cable will help to eliminate this problem.

16 Whenever the distributor cap is removed wipe it clean and check for thin lines between the electrodes. If evident, renew the cap as the lines are the result of tracking.

6.12 Fitting a spark plug

6.14 Plug leads are numerically marked for identification

7.1 Ignition coil

7 Coil – description and testing

1 The coil is located on the left-hand side of the engine compartment. It should be kept clean at all times to prevent possible arcing across the high tension tower (photo).

2 To ensure the correct HT polarity at the spark plugs, the LT coil leads must always be connected correctly. Refer to the wiring diagram (Section 1) for the lead colour coding.

3 The coil may be tested by using an ohmmeter. Connect the ohmmeter across the two LT terminals on the coil to check the primary winding resistance, and across the negative LT terminal and central HT tower to check the secondary winding resistance. If the readings are not as given in the Specifications, renew the coil. All wiring should be disconnected while checking the coil (Figs. 4.9 and 4.10).

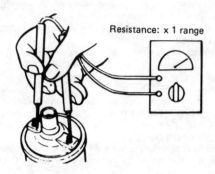

Fig. 4.9 Ignition coil primary circuit test method (Sec 7)

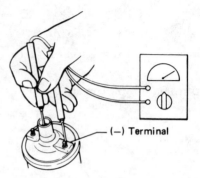

Fig. 4.10 Ignition coil secondary circuit test method (Sec 7)

8 Fault diagnosis – ignition system

Symptom	Reason(s)

If the engine fails to start due to either damp HT leads or damp distributor cap, a moisture dispersant, such as Holts Wet Start, can be very effective. To prevent the problem recurring, Holts Damp Start can be used to provide a sealing coat, so excluding any further moisture from the ignition system. In extreme difficulty, Holts Cold Start will help to start a car when only a very poor spark occurs.

Symptom	Reason(s)
Starter turns but engine will not start	Faulty or disconnected leads
	Faulty spark plug
	Air gap incorrect
	Fault in ignition coil
	Fault in pick-up/starter unit
Engine starts but runs erratically	Incorrect timing
	Fouled spark plug
	Incorrectly connected HT leads
	Crack in distributor cap or rotor
	Poor battery, engine and earth connections

Chapter 5 Clutch

For modifications, and information applicable to later models, see Supplement at end of manual

Contents

Clutch – adjustment 3
Clutch – inspection 7
Clutch – refitting 9
Clutch – removal 6
Clutch cable – renewal 4
Clutch pedal – removal and refitting 5
Clutch release bearing – removal, inspection and refitting 8
Fault diagnosis – clutch 10
General description 1
Routine maintenance 2

Specifications

Type .... Single dry plate with diaphragm spring and pressure plate, cable-operated

Driven plate
Thickness (standard) .... 3.5 mm (0.138 in)
Wear limit – lining surface to rivet .... 0.3 mm (0.012 in)
Maximum run-out .... 1.0 mm (0.039 in)
Maximum spline backlash – at disc outer edge:
   1.3 .... 0.7 mm (0.028 in)
   1.6 .... 0.8 mm (0.031 in)

Clutch cover pressure plate
Diaphragm spring finger maximum height variation .... 0.5 mm (0.020 in)

Clutch pedal and release lever
Pedal height .... 175 to 185 mm (6.89 to 7.28 in)
Pedal free travel .... 12.5 to 17.5 mm (0.492 to 0.689 in)
Release lever free play .... 2.5 to 3.5 mm (0.098 to 0.138 in)

Torque wrench settings

	Nm	lbf ft
Clutch cable locknut	3.0 to 4.0	2.2 to 3.0
Clutch cover bolts	22 to 29	16 to 21
Clutch pedal bracket nut	8 to 11	6 to 8
Fulcrum pin nut	16 to 22	12 to 16
Pedal stopper locknut	16 to 22	12 to 16

1 General description

The clutch is of single dry plate type and is cable-operated from a pendant pedal.

When the pedal is depressed, the cable pulls the release lever which forces the ball-bearing type release bearing against the diaphragm spring fingers of the cover assembly. This releases the pressure plate from the linings of the driven plate and there is then no drive between the engine and transmission.

When the pedal is released, the pressure plate is forced against the driven plate which in turn is forced against the flywheel. Drive is then transmitted from the engine, through the driven plate, and into the transmission by the input shaft.

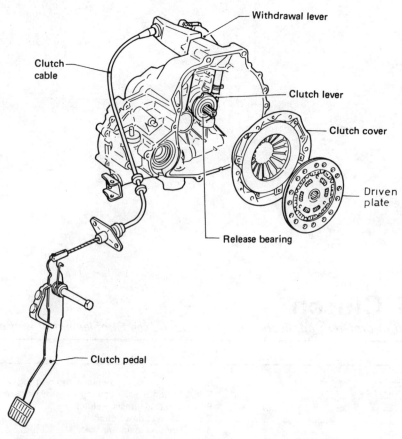

Fig. 5.1 Gearbox and clutch assembly components (Sec 1)

2   Routine maintenance

Make the following checks and adjustments at the intervals given in *Routine Maintenance* at the start of this manual.
1   Check the clutch pedal height and free play and adjust if necessary (Section 3).
2   Check the clutch release lever play and adjust the cable if necessary as described in Section 3.
3   Check that the pedal moves smoothly and lightly oil the pivot bushes.

3   Clutch – adjustment

1   Working inside the car, measure the distance from the upper surface of the clutch pedal pad to the floorpan as shown in Fig. 5.2.
2   If adjustment is required, loosen the locknut on the pedal stop bolt, adjust pedal height then tighten the locknut (photo).
3   Working in the engine compartment, check that the free play at the end of the clutch release lever is as given in Specifications. If not, loosen the locknut on the cable end fitting and turn the knurled adjuster as necessary (photo). Tighten tne locknut on completion.
4   Fully depress the clutch pedal several times and recheck the release lever free play.
5   Finally check that the clutch pedal free travel at the pad is as specified.

4   Clutch cable – renewal

1   Remove the cover from under the facia panel.
2   Release the nuts at the end of the cable at the release lever and disconnect the cable from the lever (photo).

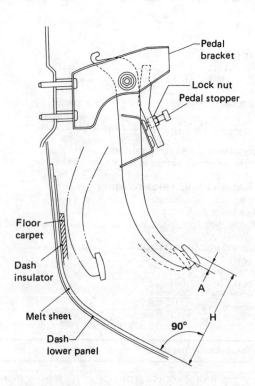

Fig. 5.2 Clutch pedal adjustment showing pedal (Sec 3)
Height (H) and free travel (A)

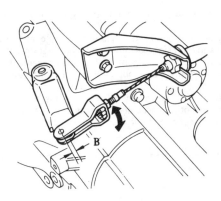

Fig. 5.3 Clutch release lever free play adjustment (Sec 3)
B Free play

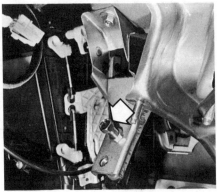

3.2 Clutch pedal and stop bolt (arrowed)

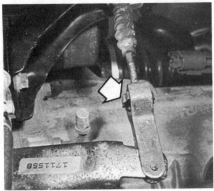

3.3 Clutch cable and release lever, with adjuster arrowed

3   Working inside the vehicle, remove the clevis pin and disconnect the cable from the clutch pedal.

4   Unscrew the two nuts which retain the cable grommet to the bulkhead and withdraw the cable from the vehicle.

5   Refit the new cable by reversing the removal operations, and then carry out the adjustments described in Section 3.

5   Clutch pedal – removal and refitting

1   Remove the cover from under the facia panel.

2   Disconnect the cable from the pedal arm.

3   Unscrew and remove the retaining nut and washer from the pedal fulcrum pin (pivot shaft).

4   Unhook the pedal return spring and slide the pedal off the pivot shaft.

5   The pivot bushes may be renewed.

6   Refitting is a reversal of removal, apply grease to the pivot shaft and bushes.

7   Adjust the pedal height and free movement, as described in Section 3.

6   Clutch – removal

1   To gain access to the clutch unit (and the release bearing components), remove the transmission as described in Chapter 6.

2   Mark the relative positions of the clutch cover to the flywheel, then unscrew each of the clutch cover bolts progressively a turn at a time until the pressure of the diaphragm spring is relieved. If the flywheel tends to turn as the bolts are unscrewed, jam the teeth of the starter ring gear using a large screwdriver or similar blade.

3   Remove the clutch cover, catching the driven plate (disc) as it is released from the flywheel.

7   Clutch – inspection

1   Examine the driven plate. If the friction linings are worn down to, or nearly down to the rivet heads, the plate should be renewed. Do not attempt to reline the plate yourself, it is unlikely to prove satisfactory.

2   If the driven plate linings are oily, the crankshaft rear oil seal and/or the gearbox input shaft oil seal are in need of renewal; refer to Chapter 1 and/or 6 as necessary. Do not attempt to clean oil or grease from the friction linings, renewal is the only satisfactory option.

3   If the linings are good for further service, check the torsion springs and the hub for cracks. Examine the splines in the driven plate hub for wear and the facings for excessive run-out (Fig. 5.6).

4   Check the clutch pressure plate cover assembly. If any parts show evidence of cracking or severe rusting, or if the fingers of the diaphragm spring are worn or stepped by contact with the release

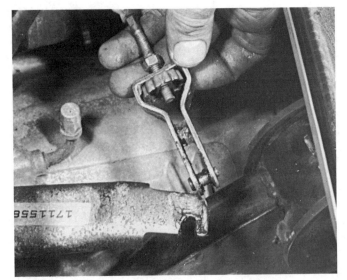

4.2 Disconnecting the clutch cable from the release lever

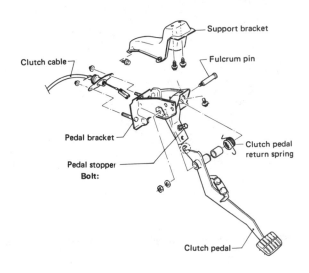

Fig. 5.4 Clutch pedal assembly components (Sec 5)

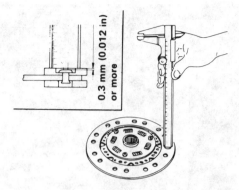

Fig. 5.5 Checking the clutch driven plate lining for wear (Sec 7)

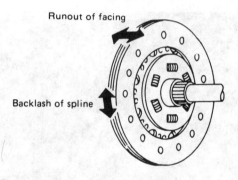

Fig. 5.6 Check clutch driven plate for run-out and excessive hub spline backlash (Sec 7)

bearing, renew the assembly. Do not attempt to dismantle the pressure plate cover.

5 Check the friction surfaces of both the pressure plate and the flywheel. If grooved, or showing signs of very fine surface cracking, the flywheel may be machined – subject to certain limitations described in Chapter 1 – but the pressure plate assembly will have to be renewed complete.

6 Prior to refitting the clutch, clean any oil from the inside of the clutch bellhousing and any other associated components. Check the clutch release bearing as described in the next Section.

8 Clutch release bearing – removal, inspection and refitting

1 Whenever the transmission is removed for clutch overhaul, check the release components and renew the bearing as a matter of routine.

2 Disconnect the springs from the release bearing and slide the release bearing off the bearing mounting sleeve.

3 Check that the release control shaft bushes are not worn. If they are, the fork-to-cross-shaft retaining pins will have to be driven out (Fig. 5.8). The return spring is released as the shaft is withdrawn. The pins can only be driven out if the cross-shaft is turned to allow the pins to pass out into the small cavities in the bellhousing.

4 Reassembly is a reversal of dismantling, apply grease to the cross-shaft bushes and to the release bearing recess.

5 Smear a little molybdenum disulphide grease onto the release bearing mounting sleeve and the input shaft splines. Make sure that the release bearing is pushed fully home until the retaining spring clips are heard to click (photo).

6 When correctly reassembled, the numbers moulded onto the release fork should be visible.

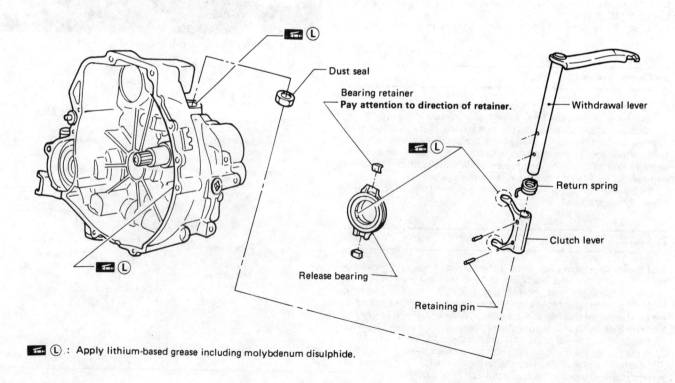

🔧 Ⓛ : Apply lithium-based grease including molybdenum disulphide.

Fig. 5.7 Clutch release bearing and lever components (Sec 8)
Lubricate as indicated

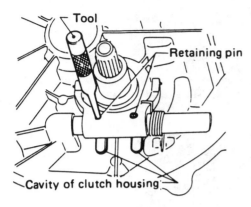

Fig. 5.8 Clutch release fork-to-cross-shaft pin removal
(Sec 8)

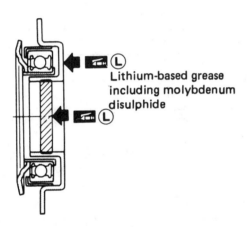

Fig. 5.9 Lubricate the release bearing as indicated (Sec 8)

9.2 Refitting the clutch driven plate and cover

9 Clutch – refitting

1 Make sure that the flywheel and pressure plate friction surfaces are clean, and free from protective grease.

2 Place the driven plate against the flywheel so that its hub has the greater projecting side away from the flywheel (photo).

3 Offer up the clutch cover (aligning the index marks made during removal if refitting the old cover), and then fit and hand tighten the retaining bolts.

4 The driven plate must now be centralised. To do this, a conventional clutch alignment tool can be used, or alternatively the splined hub of the driven plate can be centralised within the tips of the diaphragm spring fingers visually or, more accurately, by cutting a cardboard disc of outside diameter equal to the outside diameter of the clutch cover aperture. Now punch a hole centrally in the cardboard disc and then push a bar or rod through the hole in the disc and engage it in the splined hub of the driven plate (photos). The diameter of the car or rod should be such that it provides a sliding fit in the hub. A bar of incorrect diameter can be adjusted to suit by winding tape around it.

5 The driven plate should now be moved in the appropriate direction to centralise the cardboard disc. Tighten the cover bolts and remove the tool.

6 Refit the transmission with reference to Chapter 6.

8.5 Release bearing and associated fittings after reassembly

9.4A Centralising the clutch driven plate using an improvised alignment tool ...

9.4B ... inserted into the driven plate hub

---

10 Fault diagnosis – clutch

Symptom	Reason(s)
Judder when taking up drive	Loose engine or gearbox mountings Badly worn friction linings or contaminated with oil Worn splines on gearbox input shaft or driven plate hub
Clutch drag (or failure to disengage) so that gears cannot be meshed	Incorrect adjustment Rust on splines (may occur after vehicle standing idle for long periods) Damaged or misaligned pressure plate assembly Cable stretched or broken
Clutch slip (increase in engine speed does not result in increase in car speed – especially on hills)	Incorrect adjustment Friction linings worn out or oil contaminated
Noise from clutch	Worn release bearing Worn or loose components of pressure plate or driven plate

Chapter 6 Manual transmission

For modifications, and information applicable to later models, see Supplement at end of manual

Contents

Fault diagnosis – manual transmission	10	Routine maintenance	2
Final drive – adjustment	8	Transmission – dismantling	5
Gear lever and rods – removal and refitting	3	Transmission – reassembly	7
General description	1	Transmission – removal and refitting	4
Mainshaft bearing preload – adjustment	9	Transmission components – inspection	6

Specifications

Type .... Transversely mounted with four or five forward speeds and reverse. Synchromesh on all forward gears, floor-mounted gearchange

Designation
Four-speed RN4F30A
Five-speed:
   1.3 .... RS5F30A
   1.6 .... RS5F31A

Ratios
Four-speed transmission:
   1st 3.333:1
   2nd 1.955:1
   3rd 1.286:1
   4th 0.902:1
   Reverse 3.417:1
Five-speed transmission (1.3):
   1st 3.333:1
   2nd 1.955:1
   3rd 1.286:1
   4th 0.902:1
   5th 0.756:1
   Reverse 3.417:1
Five-speed transmission (1.6):
   1st 3.063:1
   2nd 1.826:1
   3rd 1.207:1
   4th 0.902:1
   5th 0.756:1
   Reverse 3.417:1
Final drive ratios:
   1.3 (four and five-speed) 4.353:1
   1.6 .... 4.167:1

Oil capacity

	Four-speed	Five-speed
Up to January 1987	2.3 litres (4.0 pints)	2.7 litres (4.8 pints)
From January 1987	2.4 litres (4.2 pints)	2.8 litres (4.9 pints)
Lubricant type/specification	Hypoid gear oil, viscosity SAE 80W/90, to API GL4 (Duckhams Hypoid 80)	

Gear endfloat

1st gear	0.18 to 0.31 mm (0.0071 to 0.0122 in)
2nd, 3rd and 4th gear	0.20 to 0.40 mm (0.0079 to 0.0157 in)
5th gear	0.18 to 0.41 mm (0.0071 to 0.0161 in)
Differential side gear-to-case clearance (maximum)	0.3 mm (0.012 in)

Torque wrench settings

	Nm	lbf ft
Clutch bellhousing to casing	20	15
Circular cover to transmission casing	8	6
Bearing retainer screws	20	15
5th/Reverse detent plug	25	18
Crownwheel bolts	80	59
Oil filler/level plug:		
Pre 1987 models (23.5 mm (diameter plug)	30	22
1987 models on (18.1 mm diameter plug)	15	11
Oil drain plug	30	22
Reverse lamp switch	25	18
Switch plug	18	13
Control rod to transaxle	20	15
Support rod to engine mounting bracket	35	26
Control lever socket to support rod	10	7
Control lever to control rod	18	13
Clutch bellhousing to engine – refer to Fig. 6.4		

1 General description

The manual transmission is of four or five-speed type, depending upon the model. On both transmissions top gear is of overdrive type.

Synchromesh is provided on all forward gears and gear selection is by means of a floor-mounted control lever.

The transmission is mounted transversely in line with the engine. Power is transmitted from the clutch through an input shaft and mainshaft to the final drive/differential which is incorporated within the transmission casing.

The four and five-speed units are so similar that their overhaul is not described separately in this Chapter as it is assumed that owners of four-speed models will be able to ignore reference to a 5th gear in the operations listed.

2 Routine maintenance

The following maintenance procedures must be carried out at the intervals given in *Routine Maintenance* at the start of this manual.
1 Check the transmission oil level and, if necessary, top up with the specified type of oil. A combined oil level/filler plug is fitted in the side of the transmission case (photos). It should be noted that models produced from January 1987 have a smaller filler plug than earlier

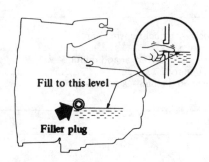

Fig. 6.1 Correct manual transmission oil level (Sec 2)

models; being 18.1 mm in diameter against 23.5 mm on earlier models. The hole size was reduced to allow for an increase in the oil capacity. Refer to the Specifications for the lubricant quantity and type required (Fig. 6.1).
2 Unscrew and remove the combined filler/level plug. The oil should be level with the bottom of the hole and just starting to dribble out. If not, top up as necessary.
3 If the car is regularly used in adverse conditions or for towing, the oil should be renewed at the specified intervals (photo).

2.1A Manual gearbox oil level/filler plug

2.1B Topping-up the oil level

2.3 Oil drain plug (arrowed)

3 Gear lever and rods – removal and refitting

1 Raise the car at the front end and support on axle stands.
2 Disconnect the exhaust downpipe from the front exhaust tube. Unbolt the front exhaust tube at its rear flange and remove it, then detach and remove the heat shield from the central tunnel (refer to Chapter 3 for details).
3 Working inside the car, unscrew the knob from the gear lever, then carefully prise free the upper dust gaiter from the console (photo). For full access to the gear lever and holder bracket remove the console (Chapter 11).
4 Remove the lower dust cover from the holder bracket (photos).
5 Working from underneath, remove the through-bolt and detach the control rod from the control lever. As they are disconnected note how the return spring, bracket and rubber are fitted.
6 Unbolt and detach the control rod at the front end and remove the

rod (photo).
7 Unbolt the support rod at the front end and remove it (photos).
8 Undo the retaining nuts from the underside and then remove the gear lever and support bracket assembly from within the car.
9 Further dismantling of the gear lever assembly can be made as required. Refer to Fig. 6.2.
10 Renew any components which are worn or damaged. The bushes are the most likely items to require replacement.
11 Refit in the reverse order of removal. Lubricate the pivot bushes as they are assembled. This includes the control rod-to-lever bolt and bushings, also the lever ball.
12 When tightening the support rod at the front end, push the rod towards the front as the bolt and nut are tightened.
13 Check for satisfactory operation of the gear lever and check that the gear lever gaiter does not interfere with the lever selection. Ensure that the gears engage in a satisfactory manner, before refitting the heat shield and exhaust.

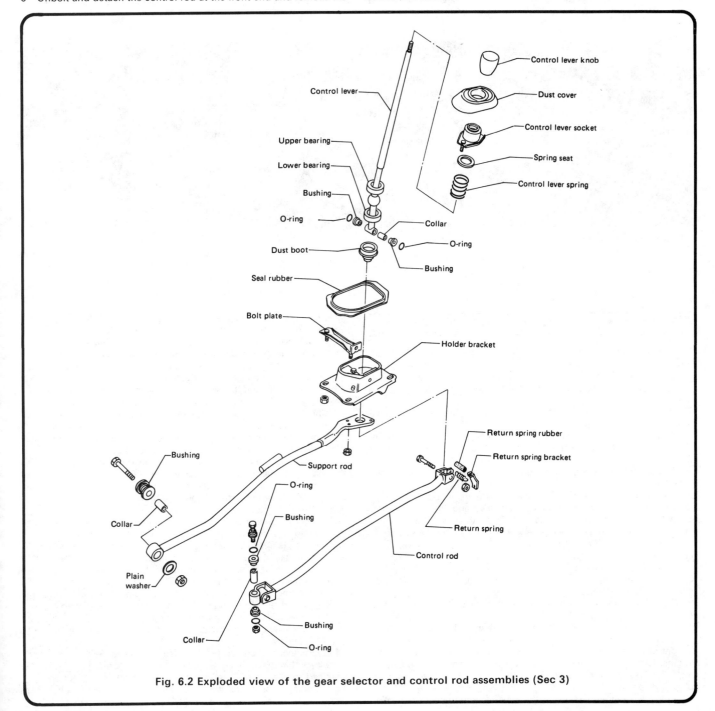

Fig. 6.2 Exploded view of the gear selector and control rod assemblies (Sec 3)

3.3 Removing the upper dust gaiter from the console

3.4A Lower gaiter removal from the lever holder bracket

3.4B General view of the gear lever holder bracket assembly

3.6 Gear control rod – front end attachment arrangement

3.7A Gear control support rod – front end attachment arrangement

3.7B Gear control and support rods disconnected

4 Transmission – removal and refitting

1 The transmission unit can be removed from the vehicle either together with the engine, as described in Chapter 1, or separate from it, as described below. In the latter instance, the transmission is disconnected from the engine and then lowered for withdrawal from underneath the vehicle.

2 Open and support the bonnet. Disconnect the battery, and remove it and its retaining bracket.

3 Drain the transmission oil into a suitable container for disposal. The drain plug is shown in photo 2.3. Refit the plug once the oil is fully drained.

4 Disconnect the clutch operating cable from the release lever (see Chapter 5).

5 Disconnect the speedometer cable from the transmission.

6 Disconnect the reversing light switch lead and the transmission earth leads (photos). Detach the reversing light switch lead at the in-line connector rather than unscrewing and removing the switch.

7 Raise and support the vehicle at the front end on axle stands, allowing sufficient clearance for the transmission to be lowered and withdrawn from underneath.

8 Remove the roadwheels and unbolt and remove the front wing side shield on the left-hand side.

9 Disconnect the gear control and support rods at their front ends (see photos 3.6 and 3.7).

10 Referring to Chapter 8, remove the left-hand driveshaft.

11 Position a jack underneath the engine and raise it to support the weight of the engine (not lift it). Insert a wooden block between the engine sump pan and the jack saddle to avoid possible damage or distortion to the sump. Do not jack up directly underneath the drain plug.

12 Position a second jack under the transmission, preferably a trolley jack, and support its weight.

13 Disconnect the front engine mounting (photo).

14 Unbolt and disconnect the transmission mounting (photo).

15 Unbolt and detach the starter motor (Chapter 12).

16 Unscrew and remove the bolts which hold the transmission bellhousing to the engine. Note the location of the coolant tube, lower protective shield ·and the sump-to-transmission reinforcement tube held by some of the bolts.

17 Check that the various transmission attachments are disconnected and out of the way.

18 If possible, enlist the aid of an assistant to help support and guide the transmission as it is lowered from the vehicle.

19 Carefully pull and withdraw the transmission from the engine so that the input shaft is clear of the clutch unit. Do not rest the weight of the transmission on the input shaft. As the transmission is withdrawn, simultaneously lever on the inboard end of the right-hand driveshaft to separate it from the transmission (see Chapter 8).

20 When the transmission is clear of the driveshaft and engine it can be lowered and removed from under the vehicle (Fig. 6.3).

21 Refitting is a reversal of removal, but observe the following points. Apply a smear of molybdenum disulphide grease to the input shaft splines. If the clutch has been dismantled, make sure that the driven plate has been centralised (Chapter 5).

22 As the transmission is refitted to the engine, align and insert the right-hand driveshaft, ensuring that it is fully engaged (Chapter 8).

23 The engine-to-transmission retaining bolts differ in length and their torque wrench settings according to location and model. Refer to Fig. 6.4 for details.

24 Reconnect and adjust the clutch cable as described in Chapter 5.

25 Check that the transmission drain plug is fitted and tightened to the specified torque, then top up the transmission oil level (Section 2).

26 On completion check the clutch and transmission for satisfactory operation.

4.6A Reverse light switch lead in-line connector

4.6B Reverse light switch

4.13 Front engine mounting

4.14 Transmission mounting

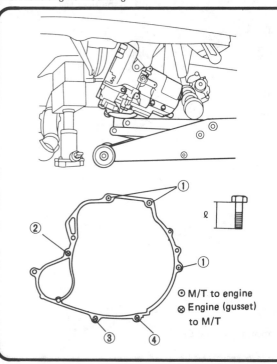

Fig. 6.3 Supporting transmission on a trolley jack for removal (Sec 4)

Fig. 6.4 Manual transmission retaining bolt identification and location, and torque setting requirements (Sec 4)

⊙ M/T to engine
⊗ Engine (gusset) to M/T

E13 engine models	Length (ℓ)	Nm	lbf ft
Bolt 1	70 mm (2.76 in)	16 to 21	12 to 15
Bolt 2	40 mm (1.57 in)	20 to 29	15 to 21
Bolt 3	25 mm (0.98 in)	16 to 21	12 to 15
Bolt 4	20 mm (0.79 in)	20 to 29	15 to 21

E16 engine models	Length (ℓ)	Nm	lbf ft
Bolt 1	70 mm (2.76 in)	23 to 27	17 to 20
Bolt 2	40 mm (1.57 in)	20 to 29	15 to 21
Bolt 3	25 mm (0.98 in)	16 to 21	12 to 15
Bolt 4	20 mm (0.79 in)	20 to 29	15 to 21

5 Transmission – dismantling

1 With the transmission removed from the vehicle, clean away external dirt using a water-soluble solvent, or paraffin, and a stiff brush. Remove the mounting brackets, noting their location.

2 Drain the transmission oil if not drained previously.

3 With the unit standing on the flange of the clutch bellhousing, unscrew the casing-to-bellhousing bolts and withdraw the casing from the bellhousing. On five-speed units, tilt the casing slightly as it is withdrawn to prevent the selector fork jamming inside the casing. If the casing is stuck, tap it off carefully to break the joint using a plastic hammer.

Transmission casing

4 Unscrew and remove the reverse lamp switch.

5 Remove the oil trough.

6 If the input shaft rear bearing is to be renewed, remove the very small welch plug from the transmission casing. Do this by drilling a hole in the plug and then screw in a self-tapping screw. The screw will probably force out the plug or its head can be used to lever it out.

7 Unbolt the circular cover from the casing, remove the O-ring seal and take out the spacer and the mainshaft bearing adjusting shim. If the mainshaft bearing is to be renewed, drive out the old outer track and fit the new one (Fig. 6.8).

8 If the differential side bearings are to be renewed, drive the bearing

outer track from the transmission casing. A new oil seal will be required.

Clutch housing

9 The clutch housing will have been left standing with the geartrains projecting from it when the transmission casing was drawn off.

10 Withdraw the selector shaft out of the 3rd, 4th and 5th selector forks. Extract the coil spring from the end of the shaft (Fig. 6.9).

11 Remove the 5th, 3rd and 4th selector forks. Retain the plastic slides from the forks. Do not lose the rectangular bushes located in the fork arm cut-outs.

12 Remove the control bracket with the 1st/2nd selector fork. Take care not to lose the small 5th speed detent ball and spring, also the shifter caps (Fig. 6.10). Extract the larger coil spring and ball from the remote control selector rod hole.

Types RS5F30A and RN4F30A

13 Remove the screws from the triangular shaped bearing retainer. One of these screws is of Torx type and will require a special bit to unscrew it. Hold the reverse idler gear up while the screw is undone. Remove the spacer from the reverse idler shaft.

14 Turn the clutch housing on its side and remove the mainshaft assembly. Remove the input shaft assembly by tapping the end of the shaft with a plastic-faced or copper hammer. Reverse idler gear will come off its shaft as the input shaft is released, but mark the idler gear as to which way up it is fitted.

15 Take out the final drive/differential.

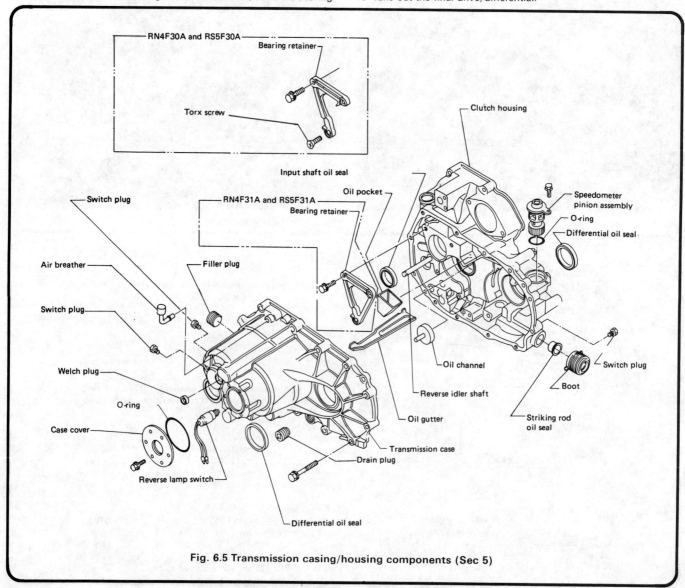

Fig. 6.5 Transmission casing/housing components (Sec 5)

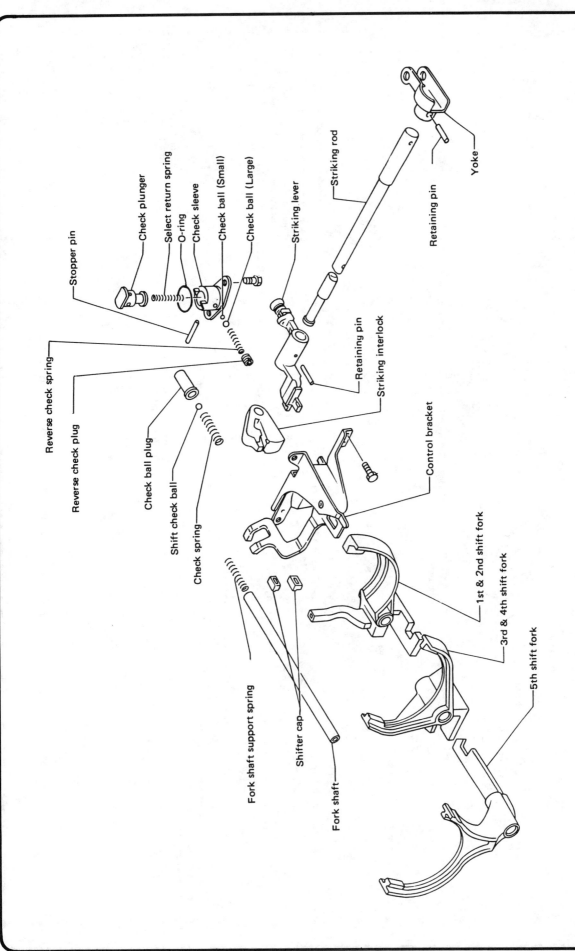

Stopper pin

Check plunger

Select return spring

O-ring

Check sleeve

Check ball (Small)

Check ball (Large)

Striking lever

Striking rod

Retaining pin

Yoke

Reverse check spring

Reverse check plug

Check ball plug

Shift check ball

Check spring

Retaining pin

Striking interlock

Control bracket

Fork shaft support spring

Shifter cap

Fork shaft

1st & 2nd shift fork

3rd & 4th shift fork

5th shift fork

Fig. 6.6 Selector components (Sec 5)

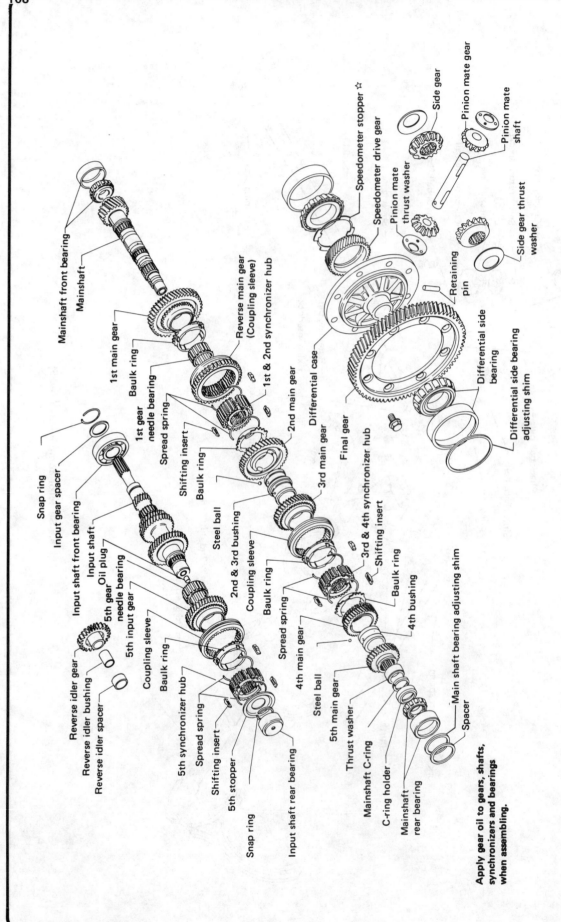

Apply gear oil to gears, shafts, synchronizers and bearings when assembling.

Fig. 6.7 Geartrain and differential components (Sec 5)

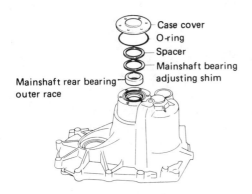

Fig. 6.8 Mainshaft rear bearing and spacer assembly components (Sec 5)

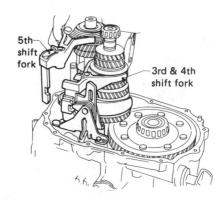

Fig. 6.9 3rd/4th and 5th selector forks (Sec 5)

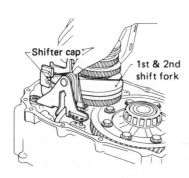

Fig. 6.10 1st/2nd selector fork and shifter bracket (Sec 5)

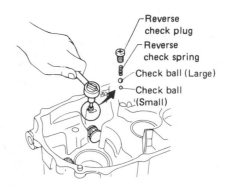

Fig. 6.11 Removing the reverse check plug, spring and balls (Sec 5)

Type RS5F31A

16 Lift out the mainshaft assembly at the same time releasing it from the input shaft gears.

17 Take out the final drive/differential.

18 Remove the bearing retainer bolts.

19 With the clutch housing on its side tap the end of the input shaft with a soft-faced hammer and remove the input shaft together with the bearing retainer and reverse idler gear. Do not remove the reverse idler shaft.

All types

20 If the plastic oil pocket must be removed then the bearing outer track which retains it must first be drawn out using a suitable extractor with thin claws. Extract the small retaining bolt and remove the speedometer drivegear.

21 Drive the roll pin from the selector rod dog then withdraw the rod, dog and interlock. When removing the rod, take care not to damage the oil seal lips.

22 Unscrew 5th/reverse detent plug, which will require a Torx type bit, and then extract the spring and balls (Fig. 6.11).

23 Remove 5th/reverse interlock plunger assembly, the screws again being of Torx type. Extract the smaller detent ball. The O-ring seal should be renewed at reassembly.

24 Remove the clutch release shaft, bearing and lever, as described in Chapter 5.

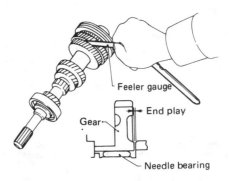

Fig. 6.12 Measuring 5th gear endfloat on the input shaft (Sec 5)

25 Remove the plastic oil channel from the transmission casing.

Input shaft

26 On five-speed units, measure and record the input shaft 5th gear endfloat. Extract the circlip and 5th gear stop plate (Fig. 6.12).

27 Remove 5th gear with the synchroniser and the split needle bearing from inside the gear.

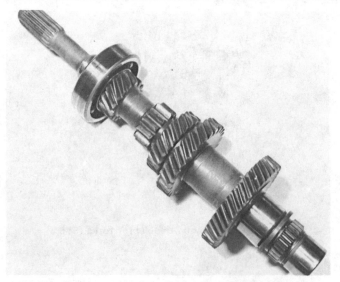

5.28 Input shaft with 5th gear and synchromesh removed

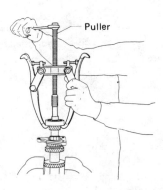

Fig. 6.13 Removing input shaft front bearing (Sec 5)

28 The input shaft (photo) cannot be dismantled further except to draw off the front bearing after having first extracted the retaining circlip and taken off the spacer. If a bearing puller is not available, support the bearing and drive the shaft from it (Fig. 6.13).

Mainshaft
29 Before dismantling the mainshaft, compare the endfloat of the gears with the specified tolerances. Inspect the components with endfloat which is outside the limits very carefully before reassembly (Fig. 6.14).
30 Remove the bearing inner races from the front and rear ends of the shaft. Use either a two-legged puller or press the shaft out of the bearings.
31 On five-speed units, remove the C-ring retainer, the C-rings and the thrust washer. Remove 5th gear, a puller will be required for this (Fig. 6.15).
32 Remove 4th gear, the gear bush and the steel locking ball (Fig. 6.16).
33 Remove the baulk ring.
34 Remove 3rd/4th synchro unit.
35 Remove 3rd gear.
36 Remove 2nd and 3rd gear bush.
37 Remove the steel locking ball.
38 Remove 2nd gear.
39 Remove the baulk ring.
40 Remove 1st/2nd synchro unit with reverse gear (straight-cut teeth on syncho sleeve) together with 1st gear as an assembly. The synchro-hub is tight on the shaft and the best way to remove the assembly is to support under 1st gear and drive the shaft downwards, using a copper-faced hammer.
41 Remove 1st gear split needle bearing.

Differential/final drive
42 Unbolt the crownwheel from the differential case.
43 Using a punch, drive out the pinion shaft lockpin and withdraw the shaft.
44 Remove the pinion and side gears together with the thrust washers.
45 Draw off the differential side bearing tracks, noting exactly how the taper of the rollers is set.
46 Remove the speedometer drivegear stop plate and the gear (Fig. 6.17).

6　Transmission components – inspection

---

1 With the transmission completely dismantled, clean all components and inspect them for wear or damage.
2 Check the gears for chipped teeth and their bushes for wear.

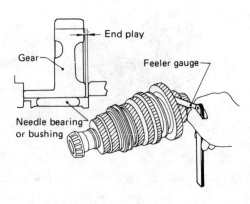

Fig. 6.14 Measure the mainshaft gear endfloat before dismantling (Sec 5)

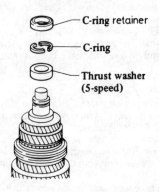

Fig. 6.15 5th gear thrust components on the mainshaft (Sec 5)

Fig. 6.16 Mainshaft 4th gear components (Sec 5)

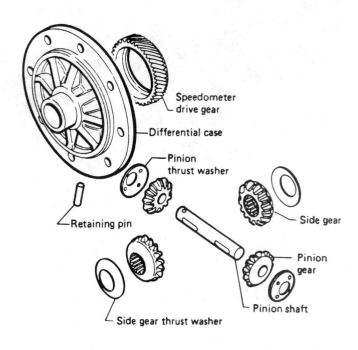

Fig. 6.17 Differential/final drive components (Sec 5)

3   Check the shafts for scoring or grooving.
4   Check the bearings for wear by spinning them with the fingers. If they shake or rattle then they must be renewed.
5   Wear in the synchronisers will usually be known about before dismantling, as a result of noisy gear changing or by the fact that the synchro action could be easily beaten during gear changing.
6   Even if the synchro is operating quietly, it is worthwhile checking the units in the following way at time of major overhaul.
7   Refer to Fig. 6.18. Extract the spreader springs, remove the sliding keys, and then push the hub from the sleeve, but not before having marked the components with quick-drying paint to ensure that their relative positions are maintained at reassembly.
8   Check the synchro components for wear or deformation. Place the baulk ring on its cone and twist it to ensure good contact between the

surfaces. Using a feeler blade, check that the gap between gear and baulk ring is not less than specified (see Fig. 6.19). If it is, renew the baulk ring.
9   When reassembling the synchro units, make sure that the spreader springs run in opposite directions, when viewed from each side of the synchro, and that the spring ends are not engaged in the same sliding keys (Fig. 6.20).
10 It is recommended that all oil seals are renewed at time of major overhaul (photos). These include those for the clutch cross-shaft, differential side bearings, gearchange control rod and the input shaft.
11 Should anything more than the slightest seepage of oil be observed during the normal operation of the vehicle the oil seals for the differential side bearings and the gearchange control rod can be renewed without having to remove the transmission from the vehicle. Refer to Chapter 7, Section 10.

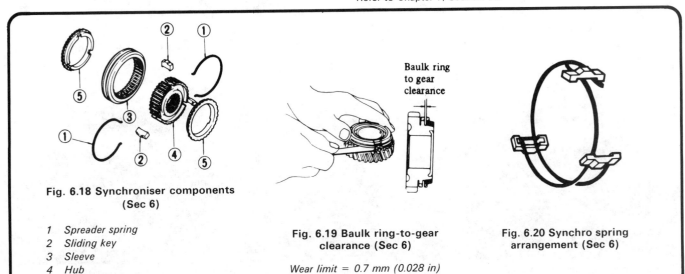

Fig. 6.18 Synchroniser components
(Sec 6)

1   Spreader spring
2   Sliding key
3   Sleeve
4   Hub
5   Baulk ring

Fig. 6.19 Baulk ring-to-gear
clearance (Sec 6)

Wear limit = 0.7 mm (0.028 in)

Fig. 6.20 Synchro spring
arrangement (Sec 6)

6.10A Interior of transmission casing

6.10B Differential bearing outer track and oil seal in transmission casing

6.10C Differential bearing outer track and oil seal in clutch bellhousing

7   Transmission – reassembly

Differential/final drive

1   Fit the speedometer worm drivegear and its stop plate to the differential case (photo).
2   Press or drive on the differential side bearing inner races (photo).
3   Into the differential case fit the pinion and side gears with thrust washers and the pinion shaft (photo). Use a dial gauge to check that the side gear-to-differential case clearance is as given in the Specifications. If necessary fit different thrust washers.
4   Drive in a new pinion shaft roll pin, making sure that it is flush with the differential case (photo).
5   Clean the threads of the crownwheel bolts and apply thread-locking fluid, then fit the crownwheel, screw them in and tighten to the specified torque.

Mainshaft

6   Oil all components liberally as they are reassembled.
7   Fit 1st gear needle bearing to the mainshaft (photos).
8   Fit 1st gear (photo).
9   Fit 1st gear baulk ring (photo).
10 Fit 1st/2nd synchro unit with reverse main gear. Ensure that the gear orientation is correct (photo and Fig. 6.22). Tap the synchro-hub down the mainshaft using a piece of tubing, but hold the synchro together with the hand in case the vibration makes it fall apart.
11 Locate the steel lock ball in its hole in the shaft. *On no account place the ball in the hole in the shaft groove* (photo).
12 Fit 2nd gear baulk ring (photo).
13 Fit 2nd gear (photo).
14 Fit 2nd/3rd gear bush, turning it slowly to engage its cut-out with the lock ball (photo).
15 Fit 3rd gear (photo).
16 Fit the baulk ring (photo).

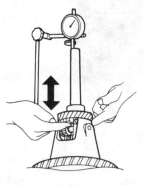

Fig. 6.21 Checking the side gear endfloat clearance (Sec 7)

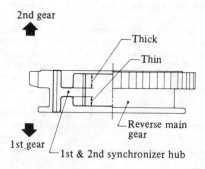

Fig. 6.22 1st/2nd synchro-hub to sleeve relationship (Sec 7)

7.1 Differential side bearing (1) stop plate (2) and speedometer worm drive gear (3)

7.2 Fitting the differential side bearing

7.3 Fitting the differential side gears and shaft

7.4 Differential pinion shaft roll pin

7.7A Mainshaft ready for reassembly

7.7B 1st gear split needle bearing

7.8 Fitting 1st gear

7.9 1st gear bulk ring

7.10 1st/2nd synchro with reverse gear

7.11 Steel ball for 2nd/3rd gear bush in the correct hole

7.12 2nd gear baulk ring

7.13 2nd gear

7.14 2nd/3rd gear bush

7.15 3rd gear

7.16 Baulk ring

17 Fit 3rd/4th synchro unit (photo) so that the engraved dashes in the sleeve are visible.
18 Using thick grease, stick the second (4th gear bush) lock ball in its shaft hole – *not the hole in the shaft groove*.
19 Fit the baulk ring (photo).
20 Fit 4th gear bush, turning it slowly to engage its cut-out with the lock ball (photo).
21 Fit 4th gear (photo).
22 If the transmission is of five-speed type, fit 5th gear (photo). Drive in onto the mainshaft using a piece of tubing (photo).
23 On five-speed models only, fit the thrust washer (photo).
24 Fit the C-ring (photo). These are supplied in various thicknesses to correct gear endfloat.
25 Fit the C-ring retainer (photo).
26 Press on new bearing inner races to both ends of the mainshaft (photo).

27 Using feeler blades check that the gear endfloat is within the specified tolerances (photo). If any endfloat measurements are outside the specified limits the shaft should be dismantled and the components re-examined.

Input shaft
28 Fit the split type needle roller bearing (photo).
29 Fit 5th gear (photo).
30 Fit the baulk ring (photo).
31 Fit the synchro unit (photo) so that the engraved dashes on the sleeve are visible.
32 To the synchro unit fit the stop plate and the circlip (photos). The circlips are available in various thicknesses to eliminate endfloat.
33 Press on a new shaft front bearing, fit the spacer and use a new circlip (photo).

7.17 3rd/4th synchro unit

7.19 4th gear baulk ring showing lock ball location

7.20 4th gear bush

7.21 4th gear

7.22A 5th gear

7.22B Driving 5th gear onto the mainshaft

7.23 5th gear thrust washer

7.24 C-rings

7.25 C-ring retainer

Clutch housing

34 Fit a new oil channel so that its relieved area is towards the oil pocket when installed (photo).

35 Press or drive the differential and mainshaft bearing outer tracks into their seats.

36 Remember that the mainshaft bearing outer track retains the oil pocket, so align the pocket correctly before fitting the bearing track.

37 Reassemble the clutch release mechanism (Chapter 5).

38 Refit the interlock plunger assembly (photo). Fit reverse/5th detent balls (small one first) the spring and plug (photos).

39 The force of the reverse detent should now be checked using a spring balance. On four-speed models the torque required to move against the detent should be 1.6 to 2.3 kgf m (11.5 to 16.6 lbf ft). On five-speed models the torque must be 0.5 to 0.8 kgf m (3.6 to 5.4 lbf ft). Use a bar clamped to the reverse detent and determine the correct pull for the spring balance according to the distance from the fulcrum point (Fig. 6.24).

40 The detent force may be increased by changing the detent plug for one of greater length. Apply locking sealant to the selector plug threads for final fitting.

41 Using new double roll pins, refit the remote control rod, striking lever and interlock (photos). The notch in the control (striking) rod should be downwards. To protect the oil seal when inserting the striking rod, tape the shouldered section of the rod, then remove the tape as the rod is passed through the casing (Fig. 6.25).

42 Refit the speedometer drive gear and screw in the lockbolt (photo).

43 Retain the differential side gears and thrust washers with rods or a bent wire clip (photo).

Types RS5F30A and RN4F30A

44 Lower the differential/final drive into position (photo).

45 Fit the input shaft and reverse idler gear simultaneously (photo). The idler gear (marked before removal) should be refitted in its original position. Use a plastic-faced or copper hammer to tap the input shaft fully home in the clutch housing.

46 Fit the spacer to the reverse idler shaft (photo).

47 Fit the triangular shaped bearing retainer (photo). Apply thread locking fluid to the screw threads and tighten them as tightly as possible (photo). Note the Torx type screw next to the idler.

48 Fit the mainshaft (photo) carefully meshing the gearteeth with those of the input shaft as the operation proceeds, push both synchro sleeves downwards and hold the reverse idler gear upwards.

Type RS5F31A

49 Fit the input shaft and reverse idler gear simultaneously, at the same time locating the gear over the shaft and the bearing retainer onto the housing. Tap the input shaft with a soft-faced hammer.

50 Insert the bearing retainer bolts and tighten them to the specified torque.

51 Fit the mainshaft while meshing the gear teeth with those of the input shaft.

52 Lower the differential/final drive into position.

All types

53 Fit the bush, the ball and the large coil spring to the hole in the remote control rod housing (photos).

54 Fit the control bracket which incorporates reverse selector fork. Make sure that 1st/2nd selector fork is located under the bracket and 5th speed detent spring and ball are placed into the hole in the remote control interlock as the assembly operations progress (photos). Tighten the control bracket screws.

55 Locate the 3rd/4th and 5th selector forks (photo). Make sure that the plastic slides (where fitted) are in position in the fork arm cut-outs (photo) also the rectangular shaped metal bushes are in the selector dog cut-outs (photo).

56 Pass the selector shaft through the forks (photo), making sure that the coil spring is located in the recess in the lower end of the shaft (photo) using grease.

Transmission casing

57 If the differential side bearings were renewed, fit the new bearing outer track now with a new oil seal.

58 If the mainshaft bearing was renewed, fit the new track into the casing now.

59 If the input shaft rear bearing was renewed, tap a new small welch plug into the hole in the casing.

Fig. 6.23 Oil pocket and channel arrangement (Sec 7)

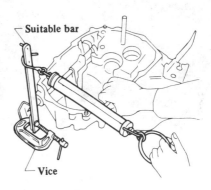

Fig. 6.24 Checking reverse detent resistance/torque (Sec 7)

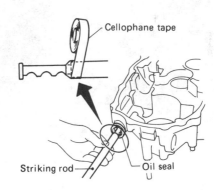

Fig. 6.25 Tape the striking rod to protect the oil seal (Sec 7)

60 Fit the plastic oil trough.

61 Screw in the reverse lamp switch.

62 With the clutch housing standing on the bench with the geartrains vertical, apply jointing compound to the mating faces of the transmission casing and clutch housing.

63 Lower the casing into position over the geartrains (photo). On five-speed units, tilt the casing as necessary to clear the selector fork.

64 Fit the connecting bolts and tighten to the specified torque (photo).

65 If the mainshaft bearing has not been changed, fit the original adjusting shim and spacer (photo). If a new bearing has been fitted, refer to Section 9 for details of mainshaft bearing adjustment.

66 Fit the new O-ring seal into its groove, then refit the circular cover. Note that one of the cover bolts also secures the reverse light switch lead in-line connector (photos).

7.26 Mainshaft bearing

7.27 Checking mainshaft gear endfloat

7.28 Input shaft split type needle roller bearing

7.29 Input shaft 5th gear

7.30 5th gear baulk ring

7.31 5th gear synchro on input shaft

7.32A Input shaft synchro unit stop plate

7.32B Input shaft stop plate circlip

7.33 Input shaft front bearing circlip

7.34 Oil channel

7.38A Using a magnet to fit the small reverse/5th detent ball

7.38B Using a magnet to fit the larger reverse/5th detent ball

7.38C Using a magnet to fit reverse/5th detent spring

7.38D Reverse/5th detent plug

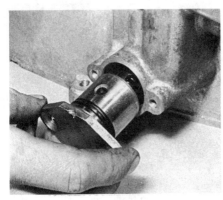
7.38E Interlock plunger assembly

7.41A Assembling remote control rod, striking lever and interlock

7.41B Striking lever roll pin (outer)

7.41C Striking lever roll pin (inner)

7.42 Speedometer drivegear

7.43 Method of retaining differential side gears

7.44 Lowering differential/final drive into clutch housing

7.45 Fitting input shaft with reverse idler gear

7.46 Reverse idler gear spacer

7.47A Fitting triangular shaped bearing retainer

7.47B Tightening the bearing retainer Torx screw

7.48 Fitting mainshaft/geartrain

7.53A Remote control housing bush

7.53B Remote control housing ball

7.53C Remote control housing spring

7.54A Detent spring (remote control interlock)

7.54B Detent ball (remote control interlock)

7.54C Remote control bracket (screw arrowed)

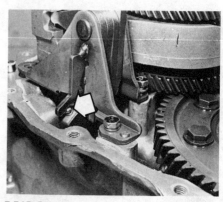

7.54D Remote control interlock detent ball correctly located (arrowed)

7.55A Selector forks

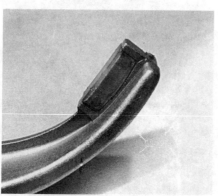

7.55B Selector fork plastic slide

7.55C Selector dog metal bushes (shifter caps) – arrowed

7.56A Fitting selector shaft into forks

7.56B Selector fork shaft coil spring

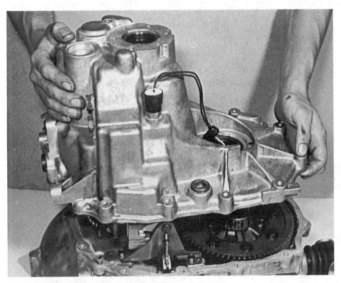

7.63 Fitting the transmission casing

7.64 Tightening the casing bolts

7.65 Mainshaft bearing adjustment shim

7.66A Locate the O-ring seal ...

7.66B ... then fit the circular cover. Note reverse switch lead connector location

8 Final drive – adjustment

1 If any of the following components of the transmission have been renewed during overhaul then you will have to take the assembly to your dealer for the final drive to be adjusted to ensure correct crownwheel-to-pinion meshing and the specified bearing preload.

Differential casing
Differential side bearing
Clutch housing
Transmission casing

2 Owing to the need for special tools, this work is not within the scope of the home mechanic.

9 Mainshaft bearing preload – adjustment

1 If any of the following components have been renewed during overhaul, then the mainshaft bearing preload must be checked and adjusted.

Mainshaft
Mainshaft bearings
Clutch housing
Transmission casing

2 Remove the circular cover from the transmission.
3 To carry out the adjustment, measure between the machined face of the transmission casing and the surface of the spacer. A shim should now be selected which is 0.2 mm (0.008 in) thicker than the dimension just taken (Fig. 6.26).
4 Fit the spacer, the selected shim and the cover and check that the input shaft turns smoothly with 4th gear selected. A special tool is available from dealers (KV38105900) which engages in the side gears and gives a torque reading for rotation of the final drive when 4th gear is selected (Fig. 6.27).
5 The correct turning torque should be between 5.9 to 13.7 Nm (4.4 to 10.1 lbf ft) with a new bearing fitted, or slightly less if using the original bearing.

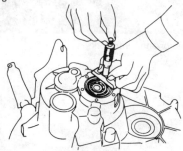

Fig. 6.26 Determining the mainshaft bearing preload shim requirements (Sec 9)

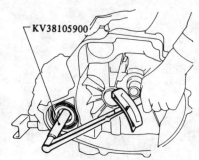

Fig. 6.27 Using special tool to check final drive turning torque (Sec 9)

10 Fault diagnosis – manual transmission

Symptom	Reason(s)
Weak or ineffective synchromesh	Syncho baulk rings worn, split or damaged Synchromesh units worn or damaged
Jumps out of gear	Gearchange mechanism worn Synchromesh units badly worn Selector fork badly worn
Excessive noise	Incorrect grade of oil in gearbox or oil level too low Gear teeth excessively worn or damaged Shaft thrust washers worn allowing excessive end play Worn bearings
Difficulty in engaging gears	Clutch pedal adjustment incorrect
Noise when cornering	Wheel bearing or driveshaft fault Differential fault

Note: *It is sometimes difficult to decide whether it is worthwhile removing and dismantling the gearbox for a fault which may be nothing more than a minor irritant. Gearboxes which howl, or where the synchromesh can be beaten by a quick gearchange, may continue to perform for a long time in this state. A worn gearbox usually needs a complete rebuild to eliminate noise because the various gears, if re-aligned on new bearings, will continue to howl when different wearing surfaces are presented to each other. The decision to overhaul, therefore, must be considered with regard to time and money available, relative to the degree of noise or malfunction that the driver has to suffer.*

Chapter 7 Automatic transmission

For information applicable to later models, see Supplement at end of manual

Contents

Brake band – adjustment	8	Inhibitor switch – adjustment	6
Differential bearing oil seals – renewal	10	Kickdown cable – adjustment and renewal	7
Fault diagnosis – automatic transmission	12	Overhaul and adjustment – general	4
Fluid level – checking, topping-up and changing	3	Routine maintenance	2
General description	1	Speed selector cable – adjustment	5
Governor shaft – removal and refitting	9	Transmission – removal and refitting	11

Specifications

Type .... RL3F01A fully automatic, with three element torque converter and two planetary geartrains. Three forward speeds and reverse. Final drive is integral

Ratios
1st	2.826:1
2nd	1.543:1
3rd	1.000:1
Reverse	2.364:1

Final drive ratios
1.3	3.737:1
1.6	3.476:1

Fluid
Capacity	6.3 litres (11.0 pints)
Type/specification	Dexron type ATF (Duckhams Uni-Matic or D-Matic)

Driveplate
Run-out	0.5 mm (0.020 in) maximum

Torque wrench settings

	Nm	lbf ft
Driveplate to torque converter	45	33
Torque converter housing to engine	20	15
Sump pan bolts	7	5
Control valve body to transmission casing	9	7
Governor valve body to shaft	7	5
Oil cooler union nut at transmission casing	48	35
Inhibitor switch	2.5	1.8

1 General description

The automatic transmission incorporates a torque converter with planetary geartrains and the final drive/differential unit.

Six speed selector control lever positions are used:

P   Park – to lock up the transmission mechanically

R   Reverse gear

N   Neutral

D   Forward speed – changing automatically up and down between 1st, 2nd and 3rd gear ratios

2   Second gear hold, will change between 1st and 2nd gears only

1   First (low) gear hold

Kickdown in D is used for rapid acceleration during overtaking, it changes down to 2nd or 1st gear, depending upon roadspeed, when accelerator is fully depressed.

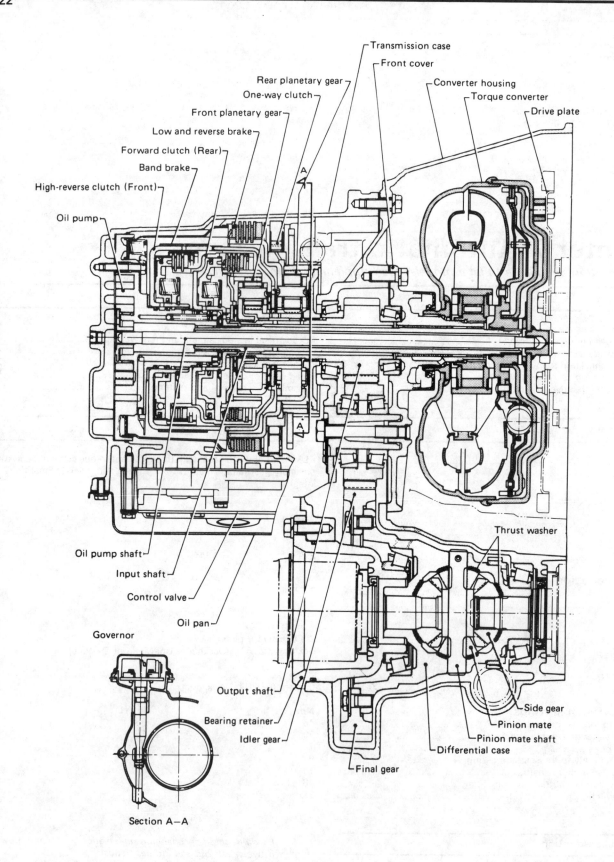

Rear planetary gear
One-way clutch
Front planetary gear
Low and reverse brake
Forward clutch (Rear)
Band brake
High-reverse clutch (Front)
Oil pump

Transmission case
Front cover
Converter housing
Torque converter
Drive plate

Oil pump shaft
Input shaft
Control valve
Oil pan

Governor

Thrust washer

Output shaft
Bearing retainer
Idler gear

Side gear
Pinion mate
Pinion mate shaft
Differential case

Final gear

Section A—A

Fig. 7.1 Sectional view of the automatic transmission showing the main components (Sec 1)

2   Routine maintenance

The following maintenance procedures must be carried out at the intervals given in *Routine Maintenance* at the start of this manual.

1   Check the transmission fluid level and top it up if necessary. At the same time check the colour of the fluid for discoloration and signs of overheating (Section 3).

2   If the fluid is noticeably discoloured, it must be drained and renewed.

3   If the vehicle is regularly used in dusty conditions, hot temperatures and/or is used regularly for towing, then the fluid should be drained and renewed at the intervals specified.

4   Periodically inspect the transmission casing for signs of fluid leakage. Any leaks must be attended to without delay.

3   Fluid level – checking, topping-up and changing

1   Check the fluid level in the automatic transmission at the intervals given in Section 2 with the car parked on level ground.

2   The precise level of the fluid will depend on the temperature of the fluid at the time of checking. The dipstick is marked with 'cold' and 'hot' fluid level markings and these, together with their respective fluid temperature ranges, are shown in Fig. 7.2. The hot range should be used when checking the fluid level directly after the vehicle has been driven in 'traffic conditions' for a minimum period of 10 minutes.

3   To make the fluid level check, first ensure that the handbrake is fully applied, then start the engine and allow it to run at its normal idle speed, move the selector lever through the full range of gears, bring it to rest in the P position.

4   Leaving the engine idling, remove the transmission dipstick, wipe it clean then fully re-insert and withdraw it again. Observe the fluid level reading which must be within the appropriate temperature range.

5   If it is not as indicated in the illustrations, top up. On no account overfill the automatic transmission or run it with too low a fluid level.

Top up the transmission fluid level through the dipstick guide tube (Fig. 7.3).

6   Renewal of the automatic transmission fluid is only specified by the manufacturers if the vehicle is operated under arduous conditions – such as trailer towing. However, it would seem to make sense to change the fluid on all vehicles after a reasonably high mileage in order to remove any impurities from the system. The additives in the fluid will almost certainly have lost some of their characteristics by this time as well.

7   Before draining the fluid, have it at normal operating temperature by running on the road for a distance of at least five miles (eight kilometres).

8   Unscrew and remove the transmission drain plug and catch the fluid in a container (Fig. 7.4).

9   The condition of the fluid is an indication of the serviceability of the transmission. If it is very dark or nearly black and smells of burning, suspect worn friction components within the transmission. If there is no odour then the discoloration may be due to a small leak of coolant coming from the fluid cooler within the radiator.

10   If the fluid is an opaque pink in colour this will be due to a coolant leak or flood water contamination.

11   If the fluid is dark brown in colour and sticky, this will probably be due to overheating by under or over filling.

12   Refit the drain plug, withdraw the dipstick and pour the fresh fluid into the transmission through the dipstick guide tube.

13   Check the fluid level, as previously described.

4   Overhaul and adjustment – general

1   Owing to the need for special tools and equipment, operations to the automatic transmission should be limited to the in-vehicle work described in the following Sections.

2   Where more extensive overhaul is required, it is best to leave this to your dealer, or, where necessary, remove the transmission for professional repair or renewal, as described in Section 11.

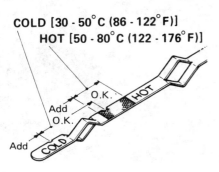

Fig. 7.2 Automatic transmission fluid level dipstick markings and temperature ranges (Sec 3)

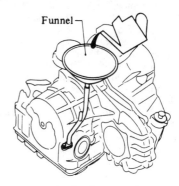

Fig. 7.3 Use a clean funnel to top up the automatic transmission fluid level (Sec 3)

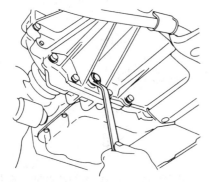

Fig. 7.4 Removing the drain plug from the automatic transmission (Sec 3)

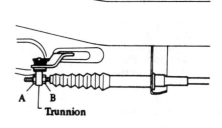

Fig. 7.5 Selector cable at transmission (Sec 5)

A   Locknut   B   Locknut

5 Speed selector cable – adjustment

1   When the hand control lever is moved to all positions on the index, the individual detents should be positively felt. If this is not so, adjust in the following way.
2   Set the control lever to P.
3   Working at the selector lever on the transmission casing, disconnect the cable.
4   With the fingers, move the selector lever positively into its P detent.
5   Using the cable end fitting locknuts, adjust the cable until it applies no tension in either direction to the selector lever on the transmission. Tighten the locknuts.
6   Check that all selector positions are positively obtained.

6 Inhibitor switch – adjustment

1   The inhibitor switch controls the reversing lamps when R is selected, and also prevents operation of the starter when the hand control lever is in any position but P or N.
2   If the inhibitor switch does not operate correctly, adjust in the following way.
3   Loosen, but do not remove, the switch screws.
4   Set the hand control lever to N.
5   Push a 2.5 mm (0.098 in) diameter pin through the switch lever and switch body holes to align them. Hold the pin and tighten the switch screws. Remove the pin (Fig. 7.6).

7 Kickdown cable – adjustment and renewal

1   Release the cable locknuts at the carburettor.
2   With the throttle cable pulley held in the full throttle position move the cable end fitting in the direction T (see Fig. 7.7). Tighten nut B to eliminate any free movement.
3   Unscrew nut B between one and one and a half turns and secure it in this position by tightening nut A (see Fig. 7.8).
4   Check that the throttle cable end fitting movement L is within the specified tolerances (see Fig. 7.9).
5   To renew the cable, first remove the fluid sump pan and control valve assembly, as described in the next Section.
6   Disconnect the kickdown cable from the carburettor.
7   Disconnect the other end of the cable from the lever and then release the cable conduit from the casing by flattening the lockplate tab and unscrewing the nut.
8   Fit the new cable by reversing the removal operations. Bend up the locktab around the nut.
9   Adjust as previously described, and finally check that the rubber bellows (if fitted) on the inner cable at the carburettor end is not twisted.

8 Brake band – adjustment

1   This will normally only be required if a fault develops, indicated by one of the following symptoms.

No change from 1st to 2nd
Speed changes direct from 1st to 3rd
Severe jerk on 1st to 2nd upshift
Poor acceleration
Maximum speed not obtained
No 3rd to 2nd downshift
No kickdown when in 3rd gear
Slip in 3rd to 2nd downshift
No manual 3rd to 2nd downshift
Transmission overheats

2   Drain the transmission fluid.
3   Remove the sump pan shield, the sump pan and the gasket from the transmission.
4   Unscrew the bolts evenly and progressively and withdraw the control valve assembly.
5   Release the brake band anchor pin locknut and then, using a torque wrench, tighten the pin to between 4.0 and 6.0 Nm (3 and 4 lbf ft).

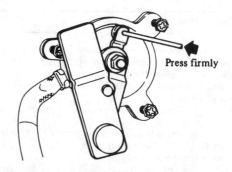

Fig. 7.6 Inhibitor switch adjustment (Sec 6)

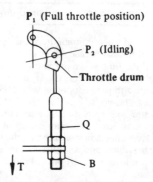

Fig. 7.7 Kickdown (throttle) cable end fitting at carburettor (Sec 7)

B Locknut	Q Cable end fitting
P1 Full throttle position	T Adjustment movement
P2 Idle position	direction

Fig. 7.8 Kickdown (throttle) cable locknuts (A and B) at the carburettor (Sec 7)

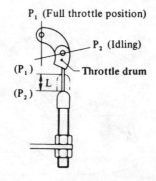

Fig. 7.9 Kickdown (throttle) cable movement diagram (Sec 7)

L = 27.4 to 31.4 mm	P1 Full throttle position
(1.079 to 1.236 in)	P2 Idle position

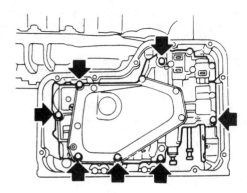

Fig. 7.10 Control valve assembly bolt locations (Sec 8)

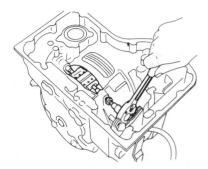

Fig. 7.11 Brake band anchor pin adjustment (Sec 8)

6   Now unscrew the anchor pin through 2$\frac{1}{2}$ complete turns. Hold the anchor pin stationary and tighten the locknut to between 16.0 and 22.0 Nm (12 and 16 lbf ft).
7   Refit the control valve assembly and tighten the bolts. Make sure that the manual and detent valves are correctly engaged – the manual valve should be set at neutral, and the groove on the detent valve should face forward.
8   Refit the sump pan together with a new gasket, followed by the shield. Fill the transmission with the specified fluid then check the level as described in Section 3.

9   Governor shaft – removal and refitting

1   Release the governor cap snap retainer then remove the cap and its seal ring.
2   If required, the governor unit can be removed, leaving the shaft in position, by undoing the four retaining bolts (Fig. 7.12).
3   To remove the governor and shaft as a unit, unscrew the lockbolt and then withdraw the governor shaft (Figs. 7.13 and 7.14).
4   The governor body may be unbolted from the shaft, and scratched or worn components renewed. The worm may be removed from the governor shaft after driving out the securing pin (Figs. 7.15 and 7.16).
5   Refitting is a reversal of removal, but make sure that the cap is located on the case protrusion correctly. Renew the seal ring (Fig. 7.17).

Fig. 7.12 Governor unit retaining bolts (Sec 9)

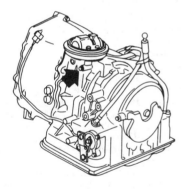

Fig. 7.13 Governor shaft lockbolt (Sec 9)

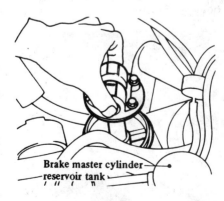

Fig. 7.14 Removing the governor shaft (Sec 9)

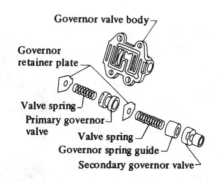

Governor valve body
Governor retainer plate
Valve spring
Primary governor valve
Valve spring
Governor spring guide
Secondary governor valve

Fig. 7.15 Governor body components (Sec 9)

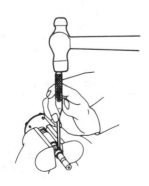

Fig. 7.16 Driving out the governor shaft worm pin (Sec 9)

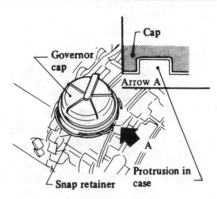

Fig. 7.17 Showing correct location of governor cap (Sec 9)

10 Differential bearing oil seals – renewal

1   The oil seals at the differential bearings into which the driveshafts engage can be renewed without removing the transmission.
2   Disconnect the driveshaft as described in Chapter 1, Section 12 paragraph 5 and Section 11, paragraphs 22 to 25.
3   Using a suitable claw-type extractor withdraw the oil seal (Fig. 7.18).
4   Apply transmission fluid to the lips of the new seal and drive it squarely into position using a piece of tubing (Fig. 7.19).
5   Reconnect the driveshaft as described in Chapter 3, Section 3, then reconnect the steering and suspension components as described in Chapter 10.

11 Transmission – removal and refitting

1   Place the vehicle over an inspection pit or raise the front end and support it securely on axle stands positioned under the side-members.
2   Disconnect the battery.
3   Remove the left-hand roadwheel.
4   Drain the transmission fluid.
5   Remove the left-hand wing shield.
6   Remove the driveshafts as described in Chapter 8.
7   Disconnect the speedometer cable from the transmission.
8   Disconnect the throttle (kickdown) cable from the carburettor and the leads from the inhibitor switch.
9   Disconnect the speed selector cable from the transmission lever, and the cable support bracket from the transmission casing.
10 Remove the dipstick guide/fluid filler tube.
11 Support the engine on a jack with a block of wood as an insulator.
12 Support the transmission on a second jack – preferably of trolley type.
13 Disconnect and plug the oil cooler pipes.
14 Unbolt and remove the starter motor unit (Chapter 12).
15 Mark the relationship of the torque converter to the driveplate using a dab of quick-drying paint.
16 Unscrew the torque converter-to-driveplate connecting bolts. The crankshaft will have to be turned to bring each bolt into view within the cut-out of the torque converter housing before a spanner or socket wrench can be used (Fig. 7.20).
17 Withdraw the automatic transmission flexible mounting pivot bolts.
18 Unscrew and remove the torque converter housing-to-engine connecting bolts. Record the location of the coolant tube and mounting brackets held by some of these bolts. Unbolt the engine-to-transmission reinforcement strut.
19 Withdraw the transmission from under the front wing, having an assistant hold the torque converter in full engagement with the oil pump driveshaft to prevent loss of fluid.
20 If the transmission is being replaced with a new or rebuilt unit, check what is fitted to the new unit before parting with the original transmission. The parts not supplied can then be removed from the old unit.
21 Before offering up the transmission to the engine, check that the

driveplate run-out is within the specified limit (Fig. 7.21).
22 Also check that the converter is pushed fully home. This can be determined if dimension A is not less than that specified (see Fig. 7.22).
23 Align the marks on the driveplate and torque converter (made before dismantling), apply thread locking fluid to clean bolt threads, and screw in and tighten the bolts to the specified torque.
24 Bolt on the starter motor.
25 Fit the engine-to-transmission connecting bolts, making sure to locate the coolant tube and mounting brackets under their correct bolts. Refit the mounting pivot bolts. Refit the reinforcement strut.
26 Reconnect the speed selector control cable, and adjust if necessary (Fig. 7.23).
27 Reconnect the inhibitor switch leads.
28 Reconnect the fluid cooler hoses.
29 Refit the wing protective shield.
30 Refit the dipstick guide/fluid filler tube.
31 Reconnect the throttle (kickdown) cable and adjust it as described in Section 7.
32 Reconnect the speedometer drive cable.
33 Reconnect the driveshafts, as described in Chapter 8.
34 Refit the left-hand roadwheel.
35 Reconnect the battery.
36 Fill the transmission with the specified fluid then check the level as described in Section 3.

Fig. 7.18 Using a puller to extract a differential bearing oil seal (Sec 10)

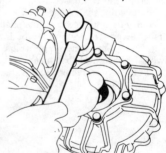

Fig. 7.19 Driving a new differential bearing oil seal into its housing (Sec 10)

Fig. 7.20 Torque converter-to-driveplate bolts are accessible through aperture (Sec 11)

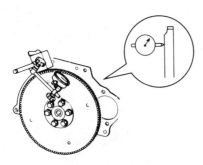

Fig. 7.21 Check the driveplate run out with a dial gauge
(Sec 11)

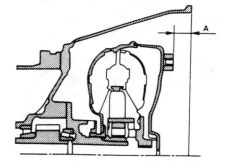

Fig. 7.22 Diagram showing torque converter fully installed
dimension (Sec 11)

A = Not less than 21.1 mm (0.831 in)

12 Fault diagnosis – automatic transmission

1   As has been mentioned elsewhere in this Chapter, no service repair work should be considered by anyone without the specialist knowledge and equipment required to undertake this work. This is also relevant to fault diagnosis. If a fault is evident, carry out the various adjustments previously described, and if the fault still exists consult the local garage or specialist.

2   Before removing the automatic transmission for repair, make sure that the repairer does not require to perform diagnostic tests with the transmission installed.

3   Most minor faults will be due to incorrect fluid level, incorrectly adjusted selector control or throttle cables and the internal brake band being out of adjustment (refer to Section 8).

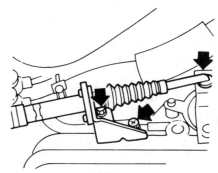

Fig. 7.23 Speed selector cable and bracket fixings at the
transmission (Sec 11)

Chapter 8 Driveshafts

For modifications, and information applicable to later models, see Supplement at end of manual

Contents

Driveshaft – checking, removal and refitting 3	General description 1
Driveshaft joints and bellows – removal, inspection and refitting . 4	Routine maintenance 2
Fault diagnosis – driveshafts 5	

Specifications

Type .... Open shafts with spider and cage type CV joints at each end

Torque wrench settings

	Nm	lbf ft
Lower balljoint to arm nut	65	48
Wheel bearing/driveshaft nut	196 to 275	145 to 203
Caliper torque member	54 to 64	40 to 47
Roadwheel nut	98 to 118	72 to 87

1 General description

The driveshafts are of the open type, transmitting the power from the final drive/differential within the transmission to the front roadwheels.

A Rzeppa constant velocity type joint is fitted to the inner ends of the driveshafts, and a ball type constant velocity joint is fitted to the outer ends. The joints are lubricated and sealed for life (photos).

The driveshaft joint units cannot be dismantled or repaired – only renewed as assemblies after removal from the shaft.

2 Routine maintenance

The following maintenance procedures must be carried out at the intervals given in *Routine Maintenance* at the start of this manual.

1 Make a visual inspection of the driveshaft bellows for any signs of damage, cracks and/or leakage. If any are found, they must be repaired as soon as possible.

2 Check the driveshaft joints for wear by gripping them near each joint in turn and twisting the shaft, then push and pull it in each direction. Any excessive movement indicates the need for renewal. Refer to Section 3 for further details.

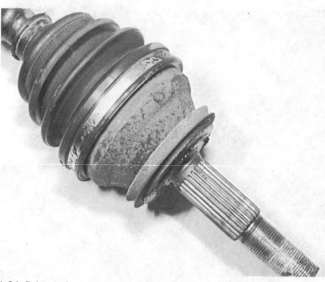

1.2A Driveshaft outer constant velocity joint

1.2B Driveshaft inner constant velocity joint

3 Driveshaft – checking, removal and refitting

1   Jack up the front of the car and support on axle stands. Apply the handbrake.

2   Grip the driveshaft and attempt to turn it in alternate directions against the rotation of the roadwheel. If possible, have an assistant depress the brake pedal during the check. If any play is evident, the joint must be renewed (Section 4) or the complete driveshaft replaced.

3   On automatic transmission models it is necessary to remove the right-hand driveshaft first before the left-hand driveshaft can be removed.

4   To remove the driveshaft first remove the roadwheel.

5   Extract the split pin, take off the nut retainer (photo), and loosen the driveshaft-to-hub retaining nut. In order to hold the hub against rotation, either refit the roadwheel and lower the vehicle to the ground, have an assistant apply the brakes, or use a length of steel rod or bar placed between two roadwheel studs as a lever. Take steps to prevent damage to the stud threads by screwing on the nuts.

6   Unbolt the brake caliper and tie it up out of the way. There is no need to disconnect the hydraulic line.

7   Extract the split pin, unscrew the nut, and detach the steering tie-rod from the steering knuckle using a separator tool (see Chapter 10).

8   Pull the hub/knuckle unit outwards and withdraw it from the driveshaft. If necessary, refit the nut to the outer end of the driveshaft, so that it is flush with the outer end, then using a soft-headed mallet drive the shaft out whilst simultaneously pulling the hub/knuckle outwards to separate them (photo). As the shaft is withdrawn take care not to damage the joint gaiters (bellows).

9   On manual transmission models prise free the driveshaft from the transmission using a suitable lever as shown in Figs. 8.2 and 8.3 according to side.

10 On automatic transmission models remove the right-hand driveshaft as shown in Fig. 8.2, then pass a suitable screwdriver or drift through the differential from the right-hand side and carefully drive out the left-hand driveshaft (Fig. 8.4). Take care not to damage the pinion mating shaft and side gears.

11 It is recommended that a new oil seal is fitted to the transmission whenever the driveshaft is removed. Refer to Chapter 7 for the procedure.

12 Refitting is a reversal of removal, but use a new circlip when fitting the inboard end of the driveshaft. Lubricate the oil seal lips.

13 If available, use the special tool fitted as shown to protect the oil seal (Fig. 8.5).

14 Push the driveshaft fully home in the side gear so that the circlip is felt to engage into the groove in the side gear.

15 Remove the special guide tool by pulling it out and down then pull on the shaft joint cover to check that the circlip is positively engaged. The flange of the joint casing may be tapped with a plastic-faced

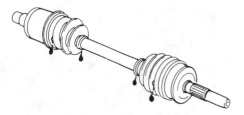

Fig. 8.1 Check the driveshaft bellows for leaks and damage (Sec 2)

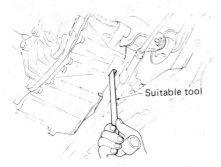

Fig. 8.2 Levering the right-hand driveshaft from the transmission (Sec 3)

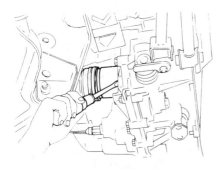

Fig. 8.3 Levering the left-hand driveshaft from the transmission – manual transmission models (Sec 3)

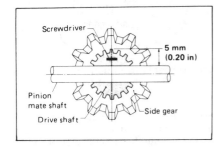

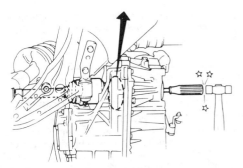

Fig. 8.4 Left-hand driveshaft removal method on automatic transmission models (Sec 3)

3.5 Removing the hub nut retainer

3.8 Separating the hub and driveshaft

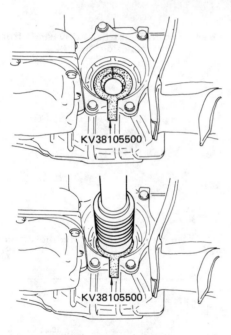

Fig. 8.5 Special oil seal protection tool used when inserting the driveshaft (Sec 3)

hammer if necessary to drive the shaft fully home.

16 Tighten all nuts and bolts to the specified torque settings and fit a new split pin to the hub nut. Refer to Chapters 9 and 10 as necessary for further details.

17 Top up the transmission oil/fluid as necessary (Chapter 6 or 7).

18 Finally, depress the brake pedal several times to set the disc pads in their normal position.

---

4 Driveshaft joints and bellows – removal, inspection and refitting

Inboard end joint – removal

1 Remove the driveshaft unit as described in the previous Section. Remove and discard the bellows securing bands (Fig. 8.6).

2 Draw back the bellows from the driveshaft joint, clean and dry the joint, then using quick-drying paint put alignment index marks on the shaft and joint (Fig. 8.7).

3 Remove the circlip (snap-ring) from the end of the shaft, then

withdraw the joint spider unit from the shaft (Fig. 8.8). Do not attempt to dismantle the spider unit.

4 Tape the splined section of the shaft to protect the bellows then withdraw the bellows from the driveshaft.

Outboard end joint – removal

5 The procedure is similar to that described for the inboard (transmission) end, but to withdraw the outer joint assembly fit the wheel hub nut to the end of the shaft then attach a puller/slide hammer or similar tool as shown and withdraw the outer joint assembly (Fig. 8.9).

Inspection

6 Clean all parts thoroughly prior to individual inspection of each component.

7 Check the driveshaft for cracks or distortion.

8 Check the joint assemblies for damage or excessive wear. They cannot be renewed separately, only as an assembly.

9 Check the condition of the bellows. Unless they are known to be fairly new and in good condition, they should be renewed.

Outboard end joint – refitting

10 Before fitting the bellows onto the shaft, ensure that the splines are fully covered with tape to protect the bellows from damage (Fig. 8.10).

11 Slide the bellows onto the shaft.

12 Fit the wheel bearing hub nut onto the driveshaft so that it is flush to the outboard end face, align the joint and shaft index alignment marks made during removal, then carefully drive the joint into position (the nut is fitted to protect the threads) (Fig. 8.11).

13 On assembly, check that the index marks align, then pack the joint and bellows with the special grease supplied with the driveshaft joint repair kit. The quantity is dependent on type as follows:

ZF80TS70C	*130 to 150 grams (4.59 to 5.29 oz)*
ZF90TS79C	*155 to 175 grams (5.47 to 6.17 oz)*

14 Set the bellows length (Fig. 8.12) according to type and check for correct fitting. The bellows must be seated correctly with no swelling, twisting or deformity. Fit the new securing bands and tighten them using a screwdriver and pliers. Bend the excess back over and secure with the retaining tabs as shown (Fig. 8.13).

Inboard end joint – refitting

15 Fit the bellows onto the shaft as described in paragraphs 10 and 11, then fit the spider unit ensuring that the index marks made during removal align.

16 Fit a new circlip into the groove on the shaft to secure the spider unit.

17 Pack the driveshaft and joint bellows with the special grease supplied with the driveshaft joint repair kit. The quantity is dependent on type as follows:

ZF80TS70C	*180 to 200 grams (6.35 to 7.05 oz)*
ZF90TS79C	*220 to 240 grams (7.76 to 8.47 oz)*

18 Refit the sliding joint housing then locate the bellows so that they are set at the length shown in Fig. 8.14. Check that the bellows are

seated correctly with no swelling, twisting or deformity, then fit the new securing bands. Tighten them using a screwdriver and pliers. Bend back the excess band section and secure with the retaining tabs as shown in Fig. 8.13.

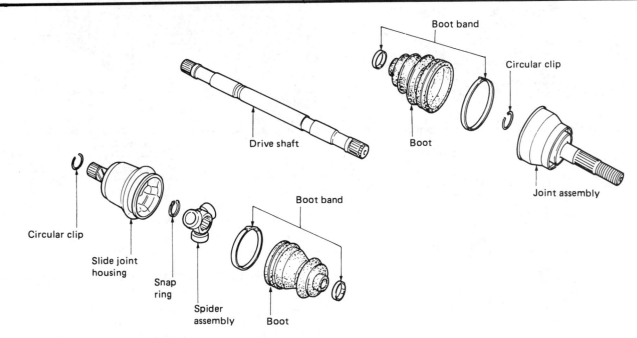

Fig. 8.6 Driveshaft and CV joint components (Sec 4)

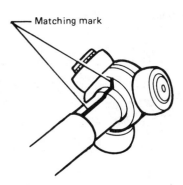

Fig. 8.7 Mark relative fitted positions of shaft and spider housing (Sec 4)

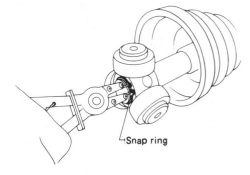

Fig. 8.8 Remove the spider retaining clip (Sec 4)

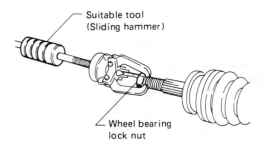

Fig. 8.9 Outboard driveshaft CV joint removal method (Sec 4)

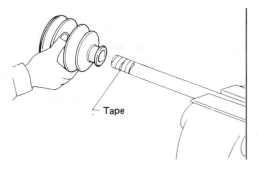

Fig. 8.10 Protective tape wound over splines (Sec 4)

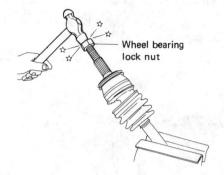

Fig. 8.11 Drive joint onto shaft – note location of nut to
protect thread (Sec 4)

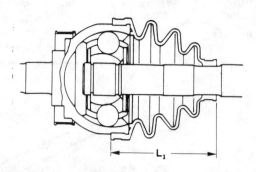

Fig. 8.12 Reassembled driveshaft, joint and bellows –
outboard end (Sec 4)

L1 = 96.0 to 98.0 mm (3.78 to 3.86 in) – E16S engine models
L1 = 90.5 to 92.5 mm (3.56 to 3.64 in) – other models

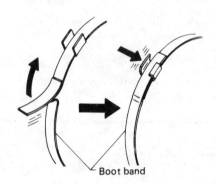

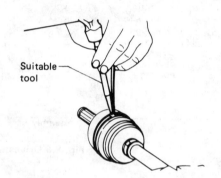

Fig. 8.13 Bellows securing bands arrangement (Sec 4)

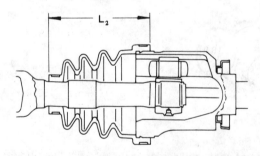

Fig. 8.14 Reassembly of driveshaft joint and bellows – inboard end (Sec 4)

L2 = 101.5 to 103.5 mm (4.00 to 4.07 in) – E16S engine models
L2 = 95.5 to 97.5 mm (3.76 to 3.84 in) – other models

5 Fault diagnosis – driveshafts

Symptom	Reason(s)
Vibration	Worn joints
	Worn wheel or differential bearings
Noise on taking up drive	Worn driveshaft splines
	Worn joints
	Loose driveshaft nut

Chapter 9 Braking system

For modifications, and information applicable to later models, see Supplement at end of manual

Contents

Brake drum – inspection and renovation	8	Hydraulic pipes and hoses – general	11
Brake pedal – removal, refitting and adjustment	17	Hydraulic system – bleeding	12
Caliper – removal, overhaul and refitting	5	Master cylinder – removal, overhaul and refitting	9
Disc – inspection and renovation	6	Pressure regulating valve – general	10
Disc pads – inspection and renewal	3	Rear brake lining – inspection and renewal	4
Fault diagnosis – braking system	18	Rear wheel cylinder – removal, overhaul and refitting	7
General description	1	Routine maintenance	2
Handbrake – adjustment	15	Vacuum servo unit – description and maintenance	13
Handbrake cables – renewal	16	Vacuum servo unit – removal and refitting	14

Specifications

System type .... Discs front, drums rear, vacuum servo assistance, dual hydraulic circuit
split diagonally, self-adjusting rear brakes, cable operated handbrake
on rear brakes, rear brake pressure regulating valve.

Front brake discs
Diameter .... 240.0 mm (9.45 in)
Pad wear limit (minimum thickness) .... 2.0 mm (0.079 in)
Disc maximum run-out .... 0.07 mm (0.0028 in)
Disc minimum thickness .... 10.0 mm (0.394 in)

Rear brakes
Drum inner diameter .... 180.0 mm (7.09 in)
Drum maximum inner diameter .... 181.0 mm (7.13 in)
Drum maximum run-out .... 0.05 mm (0.0020 in)
Shoe friction material minimum thickness .... 1.5 mm (0.059 in)

Master cylinder
Inner diameter:
    Large .... 23.81 mm (0.9374 in)
    Small .... 19.05 mm (0.750 in)
Control valve type .... Dual proportioning, integral with master cylinder

Vacuum servo unit
Diaphragm diameter .... 180 mm (7.09 in)

Brake fluid type/specification .... Hydraulic fluid to FMVSS 116 DOT 3 (Duckhams Universal Brake and
Clutch Fluid)

Brake pedal
Free height:
    Manual transmission .... 155 to 165 mm (6.10 to 6.50 in)
    Automatic transmission .... 164 to 174 mm (6.46 to 6.85 in)
Pedal free play .... 1.0 to 3.0 mm (0.04 to 0.12 in)
Depressed pedal height (engine running, force of 50 kg/110 lb):
    Manual transmission .... 75.0 mm (2.95 in) minimum
    Automatic transmission .... 80.0 mm (3.15 in) minimum
Stop-lamp switch clearance .... 0.3 to 1.0 mm (0.012 to 0.039 in)

Handbrake
Warning light illumination movement .... 1 to 2 notches
Full brake application movement .... 7 to 11 notches

Torque wrench settings

	Nm	lbf ft
Bleed screw	7 to 9	5 to 7
Stop-lamp switch locknut	12 to 15	9 to 12
Servo input locknut	16 to 22	12 to 16
Pedal bracket bolt	8 to 11	6 to 8
Hydraulic pipe union	11 to 13	15 to 18
Hydraulic connector union mounting bolt	4 to 5	2.9 to 3.6
Brake tube connector nut	15 to 18	11 to 13
Servo unit to master cylinder	8 to 11	6 to 8
Disc brake union bolt	17 to 20	3 to 5
Caliper torque member retaining bolt	54 to 64	40 to 47
Cylinder pin bolt	22 to 31	16 to 23
Rear brake cylinder (to backplate)	6 to 8	4 to 6
Rear brake backplate bolts	33 to 39	24 to 29
Handbrake lever to body bolts	8 to 11	6 to 8
Adjuster locknut	3.1 to 4.3	2.2 to 3.2
Handbrake cable clamp to body	8 to 11	6 to 8
Roadwheel nuts	98 to 118	72 to 87

1 General description

The braking system is of dual-line four wheel hydraulic type with servo assistance. The hydraulic circuit is split diagonally.

A pressure regulating valve is incorporated in the hydraulic circuit to prevent the rear wheels locking up during heavy applications of the brake pedal.

The handbrake operates mechanically on the rear wheels and incorporates an 'on' warning lamp switch.

2 Routine maintenance

The following maintenance procedures must be carried out at the intervals given in *Routine Maintenance* at the start of this manual.

1 Check that the fluid level in the brake fluid reservoir is between the MAX and MIN markings (Fig. 9.2). Top up the fluid level if required (photo). Note that slight variations of level will occur according to the wear of the brake linings, but, if the level drops considerably the complete hydraulic system should be checked for leaks.

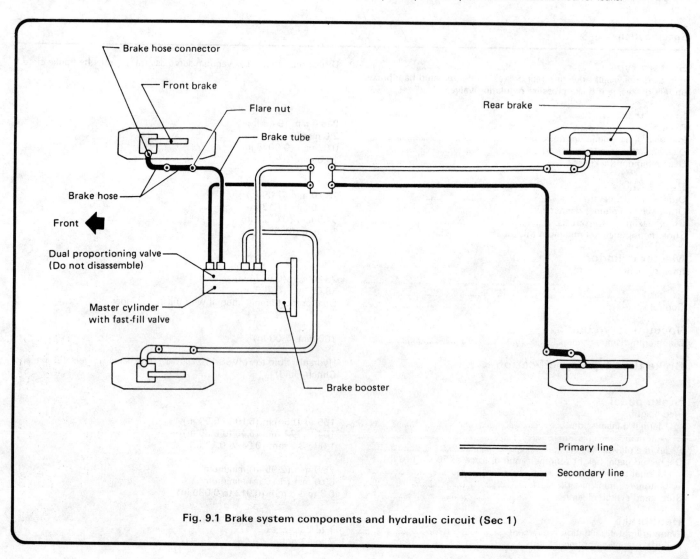

Fig. 9.1 Brake system components and hydraulic circuit (Sec 1)

2.1 Topping-up the brake fluid level

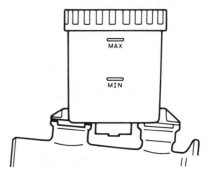

Fig. 9.2 Brake fluid reservoir showing fluid level markings (Sec 2)

2   Check the front brake disc pads for wear, and renew if necessary, (Section 3).
3   Remove the brake drums from the rear brakes and inspect the linings and associated components for wear. At the same time check the wheel cylinder for any sign of leakage. Make any repairs as necessary.
4   Check the brake system lines and hoses for any sign of leaks, damage or corrosion and make any repairs as necessary (Section 11).
5   Check the hand and foot brakes for satisfactory operation.
6   Check the servo unit and hose for condition and security.
7   Renew the brake system hydraulic fluid at the specified intervals or before if the vehicle is regularly used in adverse conditions such as city driving.

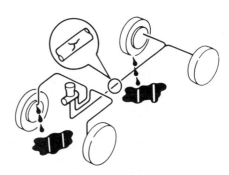

Fig. 9.3 Check the hydraulic system lines and component connections for any signs of leaks (Sec 2)

3   Disc pads – inspection and renewal

1   Raise the front of the vehicle, support it securely, and remove the roadwheels.
2   Check the thickness of the friction material. This must not be less than that specified (Fig. 9.4).
3   If the thickness is less than that figure the pads must be renewed as an axle set (four pads).
4   Unscrew and remove the caliper lower pin bolt (photo).
5   Swivel the caliper/cylinder body upwards (Fig. 9.7).
6   Remove the anti-squeal shims (photos).
7   Take out the pads (photo).
8   The retaining springs can be prised out, if required (photo).

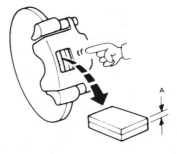

Fig. 9.4 Check disc pad lining thickness (A) (Sec 3)

3.4 Removing caliper lower pin bolt

3.6A Removing the outer shim and pad

3.6B Removing the inner shim and pad

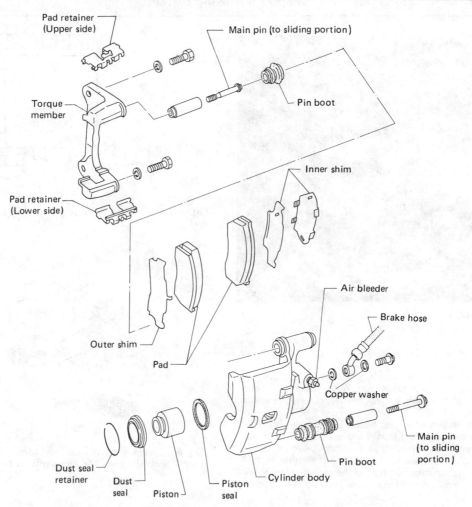

Fig. 9.5 Exploded view of the AD18B type brake unit (Sec 3)

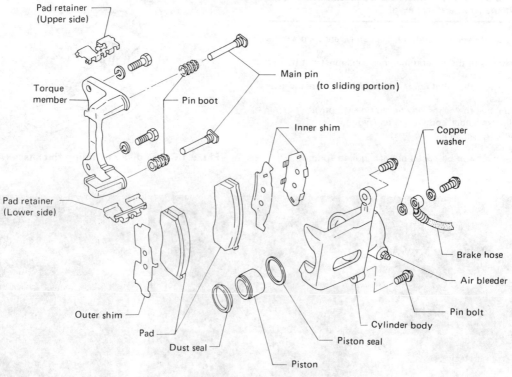

Fig. 9.6 Exploded view of the CL18B type brake unit (Sec 3)

3.7 Pads and shims removed

3.8 Removing a retaining spring

Fig. 9.7 Swivel caliper body upwards for access to the brake pads (Sec 3)

9   Brush away dirt and dust. *Avoid inhaling it as it is injurious to health.* Do not depress the brake pedal while the pads are out of the caliper.
10   Smear a trace of high-melting-point grease onto the pad backplates and then locate the pads (friction surface to disc) and the new anti-squeal shims.
11   The piston must now be fully depressed into the cylinder in order to accommodate the increased thickness of the new pads. Depressing the piston will cause the fluid level to rise in the master cylinder reservoir, so anticipate this by syphoning out some fluid using a clean battery hydrometer or meat baster.
12   Swivel the caliper/cylinder body downwards then fit and tighten the lower pin bolt. Check the tightness of both pin bolts.
13   Renew the pads on the opposite side, refit the roadwheels and lower the vehicle.
14   Apply the brakes hard to position the pads against the disc.
15   Check the fluid level, and top up the reservoir if necessary.

4   Rear brake lining – inspection and renewal

1   Chock the front wheels. Raise the rear of the vehicle, support it securely and remove the roadwheels. Release the handbrake.
2   Prise off the hub grease cap, extract the cotter pin, take off the nut retainer and unscrew and remove the nut (Fig. 9.9).
3   Pull off the brake drum, catching the outboard bearing which will be displaced. It is possible for the brake drum to be held on the axle due to the brake shoes being locked in grooves which have been worn in the drum. Should this occur, prise the plug from the brake backplate and, using a screwdriver, lift the toggle lever from the automatic adjuster star wheel and turn the star wheel to contract the shoes.
4   Inspect the shoe linings. If their thickness is less than that specified the shoes must be renewed as an axle set (four shoes) (Fig. 9.10).
5   It is recommended that new shoes are purchased complete with linings. Attempting to reline old shoes yourself seldom proves satisfactory.

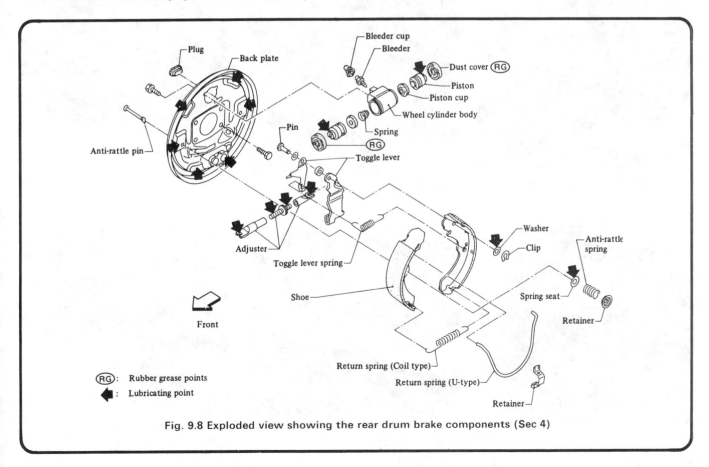

Fig. 9.8 Exploded view showing the rear drum brake components (Sec 4)

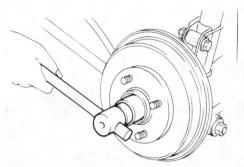
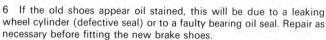

Fig. 9.9 Unscrew the rear brake drum/hub nut (Sec 4)

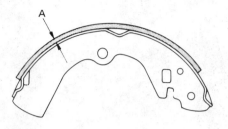

Fig. 9.10 Measure brake lining thickness (A) (Sec 4)

6   If the old shoes appear oil stained, this will be due to a leaking wheel cylinder (defective seal) or to a faulty bearing oil seal. Repair as necessary before fitting the new brake shoes.

7   Remove the shoe anti rattle springs. To do this, grip the edges of the spring retainer with a pair of pliers (photo), depress it against pressure of the coil spring and turn it through 90°. Release the spring retainer and take off the spring (photo).

8   Note the location of the shoes on the backplate with respect to the leading and trailing ends, as the lining material does not cover both ends of the shoes equally. Also note the spring location points on the shoes.

9   Prise off the shoe return spring retainer (photo), and then release the shoe return spring. This is a U-shaped spring and one arm should be gripped and levered towards the other arm to release it from the hole in the shoe (photos). It is recommended that a rag is placed over the spring to prevent it flying out accidentally.

10 Pull the upper ends of the shoes apart and remove the adjuster strut (photo).

11 Unhook and remove the lower return spring and at the same time

remove the shoes (photo). As they come away, disconnect the handbrake cable. Do not depress the brake pedal while the shoes are removed.

12 The handbrake and automatic adjuster toggle levers (photo) must be removed from the old shoe and fitted to the new one using the pin, washer, spring and U-shaped clip.

13 Apply a smear of grease to the shoe contact high spots on the brake backplate and to the ends of the wheel cylinder pistons.

14 Fit the new shoes by reversing the removal operations, but before fitting the automatic adjuster strut turn the star wheel to contact the strut fully (photo).

15 Refit the brake drum and set the bearing, as described in Chapter 10.

16 Repeat the operations on the opposite brake.

17 Apply the handbrake several times to actuate the automatic adjuster and to position the shoe linings as close as possible to the drum.

18 Refit the roadwheels and lower the vehicle.

4.7A Removing a shoe antirattle spring retainer ...

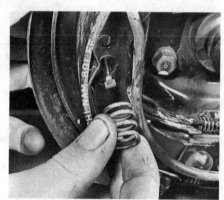

4.7B ... and spring

4.9A Prising off shoe return spring retainer

4.9B Prising off shoe return spring

4.10 Removing the automatic adjuster strut

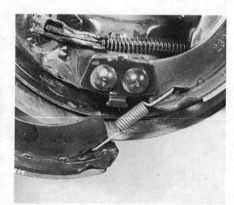

4.11 Shoe lower return spring

4.12 Handbrake and automatic adjuster toggle lever and spring

4.14 Brake shoe components reassembled

5.14 Refitting the caliper (cylinder) body

5 Caliper – removal, overhaul and refitting

1 Raise the front of the vehicle and support it securely. Remove the roadwheel. Fit a suitable clamp to the flexible hydraulic hose or alternatively tighten the fluid reservoir filler cap onto a sheet of polythene to prevent the loss of brake fluid, then disconnect the hydraulic hose from the caliper by unscrewing the hollow bolt from the banjo union. Note the copper washers, one each side of the union.

2 Unscrew the caliper mounting bolts and remove the caliper.

3 Clean away external dirt, *avoiding inhaling any dust*. Remove the pads (Section 3).

4 Unscrew the remaining pin bolt, and separate the cylinder body from the caliper bracket (torque member). Remove the pins.

5 Prise free the dust seal retainer using a screwdriver as a lever (Fig. 9.11) then apply air pressure (such as generated by a foot-operated pump) to the fluid entry hole in the caliper and eject the piston and dust excluder (Fig. 9.12).

6 Inspect the surfaces of the piston and cylinder bore. If pitted or corroded, reassemble the caliper and renew it complete.

7 If the piston and cylinder are in good condition, use a sharp instrument to pick the piston seal out of its groove and discard it.

8 Wash all components in methylated spirit or clean hydraulic fluid and obtain a repair kit which will contain all the necessary new seals and other renewable items.

9 Commence reassembly by manipulating the new piston seal into its groove using the fingers only.

10 Push the piston part way into its bore, having first lubricated it with hydraulic fluid.

11 Fit the dust excluder and its retainer (Fig. 9.13).

12 Smear the main pins with a little rubber grease and locate them in the torque member together with their dust covers.

13 Connect the cylinder body to the torque member then insert and tighten the torque member pin (upper) bolt.

14 Loosely connect the hydraulic hose to the caliper (cylinder) then depress the piston fully. Locate the pads, shims and retainers and lower the caliper unit (photo). Insert and tighten the pin (lower) bolt.

15 Support the hydraulic hose clear of adjacent components then tighten its union bolt. Bleed the hydraulic system as described in Section 12, then apply the brakes several times to position the pads on the door.

6 Disc – inspection and renovation

1 Whenever the disc pads are inspected for wear, take the opportunity to examine the disc for deep scoring, grooving or cracks. Light scoring is normal.

2 The disc should not run out-of-true by more than the specified tolerance (see Specifications). This may be checked using a dial gauge or feeler blades between the disc and a fixed point as the disc is rotated (Fig. 9.14).

3 Provided the thickness of the brake disc will not be reduced below the specified minimum, a scored disc may be reground for further use (Fig. 9.15).

Fig. 9.11 Prise free the dust seal retainer (Sec 5)

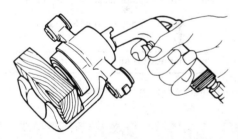

Fig. 9.12 Piston removal method using compressed air (Sec 5)

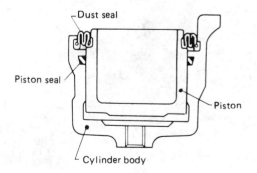

Fig. 9.13 Piston, cylinder body and seals arrangement (Sec 5)

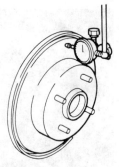

Fig. 9.14 Check the disc run-out (Sec 6)

Fig. 9.15 Check the disc thickness (Sec 6)

4   To remove the disc, first remove the caliper torque member and pull the disc from the hub.
5   Before refitting the hub, clean the mating faces then reverse the removal procedure.

7   Rear wheel cylinder – removal, overhaul and refitting

1   Remove the brake shoes, as described in Section 4.
2   Disconnect the hydraulic line from the cylinder.
3   Unbolt the wheel cylinder from the brake backplate (photo).
4   Clean away external dirt and pull off the dust covers.
5   Eject the internal components by tapping the cylinder on a block of wood or by applying air pressure from a foot-operated tyre pump to the fluid entry hole. Note which direction the seal lips face.
6   Examine the surface of the pistons and cylinder bore. If scored or corroded, renew the wheel cylinder complete.
7   If these components are in good condition, clean everything in either methylated spirits or hydraulic fluid, nothing else.
8   Discard the old seals and fit the new ones. These are contained in a repair kit, together with other renewable items.
9   Assemble the cylinder, applying hydraulic fluid as a lubricant as work progresses.
10 Refit the cylinder to the backplate, connect the fluid line and fit the brake shoes.
11 Bleed the brake circuit, as described in Section 12.

8   Brake drum – inspection and renovation

1   Whenever the brake drum is removed to inspect the wear of the

shoe linings, take the opportunity to examine the interior friction surface of the drum.
2   If it is badly scored or grooved it is possible to have it machined, provided the internal diameter will not exceed the maximum specified dimension (see Specifications).

9   Master cylinder – removal, overhaul and refitting

1   Disconnect the fluid lines from the master cylinder and allow the fluid to drain into a suitable container.
2   Unbolt the master cylinder from the front face of the vacuum servo unit (photo). Disconnect the low fluid switch wiring.
3   Withdraw the master cylinder, taking care not to spill hydraulic fluid on the paintwork.
4   Clean away external dirt.
5   Prise off the stopper end cap and be prepared for the primary piston to be ejected.
6   Where applicable slightly depress the secondary piston and unscrew and remove the stop screw.
7   Shake out the secondary piston. Note the direction in which all seal lips face.
8   Inspect the surfaces of the pistons and the cylinder bore. If they are scored or corroded, renew the master cylinder complete.
9   If these components are in good condition, clean them in either methylated spirit or hydraulic fluid, nothing else. Discard the seals, and obtain a repair kit which will contain all the necessary new seals and other renewable components.
10 Manipulate the new seals into position with the fingers only.

7.3 Rear wheel cylinder mounting bolt location

9.2 Master cylinder located on the front of the servo unit

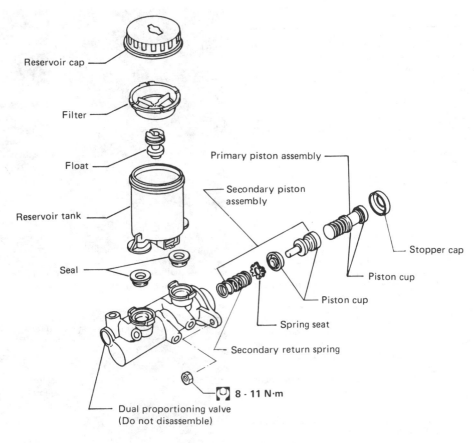

Fig. 9.16 Master cylinder components (Sec 9)

11 Renew the reservoir seals.
12 As reassembly progresses, lubricate the components with clean hydraulic fluid.
13 Insert the secondary piston spring and then the assembled secondary piston into the cylinder.
14 Where applicable, depress the secondary piston slightly with a rod and screw in the stop screw.
15 Fit the primary piston spring and the primary piston assembly and stake a new stop cap into position (Fig. 9.18).
16 Fit the master cylinder to the front face of the vacuum servo unit.
17 Reconnect the fluid pipelines and wiring as applicable.
18 Bleed the complete system, as described in Section 12.
19 Top up the reservoir and keep it full during the procedure.
20 Disconnect the primary line (nearest the servo), place a container beneath the master cylinder, then fully depress the brake pedal.
21 Release the pedal and wait five seconds.
22 Repeat until clear fluid emerges from the master cylinder, then refit and tighten the primary line.
23 While an assistant depresses the brake pedal loosen the primary line union to bleed the remaining air then tighten the union. If air is still present release the pedal, wait five seconds, and bleed out the remaining air.
24 Bleed the secondary line in a similar manner.
25 After bleeding the master cylinder, depress the brake pedal and check that it feels firm. If it feels 'spongy', air must be present in another section of the hydraulic circuit and the complete system should then be bled.

10 Pressure regulating valve – general

1 This valve (also referred to as a dual proportioning valve) is located in the master cylinder unit.
2 It is a non-repairable item and, therefore, if it develops a fault, the complete unit must be renewed.

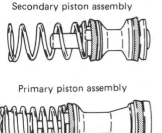

Secondary piston assembly

Primary piston assembly

Fig. 9.17 Primary and secondary piston units (Sec 9)

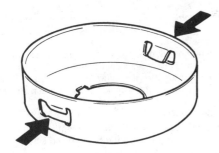

Fig. 9.18 Stake the new stopper cap at points indicated (Sec 9)

11 Hydraulic pipes and hoses – general

1   Periodically inspect the condition of the flexible brake hoses. If they appear swollen, chafed or when bent double with the fingers tiny cracks are visible, they must be renewed.
2   Always uncouple the rigid pipe from the flexible hose first, then release the end of the flexible hose from the support bracket (photos). To do this, pull out the lockplate using a pair of pliers.
3   Now unscrew the flexible hose from the caliper or connector. On calipers, a banjo type hose connector is used. When installing the hose, always use a new sealing washer.
4   When installation is complete, check that the flexible hose does not rub against the tyre or other adjacent components. Its attitude may be altered to overcome this by pulling out the clip at the support bracket and twisting the hose in the required direction by not more than one quarter turn.
5   Bleed the hydraulic system (Section 12).
6   At regular intervals wipe the steel brake pipes clean and examine them for signs of rust or denting caused by flying stones.
7   Examine the fit of the pipes in their insulated securing clips and bend the tongues of the clips if necessary to ensure a positive fit.
8   Check that the pipes are not touching any adjacent components or rubbing against any part of the vehicle. Where this is observed, bend the pipe gently away to clear.
9   Any section of pipe which is rusty or chafed should be renewed. Brake pipes are available to the correct length and fitted with end unions from most dealers and they can also be made to pattern by many accessory suppliers. When installing the new pipes use the old pipes as a guide to bending and do not make any bends sharper than is necessary.
10   The system will of course have to be bled when the circuit has been reconnected.

12 Hydraulic system – bleeding

1   The two independent hydraulic circuits are as follows:

    (a)   Front right-hand caliper and left rear wheel cylinder
    (b)   Front left-hand caliper and right rear wheel cylinder

The brake system components and hydraulic circuits layout are as shown in Fig. 9.1. When bleeding the system the following sequence should be followed.

    Left rear wheel cylinder
    Right front caliper
    Right rear wheel cylinder
    Left front caliper

2   If the master cylinder or the pressure regulating valve has been disconnected and reconnected then the complete system (both circuits) must be bled.
3   If the component of only one circuit has been disturbed then only the particular circuit need be bled.
4   Owing to the design of the hydraulic system and pipeline layout, it will be found easier to bleed the system using a pressure bleeding kit. Unless the pressure bleeding method is being used, do not forget to keep the fluid level in the master cylinder reservoir topped-up to prevent air from being drawn into the system which would make any work done worthless.
5   Before commencing operations, check that all system hoses and pipes are in good condition with all unions tight and free from leaks.
6   Take great care not to allow hydraulic fluid to come into contact with the vehicle paintwork as it is an effective paint-stripper. Wash off any spilled fluid immediately with cold water.
7   As the system incorporates a vacuum servo, destroy the vacuum by giving several applications of the brake pedal in quick succession.

Bleeding – two-man method

8   Gather together a clean glass jar and a length of rubber or plastic tubing which will be a tight fit on the brake bleed screws.
9   Engage the help of an assistant.
10   Push one end of the bleed tube onto the first bleed screw and immerse the other end in the glass jar which should contain enough hydraulic fluid to cover the end of the tube.

11.2A Flexible hose-to-rigid pipe connection on suspension strut

11.2B Flexible hose-to-rigid pipe connection at chassis

12.13 Right-hand front brake unit with bleed screw indicated (arrow). Note dust cap

11 Open the bleed screw one half turn and have your assistant depress the brake pedal fully then slowly release it. Tighten the bleed screw at the end of each pedal downstroke to obviate any chance of air or fluid being drawn back into the system.

12 Wait 5 seconds then repeat the operations as many times as is necessary until clean hydraulic fluid, free from air bubbles can be seen coming through into the jar.

13 Tighten the bleed screw at the end of a pedal downstroke and remove the bleed tube. Bleed from the remaining screws in a similar way (photo).

Bleeding – using one-way valve kit

14 There are a number of one-man, one-way brake bleeding kits available from motor accessory shops. It is recommended that one of these kits is used wherever possible, rather than just a tube, as it will greatly simplify the bleeding operation and reduce the risk of air or fluid being drawn back into the system, quite apart from being able to do the work without the help of an assistant.

15 To use the kit, connect the tube to the bleed screw and open the screw one half turn.

16 Depress the brake pedal fully and slowly release it. The one-way valve in the kit will prevent expelled air from returning at the end of each pedal downstroke. Repeat this operation several times to be sure of ejecting all air from the system. Some kits include a translucent container which can be positioned so that the air bubbles can actually be seen being ejected from the system.

17 Tighten the bleed screw, remove the tube and repeat the operations in the remaining brakes.

18 On completion, depress the brake pedal. If it feels spongy repeat the bleeding operations as air must still be trapped in the system.

Bleeding – using a pressure bleeding kit

19 These kits are available from motor accessory shops and are usually operated by air pressure from the spare tyre.

20 By connecting a pressurised contained to the master cylinder fluid reservoir, bleeding is then carried out by simply opening each bleed screw in turn and allowing the fluid to run out, rather like turning on a tap, until no air is visible in the expelled fluid.

21 By using this method, the large reserve of hydraulic fluid provides a safeguard against air being drawn into the system during bleeding which often occurs if the fluid level in the reservoir is not maintained.

22 Pressure bleeding is particularly effective when bleeding 'difficult' systems or when bleeding the complete system at a time of routine fluid renewal.

All methods

23 When bleeding is completed, check and top up the fluid level in the master cylinder reservoir.

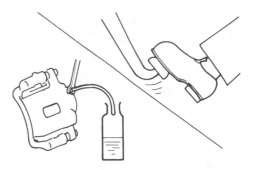

Fig. 9.19 Brake bleeding method (Sec 12)

24 Check the feel of the brake pedal. If it feels at all spongy, air must still be present in the system and further bleeding is indicated. Failure to bleed satisfactorily after a reasonable repetition of the bleeding operations may be due to worn master cylinder seals.

25 Discard brake fluid which has been expelled. It is almost certain to be contaminated with moisture, air and dirt, making it unsuitable for further use. Clean fluid should always be stored in an airtight container as it absorbs moisture readily (hygroscopic) which lowers its boiling point and could affect braking performance under severe conditions.

13 Vacuum servo unit – description and maintenance

1 The vacuum servo unit is fitted into the brake hydraulic circuit in series with the master cylinder to provide assistance to the driver when the brake pedal is depressed. This reduces the effort required by the driver to operate the brakes under all braking conditions.

2 The unit operates by vacuum obtained from the induction manifold and comprises, basically, a booster diaphragm and check valve. The servo unit and hydraulic master cylinder are connected together so that the servo unit piston rod acts as the master cylinder pushrod. The driver's effort is transmitted through another pushrod to the servo unit piston and its built-in control system. The servo unit piston does not fit tightly into the cylinder, but has a strong diaphragm to keep its edges in constant contact with the cylinder wall, so assuring an airtight seal between two parts. The forward chamber is held under vacuum conditions created in the inlet manifold of the engine and, during periods when the brake pedal is not in use, the controls open a passage to the rear chamber so placing it under vacuum conditions as well. When the brake pedal is depressed, the vacuum passage to the rear

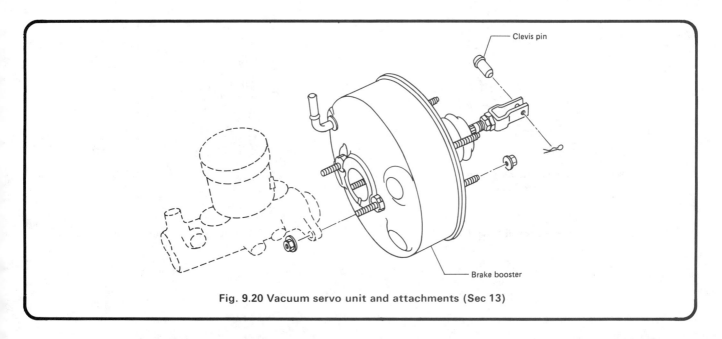

Fig. 9.20 Vacuum servo unit and attachments (Sec 13)

chamber is cut off and the chamber opened to atmospheric pressure. The consequent rush of air pushes the servo piston forward in the vacuum chamber and operates the main pushrod to the master cylinder.

3   The controls are designed so that assistance is given under all conditions and when the brakes are not required, vacuum in the rear chamber is established when the brake pedal is released. All air from the atmosphere entering the rear chamber is passed through a small air filter.

4   Under normal operating conditions the vacuum servo unit is very reliable and does not require overhaul except at very high mileages. In this case it is far better to obtain a service exchange unit, rather than repair the original unit.

5   It is emphasised that the servo unit assists in reducing the braking effort required at the foot pedal and, in the event of its failure, the hydraulic braking system is in no way affected except that the need for higher pedal pressure will be noticed.

6   Periodically inspect the condition of the vacuum hose in which is incorporated a non-return valve. Renew the hose if it is split or has hardened. (Fig. 9.21).

7   To check the non-return valve for satisfactory operation, remove it from the vacuum hose (noting fitted direction – Fig. 9.22).

8   Blow through the valve from the servo unit side and if the valve fails to open, renew the valve (Fig. 9.23).

14 Vacuum servo unit – removal and refitting

1   Remove the master cylinder, as described in Section 9.

2   Disconnect the vacuum hose from the servo unit.

3   Working inside the vehicle, disconnect the pushrod from the brake pedal.

4   Unbolt the brake servo unit from the bulkhead and remove it (photo).

5   Refitting is a reversal of removal. The length of the output rod is set during production and must not be re-adjusted (Fig. 9.24).

6   When the master cylinder is refitted, bleed the brake system (Section 12) and then depress the brake pedal a few times, checking that the pedal stroke remains the same. Hold the pedal depressed, start the engine and if the pedal depresses a fraction further it is quite normal.

7   To check the servo unit for efficiency, stop the engine after a couple of minutes running at idle speed. Depress the brake pedal a few times slowly and check that the pedal goes down further the first time, but progressively rises each subsequent time it is depressed. This indicates that the servo unit is airtight. This can be further checked by depressing the pedal with the engine running. Stop the engine with the pedal depressed and check that the pedal stroke remains the same for 30 seconds.

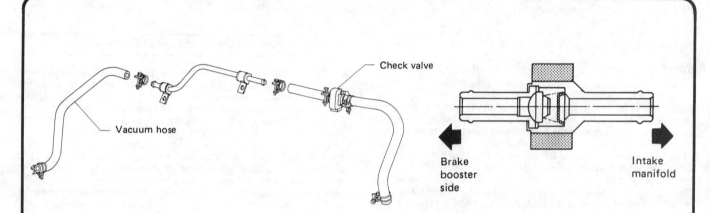

Fig. 9.21 Vacuum hose and check (non-return) valve (Sec 13)

Fig. 9.22 Check valve fitting direction is critical (Sec 13)

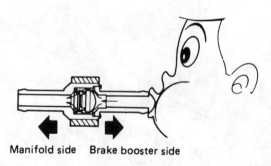

Fig. 9.23 Testing the check valve (Sec 13)

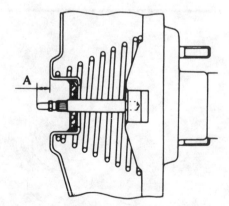

Fig. 9.24 Vacuum servo unit to master cylinder output rod length (Sec 14)

A must not be adjusted

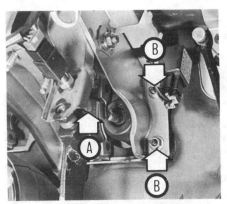

14.4 Brake pedal pushrod (A), and some vacuum servo unit mounting nuts (B)

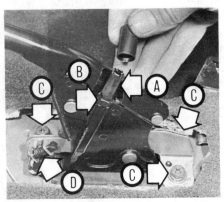

15.4 View showing handbrake adjuster (A), locknut (B), lever mounting bolts (C) and warning lamp switch (D)

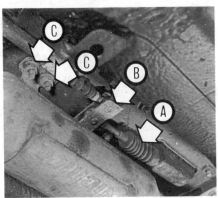

16.3 View showing front handbrake cable (A), rear handbrake cable (right-hand) (B) and rear cable retaining bracket nuts (C)

15 Handbrake – adjustment

1   The handbrake is adjusted by the action of the rear shoe automatic adjuster and will require no further attention unless the cable stretches, normally only after a high mileage has been covered.

2   The handbrake should be fully applied with the rear wheels locked if the handbrake control lever is pulled up 7 to 11 notches (clicks) of the ratchet.

3   If the lever moves over an excessive number of notches, then adjustment is necessary.

4   To gain access to the handbrake adjuster, remove the console from the handbrake as described in Chapter 11, then loosen the adjuster locknut and turn the adjuster as required, then retighten the locknut (photo).

5   Check that the handbrake warning light switch is activated when the lever is applied 1 to 2 notches. If the light fails to illuminate, check the switch and wiring connections, also the warning lamp bulb. If the switch is in need of adjustment, bend the switch mounting plate to suit.

6   Refit the handbrake console.

16 Handbrake cables – renewal

1   The handbrake cables and their attachments are shown in Fig. 9.25.

2   When removing any of the brake cables, the car must be raised at the rear and supported on axle stands. When the car is in the raised position, fully release the handbrake.

Rear cables

3   Unbolt the cable at the forward end and detach it from the forward cable (photo).

4   Unbolt the cable at its other underfloor attachment points.

5   Remove the rear wheel and brake drum on the side concerned, then disengage the cable from the handbrake operating lever on the brake shoe mechanism (see Section 4). Remove the brake cable.

6   Refit in the reverse order of removal, then readjust the handbrake as described in Section 15.

Front cable

7   Disconnect each rear cable from the front cable (see paragraph 3).

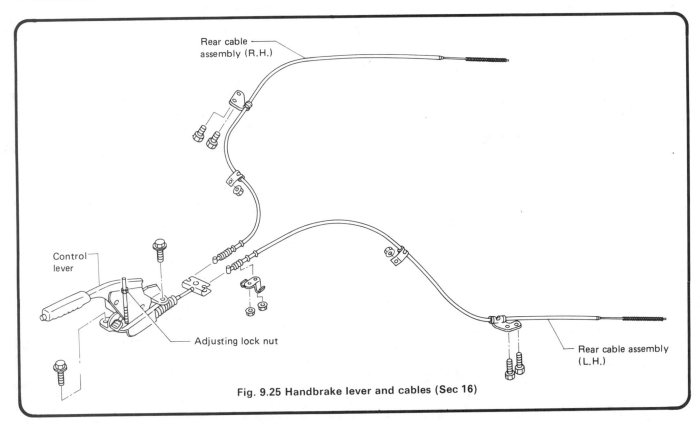

Fig. 9.25 Handbrake lever and cables (Sec 16)

8   Refer to photo 15.4, remove the adjuster cap, loosen the adjuster locknut, then unscrew and remove the adjuster and locknut.
9   Withdraw the front cable from underneath the car.
10 Refitting is a reversal of the removal procedure. Adjust the handbrake on completion as described in Section 15.

17 Brake pedal – removal, refitting and adjustment

1   Remove the driver's side lower facia panel and any items adjacent to the pedal (switches or relays) which may interfere with pedal removal.
2   Disconnect the pushrod from the brake pedal by extracting the clip and withdrawing the clevis pin (Fig. 9.26).
3   Unscrew and remove the pedal fulcrum shaft nut and then withdraw the shaft. Remove the brake pedal.
4   Refitting is a reversal of the removal procedure, but apply grease to the pedal shaft and check the pedal height as follows.
5   Measure the distance from the upper surface of the brake pedal to the floorpan as indicated by H in Fig. 9.27.
6   If the dimension is not as specified, loosen the locknut and turn the pedal pushrod as required making sure that the end of the rod protrudes into the clevis (Fig. 9.28). Tighten the locknut after adjusting the rod.
7   With the pedal fully released check that the specified clearance exists between the pedal and the stop-lamp switch. If not, loosen the locknut and adjust the stop-lamp as necessary, then tighten the locknut (photo).

17.7 Brake pedal stop-lamp switch (arrowed)

8   Finally run the engine and check that the depressed height of the pedal is as specified. If below the minimum amount check the hydraulic system for leaks or accumulation of air.

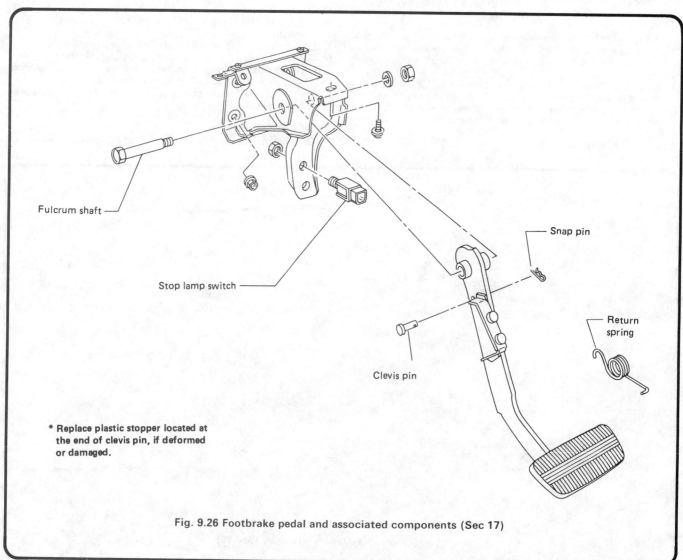

Fulcrum shaft

Stop lamp switch

Snap pin

Return spring

Clevis pin

* **Replace plastic stopper located at
   the end of clevis pin, if deformed
   or damaged.**

Fig. 9.26 Footbrake pedal and associated components (Sec 17)

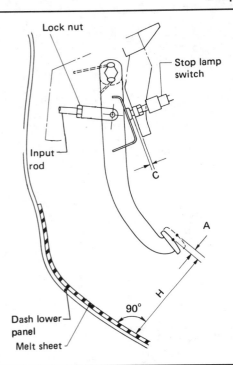

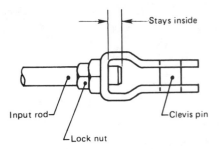

◄ **Fig. 9.27 Brake pedal adjustment (Sec 17)**

   A Free play
   C Pedal to stop-lamp switch clearance
   H Free height

Fig. 9.28 Rod protrustion within clevis is essential (Sec 17)

18 Fault diagnosis – braking system

Symptom	Reason(s)
Pedal travels a long way before the brakes operate	Incorrect pedal adjustment Brake shoes set too far from the drums (seized adjuster)
Stopping ability poor, even though pedal pressure is firm	Linings, discs or drums badly worn or scored One or more wheel hydraulic cylinders seized, resulting in some brake shoes not pressing against the drums (or pads against disc) Brake linings contaminated with oil Wrong type of linings fitted (too hard) Brake shoes wrongly assembled Servo unit not functioning
Car veers to one side when the brakes are applied	Brake pads or linings on one side are contaminated with oil Hydraulic wheel cylinder on one side partially or fully seized A mixture of lining materials fitted between sides Brake disc not matched Unequal wear between sides caused by partially seized wheel cylinders
Pedal feels spongy when the brakes are applied	Air is present in the hydraulic system
Pedal feels springy when the brakes are applied	Brake linings not bedded in (after fitting new ones) Master cylinder or brake backplate mounting bolts loose Severe wear in brake drums causing distortion when brakes are applied Discs out of true
Pedal travels right down with little or no resistance and brakes are virtually non-operative	Leak in hydraulic system resulting in lack of pressure for operating wheel cylinders If no signs of leakage are apparent the master cylinder internal seals are failing to sustain pressure
Binding, juddering, overheating	One or a combination of reasons given above Shoes installed incorrectly with reference to leading and trailing ends Broken shoe return spring Disc worn Drum distorted Incorrect pedal adjustment
Lack of servo assistance	Vacuum hose disconnected or leaking Non-return valve defective or incorrectly fitted Servo internal defect

Chapter 10 Suspension and steering

For modifications, and information applicable to later models, see Supplement at end of manual

Contents

Fault diagnosis – suspension and steering 26
Front hub/knuckle unit – removal, bearing replacement and
refitting 6
Front suspension strut – removal, overhaul and refitting 4
Front suspension transverse link arm – removal and refitting 5
General description 1
Manual steering gear – removal and refitting 19
Parallel links – removal and refitting 9
Power-assisted steering – fluid level and bleeding 23
Power-assisted steering gear – removal and refitting 20
Power steering pump – removal and refitting 22
Radius rod – removal and refitting 10
Rear hub bearings – renewal 7
Rear suspension knuckle – removal and refitting 8

Rear suspension strut – removal and refitting 11
Routine maintenance 2
Stabilizer (anti-roll bar) – removal and refitting 3
Steering angles and wheel alignment – general 24
Steering column – inspection and overhaul 16
Steering column – removal and refitting 15
Steering gear unit – overhaul 21
Steering lock/ignition switch – removal and refitting 18
Steering rack bellows – renewal 12
Steering wheel – removal and refitting 14
Tie-rod end balljoint – renewal 13
Tilt steering column – adjustment 17
Wheels and tyres – general care and maintenance 25

Specifications

Front suspension
Type .... MacPherson strut with stabilizer (anti-roll) bar

Steering
Type .... Rack and pinion with a universally-jointed column. A tilt column and power-assisted steering are optional

Saloon and Hatchback

Steering angles – N13:
    Camber .... −50′ to 40′
    Caster .... 35′ to 2° 05′
    Kingpin inclination .... 13° 05′ to 14° 35′

	Coupe	**Estate**
Steering angles – B12:		
Camber	−1° 05′ to 25′	−50′ to 40′
Caster	45′ to 2° 15′	35′ to 2° 05′
Kingpin inclination	13° 25′ to 14° 55′	13° to 14° 35′

Toe-in (all models) .... −0.5 to 1.5 mm (0.020 to 0.059 in) [−3′ to 9′]

Steering wheel turns, lock to lock:
    Manual steering .... 3.88 or 4.08
    Power steering 3.06
Steering wheel axial play .... Nil
Steering wheel play (maximum) .... 35.0 mm (1.38 in)
Power steering fluid .... Dexron type ATF (Duckhams Uni-Matic or D-Matic)

Tie-rod balljoints – axial endplay:
    Outer balljoint .... 1.3 mm (0.051 in) maximum
    Inner balljoint .... Nil

Front wheel bearing axial play	0.05 mm (0.002 in) maximum
Link arm-to-knuckle lower balljoint axial endplay (under force of 100 kg/221 lb)	0.7 mm (0.028 in) maximum

Rear suspension

Type	Trailing arm, telescopic shock absorbers and coil springs
Rear wheel alignment (unladen):	
Camber – Coupe 1.6	−1° 55' to −25'
Camber – other models	−1° 45' to −15'
Toe-out (total):	
Coupe 1.6	−0.5 to 3.5 mm (−0.020 to 0.138 in)
Other models	0 to 4 mm (0 to 0.16 in)
Rear wheel bearing axial endplay	0.05 mm (0.0020 in) maximum

Roadwheels

Type	Pressed steel or alloy
Size:	
Steel:	
Standard	5Jx13, 5^1/2JJx14 or 4^1/2Jx13
Optional	4Tx14 or 4Tx15
Alloy	5Jx13 or 5^1/2JJx14

Tyres

Tubeless radial sizes	175/70 SR 13, 155 SR 13 or 185/60 R14 82H
Tubeless bias sizes (conventional)	6.15-13-4PR or 6.45-13-4PR
Tubeless bias sizes (T type) – optional	T 115/70 D14
Tyre pressures	Refer to pressure recommendation decal on driver's door pillar

Torque wrench settings

	Nm	lbf ft
Roadwheel nuts	98 to 118	72 to 87

Steering components

	Nm	lbf ft
Steering wheel nut	29 to 39	21 to 29
Lower joint to column	24 to 29	18 to 21
Lower joint to steering gear	24 to 29	18 to 21
Hole cover to dash panel	3.4 to 4.4	2.5 to 3.2
Lower bracket to pedal bracket	13 to 18	10 to 13
Steering column clamp to bracket	13 to 18	10 to 13
Tilt lever retaining bolt	8 to 11	6 to 8
Tie-rod to knuckle	29 to 39	21 to 29
Tie-rod locknut	37 to 46	27 to 34
Tie-rod to steering gear	78 to 98	58 to 72
Steering gear unit clamp bolts	73 to 97	54 to 72
Power steering fluid tank bracket bolt	3.1 to 4.3	2.3 to 3.2
Power steering pump pulley locknut	31 to 42	23 to 31
High pressure line to steering gear	15 to 25	11 to 18
Low pressure connector to steering gear	27 to 39	20 to 29
Oil pump, tank and hoses connector bolt	69 to 78	51 to 58

Front axle/suspension components

	Nm	lbf ft
Wheel bearing/hub locknut	196 to 275	145 to 203
Transverse link (suspension arm) retaining bolt	78 to 98	58 to 72
Transverse link retaining nut	98 to 118	72 to 87
Stabilizer bar clamp	16 to 21	12 to 15
Connecting rod to transverse link	16 to 21	12 to 15
Stabilizer bar to balljoint	34 to 44	25 to 32
Transverse link to knuckle lower balljoint	59 to 74	44 to 55
Knuckle to strut	98 to 118	72 to 87
Strut to body	25 to 29	18 to 21
Strut piston rod self-locking nut	62 to 72	46 to 53
Side rod locknut	37 to 46	27 to 34
Side rod stud nut	29 to 39	21 to 29

Rear axle/suspension components

	Nm	lbf ft
Wheel bearing/hub locknut:		
Up to August 1986	186 to 255	137 to 188
From August 1986	186 to 216	137 to 159
Radius rod to knuckle	64 to 83	47 to 61
Radius rod bracket to body	88 to 108	65 to 80
Parallel link to suspension	98 to 118	72 to 87
Parallel link to knuckle	98 to 118	72 to 87
Strut to body	25 to 29	18 to 21
Strut to knuckle	98 to 118	72 to 87
Piston rod self-locking nut	62 to 72	46 to 53

1 General description

The front suspension is of MacPherson strut type, having coil springs, a transverse link arm and an anti-roll (stabilizer) bar.

The rear suspension comprises vertical struts with coil springs, parallel link arms and a radius rod.

The steering gear is of rack and pinion type, with a universally-jointed steering column. The column is adjustable for height on some models. Power-assisted steering is available as a factory-fitted option.

Note: *Whenever any parts of the front or rear suspension and steering assemblies are removed and refitted, the fastenings for the flexibly mounted components (eg stabilizer bar) should not be fully tightened to their respective torque wrench settings until after the vehicle is lowered to the ground and is free-standing*

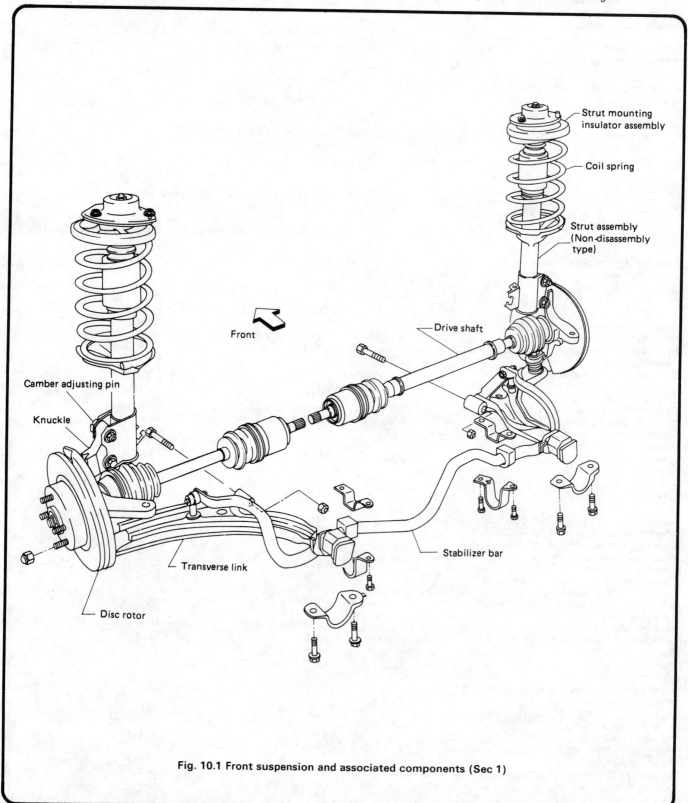

Fig. 10.1 Front suspension and associated components (Sec 1)

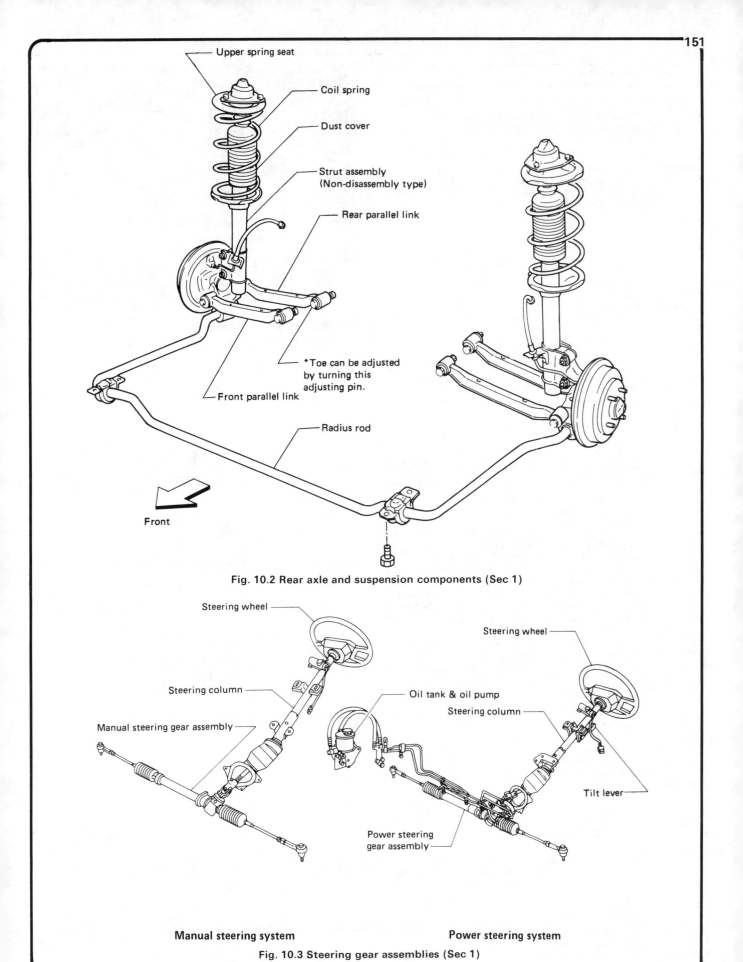

Upper spring seat

Coil spring

Dust cover

Strut assembly
(Non-disassembly type)

Rear parallel link

*Toe can be adjusted
by turning this
adjusting pin.

Front parallel link

Radius rod

Front

Fig. 10.2 Rear axle and suspension components (Sec 1)

Steering wheel

Steering column

Manual steering gear assembly

Oil tank & oil pump

Steering wheel

Steering column

Tilt lever

Power steering
gear assembly

Manual steering system

Power steering system

Fig. 10.3 Steering gear assemblies (Sec 1)

2   Routine maintenance

The following checks and maintenance procedures concerning the suspension and steering should be carried out at the intervals specified in *Routine Maintenance* at the start of this manual.

Tyres

1   Check the tyre pressures and correct if necessary.
2   Thoroughly examine the tyres for wear, damage and deterioration. Renew if necessary. See Section 25 for further information.

Front suspension and steering

3   Raise and securely support the front of the car.
4   Visually inspect the transverse link arm balljoint dust covers for splits or deterioration and renew the balljoint assembly, as described in Section 13, if any damage is apparent.
5   Grasp the roadwheel at the 12 o'clock and 6 o'clock positions and try to rock it. Very slight free play may be felt, but if the movement is appreciable further investigation is necessary to determine the source. Continue rocking the wheel while an assistant depresses the footbrake. If the movement is now eliminated or significantly reduced, it is likely that the hub bearings are at fault. If the free play is still evident with the footbrake depressed, then there is wear in the suspension joints or mountings. Pay close attention to the link arm balljoint and link arm inner mounting. Renew any worn components, as described in the appropriate Sections of this Chapter (Fig. 10.4).
6   Using a large screwdriver or flat bar, check for wear in the stabilizer bar mountings and link arm inner mountings by carefully levering against these components. Some movement is to be expected as the mountings are made of rubber, but excessive wear should be obvious. Renew any bushes that are worn.
7   Check the strut (shock absorber) each side for any sign of fluid leakage. Also check the upper and lower suspension and steering component mountings for security (photo).
8   Carefully inspect the rubber bellows which protect the steering gear. If they are cut, split or otherwise damaged they should be renewed, as described in Section 12. Neglect of damaged bellows may lead to damage to the steering gear itself.
9   Observe the tie-rod balljoints while an assistant turns the steering wheel back and forth through an arc of about 20°. If there is any side to side movement of the balljoints as the steering is turned they should be renewed, as described in Section 13. Renewal is also necessary if the rubber dust covers around the balljoints are split or damaged, or show any signs of deterioration.
10   Also inspect the condition of the flexible rubber coupling at the base of the steering column and renew this component if the rubber shows signs of deterioration or swelling, or if any cracks or splits are apparent. Full details will be found in Section 16.
11   On models with power steering, carry out the following additional work.
12   Check the power steering fluid level, using the dipstick built into the reservoir cap. Refer to Section 23 for details on level checking and topping-up.
13   Check the condition and tension of the power steering pump drivebelt (see Chapter 2 for details).
14   In the event of abnormal front tyre wear, check the front toe setting (Section 24).

Rear suspension

15   Raise and securely support the car at the rear (under the body side-members). Release the handbrake.
16   Visually inspect the rear suspension components, attachments and linkages for any obvious signs of excessive wear, damage or insecurity.
17   Grasp the roadwheel at the 12 o'clock and 6 o'clock positions and try to rock it. Any excess movement here indicates incorrect adjustment or wear in the rear hub bearings. Wear may also be accompanied by a rumbling sound when the wheel is spun, or a noticeable roughness if the wheel is turned slowly. Adjustment and repair procedures are described in Section 7.
18   Check the strut (rear shock absorber) for any sign of fluid leakage. Renew if necessary.

2.7 Check at points indicated for security and signs of leakage

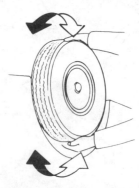

Fig. 10.4 Wheel bearing and suspension joint wear check method (Sec 2)

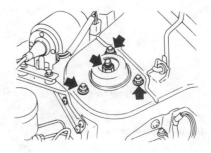

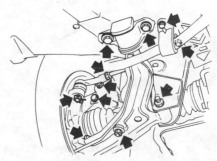

Fig. 10.5 Check points indicated for security on the front suspension (Sec 2)

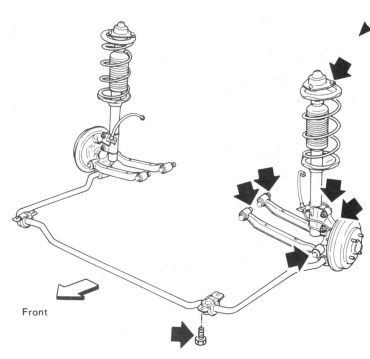

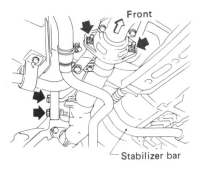

Fig. 10.6 Check points indicated for security and wear on the rear suspension (Sec 2)

Fig. 10.7 Detach exhaust downpipe at points indicated (Sec 3)

3 Stabilizer (anti-roll) bar – removal and refitting

1   Raise the vehicle at the front and support on safety stands.
2   Unbolt the exhaust downpipe from the lower coupling flange (Fig. 10.7).
3   Unbolt and disconnect the stabilizer bar saddle clamp each side (photo).
4   Unbolt the stabilizer bar at each end, either at the connecting rod or on the underside of the suspension link arm (transverse link) (photos).
5   Withdraw the stabilizer bar. Pull or lever down on the exhaust pipe to provide the necessary clearance.
6   Refitting is a reversal of removal, but if the vehicle was jacked up to remove the bar do not fully tighten the anti-roll bar nuts and bolts until the weight of the vehicle has been lowered onto the roadwheels. When securing the stabilizer bar at each end, ensure that the bar is correctly positioned at the balljoint connection as shown in Fig. 10.8.

4 Front suspension strut – removal, overhaul and refitting

1   Raise the front of the vehicle and support it securely on axle stands placed under the side-members.

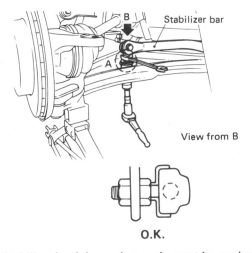

Fig. 10.8 Stabilizer bar joint socket angle must be as shown when viewed from top down (B). Secure at (A) when removing/refitting (Sec 3)

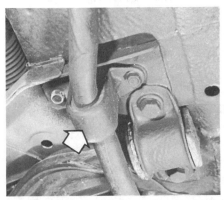

3.3 Stabilizer saddle clamp (arrowed). The transverse link arm clamp is also shown

3.4A Stabilizer-to-link arm connection viewed from underneath

3.4B Stabilizer/connecting rod connection to link arm viewed from above

154

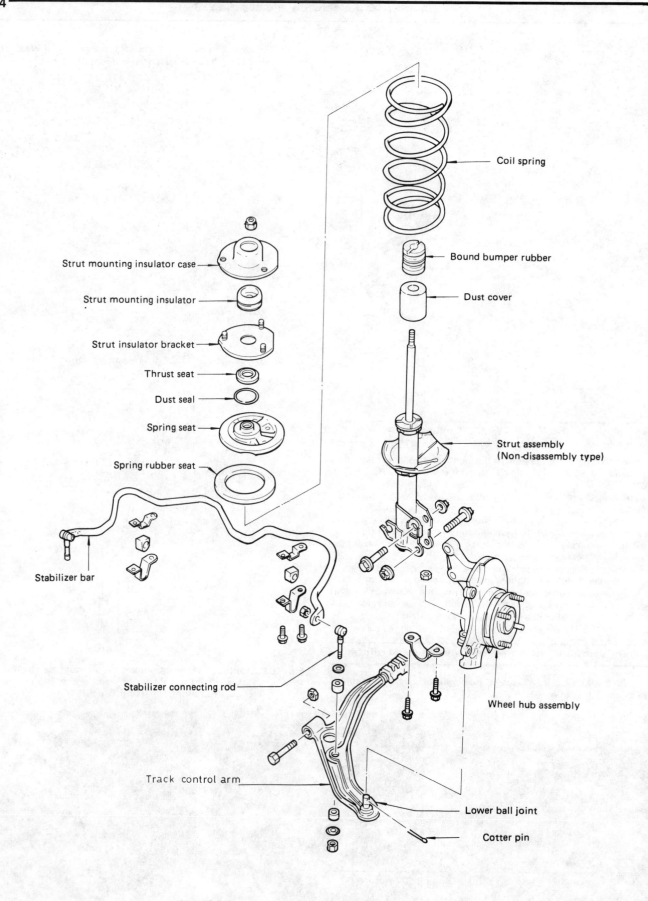

Coil spring

Bound bumper rubber

Dust cover

Strut mounting insulator case

Strut mounting insulator

Strut insulator bracket

Thrust seat

Dust seal

Spring seat

Spring rubber seat

Strut assembly
(Non-disassembly type)

Stabilizer bar

Stabilizer connecting rod

Wheel hub assembly

Track control arm

Lower ball joint

Cotter pin

Fig. 10.9 Front suspension strut components (Sec 4)

4.5 Strut-to-steering knuckle bolts. Top bolt adjusts camber angle, each graduation mark equals 15'

4.7 Front suspension strut top mounting

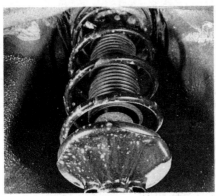

4.8 Removing the front suspension strut from the wing underside

2 Remove the roadwheel.
3 Disconnect the hydraulic brake pipe from the suspension strut where applicable.
4 Support the transverse link (suspension) arm on a jack.
5 Before detaching the strut from the steering knuckle it is essential that the upper retaining bolt position of fitting (relative to the strut) is marked, as this bolt acts as an adjusting pin when setting the camber angle during production. Marking its position is essential to ensure correct realignment when refitting (photo).
6 Unscrew and remove the strut-to-knuckle bolts and nuts noting their fitting directions.
7 Working at the top of the inner wing within the engine compartment, unscrew and remove the three nuts which secure the strut top mounting (photo). Do not undo the piston rod locknut at this stage.
8 Support the strut assembly and withdraw it from under the wing (photo).
9 Unless coil spring compressors are available do not carry out any further dismantling.
10 Where compressors are available (they can be purchased at most motor accessory stores) fit them to the strut coil spring and compress the spring just sufficiently to be able to turn the strut upper mounting insulator by hand.
11 Unscrew the self-locking nut from the top of the piston rod. Flats are machined on the rod so that an open-ended spanner can be used to prevent the rod rotating while the unit is unscrewed.
12 Take off the mounting insulator, the thrust seat, the dust seal, the spring upper seat, the spring rubber seat, coil spring (with compressors), and the rebound rubber and dust cover.
13 Unless the coil spring is to be renewed, the compressors can remain on the spring for reassembly.
14 If the strut is distorted, leaking or has lost its damping qualities, then the strut tube must be renewed; no repair being possible. The renewal of both struts is advised.
15 Reassemble the strut by fitting the spring in its compressed state followed by the upper mounting components in their originally fitted sequence (Figs. 10.11 and 10.12). Apply grease to the underside of the thrust plate.
16 Tighten the piston rod self-locking nut to the specified torque and then gently remove the spring compressors. Make sure that the spring lower end is in full contact with the abutment on the lower seat.
17 Offer the strut to its mounting under the wing. Screw on the nuts finger tight.
18 Reconnect the base of the strut with the stub axle carrier, and align the upper bolts as noted during removal.
19 Reconnect the brake pipe to the strut where applicable.
20 Refit the roadwheel and lower the vehicle to the ground.
21 Tighten all nuts and bolts to the specified torque.

5 Front suspension transverse link arm – removal and refitting

1 Raise and support the vehicle at the front, positioning the safety stands under the side-members.

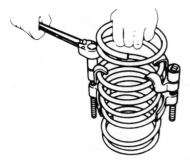

Fig. 10.10 Compressor tools fitted to the front coil spring (Sec 4)

Top

Bottom

Fig. 10.11 Coil spring fitting orientation (Sec 4)

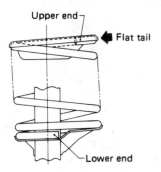

Upper end

Flat tail

Lower end

Fig. 10.12 Coil spring seating arrangement (front strut) (Sec 4)

2 Remove the front roadwheel(s).
3 Unbolt and separate the steering tie-rod end balljoint from the steering knuckle (Section 13).
4 Remove the hub nut and withdraw the hub/knuckle unit from the driveshaft as described in Chapter 8. The driveshaft can be left attached to the transmission at the inboard end, but support the weight of the driveshaft to avoid damaging its joints and gaiters.
5 Loosen the link arm-to-knuckle balljoint nut (photo) (having extracted the cotter pin), then using a balljoint separator, disconnect the two (Fig. 10.13).
6 Unbolt and disconnect the stabilizer (anti-roll) bar from the link arm, and undo the link arm at its pivot points (photo).
7 Withdraw the transverse link arm.
8 The flexible bushes may be renewed. Do this by pressing them out or by drawing them out using a bolt, nut, washers and tubular spacers. Smear the new bushes with liquid soap to make fitting easier.
9 Inspect the lower balljoint for excessive wear. If the ball-stud of the joint proves hard to turn or has excessive axial play, the joint unit must be renewed. If in doubt, have the joint inspected by a Nissan dealer. Using special tools, he will be able to assess if the balljoint turning force is correct, also the axial endplay.
10 The balljoint unit is an integral part of the link arm and they must, therefore, be renewed as a unit. This being the case, it is advisable to renew the link arm and balljoint on the opposing side of the front suspension at the same time.
11 Refit the transverse link arm by reversing the removal procedures. Note that the rear pivot saddle clamp must be fitted in the direction shown in Fig. 10.15.
12 Refer to Chapter 8 when refitting the driveshaft to the knuckle hub.
13 Do not fully tighten the retaining nuts and bolts to the specified torques until the weight of the vehicle is on the roadwheels.

6 Front hub/knuckle unit – removal, bearing replacement and refitting

1 Raise and support the vehicle at the front (positioning the safety stand under the side-members).
2 Remove the front roadwheel(s).
3 Unbolt and disconnect the brake caliper unit from the hub/knuckle unit, leaving the hydraulic line attached. Support the weight of the caliper by suspending from a suitable point using a length of wire or cord.
4 Disconnect the steering tie-rod end balljoint from the knuckle as described in Section 13.
5 Undo the hub nut and separate the driveshaft from the hub/knuckle unit as described in Chapter 8. The driveshaft can be left attached to the transmission at its inboard end, but support its weight whilst detached from the hub unit.
6 Remove the cotter pin and unscrew the hub/knuckle-to-transverse link arm balljoint nut so that a suitable separator can be fitted. Detach the link arm and balljoint from the knuckle.
7 Disconnect the hub/knuckle unit from the suspension strut as described in Section 5, paragraphs 5 and 6. Remove the hub/knuckle unit.

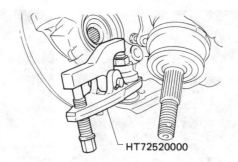

Fig. 10.13 Detaching the knuckle balljoint with special separator tool (Sec 5)

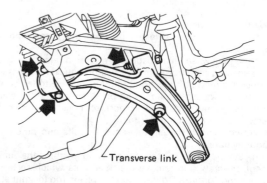

Fig. 10.14 Detach the link arm at points indicated (Sec 5)

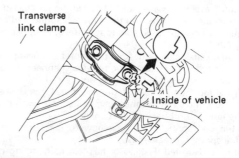

Fig. 10.15 Transverse link rear pivot clamp orientation (Sec 5)

5.5 Transverse link arm balljoint unit

5.6 Transverse link arm pivot bolt

6.8 Inboard side of hub/knuckle unit showing oil seal

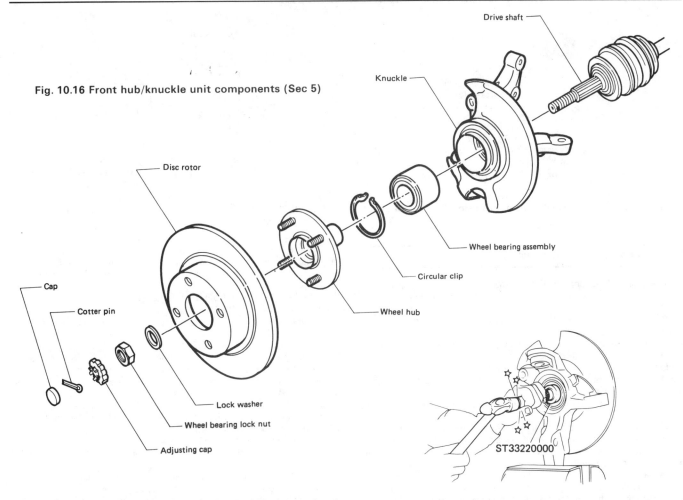

Fig. 10.16 Front hub/knuckle unit components (Sec 5)

Labels: Drive shaft, Knuckle, Disc rotor, Wheel bearing assembly, Circular clip, Wheel hub, Cap, Cotter pin, Lock washer, Wheel bearing lock nut, Adjusting cap

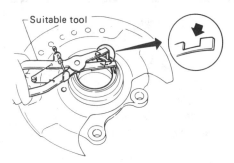

Fig. 10.17 Hub and wheel bearing removal (Sec 6)

ST33220000

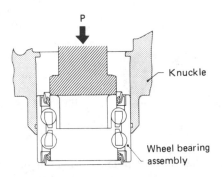

Fig. 10.18 Circlip removal from hub (Sec 6)

Suitable tool

8 If separating the hub from the knuckle the wheel bearings and seal must be renewed (photo).

9 Support the knuckle unit in a vice and then drive out the hub, complete with the outer inner bearing race, using a suitable drift or the special tool shown if available (Fig. 10.17).

10 Withdraw the inner race from the hub using a press or suitable puller.

11 Remove the inboard side inner race from the hub bearing in a similar manner.

12 Extract the circlip from the hub using suitable circlip pliers then temporarily refit the bearing inner race from the bearing and press out the bearing unit from the knuckle (Figs. 10.18 and 10.19).

13 Check the hub and knuckle for signs of damage or cracks, and renew if necessary. Renew the hub bearings and, if distorted or damaged, the retaining circlip.

14 Check that the bearing housing is clean and dry before fitting the new bearing. Press or drift the new bearing into position from the outside, but do not press directly on the bearing inner race. The outer bearing contact surfaces must not be lubricated prior to fitting. Support the underside of the knuckle with a suitable tube or the special tool shown (Fig. 10.20). Take particular care not to damage the grease seal at each end (Fig. 10.21).

15 Insert the circlip into the knuckle groove to secure the bearing, then smear some multi-purpose grease onto the seal lips.

16 Align the hub squarely to the bearing bore, then drift or press the hub into position. If pressing the hub into position do not exceed a loading of 29 kN (3.0 Imp ton).

17 With bearing and hub assembly complete, check that the hub spins smoothly and freely without binding or slackness. If a press is available check that the hub spins freely under a preloading of 44.1 kN (4.4 Imp ton).

18 The steering hub/knuckle unit can now be refitted to the vehicle. Reverse the removal procedures, referring to Chapters 8 and 9 when refitting the driveshaft and brake caliper unit. Refer to Sections 5 and 13 in this Chapter when reconnecting the transverse link and tie-rod.

P

Knuckle

Wheel bearing assembly

Fig. 10.19 Bearing removal from hub (Sec 6)

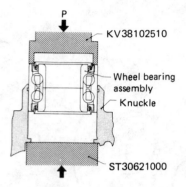

Fig. 10.20 Bearing refitting into hub using Nissan special tools (Sec 6)

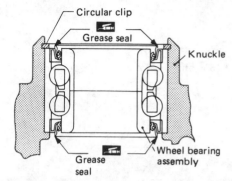

Fig. 10.21 Hub seals showing orientation and lubrication points when fitting (Sec 6)

7   Rear hub bearings – renewal

1   The rear hub is combined with the brake drum and this unit, together with the bearings, can be removed from the knuckle spindle as follows.

2   Raise and support the vehicle at the rear on safety stands.

3   Remove the rear roadwheel(s).

4   Using a suitable screwdriver as a lever, prise free the hub cap, then clean away the grease from the hub.

5   Extract the cotter pin and withdraw the adjuster cap from the hub nut. Unscrew the hub nut. This is tightened to a considerable force so when freeing it check that the car is securely supported and, if necessary, use an extension bar. Remove the hub nut and special washer (photos).

6   Fully release the handbrake, then withdraw the brake drum. As it is withdrawn collect the hub bearing cone from the outboard side and place it to one side for cleaning and inspection (photo). If the hub/drum unit is reluctant to be withdrawn, it is probable that the brakes are holding it. To retract the brake adjuster, extract the rubber inspection plug (this is oblong in shape) from the brake backplate, then reach through with a screwdriver and unwind the automatic brake adjuster.

7   Clean and inspect the hub, bearings and oil seal for excessive wear or damage. When the seal and bearing assemblies are removed from the hub, they must be renewed. If required remove them as follows (photo).

8   Prise free the oil seal from the hub using a suitable screwdriver as a lever as shown (Fig. 10.23).

9   Contract and release the bearing retaining circlip (Fig. 10.24).

10   Using a tube drift of suitable diameter, press or drive out the bearing from the hub (Fig. 10.25).

11   Clean the hub/drum unit and check for excessive wear and/or damage. Check that the inner diameter of the brake drum does not exceed the maximum allowable specified diameter (see Specifications in Chapter 9). Renew the hub/drum unit if necessary.

12   Ensure that the bearing aperture in the hub is clean and dry.

13   Press or drive the new bearing into position in the hub (Fig. 10.26).

14   Lubricate the inner and outer bearing cones with a multi-purpose grease, then fit the inner race.

15   Refit the circlip into the groove in the hub, ensuring that it is fully located.

16   Carefully drift the new oil seal into the hub so that it is fitted as shown (Fig. 10.27). Smear the seal lip with grease.

17   Insert the outboard side bearing cone into position in the hub, then relocate the hub unit onto the spindle.

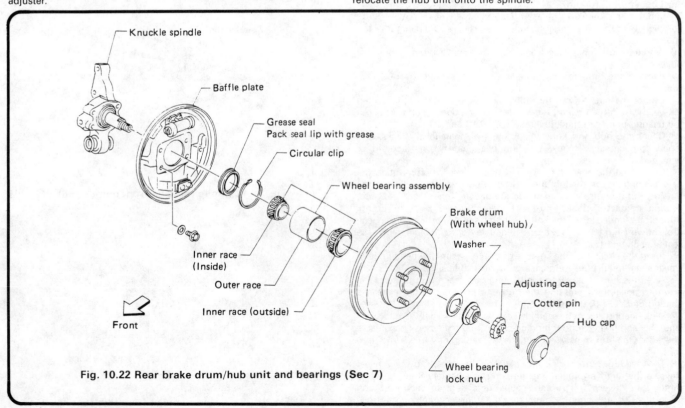

Fig. 10.22 Rear brake drum/hub unit and bearings (Sec 7)

18 Fit the special washer and screw on the hub nut. As the nut is being tightened to the specified torque setting (see Specifications), rotate the drum/hub unit to ensure that smooth rotation is maintained (photo).

19 When then nut is tightened to the specified torque, check the hub/drum axial endplay using a clock gauge. No bearing preload or hub adjustment is possible and, therefore, if incorrect it will be necessary to investigate and rectify the fault before proceeding further.

20 Refit the adjuster cap over the nut so that the cotter pin can be fitted. Use a new cotter pin and peen over the ends to secure (photo).

21 Refit the roadwheel(s) then check the brakes for satisfactory operation.

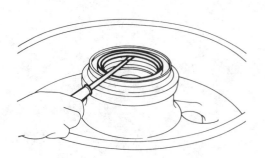

Fig. 10.23 Levering out the oil seal for renewal (Sec 7)

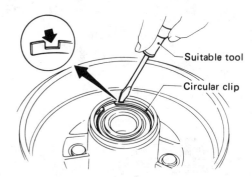

Fig. 10.24 Remove the bearing circlip (Sec 7)

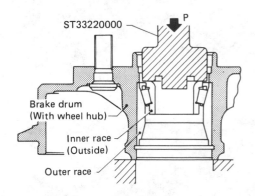

Fig. 10.25 Bearing removal from drum/hub using Nissan special tool (Sec 7)

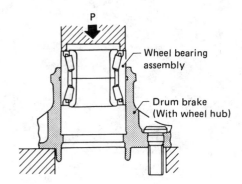

Fig. 10.26 Bearing refitting to drum/hub (Sec 7)

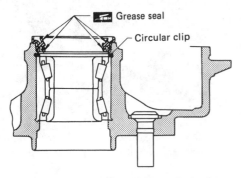

Fig. 10.27 Oil seal orientation in drum/hub. Grease seal at points indicated (Sec 7)

7.5A Rear brake drum/hub unit showing adjuster cap and retaining pin

7.5B Withdrawing the special hub washer

7.6 Rear hub bearing cone removal

7.7 Brake drum/hub inboard seal and bearing

7.18 Tighten the hub nut to the specified torque setting

7.20 Align the adjuster cap with the cotter pin hole

8.7 General view of the rear suspension knuckle showing strut (A), knuckle (B), parallel link – rear (C), radius rod (D) and parallel link – front (E)

8 Rear suspension knuckle – removal and refitting

1   Raise and support the vehicle at the rear on safety stands.
2   Remove the rear roadwheel.
3   Remove the brake drum and hub unit as described in Section 7.
4   Disconnect the brake hydraulic line from the wheel cylinder and the handbrake cable from the brake unit. Refer to Chapter 9 for details.
5   Undo the four retaining bolts and remove the brake backplate (with brake assembly attached) from the knuckle unit.
6   Unscrew and remove the radius rod end nut on the side concerned. Remove the washers and rear end bush from the rod.
7   Unbolt and disconnect the parallel link arms from the knuckle (photo).
8   Undo the two retaining nuts and extract the strut-to-knuckle clamp bolts (noting their fitting direction). Detach the knuckle from the strut and withdraw it from the end of the radius rod to remove it.
9   Refitting is a reversal of the removal procedure. Do not fully tighten the radius rod nut and the parallel link arm nuts to their specified torques until later when the vehicle is lowered and free standing under its own weight.
10 Reconnect the brake components and top up and bleed the hydraulic system as described in Chapter 9.

9 Parallel links – removal and refitting

1   Raise and support the vehicle under each side lift point at the rear with safety stands.
2   Undo and remove the pivot bolt from the outboard and inboard end of the link concerned (photos). Before removing the bolt from the inboard end of the rearmost link arm on each side, mark the relative fitted position of the bolt to the link as the position of this bolt is set during production to adjust the toe setting.
3   Remove the parallel link(s). If both links each side are being removed keep them separate and identified. The front and rear links differ and are colour-coded, pink to the front link, green to the rear link (Fig. 10.29).
4   The flexible bushes may be renewed. Do this by pressing or drawing them out using a bolt, nut washer and tubular spacers. Smear the new bushes with liquid soap to ease insertion, then fit the new bushes, reversing the removal procedure.
5   Refit the parallel link(s) in the reverse order of removal. Do not fully tighten the retaining nut(s) to the specified torque wrench setting until after the vehicle is lowered and is free standing under its own weight. Ensure that the links are correctly located and that the toe setting pin

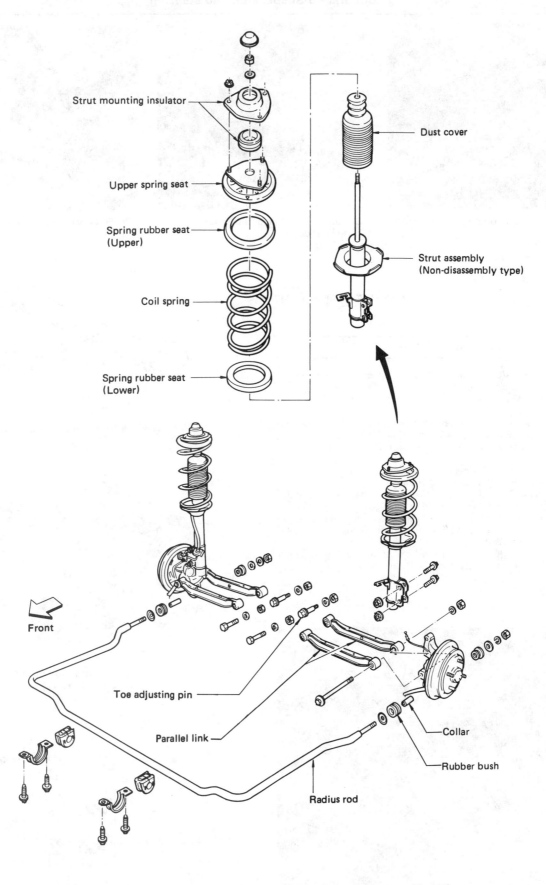

Strut mounting insulator

Upper spring seat

Spring rubber seat
(Upper)

Coil spring

Spring rubber seat
(Lower)

Dust cover

Strut assembly
(Non-disassembly type)

Front

Toe adjusting pin

Parallel link

Collar

Rubber bush

Radius rod

Fig. 10.28 Exploded view of the rear suspension components (Sec 8)

9.2A Toe setting bolt on inner end of rear parallel link arm(s)
Each index graduation mark equals 2 mm (0.08 in) of toe per side – mark original position before removal

9.2B Rear parallel link outboard retaining nut (to knuckle)

9.2C Front parallel link outboard retaining bolt (pivot pin)

bolt is correctly realigned with the index match mark made during removal.

10 Radius rod – removal and refitting

1   Raise and support the vehicle at the rear, supporting it under the sill lift point each side with axle stands.
2   Disconnect the exhaust system at the rear so that the radius rod can be withdrawn.
3   Unscrew and remove the retaining nuts and washers from the rearward end of the radius rod each side (Fig. 10.30 and photo).
4   Undo the bolts securing the radius rod clamps to the floor each side. Note the orientation of the clamps as they are removed.
5   Move the radius rod forwards to disengage it from the knuckle, then withdraw it from the underside of the vehicle.
6   Renew the radius rod bushes if they are perished or badly worn. Renew the radius rod if it is deformed or damaged.
7   Refit in the reverse order of removal, but ensure that the end bushes are fitted as shown (Fig. 10.31), and the saddle clamps are orientated as noted during removal (Fig. 10.32).
8   Do not fully tighten the retaining bolts to their specified torque settings until after the vehicle is lowered and free standing.

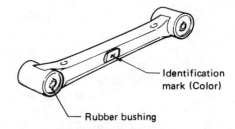

Fig. 10.29 Code mark location on parallel link (Sec 9)

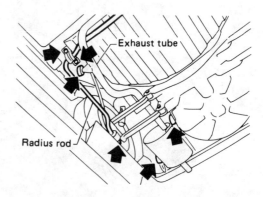

Fig. 10.30 Disconnect at points indicated to remove the radius rod (Sec 10)

10.3 Radius rod-to-knuckle connection

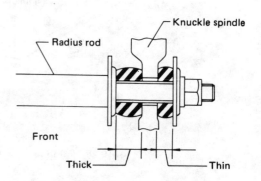

Fig. 10.31 Radius rod-to-knuckle bush orientation (Sec 10)

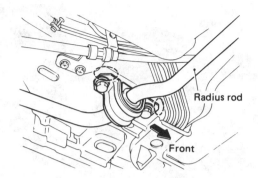

Fig. 10.32 Radius rod saddle clamp orientation (Sec 10)

11 Rear suspension strut – removal and refitting

1 Remove the interior side trim in the luggage compartment to allow access to the top mounting nuts of the strut on the side concerned (photo).
2 Raise and support the vehicle at the rear, supporting it under the sill lift points each side with axle stands.
3 Unbolt and remove the roadwheel(s).
4 Unbolt and remove the exhaust system rear of the downpipe.
5 Remove the radius rod as described in Section 10.
6 Disconnect the brake hydraulic line at the support bracket on the strut (see Chapter 9).
7 Disconnect the handbrake cable from the front cable connection (equaliser), and from the underside location points on the side concerned (Chapter 9).
8 Unbolt and disconnect the parallel link arms at their outboard (knuckle) end. If unbolting the link arms at the inboard mounting points, note the special removal procedure before removing the rearward pivot bolt, described in Section 9, paragraph 2.
9 Support the weight of the knuckle and strut assembly by positioning a jack under the knuckle/hub unit, then unscrew the three upper mounting nuts from within the vehicle, and carefully lower the strut unit from under the vehicle. If preferred, the knuckle can be unbolted from the strut before it is removed.
10 Strut inspection and coil spring removal are the same as those described in Section 4 for the front suspension (paragraphs 9 to 16 inclusive) (Fig. 10.33).
11 To refit the strut, offer it to the mounting under the car, ensuring that the upper spring seat faces the front as it is fitted, then hand tighten the retaining nuts (Fig. 10.34).
12 Reconnect the knuckle to the base of the strut, and tighten the retaining bolts to the specified torque.
13 Reconnect the brake hydraulic line and the handbrake cable, referring to Chapter 9 for details.
14 Reconnect the parallel links and the radius rod with reference to Sections 9 and 10, but do not fully retighten their fastenings until after the vehicle is lowered to the ground. The same applies to the strut upper mounting nuts.
15 Reconnect the exhaust pipe with reference to Chapter 3.

12 Steering rack bellows – renewal

1 The steering rack bellows should be inspected periodically for splits. Have an assistant turn the steering to full lock while doing this, otherwise the split will not be immediately apparent.
2 Unscrew the nut from the balljoint taper pin and, using an extractor, separate the balljoint from the eye of the steering arm (photo).
3 Grip the square end of the balljoint tie-rod to prevent it turning, then loosen the locknut from its inner end. Now grip the tie-rod and unscrew the balljoint from the tie-rod, counting the number of turns required to remove it. Unscrew the nut from the tie-rod.
4 Release the bellows securing bands and pull the bellows from the rack housing and off the tie-rod (on power steering models also detach the interconnecting breather tube).

11.1 Rear suspension strut top end viewed through trim panel support (Hatchback)

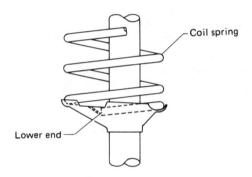

Fig. 10.33 Coil spring seating arrangement – rear strut (Sec 11)

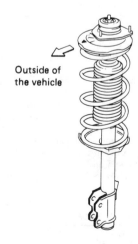

Fig. 10.34 Rear strut unit orientation (Sec 11)

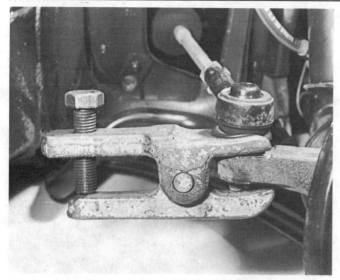

12.2 Tie-rod balljoint separation method using extractor

14.3 Steering wheel retaining nut. Note earth wire connection

5   If the bellows have been split for some time and dirt has entered, wipe away all the old lubricant and smear the rack (extended) and the rack end balljoint with a suitable grease.
6   Slide on the new bellows and fit the securing bands. Lubricate the contact surfaces of the bellows and the gear housing to ease assembly.
7   Fit the securing wire bands as shown (Fig. 10.35) and bend the protruding twisted section downwards so that they are out of the way of adjacent parts.
8   Locate the locknut onto the tie-rod at the distance noted during removal, then reconnect the tie-rod end balljoint to the steering tie-rod and knuckle. Before fully tightening the locknut and balljoint castle nut, check and if necessary adjust the steering toe-in setting as described in Section 24. When the castle nut is tightened to the specified torque further tighten it as necessary to align the split pin hole, then insert a new split pin and bend it open to secure. Tighten the locknut against the tie-rod end (Fig. 10.36).

13 Tie-rod end balljoint – renewal

1   The removal and refitting of a balljoint is covered in the preceding Section.
2   Always check the front wheel alignment after having fitted a new balljoint – refer to Section 24.

14 Steering wheel – removal and refitting

1   Disconnect the battery earth lead.
2   Remove the centre pad from the steering wheel by undoing the retaining screws on the underside of the wheel, then prising free and withdrawing the pad.
3   Centralize the steering, then unscrew and remove the retaining nut (photo).
4   Before withdrawing the steering wheel, make an alignment marking on the wheel centre and column end face to ensure correct refitting position. Pull free the steering wheel from the column.
5   Refit in the reverse order of removal. Ensure correct realignment of the steering wheel and tighten the nut to the specified torque setting. Lubricate the indicator cancel pin and horn contact stop-ring with a small amount of multi-purpose grease (Fig. 10.37).

15 Steering column – removal and refitting

1   Disconnect the battery earth lead.
2   Remove the steering column shrouds and the lower facia trim panels adjacent to the column.

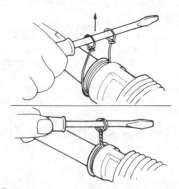

Fig. 10.35 Pull on securing bands as they are twisted to secure the bellows (Sec 12)

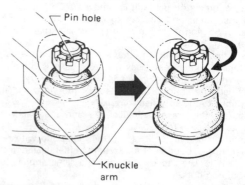

Fig. 10.36 Tie-rod balljoint nut tightening method (Sec 12)

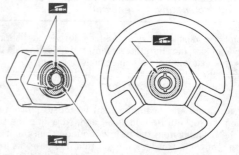

Fig. 10.37 Lubricate points indicated, indicator cancel pin (each portion) and horn contact slip-ring with multi-purpose grease (Sec 14)

15.4 Steering column shaft, universal joint and pinion shaft connection

15.5A Steering column upper mounting

15.5B Steering column lower mounting

3 Disconnect the wiring harness connectors from the column switches.

4 Centralize the steering, then from the engine side of the bulkhead, unscrew and remove the through-bolt securing the column to the lower universal joint unit (photo).

5 Support the weight of the column and undo the upper and lower mounting bolts to the retaining brackets within the vehicle (photos).

6 Lower the column and withdraw it rearwards from within the vehicle, disengaging the lower splined end from the universal joint and the grommet from the bulkhead aperture. As the column is lowered from its mountings, recover any spacer plates; noting their locations

and orientation for correct replacement on reassembly.

7 Refitting is a reversal of the removal procedure. Ensure that the spacer plates are correctly located as noted during removal. Initially fit the mounting bolts finger tight only, then when the column is fully located, tighten the bolts to the specified torque settings with no undue stress placed on the column.

8 Ensure that the wiring harness connections to the column switches are securely made. Check the switches for satisfactory operation on completion.

9 Check the steering for a satisfactory action, with an even amount of movement from the centre position to full lock on each side.

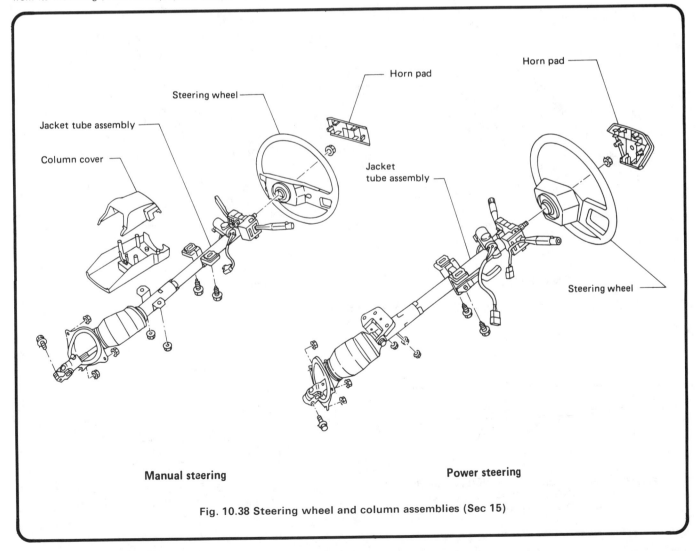

Manual steering

Power steering

Fig. 10.38 Steering wheel and column assemblies (Sec 15)

16 Steering column – inspection and overhaul

1   To check the steering column (tilt or non tilt type), first remove it from the vehicle as described in the previous Section.

2   Unlock the steering using the ignition key, then move the steering wheel from lock to lock. The steering action must be smooth with no binding or slackness felt. If the action is suspect, the column will need further inspection.

3   If not already removed, withdraw the lower bracket (bulkhead grommet) and gaiter (boot). The boot is secured by a nylon band at each end which can be cut free.

4   To remove the steering wheel, support the column by gripping the upper mounting bracket in a vice and relock the steering lock. Remove the steering wheel as described in Section 14.

5   Unlock the column, then remove the snap-ring and washers (note order of fitting) from the upper end of the shaft. Withdraw the column shaft from the lower end of the jacket tube.

6   If the column bearings are damaged or are excessively worn the column unit must be renewed. If they are serviceable, clean and lubricate them with a multi-purpose grease. Inspect the jacket tube for damage or deformity, and renew if necessary. With the column shaft inserted into its normal position in the jacket tube, the length L measured between the points indicated in Fig. 10.40 should be as specified. When making this check, ensure that the lower snap-ring at the upper end of the column shaft is flush against the upper bearing as shown (Fig. 10.41). This check is particularly important if the vehicle has suffered collision damage.

7   Renew the column shaft and/or the jacket tube if necessary.

8   If required the steering lock can be renewed as described in Section 18.

9   Reassemble in the reverse order of removal. Lubricate the bearings and bushes with a multi-purpose grease then push the shaft into the jacket. Ensure that the snap-ring which is located beneath the upper bearing is correctly fitted with its rounded face towards the bearing (Fig. 10.41).

10   Fit the upper snap-ring as shown using a suitable ring spanner (Fig. 10.42).

11   When refitting the universal joint boot align it as shown in Fig. 10.43 and secure using new nylon bands.

12   Where applicable, if the tilt steering mechanism is dismantled, lubricate the tilt lever and adjuster bolt during reassembly. When the column is refitted check the tilt mechanism operation and adjustment.

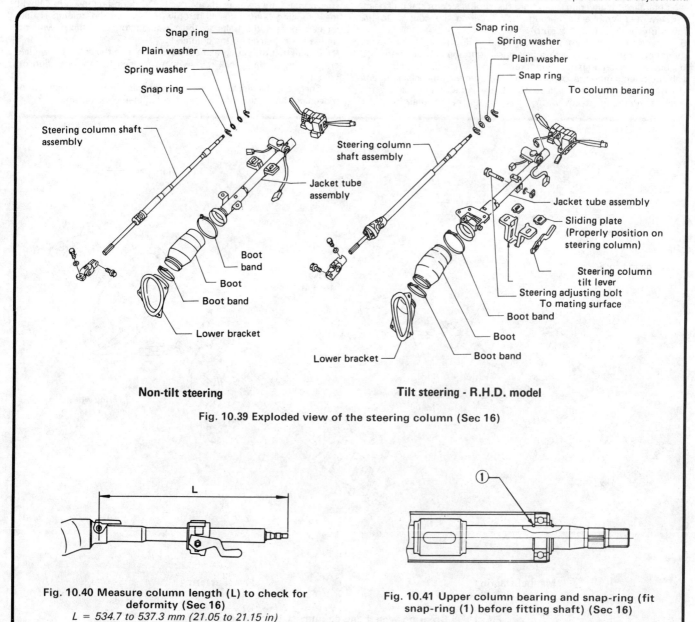

Non-tilt steering   **Tilt steering - R.H.D. model**

Fig. 10.39 Exploded view of the steering column (Sec 16)

Fig. 10.40 Measure column length (L) to check for deformity (Sec 16)
L = 534.7 to 537.3 mm (21.05 to 21.15 in)

Fig. 10.41 Upper column bearing and snap-ring (fit snap-ring (1) before fitting shaft) (Sec 16)

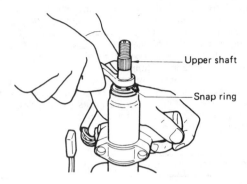

Fig. 10.42 Locating the upper column snap-ring (Sec 16)

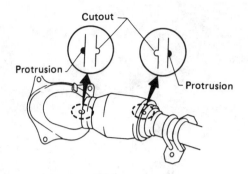

Fig. 10.43 Column universal joint boot alignment – cut-out to protrusion (Sec 16)

17 Tilt steering column – adjustment

1   Loosen the tilt adjuster bolt and move the lever so that it contacts the flange position, then tighten the adjustment bolt to the specified torque setting.
2   Move the lever downwards through an arc of 70° to ensure that the column moves freely without binding (Fig. 10.44).
3   Now move the lever back to its original position and ensure that there is no free play at the column when the steering wheel is moved down under pressure (photo).

18 Steering lock/ignition switch – removal and refitting

1   Disconnect the battery earth lead.
2   Undo the retaining screws and remove the steering column shrouds.
3   Disconnect the wiring from the ignition switch.
4   The lock/switch unit is secured to the steering column by self-shear type screws. These screws must be drilled out or removed using a proprietary tool (photo).
5   The ignition switch barrel is secured in the lock housing by a retaining pin (photo).
6   To refit the lock, align it with the hole in the outer column, locate the clamp plate and insert the shear screws finger tight.
7   Check that the lock operates correctly, then tighten the retaining screws until their heads break off.
8   Reconnect the wiring, refit the shrouds and check the operation of the switch/lock and the various column switches to ensure satisfactory operation.

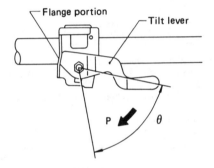

Fig. 10.44 Tilt lever angle of 70° (Sec 17)

17.3 Tilt steering column and adjustment lever

18.4 Steering column lock shear screws (arrowed)

18.5 Ignition switch retaining pin in column lock housing (arrowed)

19 Manual steering gear – removal and refitting

1   Raise the front of the vehicle and support it securely using axle stands under the side-members. Apply the handbrake and remove the front roadwheels.

2   Disconnect both tie-rod balljoints from the steering knuckle each side.

3   Unscrew and remove the bolt securing the lower joint to the steering gear pinion.

4   Unscrew the rack housing mounting bolts each side whilst supporting the weight of the unit, then lower it from the bulkhead, withdrawing the pinion shaft from the joint. Once separated the steering gear unit can be withdrawn from the side.

5   Refitting is a reversal of the removal procedures. Centralise the steering movement of the rack and the column prior to reconnecting the pinion shaft to the lower joint.

6   Do not tighten the retaining bolts and nuts until the unit is fully located, then tighten them to their specified torque settings and insert new split pins to secure the tie-rod end nuts (see Section 12).

7   On completion, check that the steering action is positive and smooth through its full movement.

20 Power assisted steering gear – removal and refitting

1   Raise the front of the vehicle and support it on axle stands. Check that the handbrake is fully applied and then remove the front roadwheels.

2   Disconnect the tie-rod end balljoints from the steering knuckle each side, as described in Section 12.

3   Disconnect the hydraulic hoses from the steering gear unit. Allow for fluid leakage as the fluid lines are detached. Plug them, as they may continue to leak and it will prevent the ingress of dirt (photos).

4   The remainder of the steering gear removal and subsequent refitting details are similar to those described for the manual type in Section 19. Detach the breather and hydraulic lines from the retaining clips to the bulkhead and at their union connections as necessary to allow removal. Do not allow any dirt to enter the hyraulic lines or their connections whilst disconnected.

5   Refitting is a reversal of the removal process. Locate and fit the steering unit in the same manner described for the manual steering gear unit (Section 19).

6   When reconnecting the hydraulic lines, ensure that the plugs are removed and that the lines and their connections are perfectly clean. Tighten the hose unions to the specified torque setting. If overtightened, the threads and/or the O-ring seals will be damaged.

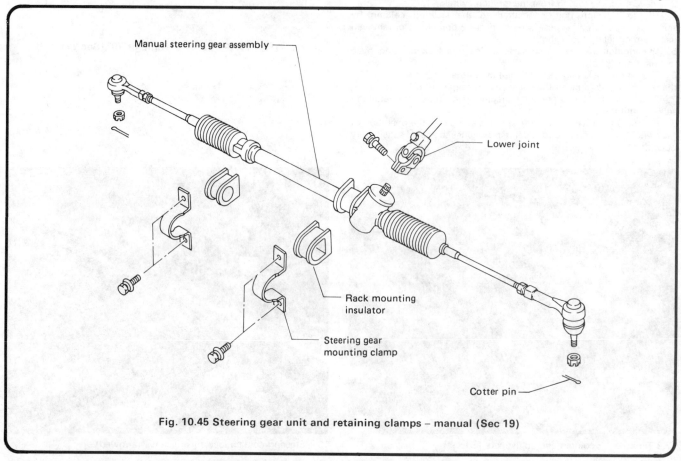

Fig. 10.45 Steering gear unit and retaining clamps – manual (Sec 19)

20.3A Power-assisted steering gear unit showing hydraulic hose connections and mounting strap at pinion housing end

20.3B Power-assisted steering gear unit showing hydraulic hose connections and mounting strap at left-hand end

Note that the O-ring seal in the low pressure (return) pipe connection is larger than the one fitted to the high pressure (supply) pipe connector.

7 Top up and bleed the power steering system as described in Section 23, then check the steering for satisfactory operation.

8 Check and if necessary adjust the front wheel alignment as described in Section 24.

9 Finally check the hydraulic line connections for any signs of leakage.

21 Steering gear unit – overhaul

1 It is not recommended that the manual or power-assisted steering gear (or the power steering pump) are overhauled.

2 Due to the precise nature of the assembly work and the need for special tools for measuring turning torque, it is preferable to purchase a new or factory-reconditioned unit when the original one becomes worn or develops a fault.

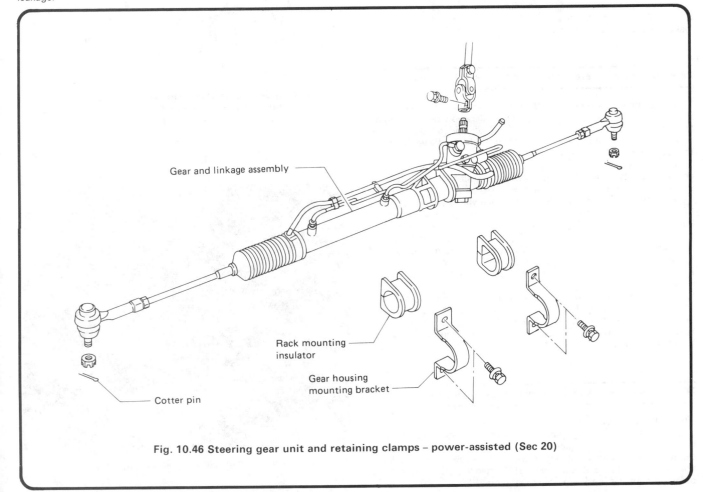

Gear and linkage assembly

Rack mounting insulator

Gear housing mounting bracket

Cotter pin

Fig. 10.46 Steering gear unit and retaining clamps – power-assisted (Sec 20)

22.1 Power steering pump drivebelt adjuster

22.4 Power steering pump unit retaining bolts and support bracket

22.5 Power steering supply and return hose-to-pipe connections and support bracket in engine compartment

22 Power steering pump – removal and refitting

1   Release the pump drivebelt adjuster link lockbolt and turn the adjuster bolt to release the tension on the belt. Slip the belt from the pulleys (photo).
2   Disconnect the pressure hose from the pump by unscrewing the banjo union bolt. Allow the fluid to drain into a suitable container.
3   Take off the return hose clamp.
4   Unbolt and remove the pump (photo).
5   If the connecting lines are to be removed, unscrew the union nuts and hose clips (photo).
6   Refitting and reconnection are reversals of disconnection and removal.
7   Tension the pump drivebelt, as described in Chapter 2.
8   Fill and bleed the system, as described in Section 23.
9   Check the hydraulic hose connections at the pump for signs of leakage (with the engine running).

23 Power-assisted steering – fluid level and bleeding

1   At the intervals specified in *Routine Maintenance* at the start of this manual, unscrew the power steering pump filler cap when the engine and pump are cold and observe the level of fluid on the dipstick (photo). Add fluid of the correct type to bring the fluid level between the low and high marks (Fig. 10.47).
2   If the system pipelines have been disconnected or new components fitted then, after reassembly, the system must be bled.
3   Fill the pump reservoir with fluid.
4   Raise the front of the vehicle until the roadwheels are off the floor.
5   Turn the steering from lock to lock ten times and then top up the fluid in the reservoir so that it is at the correct level on the dipstick.
6   Start the engine and turn the steering wheel left and right lock until the fluid becomes hot to the touch (60 to 80°C – 140 to 176°F).
7   Switch off the engine and top up the reservoir, if necessary.
8   Start the engine and run for five seconds. Switch off and top up the fluid, if necessary.
9   If air is still present in the system, which will be indicated by the steering wheel being stiff to turn, repeat the operations as previously described. When turning the steering from lock to lock during bleeding, do not hold it at full lock for more than fifteen seconds while the engine is running.

24 Steering angles and wheel alignment – general

Front wheel alignment

1   Accurate front wheel alignment is essential to good steering and for even tyre wear. Before considering the steering angles, check that the tyres are correctly inflated, that the front wheels are not buckled, the hub bearings are not worn and that the steering linkage is in good order, without slackness or wear at the joints.

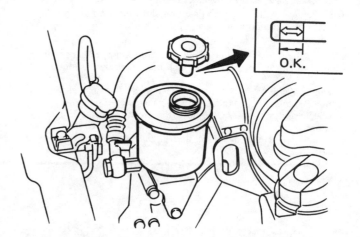

Fig. 10.47 Power-assisted steering pump reservoir filler cap and dipstick markings – check level when fluid is cold (Sec 23)

O.K.

23.1 Power steering pump reservoir and level/filler cap

2   Wheel alignment consists of four factors:

Camber, is the angle at which the roadwheels are set from the vertical when viewed from the front or rear of the vehicle. Positive camber is the angle (in degrees) that the wheels are tilted outwards at the top from the vertical. The camber angle is set by the position of the strut-to-knuckle pin (see photo 4.5).

Castor, is the angle between the steering axis and a vertical line when viewed from each side of the vehicle. Positive castor is indicated when the steering axis is inclined towards the rear of the vehicle at its upper end. This angle is not adjustable.

Steering axis inclination (kingpin inclination), is the angle, when viewed from the front or rear of the vehicle, between the vertical and an imaginary line drawn between the upper and lower front suspension strut mountings. This angle is not adjustable.

Toe, is the amount by which the distance between the front inside edges of the roadwheel rim differs from that between the rear inside edges. If the distance between the front edges is less than that at the rear, the wheels are said to toe-in. If the distance between the front inside edges is greater than that at the rear, the wheels toe-out.

3   Owing to the need for precision gauges to measure the small angles of the steering and suspension settings, it is preferable that checking of camber and castor is left to a service station having the necessary equipment. Camber and castor are set during production of the vehicle, and any deviation from the specified angle will be due to accident damage or gross wear in the suspension mountings.

4   To check the front wheel alignment, first make sure that the lengths of both tie-rods are equal when the steering is in the straight-ahead position. The tie-rod lengths can be adjusted for length if necessary by releasing the locknuts from the balljoint ends and rotating the rods. Flats are provided on the rods in order to hold them still with an open-ended spanner when the locknut is undone.

5   Obtain a tracking gauge. These are available in various forms from accessory stores, or one can be fabricated from a length of steel tubing suitably cranked to clear the sump and transmission, and having a setscrew and locknut at one end.

6   With the gauge, measure the distances between the two wheel inner rims (at hub height) at the rear of the wheel. Push the vehicle forward to rotate the wheel through 180° (half a turn) and measure the distance between the wheel inner rims, again at hub height, at the front of the wheel. This last measurement should differ from the first by the appropriate toe-in which is given in the Specifications. The vehicle must be on level ground.

7   Where the toe-in is found to be incorrect, release the tie-rod balljoint locknut and turn the tie-rods equally. Only turn them a quarter of a turn at a time before re-checking the alignment. Do not grip the threaded part of the tie-rod during adjustment, but use an open-ended spanner on the flats provided. It is important not to allow the tie-rods to become unequal in length during adjustment, otherwise the alignment of the steering wheel will become incorrect and tyre scrubbing will occur on turns (Fig. 10.48).

8   On completion tighten the locknuts without disturbing the setting. Check that the balljoint is at the centre of its arc of travel.

Rear wheel alignment

9   The general information given in paragraph 1 applies to the rear wheels also.

10   Rear wheel alignment consists of two factors, the camber angle and the toe, each of which are described in paragraph 2.

11   The rear wheel camber is preset during manufacture and cannot be adjusted.

12   The toe angle for the rear wheels is adjustable and can be set by turning the inboard rear parallel link pivot pin as required. The head of the pivot pin has graduated index marks on it, each graduation being equal to 2 mm (0.08 in) toe variance for the side in question. This adjustment is not normally required.

13   When checking the rear wheel alignment the vehicle should be in its unladen state (no passengers or luggage).

14   To check the rear wheel toe-out, raise the rear of the vehicle and mark a base line around the periphery of the tread as shown (Fig. 10.49). Repeat the procedure with the opposite side wheel.

15   Mark a line on the ground each side parallel to the centre line of the vehicle, to the front and rear of each wheel.

16   Lower the vehicle to the ground, then 'bounce' it at the rear to settle the suspension. Now measure the difference between the base line mark and the parallel index line at hub centre height, to the front and rear of each rear wheel (Fig. 10.50).

17   Check the measured distances against the specified toe setting for the model concerned and, if necessary, adjust by turning the inboard parallel link pin to suit (see Figs. 10.51 and 10.52).

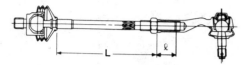

Fig. 10.48 Tie-rod length settings to be equal each side (Sec 24)
L = 176.4 mm (6.94 in)   ℓ = at least 25.0 mm (0.98 in)

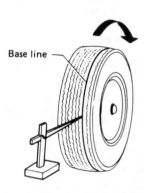

Fig. 10.49 Rear wheel toe-out check base line (Sec 24)

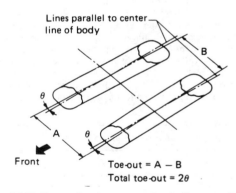

Fig. 10.50 Rear wheel toe-out check diagram (Sec 24)

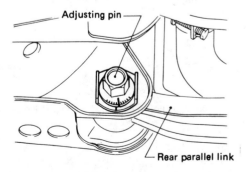

Fig. 10.51 Rear wheel toe-out adjuster on inboard end of parallel link arm. Each graduation = 2 mm (0.08 in) at base line of wheel on side concerned (Sec 24)

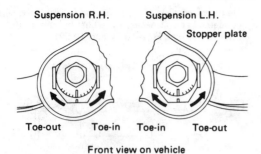

Fig. 10.52 Rear wheel toe-out setting must be equal on both sides (Sec 24)

25 Wheels and tyres – general care and maintenance

Wheels and tyres should give no real problems in use provided that a close eye is kept on them with regard to excessive wear or damage. To this end, the following points should be noted.

Ensure that tyre pressures are checked regularly and maintained correctly. Checking should be carried out with the tyres cold and not immediately after the vehicle has been in use. If the pressures are checked with the tyres hot, an apparently high reading will be obtained owing to heat expansion. Under no circumstances should an attempt be made to reduce the pressures to the quoted cold reading in this instance, or effective underinflation will result.

Underinflation will cause overheating of the tyre owing to excessive flexing of the casing, and the tread will not sit correctly on the road surface. This will cause a consequent loss of adhesion and excessive wear, not to mention the danger of sudden tyre failure due to heat build-up.

Overinflation will cause rapid wear of the centre part of the tyre tread coupled with reduced adhesion, harsher ride, and the danger of shock damage occurring in the tyre casing.

Regularly check the tyres for damage in the form of cuts or bulges, especially in the sidewalls. Remove any nails or stones embedded in the tread before they penetrate the tyre to cause deflation. If removal of a nail *does* reveal that the tyre has been punctured, refit the nail so that its point of penetration is marked. Then immediately change the wheel and have the tyre repaired by a tyre dealer. Do *not* drive on a tyre in such a condition. In many cases a puncture can be simply repaired by the use of an inner tube of the correct size and type. If in any doubt as to the possible consequences of any damage found, consult your local tyre dealer for advice.

Periodically remove the wheels and clean any dirt or mud from the inside and outside surfaces. Examine the wheel rims for signs of rusting, corrosion or other damage. Light alloy wheels are easily damaged by 'kerbing' whilst parking, and similarly steel wheels may become dented or buckled. Renewal of the wheel is very often the only course of remedial action possible.

The balance of each wheel and tyre assembly should be maintained to avoid excessive wear, not only to the tyres but also to the steering and suspension components. Wheel imbalance is normally signified by vibration through the vehicle's bodyshell, although in many cases it is particularly noticeable through the steering wheel. Conversely, it should be noted that wear or damage in suspension or steering components may cause excessive tyre wear. Out-of-round or out-of-true tyres, damaged wheels and wheel bearing wear/maladjustment also fall into this category. Balancing will not usually cure vibration caused by such wear.

Wheel balancing may be carried out with the wheel either on or off the vehicle. If balanced on the vehicle, ensure that the wheel-to-hub relationship is marked in some way prior to subsequent wheel removal so that it may be refitted in its original position.

General tyre wear is influenced to a large degree by driving style – harsh braking and acceleration or fast cornering will all produce more rapid tyre wear. Interchanging of tyres may result in more even wear, but this should only be carried out where there is no mix of tyre types on the vehicle. However, it is worth bearing in mind that if this is completely effective, the added expense of replacing a complete set of tyres simultaneously is incurred, which may prove financially restrictive for many owners.

Front tyres may wear unevenly as a result of wheel misalignment. The front wheels should always be correctly aligned according to the settings specified by the vehicle manufacturer.

Legal restrictions apply to the mixing of tyre types on a vehicle. Basically this means that a vehicle must not have tyres of differing construction on the same axle. Although it is not recommended to mix tyre types between front axle and rear axle, the only legally permissible combination is crossply at the front and radial at the rear. When mixing radial ply tyres, textile braced radials must always go on the front axle, with steel braced radials at the rear. An obvious disadvantage of such mixing is the necessity to carry two spare tyres to avoid contravening the law in the event of a puncture.

In the UK, the Motor Vehicles Construction and Use Regulations apply to many aspects of tyre fitting and usage. It is suggested that a copy of these regulations is obtained from your local police if in doubt as to the current legal requirements with regard to tyre condition, minimum tread depth, etc.

26 Fault diagnosis – suspension and steering

Symptom	Reason(s)
Front suspension	
Vehicle wanders	Incorrect wheel alignment
	Worn front transverse link balljoints
Heavy or stiff steering	Incorrect front wheel alignment
	Incorrect tyre pressures
Wheel wobble or vibration	Roadwheels out of balance
	Roadwheel buckled
	Incorrect front wheel alignment
	Faulty strut
	Weak coil spring
Excessive pitching or rolling on corners or during braking	Faulty strut
	Weak or broken coil spring
Tyre squeal when cornering	Incorrect front wheel alignment
	Incorrect tyre pressures
Abnormal tyre wear	Incorrect tyre pressures
	Incorrect front wheel alignment
	Worn hub bearing

Rear suspension

Poor roadholding and wander

Faulty shock absorber
Weak coil spring
Worn or incorrectly adjusted hub bearing
Worn radius rod bushes
Worn parallel link bushes

Manual steering gear

Stiff action

Lack of rack lubrication
Seized tie-rod end balljoint
Seized transverse link balljoint

Free movement at steering wheel

Wear in tie-rod balljoint
Wear in rack teeth
Wear in column universal joint(s)

Knocking when traversing uneven surface

Incorrectly adjusted rack slipper

Power-assisted steering gear

The symptoms and reasons applicable to manual steering gear will apply, plus the following:

Stiff action or no return action

Slipping pump drivebelt
Air in fluid
Steering column out of alignment
Castor angle incorrect due to damage or gross wear in bushes and mountings

Steering effort on both locks unequal

Leaking seals in steering gear
Clogged fluid passage within gear assembly

Noisy pump

Loose pulley
Kinked hose
Clogged filter in fluid reservoir
Low fluid level

Chapter 11 Bodywork and fittings

For modifications, and information applicable to later models, see Supplement at end of manual

Contents

Bonnet – removal and refitting	6
Bonnet lock – removal, refitting and adjustment	8
Bonnet release cable – removal and refitting	7
Boot lid – removal and refitting	15
Bumpers – removal and refitting	9
Door lock and fittings – removal and refitting	13
Doors – removal and refitting	11
Door trim panel – removal and refitting	12
Door window and regulator – removal and refitting	14
Exterior trim and mouldings – general	21
Facia and associated panels – removal and refitting	25
General description	1
Interior trim and mouldings – general	20
Maintenance – bodywork and underframe	2

Maintenance – upholstery and carpets	3
Major body damage – repair	5
Minor body damage – repair	4
Radiator grille – removal and refitting	10
Rear view mirrors – removal and refitting	24
Seat belts – general	23
Seats – removal and refitting	22
Sunroof (electric) – removal and refitting	27
Sunroof (manual) – removal and refitting	26
Tailgate – removal and refitting	16
Tailgate or boot lid lock/fuel filler lid remote control – removal and refitting	18
Tailgate strut – removal and refitting	17
Windscreen and rear window glass – removal and refitting	19

1 General description

The bodywork on all versions is of welded steel, unitary construction. In the interests of economical repair, the front wings are readily detachable, but other body panels are not.

The vehicles are protected against corrosion by dipping and also by the provision of stone guards under the front wings.

All models in the range are well-equipped and certain factory-fitted options are also available.

2 Maintenance – bodywork and underframe

1 The general condition of a vehicle's bodywork is the one thing that significantly affects its value. Maintenance is easy but needs to be regular. Neglect, particularly after minor damage, can lead quickly to further deterioration and costly repair bills. It is important also to keep watch on those parts of the vehicle not immediately visible, for instance the underside, inside all the wheel arches and the lower part of the engine compartment.

2 The basic maintenance routine for the bodywork is washing – preferably with a lot of water, from a hose. This will remove all the loose solids which may have stuck to the vehicle. It is important to flush these off in such a way as to prevent grit from scratching the finish. The wheel arches and underframe need washing in the same way to remove any accumulated mud which will retain moisture and tend to encourage rust. Paradoxically enough, the best time to clean the underframe and wheel arches is in wet weather when the mud is thoroughly wet and soft. In very wet weather the underframe is usually cleaned of large accumulations automatically and this is a good time for inspection.

3 Periodically, except on vehicles with a wax-based underbody protective coating, it is a good idea to have the whole of the underframe of the vehicle steam cleaned, engine compartment included, so that a thorough inspection can be carried out to see what minor repairs and renovations are necessary. Steam cleaning is available at many garages and is necessary for removal of the accumulation of oily grime which sometimes is allowed to become thick in certain areas. If steam cleaning facilities are not available, there are one or two excellent grease solvents available, such as Holts Engine Cleaner or Holts Foambrite, which can be brush applied. The dirt can then be simply hosed off. Note that these methods should not be used on vehicles with wax-based underbody protective coating or the coating will be

removed. Such vehicles should be inspected annually, preferably just prior to winter, when the underbody should be washed down and any damage to the wax coating repaired using Holts Undershield. Ideally, a completely fresh coat should be applied. It would also be worth considering the use of such wax-based protection for injection into door panels, sills, box sections, etc, as an additional safeguard against rust damage where such protection is not provided by the vehicle manufacturer.

4 After washing paintwork, wipe off with a chamois leather to give an unspotted clear finish. A coat of clear protective wax polish, like the many excellent Turtle Wax polishes, will give added protection against chemical pollutants in the air. If the paintwork sheen has dulled or oxidised, use a cleaner/polisher combination such as Turtle Extra to restore the brilliance of the shine. This requires a little effort, but such dulling is usually caused because regular washing has been neglected. Care needs to be taken with metallic paintwork, as special non-abrasive cleaner/polisher is required to avoid damage to the finish. Always check that the door and ventilator opening drain holes and pipes are completely clear so that water can be drained out (photos). Bright work should be treated in the same way as paint work. Windscreens and windows can be kept clear of the smeary film which often appears by the use of a proprietary glass cleaner like Holts Mixra. Never use any form of wax or other body or chromium polish on glass.

5 The locks, hinges and latches of the doors, boot/tailgate and bonnet should be lubricated annually with a light oil to prevent wear, rattles and squeaks (Fig. 11.1).

3 Maintenance – upholstery and carpets

Mats and carpets should be brushed or vacuum cleaned regularly to keep them free of grit. If they are badly stained remove them from the vehicle for scrubbing or sponging and make quite sure they are dry before refitting. Seats and interior trim panels can be kept clean by wiping with a damp cloth and Turtle Wax Carisma. If they do become stained (which can be more apparent on light coloured upholstery) use a little liquid detergent and a soft nail brush to scour the grime out of the grain of the material. Do not forget to keep the headlining clean in the same way as the upholstery. When using liquid cleaners inside the vehicle do not over-wet the surfaces being cleaned. Excessive damp could get into the seams and padded interior causing stains, offensive odours or even rot. If the inside of the vehicle gets wet accidentally it is worthwhile taking some trouble to dry it out properly, particularly where carpets are involved. *Do not leave oil or electric heaters inside the vehicle for this purpose.*

2.4A Checking a ventilator/drain hole for blockage using a rod

2.4B Checking the rear quarter panel ventilator/drain hole

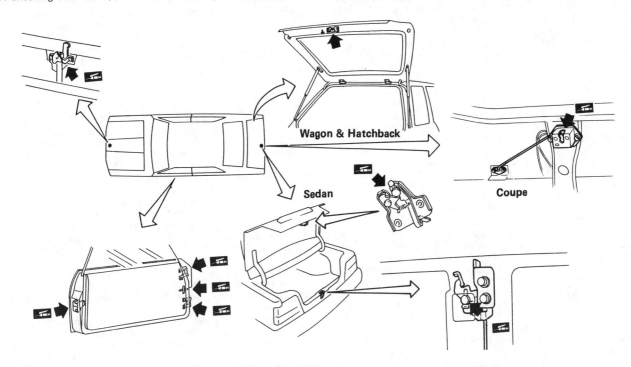

Wagon & Hatchback

Sedan

Coupe

Fig. 11.1 Lubricate the points indicated according to model (Sec 2)

4 Minor body damage – repair

The photographic sequences on pages 178 and 179 illustrate the operations detailed in the following sub-sections.

Note: For more detailed information about bodywork repair, the Haynes Publishing Group publish a book by Lindsay Porter called The Car Bodywork Repair Manual. This incorporates information on such aspects as rust treatment, painting and glass fibre repairs, as well as details on more ambitious repairs involving welding and panel beating.

Repair of minor scratches in bodywork

If the scratch is very superficial, and does not penetrate to the metal of the bodywork, repair is very simple. Lightly rub the area of the scratch with a paintwork renovator like Turtle Wax New Color Back, or a very fine cutting paste like Holts Body + Plus Rubbing Compound to remove loose paint from the scratch and to clear the surrounding bodywork of wax polish. Rinse the area with clean water.

Apply touch-up paint, such as Holts Dupli-Color Color Touch or a paint film like Holts Autofilm, to the scratch using a fine paint brush; continue to apply fine layers of paint until the surface of the paint in the scratch is level with the surrounding paintwork. Allow the new paint at least two weeks to harden: then blend it into the surrounding paintwork by rubbing the scratch area with a paintwork renovator or a very fine cutting paste, such as Holts Body + Plus Rubbing Compound or Turtle Wax New Color Back. Finally, apply wax polish from one of the Turtle Wax range of wax polishes.

Where the scratch has penetrated right through to the metal of the bodywork, causing the metal to rust, a different repair technique is required. Remove any loose rust from the bottom of the scratch with a penknife, then apply rust inhibiting paint, such as Turtle Wax Rust Master, to prevent the formation of rust in the future. Using a rubber or nylon applicator fill the scratch with bodystopper paste like Holts Body + Plus Knifing Putty. If required, this paste can be mixed with cellulose thinners, such as Holts Body + Plus Cellulose Thinners, to provide a very thin paste which is ideal for filling narrow scratches. Before the stopper-paste in the scratch hardens, wrap a piece of smooth cotton rag around the top of a finger. Dip the finger in cellulose thinners, such as Holts Body + Plus Cellulose Thinners, and then quickly sweep it across the surface of the stopper-paste in the scratch; this will ensure that the surface of the stopper-paste is slightly hollowed. The scratch can now be painted over as described earlier in this Section.

Repair of dents in bodywork

When deep denting of the vehicle's bodywork has taken place, the first task is to pull the dent out, until the affected bodywork almost attains its original shape. There is little point in trying to restore the original shape completely, as the metal in the damaged area will have stretched on impact and cannot be reshaped fully to its original contour. It is better to bring the level of the dent up to a point which is about ⅛ in (3 mm) below the level of the surrounding bodywork. In cases where the dent is very shallow anyway, it is not worth trying to pull it out at all. If the underside of the dent is accessible, it can be hammered out gently from behind, using a mallet with a wooden or plastic head. Whilst doing this, hold a suitable block of wood firmly against the outside of the panel to absorb the impact from the hammer blows and thus prevent a large area of the bodywork from being 'belled-out'.

Should the dent be in a section of the bodywork which has a double skin or some other factor making it inaccessible from behind, a different technique is called for. Drill several small holes through the metal inside the area – particulary in the deeper section. Then screw long self-tapping screws into the holes just sufficiently for them to gain a good purchase in the metal. Now the dent can be pulled out by pulling on the protruding heads of the screws with a pair of pliers.

The next stage of the repair is the removal of the paint from the damaged area, and from an inch or so of the surrounding 'sound' bodywork. This is accomplished most easily by using a wire brush or abrasive pad on a power drill, although it can be done just as effectively by hand using sheets of abrasive paper. To complete the preparation for filling, score the surface of the bare metal with a screwdriver or the tang of a file, or alternatively, drill small holes in the affected area. This will provide a really good 'key' for the filler paste.

To complete the repair see the Section on filling and re-spraying.

Repair of rust holes or gashes in bodywork

Remove all paint from the affected area and from an inch or so of the surrounding 'sound' bodywork, using an abrasive pad or a wire brush on a power drill. If these are not available a few sheets of abrasive paper will do the job just as effectively. With the paint removed you will be able to gauge the severity of the corrosion and therefore decide whether to renew the whole panel (if this is possible) or to repair the affected area. New body panels are not as expensive as most people think and it is often quicker and more satisfactory to fit a new panel than to attempt to repair large areas of corrosion.

Remove all fittings from the affected area except those which will act as a guide to the original shape of the damaged bodywork (eg headlamp shells etc). Then, using tin snips or a hacksaw blade, remove all loose metal and any other metal badly affected by corrosion. Hammer the edges of the hole inwards in order to create a slight depression for the filler paste.

Wire brush the affected area to remove the powdery rust from the surface of the remaining metal. Paint the affected area with rust inhibiting paint like Turtle Rust Master; if the back of the rusted area is accessible treat this also.

Before filling can take place it will be necessary to block the hole in some way. This can be achieved by the use of aluminium or plastic mesh, or aluminium tape.

Aluminium or plastic mesh or glass fibre matting, such as the Holts Body + Plus Glass Fibre Matting, is probably the best material to use for a large hole. Cut a piece to the approximate size and shape of the hole to be filled, then position it in the hole so that its edges are below the level of the surrounding bodywork. It can be retained in position by several blobs of filler paste around its periphery.

Aluminium tape should be used for small or very narrow holes. Pull a piece off the roll and trim it to the approximate size and shape required, then pull off the backing paper (if used) and stick the tape over the hole; it can be overlapped if the thickness of one piece is insufficient. Burnish down the edges of the tape with the handle of a screwdriver or similar, to ensure that the tape is securely attached to the metal underneath.

Bodywork repairs – filling and re-spraying

Before using this Section, see the Sections on dent, deep scratch, rust holes and gash repairs.

Many types of bodyfiller are available, but generally speaking those proprietary kits which contain a tin of filler paste and a tube of resin hardener are best for this type of repair, like Holts Body + Plus or Holts No Mix which can be used directly from the tube. A wide, flexible plastic or nylon applicator will be found invaluable for imparting a smooth and well contoured finish to the surface of the filler.

Mix up a little filler on a clean piece of card or board – measure the hardener carefully (follow the maker's instructions on the pack) otherwise the filler will set too rapidly or too slowly. Alternatively, Holts No Mix can be used straight from the tube without mixing, but daylight is required to cure it. Using the applicator apply the filler paste to the prepared area; draw the applicator across the surface of the filler to achieve the correct contour and to level the filler surface. As soon as a contour that approximates to the correct one is achieved, stop working the paste – if you carry on too long the paste will become sticky and begin to 'pick up' on the applicator. Continue to add thin layers of filler paste at twenty-minute intervals until the level of the filler is just proud of the surrounding bodywork.

Once the filler has hardened, excess can be removed using a metal plane or file. From then on, progressively finer grades of abrasive paper should be used, starting with a 40 grade production paper and finishing with 400 grade wet-and-dry paper. Always wrap the abrasive paper around a flat rubber, cork, or wooden block – otherwise the surface of the filler will not be completely flat. During the smoothing of the filler surface the wet-and-dry paper should be periodically rinsed in water. This will ensure that a very smooth finish is imparted to the filler at the final stage.

At this stage the 'dent' should be surrounded by a ring of bare metal, which in turn should be encircled by the finely 'feathered' edge of the good paintwork. Rinse the repair area with clean water, until all of the dust produced by the rubbing-down operation has gone.

Spray the whole repair area with a light coat of primer, either Holts Body + Plus Grey or Red Oxide Primer – this will show up any imperfections in the surface of the filler. Repair these imperfections with fresh filler paste or bodystopper, and once more smooth the surface with abrasive paper. If bodystopper is used, it can be mixed with cellulose thinners to form a really thin paste which is ideal for filling small holes. Repeat this spray and repair procedure until you are satisfied that the surface of the filler, and the feathered edge of the paintwork are perfect. Clean the repair area with clean water and allow to dry fully.

The repair area is now ready for final spraying. Paint spraying must be carried out in a warm, dry, windless and dust free atmosphere. This condition can be created artificially if you have access to a large indoor working area, but if you are forced to work in the open, you will have to pick your day very carefully. If you are working indoors, dousing the floor in the work area with water will help to settle the dust which would otherwise be in the atmosphere. If the repair area is confined to one body panel, mask off the surrounding panels; this will help to minimise the effects of a slight mis-match in paint colours. Bodywork fittings (eg chrome strips, door handles etc) will also need to be masked off. Use genuine masking tape and several thicknesses of newspaper for the masking operations.

Before commencing to spray, agitate the aerosol can thoroughly, then spray a test area (an old tin, or similar) until the technique is mastered. Cover the repair area with a thick coat of primer; the thickness should be built up using several thin layers of paint rather than one thick one. Using 400 grade wet-and-dry paper, rub down the surface of the primer until it is really smooth. While doing this, the work area should be thoroughly doused with water, and the wet-and-dry paper periodically rinsed in water. Allow to dry before spraying on more paint.

Spray on the top coat using Holts Dupli-Color Autospray, again building up the thickness by using several thin layers of paint. Start spraying in the centre of the repair area and then, with a single side-to-side motion, work outwards until the whole repair area and about 2 inches of the surrounding original paintwork is covered. Remove all masking material 10 to 15 minutes after spraying on the final coat of paint.

Allow the new paint at least two weeks to harden, then, using a paintwork renovator or a very fine cutting paste such as Turtle Wax

New Color Back or Holts Body + Plus Rubbing Compound, blend the edges of the paint into the existing paintwork. Finally, apply wax polish.

Plastic components

With the use of more and more plastic body components by the vehicle manufacturers (eg bumpers, spoilers, and in some cases major body panels), rectification of more serious damage to such items has become a matter of either entrusting repair work to a specialist in this field, or renewing complete components. Repair of such damage by the DIY owner is not really feasible owing to the cost of the equipment and materials required for effecting such repairs. The basic technique involves making a groove along the line of the crack in the plastic using a rotary burr in a power drill. The damaged part is then welded back together by using a hot air gun to heat up and fuse a plastic filler rod into the groove. Any excess plastic is then removed and the area rubbed down to a smooth finish. It is important that a filler rod of the correct plastic is used, as body components can be made of a variety of different types (eg polycarbonate, ABS, polypropylene).

Damage of a less serious nature (abrasions, minor cracks etc) can be repaired by the DIY owner using a two-part epoxy filler repair material like Holts Body + Plus or Holts No Mix which can be used directly from the tube. Once mixed in equal proportions (or applied direct from the tube in the case of Holts No Mix), this is used in similar fashion to the bodywork filler used on metal panels. The filler is usually cured in twenty to thirty minutes, ready for sanding and painting.

If the owner is renewing a complete component himself, or if he has repaired it with epoxy filler, he will be left with the problem of finding a suitable paint for finishing which is compatible with the type of plastic used. At one time the use of a universal paint was not possible owing to the complex range of plastics encountered in body component applications. Standard paints, generally speaking, will not bond to plastic or rubber satisfactorily, but Holts Professional Spraymatch paints to match any plastic or rubber finish can be obtained from dealers. However, it is now possible to obtain a plastic body parts finishing kit which consists of a pre-primer treatment, a primer and coloured top coat. Full instructions are normally supplied with a kit, but basically the method of use is to first apply the pre-primer to the component concerned and allow it to dry for up to 30 minutes. Then the primer is applied and left to dry for about an hour before finally applying the special coloured top coat. The result is a correctly coloured component where the paint will flex with the plastic or rubber, a property that standard paint does not normally possess.

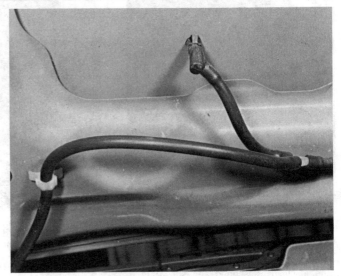

6.2 Disconnect the washer hoses from the underside of the bonnet

---

5 Major body damage – repair

This should be left to your dealer or a specialist body repairer. Special jigs and gauges will be required to check for body and underframe distortion. This must be corrected if the original steering and roadholding characteristics are to be retained.

6.4A Undo the retaining bolts at the hinges ...

---

6 Bonnet – removal and refitting

1   Open the bonnet and have an assistant support its weight.
2   Disconnect the windscreen washer hoses from the jets on the underside of the bonnet (photo).
3   Mark the position of the hinges on the underside of the bonnet with a soft pencil.
4   Unscrew the hinge bolts (photo) and then lift the bonnet from the vehicle (photo).
5   Refitting is a reversal of removal, but before fully tightening the bolts, gently close the bonnet and check its alignment. Adjust as necessary before fully tightening the bolts.
6   Now close the bonnet. If it does not shut smoothly and positively adjust the bonnet lock and striker, as described in Section 8.

---

7 Bonnet release cable – removal and refitting

1   Open and support the bonnet. If the bonnet cable has jammed or is broken release the bonnet lock by reaching up from the underside, between the radiator and the front grille, with a rod of suitable length and trip the release catch.

6.4B ... and lift the bonnet from the car

1 This photographic sequence shows the steps taken to repair the dent and paintwork damage shown above. In general, the procedure for repairing a hole will be similar; where there are substantial differences, the procedure is clearly described and shown in a separate photograph.

2 First remove any trim around the dent, then hammer out the dent where access is possible. This will minimise filling. Here, after the large dent has been hammered out, the damaged area is being made slightly concave.

3 Next, remove all paint from the damaged area by rubbing with coarse abrasive paper or using a power drill fitted with a wire brush or abrasive pad. 'Feather' the edge of the boundary with good paintwork using a finer grade of abrasive paper.

4 Where there are holes or other damage, the sheet metal should be cut away before proceeding further. The damaged area and any signs of rust should be treated with Turtle Wax Hi-Tech Rust Eater, which will also inhibit further rust formation.

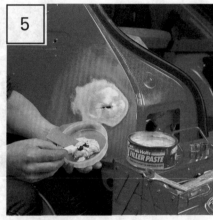

5 *For a large dent or hole* mix Holts Body Plus Resin and Hardener according to the manufacturer's instructions and apply around the edge of the repair. Press Glass Fibre Matting over the repair area and leave for 20-30 minutes to harden. Then ...

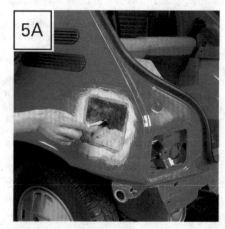

5A ... brush more Holts Body Plus Resin and Hardener onto the matting and leave to harden. Repeat the sequence with two or three layers of matting, checking that the final layer is lower than the surrounding area. Apply Holts Body Plus Filler Paste as shown in Step 5B.

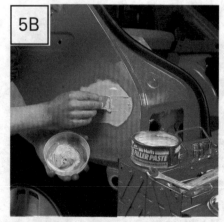

5B *For a medium dent*, mix Holts Body Plus Filler Paste and Hardener according to the manufacturer's instructions and apply it with a flexible applicator. Apply thin layers of filler at 20-minute intervals, until the filler surface is slightly proud of the surrounding bodywork.

5C *For small dents and scratches* use Holts No Mix Filler Paste straight from the tube. Apply it according to the instructions in thin layers, using the spatula provided. It will harden in minutes if applied outdoors and may then be used as its own knifing putty.

6 Use a plane or file for initial shaping. Then, using progressively finer grades of wet-and-dry paper, wrapped round a sanding block, and copious amounts of clean water, rub down the filler until glass smooth. 'Feather' the edges of adjoining paintwork.

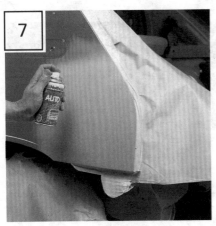

Protect adjoining areas before spraying the whole repair area and at least one inch of the surrounding sound paintwork with Holts Dupli-Color primer.

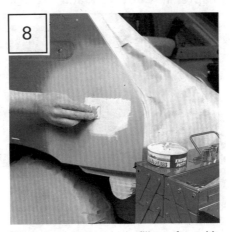

Fill any imperfections in the filler surface with a small amount of Holts Body Plus Knifing Putty. Using plenty of clean water, rub down the surface with a fine grade wet-and-dry paper – 400 grade is recommended – until it is really smooth.

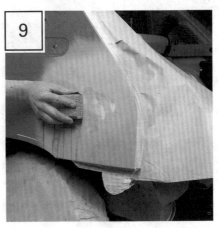

Carefully fill any remaining imperfections with knifing putty before applying the last coat of primer. Then rub down the surface with Holts Body Plus Rubbing Compound to ensure a really smooth surface.

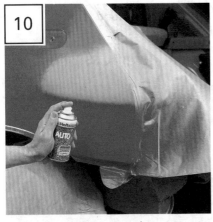

Protect surrounding areas from overspray before applying the topcoat in several thin layers. Agitate Holts Dupli-Color aerosol thoroughly. Start at the repair centre, spraying outwards with a side-to-side motion.

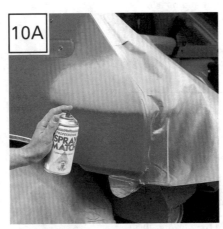

If the exact colour is not available off the shelf, local Holts Professional Spraymatch Centres will custom fill an aerosol to match perfectly.

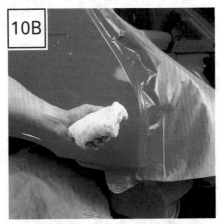

To identify whether a lacquer finish is required, rub a painted unrepaired part of the body with wax and a clean cloth.

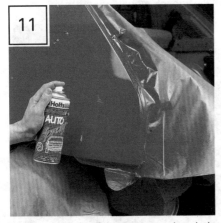

If *no* traces of paint appear on the cloth, spray Holts Dupli-Color clear lacquer over the repaired area to achieve the correct gloss level.

The paint will take about two weeks to harden fully. After this time it can be 'cut' with a mild cutting compound such as Turtle Wax Minute Cut prior to polishing with a final coating of Turtle Wax Extra.

When carrying out bodywork repairs, re-member that the quality of the finished job is proportional to the time and effort expended.

7.2 Bonnet release cable and lock

7.3 Bonnet release cable retaining screws at handle end

8.6 Lubricate the bonnet lock with grease

2   Release the inner cable nipple end from the bonnet lock and the outer cable from the retaining clamp (photo).
3   From inside the vehicle, undo the retain screw(s) and detach the bonnet release handle, then detach the cable from the retainers within the engine compartment and withdraw the cable – pulling it rearwards through the bulkhead (photo).
4   Refit in the reverse order of removal and check for satisfactory operation.

8   Bonnet lock – removal, refitting and adjustment

1   Open and support the bonnet.
2   Unscrew the lock retaining bolts, withdraw the lock from its mounting and detach the release cable from the lock.
3   Refit in the reverse order of removal. Adjust the position of the bonnet lock so that when the bonnet is closed it is 1.0 to 1.5 mm (0.039 to 0.059 in) lower than the wing panel each side (at the front end). When tightening the bonnet lock bolts, take care that the lock does not tilt. Also check that the striker is central to the lock.
4   Adjust the height of the rubber buffer each side by screwing them in the required direction so that their free height is 10 mm (0.39 in). If required adjust further to align the height of the bonnet along its front edge.
5   Check that the bonnet (hood) inner panel-to-secondary (safety) latch position is as shown (Fig. 11.2 or 11.3, as applicable).
6   Finally, check that the bonnet closes securely and when required, releases in a satisfactory manner. Apply a little grease to the lock lever and pivot (photo).

9   Bumpers – removal and refitting

1   The bumper types are shown in the accompanying figures. They are manufactured in urethane or polypropylene with metal fixing brackets and supports (Figs. 11.4 to 11.9 inclusive).
2   To remove the bumper(s), raise the front or rear of the vehicle as applicable and support on safety stands.
3   If the front bumper is being removed and it also contains the front indicator units (a feature of some models), it is advisable to disconnect the battery earth lead.
4   Unbolt and remove the front undershields for access to the bumper mountings and support brackets when removing the front bumper (photo).
5   Unscrew the mounting bolts and, where applicable, disconnect the wiring from the indicator lamps. Where possible clean exposed retaining bolt and screw threads with a wire brush and apply penetrating oil to them to ease their removal (photo).
6   Any repairs to the plastic moulded bumpers are restricted and are generally dealt with in Section 4 of this Chapter.
7   Refitting is a reversal of removal. Ensure correct realignment of the bumper(s) before fully tightening their fixing bolts. Where applicable, check the operation of the front indicators on completion.

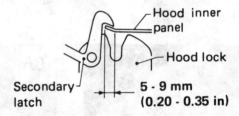

Fig. 11.2 Bonnet (hood) lock-to-safety latch adjustment – Estate and Coupe models (Sec 8)

Hood inner panel
Hood lock
Secondary latch
5 - 9 mm (0.20 - 0.35 in)

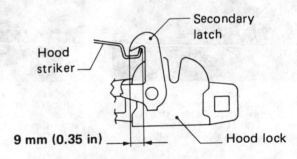

Fig. 11.3 Bonnet (hood) lock-to-safety latch adjustment – Saloon and Hatchback models (Sec 8)

Secondary latch
Hood striker
9 mm (0.35 in)
Hood lock

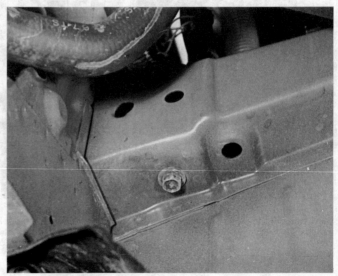

9.4 A front bumper mounting bolt

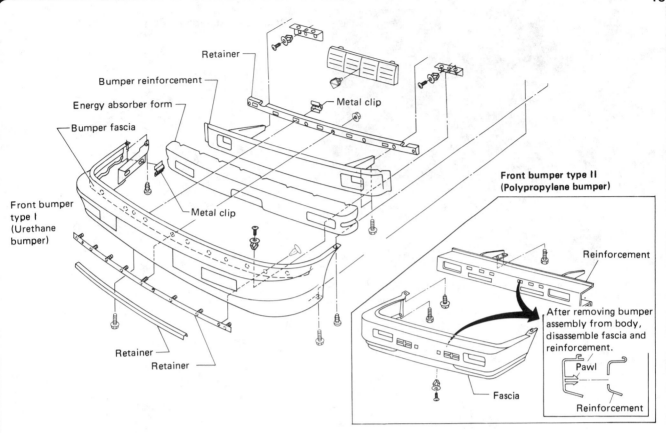

Retainer

Bumper reinforcement

Energy absorber form

Bumper fascia

Metal clip

Metal clip

Front bumper
type I
(Urethane
bumper)

Retainer

Retainer

Front bumper type II
(Polypropylene bumper)

Reinforcement

After removing bumper
assembly from body,
disassemble fascia and
reinforcement.

Pawl

Reinforcement

Fascia

Fig. 11.4 Front bumper and associated components – Estate and Coupe models (Sec 9)

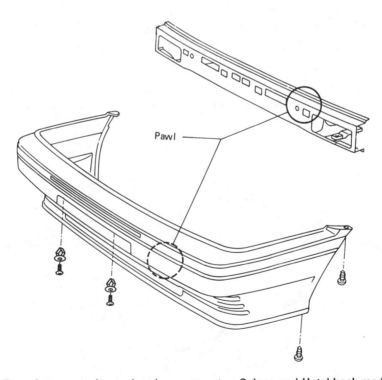

Pawl

Fig. 11.5 Front bumper and associated components – Saloon and Hatchback models (Sec 9)

Rear bumper type II (Polypropylene bumper)

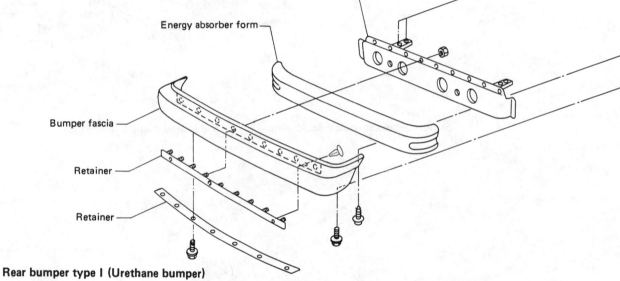

9.5 Rear bumper mounting bolts in luggage compartment
(Hatchback)

Bumper reinforcement

Bumper reinforcement

Energy absorber form

Bumper fascia

Retainer

Retainer

Bumper fascia

Rear bumper type I (Urethane bumper)

Fig. 11.6 Rear bumper and fittings – 1.6 Saloon models (Sec 9)

Pawl

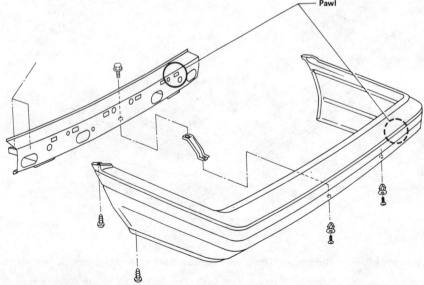

Fig. 11.7 Rear bumper and fittings – 1.3 Saloon and Hatchback models (Sec 9)

183

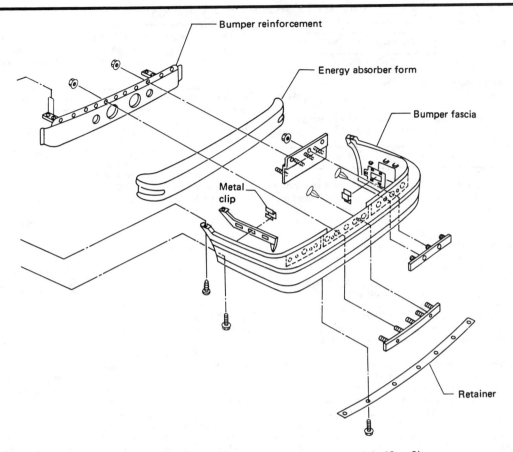

Fig. 11.8 Rear bumper and fittings – Coupe models (Sec 9)

Rear bumper type I (Urethane bumper)

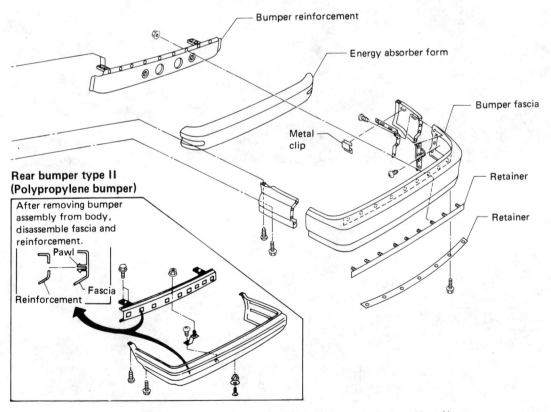

**Rear bumper type II
(Polypropylene bumper)**

After removing bumper assembly from body, disassemble fascia and reinforcement.

Pawl

Fascia

Reinforcement

Fig. 11.9 Rear bumper and fittings – Estate models (Sec 9)

10 Radiator grille – removal and refitting

1 Open the bonnet, then reach down and compress the retaining clips, one each side at the top and bottom. The lower clips are not very accessible and removal of the headlamp units may be necessary. Remove the grille.

2 Refit in the reverse order, pressing the grille and clips home.

11 Doors – removal and refitting

1 If the doors have electrical fittings (radio speakers, electric window regulators etc) disconnect the battery earth lead, remove the door trim panel (Section 12) and detach the wiring connectors as necessary within the door.

2 Open the door wide and support its lower edge on jacks or blocks with pads of rag to prevent damage to the paintwork.

3 Disconnect the check link either by removing the fixing screws or by driving out the roll pin (photo).

4 Extract the C-clips from the hinge pins then drive out the pins (photo) whilst supporting the weight of the door (an assistant would be useful in this respect). Remove the door.

5 If preferred, the door can be removed complete with the hinge. Mark the position of the hinges on the door edge with a soft pencil then support the weight of the door and remove the hinge bolts (photo).

6 Lift and withdraw the door from the vehicle, disengaging the wiring and harness tube as the door is removed.

7 Refitting is a reversal of removal. Provided the hinges are positioned within their original marked areas the door should close satisfactorily. Adjustment may be carried out by releasing the hinge bolts and moving the door.

8 The striker on the door pillar may also be adjusted to ensure smooth positive closure (photo).

9 Ensure that the electrical connections are securely made and then

check the operation of the component(s) concerned before refitting the door trim panel. Reroute and secure the wiring within the door cavity so that it is clear of the window winding mechanism.

12 Door trim panel – removal and refitting

1 Wind the door winders fully up and note the position of the regulator handle in this position (manual adjustment models).

2 If the door contains electrical fittings (eg door-mounted speaker units), disconnect the battery earth lead.

3 Carefully prise free the screw cover plugs from the door armrest and, where applicable, also prise free and disconnect the electric control switch panel (photos). Disconnect the wiring connectors from the switch panel.

4 On manual window regulator models, remove the regulator handle To do this prise a clearance between the handle and the trim panel, then reach down with a suitable hooked wire or rod and pull free the retaining spring clip (photo). Remove the regulator handle.

5 Unscrew and remove the panel retaining screws from the door pull unit. Also remove the screw from within the electrical switch panel aperture (where applicable).

6 Undo the single retaining screw and remove the plate from the inner door release (photos).

7 Prise free the door panel by inserting a flat-bladed tool between the door and trim panel, and prise it free around its periphery. Take care not to damage the door paint or the trim panel when prising it free. Any retaining clips which were broken during removal must be renewed.

8 To gain access to the inner door and components, the insulator panel will need removal. First unscrew and detach any retaining brackets and the radio speaker (if fitted), then carefully peel back the panel from the door (photos).

9 Refit in the reverse order of removal. Check the operation of the electrical components of the door on completion. The manual window regulator handle is refitted by pushing the handle home on its shaft to engage the clip.

11.3 Door check link and hinge (roll) pin

11.4 Door hinge, pin and C-clip

11.5 Door hinge and retaining bolts

11.8 Door striker plate – loosen screws to adjust its position

12.3A Prise free the cover plugs ...

12.3B ... and undo the retaining screws

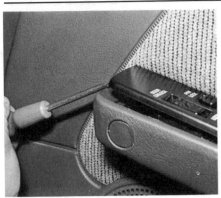

12.3C Prise free the control panel ...

12.3D ... and detach its wiring connector (where applicable)

12.4 Removing window regulator handle – manual type

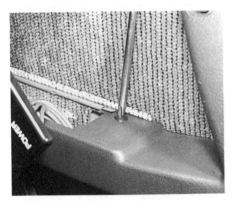

12.5 Undo door pull screws

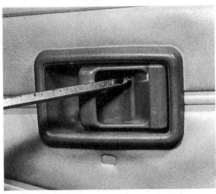

12.6A Remove door release catch plate screws ...

12.6B ... then withdraw the plate

12.8A Remove brackets and door speaker to allow insulator panel removal

12.8B General view of front door with trim and insulator panels removed (power window control and central locking type)

12.8C General view of rear door with trim and insulator panels removed

13 Door lock and fittings – removal and refitting

1   Fully raise the door windows, then remove the door trim panel as described in the previous Section.
2   Unscrew the lock plunger knob and the screws which hold the lock assembly to the door edge (photos).
3   Disconnect the control rods from the lock and withdraw the lock through the aperture in the door inner panel.
4   The door exterior handle can be removed by unscrewing its two fixing nuts by passing a tool through the hole in the upper part of the door inner panel. The lock cylinder can be removed after prising out its retaining clip.
5   On models with central locking, the lock cylinder and activating switch are a combined unit. The lock solenoid unit is removable after detaching the wires to it, undoing the two retaining bolts and detaching the connecting rod to the lock (photos).
6   To remove the interior lock release unit, fold back the foam insulator surround, undo the two retaining screws, withdraw the unit and detach the connecting rod (photo).
7   Renew any clips and/or fasteners which are worn or damaged.
8   Refitting of the various components is a reversal of the removal procedures. Adjust the outside handle as shown in Fig. 11.10 by setting the holder to rod clearance as indicated.
9   If the bellcrank was removed on the rear door, refit it as shown in Fig. 11.11. (photo).
10 On central locking models ensure that the wiring connections are secure and correctly routed within the door.
11 If required, adjust the door striker position.

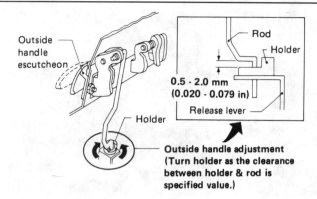

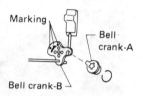

Fig. 11.10 Door outer handle adjustment – front door (Sec 13)

Fig. 11.11 Bellcrank and fitting showing orientation for left-hand rear door (Sec 13)

Fig. 11.12 Door striker adjustment (Sec 13)

14 Door window and regulator – removal and refitting

1 Remove the door trim panel as described in Section 12.
2 Position the door window so that the regulator-to-glass bolts (on the glass lower edge) are accessible through the aperture in the door (photo).
3 Undo the regulator-to-door inner panel bolts and the regulator-to-glass bolts (photos). Lower the glass and remove the regulator unit. On power window models detach the wiring connectors for full removal of the regulator.
4 To remove the door glass, undo the glass guide channel retaining bolts.
5 With the glass fully lowered, remove the inner and outer weather seal strips from the glass slot. These are held by clips and a screw (outer strip).

13.2A Front door lock unit and retaining screws

13.2B Rear door lock unit and retaining screws. This unit also incorporates a childproof lock

13.5A Door lock cylinder, connecting rods and retaining clip (central locking type)

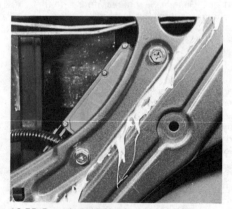

13.5B Rear door lock solenoid retaining screws (central locking)

13.6 Interior lock release and retaining screws (front door)

13.9 Rear door bellcrank

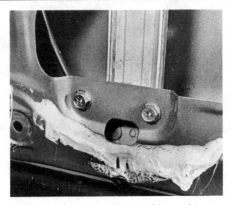

14.2 Door glass regulator to channel guide

14.3A Door glass regulator guide-to-door frame bolts at bottom end (front door)

14.3B Door window regulator-to-panel bolts

6   Pull the glass upwards, tilt it and withdraw it from the door. On rear doors the rear quarter light can be removed by pulling it forwards.
7   If a new window is being fitted, tap the base channel onto it using a wooden or plastic-faced hammer.
8   Refit by reversing the removal operations. Adjust the position of the glass guide channel before tightening it so that the window moves up and down smoothly.
9   When refitting the door slot weatherstrip, locate it as shown in Figs. 11.13 and 11.14.

15 Boot lid – removal and refitting

1   Open the boot lid and unbolt the lock and cable.
2   Mark the position of the hinges on the underside of the lid.
3   With the help of an assistant, support the lid and unscrew the bolts from the hinges (Fig. 11.15).
4   If preferred, the boot lid can be removed with the hinge by moving the hinge pin retainer out of the way and extracting the hinge pin each side (Fig. 11.16).
5   Remove the boot lid from the car.
6   Torsion rods are used to counterbalance the boot lid and they should be released gently with a suitable lever before attempting to unbolt the hinges from the body (Fig. 11.17).
7   Refitting is a reversal of removal. If adjustment is required, release the hinge bolts and move the boot lid to align it. Adjust the position of the striker to ensure smooth positive closure. Adjust the lock cable with reference to Section 18.

16 Tailgate – removal and refitting

1   Disconnect the battery negative lead.
2   Fully open the tailgate then disconnect the wiring and pull the harness from the rear pillars (Figs 11.18 and 11.19).
3   With an assistant supporting the tailgate mark the positions of the struts and unscrew the stud balljoints (photo).
4   Unscrew the hinge bolts after also marking the hinge positions, then withdraw the tailgate from the car (photo).
5   Refitting is a reversal of removal, but check that the tailgate is positioned centrally in the body aperture. Adjustment is made by loosening the hinge nuts on the body and moving the tailgate as required. Adjustment of the striker will also be necessary to ensure smooth operation of the lock (photo) and the lock can also be adjusted within the elongated mounting holes.

17 Tailgate strut – removal and refitting

1   Open the tailgate and, if both tailgate support struts are to be removed, prop the tailgate open by an independent method.
2   Undo the strut stud ball at each end and remove the strut.
3   If a strut is damaged or has lost its compression it must be renewed. Do not attempt to dismantle or repair a strut – they are gas-filled.
4   Refit in the reverse order of removal.

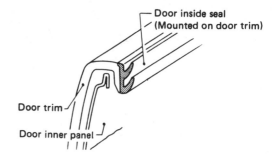

Fig. 11.13 Door/glass weatherstrip seal – inner (Sec 14)

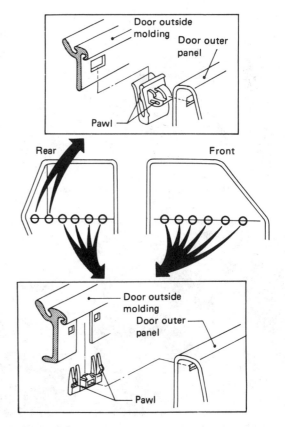

Fig. 11.14 Door/glass weatherstrip seal – outer (Sec 14)

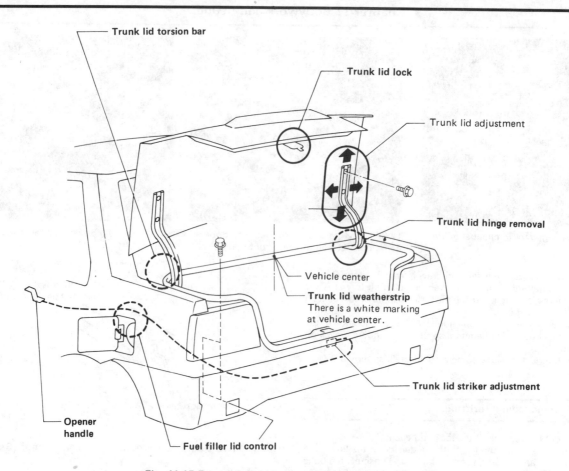

Trunk lid torsion bar

Trunk lid lock

Trunk lid adjustment

Trunk lid hinge removal

Vehicle center

Trunk lid weatherstrip
There is a white marking
at vehicle center.

Trunk lid striker adjustment

Opener
handle

Fuel filler lid control

Fig. 11.15 Boot lid and hinges – Saloon models (Sec 15)

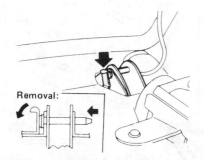

Removal:

Fig. 11.16 Boot lid hinge pin removal – Saloon models
(Sec 15)

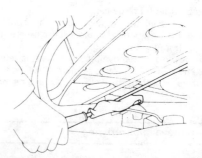

Fig. 11.17 Boot lid torsion bar removal (Sec 15)

16.3 Tailgate strut balljoint

16.4 Tailgate hinge and bolts

16.5 Tailgate striker plate (Hatchback)

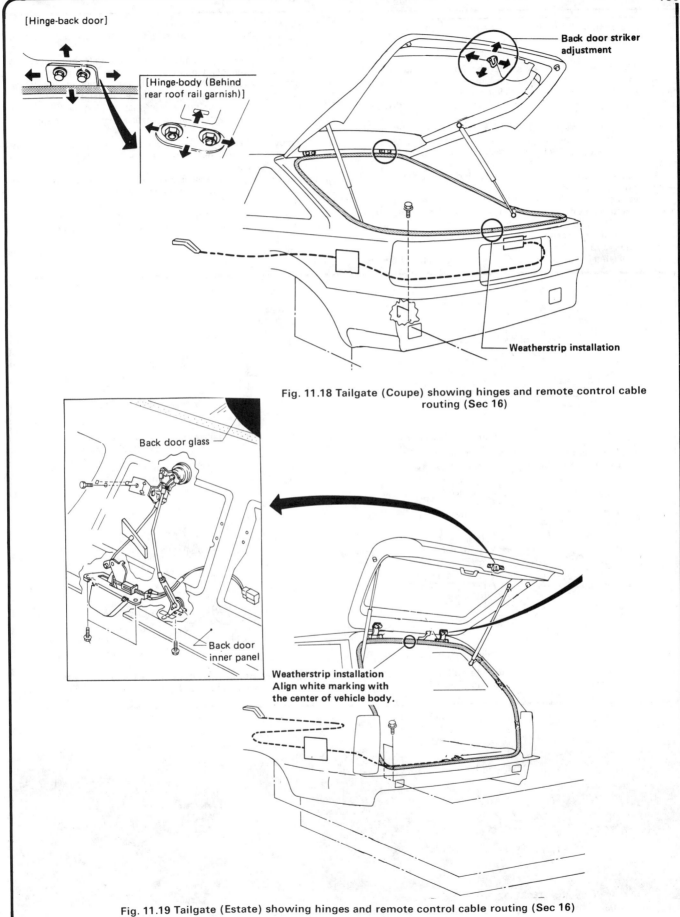

[Hinge-back door]

[Hinge-body (Behind rear roof rail garnish)]

Back door striker adjustment

Weatherstrip installation

Fig. 11.18 Tailgate (Coupe) showing hinges and remote control cable routing (Sec 16)

Back door glass

Back door inner panel

Weatherstrip installation
Align white marking with
the center of vehicle body.

Fig. 11.19 Tailgate (Estate) showing hinges and remote control cable routing (Sec 16)

18 Tailgate or boot lid lock/fuel filler lid remote control – removal, refitting and adjustment

1   The remote control cable runs from the handle along the floor adjacent to the right-hand sill, then runs across the vehicle under the rear seat and is routed up through the left-hand rear side cavity to the fuel filler lip opener and control, and on round to the boot lid/tailgate lock release.

2   If removing the cable, detach the sill trim adjacent to the opener handle and fold back the carpet over the handle for access to the retaining bolts. Undo the bolt and detach the cable from the handle (photo).

3   Remove the rear seat and fold back the floor coverings for access to the cable where it crosses the floor.

4   Remove the rear trim panel and the trim panel from the luggage area on the left-hand side for access to the cable run and fittings at the rear. Removal of the rear light unit on the left-hand side also allows access through the body aperture to the fuel lid control unit and the cable attachment to it (photo).

5   Undo the retaining screw and detach the cable from the boot/tailgate lock (photo).

6   Detach the cable from the fuel filler lid control then pull and feed the cable through the car to the rear for removal.

7   To remove the lock unit, undo the retaining bolts, disconnect the connecting rod to the lock barrel and remove the unit (photo).

8   To remove the lock barrel unit, prise free the retaining clip, detach the connecting rod (if attached) and remove the barrel (photo).

9   To remove the striker unit, mark its fitted position by outlining its periphery on the body with a soft lead pencil, then undo the retaining bolts and lift it clear.

10 To remove the fuel filler lid control unit, detach the main cable (if still attached) then undo the retaining nut and withdraw the unit from the luggage area side.

11 Refitting of all components is a reversal of the removal procedure. Ensure that the cable routing is correct without any sharp bends. Lubricate the pivot mechanisms with a general purpose grease.

12 If removed, realign the striker plate with the outline marking made during removal, but note that it may require further adjustment. The striker and opener cable adjustment must be set as shown according to model (Fig. 11.20, 11.21, 11.22 and 11.23). Check for satisfactory operation on completion.

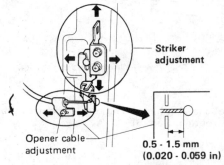

Fig. 11.20 Remote control cable and lock striker adjustment for the Saloon models (Sec 18)

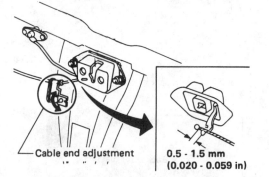

Fig. 11.21 Remote control cable-to-tailgate lock adjustment for Coupe models (Sec 18)

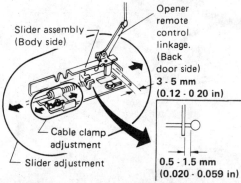

Fig. 11.22 Remote control cable-to-tailgate lock adjustment for Estate models (Sec 18)

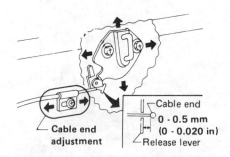

Fig. 11.23 Remote control cable-to-tailgate lock adjustment for Hatchback models (Sec 18)

18.2 Remote control cable handle and retaining bolt

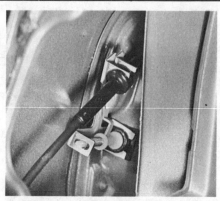

18.4 Remote control cable connection to the fuel filler cap

18.5 Remote control cable to tailgate lock (Hatchback)

19 Windscreen and rear window glass – removal and refitting

1   The renewal of both the windscreen and rear window glass on all variants are tasks which are best entrusted to a professional body repair fitter. In each case some specialised tools and knowledge of the safe and successful fitting of these glass panels are essential. Unless correctly fitted, they may well leak and at worst prove dangerous, therefore entrust renewal to a specialist.

2   The rear quarter window in the Estate and Coupe models are also best renewed by a specialist.

20 Interior trim and mouldings – general

1   Most of the interior trim and mouldings are of plastic construction and care should be exercised when removing or refitting.

2   Clips are used extensively to fix the trim, with self-tapping screws in certain positions. Most of the interior trim and facia panel retaining screws are the same length and diameter. This helps to avoid confusion when reassembling.

3   Most plastic clips and fasteners can be prised free using a flat-bladed screwdriver. Suitable pliers will also assist in their removal in some instances (Fig. 11.24).

4   Removal of the headlining is best left to an expert.

18.7 Tailgate lock unit and retaining bolts

18.8 Tailgate lock cylinder, retaining clip and connecting rod (Hatchback)

Fig. 11.24 Typical trim retaining clips and their removal methods (Sec 20)

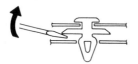

Removal:
Remove by bending up with a flat-bladed screwdriver.

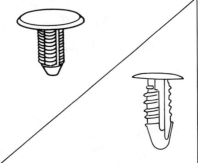

Removal:
Pull up by rotating

Removal:
Tilt clip as indicated by arrow, then draw out.

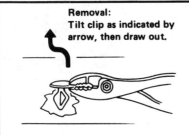

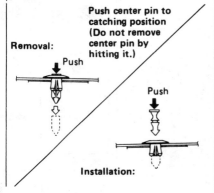

Push center pin to catching position (Do not remove center pin by hitting it.)

Removal: Push

Push

Installation:

21 Exterior trim and mouldings – general

1   The exterior body trim is either clipped in position or retained by double-sided adhesive tape.

2   Side guard mouldings are also fixed with screws on B12 Series models.

3   The accompanying illustrations show the fixing types and their locations (Figs. 11.25 and 11.26).

4   When removing a moulding secured by tape, preheating the moulding with a hot air gun (a portable hair drier will suffice) will ease its removal. Heat the moulding to a temperature of 30 to 40°C (86° to 104°F) and carefully peel back the moulding and cut the bonding agent free. Clean the body panel(s) before fitting the new mouldings. Heat the panel and moulding again to the temperature specified for removal, then carefully fit the moulding.

5   When prising free a moulding from retaining clips, use a flat-bladed tool and lever against a piece of protective cloth or cardboard to prevent marking the adjacent body panels.

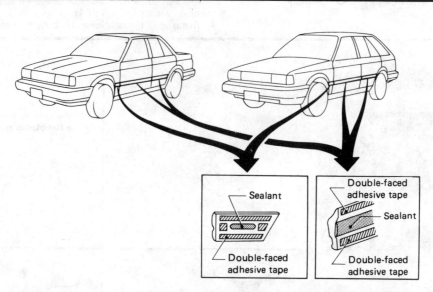

Fig. 11.25 Body side moulding types – Saloon, Estate and Hatchback models (Sec 21)

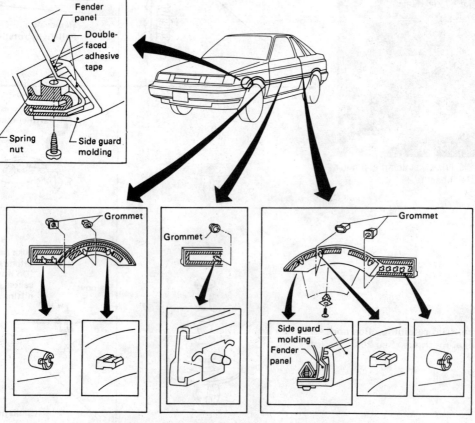

Fig. 11.26 Body side moulding types – Coupe models (Sec 21)

22 Seats – removal and refitting

Front seats

1 Push the seat rearwards and undo and remove the front seat-to-floor retaining bolt each side (photo).

2 Push the seat frontwards then undo the seat runner-to-floor bolts. Note that one bolt on the inner runner is screwed into the side of the centre tunnel (photos).

3 Remove the seat complete with runners from the car.

4 Refit in the reverse order of removal.

Rear seat

5 The rear seat types vary according to model. To remove the seat cushion, either raise and lift the seat out, disengaging the slotted fasteners, or undo the hinge-to-floor retaining bolts, as applicable (photo).

6 To remove the backrest, hinge it forwards and disengage it from its hinges. On some models it will be necessary to undo the hinge retaining bolts.

7 Refit in the reverse order of removal.

23 Seat belts – general

1 Regularly check the condition of the seat belts. If they are frayed or cut, they must be renewed (Fig. 11.27).

2 Clean the webbing by wiping it with warm water and a mild detergent only. Leave the belts unretracted until quite dry.

3 Never alter the attachment points of the belts and, if removed, make quite sure that the original sequence of fitting of the anchor bolt, spacers, washers and connecting plate is retained.

4 Access to the seat belt anchorage and retractor units is gained after removing the appropriate trim panel(s) (photos).

22.1 Front seat/runner retaining bolt (at the front)

22.2A Front seat/runner retaining bolt (at the rear outboard side)

22.2B Front seat/runner retaining bolt (at rear lower inboard side)

22.2C Front seat/runner retaining bolt (at rear upper inboard side)

22.5 Rear seat hinge (Hatchback)

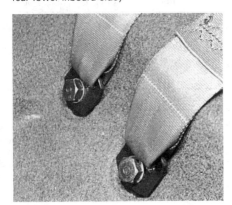

23.4A Seat belt anchorage bolts to floor

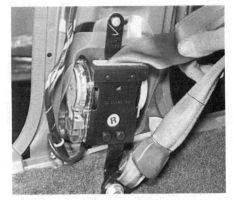

23.4B Front seat belt retracter unit and anchorage arrangement (trim removed)

23.4C Rear seat belt retracter unit

23.4D Front seat belt anchor bolt at height adjuster unit

23.4E Front seat belt height adjuster (trim and belt detached)

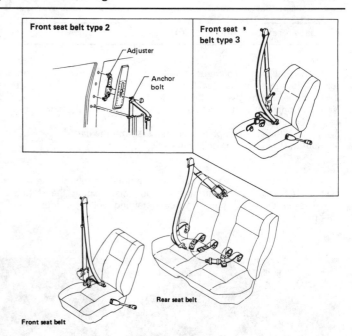

Fig. 11.27 Seat belt arrangements (Sec 23)

24 Rear view mirrors – removal and refitting

Interior mirror
1   Prise free the trim cover from the mirror mounting.
2   Undo the retaining screws and remove the mirror.
3   Refit in the reverse order of removal, then adjust the mirror to suit.

Door mirror
4   Prise free the triangular trim cover from the door (photo).
5   Support the mirror and undo the three retaining screws. Withdraw the mirror from the door. On models fitted with an electrically adjusted door mirror, disconnect the wiring connector (photos).
6   Refitting is a reversal of the removal procedure. Adjust the mirror to suit on completion.

25 Facia and associated panels – removal and refitting

1   One of two types of facia panel will be fitted according to model. The two types, together with their associated sub-assemblies and fixing methods are shown in the accompanying Figs. 11.28 and 11.29.
2   The self-tapping type screws used are all of the same length and gauge. Some of the sub-panels are secured by screws and clips. Some screws are concealed beneath plastic covers.

3   The extent to which the facia panels are to be removed is dependent on the task to be performed. Always disconnect the battery earth if electrical components are to be detached and, as their wiring connectors are disconnected, note the routing of the various sub-harnesses to the switches and controls. This will help avoid confusion when reassembling.
4   Remove the instrument panel, switches, radio and cigarette lighter as described in the relevant sections in Chapter 12. The central facia panels are removed after removing the retaining screws (photos).
5   To remove the heater control unit refer to Chapter 2.
6   If removing the centre console, unscrew the gear lever knob (manual gearbox) or undo the two retaining screws and remove the selector lever knob (automatic transmission). Lift out the ashtray unit (at the rear of the handbrake) and prise free the rectangular plastic cover from the recessed area between the handbrake lever and the gear control lever for access to the respective retaining screws (photos).
7   When removing the main facia panel, the screen demister vents must be removed to gain access to the upper retaining bolts. Carefully prise free the demister vent grilles as shown, using a rag to protect the facia (photos).
8   When withdrawing the main facia, ensure that all wiring and heating/ventilation ducts are disconnected (photo).
9   Refitting is a reversal of removal. Ensure that all wiring connections are securely made and on completion check that all switches and controls function in a satisfactory manner.

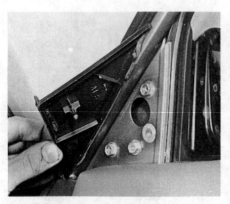

24.4 Remove the door mirror trim ...

24.5A ... undo the retaining bolts

24.5B ... withdraw the mirror and detach the wiring connector

25.4A Centre facia panel lower retaining screw removal

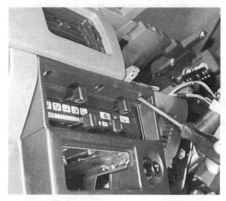

25.4B Centre facia panel upper retaining screw removal

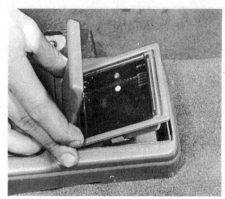

25.6A Remove the floor console ashtray ...

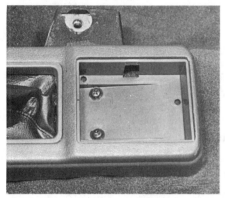

25.6B ... for access to the rear screws

25.6C Prise free the trim cover from the floor console ...

25.6D ... for access to the central screws

25.7A Prise free the demister vent grill at the rear ...

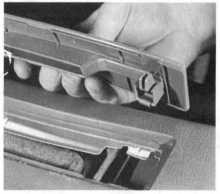

25.7B ... then push it forwards to release retaining clips

25.7C Facia panel upper retaining bolt viewed through vent aperture

25.8 Facia retaining screw – lower left side

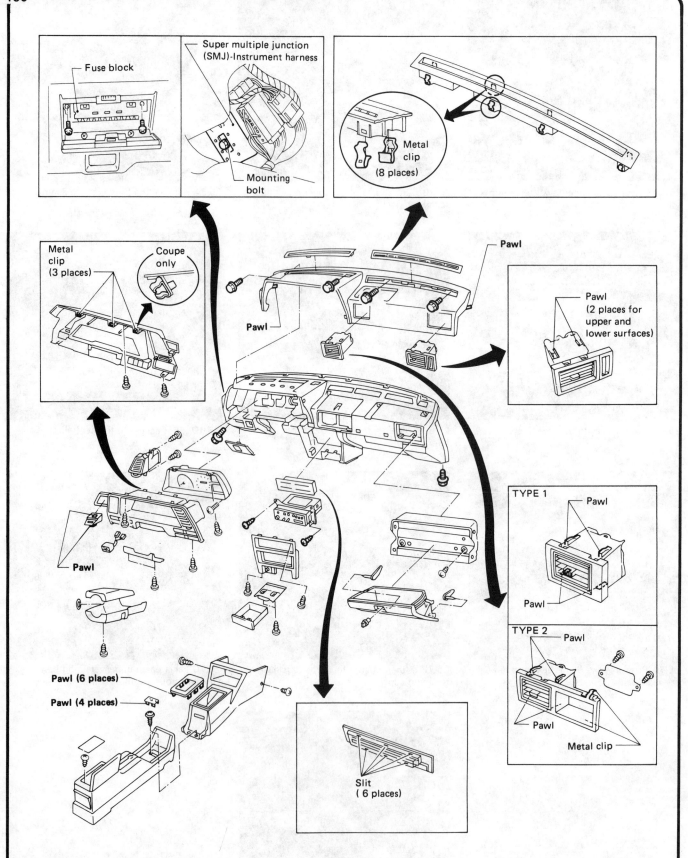

Fig. 11.28 Facia panel, and associated panels and fixings – Estate and Coupe models (left-hand drive version shown) (Sec 25)

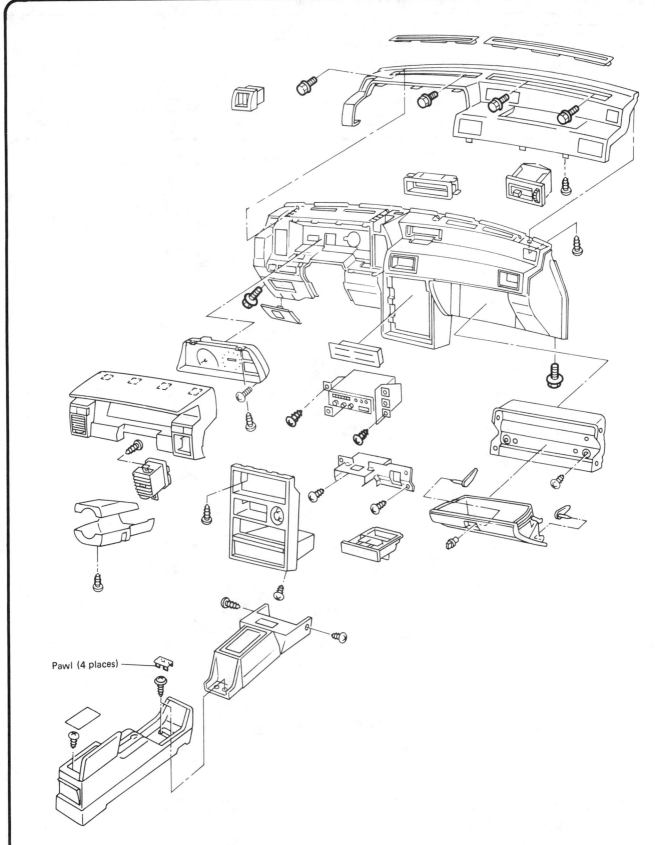

Pawl (4 places)

Fig. 11.29 Facia and associated panels and fixings – Saloon and Hatchback models (left-hand drive version shown) (Sec 25)

26 Sunroof (manual) – removal and refitting

1   The sunroof consists of a glass roof panel and a sunshade plate attached under the glass.

2   To remove the sunshade plate, hold the plate while unscrewing the retaining bolts. Pull the hooks of the plate out of their holders.

3   To remove the sunroof (always having first removed the sunshade plate), tilt the roof and push in the two buttons on the handle while pushing the sunroof upwards.

4   Raise the roof vertical then slide it to the left to disengage it from the hinges.

5   Lift the two air deflectors at the front corners of the aperture if the car is to be used with the sunroof removed. Store the sunroof in the special bag in the rear compartment.

6   Refitting is a reversal of removal. The sunroof is correctly engaged with the front hinges when the red marks are no longer visible.

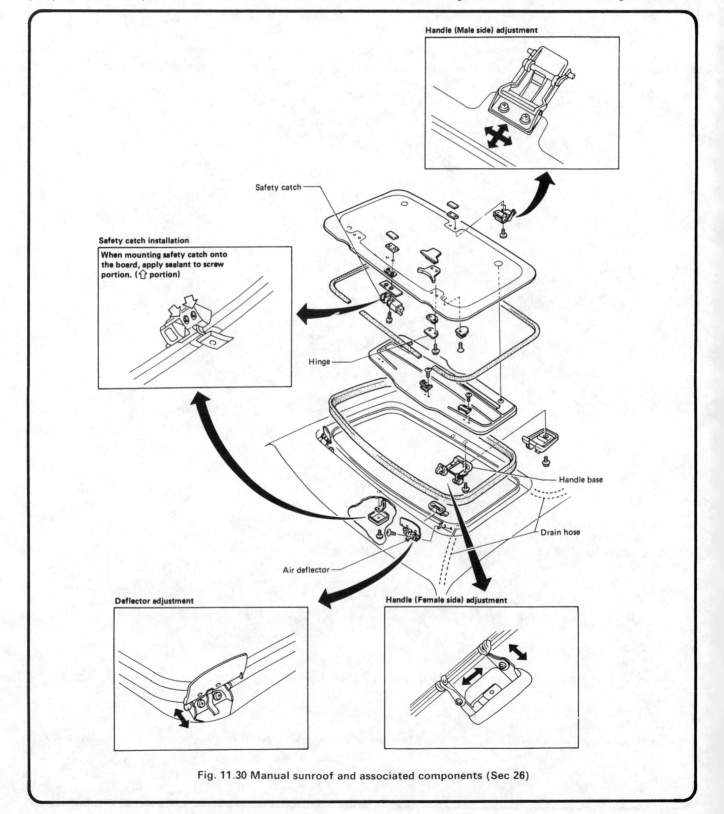

Fig. 11.30 Manual sunroof and associated components (Sec 26)

27 Sunroof (electric) – removal and refitting

1 The main components of the sunroof assembly are shown in Fig. 11.31.

2 If required, the sunroof can be hand cranked to close by undoing the switch panel screws, removing the panel and then rotating the inner shaft in a clockwise direction to the point where it stops. Now turn the outer shaft in an anti-clockwise direction to shut the roof panel (Fig. 11.32).

3 The sunroof sub-assemblies can be removed as follows.

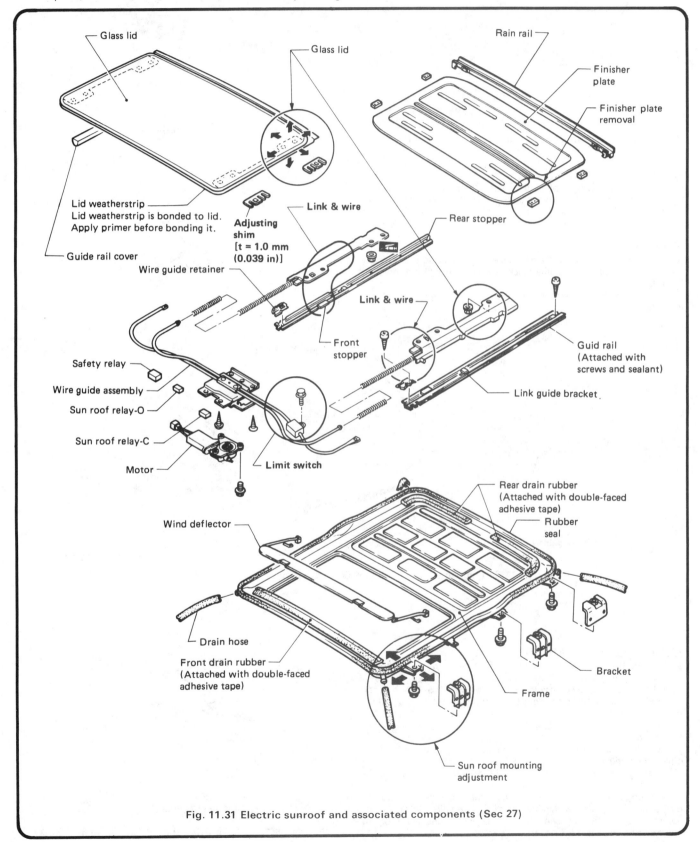

Fig. 11.31 Electric sunroof and associated components (Sec 27)

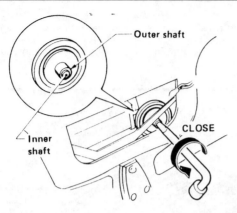

Fig. 11.32 Electric sunroof manual closure method (Sec 27)

Finisher plate

4   To remove the finisher plate, prise open the pawls on the retainer brackets, raise the finisher plate and release the brackets from the locating pins. Lift the finisher plate from the car (Fig. 13.33).
5   Refitting is a reversal of removal.

Frame assembly

6   Mark the position of the frame brackets in relation to the roof side brackets, then unbolt the frame brackets. Do not unbolt the brackets from the roof.
7   Remove the frame assembly and disconnect the drain hoses.
8   Refitting is a reversal of removal but align the previously made marks.

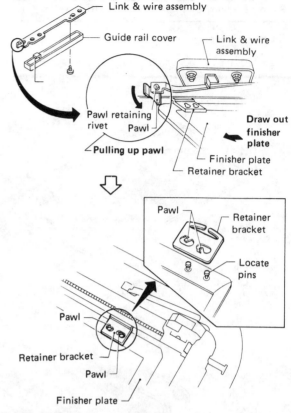

Fig. 11.33 Electric sunroof finisher plate components (Sec 27)

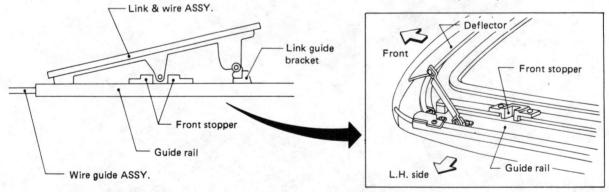

Fig. 11.34 Electric sunroof link and wire assembly components (Sec 27)

Link and guide wire assembly

9   Remove the cover from the motor, unbolt the guide rails followed by the wire guide assembly and motor.
10 When refitting apply grease to the rails and wire. Move the link and wire guide units to the lid shut position then, when fully shut, refit the sunroof motor.

Glass lid

11 With the side guide rail covers removed, mark the position of the outer lid retaining nuts with a pencil.
12 Unscrew the nuts and remove the lid, noting the location of the shims.
13 Refitting is a reversal of removal. Check that the lid is level with the roof panel and central within the aperture. Use shims to adjust the height, and if necessary centralise the lid within the limits of the mounting holes (Fig. 11.35).

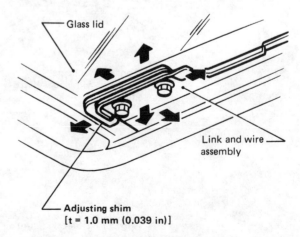

Fig. 11.35 Electric sunroof glass lid adjustment (Sec 27)

Chapter 12 Electrical system

For modifications, and information applicable to later models, see Supplement at end of manual

Contents

Alternator – description, maintenance and precautions 6
Alternator – overhaul 8
Alternator – removal and refitting 7
Battery – charging 4
Battery – maintenance 3
Battery – removal and refitting 5
Brake warning light switches – removal and refitting 32
Cigar lighter illumination bulb and unit – removal and
refitting 17
Clock – removal and refitting 23
Courtesy lamp switch – removal and refitting 15
Dim-dip lamp system 18
Facia panel mounted switches – removal and refitting 16
Fault diagnosis – electrical system 36
Fuses, fusible links and relays – general 13
General description 1
Headlamp beam alignment 19
Headlamp unit – removal and refitting 20
Heated rear window – general 30

Horn – removal and refitting 28
Instrument panel – removal and refitting 22
Lamp bulbs – renewal 21
Radio antenna (aerial) 35
Radio/cassette unit – removal and refitting 33
Routine maintenance – electrical system 2
Seat belt warning system – general 31
Speaker units – removal and refitting 34
Speedometer cable – removal and refitting 29
Starter motor – description 9
Starter motor – overhaul 12
Starter motor – removal and refitting 11
Starter motor – testing *in situ* 10
Steering column combination switch – removal and
refitting 14
Tailgate wiper motor – removal and refitting 26
Washer system – general 27
Windscreen wiper motor/linkage – removal and refitting 25
Wiper arms and blades – removal and refitting 24

Specifications

System type .... 12 volt, negative earth

Battery
Type/identification code Maintenance-free/55D23L-MF
Capacity .... 60 amp hr

Alternator
Make/type number .... Hitachi/LR-160-715 or Mitsubishi/A5T41592
Rating .... 60 amp
Regulated output .... 14.1 to 14.7 volts
Minimum brush wear limit (length):
  Hitachi .... 7.0 mm (0.276 in)
  Mitsubishi .... 8.0 mm (0.315 in)
Minimum slip-ring diameter:
  Hitachi .... 30.6 mm (1.025 in)
  Mitsubishi .... 22.2 mm (0.874 in)

Starter motor
Make/type:
  Manual transmission models .... Hitachi/S114-316 (non-reduction gear type)
  Automatic transmission models:
    1.3 .... Hitachi/S114-317A (reduction gear type)
    1.6 .... Hitachi/S114-345A (reduction type)
Minimum allowable brush length .... 11.0 mm (0.43 in)
Minimum allowable commutator diameter .... 39.0 mm (1.54 in)
Bearing-to-armature shaft clearance .... 0.2 mm (0.008 in) – maximum
Pinion front face-to-pinion stopper clearance (I) (S114-316 only) .... 0.3 to 2.5 mm (0.012 to 0.098 in)
Pinion height movement (I) (S114-317A and S114-345A) .... 0.3 to 2.5 mm (0.012 to 0.098 in)

Bulbs

	Wattage
Headlamps	60/55
Front direction indicator	21
Front side turn indicator	5
Front sidelamp	5
Rear direction indicators	21
Stop/tail lamp	21/5
Reverse lamp	21
Rear foglamp	21
Number plate lamps:	
Estate and Coupe	5
Others	7.5 (10 if bumper-mounted)
Interior lamps	10

Fuses (typical)

Circuits protected:	Rating (amps)
Warning lamps, meter, gauge, indicator, seat belt timer, reversing lamp, buzzer, check connector, 10 km/hr amplifier	10
Heated rear window	20
Fuel-cut solenoid valve, automatic choke, inhibitor relay (A/T) throttle opener, vacuum switching valve	20
Front wiper and washer	20
Rear wiper/washer, audio equipment	10
Blower motor, air conditioner	20
No plate and tail lights, front foglamp, side clearance lights	20
Cigarette lighter, clock, mirror control, headlamp wash/wiper	15
Radiator fan, automatic choke relay	20
Left-hand headlamp, rear foglamp	15
Right-hand headlamp	15
Left-hand tail lamp	10
Number plate, right-hand tail lamp, front foglamp, illumination lamps	10
Hazard warning	10
Horn	10
Stop lights	10
Interior lamps, clock, radio illumination control switch, rear foglamp	10
Door locking system, front foglamp	20
Air conditioner, condenser fan	20

Wiper blades

All models (front)	Champion X-4503
All models (rear)	Champion X-4103

1 General description

The major components of the 12 volt negative earth system consist of a 12 volt battery, an alternator (driven from the crankshaft pulley), and a starter motor.

The battery supplies a steady amount of current from the ignition, lighting and other electrical circuits and provides a reserve of power when the current consumed by the electrical equipment exceeds that being produced by the alternator.

The alternator has its own regulator which ensures a high output if the battery is in a low state of charge and the demand from the electrical equipment is high, and a low output if the battery is fully charged and there is little demand from the electrical equipment.

When fitting electrical accessories to cars with a negative earth system it is important, if they contain silicon diodes or transistors, that they are are connected correctly, otherwise serious damage may result to the components concerned. Items such as radios, tape players, electronic ignition systems, electronic tachometer, automatic dipping etc, should all be checked for correct polarity.

2 Routine maintenance – electrical system

Carry out the following procedures at the intervals given in *Routine Maintenance* at the beginning of this manual.

Battery
1   Check the condition of the battery and its terminals, as described in Section 3.

Alternator
2   Check the general condition of the alternator drivebelt. If it shows signs of excessive wear and/or cracking, it must be renewed. Check the tension of the drivebelt and adjust if necessary as described in Chapter 2.

Washer fluid
3   Top up the washer fluid reservoir before it is allowed to empty. Use a good quality windscreen cleaner solution diluted with water in accordance with the manufacturer's instructions. Do not mix antifreeze for cooling systems into the washer fluid.

3 Battery – maintenance

1   A 'maintenance-free' type battery is fitted to all models during production (photo). This type description is somewhat misleading, however, and the following items should be periodically checked.
2   Check the condition of the battery leads and terminal connections. If the connectors and/or the terminal posts show any signs of corrosion the leads must be disconnected (see Section 5) and the posts and connectors cleaned, then smeared with petroleum jelly to prevent build-up of corrosion. Wipe the top of the battery clean and reconnect the leads as described in Section 5.
3   A plug on the top of the battery may be removed in order to check the specific gravity of the electrolyte in the normal way (photo). Note that distilled water **must not** be added through the plug aperture. Peel back the label along the perforated line, then undo each cell plug in turn using a suitable tool (Figs. 12.1 and 12.2). Add distilled water (not tap water) to bring the fluid level in each cell up to the Maximum

3.1 The maintenance-free battery fitted during production

3.3 Checking the battery electrolyte specific gravity using a hydrometer

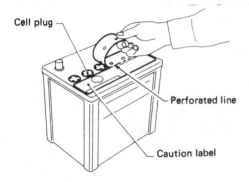

Cell plug

Perforated line

Caution label

Fig. 12.1 Remove seal strip for access to cell plugs (Sec 3)

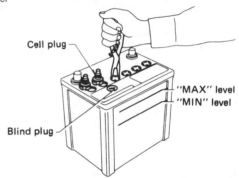

Cell plug

"MAX" level
"MIN" level

Blind plug

Fig. 12.2 View showing electrolyte level markings on battery case and cell plug removal with needle-nosed pliers (Sec 3)

line level. Do not overfill. Refit the plugs.

4   If a replacement battery of the conventional type is substituted for the original one, then carry out the following maintenance procedures.

5   Normal weekly battery maintenance consists of checking the electrolyte level of each cell to ensure that the separators are covered by 0.2 in (5 mm) of electrolyte. If the level has fallen, top up the battery using purified (distilled) water only. Do not overfill. If the battery is overfilled or any electrolyte spilled, immediately wipe away the excess as the electrolyte, which is dilute sulphuric acid, attacks and corrodes most metals it comes into contact with very quickly.

6   As well as keeping the terminals clean and covered with a light film of petroleum jelly the top of the battery, and especially the top of the cells, should be kept clean and dry. This helps prevent corrosion and ensures that the battery does not become partially discharged by leakage through dampness and dirt.

7   Every three months remove the battery and inspect the support tray, the battery clamp and the battery terminals for corrosion. This has the appearance of white fulffy deposits and if it exists it should be cleaned off using warm water to which a little ammonia or baking soda has been added. Treat the battery terminals with petroleum jelly and other metal work with rust preventative paint.

8   If topping-up the battery becomes excessive and there has been no leakage of electrolyte then it is likely that the battery is being overcharged and it will have to be checked by an auto-electrician. An elderly battery may need more frequent topping-up than a new one because it will take a bigger charge. There is no need to worry about this provided that it gives good service.

9   At the three monthly interval check, measure the specific gravity of the electrolyte with a hydrometer to determine the state of charge and condition of the electrolyte. There should be very little variation between individual cells and if a variation in excess of 0.025 exists it will be due to either:

(a) Loss of electrolyte from the battery at some time caused by spillage or a leak, resulting in a drop in the specific gravity of the electrolyte when the deficiency was made up with purified water instead of fresh electrolyte

(b) An internal short circuit caused by buckling of the plates or similar malady pointing to the likelihood of total battery failure in the near future.

10   The specific gravity of the electrolyte for fully charged and fully discharged conditions at different temperatures of the electrolyte is given below:

Fully discharged	Electrolyte temperature	Fully charged
1.098	38°C (100°F)	1.268
1.102	32°C (90°F)	1.272
1.106	27°C (80°F)	1.276
1.110	21°C (70°F)	1.280
1.114	16°C (60°F)	1.284
1.118	10°C (50°F)	1.288
1.122	4°C (40°F)	1.292
1.126	−1.5°C (30°F)	1.296

11   Do not attempt to add acid to a battery. If it is known that electrolyte has been spilled from a cell, leave the mixing of fresh electrolyte and replenishment to your dealer or service station.

Jump starting

12   If the battery condition is so low that it will not start the vehicle, the jump start method can be employed if suitable heavy duty leads and another battery in good condition are available. The battery in another vehicle can also be used. Run one booster cable between the positive terminals of both batteries. Connect the remaining booster cable

between the negative terminal of the rescue vehicle battery and the discharged vehicle's battery negative terminal or bodywork. A diagram showing the jump start lead connections is shown in the general *Fault Diagnosis* section at the start of this Manual.

13 When the vehicle has started, disconnect the negative booster cable first.

4 Battery – charging

1 The need for charging a battery from the mains has largely been eliminated with the advent of the alternator.

2 If short daily journeys are made, with much use of the starter and electrical accessories, it is still possible for the battery to become discharged as the alternator is not in use long enough to replace the current being used.

3 A trickle charger can safely be used overnight at a charging rate of 1.5A.

4 Specially rapid 'boost' charges which are claimed to restore the power of the battery in one to two hours should be avoided as they can cause serious damage to the battery plates through overheating.

5 While charging the battery note that the temperature of the electrolyte should never exceed 38°C (100°F) and remember that the gas produced in the cells contains hydrogen which is flammable and explosive, so do not smoke or bring naked lights near the top of the battery.

6 Always disconnect the battery leads (negative lead first), before connecting the mains charger to the battery.

5 Battery – removal and refitting

1 Open the bonnet and disconnect the negative and then the positive battery leads (photos).

2 Unscrew the nuts which hold the battery retainer in place. Lift off the crossbar and unhook the clamp rods.

3 Lift out the battery, taking care not to tilt it.

4 Refitting is a reversal of removal, but make sure that it is located on the battery tray correctly with respect to the positive and negative lead connections to the battery.

5 Smear the terminals with petroleum jelly and be sure to reconnect the negative terminal lead last.

6 Alternator – description, maintenance and precautions

1 The alternator is mounted on the crankcase at the timing belt end of the engine.

2 The unit is driven by a belt from the crankshaft pulley. A voltage regulator is integral with the brush holder plate.

3 Keep the drivebelt correctly tensioned (see Chapter 2) and the electrical connections tight.

4 Keep the outside of the alternator free from grease and dirt.

5 It is important that the battery leads are always disconnected if the battery is to be charged. Also, if body repairs are to be carried out using electrical welding equipment, the alternator must be disconnected otherwise serious damage can be caused.

6 Do not stop the engine by pulling a lead from the battery.

7 Alternator – removal and refitting

1 Disconnect the battery and, where necessary, remove the air cleaner.

2 Disconnect the leads from the rear of the alternator (photo).

3 Release the alternator mounting and adjuster link bolts, push the unit fully in towards the engine and slip the drivebelt off the pulley (photo).

4 Remove the alternator-to-mounting and adjuster link bolts, and remove the alternator. Note the spacer location between the alternator and mounting bracket. Also note the bolt fitting direction.

5 Refit in the reverse order of removal. Adjust the drivebelt tension as described in Chapter 2.

5.1A Disconnect the battery earth (-) lead ...

5.1B ... then the positive (+) lead

7.2 Disconnect the alternator leads

7.3A Alternator adjuster link bolt

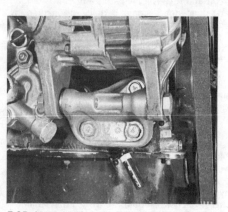
7.3B Alternator lower mounting bolt

8 Alternator – overhaul

1 In the event of the charge (ignition) warning lamp not going out after the engine has started or if the battery is being overcharged, indicated by frequent topping-up, the following operations may be carried out to rectify worn brushes or a faulty voltage regulator. If more extensive overhaul is required, or if the alternator has had a long service life, it is recommended that a new or factory-build unit is obtained.

2 Remove the alternator and clean away the external dirt. Identify the alternator type fitted and refer to the appropriate exploded diagram (Fig. 12.3 or 12.4).

3 Mark the relative position of the rear cover to the front (drive end) cover by scribing a line on them.

4 Unscrew the retaining nuts and bolts as applicable from the rear cover. If a suppressor is fitted, unbolt this also (photo).

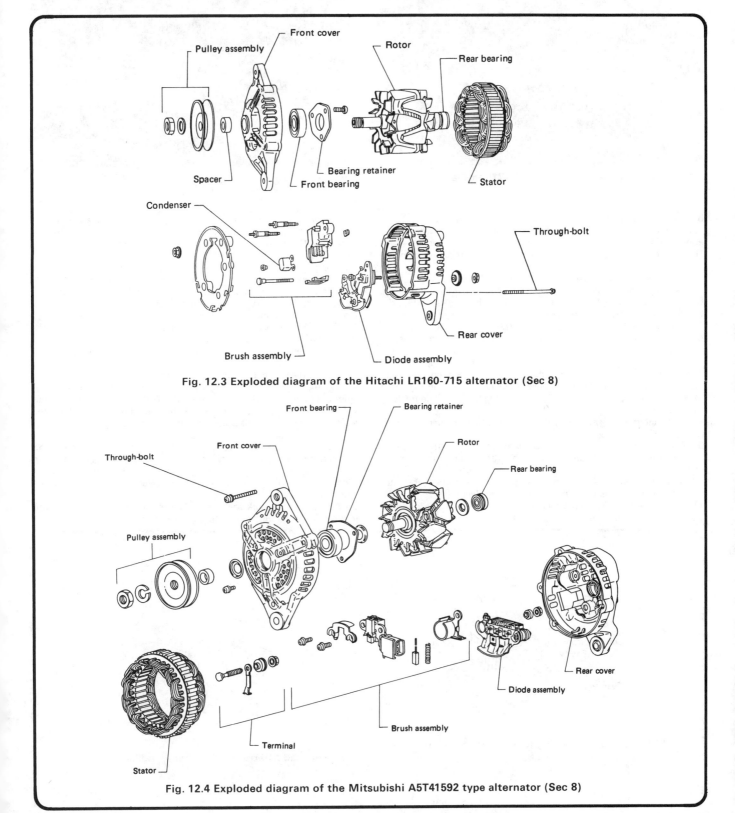

Fig. 12.3 Exploded diagram of the Hitachi LR160-715 alternator (Sec 8)

Fig. 12.4 Exploded diagram of the Mitsubishi A5T41592 type alternator (Sec 8)

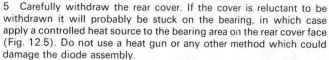

8.4 Rear cover view of the Hitachi LR160-715 alternator

8.6 View of brushes, slip-ring and rear bearing – LR160-715 alternator with rear cover removed

5   Carefully withdraw the rear cover. If the cover is reluctant to be withdrawn it will probably be stuck on the bearing, in which case apply a controlled heat source to the bearing area on the rear cover face (Fig. 12.5). Do not use a heat gun or any other method which could damage the diode assembly.

6   With the cover removed, an initial check of the condition of the brushes and their contact with the slip-ring can be made (photo). The brushes have a wear limit line (Fig. 12.6). If this line is visible, the brushes are in need of renewal.

7   Remove the brush holder unit for further examination, and if the brush length is less than the specified minimum the brushes must be renewed. To do this, the brush leads must be unsoldered. The new brushes must be attached quickly to prevent the heat leaking away and damaging adjacent components. When locating the new brushes, note that the brushes must extend from their holders as shown in Fig. 12.7, 12.8 or 12.9, according to type. Ensure that the brushes slide freely in their holders.

8   If an ohmmeter is available, the following further checks can be made.

9   Connect the ohmmeter probes as shown (Fig. 12.10) and check the slip-rings for continuity. Renew the rotor unit if there is no continuity.

10   Connect the ohmmeter as shown (Fig. 12.11) and check the rotor slip-ring for insulation. If a continuity reading is given, renew the rotor.

11   Use calipers or a suitable micrometer and measure the slip-ring diameter. If worn beyond the specified diameter renew the rotor.

12   To check the stator, note their respective connections and unsolder the connecting wires, but do not apply any more heat than is necessary. On the Mitsubishi alternator use long-nosed pliers as a heat sink (Figs. 12.12 and 12.13).

13   Connect the ohmmeter to the stator leads and check that continuity exists beteeen them (Fig. 12.14). If not renew the stator.

14   Connect the ohmmeter to the stator core and wire as shown (Fig. 12.15) and check that there is no continuity. If there is continuity renew the stator unit.

15   The main diodes can be checked using an ohmmeter in accordance with the continuity checks shown in Fig. 12.16 or 12.17.

16   Check the sub-diodes for continuity using an ohmmeter as shown in Fig. 12.18.

17   Renew the diode unit if any of the diodes are found to be defective.

18   The rear bearing must be renewed if it is excessively worn or is not smooth in action. Withdraw it using a suitable puller. When pressing the new bearing into position, the ring must be fitted so that it has the least possible amount of protrusion in the eccentric groove (see Fig. 12.19).

19   Refitting is a reversal of the dismantling procedure. When fitting the rear cover into position, raise the brush and support in this position with the aid of a lift wire (welding rod) as shown in Fig. 12.20. Withdraw the lift wire once the front and rear housings are reconnected.

20   If an alignment mark was not made across the housing faces during removal, align the retaining bolt lug holes.

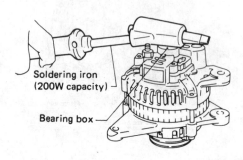

Fig. 12.5 Heating the bearing to ease rear cover removal (Sec 8)

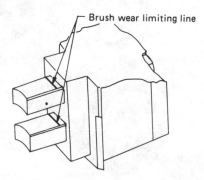

Fig. 12.6 Alternator brush wear indicator (Sec 8)

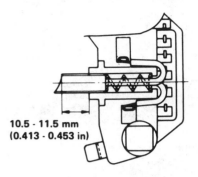

Fig. 12.7 Alternator brush/lead fitting showing required brush protrusion from holder – Hitachi alternator (Sec 8)

10.5 - 11.5 mm
(0.413 - 0.453 in)

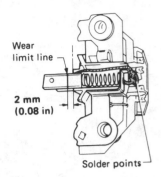

Fig. 12.8 Alternator brush/lead fitting showing required brush protrusion from holder – Mitsubishi alternator (Sec 8)

Wear limit line

2 mm (0.08 in)

Solder points

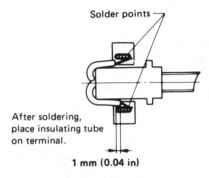

Solder points

After soldering, place insulating tube on terminal.

1 mm (0.04 in)

Fig. 12.9 Brush lead solder points (coil 1½ times round groove of terminal) (Sec 8)

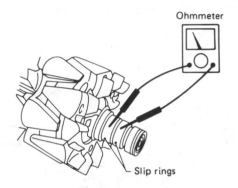

Ohmmeter

Slip rings

Fig. 12.10 Alternator slip-ring continuity check (Sec 8)

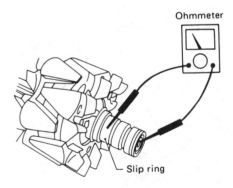

Ohmmeter

Slip ring

Fig. 12.11 Alternator rotor insulation check (Sec 8)

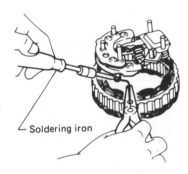

Soldering iron

Fig. 12.12 Unsoldering the stator wires – Hitachi alternator (Sec 8)

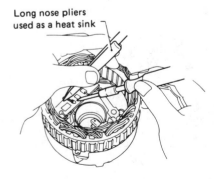

Long nose pliers used as a heat sink

Fig. 12.13 Unsoldering the stator wires – Mitsubishi alternator (Sec 8)

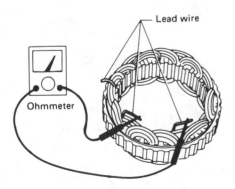

Lead wire

Ohmmeter

Fig. 12.14 Checking the stator for continuity (Sec 8)

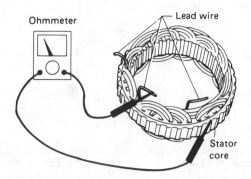

Fig. 12.15 Checking the stator earth (Sec 8)

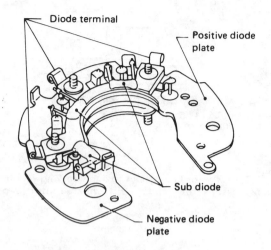

Fig. 12.16 Hitachi diode plate layout (Sec 8)
Refer to Fig. 12.17 for continuity checks

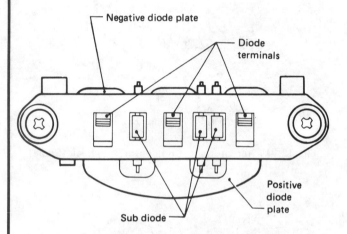

Fig. 12.17 Mitsubishi diode plate layout (Sec 8)

	Ohmmeter probes		Cont.
	Positive '+'	Negative '−'	
Diodes check ('+' side)	'+' diode plate	Diode term	Yes
	Diode term	'+' diode plate	No
Diodes check ('−' side)	'−' diode plate	Diode term	No
	Diode term	'−' diode plate	Yes

[MITSUBISHI make]

[HITACHI make]

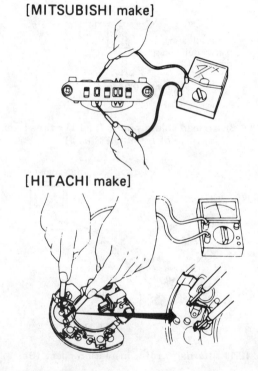

Fig. 12.18 Alternator sub-diode check method (Sec 8)

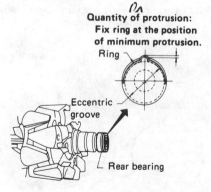

Fig. 12.19 Alternator rear bearing fitting location (Sec 8)

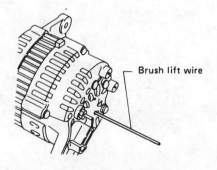

Fig. 12.20 Insert wire to lift the brush when fitting rear cover (Sec 8)

9 Starter motor description

1 The starter motor is of pre-engaged type.
2 When the starter switch is operated, current flows from the battery to the solenoid switch which is mounted on the starter body. The plunger in the solenoid moved inwards, so causing a centrally pivoted lever to push the drive pinion into mesh with the starter ring gear. When the solenoid plunger reaches the end of its travel, it closes an internal contact and full starting current flows to the starter field coils. The armature is then able to rotate the crankshaft, so starting the engine.
3 A special freewheel clutch is fitted to the starter drive pinion so that as soon as the engine fires and starts to operate on its own it does not drive the starter motor.
4 When the starter switch is released, the solenoid is de-energised and a spring moves the plunger back to its rest position. This operates the pivoted lever to withdraw the drive pinion from engagement with the starter ring.
5 On automatic transmission models, an idler gear is incorporated at the drive end of the starter motor.

10 Starter motor – testing *in situ*

1 If the starter motor fails to turn the engine when the switch is operated there are five possible causes:

  (a) The battery is faulty
  (b) The electrical connections between the switch, solenoid battery and starter motor are somewhere failing to pass the necessary current from the battery through the starter to earth
  (c) The solenoid switch is faulty
  (d) The starter motor is mechanically or electrically defective
  (e) The starter motor pinion and/or flywheel ring gear is badly worn and in need of replacement.

2 To check the battery, switch on the headlights. If they dim after a few seconds the battery is in a discharged state. If the lights glow brightly, operate the starter switch and see what happens to the lights. If they dim then you know that power is reaching the starter motor but failing to turn it. If the starter turns slowly when switched on, proceed to the next check.
3 If, when the starter switch is operated, the lights stay bright, then insufficient power is reaching the motor. Remove the battery connections, starter/solenoid power connections and the engine earth strap and thoroughly clean them and refit them. Smear petroleum jelly around the battery connections to prevent corrosion. Corroded connections are the most frequent cause of electric system malfunctions.
4 When the above checks and cleaning tasks have been carried out, but without success, you will possibly have heard a clicking noise each time the starter switch was operated. This was the solenoid switch operating, but it does not necessarily follow that the main contacts were closing properly (if no clicking has been heard from the solenoid, it is certainly defective). The solenoid contact can be checked by putting a voltmeter or bulb across the main cable connection on the starter side of the solenoid and earth. When the switch is operated, there should be a reading or lighted bulb. If there is no reading or lighted bulb, the solenoid unit is faulty and should be renewed.
5 If the starter motor operates but doesn't turn the engine over then it is most probable that the starter pinion and/or flywheel ring gear are badly worn, in which case the starter motor will normally be noisy in operation.
6 Finally, if it is established that the solenoid is not faulty and 12 volts are getting to the starter, then the motor is faulty and should be removed for inspection.

11 Starter motor – removal and refitting

1 Disconnect the battery.
2 Disconnect the leads from the starter motor and solenoid terminals (photo).
3 Unscrew the starter motor fixing bolts and lift the unit from the engine (photo).
4 Refitting is a reversal of removal.

12 Starter motor – overhaul

1 Such is the inherent reliability and strength of the starter motors fitted, it is very unlikely that a motor will need dismantling until it is totally worn out and in need of replacement as a whole.
2 If, however, the motor is only a couple of years old and a pinion carriage, solenoid system or brush fault is suspected then remove the motor from the engine and dismantle as described in the following paragraphs.
3 Extract the screws and remove the solenoid by tilting it to release its plunger from the shift lever. Retain the torsion spring and adjusting plate.
4 Prise off the rear cover dust cap.

11.2 Detach the leads from the starter motor solenoid

11.3 Unbolt and remove the starter motor

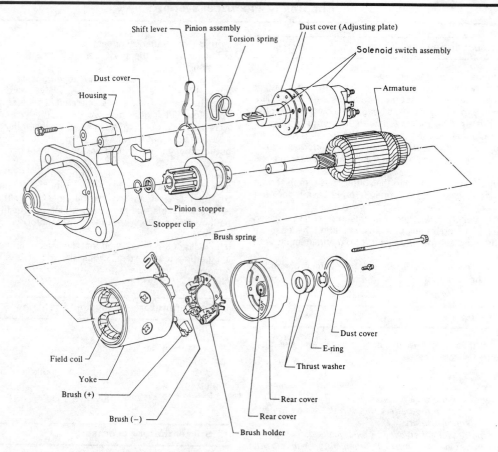

Shift lever — Pinion assembly
Torsion spring
Dust cover (Adjusting plate)
Solenoid switch assembly
Dust cover
Housing
Armature
Pinion stopper
Stopper clip
Brush spring
Field coil
Yoke
Brush (+)
Brush (−)
Brush holder
Rear cover
Rear cover
Thrust washer
E-ring
Dust cover

Fig. 12.21 Exploded view of starter motor type S114-316 (Sec 12)

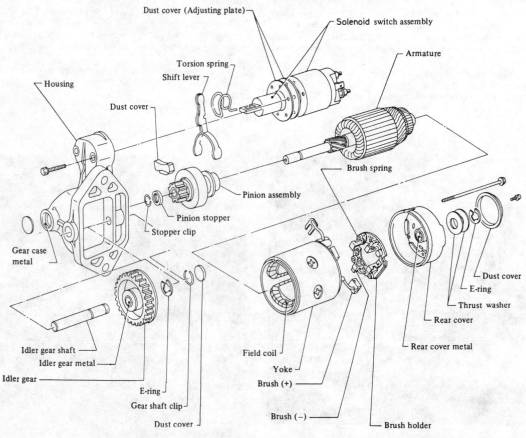

Dust cover (Adjusting plate)
Solenoid switch assembly
Torsion spring
Shift lever
Housing
Armature
Dust cover
Brush spring
Pinion assembly
Pinion stopper
Stopper clip
Gear case metal
Dust cover
E-ring
Rear cover
Rear cover metal
Thrust washer
E-ring
Dust cover
Idler gear shaft
Idler gear metal
Idler gear
E-ring
Gear shaft clip
Dust cover
Field coil
Yoke
Brush (+)
Brush (−)
Brush holder

Fig. 12.22 Exploded view of starter motor type S114-317A/345A (Sec 12)

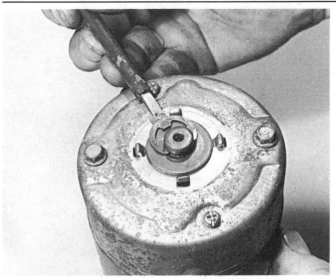

12.5 Remove the E-ring and washers ...

12.6 ... and remove the starter motor rear cover

12.7A Pull up on the brush retainer spring (arrowed) ...

12.7B ... then extract the brush from holder. Spring will retain brush in partially retracted position (arrowed)

5   Prise off the E-ring (photo), and remove the thrust washers.
6   Remove the brush holder screws and the tie-bolts, and withdraw the rear cover (photo).
7   Remove the brush holder. To do this, pull the brush springs upwards and partially withdraw the brushes. If the springs are now released they will apply pressure to the side of the brushes and retain them in the partially withdrawn position (photos).
8   Withdraw the yoke.
9   Withdraw the armature and shift lever from the drive end housing.
10 To remove the drive assembly from the armature shaft, tap the stop-ring down the shaft to expose the circlip.
11 Prise the circlip from its groove, pull the stop-ring off the shaft.
12 Remove the drive pinion assembly from the shaft.
13 On automatic transmission models remove the idler gear by prising out the E-ring and dust cap and driving out the idler shaft. Note which way round the gear is fitted.
14 With the motor dismantled, inspect all the components for wear.
15 If the commutator appears dirty or burned, clean it with a solvent-soaked rag and, if necessary, burnish it with very fine glass paper.
16 If the segment insulators are flush with the surface of the segments, then the insulators must be undercut, as shown in Fig. 12.23. Use a

thin hacksaw blade, or similar, and make sure that the undercut corners are square.
17 If an ohmmeter is available, test the armature for continuity between adjacent segments. The insulation can be tested by placing one probe of the test instrument on the armature shaft and the other on each segment in turn. If continuity is found to exist, the armature must be renewed (Fig. 12.24 and 12.25).
18 Now check for continuity between the field coil positive terminal and the positive brush. If it does not exist, the field coils will have to be renewed (Fig. 12.26).
19 Check the insulation by connecting one probe of the test instrument to the field coil positive terminal and the yoke. If continuity exists, the field coil must be renewed.
20 Renewal of the starter motor field coils ia a job best left to your dealer or auto-electrical agent due to the need for a pressure screwdriver and other equipment.
21 Check the brushes for wear. If they have worn down to the minimum specified length, renew them by removing the old brush lead and soldering on the new. Carry out the work quickly to avoid the spread of heat to the field coils, and do not allow the solder to seep down the lead or its flexibility will be impaired.
22 The brush holder can be checked for insulation breakdown by

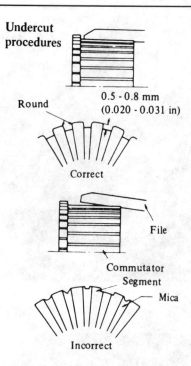

Undercut procedures

0.5 - 0.8 mm
(0.020 - 0.031 in)

Round

Correct

File

Commutator Segment

Mica

Incorrect

Fig. 12.23 Starter motor commutator insulator undercut (Sec 12)

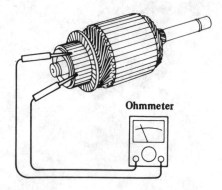

Ohmmeter

Fig. 12.24 Testing armature for continuity (Sec 12)

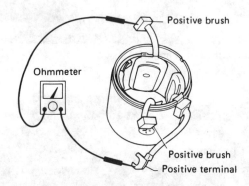

Positive brush

Ohmmeter

Positive brush
Positive terminal

Fig. 12.26 Testing starter field coil to positive brush insulation (Sec 12)

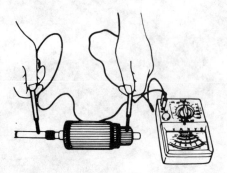

Fig. 12.25 Testing armature insulation (Sec 12)

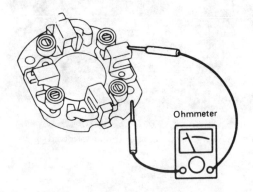

Ohmmeter

Fig. 12.27 Testing starter brush holder insulation (Sec 12)

placing one probe of the tester on the positive side of the brush holder and the other one on the negative (baseplate) side. If continuity is indicated, renew the brush holder (Fig. 12.27).

23 The solenoid switch can be checked for continuity by connecting the test instrument between the S terminal and the switch body. If no continuity is indicated, renew the switch.

24 Now place the probes of the tester on the S and M terminals of the switch. If no continuity is indicated, renew the switch.

25 Finally check the teeth of the drive pinion and idler gear (where applicable). If they are worn or chipped renew the component. Test the pinion/clutch assembly for correct operation. It should turn smoothly in the drive direction and lock when turned in the reverse direction.

26 Reassemble by reversing the dismantling procedure. Lightly grease the friction surfaces, bushes, bearings and pivots as work proceeds.

27 On automatic transmission models, make sure that the idler gear is fitted the right way round with its collar opposite the groove in the pinion.

28 The pinion projection should now be checked by connecting the solenoid to a 12V battery to actuate it.

29 *On Manual transmission models,* the clearance between the face of the pinion and the stop plate should be as specified in the Specifications at the beginning of this Chapter. If it is not, change the adjustment plate under the solenoid switch for one of different thickness. The plates are available in thicknesses of 0.5 mm (0.020 in) and 0.8 mm (0.031 in) (Figs. 12.28, 12.29 and 12.30).

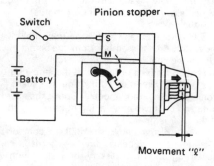

Switch   Pinion stopper

S
M

Battery

Movement "ℓ"

Fig. 12.28 Starter motor pinion protrusion – type S114-316 (Sec 12)

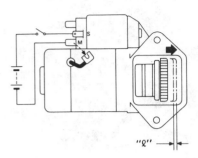

Fig. 12.29 Starter motor pinion protrusion – type
S114-317A (Sec 12)

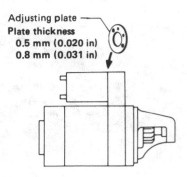

Fig. 12.30 Solenoid adjuster plate location (Sec 12)

30 *On automatic transmission models,* with the solenoid actuated, measure the projection of the front face of the idler gear. Now measure again when the idler gear is pulled out by hand. The difference between the two measurements should be within the specified tolerance. If it is not, change the adjusting plate for one of suitable thickness.

13 Fuses, fusible links and relays – general

Fuses

1 The fusebox is located inside the vehicle under the right-hand side of the facia panel.
2 Place the fingers under the fusebox cover and pull it off.
3 The fuses are of 10 to 20A rating according to the circuit which is protected (photo).
4 A blown fuse can be detected visually and should be renewed with one of similar amperage (Fig. 12.31).
5 If the new fuse blows immediately, suspect a short circuit, probably faulty insulation, which should be rectified at once.
6 Never substitute a fuse of higher amperage, or a piece of wire or foil as a means of preventing a fuse blowing, this could lead to a fire or severely damage the components of the circuit.

Fusible links

7 These are designed to melt in the event of a short in a major current carrying circuit (Fig. 12.32).
8 The links must never be taped up or placed in contact with adjacent wiring, plastic or rubber parts.
9 Before renewing a melted fusible link, rectify the cause or have a thorough check carried out on the vehicle wiring harness.
10 The circuits which the fusible links supply are shown in the wiring diagrams at the end of the manual.

Relays

11 The number and purpose of the relays fitted depends upon the particular model vehicle and its equipment.
12 The flasher unit is located under the facia panel next to the steering column (photo).
13 The ignition and accessory relays are located on top of the fusebox.
14 Within the engine compartment relays may be located which activate the following.

Horn(s)
Automatic choke/lamp check
Radiator fan relay
Inhibitor (transmission switch)
Cooling fan motor
Sunroof and power windows
Dim-dip unit (Fig. 12.33)

15 Most relay units in the engine compartment are contained in a common mounting blocks each side and the respective relay unit functions labelled on the covers (photos).

13.3 Fuse and relay box unit (shown with facia removed)

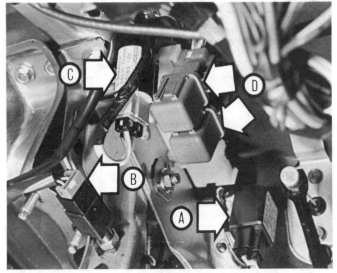

13.12 Under facia relays (D), circuit breaker (C), brake stop-lamp switch (B) and the combination flasher unit (A)

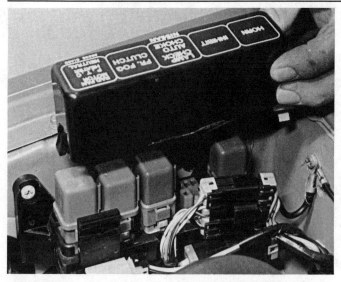

13.15A Relay block – engine compartment right-hand side

13.15B Relay block – engine compartment left-hand side

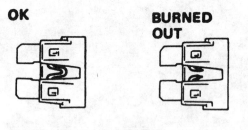

Fig. 12.31 Fuse conditions (Sec 13)

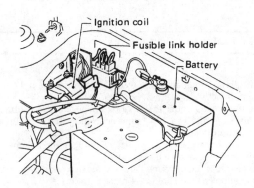

Fig. 12.32 Fusible link location (Sec 13)

14 Steering column combination switch – removal and refitting

1   Disconnect the battery earth lead.
2   Remove the upper and lower column shrouds. These are secured by screws recessed within the lower shroud (photos).
3   Undo the switch retaining screws, partially remove the switch then detach the wiring harness connector on the lower side of the column. Remove the switch (photos).
4   If the switch is defective it must be renewed; no repairs are possible.
5   Refit in the reverse order of removal and check the function of the switch on completion to ensure that it operates in a satisfactory manner.

15 Courtesy lamp switch – removal and refitting

1   The courtesy lamp switch is located on the front door pillar (photo).
2   To remove the switch, extract the screw and pull the switch with leads from its hole.
3   If the leads are to be disconnected, tape them to the body panel to prevent them from slipping inside the body cavity.

4   Smear the switch contacts and plunder with petroleum jelly before fitting as an aid to preventing corrosion.

16 Facia panel mounted switches – removal and refitting

1   Before removing any switches, first disconnect the battery.
2   The facia mounted switches are secured in position by plastic clips/tabs on their underside. In some instances the switch can be released and withdrawn from its aperture by carefully prising it free on one side using a suitable flat bladed too. If, however, the switch is reluctant to move using this method, reach behind the switch and compress the retaining clips each side. Removal of either the adjacent panels or the switch panel itself will probably be necessary to gain access to the switch underside (photos).
3   With the instrument surround switches, undo the six retaining screws and withdraw the surround panel from the facia for access to the switches and their wiring connectors.
4   Detach the wiring connector and remove the switch.
5   If a switch operates in a satisfactory manner, but its bulb has blown, it will be necessary to renew the switch unit complete. The bulb cannot be renewed separately.
6   Refitting is a reversal of the removal procedure. Ensure that the wiring connection is securely made then press the switch into its aperture. Check for satisfactory operation when the battery is reconnected.

14.2A Removing the steering column upper ...

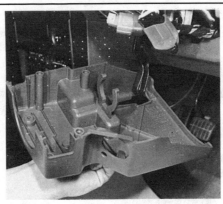

14.2B ... and lower shrouds

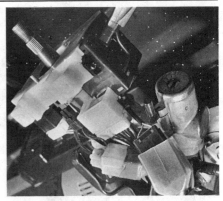

14.3A Steering column switch lead connectors

14.3B Undoing a column combination switch retaining screw

15.1 Door courtesy lamp switch

16.2A Prising free a facia panel switch

16.2B Withdrawing a facia panel switch and its wiring connector

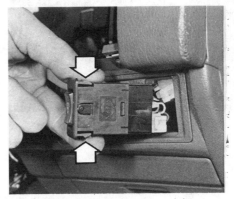

16.2C This switch type has the retaining clips at the top and bottom (arrows)

17 Cigar lighter illumination bulb and unit – removal and refitting

1   Disconnect the battery earth lead.

Bulb renewal

2   Access to the bulb for renewal is best gained by removing the lower centre facia panel. Refer to Chapter 11, Section 25 for details.
3   Pull free the bulb holder from the rear of the cigar lighter, then extract the bulb (photos). Refit in the reverse order of removal.

Cigar lighter unit

4   Proceed as described in paragraphs 1 and 2 above.
5   Withdraw the lighter from its holder socket, then use a suitable small screwdriver or similar implement, depress the plastic retainer each side through the square holes and withdraw the unit (photos). Disconnect the wiring connectors.
6   Refit in the reverse order of removal and check for satisfactory operation.

18 Dim-dip lamp system

This is a safety system designed to ensure that the vehicle cannot be driven with only the side (parking) lights on. When the lighting control switch is moved to the first position with the ignition switched off, the normal parking lights, tail lights and instrument illumination lights are switched into operation.

When the lighting control switch is moved to the first position and

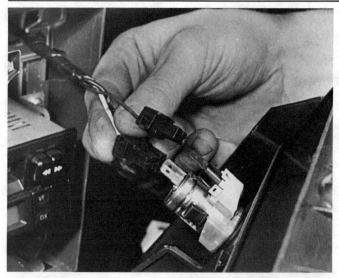

17.3A Detaching the cigar lighter wiring connectors

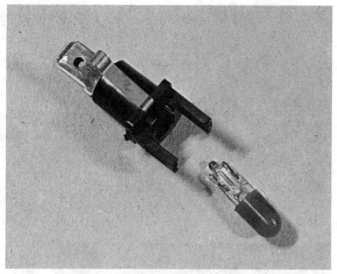

17.3B Cigar lighter bulb and holder

17.5A Compress the lugs (arrowed) ...

17.5B ... and withdraw the cigar lighter unit

the ignition is switched on, the headlights will operate at reduced power. When the headlights are switched to their normal on position they will operate at full power.

The dim-dip mode is actuated by a switch unit in the engine compartment, attached to the left-hand suspension strut mounting panel (Fig. 12.33).

19 Headlamp beam alignment

1   It is recommended that this work is left to your dealer or a service station with the necessary optical beam setting equipment.
2   In an emergency the beams can be set in the following way.
3   Position the vehicle square to a wall or screen during the hours of darkness at the distance shown in Fig. 12.34.
4   Measure the height and separation of the centres of the headlamps and then transpose the measurements onto the wall.
5   Switch the headlamps to dipped beam and adjust the beam so that they are set as indicated. The adjustment screws are in the locations shown according to model (Fig. 12.35).
6   Holts Amber Lamp is useful for temporarily changing the headlight colour to conform with the normal usage on Continental Europe.

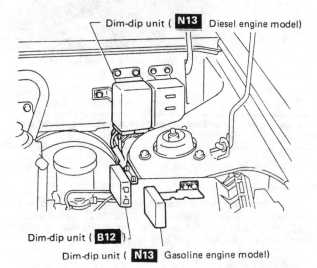

Dim-dip unit (N13   Diesel engine model)

Dim-dip unit (B12)

Dim-dip unit (N13   Gasoline engine model)

Fig. 12.33 Dim-dip unit location (depending on model)
(Sec 13)

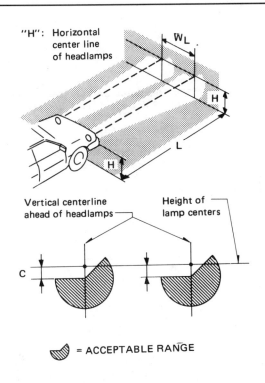

Fig. 12.34 Headlamp beam adjustment diagram (Sec 19)

C   = 50 mm (1.97 in)
H   Headlamps centre line
L   = 5.0 m (16.5 ft approx)
WL   Distance between headlamp centres
Pattern should be reversed for right-hand drive

20 Headlamp unit – removal and refitting

1   Disconnect the battery earth lead.

Saloon and Hatchback

2   Remove the headlamp and sidelamp bulbs (Section 21).
3   Remove the front direction indicator lamp (Section 21).
4   Remove the front grille panel. This is secured by plastic clips, one each side of the top and bottom of the grille and accessible from the rear. Compress the clips and pull the grille forwards.
5   Undo the headlight unit retaining screws and withdraw the unit (photo).
6   Refitting is a reversal of the removal, but check for satisfactory operation and adjust the beam alignment (Section 19).

Coupe and Estate

7   The procedures are similar to those described for the Saloon models, but note the differences given below and refer to the appropriate illustration (Fig. 12.37 or 12.38).
8   When removing the headlamp unit, disconnect the tension spring.
9   On Coupe models, remove the side marker lamp (not the indicator lamp). The removal details for the side marker unit on Coupe models is the same as that for the indicator lamp unit on other models (Section 21).
10   Refitting is a reversal of the removal procedure, but check for satisfactory operation on completion and adjust the beam alignment (Section 19).

21 Lamp bulbs – renewal

1   Before removing any bulb for inspection and replacement, the battery should be disconnected.

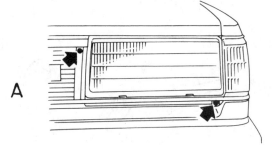

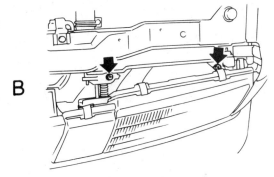

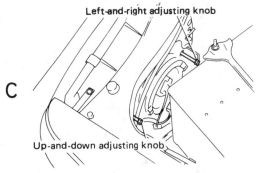

Fig. 12.35 Headlamp adjuster screw locations (Sec 19)

A   Estate
B   Coupe
C   Saloon and Hatchback

20.5 Side view of headlamp showing retaining screws (Hatchback)

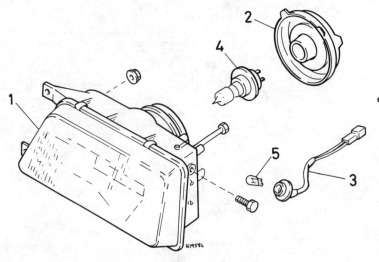

Fig. 12.36 Headlamp unit and associated
components – Saloon and Hatchback (Sec 20)

1   Lamp unit
2   Rubber cap
3   Wiring lead and connector
4   Headlamp bulb
5   Sidelamp bulb

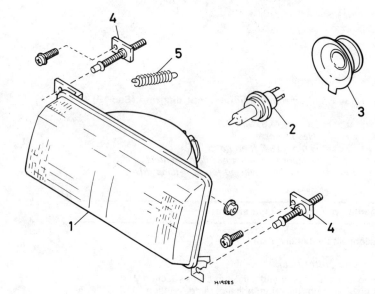

Fig. 12.37 Headlamp unit and associated
components – Saloon (alternative) and Estate
(Sec 20)

1   Lamp unit
2   Headlamp bulb
3   Rubber cap
4   Adjuster screws
5   Spring

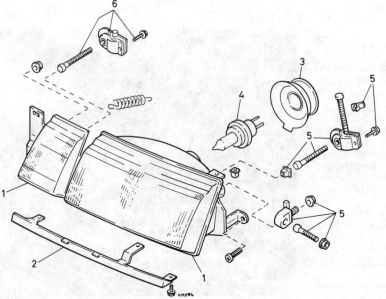

Fig. 12.38 Headlamp unit and associated
components – Coupe (Sec 20)

1   Headlamp units
2   Moulding strip
3   Rubber cap
4   Bulb
5   Outboard adjusters
6   Inboard adjusters

21.4 Headlamp and sidelamp bulb lead connectors (Hatchback)

21.5A Release the headlamp bulb holder retaining clip ...

21.5B ... and withdraw the bulb and holder

21.7 Sidelamp bulb and holder removal – Saloon and Hatchback

21.8A Undo the three side retaining screws ...

21.8B ... and the top screw ...

Headlamp bulb

2 The headlamp units are semi-sealed beam type which use a halogen type bulb. During removal and refitting avoid touching the bulb glass with the fingers as moisture and/or residual grease will shorten the life of the bulb.
3 The bulbs are removed from the rear of the headlamp units, access being from the engine compartment side.
4 Open the bonnet, pull the wiring connector from the rear of the light unit (photo).
5 Prise back the rubber dust cover, then release the spring clips and withdraw the bulb (photos).
6 Refit by reversing the removal operations. If applicable, ensure that the up marking on the dust cover is fitted to the top. Check for satisfactory operation.

Sidelamp bulb (in-headlamp type)

7 Proceed as described in paragraphs 3 and 4, then withdraw the bulb and holder (photo). Refit in the reverse order and check for satisfactory operation.

Front indicator (Saloon, Hatchback and Estate)

8 Remove the lens retaining screws, three at the side and one on top (photos).
9 Extract the bulb and holder from the rear of the unit (photo).
10 Refit in the reverse order and check for satisfactory operation.

Front/side clearance lamp (Coupe)

11 Proceed as described in paragraphs 8, 9 and 10 above.

Side marker/indicator lamp

12 With the circular type lamp unit, unscrew and withdraw the lamp unit, then remove the bulb and holder (Fig. 12.39). With the square type lamp unit, push the lens forward to remove it, then detach the bulb as shown in Fig. 12.40.

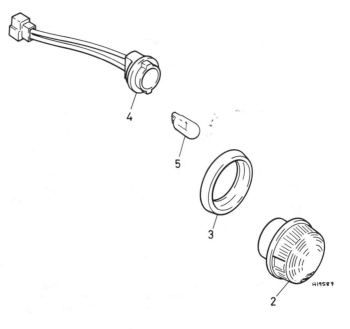

Fig. 12.39 Side marker (indicator) lamp components (circular type) (Sec 21)

2 Lens
3 Lens retainer packing piece
4 Lead and bulb holder
5 Bulb

21.9 ... to remove the side indicator lamp unit (Saloon, Hatchback and Estate)

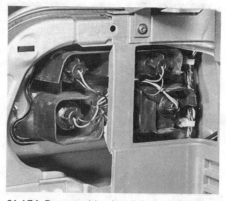

21.17A Rear combination light bulb holders (Hatchback)

21.17B Bulb and holder removed from rear combination light

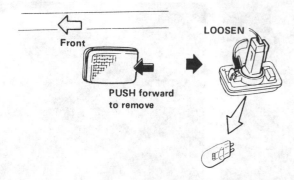

Fig. 12.40 Side marker (indicator) lamp bulb renewal (square type) (Sec 21)

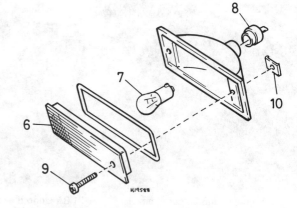

Fig. 12.41 Front indicator lamp unit components – Coupe (Sec 21)

| 6 Lens | 8 Bulb holder | 10 Captive nut |
| 7 Bulb | 9 Lens screw | |

13 Refit in the reverse order of removal and check for satisfactory operation.

Front indicator lamp (Coupe)

14 Undo the two retaining screws and remove the lens. If the seal breaks or is in poor condition, renew it.
15 Untwist and remove the bulb (Fig. 12.41).
16 Refit in the reverse order of removal and check for satisfactory operation.

Rear combination light

17 Unclip and remove the plastic trim cover from the side concerned in the luggage area, then untwist and withdraw the bulb holder from the lamp unit. Remove the bulb from its holder for inspection/renewal (photos).
18 If the light unit is to be removed, detach all bulb holders then undo the retaining nuts on the inner face. An adhesive type seal is used, and to remove the lamp unit the seal area will need to be warmed using a suitable hot air gun (or hair dryer). If required a new bead of butyl seal should be applied on refitting. Warm up the seal area to about 55°C (131°F) before fitting (Fig. 12.42).

Rear number plate lamps

19 These lamp units are either mounted in the bumper or the tailgate, according to model. Some are integral with the reversing lamp.
20 The bumper mounted type lamp bulb is accessible after removing the lens, and this is secured by two screws from underneath as shown in Fig. 12.43.
21 The tailgate mounted type lamp bulb is accessible through the aperture in the tailgate. Remove the trim panel on the side concerned, reach through the aperture, withdraw the bulb holder, then extract the bulb (photo).
22 If the reversing lamps and/or number plate lamps are not integral with the rear combination lamp, they are removed as follows.
23 Remove the trim panel from the aperture in front of the unit in the luggage area, undo the cover retaining screw and remove the cover

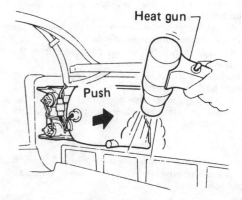

Fig. 12.42 Rear combination lamp unit removal method (Sec 21)

from the lamp unit. Remove the bulb from its holder (Figs. 12.44 and 12.45).
24 Refitting of all types is a reversal of the removal procedure, but check for satisfactory operation on completion.

Luggage compartment lamp

25 Untwist or prise free the lens unit (according to type), then pull free the bulb from its holder. The lamp unit can be removed by releasing its clips, withdrawing the unit and detaching the wiring connector (photo).
26 Refit in the reverse order of removal.

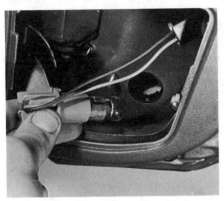

21.21 Tailgate mounted number plate lamp bulb and holder removal

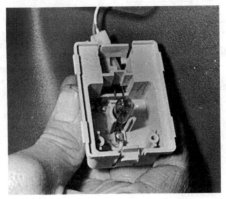

21.25 Luggage compartment lamp unit removal

21.27 Interior light unit with lens removed (circular type)

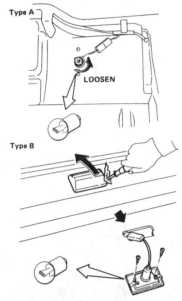

Fig. 12.43 Number plate lamp removal – bumper mounted type (Sec 21)

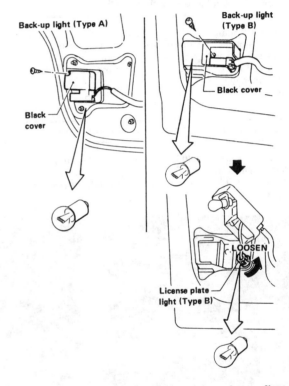

Fig. 12.44 Reversing lamps/number plate lamp fitted to Saloon, Hatchback and Coupe (Sec 21)

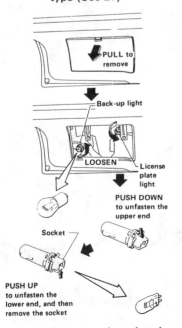

Fig. 12.45 Reversing lamp/number plate lamp fitted to Estate (Sec 21)

Interior lamp

27 Untwist the circular type or unclip the square type lens (as applicable) then, with the lens withdrawn, pull the festoon type bulb from its holder (photo).
28 Refit in the reverse order of removal and check for satisfactory operation.

Instrument panel lamps

29 Refer to Section 22 and remove the instrument panel from the facia.
30 Untwist and remove the bulb holder concerned from the rear face of the panel, then extract the bulb from its holder (see photo 22.3D).
31 Refit in the reverse order of removal. Check that the various instrument panel functions operate in a satisfactory manner on completion.

Heater control panel lamp

32 Remove the heater control panel as described in Section 12 of Chapter 2. Remove and renew the bulb.
33 Refit in the reverse order of removal.

22 Instrument panel – removal and refitting

1   Disconnect the battery earth lead.
2   Undo the retaining screws and withdraw the instrument panel surround lid cluster (photo). As the cluster unit is withdrawn, detach the wiring connectors from the switches in the cluster.
3   Undo the four screws retaining the instrument panel and carefully withdraw it to the point where the wiring connections can be detached from it. Take care not to damage the printed circuit on the rear face of the instrument panel unit (photos).
4   Dismantling of the instrument panel (combination meter) is not recommended and, therefore, if any of its integral components are faulty, have them replaced by your Nissan dealer or local instrument repair specialist.
5   Refitting is a reversal of the removal procedure. Check the operation of the various panel components on completion.

23 Clock – removal and refitting

1   The facia mounted quartz digital clock is held by compression clips each side. Carefully prise free the clock from the facia on one side, then withdraw the unit and detach the wiring connectors from it (photo). If the clock will not release on one side, remove the facia to release the clips (Chapter 11).
2   Refit in the reverse order and reset the clock.

24 Wiper arms and blades – removal and refitting

1   The wiper blades should be renewed as soon as they cease to wipe the glass cleanly.
2   The complete blade assembly or just the rubber insert are available as replacements.

3   Pull the wiper arm from the glass until it locks.
4   Depress the small tab and slide the blade off the arm (photo).
5   Refitting is a reversal of removal.
6   Before removing a wiper arm, it is worthwhile sticking a strip of masking tape on the glass against the edge of the wiper blade as a guide to wiper arm setting when refitting.
7   Lift up the cap to expose the nut which holds the wiper arm to the driving spindle (photos) (if applicable).
8   Unscrew the nut and pull the arm/blade assembly from the spindle splines (photo).
9   Refit by reversing the removal operations.
10 Wet the glass and operate the wipers to check their arc of travel. If it is incorrect, remove the arm and move it a spline or two in the required direction (Figs. 12.46 and 12.47).

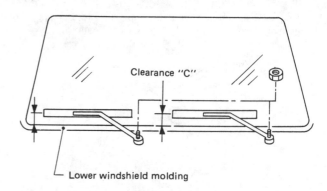

Fig. 12.46 Windscreen wiper blade park position (Sec 24)

C = 30 mm (1.18 in)

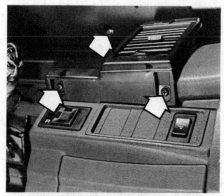

22.2 Underside view of instrument panel showing surround retaining screws (arrowed) on the right-hand side

22.3A Instrument panel retaining screws (upper and lower on the right-hand side)

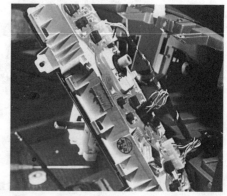

22.3B Instrument panel removal

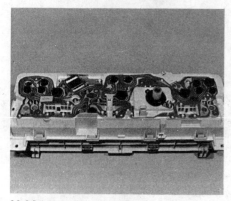

22.3C Instrument panel rear face showing printed circuit and bulb holders

22.3D Bulb and holder removal from instrument panel

22.3E General view of facia with the instrument panel removed showing wiring connectors and their locations in the facia

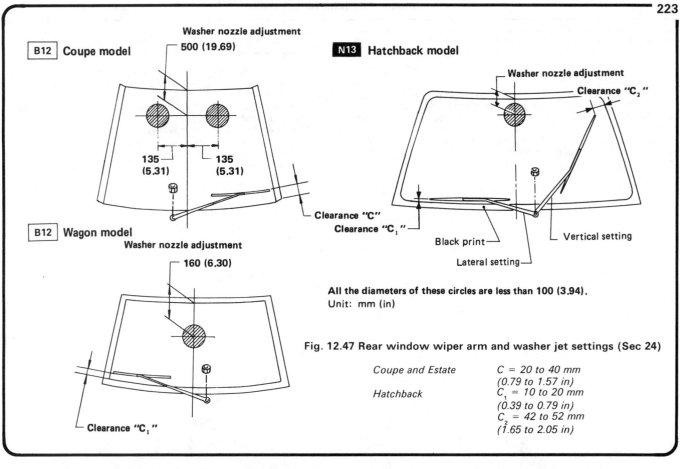

B12 Coupe model

Washer nozzle adjustment
500 (19.69)

135 (5.31)   135 (5.31)

Clearance "C"
Clearance "C₁"

B12 Wagon model

Washer nozzle adjustment
160 (6.30)

Clearance "C₁"

N13 Hatchback model

Washer nozzle adjustment
Clearance "C₂"

Black print
Lateral setting
Vertical setting

All the diameters of these circles are less than 100 (3.94).
Unit: mm (in)

Fig. 12.47 Rear window wiper arm and washer jet settings (Sec 24)

Coupe and Estate	C = 20 to 40 mm (0.79 to 1.57 in)
Hatchback	C₁ = 10 to 20 mm (0.39 to 0.79 in)
	C₂ = 42 to 52 mm (1.65 to 2.05 in)

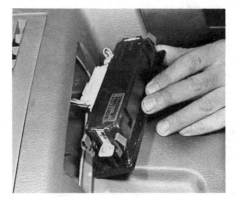

23.1 Clock unit withdrawn from facia showing wiring connector and retaining clip positions

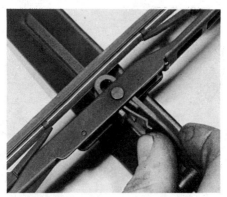

24.4 Wiper blade removal from wiper arm depress clip as shown

24.7A Wiper arm retaining nut – windscreen

24.7B Wiper arm retaining nut – tailgate

24.8 Removing the windscreen wiper arm from the spindle splines

25 Windscreen wiper motor/linkage – removal and refitting

1   Remove the wiper arms, as described in the preceding Section, then disconnect the battery.
2   Open the bonnet and disconnect the wiper motor wiring (photo).
3   Detach and remove the grille forward of the windscreen.
4   Disconnect the wiper motor crank-arm then unscrew the mounting bolts and withdraw the wiper motor.
5   Unscrew the nuts from the wiper drive spindle units.
6   Remove the linkage (Fig. 12.48).
7   Refitting is a reversal of removal.

26 Tailgate wiper motor – removal and refitting

1   The tailgate wiper motor is of direct drive type, without linkages.
2   The wiper arm/blade is removed as described for the windscreen wiper in Section 24.
3   Open the tailgate and remove the trim panel by carefully prising out the clips. Disconnect the battery.
4   Disconnect the wiper motor wiring (photo).
5   Prise off the cap and unscrew the drive spindle nut.
6   Unbolt and remove the wiper motor.
7   Refitting is a reversal of removal.

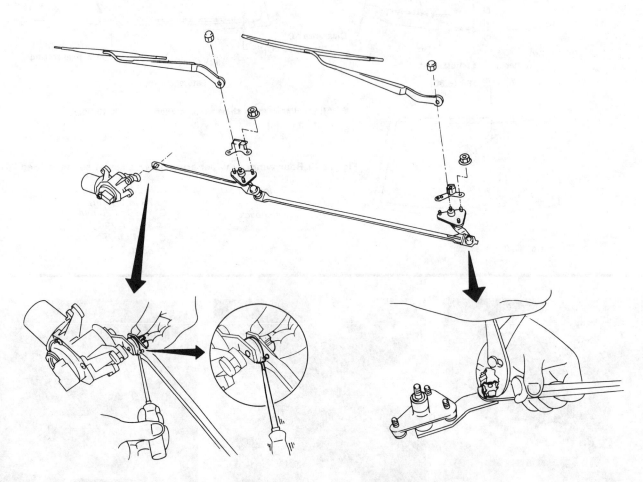

Fig. 12.48 Windscreen wiper motor linkage components showing removal and refitting method – LH drive shown (Sec 25)

25.2 Windscreen wiper motor and wiring connector

26.4 Tailgate wiper motor and wiring connection (Hatchback)

27.4 Washer fluid reservoir and pump unit

27 Washer system – general

1   All models are equipped with a windscreen washer.
2   The washer reservoir is located within the front right-hand wheel arch at the front. A filler spout is located in the engine compartment front right-hand corner. The filler cap has a fluid level tube attached. When removing the cap place a finger over the air hole and fully withdraw the level indicator tube.
3   If topping-up is required, use a good quality screen wash product. Never use cooling system antifreeze as it will damage the paintwork. Do not operate the washer pump if the reservoir has run dry.
4   Access to the pump(s) and reservoir can be gained after removing the undershield from the right-hand wheel arch (photo).
5   Disconnect the fluid tube(s) from the pump(s), also the wiring connectors. Undo the reservoir retaining screws and lower it so that the filler tube can be detached, then withdraw it.
6   Refit in the reverse order of removal, top up the fluid level, then check for satisfactory operation.
7   If required, the washer nozzles can be adjusted by inserting a square tool into the adjusting hole in the nozzle face (Fig. 12.49). Adjust as shown in Fig. 12.50.
8   If the check valve in the fluid line is removed any time, ensure that it is refitted correctly (Fig. 12.51).

28 Horn – removal and refitting

1   Unclip and remove the radiator grille.
2   Unbolt the horn from the bracket and disconnect the wiring (photo).
3   Refitting is a reversal of the removal procedure. Check for satisfactory operation before refitting the grille.

29 Speedometer cable – removal and refitting

1   The speedometer cable must be renewed as an assembly if it breaks.
2   Remove the instrument panel as described in Section 22.
3   Disconnect the speedometer cable at the transmission by unscrewing the knurled nut (photo).
4   Disconnect the cable at the engine compartment rear bulkhead.
5   Disconnect the cable from its location slot at the facia then withdraw the cable through the bulkhead. Note the routing of the cable as it is withdrawn (photo).
6   Refit in the reverse order of removal.

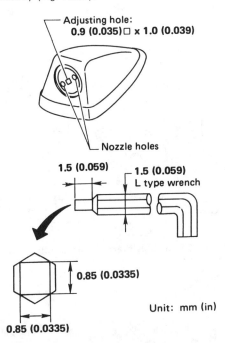

Fig. 12.49 Washer nozzle adjuster tool dimensions – mm (in) (Sec 27)

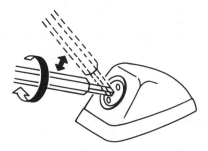

Fig. 12.50 Washer nozzle adjustment method (Sec 27)

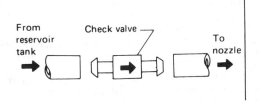

Fig. 12.51 Washer system check valve fitting direction (Sec 27)

28.2 Horn and mounting bracket

29.3 Speedometer cable attachment at transmission

29.5 Speedometer cable location at facia

30 Heated rear window – general

1 Care should be taken to avoid damage to the element for the heated rear window or tailgate.
2 Avoid scratching with rings on the fingers when cleaning, and do not allow luggage to rub against the glass.
3 Do not stick labels over the element on the inside of the glass.
4 If the element grids do become damaged, a special conductive paint is available from most motor factors to repair it.
5 Do not leave the heated rear window switched on unnecessarily as it draws a high current from the electrical system.
6 It should be noted that some models also incorporate the radio antenna (aerial) in the rear window. Similar principles apply for its care and repair as that described above for the heated rear window element (photo).

31 Seat belt warning system – general

1 On certain models the seat belt on the driver's side incorporates a visual and audible warning as a reminder that the belt is not connected when starting the vehicle.
2 The warnings are given for a six second period if the ignition key is turned ON without the seat belt having been fastened.
3 If required, the timer can be checked using a test lamp connected in accordance with the diagram shown in Fig. 12.52. With the test lamp connected as shown, it should light and the chimes operate for a period of 4 to 8 seconds. If not renew the unit.

32 Brake warning light switches – removal and refitting

Stop-lamp switch

1 This switch is attached to the brake pedal support bracket. Remove the lower facia trim panel for access.
2 Disconnect the switch wire, loosen the locknut and then unscrew the switch (photo).
3 Refit in the reverse order of removal but adjust the switch as described in Section 17 of Chapter 9.

Handbrake warning light switch

4 This switch is attached to the handbrake mounting bracket. To remove the switch, first remove the centre console rear section from the handbrake.
5 Disconnect the wiring connector from the handbrake warning switch, undo the retaining screw and remove the switch.
6 Refit in the reverse order of removal and adjust the switch as described in Section 15 of Chapter 9.

33 Radio/cassette unit – removal and refitting

1 Disconnect the battery earth lead.
2 Remove the ashtray and the lower centre facia as described in Chapter 11.
3 Undo the two radio/cassette retaining screws each side and withdraw the unit (photo).
4 Disconnect the wiring and antenna lead connectors from the rear of the unit (photo).
5 Refit in the reverse order of removal. If a new receiver has been fitted, the aerial should be trimmed in the following way.
6 Extend the aerial fully, switch on the radio and turn to maximum volume.
7 Tune to a station which is barely audible and is found at around 1400 kHz.
8 Turn the trim screw in the front of the receiver until the signal is at its strongest. The screw should not be turned more than one half turn in either direction (Fig. 12.53).

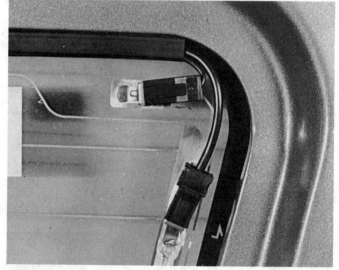
30.6 Lead connections to the heated rear window element and the radio antenna

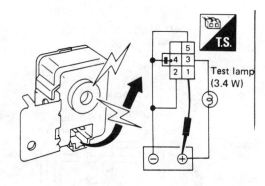
Fig. 12.52 Seat belt warning timer check (Sec 31)

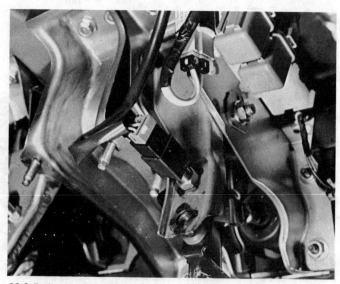
32.2 Brake warning lamp switch and wiring connector

33.3 Radio/cassette unit and retaining screws each side

33.4 Wiring and antenna connections on rear face of radio/cassette unit

34.1A Door mounted speaker unit

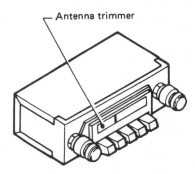

Fig. 12.53 Radio antenna trimmer screw location (Sec 33)

34 Speaker units – removal and refitting

1   The number and location of speaker units fitted is dependent on model. Speaker units can be located in the facia unit, the door trim panels and/or at the rear, each side of the parcel shelf (photos).
2   To remove a speaker unit, first detach and remove the facia panel, door trim panel or rear luggage area trim panel, as applicable (Chapter 11).
3   Undo the speaker unit retaining screws, disconnect the wiring connector at the speaker, then withdraw the speaker unit from its mounting.
4   Refit in the reverse order of removal.

34.1B Rear parcel shelf mounted speaker unit

35 Radio antenna (aerial)

1   The standard radio antenna fitted will either be mounted in the driver's side windscreen pillar or will be a ribbon type in the rear window (see photo 30.6).
2   To remove the windscreen pillar type, disconnect the antenna lead from the rear of the radio receiver unit. Remove the radio for access (see Section 33).
3   Remove the lower facia and driver's well side trim panels as necessary for cable withdrawal.
4   Undo the antenna fixing screws to the windscreen pillar and carefully withdraw the antenna and lead.
5   Refit in reverse order of removal.
6   The rear window antenna repair or renewal must be entrusted to your Nissan dealer. The cautionary notes for the antenna are the same as those for the rear window demister element (see Section 30).

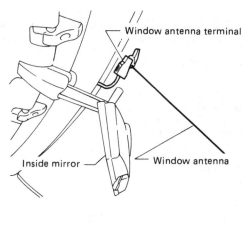

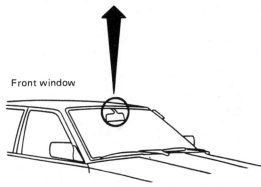

Fig. 12.54 Windscreen mounted antenna and lead terminal – all models except Coupe can have this type fitted (Sec 35)

36 Fault diagnosis – electrical system

Symptom	Reason(s)
No voltage at starter motor	Battery discharged
	Battery defective internally
	Battery terminals loose or earth lead not securely attached to body
	Loose or broken connections in starter motor circuit
	Starter motor switch or solenoid faulty
Voltage at starter motor – faulty motor	Starter brushes badly worn, sticking, or brush wires loose
	Commutator dirty, worn or burnt
	Starter motor armature faulty
	Field coils earthed
Starter motor noisy or rough in engagement	Pinion or flywheel gear teeth broken or worn
	Starter motor retaining bolts loose
Alternator not charging*	Drivebelt loose and slipping, or broken
	Brushes worn, sticking, broken or dirty
	Brush springs weak or broken

If all appears to be well but the alternator is still not charging, take the car to an automobile electrician for checking of the alternator

Battery will not hold charge for more than a few days	Battery defective internally
	Electrolyte level too low or electrolyte too weak due to leakage
	Plate separators no longer fully effective
	Battery plates severely sulphated
	Drivebelt slipping
	Battery terminal connections loose or corroded
	Alternator not charging properly
	Short in lighting circuit causing continual battery drain
Ignition light fails to go out, battery runs flat in a few days	Drivebelt loose and slipping, or broken
	Alternator faulty

Failure of individual electrical equipment to function correctly is dealt with alphabetically below

Fuel gauge gives no reading	Fuel tank empty
	Electric cable between tank sender unit and gauge earthed or loose
	Fuel gauge case not earthed
	Fuel gauge supply cable interrupted
	Fuel gauge unit broken
Fuel gauge registers full all the time	Electric cable between tank unit and gauge broken or disconnected
Horn operates all the time	Horn push either earthed or stuck down
	Horn cable to horn push earthed
Horn fails to operate	Blown fuse
	Cable or cable connection loose, broken or disconnected
	Horn has an internal fault
Horn emits intermittent or unsatisfactory noise	Cable connections loose
	Horn incorrectly adjusted
Lights do not come on	If engine not running, battery discharged
	Light bulb filament burnt out or bulbs broken
	Wire connections loose, disconnected or broken
	Light switch shorting or otherwise faulty
Lights come on but fade	If engine not running, battery discharged
Lights give very poor illumination	Lamp glasses dirty
	Reflector tarnished or dirty
	Lamps badly out of adjustment
	Incorrect bulb with too low wattage fitted
	Existing bulbs old and badly discolored
	Electrical wiring too thin not allowing full current to pass
Lights work erratically, flashing on and off, especially over bumps	Battery terminals or earth connections loose
	Lights not earthing properly
	Contacts in light switch faulty

Wiper motor fails to work

Blown fuse
Brushed badly worn
Wire connections loose, disconnected or broken
Armature worn or faulty
Field coils faulty

Wiper motor works very slowly and takes excessive current

Commutator dirty, greasy or burnt
Drive to spindles bent or unlubricated
Drive spindle binding or damaged
Armature bearings dry or misaligned
Armature badly worn or faulty

Wiper motor works slowly and takes little current

Brushes badly worn
Commutator dirty, greasy or burnt
Armature badly worn or faulty

Wiper motor works but wiper blades remain static

Linkage disengaged or faulty
Drive spindle damaged or worn
Wiper motor gearbox parts badly worn

Wiring diagrams commence overleaf

WIRING DIAGRAM

Symbols used in WIRING DIAGRAM are shown below.

Example

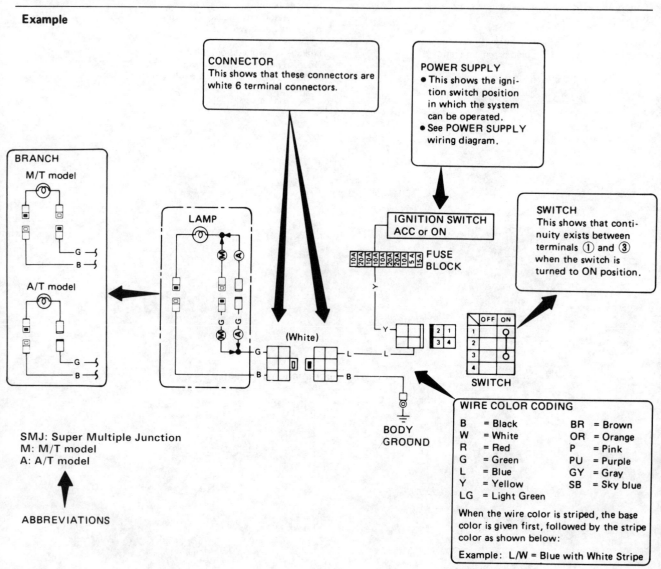

Fig. 12.55 How to use the wiring diagrams

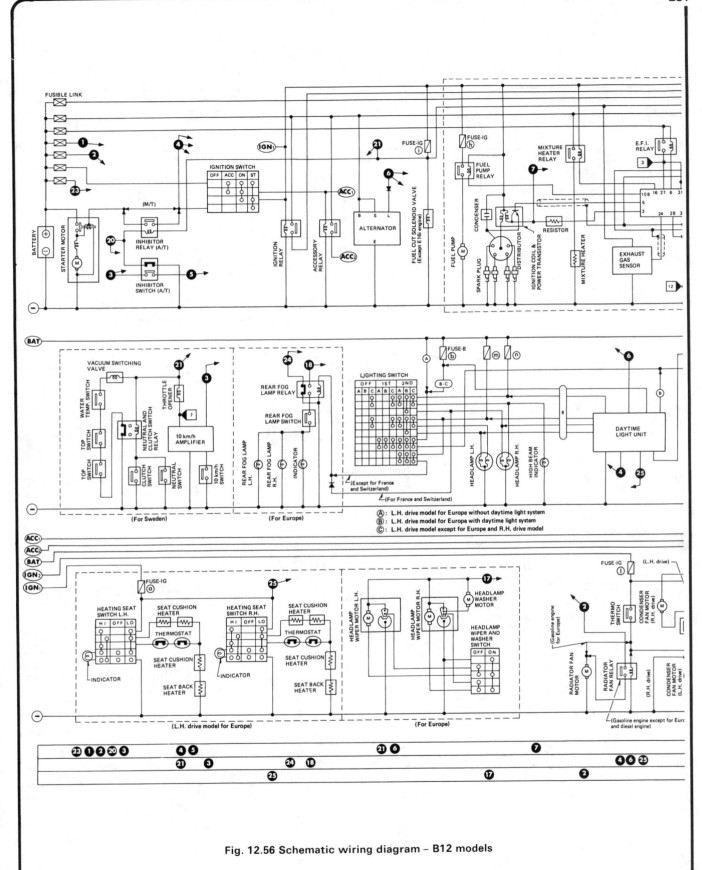

Fig. 12.56 Schematic wiring diagram – B12 models

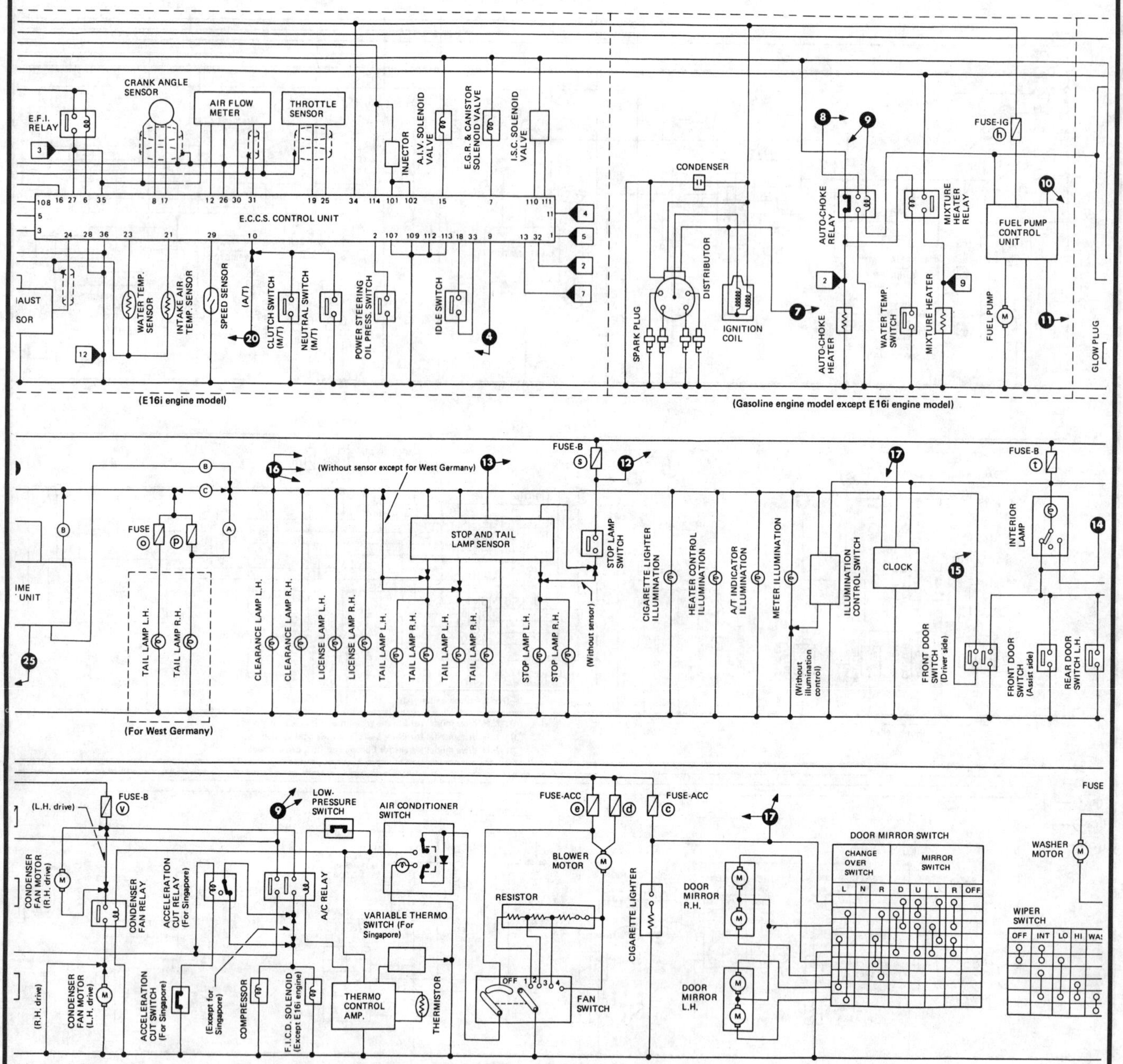

CRANK ANGLE SENSOR
AIR FLOW METER
THROTTLE SENSOR
E.F.I. RELAY
A.I.V. SOLENOID VALVE
E.G.R. & CANISTOR SOLENOID VALVE
I.S.C. SOLENOID VALVE
INJECTOR
CONDENSER
FUSE-IG

E.C.C.S. CONTROL UNIT

WATER TEMP. SENSOR
INTAKE AIR TEMP. SENSOR
SPEED SENSOR
CLUTCH SWITCH (M/T)
NEUTRAL SWITCH (M/T)
POWER STEERING OIL PRESS. SWITCH
IDLE SWITCH
EXHAUST SENSOR

SPARK PLUG
DISTRIBUTOR
IGNITION COIL

AUTO-CHOKE RELAY
MIXTURE HEATER RELAY
FUEL PUMP CONTROL UNIT

AUTO-CHOKE HEATER
WATER TEMP. SWITCH
MIXTURE HEATER
FUEL PUMP
GLOW PLUG

(E16i engine model)
(Gasoline engine model except E16i engine model)

FUSE
TIME UNIT
TAIL LAMP L.H.
TAIL LAMP R.H.
(For West Germany)

(Without sensor except for West Germany)
STOP AND TAIL LAMP SENSOR
STOP LAMP SWITCH
FUSE-B

CLEARANCE LAMP L.H.
CLEARANCE LAMP R.H.
LICENSE LAMP L.H.
LICENSE LAMP R.H.
TAIL LAMP L.H.
TAIL LAMP R.H.
TAIL LAMP L.H.
TAIL LAMP R.H.
STOP LAMP L.H.
STOP LAMP R.H.
(Without sensor)

CIGARETTE LIGHTER ILLUMINATION
HEATER CONTROL ILLUMINATION
A/T INDICATOR ILLUMINATION
METER ILLUMINATION
(Without illumination control)
ILLUMINATION CONTROL SWITCH
CLOCK
FRONT DOOR SWITCH (Driver side)
INTERIOR LAMP
FUSE-B
FRONT DOOR SWITCH (Assist side)
REAR DOOR SWITCH L.H.

(L.H. drive)
FUSE-B
LOW-PRESSURE SWITCH
AIR CONDITIONER SWITCH
FUSE-ACC
FUSE-ACC
FUSE
WASHER MOTOR

CONDENSER FAN MOTOR (R.H. drive)
CONDENSER FAN RELAY
ACCELERATION CUT RELAY (For Singapore)
A/C RELAY
VARIABLE THERMO SWITCH (For Singapore)
BLOWER MOTOR
RESISTOR
CIGARETTE LIGHTER
DOOR MIRROR R.H.
DOOR MIRROR SWITCH

(R.H. drive)
CONDENSER FAN MOTOR (L.H. drive)
ACCELERATION CUT SWITCH (For Singapore)
(Except for Singapore)
COMPRESSOR
F.I.C.D. SOLENOID (Except E16i engine)
THERMO CONTROL AMP.
THERMISTOR
OFF 1 2 3 4
FAN SWITCH
DOOR MIRROR L.H.

CHANGE OVER SWITCH
MIRROR SWITCH
L N R D U L R OFF

WIPER SWITCH
OFF INT LO HI WAS

engine except for Europe engine)

Fig. 12.56 Schematic wiring diagram – B12 models (continued)

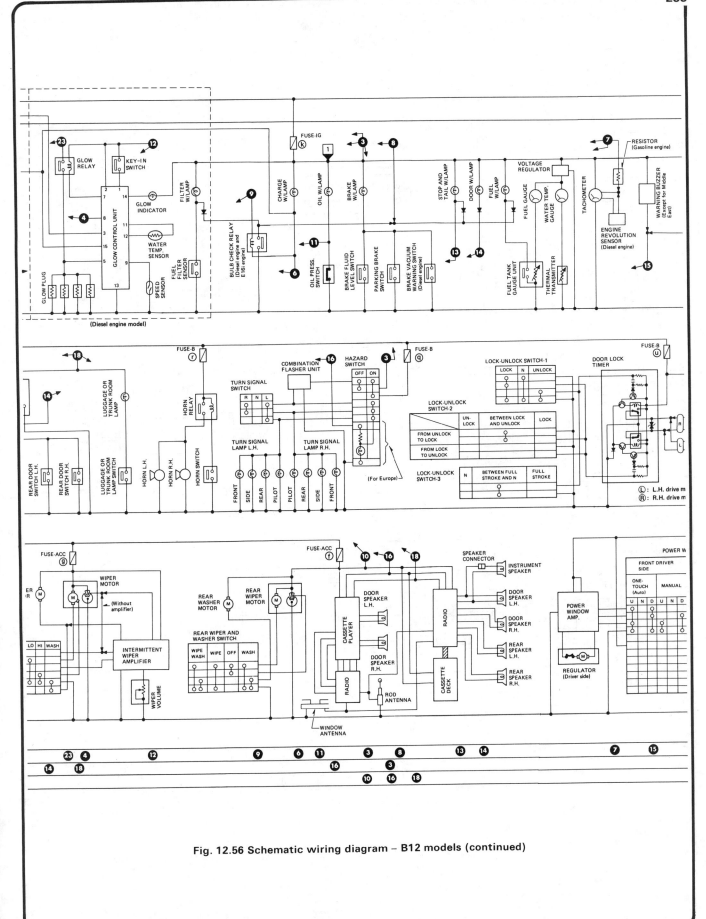

Fig. 12.56 Schematic wiring diagram – B12 models (continued)

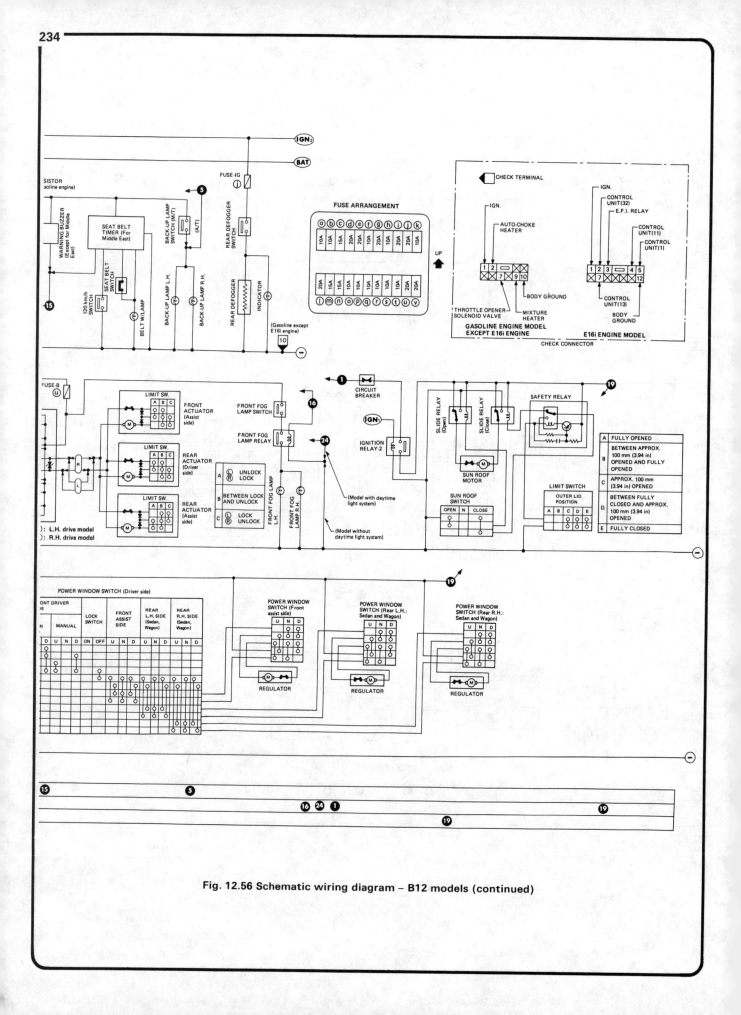

Fig. 12.56 Schematic wiring diagram – B12 models (continued)

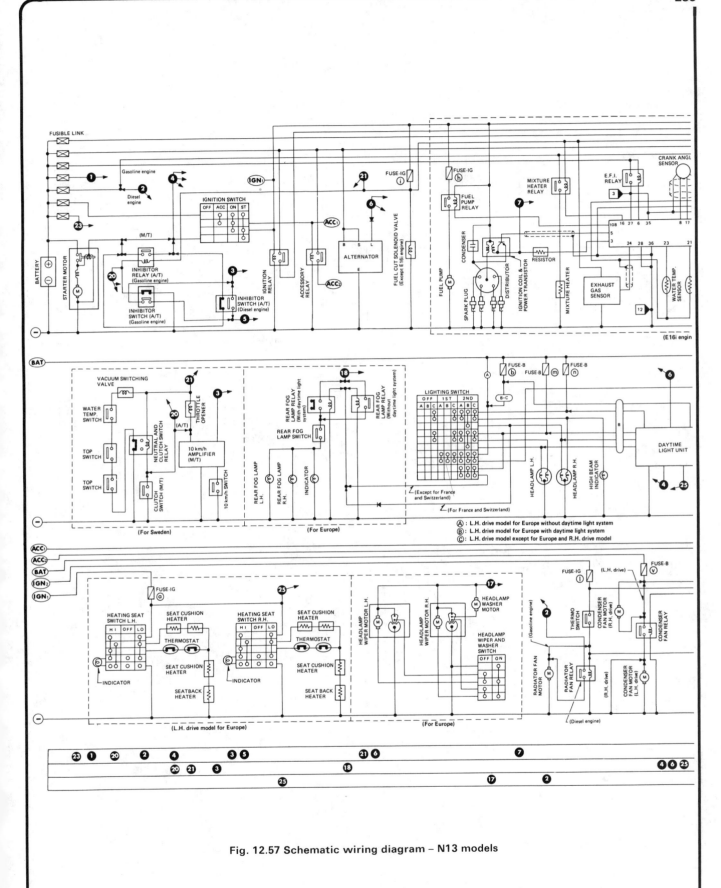

Fig. 12.57 Schematic wiring diagram – N13 models

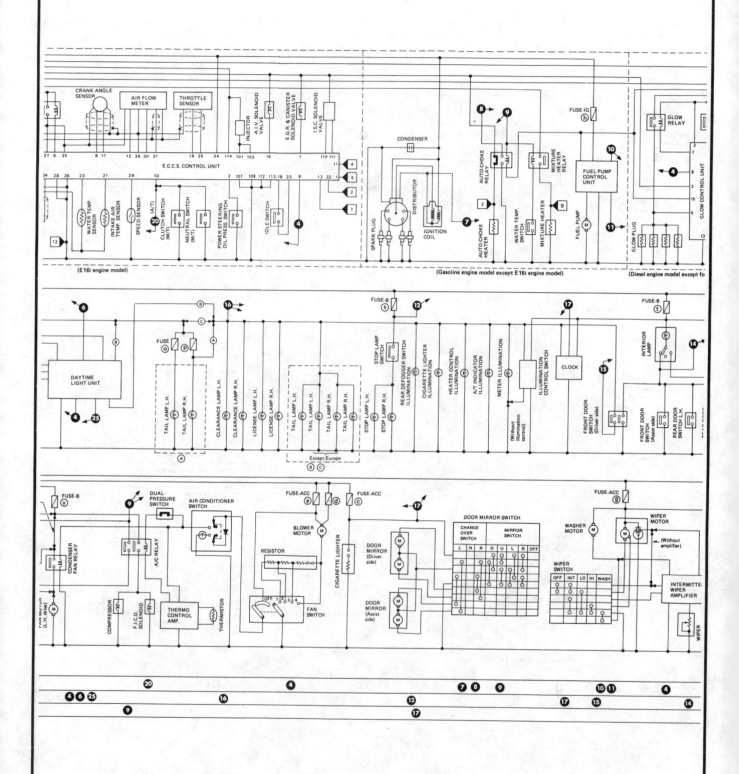

Fig. 12.57 Schematic wiring diagram – N13 models (continued)

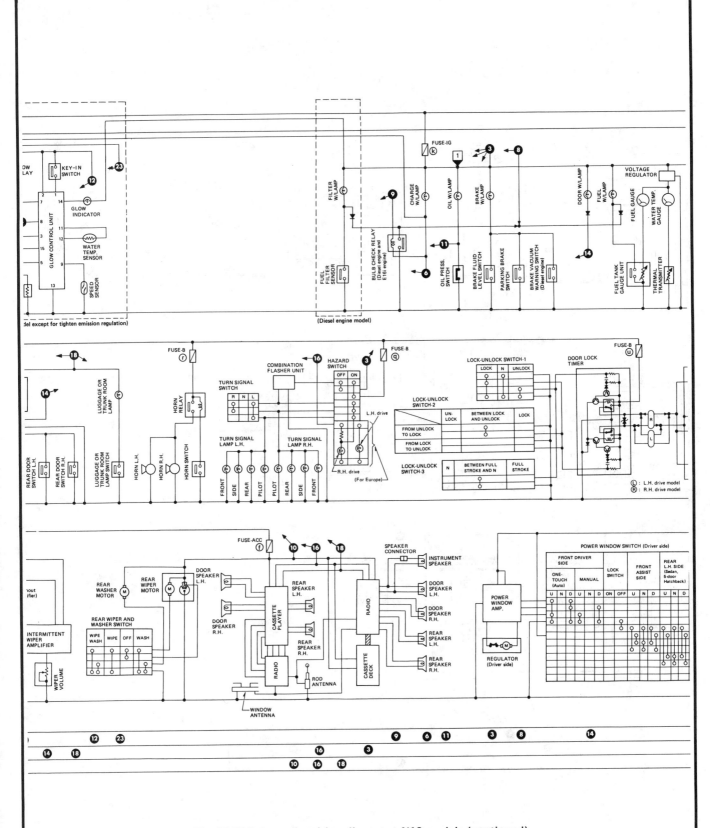

Fig. 12.57 Schematic wiring diagram – N13 models (continued)

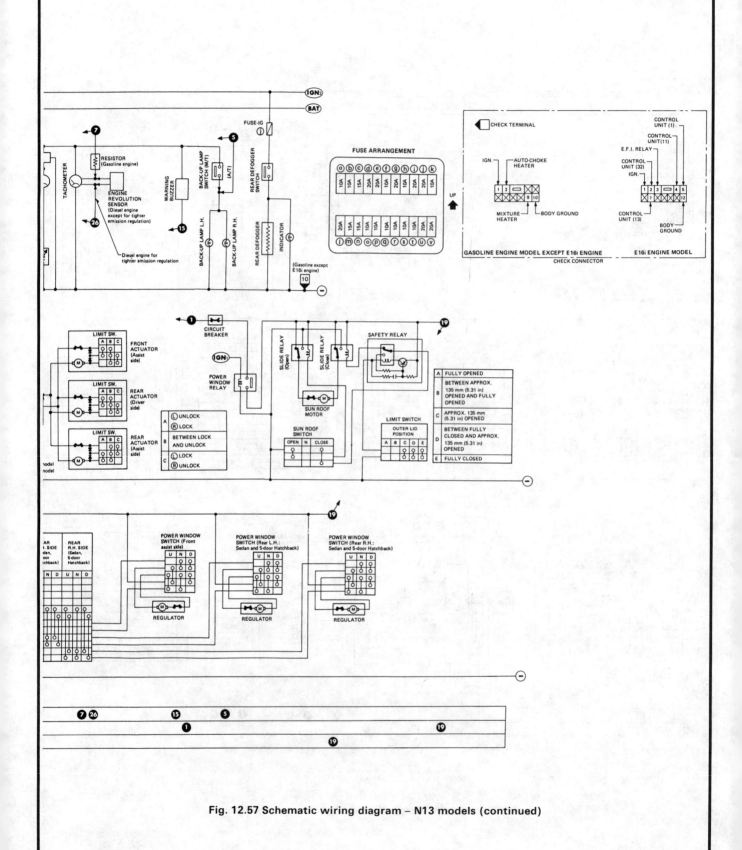

Fig. 12.57 Schematic wiring diagram – N13 models (continued)

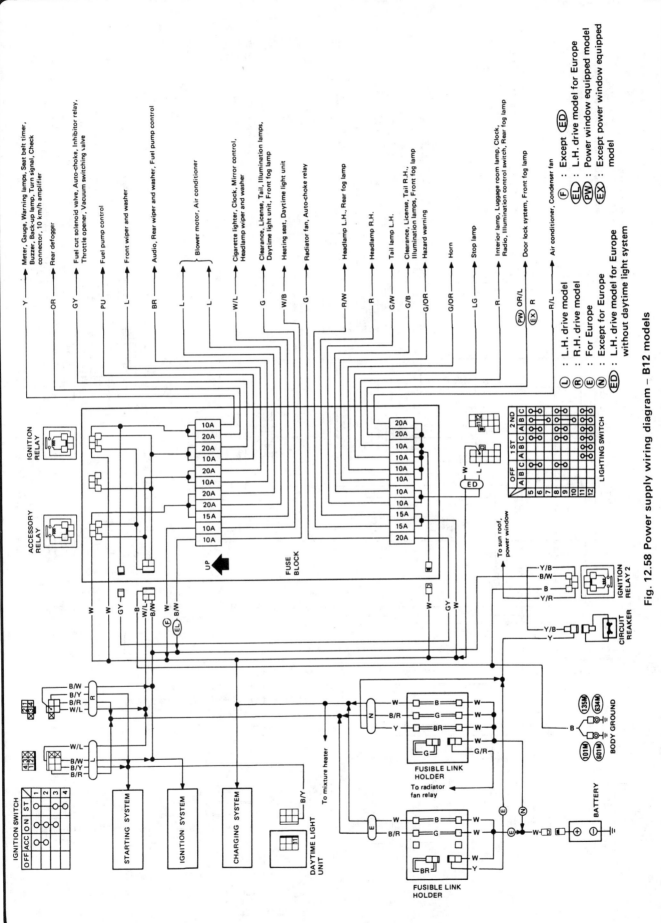

Fig. 12.58 Power supply wiring diagram – B12 models

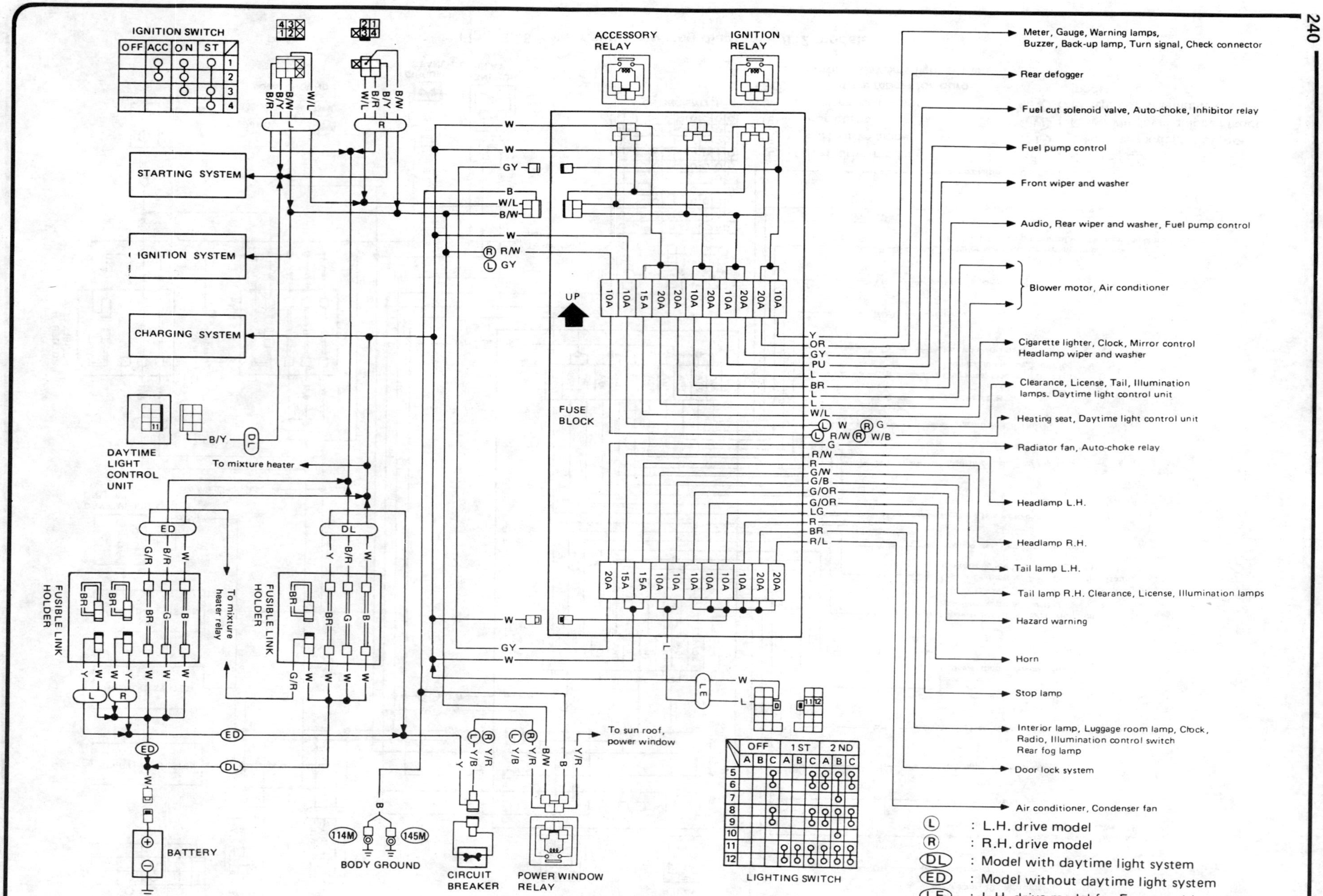

Fig. 12.59 Power supply wiring diagram – N13 models

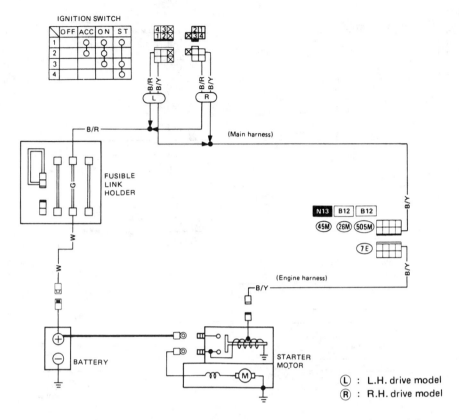

Fig. 12.60 Starting system wiring diagram – all manual transmission models

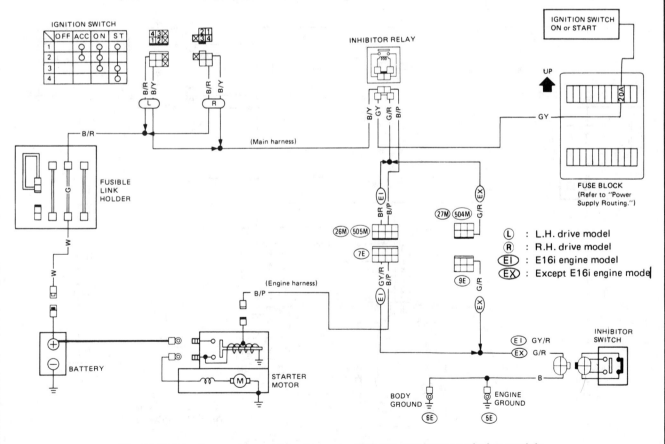

Fig. 12.61 Starting system wiring diagram – B12 automatic transmission models

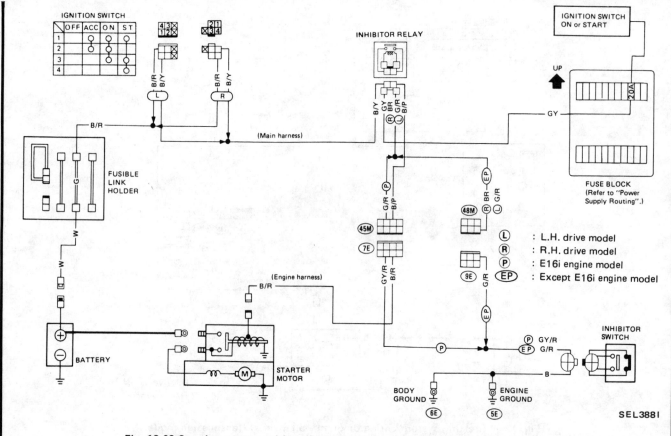

Fig. 12.62 Starting system wiring diagram – N13 automatic transmission models

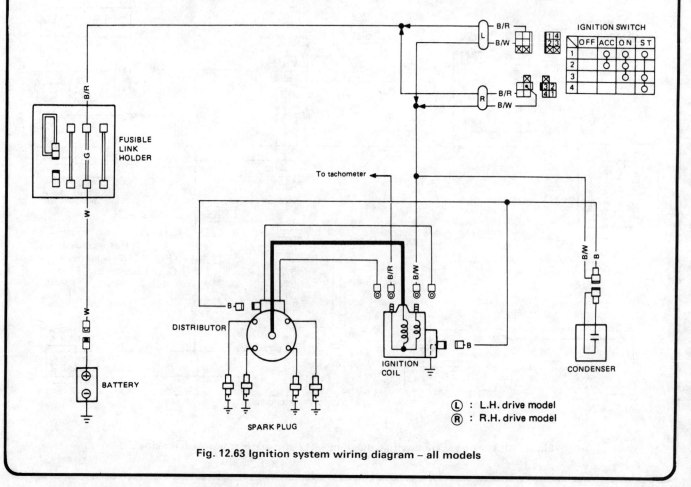

Fig. 12.63 Ignition system wiring diagram – all models

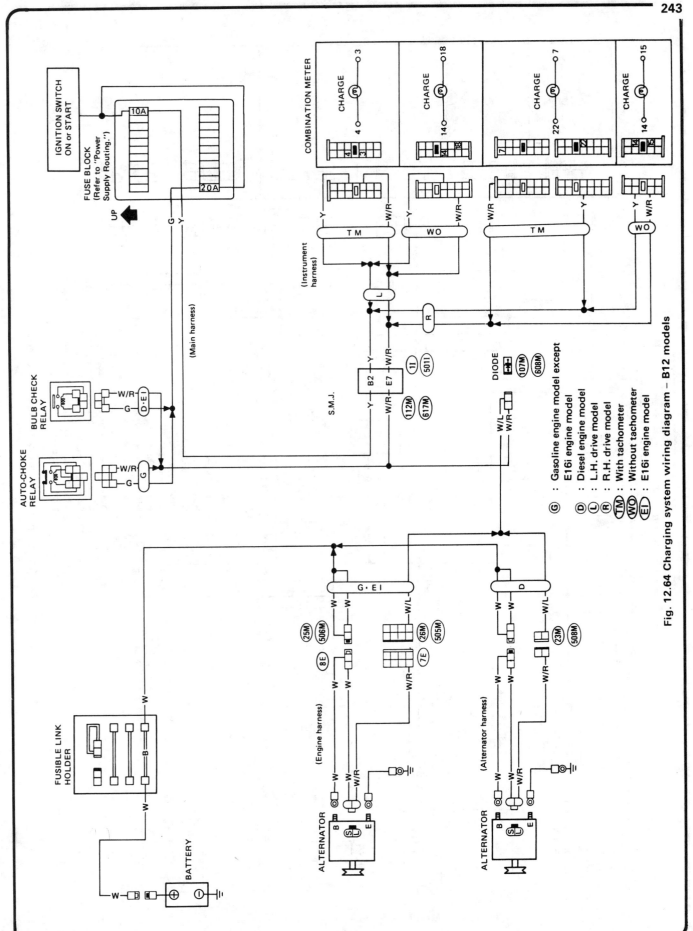

Fig. 12.64 Charging system wiring diagram – B12 models

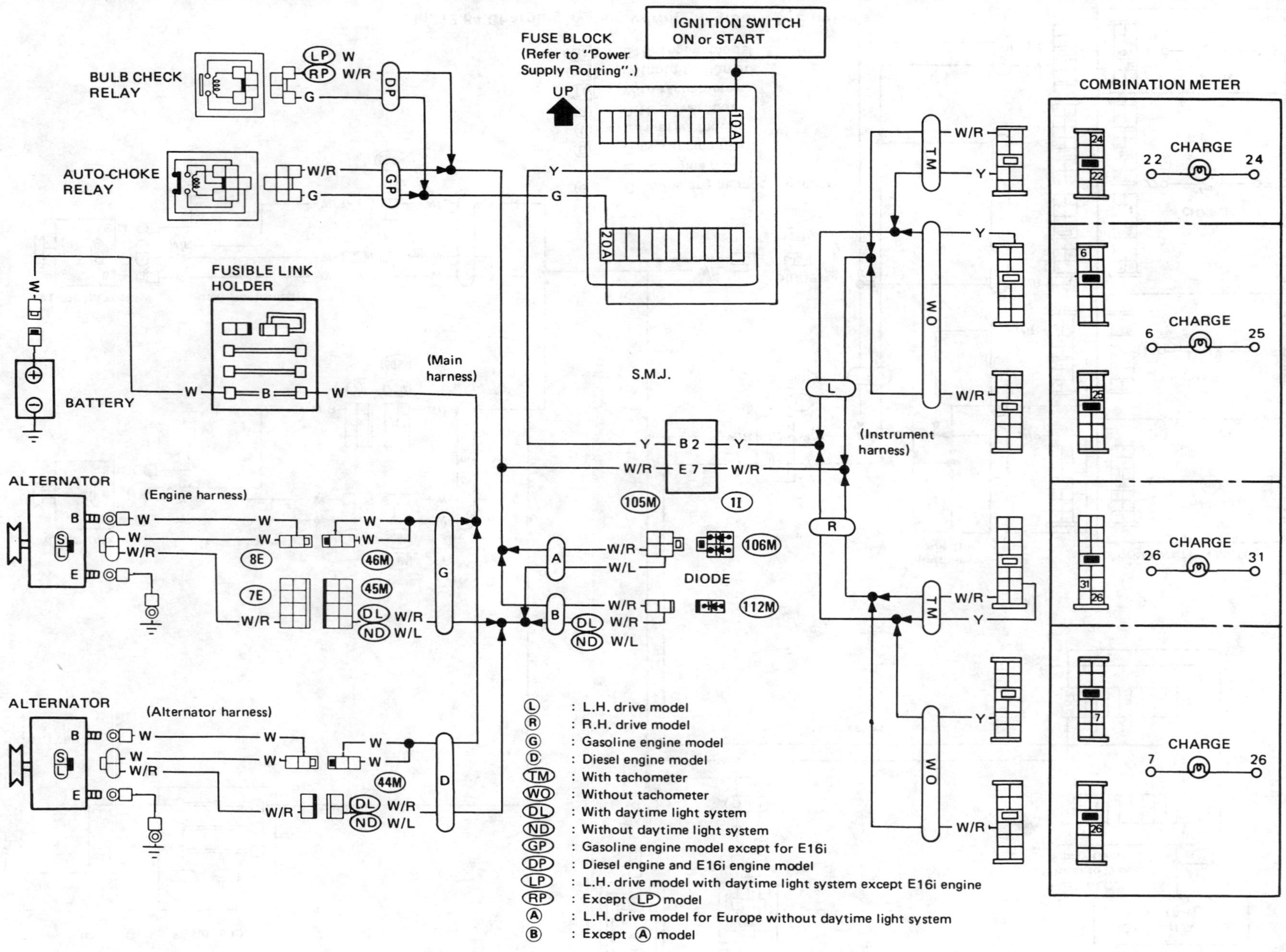

Fig. 12.65 Charging system wiring diagram – N13 models

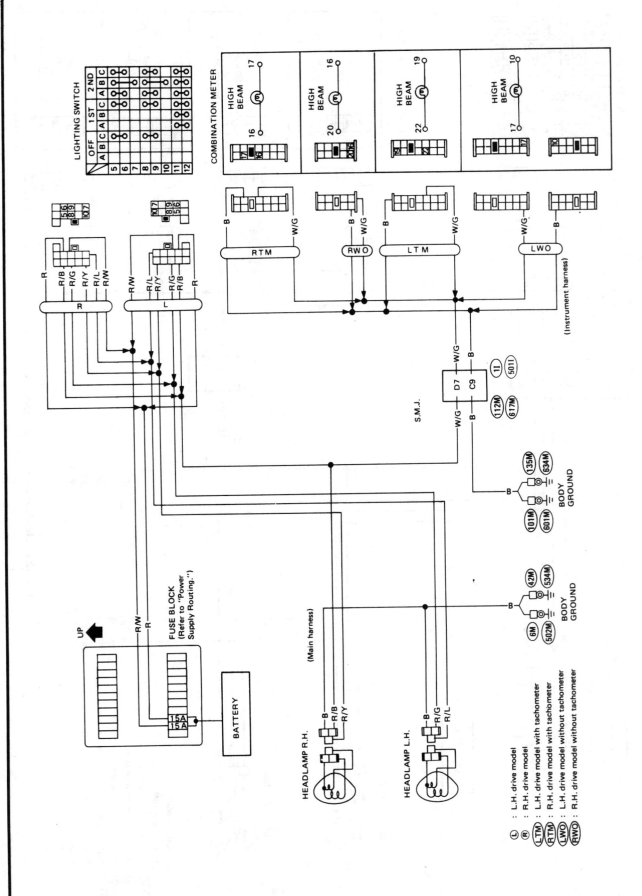

Fig. 12.66 Headlamps wiring diagram – B12 models

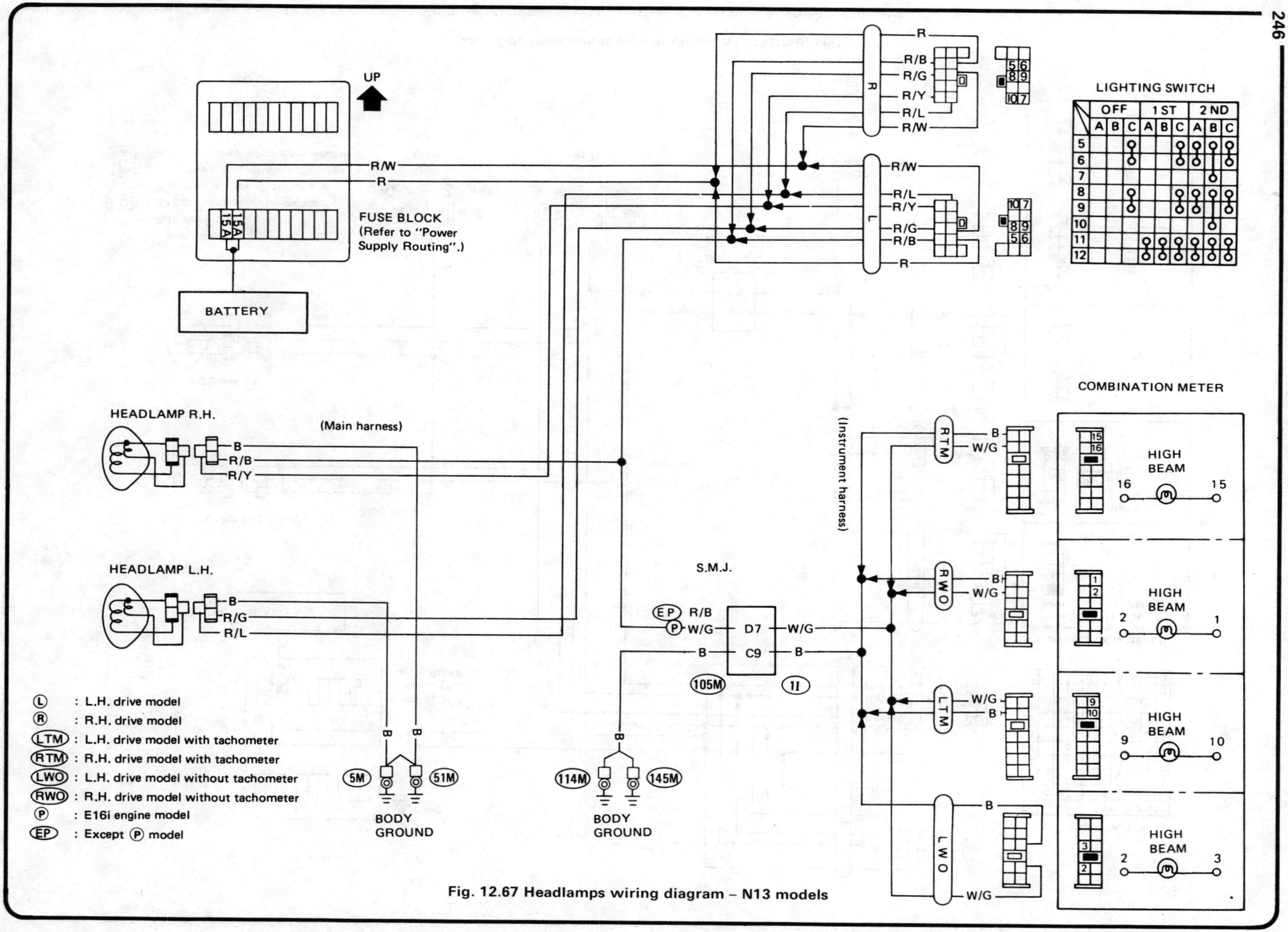

Fig. 12.67 Headlamps wiring diagram – N13 models

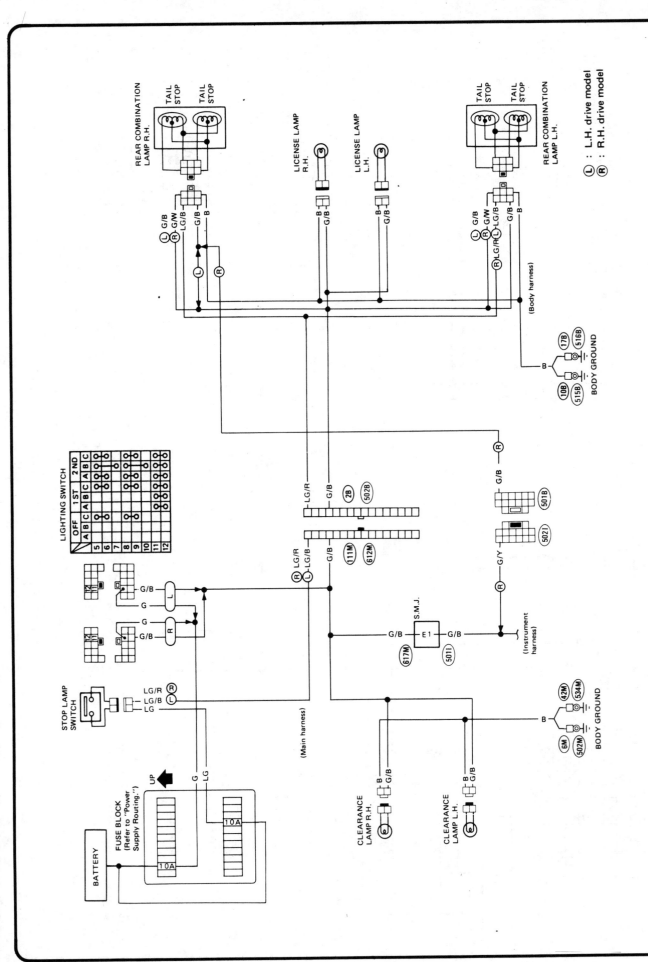

Fig. 12.68 Exterior lamps wiring diagram – B12 models

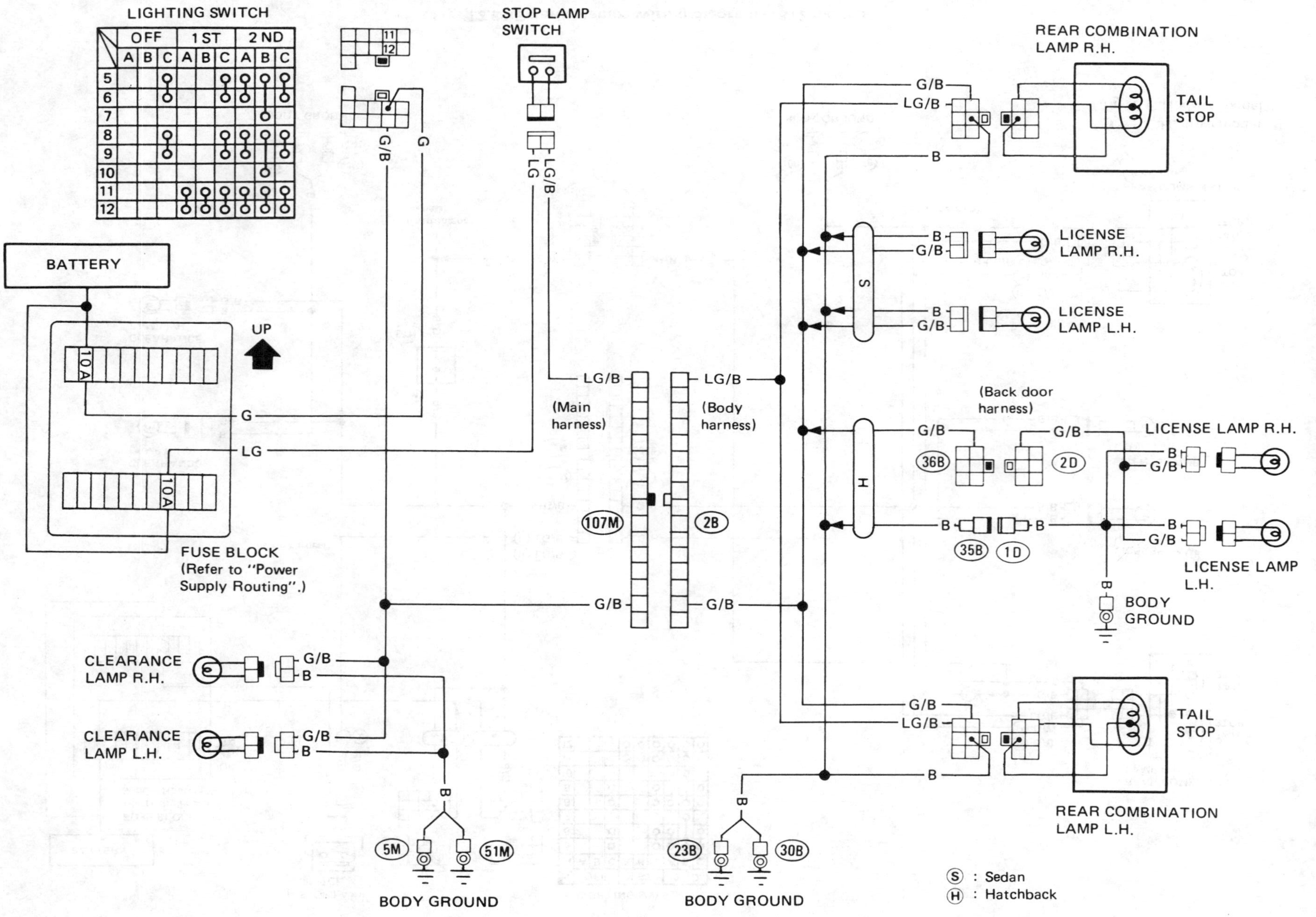

Fig. 12.69 Exterior lamps wiring diagram – N13 models

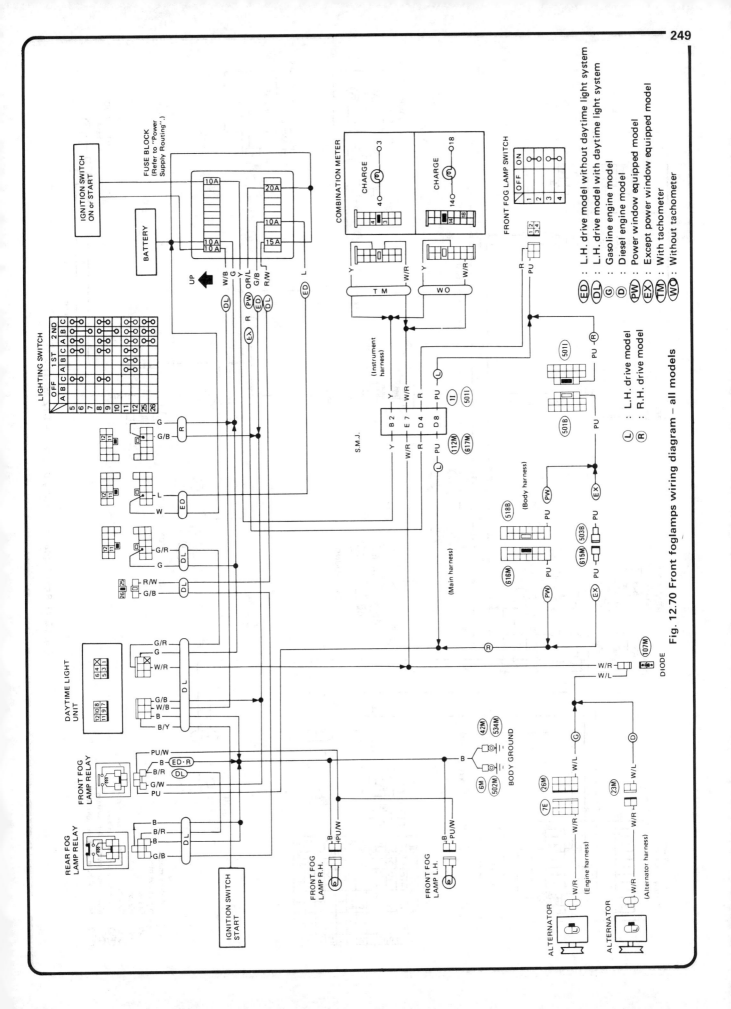

Fig. 12.70 Front foglamps wiring diagram – all models

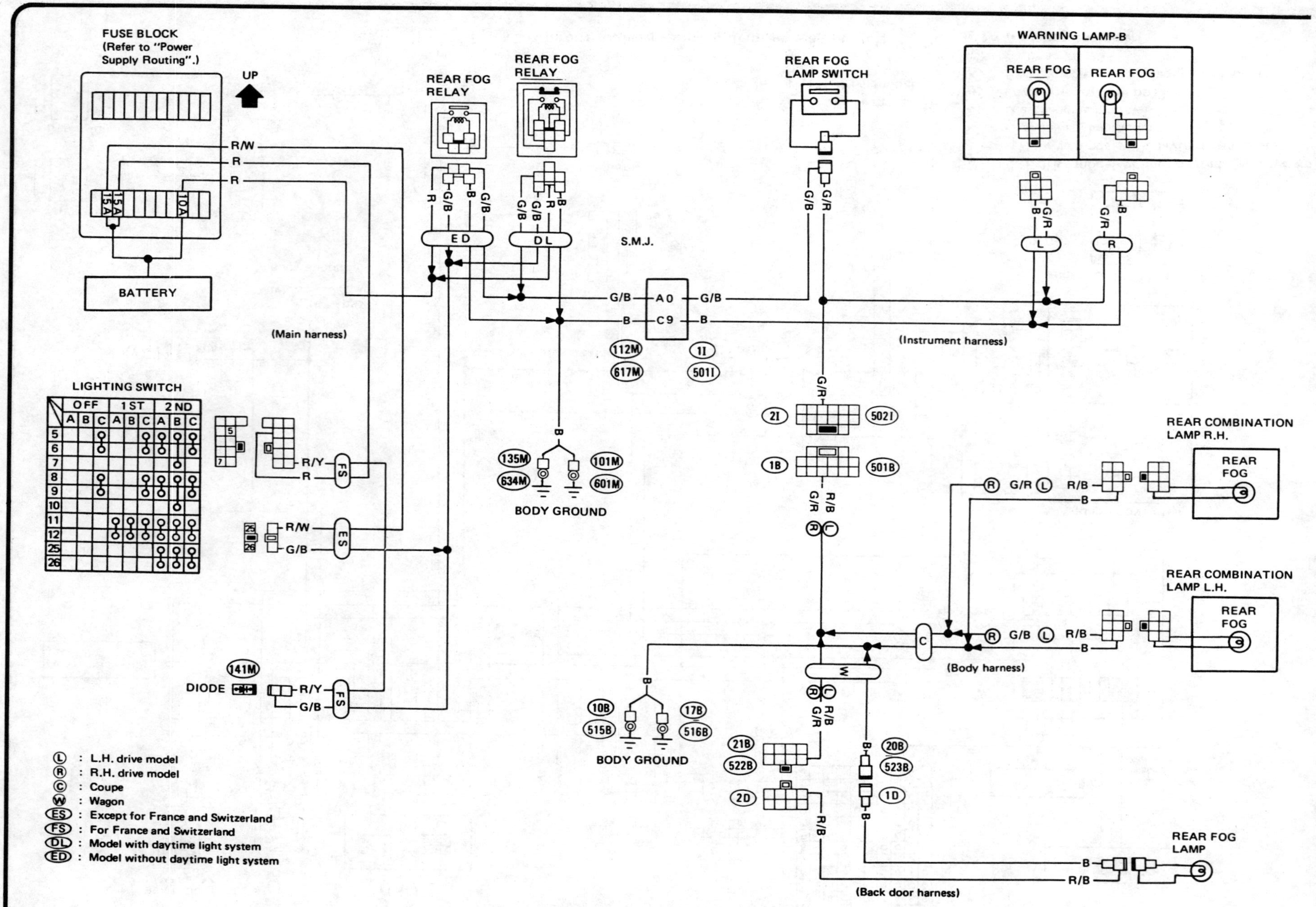

Fig. 12.71 Rear foglamps wiring diagram – B12 models

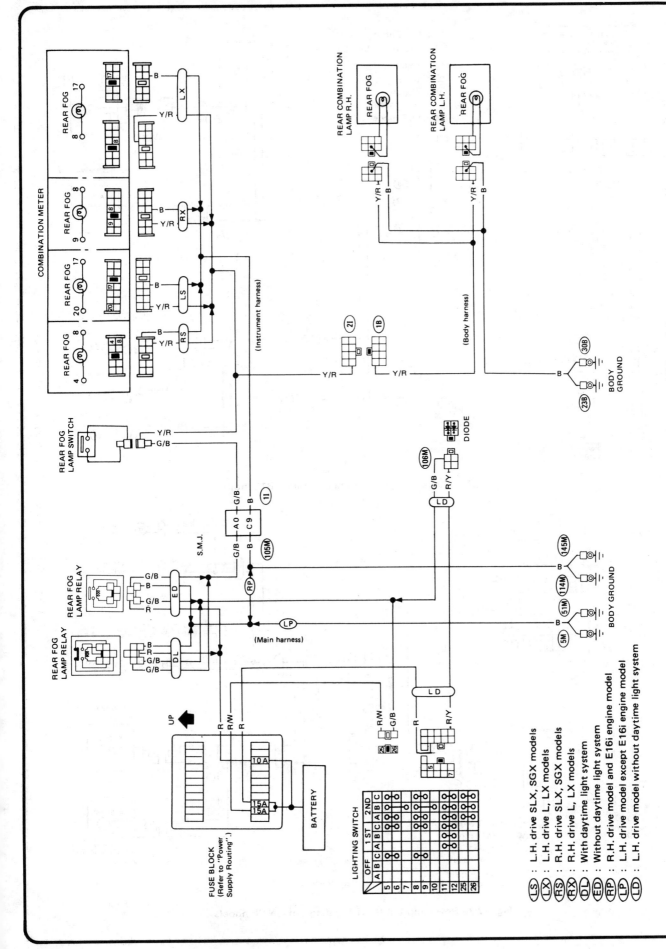

Fig. 12.72 Rear foglamps wiring diagram – N13 models

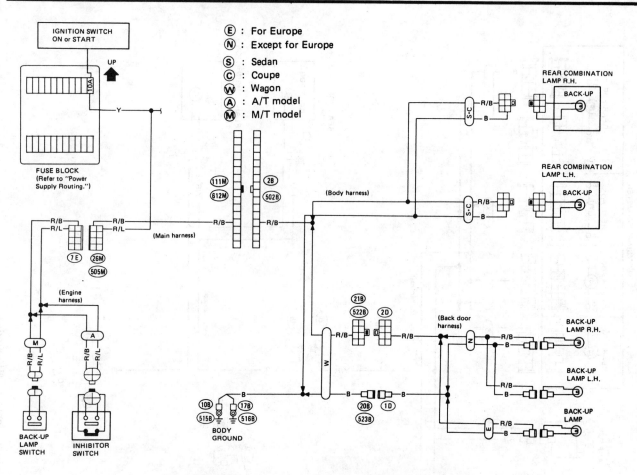

Fig. 12.73 Reversing lights wiring diagram – B12 models

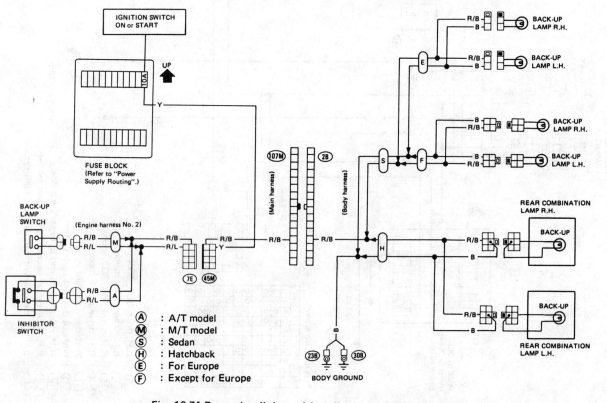

Fig. 12.74 Reversing lights wiring diagram – N13 models

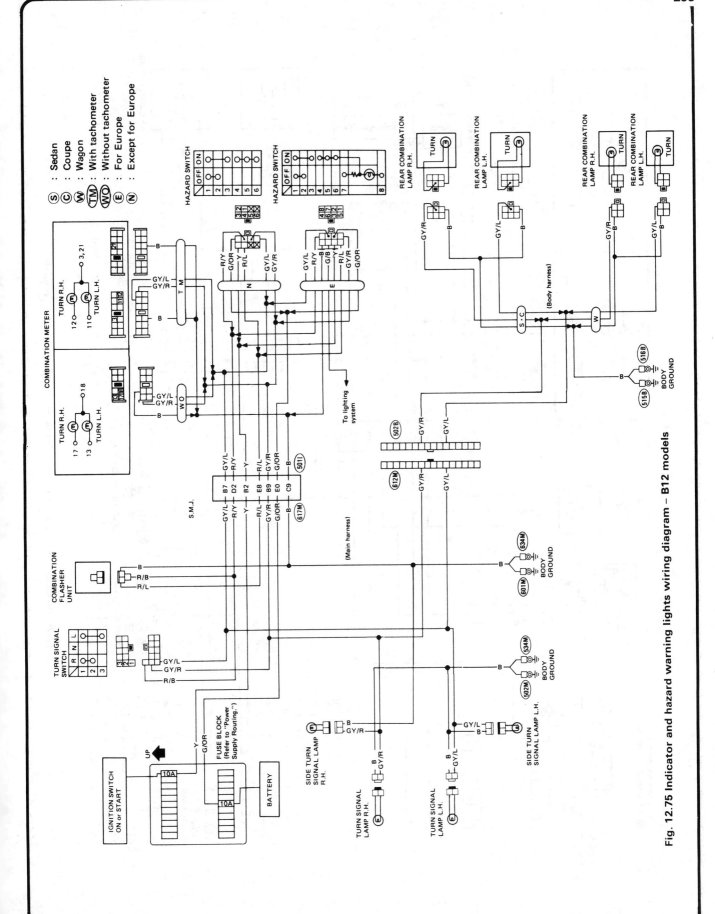

Fig. 12.75 Indicator and hazard warning lights wiring diagram – B12 models

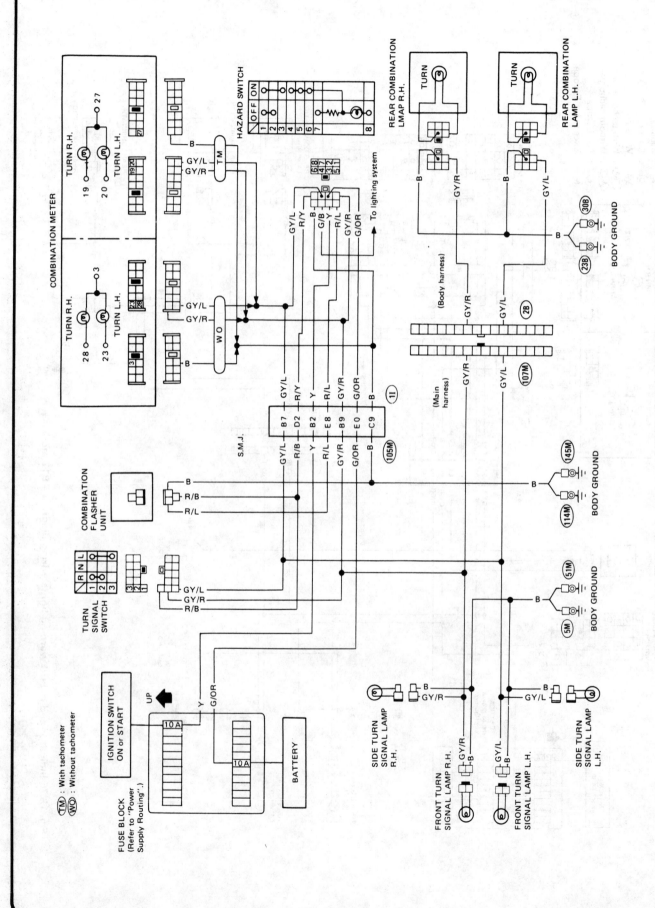

Fig. 12.76 Indicator and hazard warning lights wiring diagram – N13 models

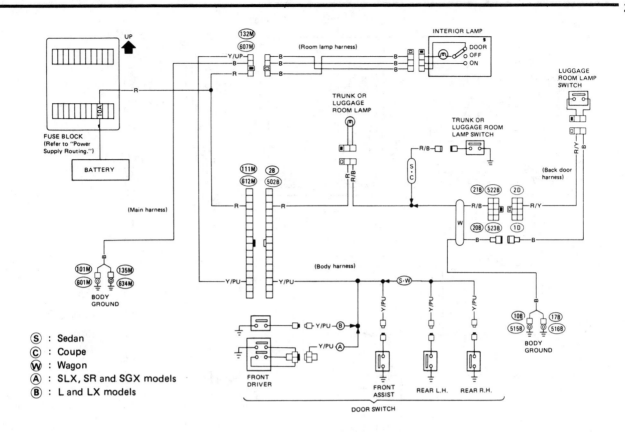

Fig. 12.77 Interior and luggage compartment lights wiring diagram – B12 models

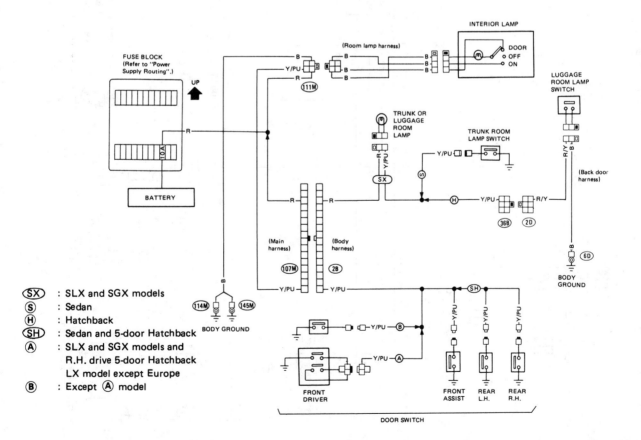

Fig. 12.78 Interior and luggage compartment lights wiring diagram – N13 models

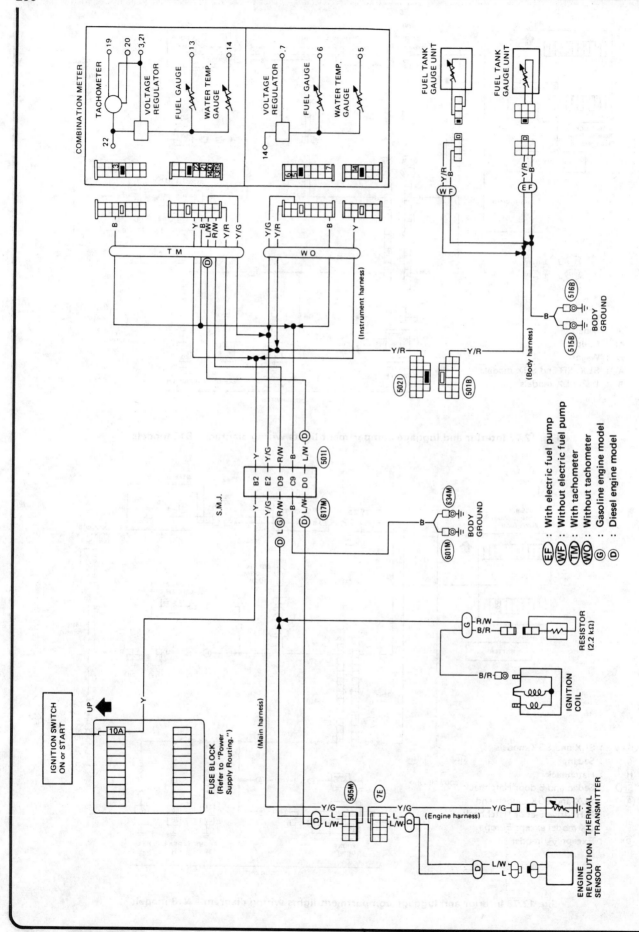

Fig. 12.79 Tachometer, fuel and water temperature gauges wiring diagram – B12 models

257

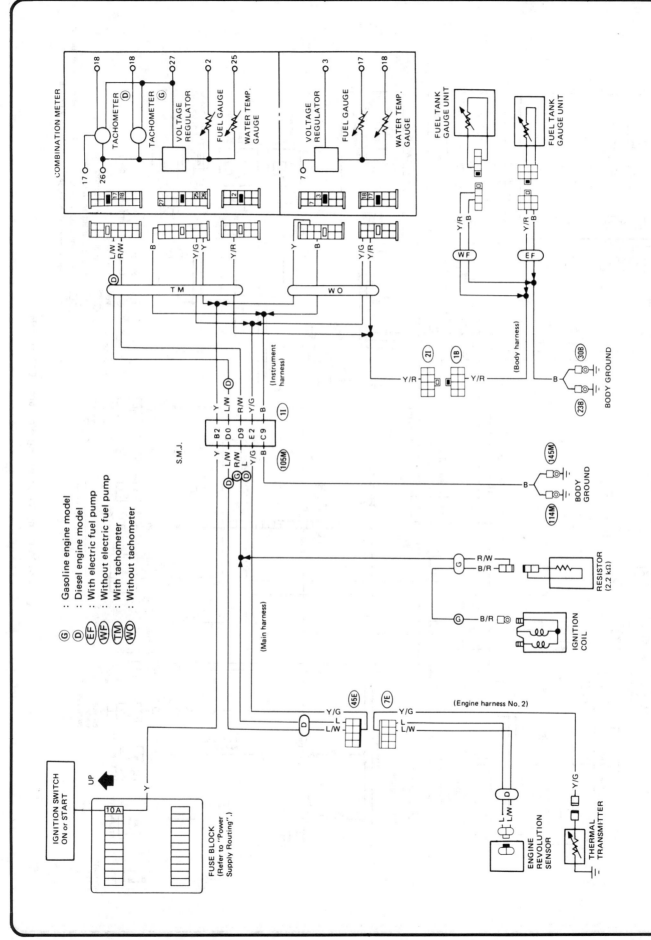

Fig. 12.80 Tachometer, fuel and water temperature gauges wiring diagram – N13 models

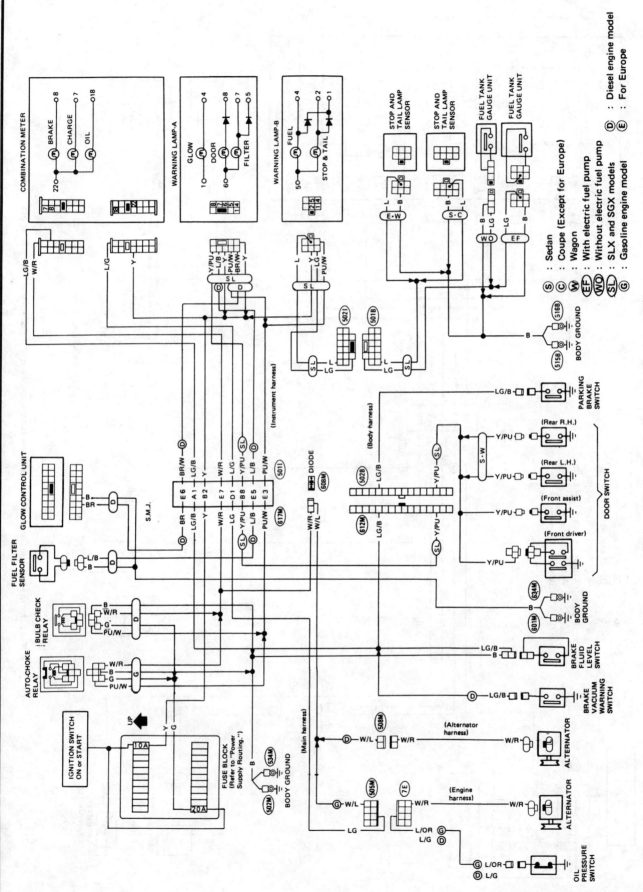

Fig. 12.81 Warning lamps wiring diagram – B12 models

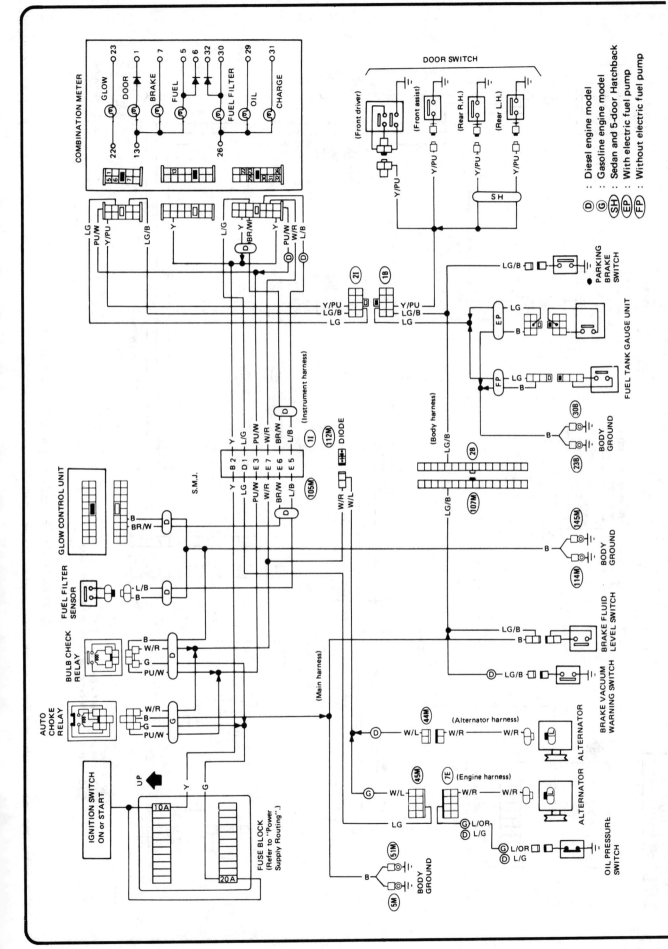

Fig. 12.82 Warning lamps wiring diagram – N13 models

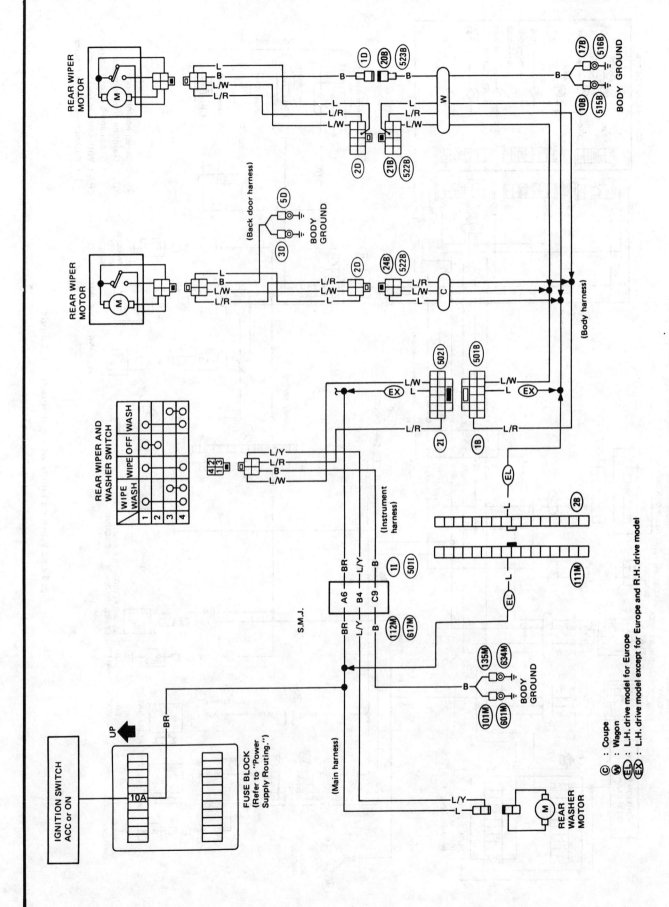

Fig. 12.83 Rear wash/wipe wiring diagram – B12 models

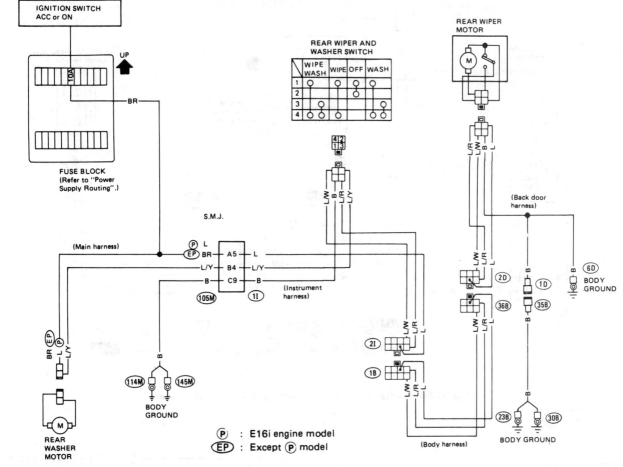

Fig. 12.84 Rear wash/wipe wiring diagram – N13 models

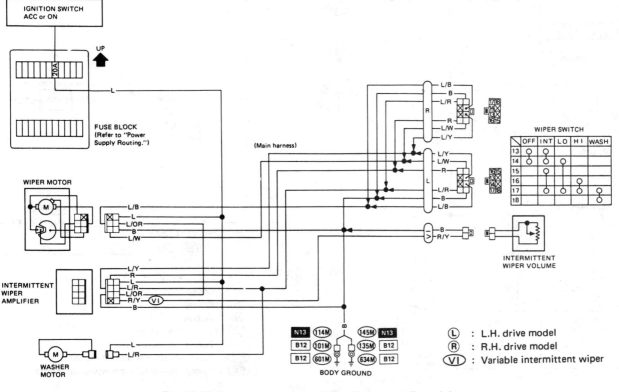

Fig. 12.85 Front wash/wipe wiring diagram – all models

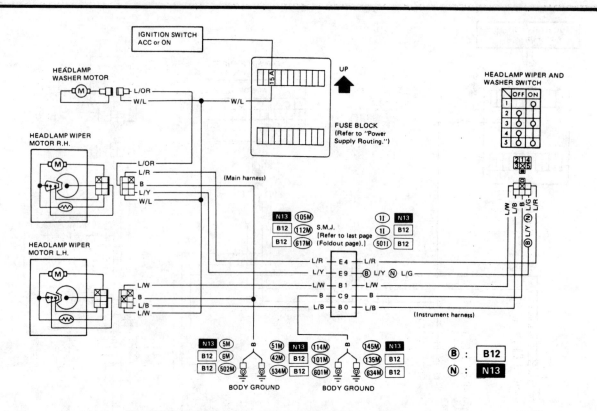

Fig. 12.86 Headlamp wash/wipe wiring diagram – all models

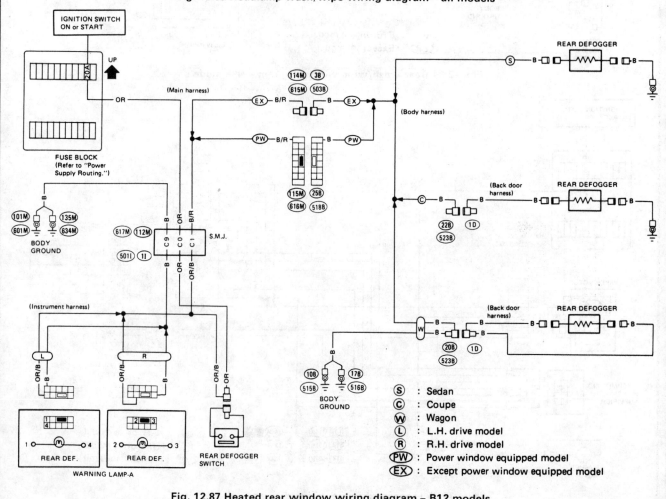

Fig. 12.87 Heated rear window wiring diagram – B12 models

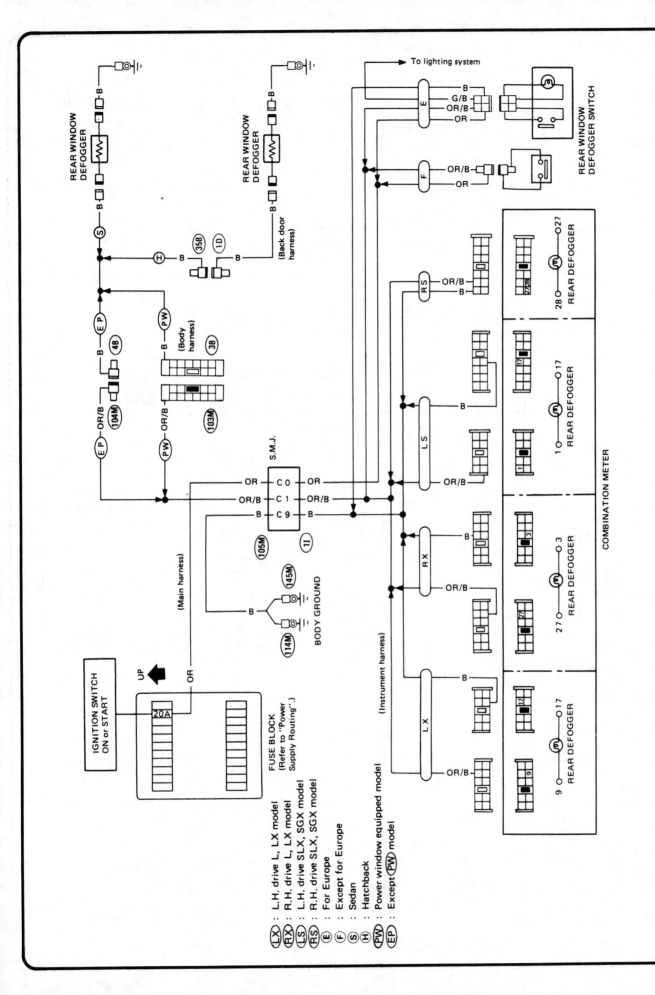

Fig. 12.88 Heated rear window wiring diagram – N13 models

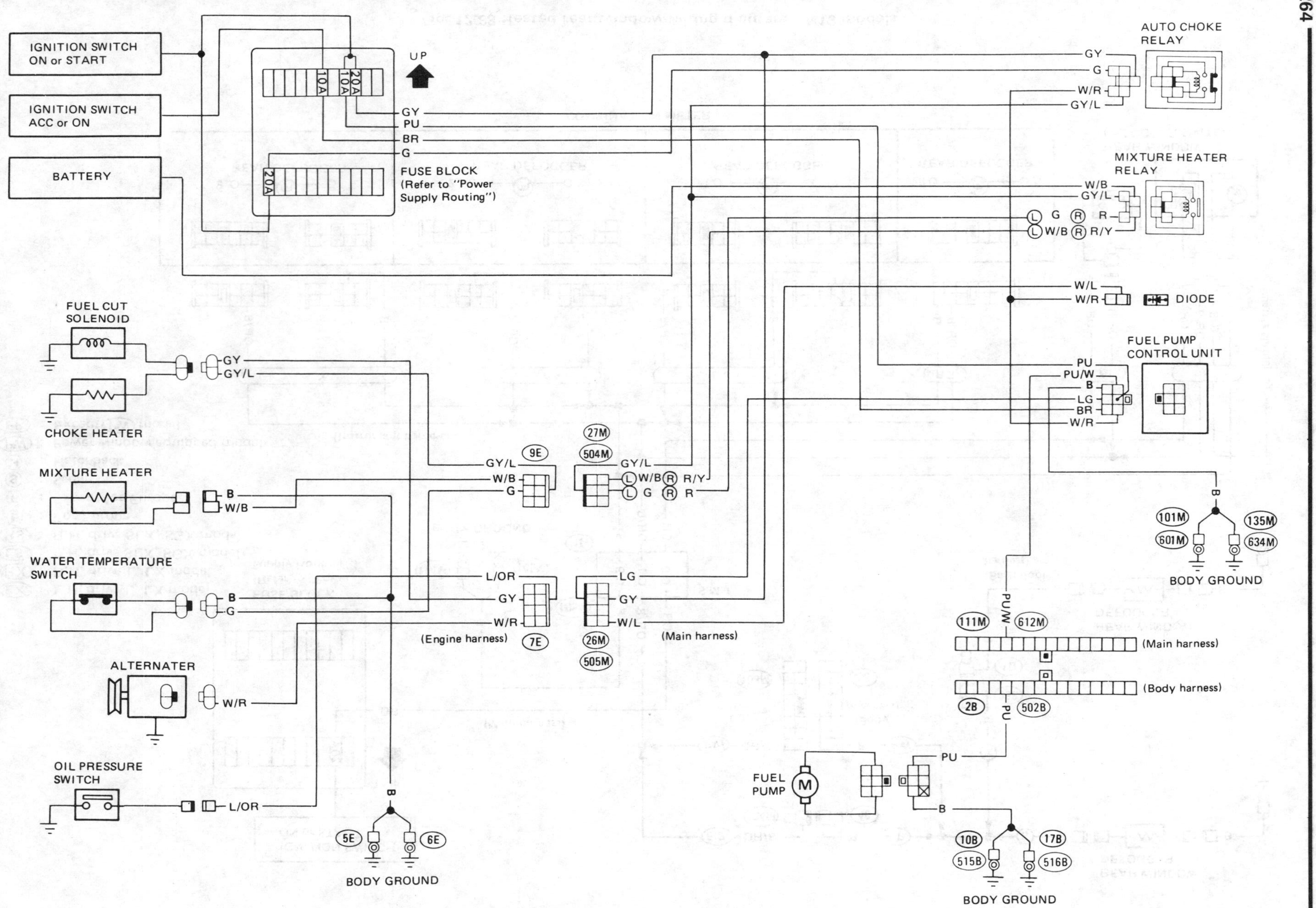

Fig. 12.89 Engine electrics wiring diagram – B12 models

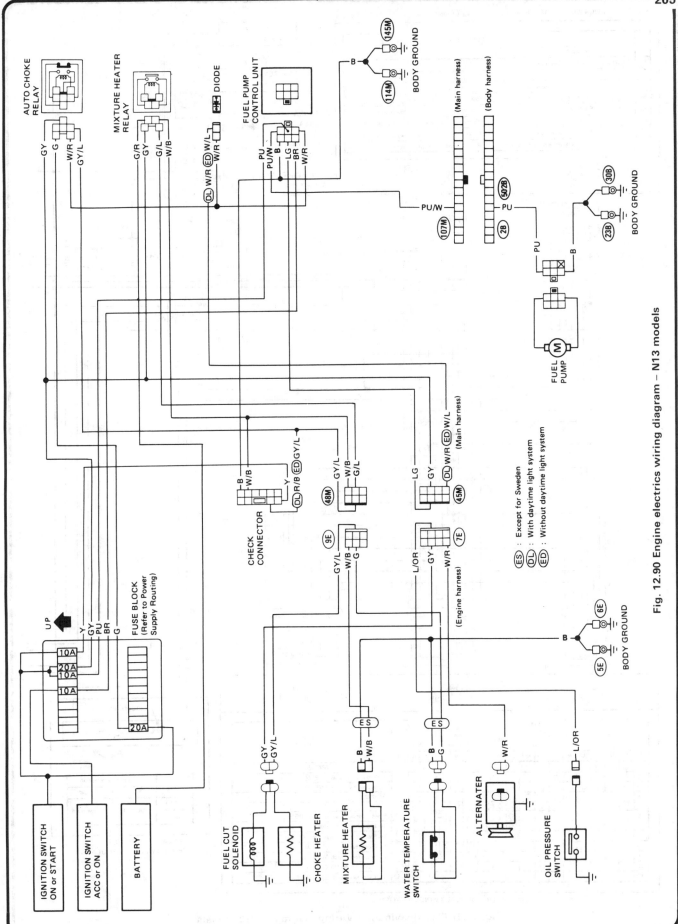

Fig. 12.90 Engine electrics wiring diagram – N13 models

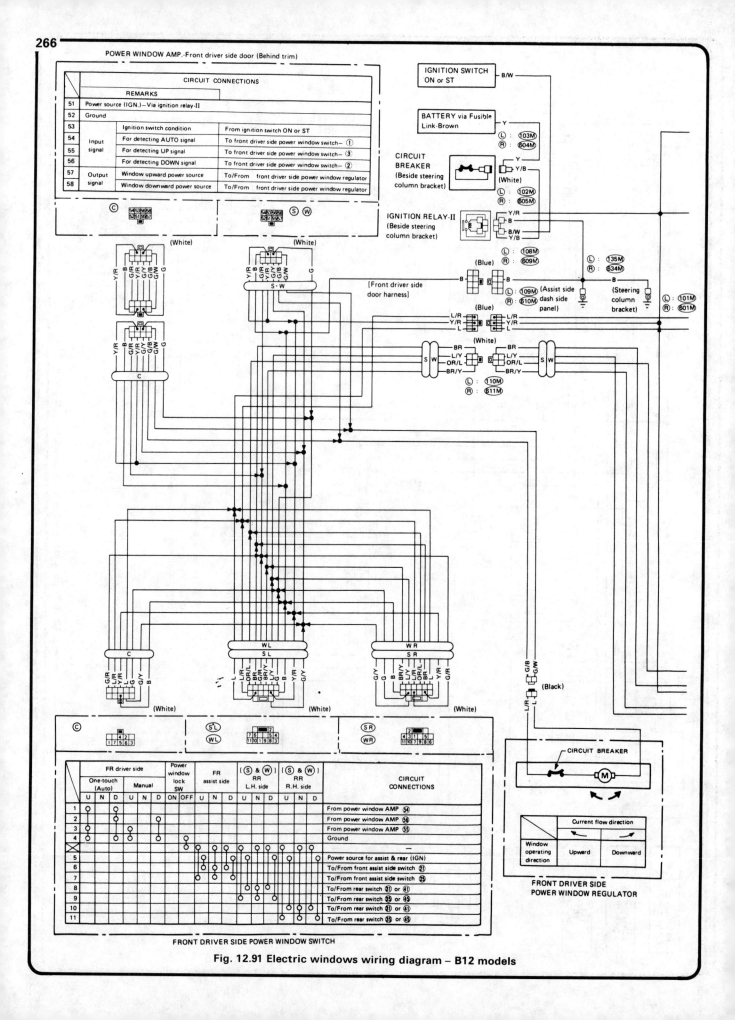

266

Fig. 12.91 Electric windows wiring diagram – B12 models

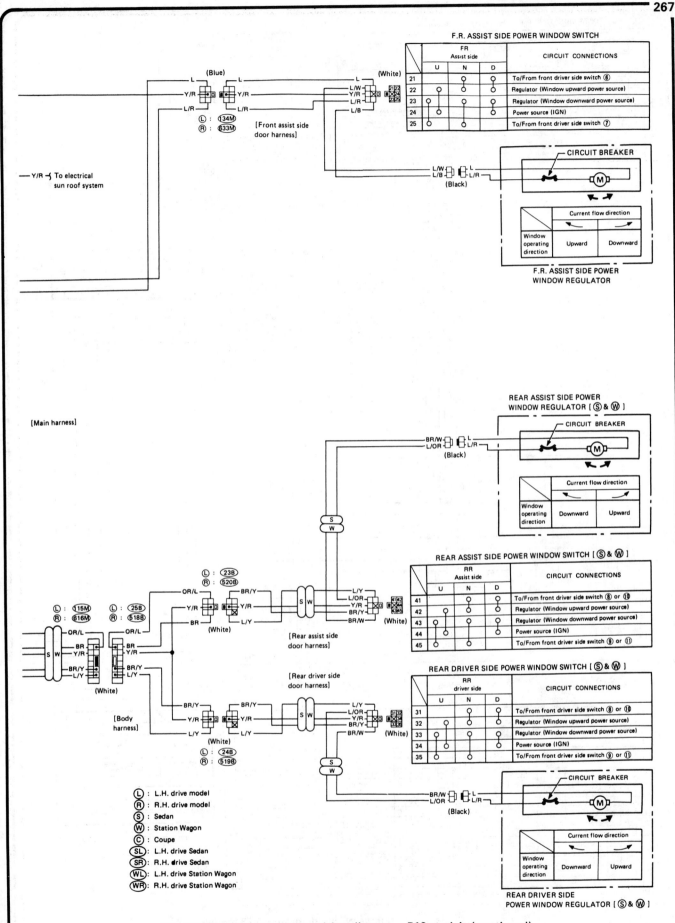

Fig. 12.91 Electric windows wiring diagram – B12 models (continued)

POWER WINDOW AMP.-Front driver side door (Behind trim)

		CIRCUIT CONNECTIONS	
		REMARKS	
51		Power source (IGN.)–Via ignition relay-II	
52		Ground	
53		Ignition switch condition	From ignition switch ON or ST
54	Input signal	For detecting AUTO signal	To front driver side power window switch– ①
55		For detecting UP signal	To front driver side power window switch– ③
56		For detecting DOWN signal	To front driver side power window switch– ②
57	Output signal	Window upward power source	To/From front driver side power window regulator
58		Window downward power source	To/From front driver side power window regulator

54 55 56 58
52 51 55 57

(White)

IGNITION SWITCH ON or ST — B/W

BATTERY via Fusible Link-Brown — Y

(115M)

CIRCUIT BREAKER (Beside steering column bracket)

Y
Y/B (White)

(116M)

IGNITION RELAY-II (Beside steering column bracket)

Y/B
B/W
B
Y/R

Y/R B G/R Y/R G/B G (White)
       Y/R G/Y G/W

[Front driver side door harness]

(109M)
L/R
B
Y/R
L
(Blue)

(Assist side dash side panel) (114M)

B (Steering column bracket)

(145M)

S F
BR
L/Y
OR/L
BR/Y

(108M) (White)

S F
BR
L/Y
OR/L
BR/Y

T L   T R   F L   F R
       S L   S R

L/R L Y/R G G/Y   G/Y B L/R Y/R L G/R
(White) L BR/Y G/R OR/L BR B Y/R G/Y
                                    G/Y B BR/Y L/R OR/L BR L Y/R G/R
(White)   (White)

L/R L G/B G/W (Black)

| 7 6 | | 5 4 | T L | | 2 | 6 | T R | | 7 6 | | 5 4 | S L |
| | 1 | | | 4 3 1 5 | | | 1 10 19 8 3 | F L |

SR FR
4 3 1 5
11 10 7 9 8 6

CIRCUIT BREAKER

(M)

FRONT DRIVER SIDE POWER WINDOW REGULATOR

	FR driver side					Power window lock SW		FR assist side			(S) & (F) RR L.H. side			(S) & (F) RR R.H. side			CIRCUIT CONNECTIONS
	[(S) & (D)] One-touch (Auto)		Manual			ON	OFF	U	N	D	U	N	D	U	N	D	
	U	N	D	U	N	D												
1	O		O														From power window AMP ⑤④
2			O		O												From power window AMP ⑤⑥
3	O			O		O											From power window AMP ⑤⑤
4		O		O		O	O										Ground
✕																	—
5								O	O	O	O	O	O	O	O	O	Power source for assist & rear (IGN)
6								O	O	O							To/From front assist side switch ㉑
7								O		O							To/From front assist side switch ㉕
8											O	O	O				To/From rear switch ㉛
9											O		O				To/From rear switch ㉟
10														O	O	O	To/From rear switch ㊶
11														O		O	To/From rear switch ㊺

(S) & (F)

FRONT DRIVER SIDE POWER WINDOW SWITCH

Window operating direction	Current flow direction	
	←	→
	Upward	Downward

Fig. 12.92 Electric windows wiring diagram – N13 models

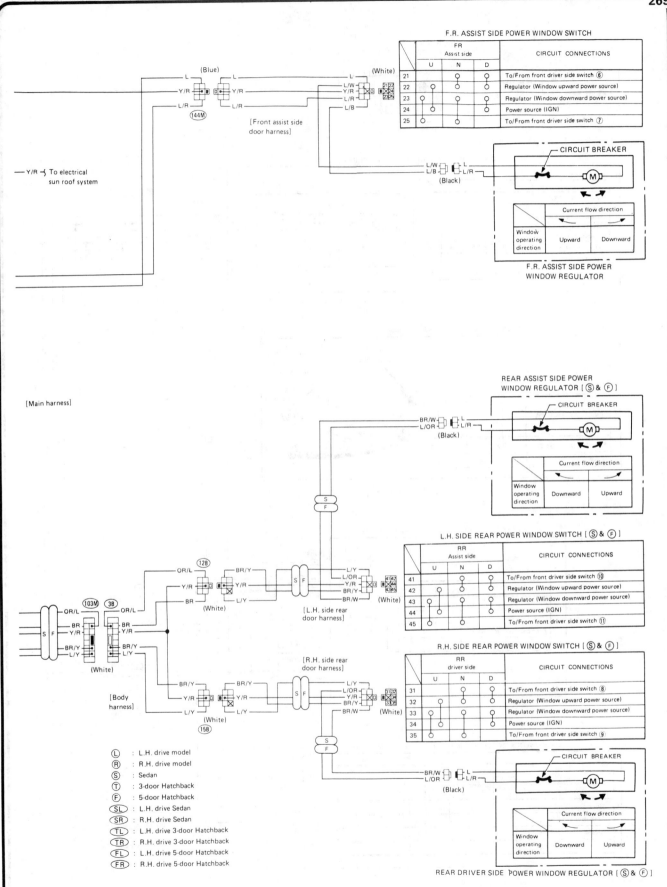

Fig. 12.92 Electric windows wiring diagram – N13 models (continued)

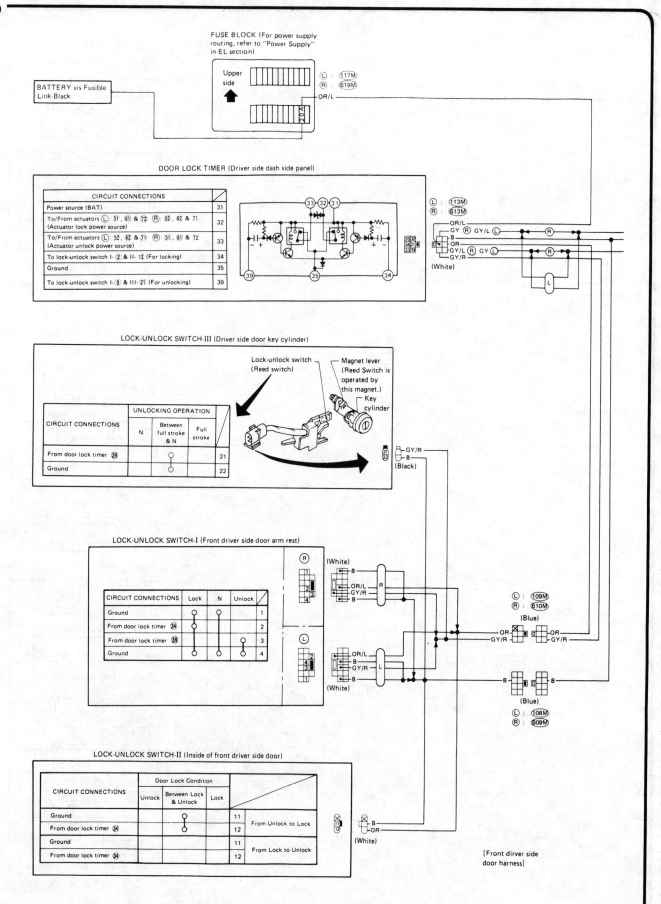

Fig. 12.93 Central locking wiring diagram – B12 models

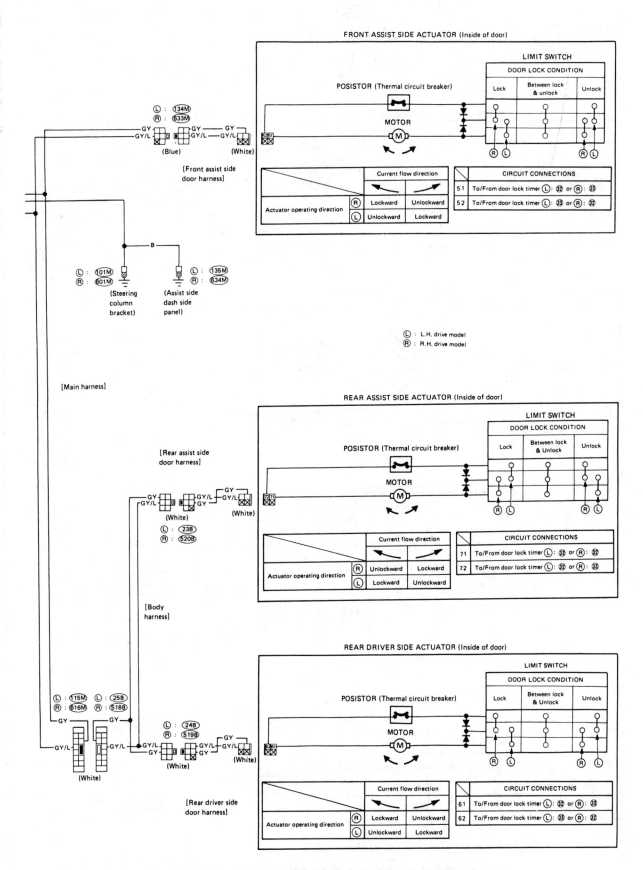

Fig. 12.93 Central locking wiring diagram – B12 models (continued)

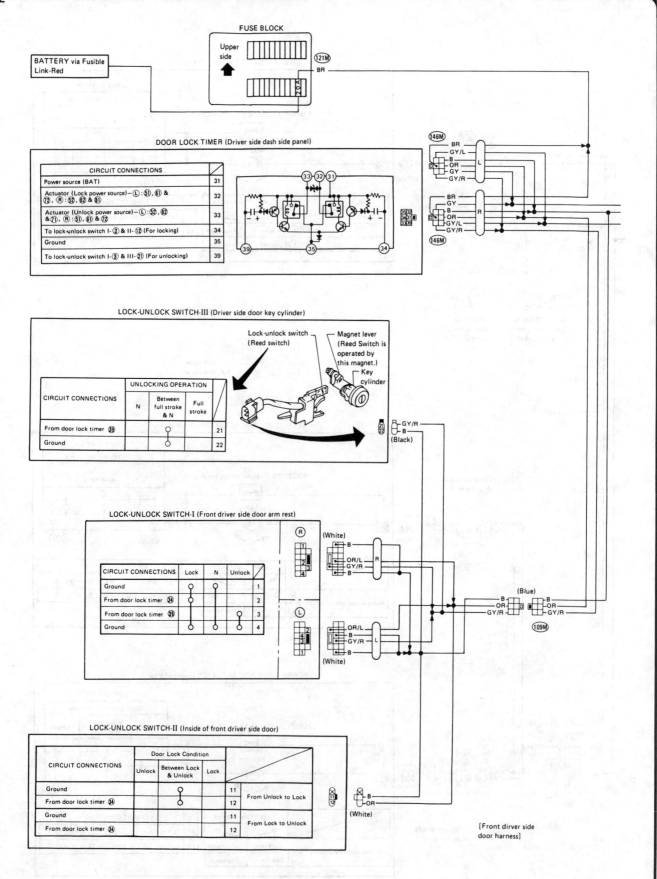

Fig. 12.94 Central locking wiring diagram – N13 models

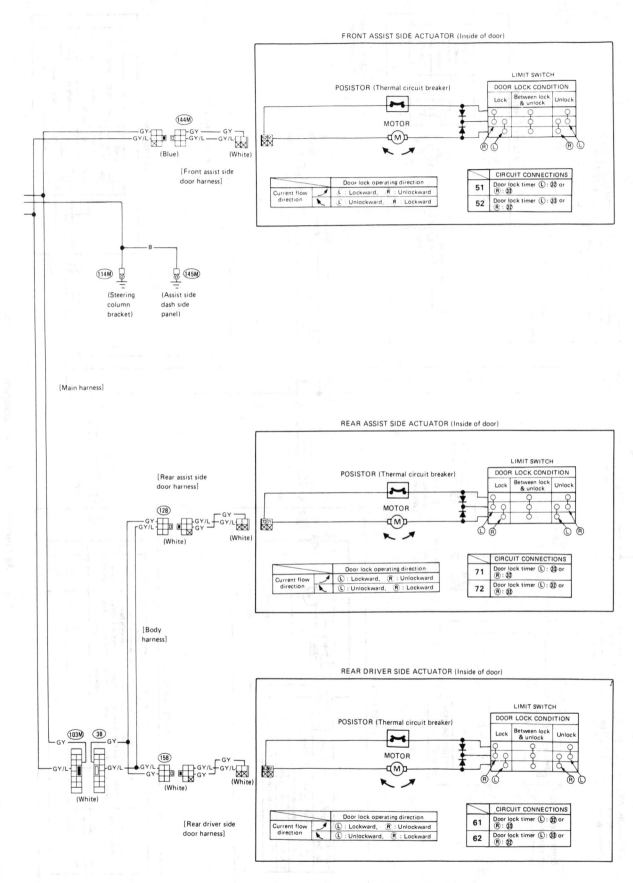

Fig. 12.94 Central locking wiring diagram – N13 models (continued)

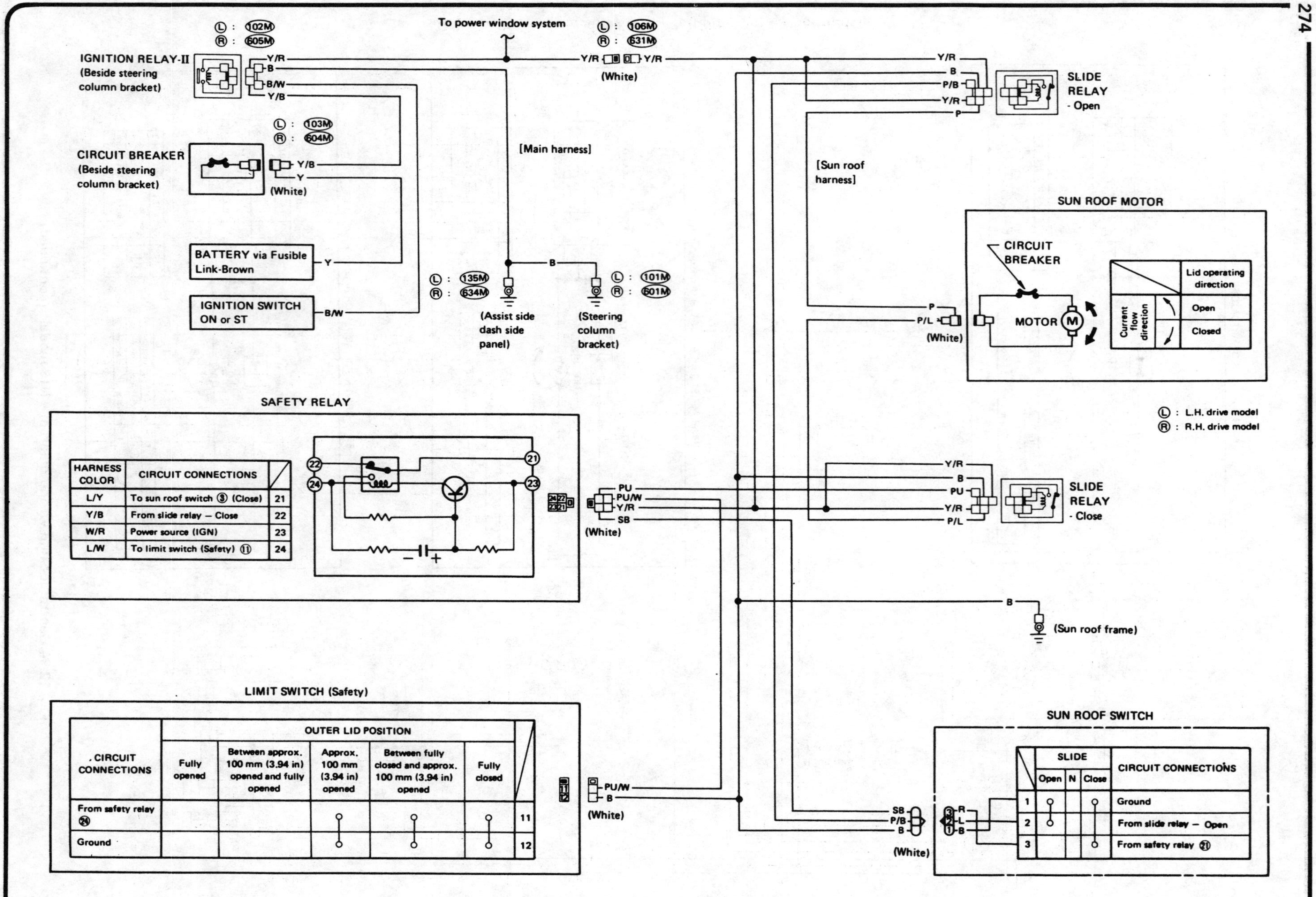

SLIDE RELAY - Open

SUN ROOF MOTOR

Ⓛ : L.H. drive model
Ⓡ : R.H. drive model

		Lid operating direction
	Open	
	Closed	

Current flow direction

CIRCUIT BREAKER

MOTOR

SLIDE RELAY - Close

(Sun roof frame)

SUN ROOF SWITCH

SLIDE		CIRCUIT CONNECTIONS
Open	N	Close	
			Ground	1
			From slide relay – Open Ⓐ	2
			From safety relay Ⓐ	3

Y/R

B
P/B

(White)

S8
P/B
B

(White)

[Sun roof harness]

Y/R
B
P/U
Y/R
P/L

P
P/L
(White)

Y/R
B

Ⓛ : Ⓐ⁰⁶ᴹ
Ⓡ : Ⓐ³¹ᴹ Y/R

Y/R ⟶ Y/R
(White)

Ⓛ : Ⓐ⁰¹ᴹ
Ⓡ : Ⓐ⁰¹ᴹ

(Steering column bracket)

B

To power window system

[Main harness]

PU
PU/W
Y/R
S8
(White)

B

(Assist side dash side panel)

Ⓛ : Ⓐ³⁵ᴹ
Ⓡ : Ⓐ³⁴ᴹ

PU/W
B
(White)

IGNITION RELAY-II
(Beside steering column bracket)

Ⓛ : Ⓐ⁰²ᴹ
Ⓡ : Ⓐ⁰⁵ᴹ

Y/R
B
B/W
Y/B

CIRCUIT BREAKER
(Beside steering column bracket)

Ⓛ : Ⓐ⁰³ᴹ
Ⓡ : Ⓐ⁰⁴ᴹ

Y/B
Y
(White)

BATTERY via Fusible Link-Brown   Y

IGNITION SWITCH ON or ST   B/W

SAFETY RELAY

HARNESS COLOR	CIRCUIT CONNECTIONS	
L/Y	To sun roof switch ③ (Close)	21
Y/B	From slide relay – Close	22
W/R	Power source (IGN)	23
L/W	To limit switch (Safety) Ⓐ	24

LIMIT SWITCH (Safety)

CIRCUIT CONNECTIONS	OUTER LID POSITION				
	Fully opened	Between approx. 100 mm (3.94 in) opened and fully opened	Approx. 100 mm (3.94 in) opened	Between fully closed and approx. 100 mm (3.94 in) opened	Fully closed
From safety relay Ⓐ					11
Ground					12

Fig. 12.95 Electric sunroof wiring diagram – B12 models

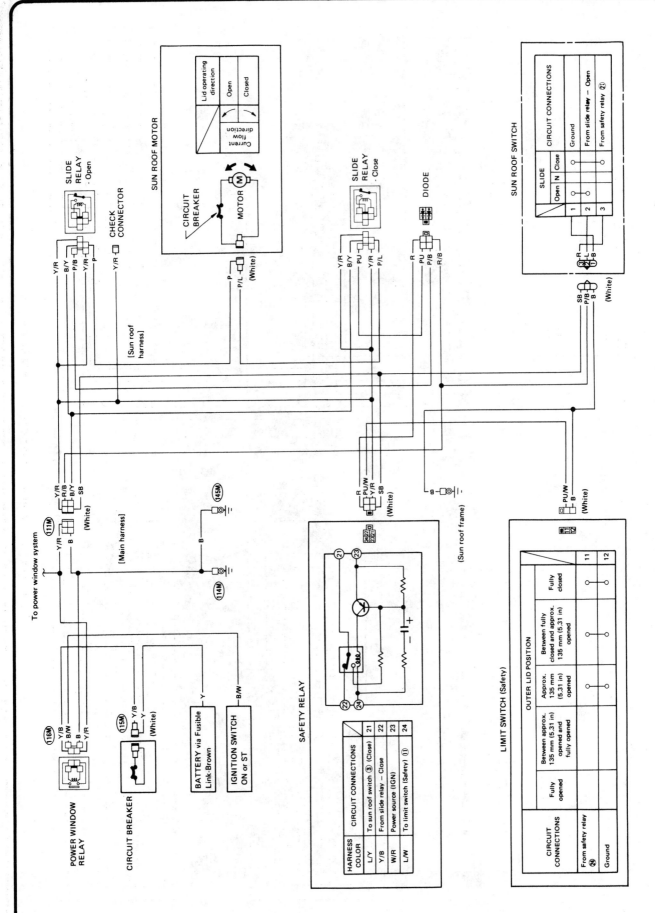

Fig. 12.96 Electric sunroof wiring diagram – N13 models

Nissan Sunny ZX Coupe

Chapter 13 Supplement:
Revisions and information on later models

Contents

Introduction 1
Specifications 2
Routine maintenance 3
Engine (1.4 and 1.6 twelve-valve) 4
    General description
    Valve clearances (GA14S engine) – checking and adjustment
    Timing chain – removal and refitting
    Cylinder head – removal and refitting
    Cylinder head – dismantling, overhaul and reassembly
    Sump – removal and refitting
    Oil pump – removal, checking and refitting
    Cylinder block – dismantling and reassembly
    Pistons – disconnecting from connecting rods
    Engine and manual transmission – removal and refitting
    Engine and automatic transmission – removal and refitting
Engine (1.6 and 1.8 sixteen-valve) 5
    General description
    Timing belt – removal and refitting
    Cylinder head – removal and refitting
    Cylinder head – dismantling, overhaul and reassembly
    Sump – removal and refitting
    Oil pump – removal, checking and refitting
    Cylinder block – dismantling and reassembly
    Pistons – disconnecting from connecting rods
    Engine and manual transmission – removal and refitting
Cooling system (twelve and sixteen-valve engines) 6
    General description
    Thermostat – removal, testing and refitting
    Radiator – removal, repair and refitting
    Water pump (twelve-valve engine) – removal and refitting
    Water pump (sixteen-valve engine) – removal and refitting
    Drivebelts – removal, refitting and adjustment
    Cooling fan thermoswitch – removal, testing and refitting
Fuel, exhaust and emission control systems (twelve-valve
engines) 7
    General description
    Fuel pump – removal and refitting
    Carburettor – description
    Carburettor – checks and adjustments
    Carburettor – idle speed and mixture adjustment
    Manifolds and exhaust systems – general
Fuel, exhaust and emission control systems (sixteen-valve
engines) 8
    General description and precautions
    Air cleaner element and body – removal and refitting
    Fuel pump – removal and refitting
    Idle speed and mixture – adjustment
    Releasing the ECCS fuel pressure
    Checking the fuel pressure (using a pressure gauge)
    Fuel injectors – removal and refitting
    Fuel filter – removal and refitting
    Self-diagnosis system – description and operation
    ECCS ECU voltage supply – checking
    Injectors – checking

    Manifolds and exhaust system – general
    Inlet manifold – removal and refitting
Ignition system (twelve and sixteen-valve engines) 9
    General description
    Thermal vacuum valve (twelve-valve engines) – testing
    Distributor (twelve-valve engine) – overhaul
    Ignition timing
    Spark plugs (sixteen-valve engines) – removal and refitting
Clutch (twelve and sixteen-valve engines) 10
    General description
    Clutch pedal (CA18DE engine) – adjustment
    Clutch hydraulic system (CA18DE engine) – bleeding
    Clutch slave cylinder (CA18DE engine) – removal, overhaul
    and refitting
    Clutch master cylinder (CA18DE engine) – removal, overhaul
    and refitting
    Clutch pedal (CA18DE engine) – removal and refitting
    Clutch release bearing and fork (CA18DE engine) – removal
    and refitting
Manual transmission (twelve and sixteen-valve engines) ... 11
    General description
    Transmission (RS5F50A and RS5F50V) – dismantling
    Transmission components (RS5F50A and RS5F50V) –
    inspection
    Transmission (RS5F50A and RS5F50V) – reassembly
Driveshafts 12
    General description
    Driveshaft (sixteen-valve engine models) – removal and
    refitting
    Driveshaft joints and bellows (sixteen-valve engine models) –
    removal, inspection and refitting
Braking system (sixteen-valve engine models) 13
    General description
    Front disc pads – inspection and renewal
    Rear disc pads – inspection and renewal
    Rear brake caliper – removal, overhaul and refitting
Suspension and steering (sixteen-valve engines) 14
    General description
    Rear hub bearings – renewal
    Rear suspension knuckle – removal and refitting
    Power steering system – modifications
Bodywork and fittings 15
    General description
    Bonnet lock (March 1989-on) – removal, refitting and
    adjustment
    Door trim panel (March 1989-on) – removal and refitting
    Facia panel (March 1989-on) – description
    Door mirror glass –renewal
Electrical system 16
    General description
    Alternators (later models) – description
    Starter motor (later models) – description
    Starter motor (later models) – overhaul
    Starter motor (sixteen-valve engine) – removal and refitting

1   Introduction

This Supplement contains information which has become available since the manual was first written. This includes the introduction of the 1.4 and 1.6 twelve-valve engines, and the 1.6 and 1.8 sixteen-valve engines. The twelve-valve engines are fitted with Hitachi carburettors and the sixteen-valve engines are fitted with the ECCS fuel injection system. The facelift introduced in March 1989 was mainly cosmetic and therefore does not affect the procedures given in the preceding Chapters of this manual.

In order to use the Supplement to the best advantage it is suggested that it is referred to before the main Chapters of the manual. This will ensure that any relevant information can be noted and incorporated within the procedures given in Chapters 1 to 12. Time and cost will therefore be saved and the particular job will be completed correctly.

2   Specifications

The Specifications below are revisions of, or supplementary to, those at the beginning of the preceding Chapters

Engine (1.4 and 1.6 twelve-valve)

General

Type	Four-cylinder, in-line, single over-head camshaft, mounted transversely
Designation and capacity:	
GA14S	1392 cc (84.94 cu in)
GA16S	1597 cc (97.45 cu in)
Bore	
GA14S	73.6 mm (2.899 in)
GA16S	76.0 mm (2.992 in)
Stroke:	
GA14S	81.8 mm (3.220 in)
GA16S	88.0 mm (3.465 in)
Compression ratio:	
GA14S	9.4 to 1
GA16S	9.8 to 1
Compression pressure – bar (lbf/in^2) at 350 rpm:	
Normal	13.04 (189)
Minimum	11.08 (161)
Maximum difference between cylinders	0.98 (14)
Firing order	1-3-4-2 (No 1 at timing end)

Cylinder block

Material	Cast iron
Maximum bore out-of-round	0.015 mm (0.0006 in)
Maximum taper of bore	0.010 mm (0.0004 in)

Crankshaft

Number of main bearings	5
Main journal diameter:	
Grade 0	49.956 to 49.964 mm (1.9682 in to 1.9685 in)
Grade 1	49.948 to 49.956 mm (1.9679 in to 1.9682 in)
Grade 2	49.940 to 49.948 mm (1.9676 in to 1.9679 in)
Crankpin diameter	30.056 to 39.974 mm (1.1842 in to 1.5749 in)
Maximum journal and crankpin out-of round	0.005 mm (0.000197 in)
Maximum journal and crankpin taper	0.002 mm (0.0001 in)
Endfloat	
Standard	0.060 to 0.180 mm (0.0024 to 0.0071 in)
Wear limit	0.30 mm (0.012 in)
Main bearing running clearance:	
Standard	0.020 to 0.042 mm (0.0008 to 0.0017 in)
Wear limit	0.1 mm (0.004 in)
Main bearing undersizes	0.25 mm (0.0098 in) and 0.50 mm (0.0197 in)

Connecting rods

Side play at big-ends:	
Standard	0.20 to 0.47 mm (0.0079 to 0.0185 in)
Wear limit	0.52 mm (0.0205 in)
Big-end bearing running clearance:	
Standard	0.016 to 0.041 mm
Wear limit	0.1 mm
Big-end bearing undersizes	0.08, 0.12, and 0.25 mm

Gudgeon pin

Interference fit in piston	0.004 to 0 mm (0.0002 to 0 in)
Pin-to-small end clearance	0.005 to 0.017 mm (0.0002 to 0.0007 in)

Piston rings
Side clearance in piston groove:
    Top .... 0.040 to 0.080 mm (0.0016 to 0.0031 in)
    Second .... 0.030 to 0.070 mm (0.0012 to 0.0028 in)
    Wear limit .... 0.2 mm (0.008 in)
End gap:
    Top .... 0.20 to 0.35 mm (0.0079 to 0.0138 in)
    Second .... 0.37 to 0.52 mm (0.0146 to 0.0205 in)
    Oil .... 0.20 to 0.60 mm (0.0079 to 0.0236 in)
    Wear limit .... 1.0 mm (0.039 in)

Pistons (GA14S engine)
Standard diameter (at skirt):
    Grade 1 .... 73.575 to 73.585 mm (2.0966 to 2.8970 in)
    Grade 2 .... 73.585 to 73.595 mm (2.8970 to 2.8974 in)
    Grade 3 .... 73.595 to 73.605 mm (2.8974 to 2.8978 in)
Oversizes .... 0.5 and 1.0 mm (0.020 and 0.039 in)
Piston to bore clearance .... 0.015 to 0.035 mm (0.0006 to 0.0014 in)

Pistons (GA16S engine)
Standard diameter (at skirt):
    Grade 1 .... 75.975 to 75.985 mm (2.9911 to 2.9915 in)
    Grade 2 .... 75.985 to 75.995 mm (2.9915 to 2.9919 in)
    Grade 3 .... 75.995 to 76.005 mm (2.9919 to 2.9923 in)
Oversizes .... 0.5 and 1.0 mm (0.020 and 0.039 in)
Piston to bore clearance .... 0.015 to 0.035 mm (0.0006 to 0.0014 in)

Camshaft
Cam lobe wear limit .... 0.20 mm (0.0079 in)
Running clearance:
    Standard .... 0.045 to 0.090 mm (0.0018 to 0.0035 in)
    Wear limit .... 0.15 mm (0.0059 in)
Maximum run-out .... 0.1 mm (0.004 in)
Maximum end-play .... 0.20 mm (0.0079 in)

Cylinder head
Material .... Aluminium
Surface out-of-true (limit) .... 0.10 mm (0.004 in)
Height .... 120.60 to 120.80 mm (4.7480 to 4.7559 in)
Resurfacing limit (including block) .... 0.2 mm (0.008 in)

Valves
Seat angle .... 45° 15′ to 45° 45′
Valve clearances (GA14S only):
    Inlet:
        Hot .... 0.20 to 0.30 mm (0.008 to 0.012 in)
        Cold .... 0.15 (0.006 in)
    Exhaust:
        Hot .... 0.25 to 0.35 mm (0.010 to 0.014 in)
        Cold .... 0.20 mm (0.008 in)
Maximum valve deflection in guide .... 0.2 mm (0.008 in)
Valve spring free length:
    Inlet .... 52.6 mm (2.071 in)
    Exhaust:
        GA14S .... 52.3 mm (2.059 in)
        GA16S .... 54.7 mm (2.154 in)

Valve guides
Interference fit of guide in head .... 0.027 to 0.049 mm (0.0011 to 0.0019 in)
Stem-to-guide clearance:
    Inlet .... 0.020 to 0.050 mm (0.0008 to 0.0020 in)
    Exhaust .... 0.030 to 0.057 mm (0.0012 to 0.0022 in)

Valve timing

	GA14S	GA16S
Inlet opens	2° BTDC	10° BTDC
Inlet closes	40° ABDC	46° ABDC
Exhaust opens	50° BBDC	55° BBDC
Exhaust closes	6° ATDC	15° ATDC

Lubrication
Oil capacity:
    With filter change .... 3.2 litres (5.6 pints)
    Without filter change .... 2.8 litres (4.93 pints)
Oil filter .... Champion C109

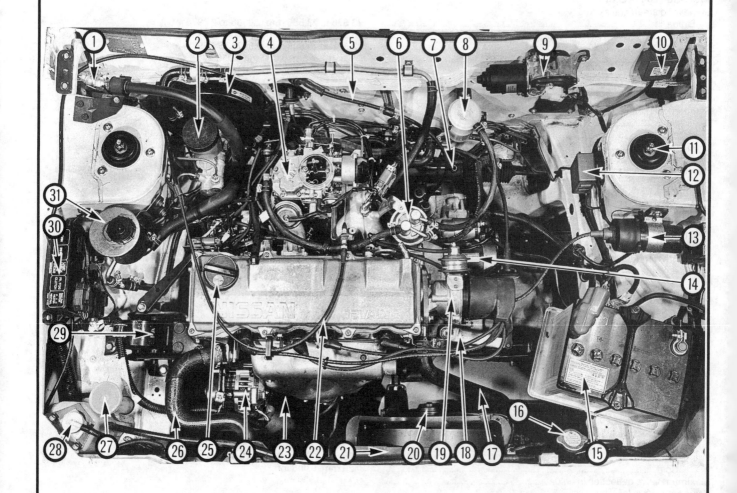

Engine compartment (GA16S) – air cleaner removed

1	Power steering pressure switch	9	Windscreen wiper motor
2	Brake fluid reservoir	10	Transfer control relay
3	Brake vacuum servo unit	11	Front suspension strut top mounting
4	Carburettor	12	Fusible link holder
5	Speedometer cable	13	Ignition coil
6	Fuel pump	14	Starter motor
7	Steering gear	15	Battery
8	Fuel filter	16	Radiator filler cap

17	Bottom hose	26	Top hose
18	Clutch release lever	27	Washer fluid reservoir
19	Distributor	28	Radiator expansion tank
20	Electric cooling fan motor	29	Engine mounting
21	Radiator	30	Relay cover
22	Accelerator cable	31	Power steering fluid reservoir
23	Engine oil level dipstick		
24	Alternator		
25	Engine oil filler cap		

Lubrication (continued)

Oil pressure (hot):
- Idle speed.. 0.49 to 1.86 bar (7 to 27 lbf/in²)
- 3000 rpm.. 3.92 to 4.90 bar (57 to 71 lbf/in²)

Oil pump clearances:
- Body to outer gear... 0.114 to 0.200 mm (0.0045 to 0.0079 in)
- Inner gear to crescent... 0.217 to 0.327 mm (0.0085 to 0.0129 in)
- Outer gear to crescent.. 0.21 to 0.32 mm (0.0083 to 0.0126 in)
- Body to inner gear... 0.05 to 0.09 mm (0.0020 to 0.0035 in)
- Body to outer gear... 0.05 to 0.11 mm (0.0020 to 0.0043 in)
- Inner gear to brazed housing.. 0.045 to 0.091 mm (0.0010 to 0.0036 in)

Torque wrench settings

	Nm	lbf ft
Sump drain plug...	29 to 39	22 to 29
Inlet manifold...	16 to 21	12 to 15
Crankshaft pulley bolt	132 to 152	98 to 112
Exhaust manifold...	16 to 21	12 to 15
Timing chain guide..	13 to 19	9 to 14
Front cover...	16 to 21	12 to 15
Camshaft sprocket bolt...	98 to 127	72 to 94
Timing chain tensioner..	13 to 19	9 to 14
Valve cover...	2 to 4	1.4 to 2.9
Rocker shaft...	37 to 41	27 to 30
Camshaft thrust plate..	6.3 to 8.3	4.6 to 6.1
Cylinder head bolts (see text):		
Stage 1...	29	22
Stage 2...	64	47
Stage 3...	Loosen all bolts completely	Loosen all bolts completely
Stage 4...	29	22
Stage 5:		
Method 1	Angle tighten bolt 1 by 80° to 85° and bolts 2 to 10 by 60° to 65°	
Method 2	59 to 69	43 to 51
Stage 6 (bolts 11 to 15 only).....................	6.3 to 8.3	4.6 to 6.1
Engine mounting bolts	39 to 54	29 to 40
Flywheel bolts	83 to 93	61 to 69
Driveplate bolts (automatic transmission)	93 to 103	69 to 76
Rear oil seal housing	7 to 8	5 to 6
Cylinder block drain plug	34 to 44	25 to 33
Main bearing cap bolts	46 to 52	34 to 38
Sump	6.3 to 8.3	4.6 to 6.1
Big-end nuts:		
Stage 1...	14 to 16	10 to 12
Stage 2:		
Method 1	Angle tighten 35° to 40°	Angle tighten 35° to 40°
Method 2	23 to 28	17 to 21
Oil pump cover:		
Screw	3 to 5	2.2 to 3.6
Bolt	5 to 7	3.6 to 5.1
Oil pump release valve plug........................	20 to 29	14 to 22

Engine (1.6 and 1.8 sixteen-valve)

General

Type.. Four-cylinder, in-line, double over-head camshaft, mounted transversely

Designation and capacity:
- CA16DE.. 1598 cc (97.51 cu in)
- CA18DE.. 1809 cc (110.39 cu in)

Bore:
- CA16DE.. 78.0 mm (3.071 in)
- CA18DE.. 83.0 mm (3.268 in)

Stroke:
- CA16DE.. 83.6 mm (3.291 in)
- CA18DE.. 83.6 mm (3.291 in)

Compression ratio:
- CA16DE.. 10.0 to 1
- CA18DE.. 10.5 to 1

Compression pressure – bar (lbf/in²) at 350 rpm:
CA16DE:
- Normal.. 13.73 (199)
- Minimum... 11.77 (171)
CA18DE:
- Normal.. 14.71 (213)
- Minimum... 10.79 (156)
Maximum difference between cylinders 0.98 (14)
Firing order... 1-3-4-2 (No 1 at timing end)

View from beneath the engine (GA16S)

1 Anti-roll bar
2 Gearchange control rod
3 Gearbox support rod
4 Exhaust system
5 Spring tensioned exhaust joint

6 Right-hand driveshaft
7 Splash shield
8 Engine oil drain plug
9 Oil filter
10 Towing eye

11 Front exhaust downpipe
12 Engine crossmember
13 Bottom hose
14 Gearbox
15 Coolant drain plug

16 Gearbox oil drain plug
17 Left-hand driveshaft
18 Track rod

Cylinder block
Material .... Cast iron
Maximum bore out-of-round.. 0.015 mm (0.0006 in)
Maximum taper of bore .... 0.010 mm (0.0004 in)

Crankshaft
Number of main bearings.. 5
Main journal diameter .... 52.951 to 52.975 mm (2.0847 to 2.0856 in)
Crankpin diameter.. 44.954 to 44.974 mm (1.7698 to 1.7706 in)
Maximum journal and crankpin out-of-round .... 0.005 mm (0.002 in)
Maximum journal and crankpin taper .... 0.005 mm (0.0002 in)
Endfloat:
    Standard... 0.05 to 0.18 mm (0.0020 in to 0.0071 in)
    Wear limit... 0.3 mm (0.012 in)
Main bearing running clearance:
    Standard... 0.021 to 0.048 mm (0.0008 to 0.0019 in)
    Wear limit... 0.1 mm (0.004 in)
Main bearing undersize... 0.25 mm (0.0098 in)

Connecting rods
Maximum big-end sideplay .... 0.4 mm (0.016 in)
Big-end bearing running clearance:
    Standard... 0.018 to 0.045 mm (0.0007 to 0.0018 in)
    Wear limit... 0.1 mm (0.004 in)
Big-end bearing undersizes .... 0.08, 0.12, and 0.25 mm (0.0031, 0.0047, and 0.0098 in)

Gudgeon pin
Interference fit in piston.. 0.004 to 0 mm (0.0002 to 0 in)
Pin-to-small end clearance... 0.005 to 0.017 mm (0.0002 to 0.0007 in)

Piston rings
Side clearance in piston groove:
  Top:
    Standard... 0.040 to 0.073 mm (0.0016 to 0.0029 in)
    Wear limit... 0.1 mm (0.004 in)
  Second:
    Standard... 0.030 to 0.063 mm (0.0012 to 0.0025 in)
    Wear limit... 0.1 mm (0.004 in)
  Oil (CA16DE):
    Standard... 0.025 to 0.085 mm (0.0010 to 0.0033 in)
    Wear limit... 0.1 mm (0.004 in)
  Oil (CA18DE):
    Standard... 0.015 to 0.185 mm (0.0006 to 0.0073 in)
    Wear limit... 0.2 mm (0.008 in)
End gap:
  Top (CA16DE):
    Standard... 0.22 to 0.39 mm (0.0087 to 0.0154 in)
    Wear limit... 1.0 mm (0.039 in)
  Top (CA18DE):
    Standard... 0.22 to 0.48 mm (0.0087 to 0.0189 in)
    Wear limit... 1.0 mm (0.039 in)
  Second (CA16DE):
    Standard... 0.19 to 0.45 mm (0.0075 to 0.0177 in)
    Wear limit... 1.0 mm (0.039 in)
  Second (CA18DE):
    Standard... 0.38 to 0.64 mm (0.0150 to 0.0252 in)
    Wear limit... 1.0 mm (0.039 in)
  Oil (rail):
    Standard... 0.20 to 0.76 mm (0.0079 to 0.0299 in)
    Wear limit... 1.0 mm (0.039 in)

Pistons (CA16DE engine)
Standard diameter (at skirt):
    Grade 1 .... 77.925 to 77.935 mm (3.0679 to 3.0683 in)
    Grade 2 .... 77.935 to 77.945 mm (3.0683 to 3.0687 in)
    Grade 3 .... 77.945 to 77.955 mm (3.0687 to 3.0691 in)
    Grade 4 .... 77.955 to 77.965 mm (3.0691 to 3.0695 in)
    Grade 5 .... 77.965 to 77.975 mm (3.0695 to 3.0699 in)
Oversizes.. 0.5 and 1.0 mm (0.020 and 0.039 in)
Piston to bore clearance .... 0.015 to 0.035 mm (0.0006 to 0.0014 in)

Pistons (CA18DE engine)
Standard diameter (at skirt):
    Grade 1 .... 82.975 to 82.985 mm (3.2667 to 3.2671 in)

Engine compartment (CA18DE engine) – air cleaner removed

1	Power steering hose	9	Windscreen wiper motor	16	Radiator filler cap	23	Alternator
2	Brake fluid reservoir	10	Dim-dip unit	17	Gearbox	24	Engine oil filler cap
3	Clutch fluid reservoir	11	Wiper control unit	18	Bottom hose	25	Top hose
4	Inlet manifold	12	Front suspension strut top mounting	19	Electric cooling fan motor	26	Washer fluid reservoir
5	Throttle valve switch			20	Radiator	27	Accelerator cable
6	AAC valve	13	Air flow meter	21	Air inlet duct	28	Relay cover
7	Fuel pressure regulator valve	14	Air cleaner	22	Exhaust manifold hot air shroud	29	Power steering fluid reservoir
8	Fuel filter	15	Battery				

Pistons (CA18DE engine) – continued

Grade 2	82.985 to 82.995 mm (3.2671 to 3.2675 in)
Grade 3	82.995 to 83.005 mm (3.2675 to 3.2679 in)
Grade 4	83.005 to 83.015 mm (3.2679 to 3.2683 in)
Grade 5	83.015 to 83.025 mm (3.2683 to 3.2687 in)
Oversizes	0.5 and 1.0 mm (0.020 and 0.039 in)
Piston to bore clearance	0.015 to 0.035 mm (0.0006 to 0.0014 in)

Camshafts

Cam lobe wear limit	0.20 mm (0.0079 in)
Running clearance:	
Standard	0.045 to 0.090 mm (0.0018 to 0.0035 in)
Wear limit	0.15 mm (0.0059 in)
Maximum run-out	0.05 mm (0.0020 in)
Endplay:	
Standard	0.07 to 0.15 mm (0.0028 to 0.0059 in)
Wear limit	0.2 mm (0.008 in)

Cylinder head

Material	Aluminium
Surface out-of-true:	
Standard	0.03 mm (0.0012 in)
Wear limit	0.1 mm (0.004 in)
Height	125.9 to 126.1 mm (4.957 to 4.965 in)
Resurfacing limit (including block)	0.2 mm (0.008 in)

Valves

Seat angle	45° 30′
Valve deflection (measured at valve head with valve raised 25 mm/1.0 in):	
CA16DE	0.10 mm (0.0039 in) maximum
CA18DE	0.20 mm (0.008 in) maximum
Valve spring free length	43.1 mm (1.697 in)

Valve guides (CA16DE engine)

Interference fit of guide in head:	
Standard:	
Inlet	0.045 to 0.074 mm (0.0018 to 0.0029 in)
Exhaust	0.027 to 0.059 mm (0.0011 to 0.0023 in)
Service	0.027 to 0.049 mm (0.0011 to 0.0019 in)
Stem to guide clearance:	
Inlet:	
Standard	0.020 to 0.053 mm (0.0008 to 0.0021 in)
Wear limit	0.1 mm (0.039 in)
Exhaust:	
Standard	0.040 to 0.073 mm (0.0016 to 0.0029 in)
Wear limit	0.1 mm (0.039 in)

Valve guides (CA18DE engine)

Interference fit of guide in head (all valves)	0.027 to 0.059 mm (0.0011 to 0.0023 in)
Stem to guide clearance:	
Inlet:	
Standard	0.020 to 0.053 mm (0.0008 to 0.0021 in)
Wear limit	0.1 mm (0.039 in)
Exhaust:	
Standard	0.040 to 0.073 mm (0.0016 to 0.0029 in)
Wear limit	0.1 mm (0.039 in)

Valve timing

	CA16DE	CA18DE
Inlet opens	15° BTDC	16° BTDC
Inlet closes	53° ABDC	52° ABDC
Exhaust opens	59° BBDC	50° BBDC
Exhaust closes	9° ATDC	18° ATDC

Lubrication

Oil capacity:	
With filter change	3.8 litres (6.7 pints)
Without filter change	3.4 litres (6.0 pints)
Oil filter	Champion C109
Oil pressure (hot):	
Idle speed	0.78 bar (11.0 lbf/in^2) minimum
2000 rpm	4.61 bar (67.0 lbf/in^2)
6000 rpm	5.88 bar (85.0 lbf/in^2)

View from beneath the engine (CA18DE)

1 Steering gear
2 Gearchange rod
3 Gearbox support rod
4 Exhaust mounting
5 Anti-roll bar
6 Right-hand driveshaft
7 Engine oil drain plug
8 Exhaust front down pipe
9 Towing eye
10 Engine crossmember
11 Electric cooling fan motor
12 Bottom hose
13 Gearbox
14 Front suspension transverse link arm

Lubrication (continued)

Oil pump clearances:

Body to outer gear	0.11 to 0.20 mm (0.0043 to 0.0079 in)
Inner gear to crescent	0.15 to 0.26 mm (0.0059 to 0.0102 in)
Outer gear to crescent	0.21 to 0.32 mm (0.0083 to 0.0126 in)
Body to inner gear	0.05 to 0.09 mm (0.0020 to 0.0035 in)
Body to outer gear	0.05 to 0.11 mm (0.0020 to 0.0043 in)
Regular valve opening pressure	4.71 to 5.10 bar (68 to 74 lbf/in²) at 2000 rpm

Torque wrench settings

	Nm	lbf ft
Timing belt tensioner nut	22 to 29	16 to 22
Timing belt idler pulley bolt	31 to 42	23 to 31
Crank angle sensor	7 to 8	5.1 to 5.8
Crank pulley bolt	142 to 152	105 to 112
Inlet manifold	20 to 25	14 to 19
Throttle housing	18 to 22	13 to 16
Air regulator valve	5 to 6	3.6 to 4.3
Exhaust manifold	37 to 48	27 to 35
Exhaust downpipe	42 to 48	31 to 35
Cylinder head bolts:		
Stage 1	29	22
Stage 2	103	76
Stage 3	Loosen all bolts completely	Loosen all bolts completely
Stage 4	29	22
State 5:		
Method 1	Angle tighten all bolts by 85° to 90°	
Method 2	103	76
Camshaft sprocket bolt	14 to 19	10 to 14
Camshaft bearing cap bolts	10 to 12	7 to 9
Main bearing cap bolts	44 to 54	33 to 40
Big-end nuts:		
Stage 1	14 to 16	10 to 12
Stage 2:		
Method 1	Angle tighten 60° to 65°	Angle tighten 60° to 65°
Method 2	41	44
Cylinder block drain plug	54 to 74	40 to 54
Sump	7 to 8	5.1 to 5.8
Sump drain plug	29 to 39	22 to 29
Flywheel bolts	83 to 93	61 to 69
Oil pump	11 to 14	8 to 10
Oil pump cover	4 to 5	2.9 to 3.6
Oil pressure regulator cap	39 to 69	29 to 51
Oil pressure switch	10 to 16	7 to 12
Engine mounting bolts	39 to 54	29 to 40
Oil separator	4 to 5	2.9 to 3.6
Rear timing cover	7 to 8	5.1 to 5.8
Crankshaft rear oil seal retainer	7 to 10	5.1 to 7.2
Oil pick-up tube:		
To block	7 to 8	5.1 to 5.8
To pump	11 to 14	8 to 10

Cooling system

General

System test pressure (twelve-valve engine only)	0.98 bar (14 lbf/in²) maximum
Thermostat (twelve-valve engine):	
Opening temperature	76.5°C (170°F)
Maximum valve lift	8 mm (0.31 in) at 90°C (194°F)
Thermoswitch operating temperature:	
Twelve-valve engine	82 to 88°C (180 to 190°F)
Sixteen-valve engine	85°C (185°F)
Cooling system capacity (later models):	
With aluminium radiator	4.3 litres (7.6 pints)
With copper radiator	4.9 litres (8.6 pints)
Sixteen-valve engines	5.2 litres (9.2 pints)

Torque wrench settings

	Nm	lbf ft
Twelve-valve engine:		
Radiator drain plug	34 to 44	25 to 33
Water pump	5 to 7	4 to 5
Water pump pulley	3 to 5	2 to 3
Thermostat housing to water pump	5 to 7	4 to 5
Thermostat cover	5 to 7	4 to 5
Cylinder head water outlet	8 to 10	6 to 7
Sixteen-valve engine:		
Cylinder block drain plug	54 to 74	40 to 54
Water pump	16 to 20	12 to 14

Torque wrench settings – continued

	Nm	lbf ft
Thermostat cover	18 to 22	13 to 16
Thermoswitch	9 to 10	7 to 8

Fuel, exhaust and emission control systems
General
System type:
E16S engine with automatic transmission	Electric fuel pump, downdraught carburettor
GA14S, GA16S	Mechanical fuel pump, downdraught carburettor
CA16DE, CA18DE	Nissan ECCS fuel injection system

Air cleaner element:
GA14S, GA16S	Champion W108

Fuel tank capacity:
Hatchback and saloon	50 litres (11 gals)
Estate and Coupe	52 litres (11.4 gals)

Fuel octane rating (minimum):
GA16S and CA18DE	Leaded or unleaded 95 octane
GA14S	Leaded or unleaded 91 octane
CA16DE	97 octane

E16S with automatic transmission
Electric fuel pump pressure	0.177 to 0.235 bar (2.6 to 3.4 lbf/in^2)
Electric fuel pump capacity	500 m/litres (17.6 fl oz) per 20 seconds

GA14S, GA16S
Fuel pump pressure	0.206 to 0.343 bar (3.0 to 5.0 lbf/in^2)

Carburettor

	GA14S	GA16S
Primary bore	28 mm	30 mm
Secondary bore	32 mm	34 mm
Primary venturi	22 mm	22 mm
Secondary venturi	30 mm	30 mm
Primary jet	96	99
Secondary main jet	155	155
Primary main air bleed	70	70
Secondary main air bleed	60	60
Primary slow jet	40	40
Secondary slow jet	70	70
Primary slow air bleed	80	80
Secondary slow air bleed (fixed)	80	80
Power jet	45	45
Fast idle speed at second cam step:		
Manual transmission	2700 ± 200 rpm	2700 ± 200 rpm
Automatic transmission	3400 ± 200 rpm	3100 ± 200 rpm
Fast idle clearance 'A':		
Manual transmission	0.75 ± 0.07 mm (0.030 ± 0.003 in)	0.71 ± 0.07 mm (0.028 ± 0.003 in)
Automatic transmission	0.93 ± 0.07 mm (0.037 ± 0.003 in)	0.89 ± 0.07 mm (0.035 ± 0.003 in)
Vacuum clearance R1	1.37 ± 0.14 mm (0.054 ± 0.006 in)	1.37 ± 0.14 mm (0.054 ± 0.006 in)
Vacuum clearance R2	2.18 ± 0.32 mm (0.086 ± 0.013 in)	2.18 ± 0.32 mm (0.086 ± 0.013 in)
Dashpot touchspeed	2800 ± 200 rpm	2800 ± 200 rpm
Idle speed:		
Manual transmission	800 ± 50 rpm	850 ± 50 rpm
Automatic transmission	850 ± 50 rpm	900 ± 50 rpm
Idle CO %	1.5 ± 0.5	1.5 ± 0.5
Float height:		
Dimension H1	8.5 to 9.5 mm (0.335 to 0.374 in)	8.5 to 9.5 mm (0.335 to 0.374 in)
Dimension H2	46.5 to 47.5 mm (1.831 to 1.870 in)	46.5 to 47.5 mm (1.831 to 1.870 in)

ECCS fuel injection system
Idle speed	800 ± 50 rpm
CO % at idle	2.0 % maximum
Thermistor resistance:	
At 20°C (68°F)	2.5 Ω
At 80°C (176°F)	0.33 Ω
Throttle switch:	
Engine speed when switch changed from off to on	Idle speed + 250 ± 150 rpm
Fuel pressure	2.5 bar (36.3 lbf/in^2)
Injector coil resistance:	
CA16DE	2.5 ohms
CA18DE	10 to 15 ohms
Air regulator circuit resistance	Approximately 75 ohms
Detonation sensor resistance	500 to 600 ohms
Auxiliary air control valve resistance	Approximately 10 ohms

Air regulator resistance	Approximately 70 ohms
Injector resistance	Approximately 2.5 ohms
Dropping resistor resistance	Approximately 6 ohms

Ignition system
General

System type:	
Twelve-valve engine	Electronic, with breakerless distributor driven from camshaft, conventional coil
Sixteen-valve engine	Integral with ECCS, no distributor, individual ignition coils fitted to each spark plug
Firing order	1-3-4-2 (No 1 at timing chain/belt end)

Spark plugs

	Type	Electrode gap
GA14S	Champion RC7YCC or RC7YC	0.9 mm (0.035 in)
GA16S	Champion RC9YCC or RC9YC	0.9 mm (0.035 in)
CA16DE	Champion RC9YCC or RC9YC4	1.0 mm (0.039 in)
CA18DE	Champion RC7YCC or RC7YC4	1.0 mm (0.039 in)

Ignition timing

Twelve-valve engines (at idle speed with distributor vacuum hose disconnected and plugged):	
GA14S	2° ± 2° ATDC
GA16S	0° ± 2° ATDC
Sixteen-valve engines	15° ± 2° BTDC at 800 ± 50 rpm

HT leads

Resistance (twelve-valve engines)	Less than 30 k ohms, and more than 9.6 k ohms/metre

Detonation sensor

Resistance	500 to 600 k ohms

Clutch
General

Type:	
GA14S, GA16S and CA16DE	As for E13S and E16S engines given in Chapter 5
CA18DE	Single dry plate with diaphragm spring and pressure plate, hydraulically operated
Driven plate diameter:	
GA14S	180 mm (7.09 in)
GA16S	190 mm (7.48 in)
CA16DE	200 mm (7.87 in)
CA18DE	215 mm (8.46 in)
Clutch plate adjustment (CA18DE)	
Pedal height	175 to 185 mm (6.89 to 7.28 in)
Pedal free-play	1.0 to 3.0 mm (0.039 to 0.118 in)

Torque wrench settings (CA18DE)

	Nm	lbf ft
Fluid reservoir	3 to 6	2 to 4
Master cylinder	8 to 12	6 to 9
Pushrod locknut	8 to 12	6 to 9
Slave cylinder	30 to 40	22 to 30
Hydraulic pipe bracket	17 to 20	12 to 14
Master cylinder stopper	1.5 to 2.9	1.1 to 2.2
Slave cylinder bleed screw	7 to 9	5 to 7

Manual transmission
Application

GA14S engine	RN4F30A (four-speed) or RS5F30A (five-speed)
GA16S engine	RN4F31A (four-speed) or RS5F31A (five-speed)
CA16DE engine	RS5F31A (five-speed)
CA18DE engine	RS5F50A or RS5F50V (both five-speed)

Ratios

GA14S:	RN4F30A	RS5F30A
1st	3.333	3.333
2nd	1.955	1.955
3rd	1.286	1.286
4th	0.902	0.902
5th	–	0.733
Reverse	3.417	3.417
Final drive	4.167	4.167

Ratios (continued)

	RN4F31A	RS5F31A
GA16S:		
1st	3.063	3.063
2nd	1.826	1.826
3rd	1.207	1.207
4th	0.902	0.902
5th	–	0.756
Reverse	3.147	3.147
Final drive	4.167	4.167
CA16DE:		
1st	3.063	
2nd	1.826	
3rd	1.286	
4th	0.975	
5th	0.810	
Reverse	3.417	
Final drive	4.471	
CA18DE:		
1st	3.285	
2nd	1.850	
3rd	1.272	
4th	0.954	
5th	0.759	
Reverse	3.428	
Final drive	4.167	

Transmission tolerances (RS5F50A and RS5F50V)

Baulk ring to gear:	
Standard	1.0 to 1.35 mm (0.0394 to 0.0531 in)
Wear limit	0.7 mm (0.028 in)
Gear endfloat:	
1st	0.23 to 0.43 mm (0.0091 to 0.0169 in)
2nd	0.23 to 0.58 mm (0.0091 to 0.0228 in)
5th	0 to 0.15 mm (0 to 0.0059 in)
Synchro hub clearance:	
3rd/4th	0 to 0.1 mm (0 to 0.004 in)
1st/2nd	0 to 0.1 mm (0 to 0.004 in)
Input shaft thrust washer clearance	0 to 0.06 mm (0 to 0.0024 in)
Clearance between side gear and differential case or viscous coupling with washer	0.1 to 0.2 mm (0.004 to 0.008 in)
Mainshaft bearing preload	0.25 to 0.31 mm (0.0098 to 0.0122 in)
Differential side bearing preload	0.40 to 0.46 mm (0.0157 to 0.0181 in)
3rd	0.23 to 0.43 mm (0.0091 to 0.0169 in)
4th	0.25 to 0.55 mm (0.0098 to 0.0217 in)
5th	0.23 to 0.48 mm (0.0091 to 0.0189 in)

Oil capacity

Type:	
RN4F30A	2.4 litres (4.2 pints)
RS5F30A	2.8 litres (4.9 pints)
RN4F31A	2.7 litres (4.8 pints)
RS5F31A	2.8 litres (4.9 pints)
RS5F30A and RS5F30V	4.7 litres (8.3 pints)

Torque wrench settings (RS5F50A and RS5F50V)

	Nm	lbf ft
Drain plug	20 to 29	14 to 22
Filler plug	25 to 34	18 to 25
Position switch	3.7 to 5.0	2.7 to 3.7
Transmission casing	16 to 21	12 to 15
Viscous coupling	3.7 to 5.0	2.7 to 3.7
Crownwheel	74 to 88	54 to 65
Reverse idler shaft bolt	16 to 21	12 to 15
Detent plug	16 to 22	12 to 16
Selector check spring	16 to 21	12 to 15
Reverse lever assembly	16 to 21	12 to 15

Automatic transmission
Final drive ratio

1.4	3.737:1

Driveshafts
Type

CA16DE and CA18DE engine models	Birfield ball type constant velocity joints, right-hand driveshaft supported by a bearing bracket on the rear of the engine cylinder block

Torque wrench settings (CA16DE and CA18DE models)

	Nm	lbf ft
RH driveshaft support bearing bracket to engine:		
Two upper	25 to 35	19 to 26
RH lower	43 to 58	32 to 43
Centre lower	30 to 40	22 to 30
RH driveshaft support bearing retainer	13 to 19	9 to 14

Braking system

Type

CA16DE and CA18DE engine models	Front and rear discs, vacuum servo assistance, dual hydraulic circuit split diagonally, self-adjusting handbrake mechanism in rear caliper, rear brake pressure regulating valve
GA14S and GA16S engine models	As for E13S and E16S given in Chapter 9 except for the following

Front brake discs

Diameter:	
CA16DE engine	240 mm (9.45 in)
CA18DE engine	254 mm (10.00 in)
Thickness:	
CA16DE engine:	
New	12 mm (0.47 in)
Minimum	9 mm (0.354 in)
CA18DE engine:	
New	20 mm (0.79 in)
Minimum	16 mm (0.630 in)
Pad wear limit (minimum thickness)	2.0 mm (0.079 in)
Disc maximum run-out	0.07 mm (0.0028 in)

Rear brake discs (CA16DE and CA18DE)

Diameter	234 mm (9.21 in)
Thickness:	
New	10 mm (0.39 in)
Minimum	9 mm (0.354 in)
Pad wear limit (minimum thickness)	2.0 mm (0.079 in)
Disc maximum run-out	0.07 mm (0.0028 in)

Vacuum servo unit

Diaphragm diameter (GA14S, GA16S, CA16DE and CA18DE)	205 mm (8.07 in)

Brake pedal

Depressed pedal height (engine running, force of 50 kg/110 lb)	80.0 mm (3.15 in) minimum

Torque wrench settings (CA16DE and CA18DE models)

	Nm	lbf ft
Front brake torque member	54 to 64	40 to 47
Flexible brake hose union bolt	17 to 20	12 to 14
Front caliper guide pin:		
CA16DE	31 to 41	23 to 30
CA18DE	22 to 31	16 to 13
Front caliper bleed screw	7 to 9	5 to 7
Rear caliper handbrake cable bracket	37 to 49	27 to 36
Rear brake torque member	38 to 52	28 to 38

Suspension and steering (sixteen-valve engines)

Rear hub bearing

Bearing end-play	0.05 mm (0.0020 in)

Wheel alignment

Front:	
Camber	–1° 05′ to 0° 25′
Caster	0° 55′ to 2° 25′
Toe-in	0.5 to 1.5 mm (0.020 to 0.059 in), equivalent to 3′ to 9′
King pin inclination	13° 05′ to 14° 35′
Toe-out on turn:	
Inside	22° 24′
Outside	20°
Rear:	
Camber	–1° 55′ to –0° 25′
Toe-out	–4′ to 20′

Torque wrench settings

	Nm	lbf ft
Rear hub (sixteen-valve engines):		
Baffle plate..	33 to 45	25 to 33
Wheel bearing locknut..................................	186 to 216	137 to 159

Electrical system
Alternator

	Standard	Optional
Type		
GA engines:		
Hitachi..	LR165-707	–
Mitsubishi..	A5T00192	–
CA16DE engines:		
Hitachi..	LR170-715B	LR170-716
Mitsubishi..	A2T48298	2T48292
CA18DE engines:		
Hitachi..	LR170-715B	LR170-716
Mitsubishi..	A2T48298	A2T48292
Rating:		
GA engines..	65 amp	
CA engines..	70 amp	
Minimum brush wear length:		
LR165-707..	6 mm (0.24 in)	
All others..	As given in Chapter 12	
Minimum slip-ring diameter:		
LR165-707..	26.8 mm (1.055 in)	
A5T00192..	22.1 mm (0.870 in)	
A2T48298/A2T48292....................................	22.4 mm (0.882 in) minimum	
LR170-715B/LR170-716................................	30.6 mm (1.205 in) minimum	
LR170-715B/LR170-716................................	30.6 mm (1.205 in) minimum	

Starter motor

	Hitachi	Mitsubishi
Make/type:		
GA engines:		
Manual transmission..............................	S114-316	M3T27781D
Automatic transmission..........................	S114-517C	M1T72081
CA16DE engine..	S114-509	M1T71681
CA18DE engine..	–	M1T70985
Minimum brush length:		
Hitachi..	11 mm (0.433 in)	
Mitsubishi:		
M3T27781D..	11.5 mm (0.453 in)	
M1T72081, M1T71681, M1T70985	12.0 mm (0.472 in)	
Minimum commutator diameter:		
Hitachi:		
S114-316, S114-517C, S114-509	32.0 mm (1.260 in)	
Mitsubishi:		
M3T27781D..	31.4 mm (1.236 in)	
M1T72081, M1T71681, M1T70985	28.8 mm (1.134 in)	
Pinion front face-to-pinion stopper clearance:		
S114-517C, S114-509	0.3 to 1.5 mm (0.012 to 0.059 in)	

Bulbs

	Wattage
Luggage compartment................................	5

---

3   Routine maintenance

The routine maintenance intervals for models manufactured from August 1987 are changed as follows:

Every 9000 miles (15 000 km) or 6 months, whichever comes first

---

Ignition system (Chapter 4)
Renew the spark plugs

Braking system (Chapter 9)
Check rear pads for wear (sixteen-valve models only)

Every 18 000 miles (30 000 km) or 12 months, whichever comes first

---

Engine (Chapter 1)
Adjust valve clearances (GA14S engine only)

Cooling system (Chapter 2)
Check the drivebelt(s) condition and tension

Every 36 000 miles (60 000 km) or 2 years, whichever comes first

---

Ignition system (Chapter 4)
No requirement to check wiring for condition and security on sixteen-valve engines

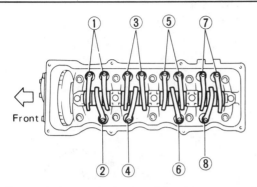

Fig. 13.1 Valve numbering for adjustment purposes (Sec 4)

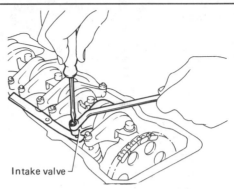

Fig. 13.2 Adjusting an inlet valve (Sec 4)

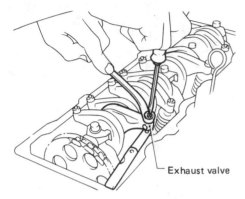

Fig. 13.3 Adjusting an exhaust valve (Sec 4)

4 Engine (1.4 and 1.6 twelve-valve)

General description

1   The 1.4 and 1.6 twelve-valve engine is of four-cylinder, in-line, single over-head camshaft type. The camshaft is driven by a timing chain from the front of the crankshaft. The engine front cover incorporates an oil pump and the water pump.
2   With the exception of the following, the procedures are the same as described in Chapter 1.

Valve clearances (GA14S engine) – checking and adjustment

3   The procedure is as described in Chapter 1, Section 4, however the clearances are different (as given in the Specifications).

Timing chain – removal and refitting

4   Drain the cooling system as described in Chapter 2. Also unscrew the plug from the front of the cylinder block and drain the coolant.

4.5A Unbolt the oil pick-up tube ...

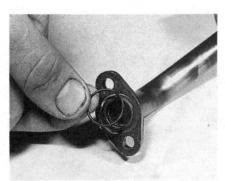

4.5B ... and recover the O-ring

4.6A Power steering pump mounting and adjusting bolts ...

4.6B ... and mounting bracket

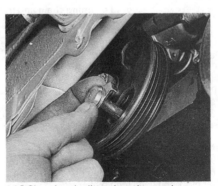

4.6C Showing the lipped washer on the power steering mounting bolt

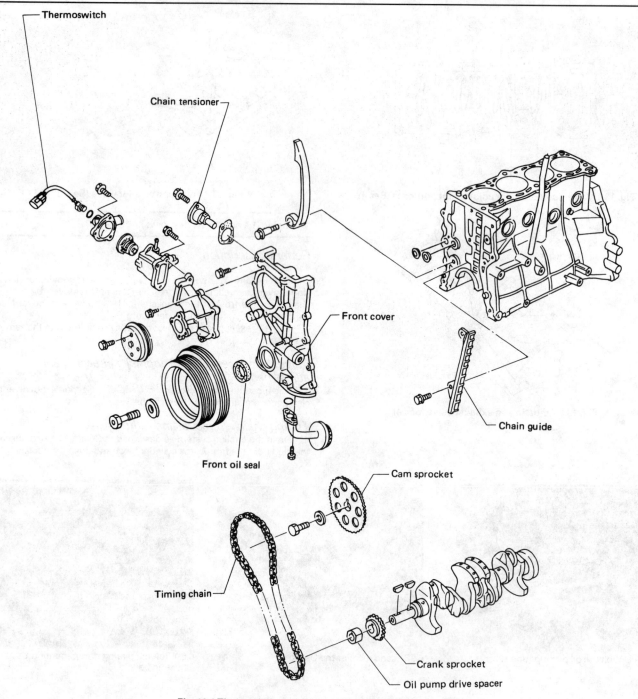

Thermoswitch

Chain tensioner

Front cover

Chain guide

Front oil seal

Cam sprocket

Timing chain

Crank sprocket

Oil pump drive spacer

Fig. 13.4 Timing chain and front engine components (Sec 4)

5   Remove the sump as described later. Also unbolt the oil pick-up tube and recover the O-ring (photos).

6   Remove the power steering pump drivebelt by unscrewing the removing the pivot and adjustment bolts (photos). Tie the pump to the bulkhead so that the fluid pipes are not strained.

7   Remove the alternator and drivebelt with reference to Chapter 12 (photo).

8   Unbolt the power steering pump bracket from the cylinder block (photo).

9   Remove the air cleaner as described in Chapter 3.

10   Using a hoist, support the right-hand end of the engine, then unscrew and remove the right-hand engine mounting bolt and unbolt the bracket from the cylinder block and head (photos).

11   Unbolt the water pump from the front cover. Refer to Section 6 if necessary.

12   Remove all of the spark plugs and turn the crankshaft clockwise with a socket on the pulley bolt until pressure can be felt through the No 1 plug hole with a finger. Continue to turn the crankshaft until the yellow TDC marks on the pulley are aligned with the timing pointer on the front cover (photo).

13   Remove the distributor cap and check that the rotor arm is pointing towards the No 1 position.

14   Unscrew the bolts and remove the timing chain tensioner from the front cover (photos). Recover the gasket.

15   Unbolt and remove the valve cover. Recover the gasket.

16   Apply the handbrake firmly then engage 4th gear in order to hold the crankshaft stationary. Alternatively (and essential on automatic transmission models) remove the starter motor and engage a wide-blade screwdriver with the teeth of the ring gear.

17   Unscrew the crankshaft pulley bolt. For better access remove the splash shield from under the right-hand wheel arch.

18   Slide off the crankshaft pulley. If it is tight use a puller (photos).

4.7 Alternator upper mounting and adjustment bolt

4.8 Power steering pump bracket removal

4.10A Right-hand engine mounting bracket lower ...

4.10B ... and upper bolts

4.12 Crankshaft pulley TDC mark aligned with the timing pointer

19 Unbolt and remove the front cover from the front of the cylinder block and from under the cylinder head extension. If it is tight it may be necessary to gently tap it from the inside with a soft headed mallet. Remove the two seals from the front of the cylinder block and discard.
20 Hold the camshaft sprocket stationary with a suitable tool engaged with the holes in the sprocket. A screwdriver may be used if

necessary. Unscrew and remove the camshaft sprocket bolt.
21 Unbolt the timing chain guides from the cylinder block.
22 Mark the timing chain and sprocket in relation to each other.
23 Lower the camshaft sprocket and withdraw the oil pump drive spacer, crankshaft sprocket and timing chain from the front of the crankshaft (photos). Leave the Woodruff keys in position. Separate the timing chain from the sprockets.
24 Do not attempt to turn the camshaft or crankshaft with the timing chain removed.
25 Examine the timing chain for excessive wear or cracking of the roller links. One way to check the chain is to hold it horizontally to detect the amount of slack in the links. Renew the chain if necessary.
26 Clean all the components and wipe dry. Make sure that all traces of liquid gasket are removed from contact surfaces.
27 Using a screwdriver prise the crankshaft front oil seal from the front cover. Clean the seating then fit a new oil seal by dipping it in clean engine oil and driving it squarely into the front cover with a suitable socket (photos).
28 Commence reassembly by engaging the camshaft and crankshaft sprockets with the timing chain so that the timing marks are aligned with the special bright links on the chain (photo).
29 Slide the sprocket onto the front of the crankshaft making sure that it engages the Woodruff key correctly (photo). Similarly fit the oil pump drive spacer.
30 Raise the camshaft sprocket through the cylinder head extension and locate it on the front of the camshaft making sure that it engages with the Woodruff key correctly.
31 Check that the timing chain bright links are aligned, then insert the sprocket bolt and washer. The chamfered side of the washer must face outwards.
32 Hold the sprocket stationary then tighten the bolt to the specified torque (photo).
33 Refit the chain guides and tighten the bolts (photo). It will be necessary to press the guides firmly inwards in order to align the bolt holes.
34 Clean the contact faces of the front cover and cylinder block and apply an even bead of liquid gasket. Fit two new seals to the front of the cylinder block (photos).

Mating mark (silver)

Mating mark

Same number link

23 links

23 links

Mating mark

Mating mark (silver)

Fig. 13.5 Timing chain alignment (Sec 4)

4.14A Unscrew the bolts ...

4.14B ... and remove the timing chain tensioner

4.18A Release the crankshaft pulley with a puller if necessary ...

4.18B ... then withdraw the pulley

4.23A Removing the oil pump drive spacer ...

4.23B ... and crankshaft sprocket

4.27A Crankshaft front oil seal removal

4.27B Fitting a new crankshaft front oil seal

4.28 Timing chain bright link and camshaft sprocket timing mark alignment

4.29 Timing chain and sprocket on the crankshaft, showing bright link and timing mark

4.32 Tightening the camshaft sprocket bolt

4.33 Refitting the timing chain guides

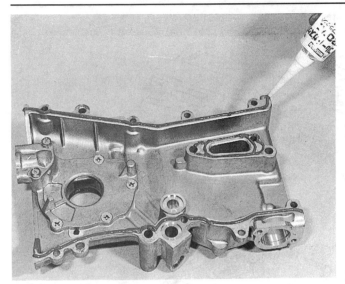

4.34A Applying liquid gasket to the front cover

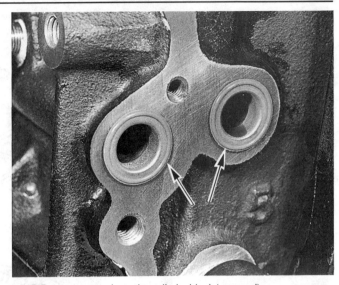

4.34B Front cover seals on the cylinder block (arrowed)

35 Fit the front cover on its dowels, then insert the bolts and tighten them progressively to the specified torque (photo). Take care not to damage the cylinder head gasket which is under the head extension.
36 Insert the timing chain tensioner together with a new gasket and tighten the bolts to the specified torque. Make sure that the cut-out in the gasket is aligned with the oil hole (photo).
37 Refit the oil pick-up tube together with a new O-ring and tighten the bolts. Refit the sump with reference to paragraphs 116 to 118.
38 Slide the crankshaft pulley onto the front of the crankshaft making sure that it engages with the Woodruff key.
39 Insert the pulley bolt and washer then tighten to the specified

torque using the method described earlier to hold the crankshaft stationary (photo).
40 Refit the splash shield under the right-hand wheel arch.
41 Refit the valve cover together with a new gasket. Insert the bolts and tighten to the specified torque.
42 Refit the distributor cap and spark plugs.
43 Refit the water pump, referring to Section 6 if necessary.
44 Refit the right-hand engine mounting bracket to the cylinder block and tighten the bolts. Align the holes then insert and tighten the bolt. Disconnect the hoist.
45 Refit the air cleaner (Chapter 3).

4.35 Refitting the front cover

4.36 Timing chain tensioner oil hole

4.39 Tightening the crankshaft pulley bolt

4.48A Topping up the radiator ...

4.48B ... and expansion tank

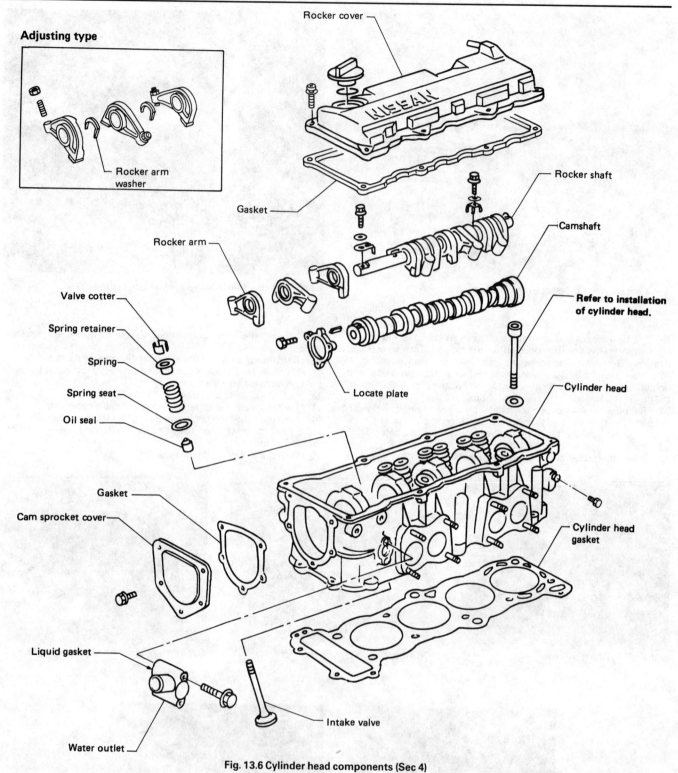

Adjusting type

Fig. 13.6 Cylinder head components (Sec 4)

46   Refit the power steering pump bracket, pump and drivebelt with reference to Chapter 10 if necessary.

47   Refit the alternator and drivebelt with reference to Chapter 12.

48   Tighten the radiator and cylinder block drain plugs, then refill the cooling system with reference to Chapter 2 (photos).

Cylinder head – removal and refitting

49   Disconnect the battery negative lead.

50   Drain the cooling system as described in Chapter 2.

51   Remove the air cleaner (Chapter 3) (photos).

52   Unscrew the nuts securing the exhaust downpipe to the exhaust manifold, lower the downpipe and remove the gasket (photo). If necessary unbolt the front exhaust mounting.

53   Unbolt the inlet manifold support stay. If necessary also unbolt the engine lifting eyes and wiring support brackets (photos).

54   Remove the distributor with reference to Chapter 4. Also unbolt the coolant pipe bracket from the cylinder head (photos).

55   Disconnect the accelerator cable from the carburettor and bracket (photos).

4.51A Release the clips ...

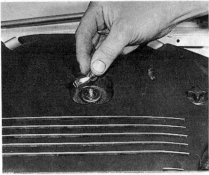

4.51B ... unscrew the wing nut ...

4.51C ... remove the cover and element ...

4.51D ... disconnect the hot air duct from the exhaust manifold ...

4.51E ... unscrew the left-hand mounting ...

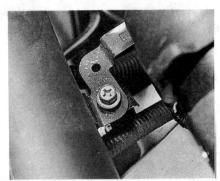

4.51F ... intermediate mounting ...

4.51G ... front mounting ...

4.51H ... disconnect the crankshaft ventilation hose ...

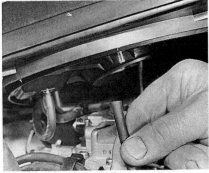

4.51I ... and vacuum hose

56   Disconnect all wiring from the cylinder head noting the routing of the harness for correct reassembly (photo).
57   Disconnect the fuel pipes from the fuel pump and carburettor (photo).
58   Disconnect the vacuum hose from the inlet manifold.
59   Remove the inlet and exhaust manifolds together with their gaskets with reference to Section 7.
60   Loosen the clip and disconnect the top hose from the cylinder head outlet.
61   Disconnect the crankshaft ventilation hose then unbolt and remove the valve cover. Remove the gasket. The rocker shaft may be removed at this stage if the cylinder head is to be subsequently dismantled. Refer to paragraph 97 (photos).
62   Unscrew and remove the spark plugs.
63   Turn the crankshaft clockwise with a socket on the pulley bolt until pressure can be felt through the No 1 plug hole with a finger. Continue to turn the crankshaft until the TDC marks on the pulley are aligned with the timing pointer on the front cover.

64   Unscrew the camshaft sprocket cover from the right-hand side of the cylinder head. Remove the gasket (photos).
65   Hold the camshaft sprocket stationary with a suitable tool engaged with the holes in the sprocket. A screwdriver may be used if necessary. Unscrew and remove the camshaft sprocket bolt (photos).
66   Mark the timing chain and sprocket in relation to each other, then withdraw and lower the sprocket onto the guides. The timing chain will not become disengaged from the crankshaft sprocket since there is a cast lug on the inner side of the engine front cover (photo).
67   Unscrew the external bolts securing the cylinder head to the front cover and cylinder block in the order shown in Fig. 13.7 (photo).
68   Progressively unscrew the cylinder head bolts in the order shown in Fig. 13.7. Remove the bolts and washers (photo).
69   Rock the cylinder head to release it from the gasket, then lift it from the cylinder block (photo).
70   Remove the gasket from the block.
71   Thoroughly clean the joint surfaces of the cylinder head, block and front cover.

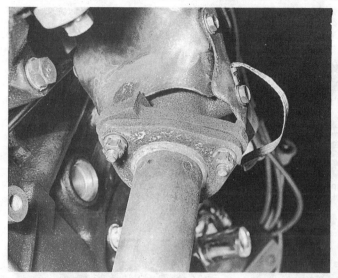

4.52 Exhaust downpipe to manifold joint

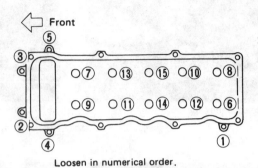

Loosen in numerical order.

Fig. 13.7 Cylinder head bolt loosening sequence (Sec 4)

72   Check that the crankshaft is still at TDC and that the location peg on the camshaft is uppermost.
73   Locate the new gasket on the cylinder block making sure that all holes are correctly aligned (photo).
74   Carefully lower the cylinder head onto the gasket making sure that the bolt holes are aligned.
75   Insert the cylinder head bolts noting that the single longer bolt (length 133 mm/5.24 in) is located in the number 1 position (photo).

76   Tighten the bolts in the order given in Fig. 13.8 and in the stages given in Specifications (photo). Do not tighten the small external bolts at this stage. Note that after the first two stages, all of the bolts must be completely loosened before proceeding (ie **not** individually loosened then tightened).
77   Tighten the small external bolts in the order given to the specified torque.

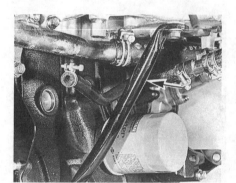

4.53A Remove the inlet manifold support stay (arrowed) ...

4.53B ... front engine lifting eye ...

4.53C ... rear engine lifting eye ...

4.53D ... and wiring support brackets (arrowed)

4.54A Remove the distributor jacket ...

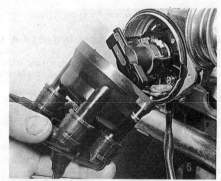

4.54B ... and cap ...

4.54C ... disconnect the vacuum hoses ...

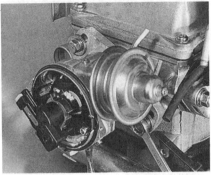

4.54D ... then unscrew the mounting bolts ...

4.54E ... and remove the distributor

4.54F Coolant pipe bracket

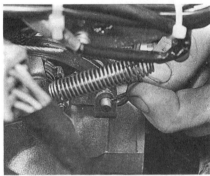

4.55A Disconnect the accelerator cable from the carburettor ...

4.55B ... and bracket

4.56 Wiring harness mounting on the rear of the cylinder head

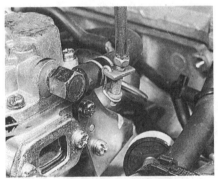

4.57 Disconnect the fuel pipe from the carburettor

4.61A Disconnect the crankshaft ventilation hose ...

4.61B ... remove the screws ...

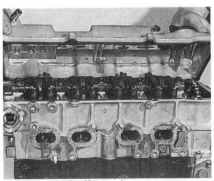

4.61C ... then lift off the valve cover ...

4.61D ... and remove the gasket

4.61E Removing the rocker shaft

4.64A Unscrew the bolts ...

4.64B ... and remove the camshaft sprocket cover

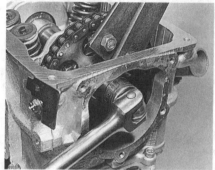

4.65A Unscrew the camshaft sprocket bolt ...

4.65B ... and remove it

4.66 Cast lug on the front cover retaining the timing chain (arrowed)

4.67 Cylinder head to front cover bolts (arrowed)

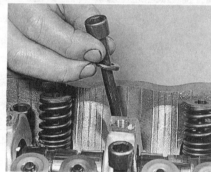

4.68 Removing the cylinder head bolts

4.69 Removing the cylinder head

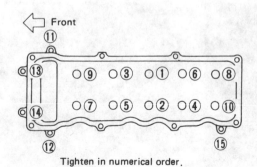

Fig. 13.8 Cylinder head bolt tightening sequence (Sec 4)

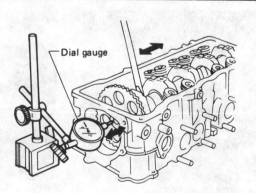

Fig. 13.9 Measuring the camshaft end play (Sec 4)

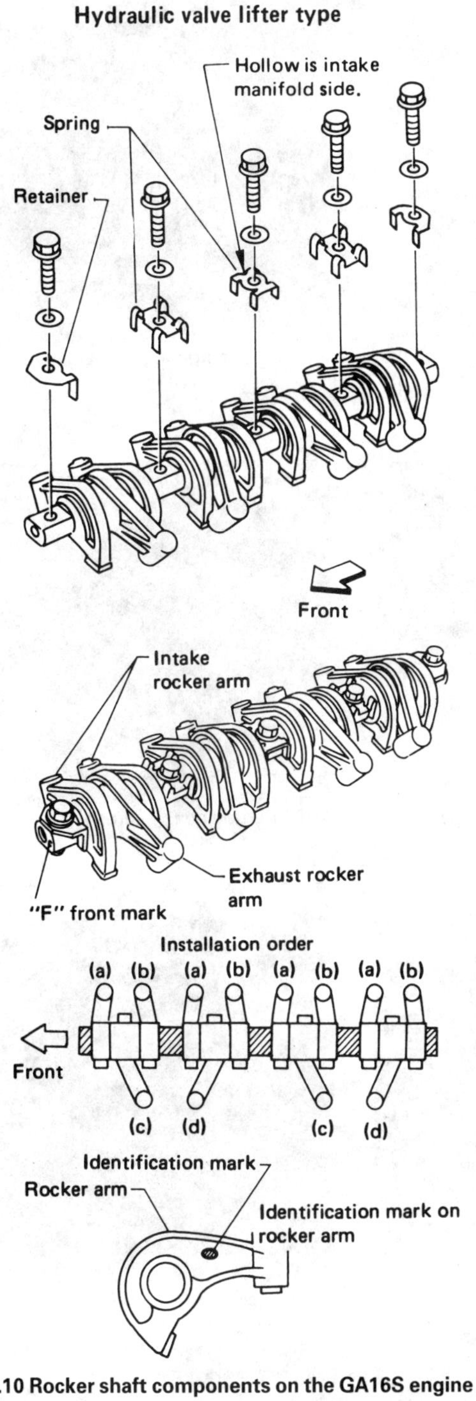

Hydraulic valve lifter type

Spring

Retainer

Hollow is intake manifold side.

Front

Intake rocker arm

Exhaust rocker arm

"F" front mark

Installation order

(a) (b) (a) (b) (a) (b) (a) (b)

Front

(c) (d) (c) (d)

Identification mark

Rocker arm

Identification mark on rocker arm

Fig. 13.10 Rocker shaft components on the GA16S engine (Sec 4)

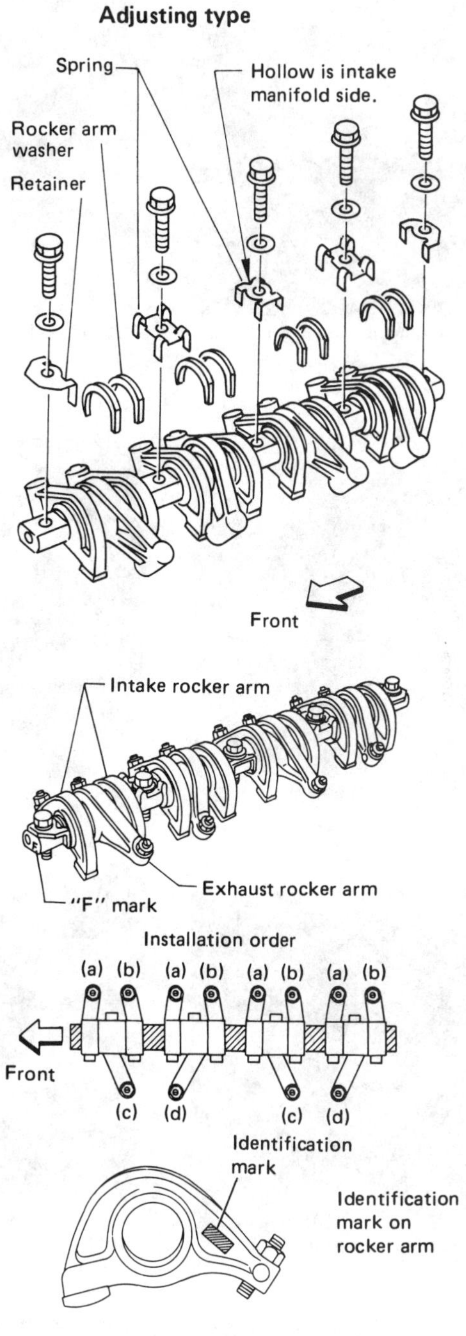

Adjusting type

Spring

Rocker arm washer

Retainer

Hollow is intake manifold side.

Front

Intake rocker arm

Exhaust rocker arm

"F" mark

Installation order

(a) (b) (a) (b) (a) (b) (a) (b)

Front

(c) (d) (c) (d)

Identification mark

Identification mark on rocker arm

Fig. 13.11 Rocker shaft components on the GA14S engine (Sec 4)

78   Make sure that the marks previously made on the timing chain and sprocket are still aligned.
79   Locate the sprocket on the camshaft making sure that it engages with the location peg. Insert the bolt.
80   Hold the camshaft sprocket stationary as previously described, then tighten the bolt to the specified torque.
81   Refit the camshaft sprocket cover together with a new gasket and tighten the bolts.
82   Refit and tighten the spark plugs. Refit the rocker shaft if it has been removed, as described in paragraph 104.
83   On the GA14S engine adjust the valve clearances with reference to paragraph 3. Refit the valve cover together with a new gasket, and tighten the bolts evenly to the specified torque. Reconnect the crankshaft ventilation hose.

84   Refit the top hose and tighten the clip.
85   Refit the inlet and exhaust manifolds together with new gaskets with reference to Section 7.
86   Refit the vacuum hose to the inlet manifold.
87   Reconnect the fuel pipes to the fuel pump and carburettor.
88   Reconnect the wiring harness.
89   Reconnect the accelerator cable and adjust it as described in Chapter 3.
90   Refit the distributor with reference to Chapter 4. Also refit the coolant pipe to the cylinder head.
91   Refit the inlet manifold support stay, wiring support brackets, and engine lifting eyes and tighten the bolts.
92   Refit the exhaust downpipe to the manifold together with a new gasket, and tighten the nuts. Reconnect the front mounting if necessary.

4.73 Cylinder head gasket located on the block

4.75 One cylinder head bolt is longer than the others

4.76 Tightening the cylinder head bolts

4.98 Checking the camshaft end play

4.99 Removing the camshaft thrust plate

4.100 Removing the camshaft

4.101A Compress the valve springs and remove the collets ...

4.101B ... then remove the cap ...

4.101C ... spring ...

4.101D ... spring seat ...

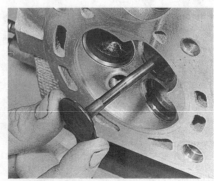

4.101E ... and valve

4.103A Front mark on the rocker shaft

4.103B Hydraulic valve lifter showing markings

4.104A Refitting a valve stem oil seal

4.104B Refitting the rocker shaft mounting bolt and spring ...

4.104C ... 1st inlet valve rocker ...

4.104D ... exhaust valve rocker ...

4.104E ... and 2nd inlet valve rocker

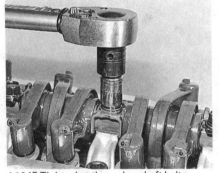

4.104F Tightening the rocker shaft bolts

93   Refit the air cleaner (Chapter 3).
94   Reconnect the battery negative lead.
95   Refill the cooling system with reference to Chapter 2.

Cylinder head – dismantling, overhaul and reassembly

96   Refer to Chapter 1, Section 17 and observe the cautionary note.
97   Progressively loosen the rocker shaft mounting bolts in two or three stages, then lift the rocker shaft assembly from the cylinder head. On the GA16S engine keep the assembly upright to prevent oil draining from the hydraulic valve lifters.
98   If necessary at this stage measure the camshaft end play to determine the amount of wear present. To do this it will be necessary to temporarily refit the camshaft sprocket to the camshaft and either use a dial gauge or feeler blade (photo).
99   With the sprocket removed, unbolt the camshaft thrust plate (photo).
100   Carefully withdraw the camshaft from the rear of the cylinder head through the distributor mounting hole (photo).
101   Refer to Chapter 1, Section 17 for details of removing the valves and overhauling the cylinder head. Since there are two inlet valves per cylinder make sure that each one is marked for correct reassembly (photos). Refer also to the Specifications in this Supplement.
102   Note that the valve springs are fitted with their narrow pitch ends towards the cylinder head.
103   The rocker shaft may be dismantled if necessary, but each item should be identified for location to ensure correct reassembly. On the GA16S engine it is important not to allow the oil to drain from the hydraulic valve lifters, and they must therefore be kept in an upright position or preferably immersed in a container of engine oil. It is not possible to dismantle the hydraulic valve lifters (photos).
104   Reassembly is a reversal of dismantling with reference also to Chapter 1, Section 17, however when refitting the rocker shaft, delay tightening the mounting bolts until the camshaft sprocket and chain have been fitted to the camshaft. With No 1 cylinder at TDC on

4.108 Engine oil drain plug

4.114 Sump bolts and nuts

4.118 Refitting the sump

4.125A Topping up the engine with oil

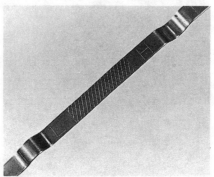
4.125B Engine oil level dipstick markings

4.127 Oil pump cover and screws

4.128A Checking the clearances for the oil pump body to outer gear ...

4.128B ... inner gear to crescent ...

4.128C ... outer gear to crescent ...

compression tighten the bolts 1 and 2 from the front of the engine, then turn the engine so that No 4 cylinder is at TDC on compression and tighten bolts 4 and 5. Finally tighten bolt 3. If this procedure is not followed the valve spring tension will make the torque setting incorrect (photos).

105   On the GA16S engine the hydraulic valve lifters may be checked for an air lock as follows. With the rocker arm on the low point of the cam lobe, press the hydraulic valve lifter onto the valve stem. If the rocker arm moves more than 1 mm (0.04 in) air is present. To purge the air the engine must be run at 1000 rpm for approximately 10 minutes, however if the rocker arm is still noisy it should be renewed.

Sump – removal and refitting

106   Apply the handbrake and chock the rear wheels, then jack up the front of the car and support on axle stands.
107   Remove the splash shield from under the engine.
108   Position a suitable container beneath the sump, then unscrew the drain plug and drain the oil (photo). Refit and tighten the plug on completion.
109   Unscrew the nuts and disconnect the exhaust downpipe from the manifold. Remove the gasket.
110   On the GA16S engine unbolt the front pipe from the exhaust system.
111   Unbolt the crossmember from under the engine and withdraw it from under the car.
112   Unbolt the strengthener between the engine and gearbox.
113   On automatic transmission models unbolt and remove the transmission front cover.
114   Unscrew the sump bolts and nuts (photo).
115   Carefully prise the sump from the block taking care not to damage the contact faces.
116   Clean all traces of sealant from the contact faces.
117   Using suitable sealant (preferably Nissan type) apply a continuous bead to the sump, making sure that the bead goes on the inner side

4.128D ... cover diameter ...

4.128E ... outer gear diameter ...

4.128F ... cover to outer gear ...

4.128G ... and cover to inner gear

4.129 Oil pump release valve removal

of bolt holes. The bead should be 3.5 to 4.5 mm (0.138 to 0.177 in) wide.
118   Offer the sump to the block in one action to prevent disturbing the carefully applied sealant, and insert the bolts (photo). Tighten the bolts evenly to the specified torque.
119   Refit the transmission front cover on automatic transmission models.
120   Refit the engine-to-gearbox strengthener.
121   Refit the engine crossmember and tighten the bolts.
122   On the GA16S engine refit the front pipe to the exhaust system.
123   Fit the downpipe to the manifold together with a new gasket and tighten the nuts.
124   Refit the engine splash shield.
125   Lower the car to the ground, then refill the engine with oil (photos).

Oil pump – removal, checking and refitting

126   Remove the engine front cover with reference to paragraphs 4 to 19.
127   Unscrew the bolts and remove the oil pump cover from the front cover (photo).
128   Using a feeler blade, vernier calipers and straight-edge check the gear clearances as given in the Specifications (photos). If outside the tolerances given, renew the gears or if necessary renew the complete front cover.
129   If necessary, unscrew the plug and check the release valve and spring for wear and damage (photo).
130   Thoroughly clean all the components. Dip the gears in clean engine oil and locate them in the front cover.
131   Refit the release valve and spring followed by the plug together

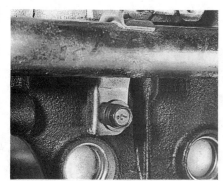

4.134A Coolant pipe to block bracket

4.134B Unscrewing the oil filter

4.134C Alternator bracket

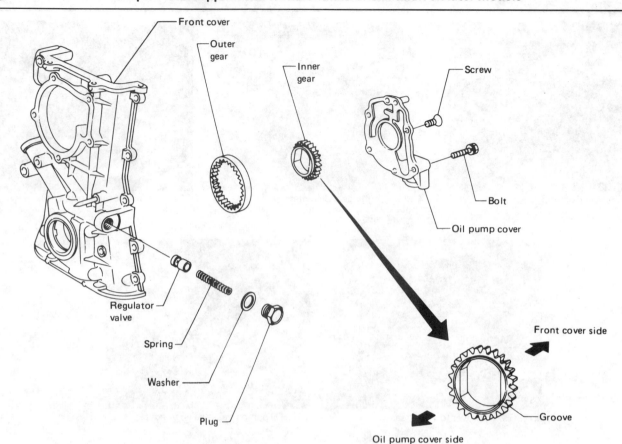

Fig. 13.12 Oil pump components (Sec 4)

with a new washer. Tighten the plug to the specified torque.

132   Fill the area around the gears with oil, then refit the cover, insert the bolts and tighten them to the specified torque.

133   Refit the engine front cover with reference to paragraphs 34 to 48.

Cylinder block – dismantling and reassembly

Note: *The following paragraphs give an outline of the procedures, however, refer to Chapter 1 for a more detailed description*

134   With the engine removed from the car, remove the cylinder head, sump and timing chain as previously described. Also unbolt the coolant pipe. If necessary unscrew the oil filter and unbolt the alternator bracket (photos).

135   Hold the flywheel/driveplate stationary using a suitable tool as shown in the photograph, then unscrew the bolts and lift off the flywheel/driveplate. Remove the rear engine plate (photos).

136   Remove the pistons from the cylinder block with reference to Chapter 1 (photos).

137   Unbolt and remove the crankshaft rear oil seal retainer (photo).

138   Check that the main bearing caps are numbered for position then unscrew the main bearing cap bolts progressively in two or three stages (photos).

139   Remove the main bearing caps taking care not to disturb the bearing shells (photo).

140   Lift the crankshaft from the cylinder block (photo).

141   Remove the bearing shells from the block (photo).

142   Reassemble the cylinder block in reverse order with reference also to Chapter 1, Section 20. Tighten the main bearing cap bolts in the sequence given in Fig. 13.14 and in two or three stages. Renew the crankshaft rear oil seal before refitting the retainer. Use a punch to drive out the old seal then clean the seating and drive in the new seal using a block of wood. Apply a bead of sealant to the retainer before refitting it. It is suggested that the timing chain is refitted before refitting the cylinder head, and therefore it will be necessary to hold the camshaft sprocket in a raised position. A block of wood can be temporarily located on the cylinder block and the sprocket held with a metal rod (photos).

4.135A Home-made tool for holding the flywheel stationary

4.135B Removing the flywheel

4.135C Rear engine plate

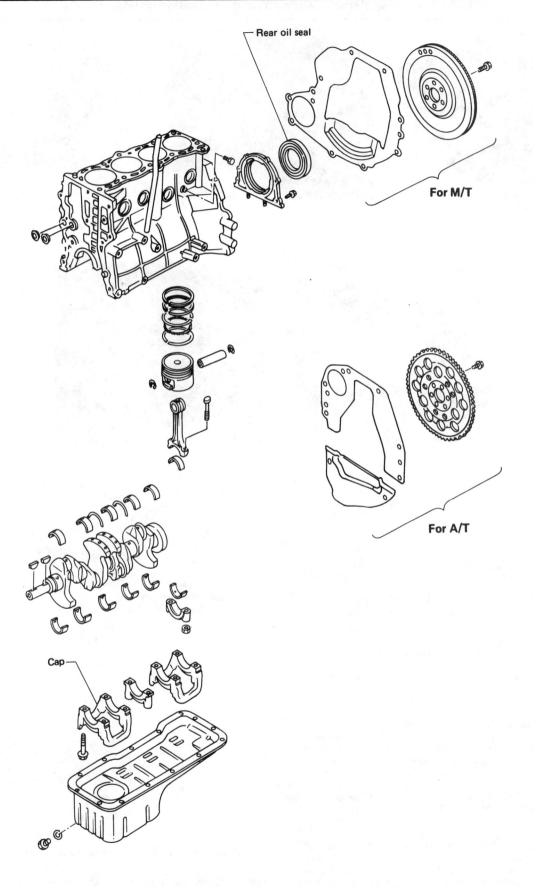

Rear oil seal

For M/T

For A/T

Cap

Fig. 13.13 Cylinder block and sump components (Sec 4)

4.136A Connecting rod/big-end cap markings

4.136B Removing a big-end cap

4.136C Removing a big-end bearing shell

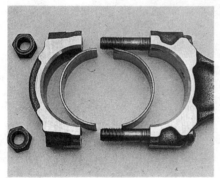

4.136D Big-end components

4.137 Removing the crankshaft rear oil seal retainer

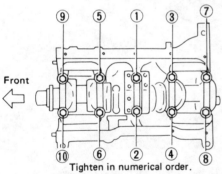

Fig. 13.14 Main bearing bolt tightening sequence (Sec 4)

Tighten in numerical order.

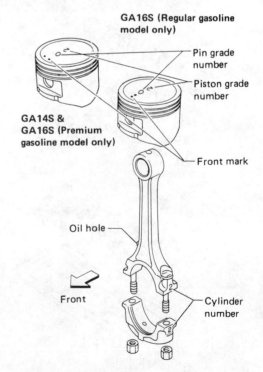

Fig. 13.15 Piston and connecting rod markings and alignment (Sec 4)

Pistons – disconnecting from connecting rods

143   Extract the circlip from one end of the gudgeon pin (photo).
144   Heat the piston in hot water to between 60° and 70°C (140° to 158°F) then push out the gudgeon pin (photo). Note which way round the piston is fitted.
145   To refit a piston first heat as for removal, then locate the piston on the connecting rod in its original position and push the gudgeon pin firmly into the piston. Refer to Fig. 13.15 (photo).
146   Refit the circlip.

Engine and manual transmission – removal and refitting

147   Open the bonnet and disconnect the washer tube. Mark the hinge positions then unbolt the bonnet and lift it from the car (photo). Nissan apply a very strong adhesive between the hinges and bonnet which is hard to break, so care is necessary to avoid damaging the bonnet while prising the hinges free.
148   Disconnect the battery leads then remove the clamp and lift out the battery. Remove the battery tray, and unbolt the platform (photos).

149   Support the front of the car on axle stands and apply the handbrake.
150   Remove the front wheels. Remove the engine splash shields including the side shields (photo).
151   Drain the cooling system (Chapter 2).

4.138A Main bearing cap numbering

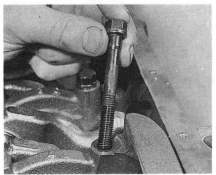
4.138B Removing a main bearing cap bolt

4.139 Removing a main bearing cap

4.140 Lifting the crankshaft from the block

4.141 Removing the main bearing shells

152   Loosen the power steering pump mounting and adjusting bolts, remove the drivebelt, then unbolt the pump from the cylinder block and tie it to one side.

153   Unscrew the nuts securing the exhaust downpipe to the exhaust manifold. On GA16S engines unbolt the downpipe at the front connection and remove it.

154   Disconnect the steering track rod ends and front suspension lower balljoints (photo).

155   Position a suitable container beneath the gearbox to catch any spilled oil then lever each driveshaft from the gearbox (photos). Tie the right-hand driveshaft forward and let the left-hand driveshaft rest on the side member.

156   Unscrew and remove the rear engine mounting bolt.

157   If necessary unbolt the crossmember from under the engine (photos). This is not strictly necessary as the engine is lifted upwards but will provide additional working room.

158   Unscrew the bolt from the front engine mounting (photo).

159   Remove the air cleaner and trunking.

160   Pull the small earth cable from the front valance (photo).

161   Disconnect the accelerator cable from the carburettor and bracket.

162   Disconnect the wiring from the engine. If major dismantling of the engine is not contemplated, leave the harness in position and disconnect the main and small multiplugs on the right-hand side, otherwise disconnect the following (photos):

Ignition coil HT lead
Multiplug by the battery mounting (after pulling from the mounting)
Battery cable from the starter solenoid
Starter solenoid and gearbox reverse switch
Battery earth lead from the starter mounting bolt
Alternator harness and bracket
Temperature sender multiplug
Earth cable from the inlet manifold
Multiplugs from the rear of the cylinder head and block
Multiplug from the clip on the inlet manifold

4.142A Refitting the main bearing shells ...

4.142B ... and thrust washers

4.142C Tightening the main bearing bolts

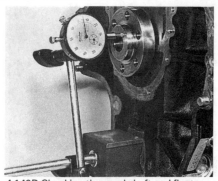

4.142D Checking the crankshaft end float with a dial gauge ...

4.142E ... and feeler blade

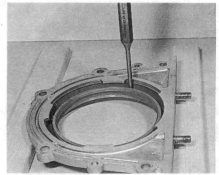

4.142F Removing the rear oil seal

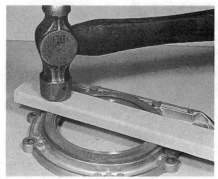

4.142G Fitting a new rear oil seal

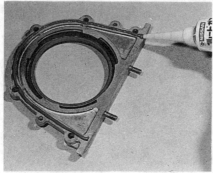

4.142H Applying sealant to the rear oil seal retainer

4.142I Tightening the rear oil seal retainer bolts

4.142J Inserting a piston in the cylinder bore

4.142K Tightening the big-end nuts with a torque wrench ...

4.142L ... and angle dial

4.142M Checking the big-end cap endfloat

4.142N Tightening the flywheel bolts

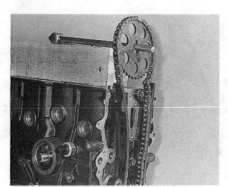

4.142O Method of retaining the timing chain before refitting the front cover

4.143 Extracting a gudgeon pin retaining circlip

4.144 Removing the gudgeon pin

4.145 Piston markings

4.147 Removing the bonnet

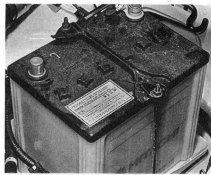

4.148A Battery and clamp

4.148B Removing the battery tray

4.150 Engine side shield

4.154 Disconnecting the front suspension lower balljoints

4.155A Lever out ...

4.155B ... and remove the driveshafts

4.157A Engine crossmember front mounting bolts ...

4.157B ... and rear mounting nuts

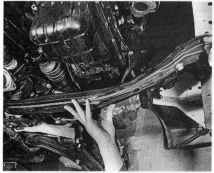

4.157C Removing the engine crossmember

4.158 Front engine mounting

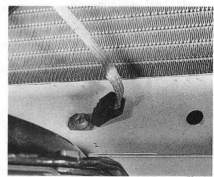

4.160 Front valance earth cable

4.162A Disconnect the ignition coil HT lead ...

4.162B ... left-hand multiplug ...

4.162C ... starter solenoid battery cable ...

4.162D ... starter solenoid trigger wire ...

4.162E ... gearbox reverse switch multiplug ...

4.162F ... alternator harness ...

4.162G ... rear multiplug ...

4.162H ... and strap ...

4.162I ... lower rear multiplug ...

4.162J ... multiplug from the clip on the inlet manifold ...

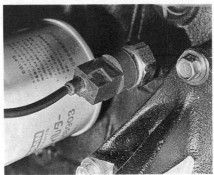

4.162K ... oil pressure switch lead ...

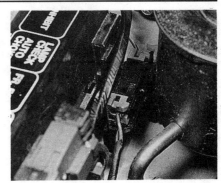

4.162L ... small ...

4.162M ... and large multiplugs from the right-hand strut tower ...

4.162N ... and the earth wire

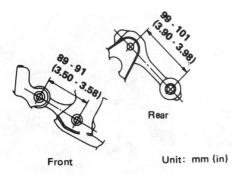

Fig. 13.16 Engine front and rear mounting buffer rod adjustment dimensions (Sec 4)

Oil pressure switch lead
Inlet manifold temperature sender leads
Right-hand strut tower multiplugs and earth wire

163   Unbolt the gearchange rod from the gearbox (photo).
164   Unbolt the rear engine support rod.
165   Loosen the clips and disconnect the top hose from the radiator and engine.
166   Loosen the clips and disconnect the bottom hose from the coolant pipe and the radiator (photo).
167   Loosen the clips and disconnect the heater hoses from the bulkhead (photo).
168   Unscrew the collar and disconnect the speedometer cable from the gearbox (photo). Note that the inner cable has a spline which engages with the drive pinion.
169   Slacken the adjuster and unhook the clutch cable from the release lever and bracket (photos).

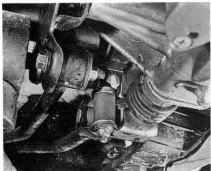

4.163 Gearchange rod connection to the gearbox

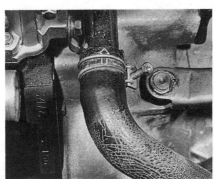

4.166 Bottom hose connection to the coolant pipe

4.167 Heater hose connections at the bulkhead

4.168 Speedometer cable connection to the gearbox

4.169A Slacken the adjuster ...

4.169B ... and unhook the clutch cable

4.171 Brake servo vacuum hose connection to the inlet manifold

4.174 Rear engine mounting bolt (arrowed)

4.175 Left-hand engine mounting bolt (arrowed)

4.177 Lifting the engine and transmission assembly from the engine compartment

4.178A Unbolt the right-hand support bar ...

4.178B ... the left-hand support bar...

4.178C ... the rear mounting bracket ...

4.178D ... and the front mounting bracket

4.178E Gearbox separated from the engine

4.179 Using a pair of grips when reconnecting the exhaust downpipe to the main exhaust

170 Identify the fuel pump pipes for position then disconnect them.
171 Disconnect the brake servo vacuum hose from the inlet manifold stub (photo).
172 Disconnect the radiator expansion hose from the left-hand side of the radiator, detach the two upper mountings, and lift the radiator from the engine compartment.
173 Connect an engine lifting hoist to the lifting eyes on the cylinder head.
174 Unscrew the rear engine mounting bolt (photo).
175 Unscrew the right and left-hand engine mounting bolts (photo). Note that the bolts are fitted with their heads towards the front.
176 For additional working room unbolt the left-hand engine mounting bracket from the body.

177 Lift the engine and transmission assembly carefully from the engine compartment taking care not to damage the surrounding body-work and components (photo).
178 To separate the engine from the gearbox, unbolt the support bars and rear mounting bracket, then unscrew the gearbox bolts. Also unbolt the front engine mounting bracket. Withdraw the gearbox from the engine (photos).
179 Refitting is a reversal of removal, but check that the front and rear engine mounting buffer rods are adjusted to the dimensions shown in Fig. 13.16. Adjust the accelerator cable with reference to Chapter 3. Top up the gearbox with oil as necessary. Refill the cooling system with reference to Chapter 2. When reconnecting the exhaust downpipe to the main exhaust on the GA16S engine it is helpful to use a pair of grips to hold the connector collar against the pressure of the spring (photo).

Engine and automatic transmission – removal and refitting

180 The procedure is similar to that for the manual transmission models but with reference also to Chapter 1, Section 12.

5 Engine (1.6 and 1.8 sixteen-valve)

General description

1 The 1.6 and 1.8 sixteen-valve engine is of four-cylinder, in-line, double over-head camshaft type. The camshafts are driven by a timing belt from the front of the crankshaft. The cylinder head is of light alloy construction and the cylinder block/crankcase of cast iron. The crankshaft is of five main bearing type. On the CA18DE engine a main bearing beam is fitted over the main bearing caps. The oil pump is mounted at the timing belt end of the crankshaft and supplies pressurised oil to all moving parts after the oil has first passed through an externally mounted full-flow cartridge type filter.

5.3 Disconnecting the top hose from the radiator

5.6A Loosen the alternator adjustment bolt ...

5.6B ... and remove the drivebelt

5.6C Removing the power steering drivebelt

5.7 Removing the water pump pulley

5.8A Unscrew the bolts ...

5.8B ... remove the crank angle sensor ...

5.8C ... and disconnect the multiplugs

5.10A Right-hand engine mounting

5.10B Removing the right-hand engine mounting bracket

5.10C Unscrew the lower bolts ...

5.10D ... and upper bolts including the dipstick bracket ...

5.10E ... and remove the upper timing belt cover

5.13A Unscrew the crankshaft pulley bolt ...

5.13B ... and remove the pulley

5.13C Using a puller to remove the crankshaft pulley

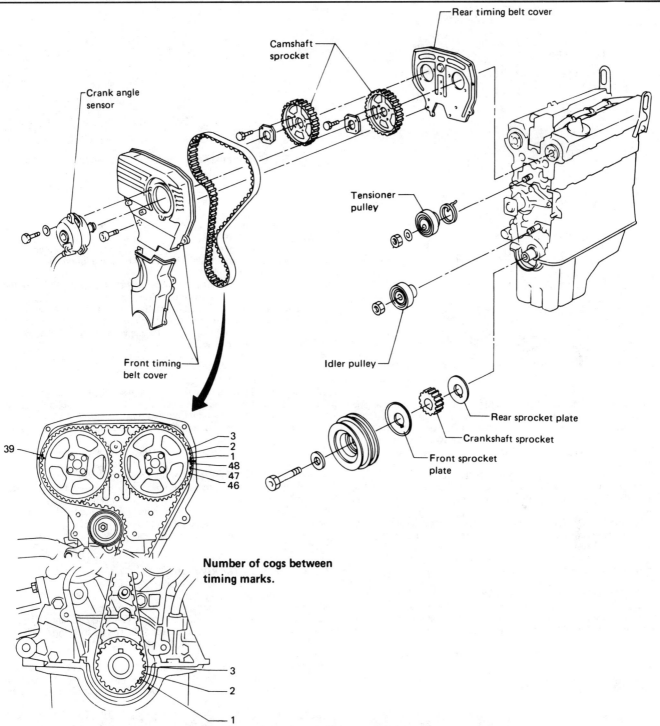

Number of cogs between timing marks.

Fig. 13.17 Timing belt and associated components (Sec 5)

Timing belt – removal and refitting

2   Disconnect the battery negative lead, then drain the cooling system with reference to Chapter 2.

3   Loosen the clips then disconnect and remove the top hose from both the engine and radiator (photo).

4   Apply the handbrake then jack up the front of the car and support on axle stands.

5   Remove the right-hand side roadwheel and the right-hand engine splash shield.

6   Remove the alternator and water pump/power steering pump drivebelts with reference to Section 6 (photos).

7   Unbolt and remove the water pump pulley (photo).

8   Mark the crank angle sensor and timing cover in relation to each other, then unscrew the mounting bolts and withdraw the sensor. Disconnect the multiplugs and remove the sensor (photos).

9   Support the weight of the engine with a hoist or with a trolley jack and block of wood beneath the right-hand side of the sump.

10   Unbolt and remove the right-hand engine mountings followed by the upper timing belt cover. An Allen key will be required to unscrew the upper timing belt cover bolts, and the dipstick support bracket must be released from one of the upper bolts (photos).

11   Turn the engine with a socket on the crankshaft pulley bolt until the timing marks on the camshaft sprockets are aligned with the marks on the rear timing belt cover and the timing cover pointer is aligned with the TDC mark on the crankshaft pulley.

12   Engage top gear and apply the handbrake, then unscrew the

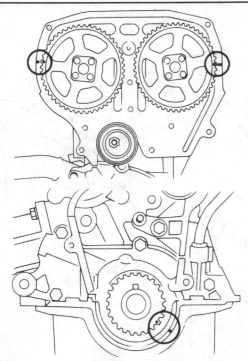

Fig. 13.18 TDC timing marks on the camshaft and crankshaft sprockets (Sec 5)

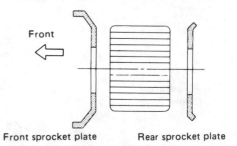

Fig. 13.19 Crankshaft sprocket plate locations (Sec 5)

21   Check that the marks on the camshaft sprockets are still aligned with the marks on the rear timing belt cover. Check also that the dot on the crankshaft sprocket is aligned with the mark on the front oil seal housing.
22   Engage the timing belt with the sprockets, tensioner and idler pulley making sure that the timing marks remain aligned. New timing belts are marked with white lines to coincide with the timing marks.
23   Loosen the tensioner pulley nut so that the spring tightens the timing belt. Do not tighten the nut at this stage.
24   Refit the lower timing belt cover, then insert and tighten the bolts.
25   Slide the pulley onto the front of the crankshaft. Insert the bolt and washer and tighten to the specified torque with top gear engaged and the handbrake applied (photo).
26   Using a socket on the crankshaft pulley bolt, turn the engine in its normal direction two complete turns. For ease of turning the engine, temporarily remove the spark plugs.
27   Tighten the tensioner pulley nut to the specified torque (photo).
28   Refit the upper timing belt cover and tighten the bolts. Note the location of the different length bolts as shown in Fig. 13.21.
29   Refit the right-hand engine mounting and tighten the bolts to the specified torque.
30   Refit the crank angle sensor, align the previously made marks, then insert and tighten the bolts to the specified torque.
31   Refit the water pump pulley and tighten the bolts.
32   Refit the water pump/power steering pump drivebelt with reference to Section 6.
33   Refit the right-hand side engine splash shield and roadwheel.
34   Lower the car to the ground.
35   Refit the top hose and refill the cooling system with reference to Chapter 2.

Cylinder head – removal and refitting
36   Release the ECCS fuel pressure as described in Section 8, then disconnect the battery negative lead.
37   Remove the timing belt as previously described.
38   Remove the air cleaner, accelerator cable, and relevant fuel injection equipment with reference to Section 8. The air trunking and lifting eye brackets may also be unbolted from the rear of the cylinder head at this stage (photos).
39   Unbolt the exhaust hot air shroud sections, and the exhaust downpipe support bracket. Unscrew the nuts securing the exhaust downpipe to the exhaust manifold, lower the downpipe and remove the gasket or sealing rings as applicable (photos).

crankshaft pulley bolt. The bolt is tightened to a high torque, and particular care will be necessary if the engine is supported on a trolley jack. If necessary, re-align the timing marks after loosening the bolt.
13   Remove the bolt and washer then slide the pulley from the front of the crankshaft. If it is tight use a puller. Remove the outer plate from the sprocket (photos).
14   Unbolt and remove the lower timing belt cover (photo).
15   Loosen the tensioner pulley nut, rotate the tensioner clockwise using an Allen key, then tighten the nut to hold the pulley in the retracted position.
16   Mark the timing belt to indicate its normal direction of rotation. Slip the belt from the crankshaft and camshaft sprockets and from the idler and tensioner pulleys (photo).
17   If required, unscrew the nut and remove the tensioner and spring, and slide off the crankshaft sprocket together with the inner plate (photo).
18   Examine the belt for damage and deterioration. Check for cracking at the base of the teeth and for excessive wear of the sides. Check for contamination by oil or coolant. The timing belt should be renewed at 60 000 mile (100 000 Km) intervals in any case, and it is recommended that it be renewed whenever removed.
19   If removed, refit the tensioner and spring and retain in the retracted position.
20   Slide the sprocket onto the front of the crankshaft together with the two plates. Make sure that the plates are fitted as shown in Fig. 13.19.

5.13D Removing the outer plate

5.14 Removing the lower timing belt cover

5.16 Crankshaft sprocket and timing belt idler

5.17 Crankshaft sprocket showing the Woodruff key

5.25 Tightening the crankshaft pulley bolt

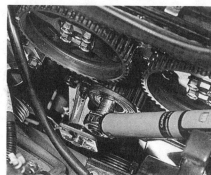

5.27 Tightening the tensioner pulley nut

5.38A Inlet air trunking bracket removal

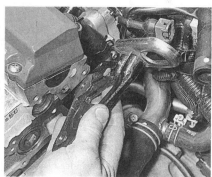

5.38B Engine lifting eye and bracket removal

5.39A Unscrew the bolts ...

5.39B ... and remove the exhaust hot air shroud upper section ...

5.39C ... and lower section ...

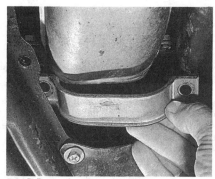

5.39D Removing the exhaust downpipe support bracket

5.40 Disconnecting the crankshaft ventilation hoses from the oil separator

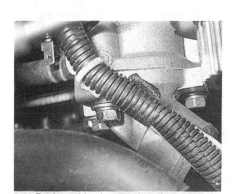

5.41 Engine wiring harness location on the right-hand side of the engine

5.42 Removing the exhaust manifold

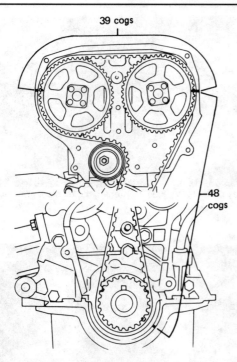

Fig. 13.20 Timing belt location diagram (Sec 5)

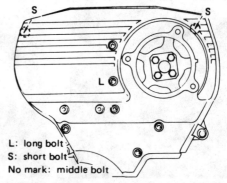

L: long bolt
S: short bolt
No mark: middle bolt

Fig. 13.21 Upper timing belt cover bolt locations (Sec 5)

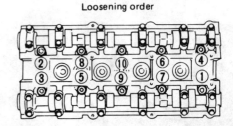

Fig. 13.22 Cylinder head bolt loosening sequence (Sec 5)

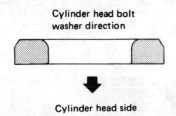

Fig. 13.23 Cylinder head bolt washer direction (Sec 5)

40   Disconnect the crankshaft ventilation hoses from the oil separator on the right-hand side of the cylinder head (photo).
41   Disconnect all wiring from the cylinder head noting the routing of the harness for correct reassembly (photo).
42   Remove the inlet and exhaust manifolds together with their gaskets with reference to Section 7 (photo).
43   Remove the spark plugs and HT wiring as described in Section 9. Also unbolt the power transistor and bracket (photos).
44   Unscrew the crosshead screws then remove the valve covers and remove the gaskets. Prise the camshaft seals from the rear of the cylinder head (photos).
45   Unbolt and remove the oil separator in order to give access to the

cylinder head bolts (photos). Also unbolt the right-hand front engine mounting bracket.
46   Progressively unscrew the cylinder head bolts in the order shown in Fig. 13.22. Remove the bolts together with their washers, taking care not to drop the washers down into the head cavity. A magnet is helpful to remove the washers (photos).
47   Rock the cylinder head to release it from the gasket, then lift it from the cylinder block (photo).
48   Remove the gasket from the block.
49   Thoroughly clean the joint surfaces of the cylinder head, block and front cover (photo).
50   Locate the new gasket on the cylinder block making sure that all holes are correctly aligned (photo).
51   Check that the camshafts are in the number 1 cylinder TDC compression position. Carefully lower the cylinder head onto the gasket making sure that the bolt holes are aligned.
52   Clean the cylinder head bolts and fit their washers noting that the chamfered side of the washers is next to the bolt heads. As it is difficult to fit the bolts with their washers already fitted, it is better to locate the washers on the cylinder head first using a screwdriver to lower them (photo).
53   Oil the threads and heat contact faces of the bolts. Insert them and tighten them in the order given in Fig. 13.24 and in the stages given in Specifications (photos). Note that after the first two stages, all of the bolts must be completely loosened before proceeding (ie **not** individually loosened then tightened).

5.43A Unscrew the lower bolts and remove the bracket ...

5.43B ... then remove the upper mounting bolts ...

5.43C ... and remove the power transistor

5.44A Unscrew the crosshead screws ...

5.44B ... and remove the valve covers ...

5.44C ... and gasket ...

5.44D ... and remove the camshaft seals

5.45A Unscrew the studs and bolts ...

5.45B ... and remove the oil separator

5.46A Removing the cylinder head bolts ...

5.46B ... and washers (using a magnet)

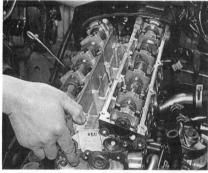

5.47 Lifting the cylinder head from the block

5.49 View of the cylinder block with the head removed

5.50 Locating the new head gasket on the block

5.52 Using a screwdriver to lower the washers onto the head

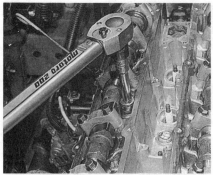

5.53A Torque tightening the cylinder head bolts

5.53B Angle tightening the cylinder head bolts

5.66A Unbolt the plates ...

5.66B ... and remove the camshaft sprockets

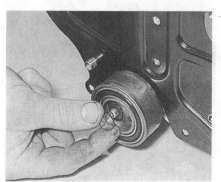

5.67A Unscrew the nut ...

5.67B ... and remove the timing belt tensioner

54   Clean the contact surfaces of the oil separator and head, then apply suitable sealant to the head. Refit the oil separator, insert the bolts and tighten them to the specified torque.

55   Clean the seal surface behind the rear ends of the camshafts and apply suitable sealant. Locate two new seals on the head.

56   Refit the valve covers together with new gaskets. Insert and tighten the bolts.

57   Refit the spark plugs and HT wiring.

58   Refit the inlet and exhaust manifolds together with new gaskets with reference to Section 7.

59   Reconnect all wiring to the cylinder head.

60   Reconnect the crankshaft ventilation hoses to the oil separator. Also refit the right-hand front engine mounting bracket and tighten the bolts.

61   Refit the exhaust downpipe to the manifold together with a new gasket and tighten the nuts.

62   Refit the fuel injection equipment and air cleaner with reference to Section 8.

63   Refit the timing belt as previously described.

64   Reconnect the battery negative lead.

Cylinder head – dismantling, overhaul and reassembly

65   Refer to Chapter 1, Section 17 and observe the cautionary note.

66   Identify for position then remove both camshaft sprockets by holding them stationary with a tool as shown in Section 4 or with a spanner on the special flats, and unscrewing the bolts. Remove the plates and pull the sprockets off the camshaft dowels (photos).

67   Unscrew the nut and remove the timing belt tensioner and spring (photos).

68   Unbolt the rear timing belt cover (photo)

69   Check that the camshaft bearing caps are numbered to ensure correct reassembly (they should be numbered from the front of the engine eg E1, E2 et seq for the exhaust caps). Progressively loosen the camshaft bearing cap bolts in the order shown in Fig. 13.25 then remove them (photos).

70   Remove the caps, then lift out the camshafts and remove the oil seals from them (photos).

71   Have ready a container of clean engine oil for the hydraulic valve lifters. As each lifter is removed, identify it for position with a tag. Remove each hydraulic valve lifter in turn starting from the front of the engine, and immerse it immediately in the oil in an upright position (photo). Do not place them upside down or on their sides as air may enter them. It is not possible to dismantle the hydraulic valve lifters.

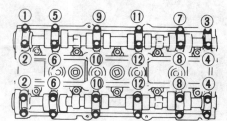

Fig. 13.24 Cylinder head bolt tightening sequence (Sec 5)

Fig. 13.25 Camshaft bearing cap bolt loosening sequence (Sec 5)

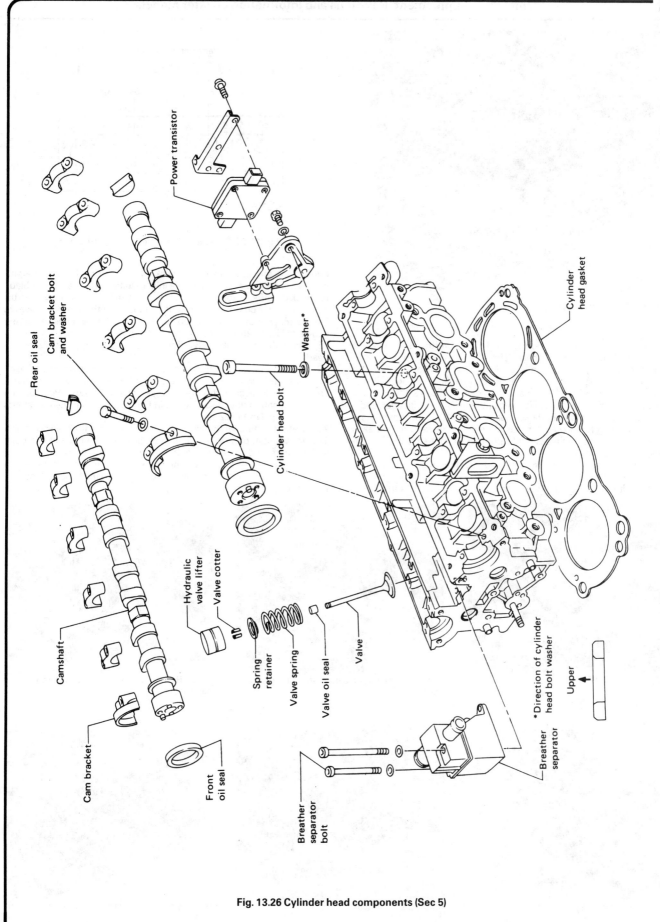

Fig. 13.26 Cylinder head components (Sec 5)

5.68 Rear timing belt cover

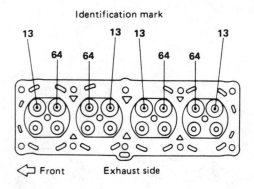

Fig. 13.27 Original inlet valve numbering (Sec 5)

72 Refer to Chapter 1, Section 17 for details of removing the valves and overhauling the cylinder head. The valves are located very deep within the cylinder head and it may be necessary to make up an adaptor to use with a valve lifter in order to remove the collets. The original inlet valves are identified with numbers as shown in Fig. 13.27, however service replacements are only supplied with the '64' identification and it is perfectly acceptable to fit these in place of the '13' type. Since there are two inlet and two exhaust valves per cylinder make sure that each one is marked for correct reassembly (photos). Refer also to the Specifications in this Supplement.

73 Note that the valve springs are fitted with their narrow pitch ends towards the cylinder head.

74 With the inlet manifold removed on the CA16DE engine, the opportunity should be taken to check it for distortion. Place a straight-edge across the contact face of the inlet manifold and use a feeler blade to check that the distortion is less than 0.1 mm (0.004 in). If outside this limit, it may be possible to adjust it by loosening the screws shown in Fig. 13.28. Do not, however, loosen the power valve adjusting screw shown in Fig. 13.29 as this is preset by the manufacturers.

75 Refit the hydraulic valve lifters in their correct positions in the head.

76 Oil the camshaft journals or bearing surfaces then locate each camshaft in its correct position. Note that the exhaust camshaft has a splined end to accept the crank angle sensor (photos). Position the sprocket location dowels as shown in Fig. 13.30 so that the camshafts are at TDC on No 1 cylinder.

77 Refit the camshaft bearing caps in their previously noted positions. The arrows stamped on the caps must face the front. Insert the bolts and washers, and initially just tighten them with the fingers.

78 Dip the new oil seals in oil and press them over the camshafts and into the front bearing caps as far as possible. Since the bolts are not fully tightened they can be pressed in by hand.

5.69A Camshaft bearing cap numbering

5.69B Removing the camshaft bearing cap bolts

5.70A Removing the camshaft bearing caps ...

5.70B ... and camshafts ...

5.70C ... and oil seals

5.71 Hydraulic valve lifters immersed in clean engine oil

5.72A Removing the hydraulic valve lifters from the cylinder head

5.72B Valve removal adaptor

5.72C Removing the cap ...

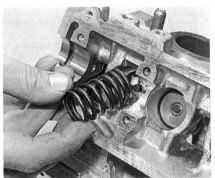

5.72D ... valve spring ...

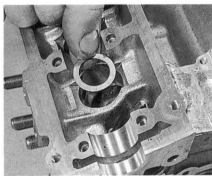

5.72E ... spring seat ...

5.72F ... and inlet valve

5.72G Valve stem oil seal located on the valve guide

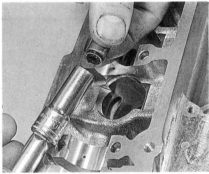

5.72H Use a suitable socket to drive the new valve stem oil seal onto the valve guide

5.72I Inserting an exhaust valve

5.72J Fitting the collets

5.72K Collets correctly fitted to the valve

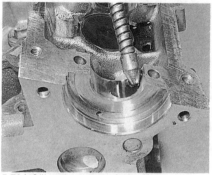

5.76A Oiling the camshaft bearing surfaces

5.76B Splined end of the exhaust camshaft to accept the crank angle sensor

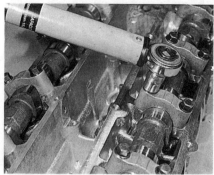

5.79 Tightening the camshaft bearing caps

79   Tighten the camshaft bearing caps to the specified torque in two or three stages in the order given in Fig. 13.31 (photo).
80   Refit the rear timing belt cover and tighten the bolts to the specified torque (photo).
81   Refit the timing belt tensioner and spring, turn the tensioner clockwise and tighten the nut (photo).
82   Refit the camshaft sprockets and plates, insert the bolts and tighten to the specified torque (photo).
83   The hydraulic valve lifters may be checked for an air lock as follows. With the cam lobe peak facing away from the lifter, press the lifter onto the valve stem. If the rocker arm moves more than 1 mm (0.04 in) air is present. To purge the air the engine must be run at 1000 rpm for approximately 10 minutes, however if the lifter is still noisy it should be renewed.

Sump – removal and refitting
84   Apply the handbrake, then jack up the front of the car and support on axle stands.

85   Remove the right-hand side and bottom splash shields from under the engine.
86   Position a suitable container beneath the sump, then unscrew the drain plug and drain the oil. Refit and tighten the plug on completion.
87   Unbolt the crossmember from under the engine and withdraw it from under the car.
88   Unscrew the nuts and disconnect the exhaust downpipe from the manifold. Remove the gasket or sealing rings as applicable (photo).
89   Unbolt the engine front mounting buffer rod and bracket.
90   Unbolt the strengtheners between the engine and gearbox.
91   Unscrew the sump bolts.
92   Carefully prise the sump from the block taking care not to damage the contact faces.
93   Clean all traces of sealant from the contact faces.
94   Using suitable sealant (preferably Nissan type) apply a continuous bead to the sump, making sure that the bead goes on the inner side of bolt holes. The bead should be 3.5 to 4.5 mm (0.138 to 0.177 in) wide.
95   Offer the sump to the block and insert the bolts. Tighten the bolts evenly to the specified torque.

Fig. 13.28 Inlet manifold distortion adjustment screws on the CA16DE engine only (Sec 5)

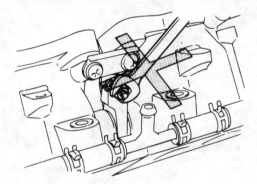

Fig. 13.29 Do not loosen the power valve adjusting screw on the CA16DE engine (Sec 5)

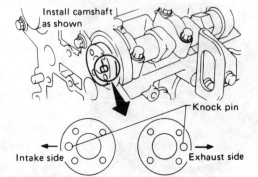

Install camshaft as shown

Knock pin

Intake side   Exhaust side

Fig. 13.30 Sprocket location dowel positions to set the camshafts at TDC (Sec 5)

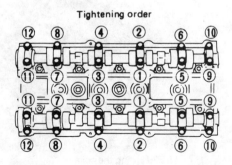

Tightening order

Fig. 13.31 Camshaft bearing cap bolt tightening sequence (Sec 5)

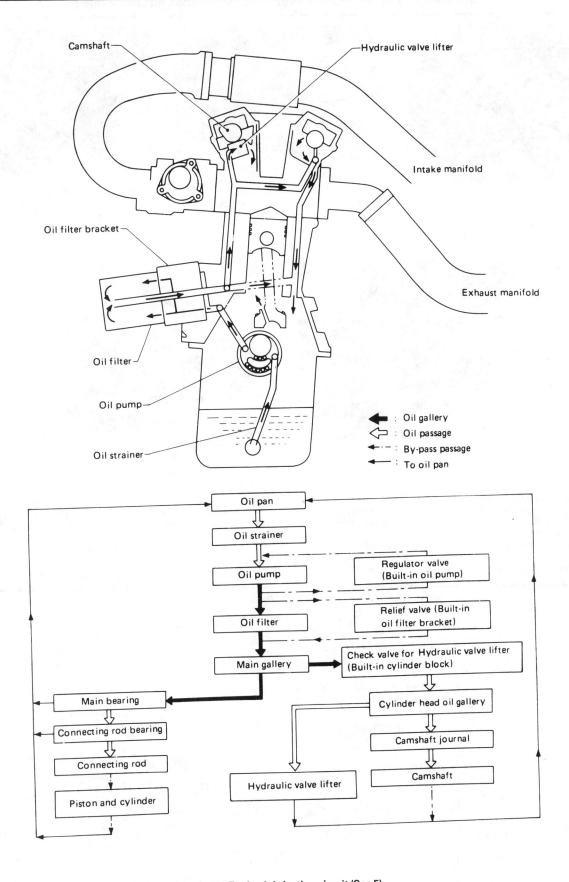

Fig. 13.32 Engine lubrication circuit (Sec 5)

5.80 Tightening the rear timing belt cover bolts

5.81 Refitting the timing belt tensioner

5.82 Tightening the camshaft sprocket bolts

5.88 Removing the exhaust downpipe sealing rings

5.103 Removing the oil pick-up pipe

96   Refit the strengtheners and tighten the bolts.
97   Refit the engine front mounting buffer rod and bracket.
98   Refit the exhaust downpipe to the manifold together with a new gasket and tighten the nuts.
99   Refit the engine crossmember and tighten the bolts.
100   Refit the splash shields.
101   Lower the car to the ground then refill the engine with oil.

Oil pump – removal, checking and refitting
102   Remove the timing belt and sump as described previously.
103   Unbolt and remove the oil pick-up pipe and strainer. Remove the O-ring (photo).
104   Unbolt and remove the oil pump from the front face of the crankcase. Discard the joint gasket.
105   Extract the screws using an impact driver, remove the cover and

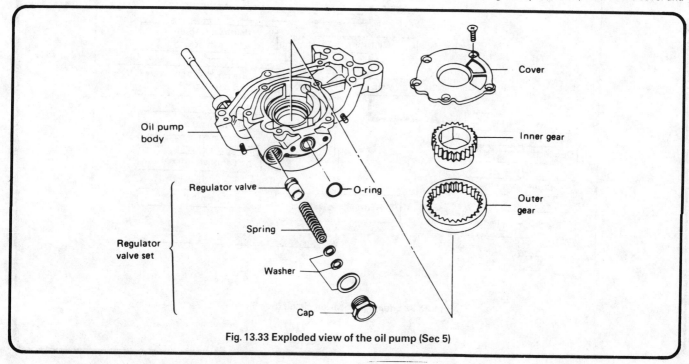

Fig. 13.33 Exploded view of the oil pump (Sec 5)

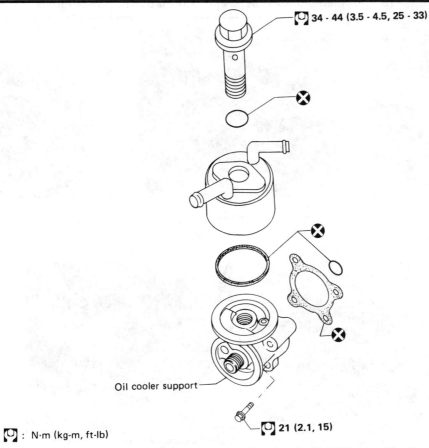

34 - 44 (3.5 - 4.5, 25 - 33)

Oil cooler support

21 (2.1, 15)

: N·m (kg-m, ft-lb)

Fig. 13.34 Oil cooler components fitted to the CA18DE engine (Sec 5)

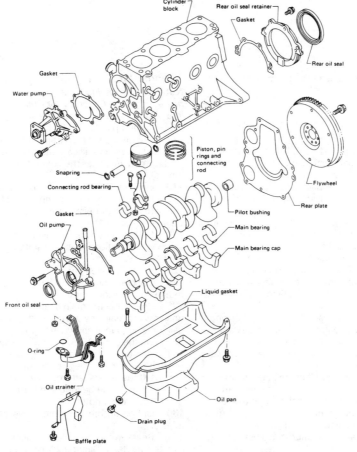

Cylinder block

Rear oil seal retainer

Gasket

Rear oil seal

Gasket

Water pump

Piston, pin rings and connecting rod

Flywheel

Snapring

Connecting rod bearing

Pilot bushing

Rear plate

Gasket

Oil pump

Main bearing

Main bearing cap

Front oil seal

Liquid gasket

O-ring

Oil strainer

Oil pan

Drain plug

Baffle plate

Fig. 13.35 Cylinder block components on the CA16DE engine (Sec 5)

5.105A Removing the oil pump cover

5.105B Checking the oil pump inner gear-to-crescent clearance ...

5.105C ... outer gear-to-crescent clearance ...

5.105D ... and outer gear-to-body clearance

5.106 Checking the oil pump gear endfloat

check the following clearances with a feeler blade and compare with the specified tolerances (photos):

   (a)   *Inner gear to crescent*
   (b)   *Outer gear to crescent*
   (c)   *Outer gear to body*

106   Now measure the gear endfloat using a feeler blade and a straight edge across the pump body. The endfloat must be within the specified tolerance (photo).

107   If any of the clearances are outside those specified, renew the components or complete oil pump as necessary, otherwise refit the cover and tighten the screws.

108   If necessary unscrew the endplug and remove the pressure regulator components (photos). Examine them for wear then clean them and refit together with a new sealing washer.

109   If it also worth checking the pressure relief valve ball at this time. To do this, remove the oil filter. If there is any indication of scoring or chipping of the ball valve, prise the valve from the oil filter mounting base and tap a new one into place with a piece of tubing. Refit the oil filter.

110   Prise out the crankshaft front oil seal from the oil pump housing, clean the seating, then dip the new seal in engine oil and press it into position using a suitable metal tube or socket (photos).

111   Clean the oil pump and block contact faces then fit a new gasket on the dowels.

112   As the oil pump is offered into position, align the inner gear with the flats on the crankshaft. Tape the shoulder on the crankshaft to prevent damage to the oil seal lips during fitting of the pump (photos). Remove the tape when the pump is in position.

113   Insert the bolts and tighten to the specified torque.

114   Refit the oil pick-up pipe and strainer together with a new O-ring and tighten the nut and bolts.

115   Refit the sump and timing belt as described previously.

Cylinder block – dismantling and reassembly

Note: *The following paragraphs give an outline of the procedures, however refer to Chapter 1 for a more detailed description*

116   With the engine remove from the car, remove the timing belt, sump, oil pump and cylinder head as previously described.

117   Unbolt the alternator and power steering pump brackets.

118   Unscrew and discard the oil filter. On the CA18DE engine disconnect the coolant hoses then unbolt and remove the oil cooler and gasket (photo).

119   Unscrew and remove the oil pressure switch.

120   Remove the water pump with reference to Section 6.

121   Remove the pistons from the cylinder block with reference to Chapter 1.

122   Mark the flywheel in relation to the crankshaft rear flange. Hold the flywheel stationary using a suitable tool then unscrew the bolts and lift it off.

123   Take off the engine rear plate (photo).

124   Unscrew the crankshaft rear oil seal retainer bolts and remove the retainer and gasket (photo).

125   Check that the main bearing caps are numbered for position then unscrew the main bearing cap bolts progressively in two or three stages using the sequence shown in Fig. 13.37. Remove the bolts.

126   On the CA18DE engine remove the main bearing beam.

127   Remove the main bearing caps taking care not to disturb the bearing shells. Keep the shells with their respective caps.

128   Lift the crankshaft from the cylinder block.

129   Remove the bearing shells from the block keeping them identified for position (photo).

130   Unbolt and remove the baffle plate from inside the crankcase (photo).

131   Reassemble the cylinder block in reverse order with reference also to Chapter 1, Section 20. Note that the upper main bearing shells have oil grooves. Tighten the main bearing cap bolts in two or three

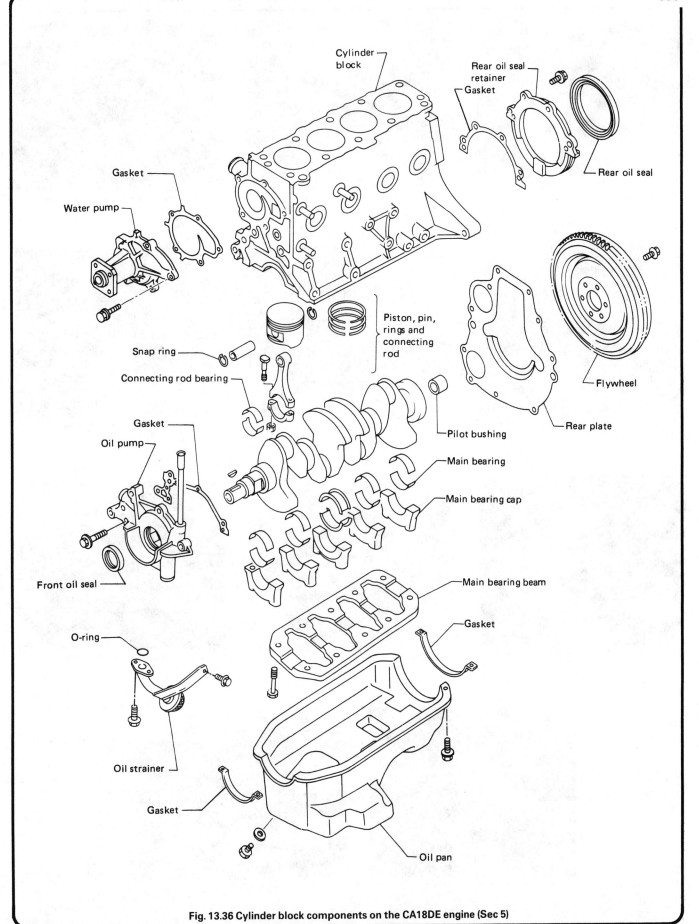

Fig. 13.36 Cylinder block components on the CA18DE engine (Sec 5)

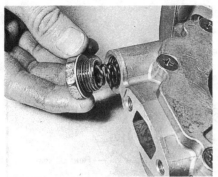

5.108A Unscrew the endplug ...

5.108B ... and remove the pressure regulator components

5.110A Prise out the crankshaft front oil seal ...

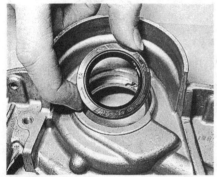

5.110B ... and remove it from the oil pump housing

5.112A Tape the crankshaft end ...

5.112B ... before fitting the oil pump

5.118 Coil cooler on the CA18DE engine

5.123 Engine rear plate

5.124 Removing the crankshaft rear oil seal retainer

5.129 Removing the main bearing shells

5.130 Crankcase oil baffle plate

5.131A Piston front mark

5.131B Driving piston into the cylinder bore

5.131C Tightening the big-end cap nuts

5.131D Fitting a new crankshaft rear oil seal in the retainer

5.139 Alternator and bracket

5.140 Front exhaust downpipe

stages in the sequence given in Fig. 13.14 for the twelve-valve engine. Renew the crankshaft rear oil seal before refitting the retainer. Use a punch to drive out the old seal then clean the seating and drive in the new seal using a block of wood (photos). Refit the rear oil seal retainer using a new gasket. Fit a new oil filter. On the CA18DE engine refit the oil cooler with a new gasket.

Pistons – disconnecting from connecting rods
132   The procedure is as described in Section 4 for the twelve-valve engines.

Engine and manual transmission – removal and refitting
133   Open the bonnet and disconnect the washer tube. Mark the hinge positions then unbolt the bonnet and lift it from the car. Nissan apply a very strong adhesive between the hinges and bonnet which is hard to break, so care is necessary to avoid damaging the bonnet while prising the hinges free.
134   Release the ECCS fuel pressure as described in Section 8.

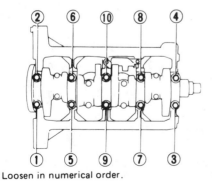
Loosen in numerical order.

Fig. 13.37 Main bearing cap bolt loosening sequence (Sec 5)

135   Disconnect the battery leads then remove the clamp. Remove the battery tray, and unbolt the platform.
136   Support the front of the car on axle stands and apply the handbrake.
137   Remove the front wheels. Remove the engine splash shields including the side shields.
138   Drain the cooling system (Chapter 2).
139   Loosen the alternator and power steering pump mounting and adjusting bolts and remove the drivebelts (photo). Unbolt the power steering pump from the cylinder block and tie it to one side.
140   Remove the front exhaust downpipe and gaskets or sealing rings with reference to Section 7 (photo).
141   Disconnect the steering track rod ends and front suspension lower balljoints.
142   Remove both front brake calipers with reference to Chapter 9, however do not disconnect the hydraulic hose. Support the caliper so that the hose is not strained or twisted.
143   Separate the steering knuckle from the front suspension strut by unscrewing the two bolts. Note that their heads face the front.
144   Position a suitable container beneath the gearbox to catch any spilled oil then lever each driveshaft from the gearbox and withdraw from the car.
145   Unscrew and remove the rear engine mounting bolt.
146   Unbolt the crossmember from under the engine.
147   Unscrew the bolt from the front engine mounting.
148   Remove the air ducting between the air cleaner and throttle housing (photos).
149   Pull the small earth cable from the front valance.
150   Disconnect the accelerator cable.
151   Disconnect the wiring from the engine. If major dismantling of the engine is not contemplated, leave the harness in position and disconnect the main and small multiplugs on the right-hand side (photo), otherwise disconnect the following:

Multiplug by the battery mounting
Battery cable from the starter solenoid
Starter solenoid and gearbox switch (photo)
Battery earth lead from the starter mounting bolt

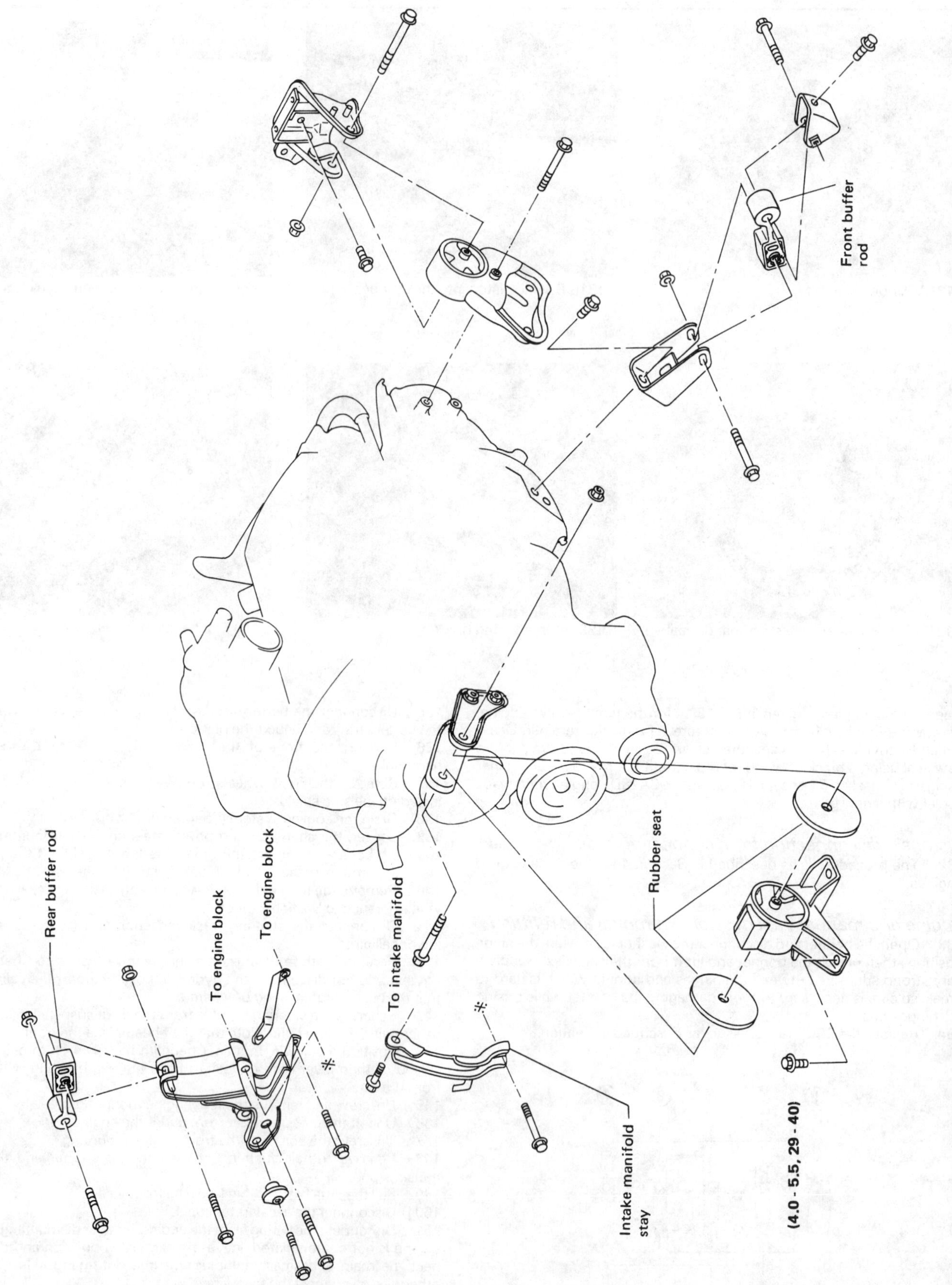

Front buffer rod

Rear buffer rod

To engine block

To engine block

To intake manifold

Rubber seat

Intake manifold stay

(4.0 - 5.5, 29 - 40)

Fig. 13.38 Engine mounting components on the CA18DE engine (Sec 5)

Note: *Mountings vary slightly on the CA16DE engine*

5.148A Loosen the clips ...

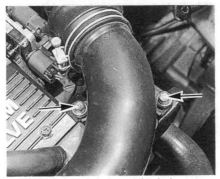

5.148B ... unscrew the mounting bolts (arrowed) ...

5.148C ... and remove the air ducting

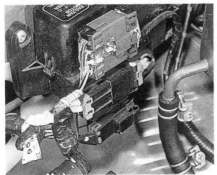

5.151A Main engine wiring harness multiplugs on the right-hand side of the engine compartment

5.151B Gearbox wiring multiplug

Alternator harness and bracket
Temperature sender multiplug
Earth cable from the inlet manifold
Multiplug from the rear of the cylinder head
Oil pressure switch lead
Right-hand strut tower earth wire

152   Unbolt the gearchange rod from the gearbox.
153   Unbolt the rear engine support rod.
154   Loosen the clips and disconnect the top hose from the radiator and engine.
155   Loosen the clips and disconnect the bottom hose from the coolant pipe and radiator.
156   Loosen the clips and disconnect the heater hoses from the bulkhead.
157   Unscrew the collar and disconnect the speedometer cable from the gearbox. Note that the inner cable has a spline which engages with the drive pinion.
158   Slacken the adjuster and unhook the clutch cable from the release lever and bracket.
159   Disconnect the fuel supply and return pipes.
160   Disconnect the brake servo vacuum hose from the inlet manifold stub.
161   Disconnect the radiator expansion hose from the left-hand side of the radiator, detach the two upper mountings, and lift the radiator from the engine compartment.
162   Connect an engine lifting hoist to the lifting eyes on the cylinder head.
163   Unbolt the rear engine mounting at the body.
164   Unbolt the right-hand engine mounting. Note that the right and left-hand engine mounting bolts are fitted with their heads towards the front.
165   For additional working room unbolt the left-hand engine mounting bracket from the body.
166   Lift the engine and transmission assembly carefully from the engine compartment taking care not to damage the surrounding bodywork and components.

167   To separate the engine from the gearbox, unbolt the support bars and front mounting bracket, then unscrew the gearbox bolts. Also unbolt the rear engine mounting bracket. Withdraw the gearbox from the engine.
168   Refitting is a reversal of removal, but check that the front and rear engine mounting buffer rods are adjusted to the dimensions shown in Fig. 13.16. Make sure that the right and left-hand engine mounting insulators are central within their brackets. Adjust the accelerator cable with reference to Chapter 3. Top up the gearbox with oil as necessary. Refill the cooling system with reference to Chapter 2.

6 Cooling system (twelve and sixteen-valve engines)

General description

1   The cooling system is as described in Chapter 2 except for the following differences. On twelve-valve engines the water pump is located on the front timing cover which incorporates channels leading to the cylinder block. The thermostat is located on the water pump. On sixteen-valve engines the water pump is fitted to the front of the cylinder block and the thermostat is located above it.

Cooling system – draining, flushing and refilling

2   Refer to Chapter 2, however note the following. On both twelve and sixteen-valve engines a cylinder block drain plug is provided on the rear right-hand side of the block, and on twelve-valve engines a vent plug is provided on the front left-hand side of the cylinder head (photos).

6.2A Cylinder block drain plug (twelve-valve engines)

6.2B Unscrewing the cooling system vent plug (twelve-valve engines)

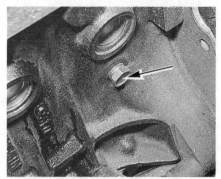

6.2C Cylinder block drain plug on the CA18DE engine (arrowed)

6.3 Thermostat housing and cover on the twelve-valve engine (arrowed)

4   The removal, testing and refitting procedures are similar to those described in Chapter 2 except that on twelve-valve engines the cover is sealed with sealant instead of a gasket (photos). This may mean that it is necessary to tap the cover gently to release it.
5   Before refitting the cover on the twelve-valve engine, thoroughly clean the contact faces then apply a bead of suitable sealant as shown in Fig. 13.42 (photo). Tighten the cover bolts to the specified torque and refill the cooling system as described earlier in this Section.

Radiator – removal, repair and refitting
6   The procedure is as given in Chapter 2, Section 6, however the top and bottom hose locations are different as shown in Figs. 13.43 and 13.44 (No A/C in UK) (photos).

Water pump (twelve-valve engine) – removal and refitting
7   Drain the cooling system as described previously.
8   Remove the alternator drivebelt and if applicable the power steering pump drivebelt as described in Chapter 2, Section 9.
9   Remove the thermostat as previously described. Note that the cooling fan thermoswitch is located in the thermostat cover (photo).
10   Unbolt the thermostat housing from the water pump.
11   Unbolt the pulley from the water pump drive flange (photo).
12   Unscrew the mounting bolts and withdraw the water pump from the engine front cover (photo).

Thermostat – removal, testing and refitting
3   On twelve-valve engines the thermostat is located beneath a cover on a housing attached to the rear of the water pump on the right-hand side of the engine (photo). On sixteen-valve engines it is located beneath a cover on the right-hand end of the cylinder head.

6.4A Removing the thermostat on the twelve-valve engine

6.4B Jiggle pin and TOP marking on the thermostat on the twelve-valve engine

6.5 Fitting the thermostat cover on the twelve-valve engine

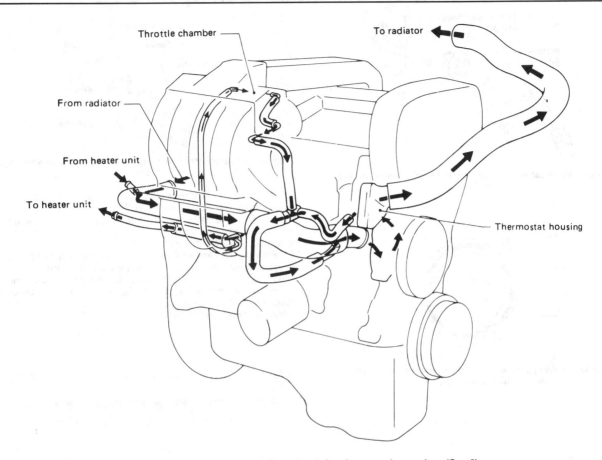

Throttle chamber

From radiator

From heater unit

To heater unit

To radiator

Thermostat housing

Fig. 13.39 Cooling system flow circuit for sixteen-valve engines (Sec 6)

6.6A Radiator drain tap (arrowed)

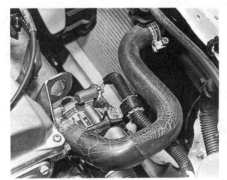

6.6B Radiator top hose

6.6C Radiator upper mounting

6.6D Removing the radiator

6.9 Cooling fan thermoswitch location on the twelve-valve engine

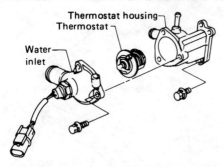

Fig. 13.40 Thermostat components on the twelve-valve engine (Sec 6)

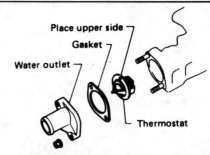

Fig. 13.41 Thermostat components on the sixteen-valve engine (Sec 6)

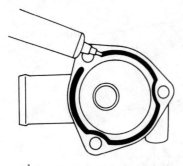

Fig. 13.42 Applying sealant to the thermostat cover on the twelve-valve engine (Sec 6)

13   It is not possible to repair the water pump, and therefore a leaking or damaged pump must be renewed. If it is to be refitted, clean all traces of sealant from the contact surfaces of the water pump and engine front cover. Make sure that the sealant is also removed from the grooves in the contact surface of the water pump.

14   Refitting is a reversal of removal but apply a bead of suitable sealant to the contact face of the water pump as shown in Fig. 13.46. Similarly clean the thermostat housing and cover faces and apply sealant. Tighten all bolts to the specified torque, and adjust the drivebelt tension with reference to Chapter 2, Section 9. Refill the cooling system as described previously (photos).

Water pump (sixteen-valve engine) – removal and refitting

15   Drain the cooling system as described previously.

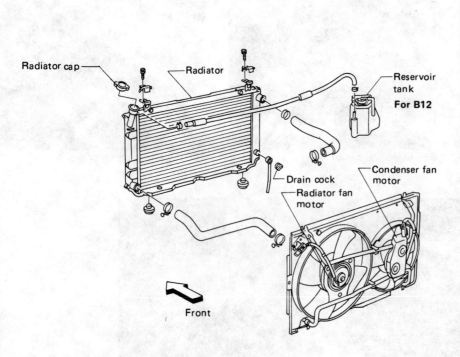

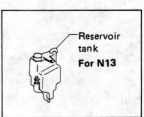

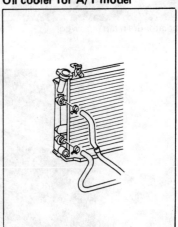

Oil cooler for A/T model

Fig. 13.43 Radiator components on the twelve-valve engine (Sec 6)

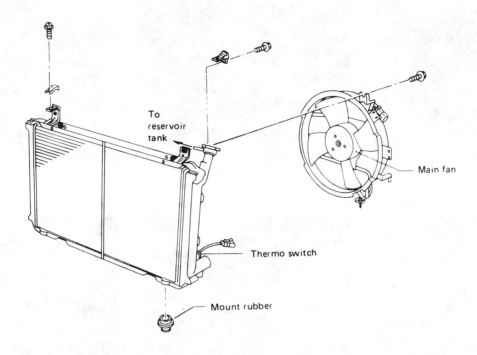

Fig. 13.44 Radiator components on the sixteen-valve engine (Sec 6)

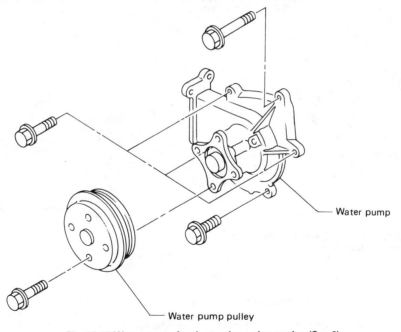

Fig. 13.45 Water pump for the twelve-valve engine (Sec 6)

6.11 Water pump pulley

6.12 Water pump removal on the twelve-valve engine

6.14A Applying sealant to the water pump on the twelve-valve engine

6.14B Refitting the water pump on the twelve-valve engine

6.14C Refitting the thermostat housing

6.23 Using a spring balance to check the alternator drivebelt deflection

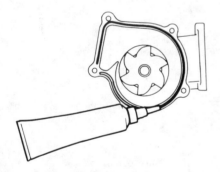

Fig. 13.46 Applying sealant to the contact face of the water pump on the twelve-valve engine (Sec 6)

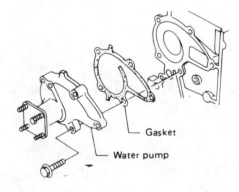

Fig. 13.47 Water pump for the sixteen-valve engine (Sec 6)

16   Remove the alternator drivebelt and if applicable the power steering pump drivebelt as described in Chapter 2, Section 9.
17   Remove the timing covers with reference to Section 5 of this Supplement.
18   Unbolt the pulley from the water pump drive flange.
19   Unscrew the water pump mounting bolts and withdraw the water pump sideways taking care not to allow the coolant to drop onto the timing belt. Remove the gasket.
20   It is not possible to repair the water pump so if it is faulty it should be renewed.
21   Clean the contact faces of the water pump and cylinder block.
22   Refitting is a reversal of removal but use a new gasket and tighten all bolts to the specified torque. Tension the drivebelts with reference to Chapter 2, Section 9. Refill the cooling system as described previously.

Drivebelts – removal, refitting and adjustment
23   Refer to Chapter 2, Section 9 and also Figs. 13.48 and 13.49. The

drivebelt deflection should be checked with a force of 98 N (22 lb) applied at the points indicated, and one way to measure this is to use a spring balance (photo).

Cooling fan thermoswitch – removal, testing and refitting
24   Drain approximately 1 litre (1.8 pints) from the cooling system as previously described.
25   Disconnect the wiring and unscrew the thermoswitch from the rear of the cylinder head (twelve-valve engine) or bottom of the radiator (sixteen-valve engine). Remove the sealing washer.
26   To test the switch, connect an ohmmeter or test lamp to the switch terminals then suspend it in water which is being heated. Check the temperature at which the internal contacts close, and renew the switch if this is not as given in the Specifications.
27   Refitting is a reversal of removal but fit a new sealing washer and tighten the switch to the specified torque. Refill the cooling system as previously described.

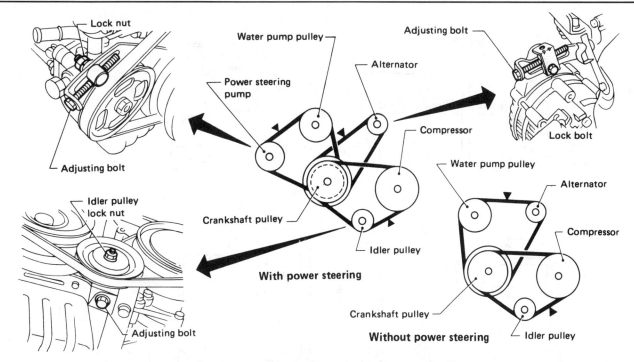

Fig. 13.48 Drivebelt configurations on the twelve-valve engine (Sec 6)

Arrows indicate tension checking points   Note A/C not fitted to UK models

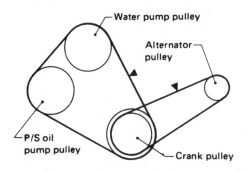

Fig. 13.49 Drivebelt configuration on the sixteen-valve engine (Sec 6)

Arrows indicate tension checking points

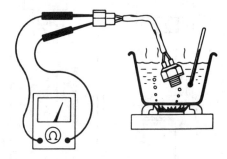

Fig. 13.50 Checking the cooling fan thermoswitch (Sec 6)

---

7   Fuel, exhaust and emission control systems (twelve-valve engines)

General description

1   On the E16S engine the fuel pump is located in the fuel tank together with the fuel level transmitter and gauge. On twelve-valve engines the fuel pump is located on the cylinder head and is operated by a lever in contact with an eccentric on the camshaft.

Fuel pump – removal and refitting

2   The procedure is similar to that described in Chapter 3 except for its location on the cylinder head (photos).

Carburettor – description

3   The carburettor fitted to the twelve-valve engine is shown in Fig. 13.52 and incorporates an automatic choke (photos). Its design is similar to the carburettor fitted to the E13 engine in Chapter 3.

Carburettor – checks and adjustments
Float level
4   Remove the carburettor from the engine and remove the cover (photos).
5   Hold the cover upside down in a horizontal position.
6   Fully raise the float then lower it until it just contacts the needle valve. Hold it in this position and use a ruler or vernier calipers to check the distance from the cover to the float – dimension H1 in Fig. 13.53 (photo). If the distance is not as given in the Specifications bend the float seat as necessary.
7   Now hold the cover upright so that the float is fully lowered, and check that the distance from the cover to the further edge of the float is as given in the Specifications – dimension H2 in Fig. 13.54.
8   With the cover refitted the level may also be checked using the sight glass as described in Chapter 3.
Automatic choke
9   Refer to Chapter 3, Section 10, paragraphs 3 to 6.
10   Start the engine then disconnect the automatic choke wiring at the multiplug. Using a voltmeter check that the voltage available at terminal 1 (Fig. 13.55) is between 9 and 12 volts. If not, suspect the relay or associated wiring.
11   With the multiplug still disconnected use an ohmmeter to check for continuity between terminal 4 and the choke housing (Fig. 13.56).
12   Run the engine to normal operating temperature. Remove the automatic choke cover and position the fast idle arm on the second step of the cam.

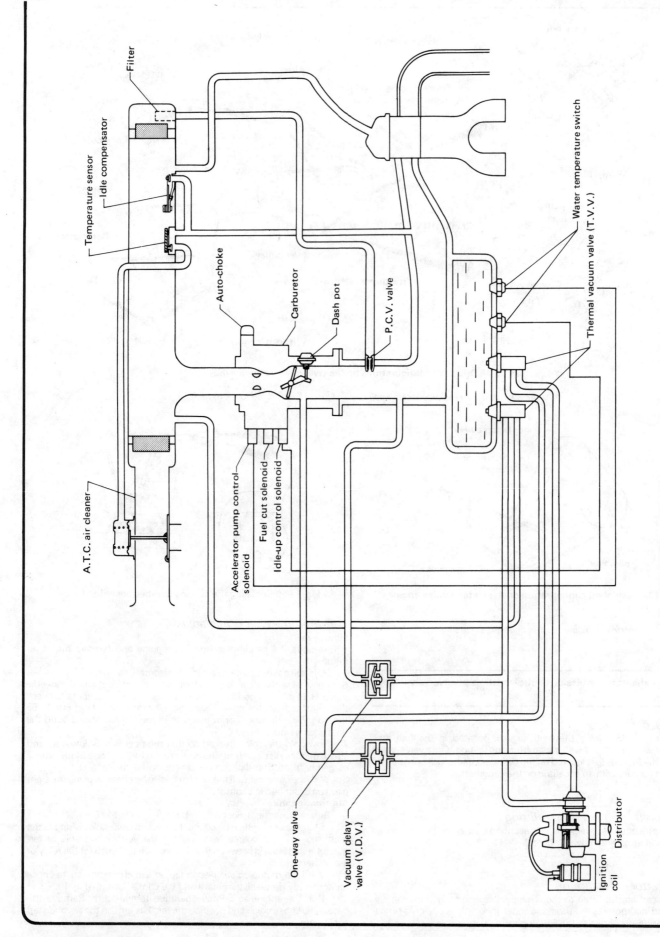

Fig. 13.51 Diagram of fuel system on twelve-valve engines (Sec 7)

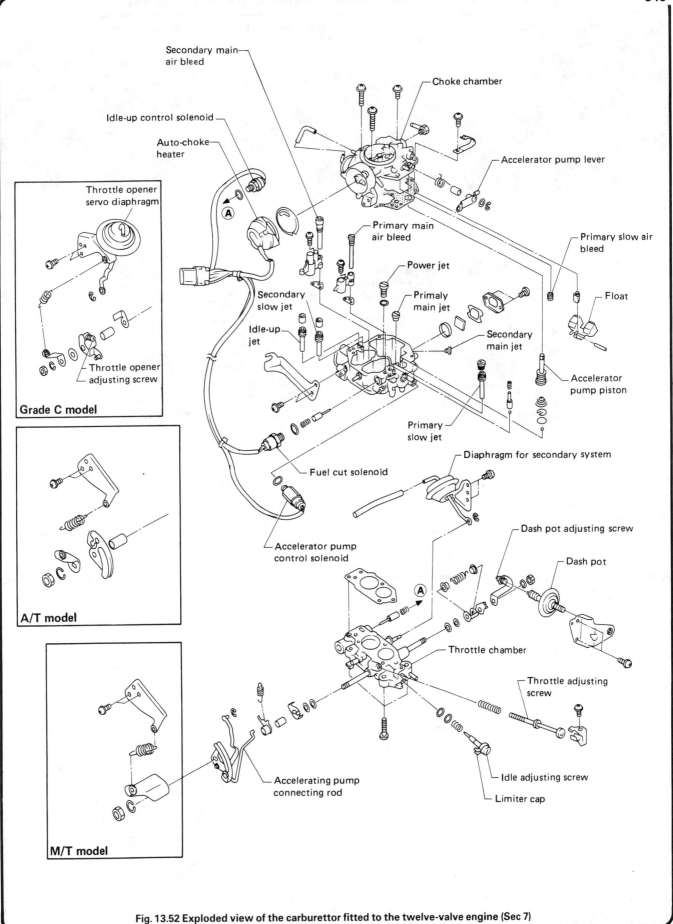

Fig. 13.52 Exploded view of the carburettor fitted to the twelve-valve engine (Sec 7)

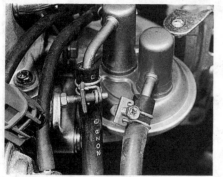
7.2A Fuel pump and hoses on the twelve-valve engine

7.2B Disconnecting a fuel pump hose

7.2C Unscrew the nuts ...

7.2D ... and remove the fuel pump ...

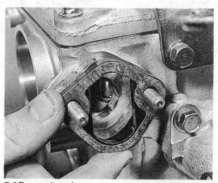
7.2E ... and gasket

13   With a tachometer connected to the engine check that the speed is as given in the Specifications. If not, remove the carburettor from the engine and position the fast idle cam on the second step of the cam.

14   Using a twistdrill check that the clearance between the throttle valve and the bore wall is as given in the Specifications. If not, turn the fast idle adjusting screw as necessary.

15   Refit the carburettor to the engine and check the fast idle speed as previously described.

Automatic temperature control accelerator pump

16   The amount of fuel injected by the accelerator pump is determined by the temperature of the coolant. A control solenoid is located below the accelerator pump lever on the side of the carburettor.

17   As an initial check, remove the air cleaner then operate the throttle fully while looking down into the carburettor. A well defined spurt of fuel should come from the jet. With the ignition switched on, the control

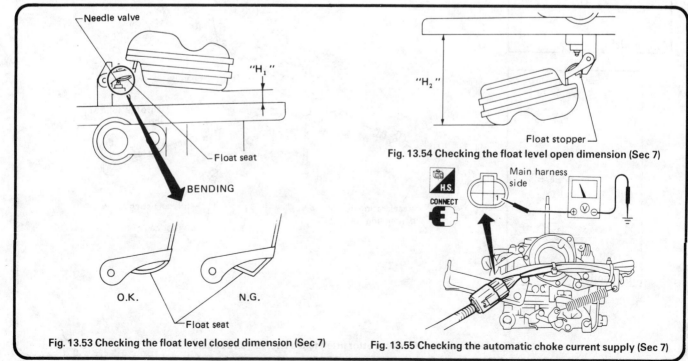

Fig. 13.53 Checking the float level closed dimension (Sec 7)

Fig. 13.54 Checking the float level open dimension (Sec 7)

Fig. 13.55 Checking the automatic choke current supply (Sec 7)

7.3A Top view of carburettor

7.3B Removing the carburettor from the inlet manifold

7.3C Carburettor front view ...

7.3D ... rear view ...

7.3E ... right-hand side view ...

7.3F ... and left-hand side view

solenoid should be on and the amount of fuel injected high, however with the ignition off the control solenoid should be off and the amount of fuel injected low.

18   To check the solenoid valve, disconnect the multiplug and connect a 12 volt supply to the solenoid terminals. The valve should be heard to click as the battery is connected and disconnected. If not, the solenoid is faulty.

Idle-up control solenoid

19   The idle-up control increases the engine speed when the head-lamps, heated rear window, heater motor, or power steering is in operation.

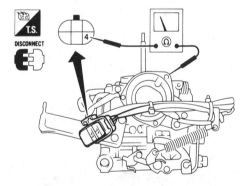

Fig. 13.56 Checking the automatic choke heater for continuity (Sec 7)

7.3G View of the inside of the carburettor

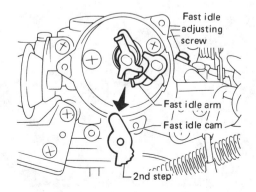

Fig. 13.57 Fast idle adjustment (Sec 7)

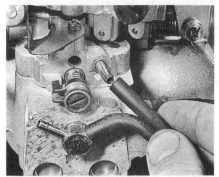

7.4A Disconnecting the vacuum hose from the carburettor

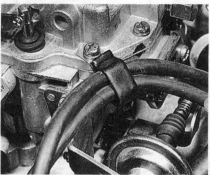

7.4B Vacuum hose clip on the carburettor

7.4C Removing a cover screw

7.4D Throttle lever on the carburettor

7.4E Removing the carburettor cover

7.6 Checking the float level dimension

20   To check the solenoid, disconnect the wiring multiplug and connect a 12 volt supply. As the battery is connected and disconnected the solenoid should be heard to click. If not, the solenoid is faulty.

Fuel cut solenoid

21   The fuel cut solenoid stops the fuel supply when the engine is switched off.

22   To check the solenoid, disconnect the multiplug and connect a 12 volt supply to the terminals. As the battery is connected and disconnected the solenoid should be heard to click. If not, it is faulty.

Dash pot

23   With the engine at normal operating temperature and the idle speed and mixture correct, run the engine at idle speed. Position the throttle so that the lever is just touching the pot plunger, then check that the engine speed is as given in the Specifications.

24   After the check release the throttle and check that the speed drops smoothly from 2000 to 1000 rpm in approximately 3 seconds.

Carburettor – idle speed and mixture adjustment

25   Refer to Chapter 3, Section 11 together with the accompanying Fig. 13.60 (photos). The starting point for the mixture adjusting screw is three complete turns instead of the two turns given in Chapter 3.

7.25A Idle speed adjustment screw

7.25B Mixture adjustment screw

7.27A Inlet manifold support stay (arrowed)

7.27B Connections to the inlet manifold

7.27C Inlet manifold mounting nuts

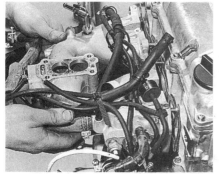

7.27D Removing the inlet manifold

7.27E Inlet manifold gasket on the cylinder head

7.27F Removing the carburettor flange gasket from the inlet manifold

7.27G Inlet manifold and carburettor assembly

7.27H Exhaust manifold hot air shroud, showing the earth cable

7.27I Removing the exhaust manifold hot air shroud

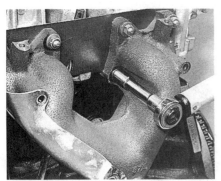

7.27J Unscrew the mounting nuts ...

7.27K ... and remove the exhaust manifold ...

7.27L ... and gasket

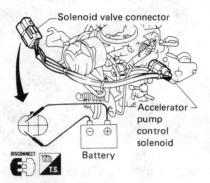

Fig. 13.58 Checking the automatic temperature control accelerator pump solenoid valve (Sec 7)

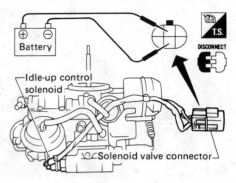

Fig. 13.59 Checking the idle-up control solenoid (Sec 7)

Fig. 13.60 Idle speed and mixture adjustment screws (Sec 7)

Manifolds and exhaust system – general

26   The exhaust manifold is on the left-hand side of the cylinder head, the inlet manifold on the right-hand side.

27   Refer to Chapter 3 for more information on removing the manifolds (photos).

28   The exhaust system on the GA14S engine is identical to that for the E13 engine shown in Chapter 3 except that a sealing ring is fitted instead of a gasket.

29   The exhaust system on the GA16S engine is identical to that for the E16 engine shown in Chapter 3 except that the front downpipe is of single instead of twin pipe construction. Further there is no heat shield fitted over the downpipe.

---

8   Fuel, exhaust and emission control systems (sixteen-valve engines)

General description and precautions

1   The electronic fuel injection system is an integral part of the ECCS system which covers both the fuel and ignition systems. The electronic control unit (ECU) incorporates a self-diagnostic system using coded flashing lamps and the unit controls the following:

(a)   *Quantity of fuel injected*
(b)   *Ignition timing*
(c)   *Idle speed*

(d)   *Fuel pump*
(e)   *Air regulator*
(f)   *Acceleration cut control*
(g)   *Self-diagnosis*

2   A crank angle sensor is located at the front of the crankshaft and monitors engine speed and piston position using light emitting and photo diodes.

3   An air flow meter measures the flow rate of the air entering the engine using a hot wire system (photo).

4   A thermistor type water temperature sensor monitors the temperature of the coolant.

5   The speed of the vehicle is monitored by a reed switch located in the speedometer.

6   A throttle valve switch is located on the throttle housing. It has two internal contacts which close when the throttle is in either the closed or open position.

7   An idle air adjusting control valve located on the inlet manifold controls the idle speed at a preset value. It is itself controlled by the ECU which processes the information from the various sensors including a neutral switch located on the gearbox. An auxiliary air control valve functions together with the idle air adjusting control valve.

8   An air regulator located on the inlet manifold provides additional air when the engine is cold in order to increase the engine speed during the warm-up period.

9   Each cylinder is provided with an injector which is activated electronically by the ECU, the amount of fuel injected depending on the length of opening time.

10   The fuel pump is located in the fuel tank and incorporates vane rollers. The motor is cooled by the fuel.

11   An in-line fuel filter is fitted in the fuel supply line (photo).

12   The ECU receives information from the various sensors and calculates the basic injection pulse width for each injector. The same ECU calculates the ignition timing.

13   On the CA16DE engine a power valve is provided on the inlet manifold which effectively increases the size of the intake passages during high engine speed or heavy load conditions. Each intake passage has two channels one of which is blocked by the power valve during normal running so increasing the velocity of the incoming air and promoting more efficient combustion.

8.3 Air flow meter

8.11 In-line fuel filter

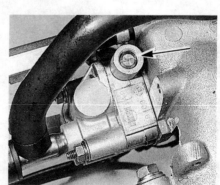

8.27 Idle speed adjusting screw (arrowed)

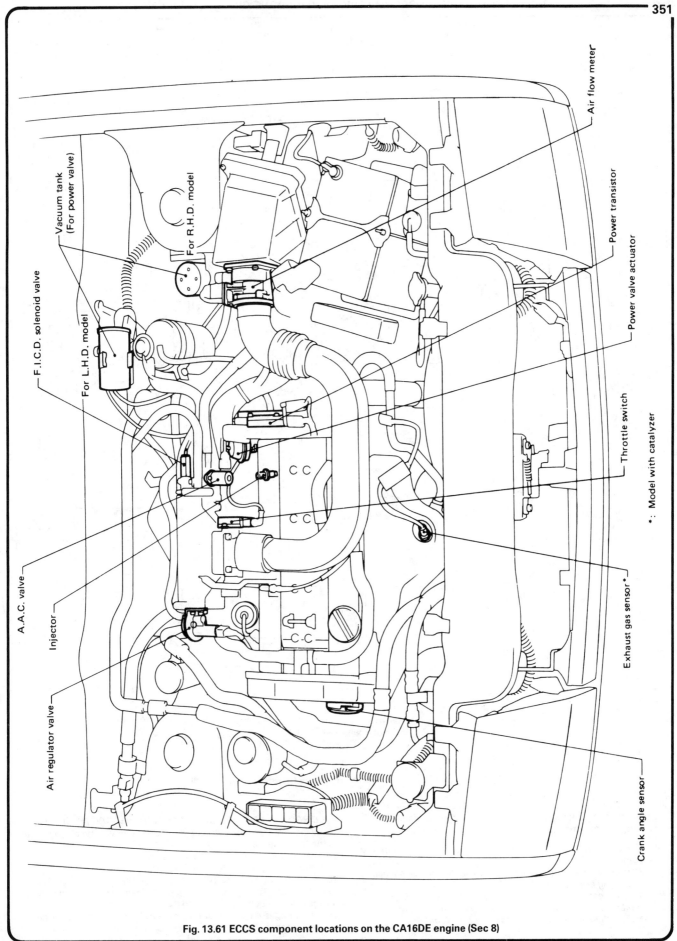

Fig. 13.61 ECCS component locations on the CA16DE engine (Sec 8)

Air flow meter

Power transistor

Power valve actuator

Throttle switch

*: Model with catalyzer

Exhaust gas sensor*

Crank angle sensor

Vacuum tank (For power valve)

For R.H.D. model

F.I.C.D. solenoid valve

For L.H.D. model

A.A.C. valve

Injector

Air regulator valve

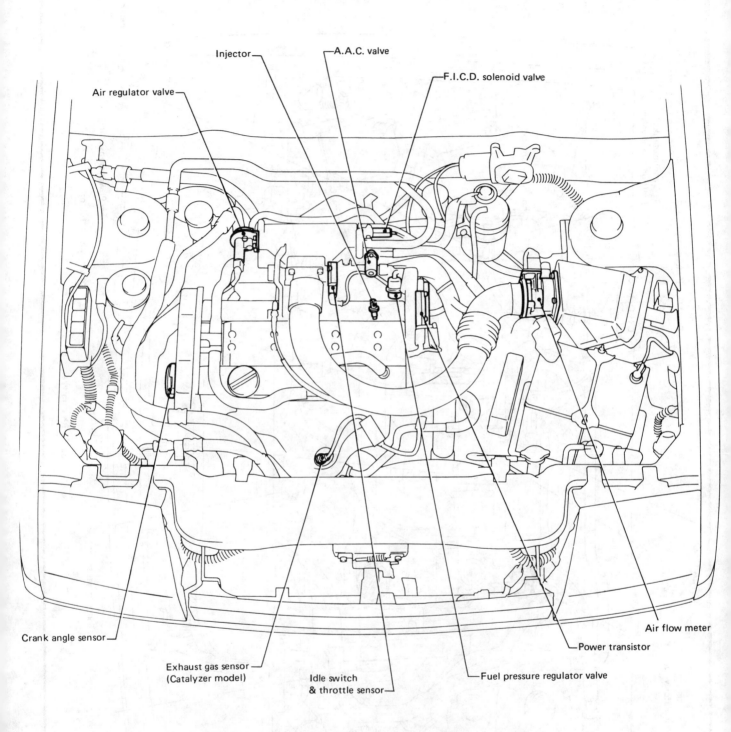

Fig. 13.62 ECCS component locations on the CA18DE engine (Sec 8)

14   Before carrying out the procedures given in this Section, observe the following precautions:

(a)   *Switch off the ignition before disconnecting wiring from any component.*

(b)   *Disconnect the battery negative terminal before disconnecting the wiring from the ECU*

(c)   *When measuring the voltage at terminals, do not allow multi-meter probes to touch each other otherwise the component will be short-circuited resulting in damage to the control unit*

Air cleaner element and body – removal and refitting

15   Unscrew the bolts securing the air cleaner cover and air flow meter to the top of the air cleaner body.

16   Lift the cover and withdraw the element.

17   Wipe clean the inside of the body and cover.

18   To remove the body, unscrew the mounting bolts and disconnect the inlet hose. The upper part of the air cleaner may be removed by unscrewing the bolts securing it to the air flow meter.

19   Refitting is a reversal of removal but fit a new flowmeter gasket where necessary.

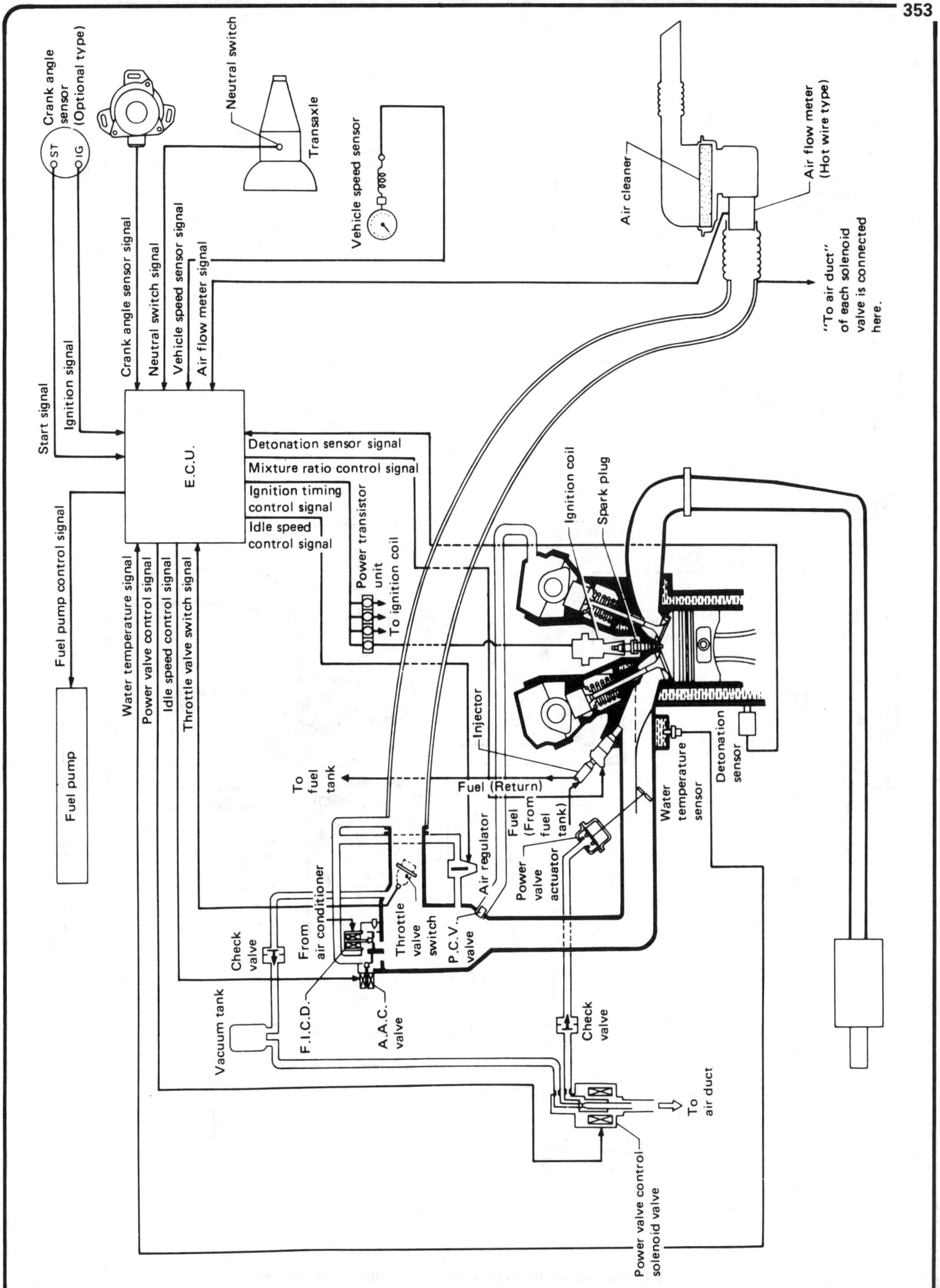

Fig. 13.63 ECCS function diagram for the CA16DE engine (Sec 8)

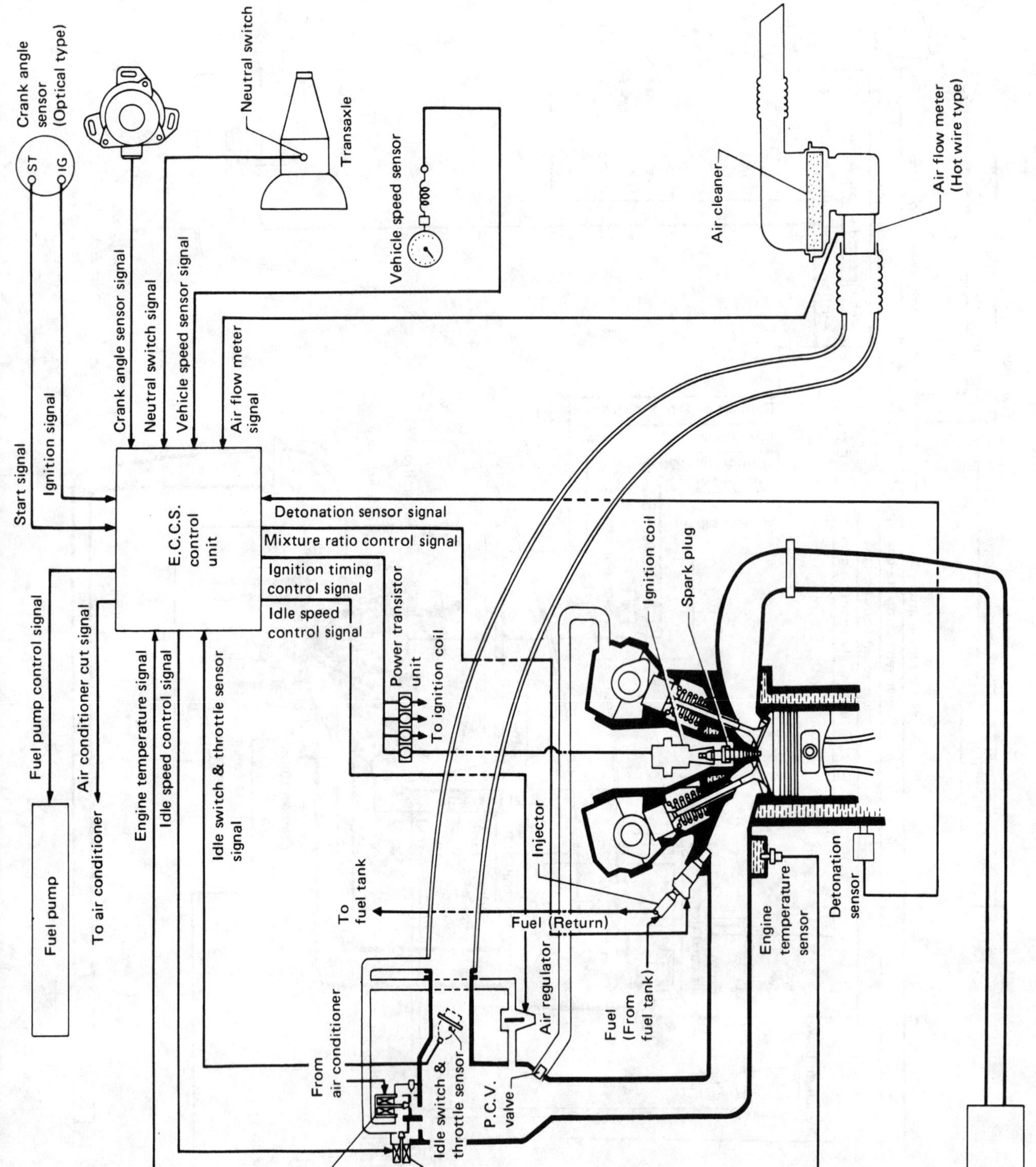

Fig. 13.64 ECCS function diagram for the CA18DE engine (Sec 8)

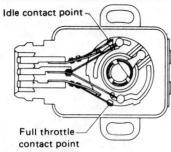

Fig. 13.65 Cut-away view of the throttle valve switch (Sec 8)

Fig. 13.67 Adjusting the CO % by turning the variable resistor on the air flow meter (Sec 8)

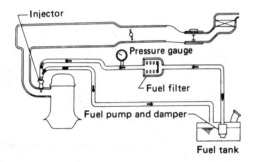

Fig. 13.69 Checking the fuel pressure of the ECCS (Sec 8)

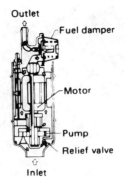

Fig. 13.66 Cut-away view of the fuel pump (Sec 8)

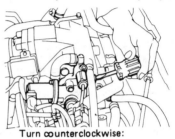

Fig. 13.68 Adjusting the idle speed (Sec 8)

Fuel pump – removal and refitting

20   The fuel pump is located in the fuel tank itself and its removal and refitting is similar to that for the fuel level transmitter and gauge described in Chapter 3.

Idle speed and mixture – adjustment

21   In order to make an accurate adjustment the engine should be in good working condition and all vacuum hoses should be secure.
22   Run the engine to normal operating temperature and make the following adjustments while the electric cooling fan is stopped.
23   Connect a tachometer and exhaust gas analyser to the engine.
24   Start the engine and rev it at 2000 to 3000 rpm two or three times, then allow it to idle.
25   Check that the CO% is as given in the Specifications. If not, use a screwdriver to adjust the variable resistor on the air flow meter until the reading is correct. If an exhaust gas analyser is not available adjust the variable resistor so that the engine runs at the highest speed, then turn the screw exactly two full turns anti-clockwise.
26   Rev the engine at 2000 to 3000 rpm two or three times, then allow it to idle.
27   Check that the idle speed is as given in the Specifications. If not, disconnect the auxiliary air control valve multiplug then turn the idle speed adjusting screw shown in Fig. 13.68 as required (photo). Repeat paragraphs 21 and 22 as necessary until the idle speed is correct.

Releasing the ECCS fuel pressure

28   Before disconnecting any of the fuel lines it is necessary to release the fuel pressure as follows. Open the fuse box and remove the fuel

pump fuse. Start the engine and run it until it stalls. Crank it two or three times to make sure that the fuel pressure is fully released, then turn off the ignition and refit the fuel pump fuse.

Checking the fuel pressure (using a pressure gauge)

29   Release the fuel pressure as previously described, then disconnect the fuel hose from the engine side of the fuel filter. Fit the pressure gauge then start the engine and allow it to idle. Check that the pressure is as given in the Specifications.
30   After making the check release the pressure as previously described, remove the pressure gauge and refit the fuel hose.

Fuel injectors – removal and refitting
CA16DE engine
31   Release the fuel pressure as previously described.
32   Remove the throttle housing and stay.
33   Remove the idle air adjusting unit.
34   Remove the inlet side rocker cover and the positive crankcase ventilation (PCV) valve.
35   Disconnect the fuel hoses and the pressure regulator vacuum hose.
36   Unscrew the injector assembly mounting bolts and lift out the assembly from the rear while tilting it and being careful not to damage the injectors or fuel rail.
37   Remove the injectors from the rail or inlet manifold (photo).
38   A 150 watt soldering iron is necessary to remove the hose from the injectors. Heat the iron and draw it along the hose to cut it from the injector tail piece. Take care not to damage the plastic socket or collar, and do not attempt to hold the injector in a vice while removing the hose.
39   Clean the tail pieces of the new injectors. Apply a little fuel to the insides of the new injectors then quickly push them fully onto the tail pieces as far as they will go.
40   Refitting is a reversal of the removal procedure, however after starting the engine check the hoses for leakage.
CA18DE engine
41   Release the fuel pressure as previously described.
42   Unscrew the injector assembly mounting bolts and nut.
43   Withdraw the injector assembly.

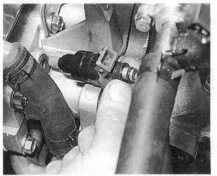

8.37 Removing an injector

8.52A Removing the ECU from under the front seat

8.52B Mode selector on the ECU

44   Disconnect the hoses then remove the injectors from the rail.

45   Clean the tail pieces of the new injectors and renew the O-rings and insulators. Smear the O-rings with engine oil before fitting them.

46   Refitting is a reversal of the removal procedure, however after starting the engine check the hoses for leakage.

Fuel filter – removal and refitting

47   Release the fuel pressure as previously described.

48   Loosen the clips at each end of the filter, place some rags under the filter then disconnect the hoses and remove the filter.

49   Fit the new filter using a reversal of the removal procedure, however make sure it is fitted the correct way round. Any fuel flow arrows should point in the direction of flow towards the engine.

Self-diagnostic system – description and operation

50   The ECU has a self-diagnosis function which uses coded flashing lights to indicate the area of a fault. For a comprehensive test it is suggested that the vehicle is taken to a Nissan dealer who will be able to diagnose the fault accurately and possibly quicker using specialised equipment, however the following procedure will enable the home mechanic to isolate the problem to a specific area.

51   The system operates in five modes as follows:

Modes 1 and 2	For models fitted with a catalytic converter only (ie no current models)
Mode 3	Self-diagnosis
Mode 4	Switch diagnosis mode for checking the on/off condition of the switches
Mode 5	Real time diagnosis for checking the system during a road test

52   Locate the ECU below the front passenger seat and pull it out to the extent of the wiring (photos). To select a particular mode first switch on the ignition. Using a screwdriver as shown in Fig. 13.73 turn the mode selector fully clockwise and wait for the lamps to flash. After the required flashes have occurred depending on the mode required, turn the mode selector fully anti-clockwise immediately. Do not turn off the ignition otherwise the mode will return to Mode 1.

53   To carry out a Mode 3 scan, first run the engine to normal operating temperature then select Mode 3 and count the number of red and green

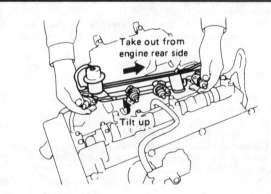

Fig. 13.70 Removing the injectors on the CA16DE engine (Sec 8)

Take out from engine rear side

Tilt up

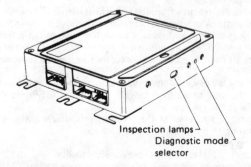

Inspection lamps
Diagnostic mode selector

Fig. 13.72 The ECCS electronic control unit (Sec 8)

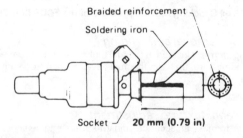

Braided reinforcement

Soldering iron

Socket   **20 mm (0.79 in)**

Fig. 13.71 Method of removing the injector hoses using a soldering iron (Sec 8)

Fig. 13.73 Selecting a mode on the ECU (Sec 8)

Unit: sec

RED L.E.D.   **3.2   3.2   3.2**

ON

OFF   1.6 1.6 1.6 1.6 1.6

Fig. 13.74 Crank angle sensor display code (Sec 8)

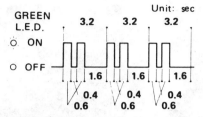

Fig. 13.75 Air flow meter display code (Sec 8)

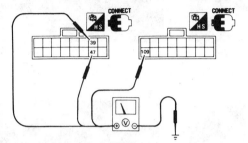

Ignition switch "ON"

Fig. 13.77 Checking the ECU voltage supply on the CA18DE engine (Sec 8)

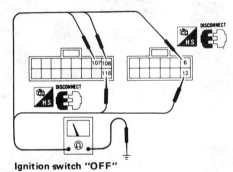

Ignition switch "OFF"

Fig. 13.79 Checking the ECU wiring resistance on the CA18DE engine (Sec 8)

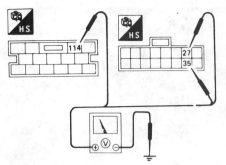

Fig. 13.76 Checking the ECU voltage supply on the CA16DE engine (Sec 8)

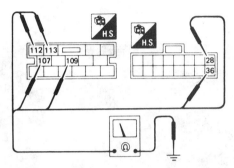

Fig. 13.78 Checking the ECU wiring resistance on the CA16DE engine (Sec 8)

43 Throttle sensor (CA18DE)
44 No malfunction found (CA16DE)
55 No malfunction found (CA18DE)

54   To erase the memory, turn the mode selector fully clockwise, wait for the lamps to flash 4 times then turn the selector fully anti-clockwise. Switch off the ignition and refit the ECU.
55   To carry out a Mode 4 scan, select mode 4 then make sure that the red lamp goes out. Now depress the accelerator pedal and check that it comes on. If not, the throttle valve or associated wiring is faulty. Operate the starter and check that the red lamp comes on. Raise the front of the vehicle and support adequately on axle stands. Apply the handbrake firmly. Start the engine and engage the gears until the speedometer registers in excess of 12 mph at which point the green lamp should come on. If not, the vehicle speed sensor or associated wiring is faulty. Switch off the ignition and refit the ECU.
56   The Mode 5 diagnosis should be used to detect malfunctions as they occur. In this mode, faults are not stored in the ECU memory. This mode is used to check for faults occurring in the crank angle sensor of airflow meter output signal. First pull out the ECU from under the passenger seat and start the engine. Select mode 5 then either run the engine at idling speed or drive the car for a total of five minutes or more. If no faults occur during this period the lamps will not flash, however the lamps should be observed closely as the faults are not consigned to

flashes. The red flashes indicate the number of tens and the green flashes indicate the number of units. The engine may be started if necessary or if it is a non-runner crank it for more than two seconds. The code indicates the following fault areas.

11   Crank angle sensor circuit
12   Air flow meter circuit
13   Water temperature sensor circuit
14   Vehicle speed sensor circuit (CA18DE)
21   Ignition signal circuit (CA18DE)
23   Idle switch circuit (CA18DE)
31   ECU (CA18DE)
34   Detonation sensor circuit (photo)

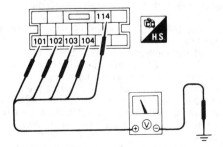

Fig. 13.80 Checking the injector voltage supply on the CA16DE engine (Sec 8)

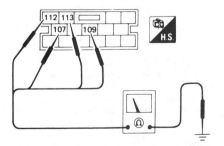

Fig. 13.81 Checking the injector wiring resistance on the CA16DE engine (Sec 8)

8.53 Detonation sensor on the cylinder block (head removed)

8.69 Removing an exhaust manifold gasket

8.75A Removing the accelerator cable ...

8.75B ... and bracket

8.76A Power transistor inner (arrowed) ...

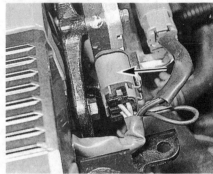

8.76B ... and outer multiplugs (arrowed)

8.76C Multiplug on the support bracket

8.77 AAC valve and multiplug

8.78 Throttle switch and multiplugs

memory and may only flash once. After making the check switch off the ignition and refit the ECU. The code indicates the following fault areas:

| Crank angle sensor | 1.6 second red pulses at 1.6 second intervals |
| Air flow meter | A 0.6 second green pulse, 0.4 second gap, 0.6 second green pulse, and 1.6 second gap |

ECCS ECU voltage supply – checking

57   Pull out the ECU from under the passenger seat, leaving it connected to the wiring.
58   Switch on the ignition.
59   Using a voltmeter, check the supply voltage with reference to Figs. 13.76 and 13.77. If battery voltage is not available check the EFI relay or wiring.
60   Switch off the ignition and check the resistance between the terminals shown in Figs. 13.78 and 13.79 and earth. In each case zero ohms should be registered. If not, check the associated wiring.

Injectors – checking
CA16DE engine
61   Disconnect the wiring multiplug from each injector and using an ohmmeter check that the resistance of each one is 2.5 ohms.
62   Reconnect the multiplugs and start the engine.
63   Refer to Fig. 13.80 and use a voltmeter to check that battery voltage exists at the ECU terminal 114. The voltage at the other terminals should vary between zero and 12 volts.
64   Switch off the ignition and check the resistance between the terminals shown in Fig. 13.81 and earth. In each case zero ohms should be registered. If not, check the associated wiring.
65   To check the dropping resistor located on the air cleaner cover, refer to Fig. 13.82 and use an ohmmeter to check that resistance between terminals a and b, a and c, a and d, and a and e is 6 ohms with the multiplug disconnected. If not, renew the resistor.
CA18DE engine
66   Disconnect the wiring multiplug from each injector and using an ohmmeter check that the resistance of each one is approximately 10 to 15 ohms. Renew the injector if not.

8.79 Injector and multiplug

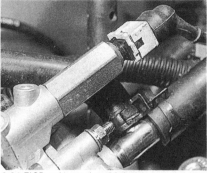

8.81 FICD valve and multiplug

8.84 Water temperature sensor and multiplug (arrowed)

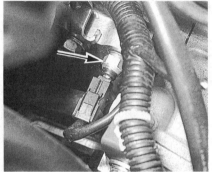

8.85 Water temperature sensor with the Lucar terminal (arrowed)

8.86 Wiring harness and air hose along the rear of the engine

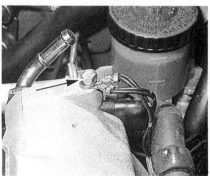

8.87 Earth cables on the inlet manifold (arrowed)

8.89 Brake servo vacuum hose on the inlet manifold (arrowed)

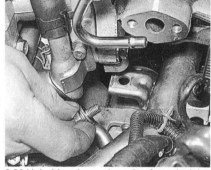

8.90 Unbolting the coolant pipe from the inlet manifold

67   Disconnect the 16 pin multiplug from the ECU. Refer to Fig. 13.83 and check that battery voltage exists at the terminals shown.

68   Refer to Fig. 13.84 and use an ohmmeter to check that the resistance between the ECU terminals shown and earth is zero. If not, check the wiring as necessary.

Manifolds and exhaust system – general

69   The exhaust manifold is on the left-hand side of the cylinder head, the inlet manifold on the right-hand side (photo).

70   The exhaust system is shown in Fig. 13.85.

71   Refer to Section 5 for details of checking the inlet manifold for distortion.

Inlet manifold – removal and refitting

72   Release the ECCS fuel pressure as described in Section 8.

73   Loosen the clips and disconnect the air inlet ducting from the air flow meter and throttle housing.

74   Disconnect the battery negative lead.

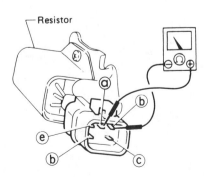

Fig. 13.82 Checking the dropping resistor resistance on the CA16DE engine (Sec 8)

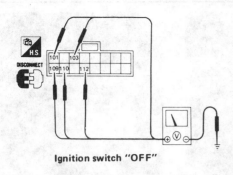

Ignition switch "OFF"

Fig. 13.83 Checking the injector voltage supply on the CA18DE engine (Sec 8)

Ignition switch "OFF"

Fig. 13.84 Checking the injector wiring resistance on the CA18DE engine (Sec 8)

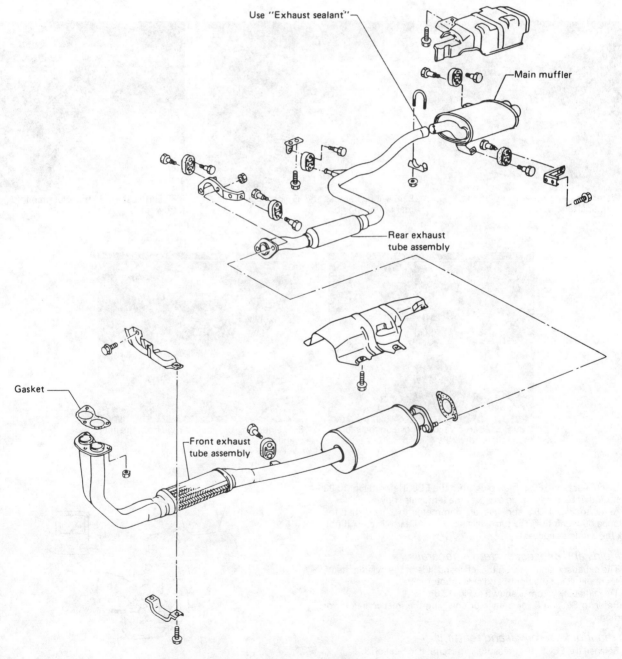

Use "Exhaust sealant"

Main muffler

Rear exhaust tube assembly

Gasket

Front exhaust tube assembly

Fig. 13.85 Exhaust system fitted to the sixteen-valve engines (Sec 8)

Note: *On the CA18DE engine the downpipe gasket is replaced by two sealing rings*

8.94A Centre inlet manifold support bracket

8.94B Left-hand inlet manifold support bracket upper bolt

8.95A Crankshaft ventilation pipe bracket and bolt (arrowed)

8.95B Disconnecting the crankshaft ventilation pipe

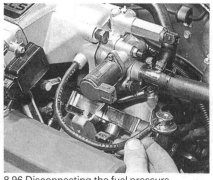

8.96 Disconnecting the fuel pressure regulator vacuum hose

75   Disconnect the accelerator cable and unbolt the bracket (photos).

76   Disconnect the multiplugs from the power transistor on the left-hand side of the cylinder head. Also release the multiplug from the support bracket by the power transistor (photos).

77   Disconnect the green block connector from the AAC valve (photo).

78   Release the cable tie, then disconnect the grey and black multiplugs from the throttle switch (photo).

79   Disconnect the grey multiplugs from Nos 1 and 2 injectors (photo).

80   Disconnect the left-hand wiring harness from the support.

81   Disconnect the pale blue multiplug from the FICD valve (photo).

82   Disconnect the blue multiplug from the air regulator valve.

83   Disconnect the grey multiplugs from No's 3 and 4 injectors.

84   Disconnect the yellow multiplug from the water temperature

sensor on the inlet manifold (photo).

85   Disconnect the Lucar plug from the water temperature sensor (photo).

86   Unscrew the screws and release the wiring harness support brackets from the inlet manifold (photo).

87   Unscrew the two screws and detach the earth cables from the inlet manifold. Note where they are fitted (photo).

88   Unclip the wiring harness from the inlet manifold and push it to the rear of the engine compartment.

89   Disconnect the brake servo vacuum hose from the inlet manifold (photo).

90   Unbolt the coolant pipe from the outer inlet manifold section using an Allen key (photo).

8.97A Fuel supply pipe (arrowed)

8.97B Fuel return pipe

8.98A Unscrew the mounting bolts ...

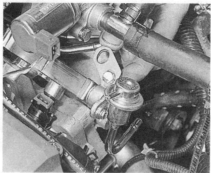

8.98B ... and support bracket ...

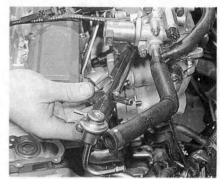

8.98C ... and withdraw the fuel rail

8.99A Unscrewing the lower throttle housing mounting bolts ...

8.99B ... left-hand bracket bolt ...

8.99C ... and right-hand bracket bolt

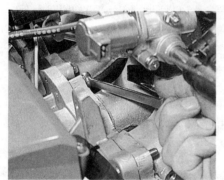

8.100 Unscrew the nuts and bolts ...

8.101A ... and remove the outer inlet manifold section ...

8.101B ... and gasket

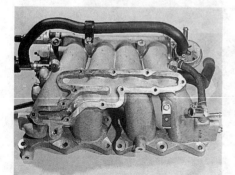

8.101C Outer inlet manifold section removed

8.102A Unscrewing the inner inlet manifold nuts and bolts

8.102B Inner inlet manifold gasket

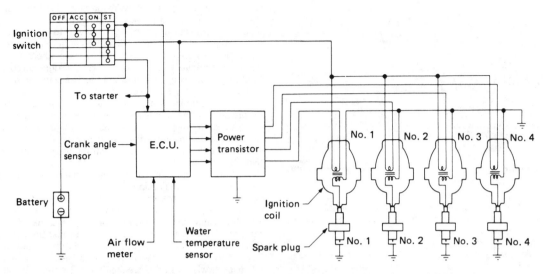

Fig. 13.86 Diagram of the ignition system fitted to sixteen-valve engine models (Sec 9)

91   Disconnect the two coolant hoses from the thermostat housing and coolant pipe.
92   Raise the car and support on axle stands. Apply the handbrake.
93   For additional working room remove the exhaust front downpipe.
94   Working from under the car unbolt the inlet manifold support brackets. One bracket must be removed completely but the other one can be moved to the rear (photos).
95   Detach the left-hand ventilation pipe and brackets (photos).
96   Disconnect the fuel pressure regulator vacuum hose (photo).
97   Disconnect the fuel supply pipe from the fuel rail and the return pipe from the pressure regulator (photos).
98   Unbolt the fuel rail and bracket from the top (photos).
99   Unscrew the lower throttle housing mounting bolts which also secure the mounting bracket. Also unscrew the bracket lower mounting bolts (photos).
100   Unscrew the bolts and nuts securing the inlet manifold outer section to the inner section (photo). The lower bolts are very difficult to remove as they are concealed by other components.
101   Remove the inlet manifold outer section and gasket, then remove the bracket (photos).
102   Unscrew the nuts and bolts then remove the inner inlet manifold and gasket from the cylinder head (photos).
103   Thoroughly clean the contact faces of the inlet manifold and cylinder head.
104   Refitting is a reversal of removal, but tighten all nuts and bolts to the specified torque and adjust the accelerator cable with reference to Chapter 3.

---

9   Ignition system (twelve and sixteen-valve engines)

General description

1   The ignition system fitted to twelve-valve engines is identical to that described in Chapter 4. On sixteen-valve engines the *direct* ignition system is controlled by the ECCS ECU together with a power transistor, and instead of a single coil, individual coils are fitted to each spark plug. A detonation sensor automatically retards the ignition when operating conditions cause instantaneous combustion as opposed to controlled combustion. There are no HT leads.
2   On twelve-valve engines a thermal vacuum valve is located in the distributor vacuum line in order to prevent vacuum advance during engine warm-up and also to improve operating performance. A delay valve is also fitted to prevent the timing from retarding when the throttle is opened quickly.

Thermal vacuum valve (twelve-valve engines) – testing

3   Drain the cooling system then unscrew the thermal vacuum valve from the inlet manifold.

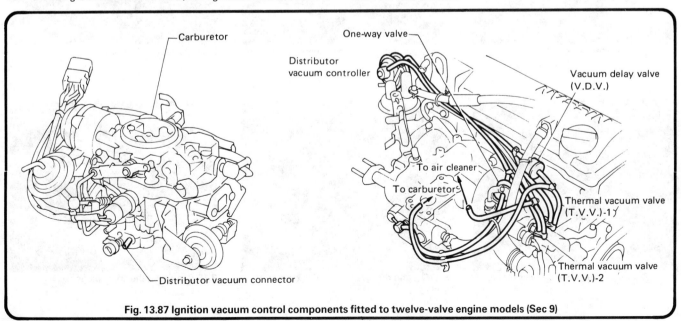

Fig. 13.87 Ignition vacuum control components fitted to twelve-valve engine models (Sec 9)

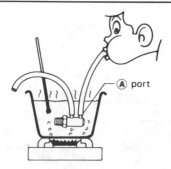

Fig. 13.88 Testing the thermal vacuum valve fitted to twelve-valve engines (Sec 9)

4   Refer to Fig. 13.88 and suspend the valve in a container of water being heated. Make sure that the hoses are fitted as shown and do not allow water to enter the valve.

5   Heat the water while attempting to blow through the hoses. The TVV2 valve should open at 20°C (68°F) and the TVV1 valve at 40°C (104°F). When cooling the valve, the TVV2 valve should close at 5°C (41°F) or over and the TVV1 valve at 30°C (86°F) or over.

6   Renew the valve if it is not functioning properly.

Distributor (twelve-valve engine) – overhaul

7   The procedure is similar to that described in Chapter 4 but with reference also to Fig. 13.89.

Ignition timing

Twelve-valve engines

8   The procedure is as described in Chapter 4.

Sixteen-valve engines

9   Because the direct type ignition does not have any HT leads some preliminary work may be necessary in order to attach the timing light to the engine. Nissan technicians use a special pulse-type timing light which is attached to a trigger wire loop from No 1 ignition coil, however the use of a standard pulse-type timing light may not give accurate results if it is not sensitive enough. One way to overcome the problem is to insert a short length of HT lead between the No 1 ignition coil and spark plug. To do this it is necessary to disconnect the air duct and air hoses and remove the cover for access to the ignition coil. If a pulse type timing light is being used, this can then be clamped onto the lead. If a voltage type timing light is being used, it should be possible to connect the end of the timing light sensor wire between the coil and the HT lead. Before starting the engine re-connect the air hoses and duct.

10   An alternative method using a voltage type timing light is to remove the cap from the diagnostic connector (Fig. 13.91), and insert a small tool or length of wire to which the timing light may be attached (Fig. 13.92).

11   With the engine at normal operating temperature and idling, point the timing light at the timing marks on the crankshaft pulley and timing cover pointer. The marks are at 5° intervals and the 15° advance mark should appear in line with the pointer.

12   If the ignition timing is not correct, the crank angle sensor on the right-hand end of the exhaust camshaft must be repositioned. To do this, loosen the three mounting bolts and turn the sensor as necessary. Turning the sensor clockwise will retard the ignition timing and turning it anti-clockwise will advance the timing. Tighten the bolts after making an adjustment and recheck the timing.

13   Switch off the engine and remove the HT lead where fitted. Reconnect all wires.

Spark plugs (sixteen-valve engines) – removal and refitting

14   Disconnect the air hose and inlet air duct.

15   Unbolt the cover to allow access to the ignition coils (photos).

16   Disconnect the coil multiplugs located on the power transistor.

17   Unbolt the ignition coil bracket, remove the wiring harness rubber seals, and remove the coils after disconnecting them from the spark plugs (photos).

18   Unscrew the spark plugs using a deep socket or box spanner (photo).

19   Refitting is a reversal of removal with reference to Chapter 4.

9.15A Unscrew the bolts ...

9.15B ... and remove the spark plug covers

9.17A Unscrew the bolts ...

9.17B ... remove the wiring harness rubber seals ...

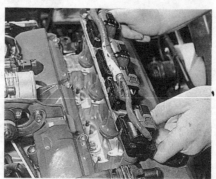

9.17C ... and remove the ignition coils and bracket

9.18 Removing the spark plugs

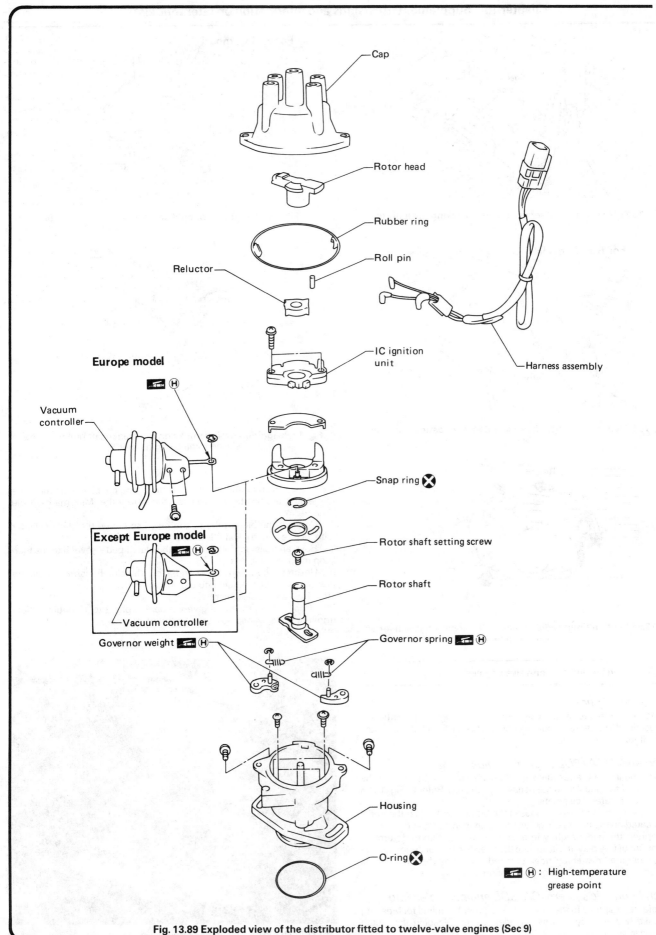

Cap

Rotor head

Rubber ring

Roll pin

Reluctor

Harness assembly

IC ignition unit

Europe model

Vacuum controller

Snap ring

Rotor shaft setting screw

Except Europe model

Vacuum controller

Rotor shaft

Governor weight

Governor spring

Housing

O-ring

⊞ (H) : High-temperature grease point

Fig. 13.89 Exploded view of the distributor fitted to twelve-valve engines (Sec 9)

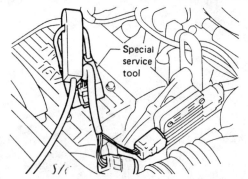

Fig. 13.90 Nissan special service tool for checking the ignition timing (Sec 9)

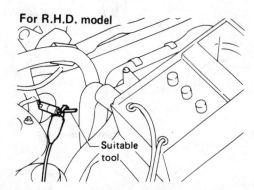

Fig. 13.92 Ignition timing light attached to diagnostic connector (Sec 9)

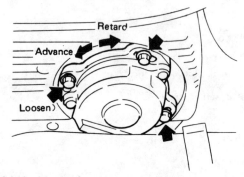

Fig. 13.94 Ignition timing adjustment on the crank angle sensor on sixteen-valve engines (Sec 9)

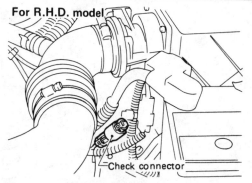

Fig. 13.91 Ignition timing diagnostic connector (Sec 9)

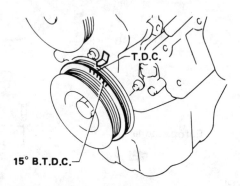

Fig. 13.93 Ignition timing marks on the crankshaft pulley on the sixteen-valve engine (Sec 9)

6   Top up the hydraulic fluid reservoir. During the bleeding procedure the level must not be allowed to drop below the 'Min' mark on the reservoir.
7   Connect the bleed tube to the bleed screw on the slave cylinder with its free end in a suitable container.
8   Have an assistant fully depress the clutch pedal several times then keep the pedal depressed.
9   Unscrew the bleed screw and allow the clutch diaphragm spring pressure to force the fluid into the container.
10   Tighten the bleed screw.
11   Repeat the procedure given in paragraphs 8 to 10 until the fluid from the slave cylinder is free of air bubbles.

---

10   Clutch (twelve and sixteen-valve engines)

General description
1   The clutch fitted to twelve-valve and CA16DE engines is identical to that described in Chapter 5, however on the CA18DE engine the clutch is of hydraulic operated type.

Clutch pedal (CA18DE engine) – adjustment
2   Working inside the car measure the distance from the floor to the upper face of the pedal with the pedal fully released. Refer to Fig. 13.96 to observe the reference points.
3   If adjustment is necessary, loosen the locknut and adjust the pedal stop located on the bracket. Tighten the locknut on completion.
4   Depress the pedal slightly from its released position to determine the amount of free play. If it is outside the specified tolerance, loosen the locknut on the master cylinder pushrod and turn the pushrod as required. Tighten the locknut on completion.

Clutch hydraulic system (CA18DE engine) – bleeding
5   Refer to Chapter 9 for details of the equipment required for bleeding the brake hydraulic system as it is identical for bleeding the clutch hydraulic system.

10.12 Clutch master cylinder and fluid reservoir

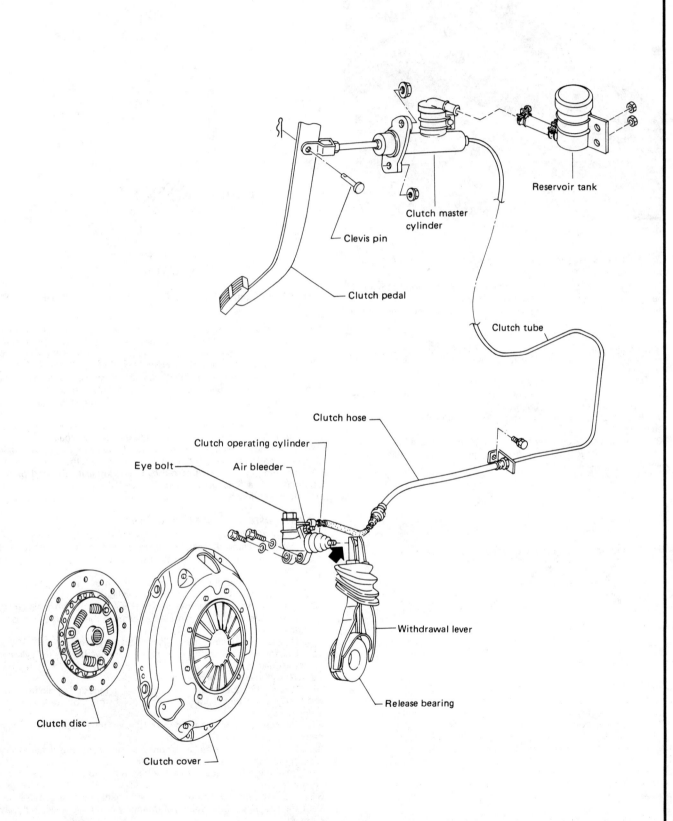

Fig. 13.95 Hydraulically operated clutch components fitted to the CA18DE engine (Sec 10)

10.13 Clutch slave cylinder

Clutch slave cylinder (CA18DE engine) – removal, overhaul and refitting

12   Remove the cap from the hydraulic fluid reservoir (photo) and fill the reservoir to the brim. Place some polythene sheeting over the reservoir and tighten the cap onto it. This will reduce the loss of fluid when the slave cylinder is disconnected.
13   Place a rag under the slave cylinder, then unscrew the union nut and disconnect the hydraulic line (photo). Plug the line.
14   Unbolt the slave cylinder from the gearbox, taking care not to spill fluid on the car paintwork.
15   Clean the exterior of the slave cylinder.
16   Prise off the rubber dust cover, then extract the pushrod followed by the piston assembly and the return spring.
17   Prise the rubber seal from the piston, noting the position of the sealing lip.
18   Clean the slave cylinder and components using a suitable solvent such as methylated spirit. Alternatively clean hydraulic fluid may be used.

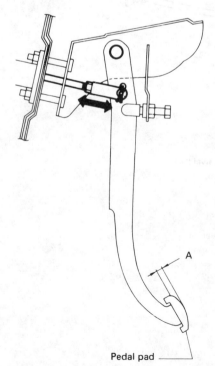

A

Pedal pad

Fig. 13.97 Clutch pedal free play adjustment on the CA18DE engine (Sec 10)

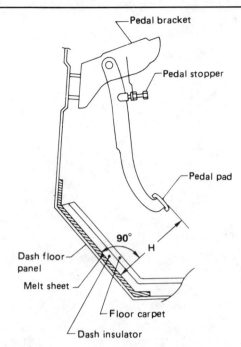

Pedal bracket

Pedal stopper

Pedal pad

90°   H

Dash floor panel

Melt sheet

Floor carpet

Dash insulator

Fig. 13.96 Clutch pedal height adjustment on the CA18DE engine (Sec 10)

19   Wipe dry the components then examine them for excessive wear and damage. Check the cylinder bore and piston for scoring and corrosion, and if excessive, renew the complete cylinder. If the components are still serviceable obtain a kit of rubber seals.
20   Commence reassembly by dipping the new seal in clean hydraulic fluid, then fit it to the piston using the fingers only to manipulate it into position. Make sure that the seal lip is facing the correct way (ie into the cylinder).
21   Locate the return spring on the piston, then insert both items into the slave cylinder bore, taking care not to damage the seal.
22   Fit the new dust cover to the pushrod, then locate the pushrod in the piston and ease the dust cover into the groove on the slave cylinder.
23   Refitting is a reversal of removal, but lubricate the end of the pushrod with a little grease. Finally bleed the hydraulic system as described previously.

Clutch master cylinder (CA18DE engine) – removal, overhaul and refitting

24   Working inside the car, reach up behind the clutch pedal and disconnect the master cylinder pushrod by extracting the spring clip and removing the clevis pin.
25   Working in the engine compartment remove the cap from the hydraulic fluid reservoir and syphon out the fluid using a pipette.
26   Place a container or rag beneath the reservoir to catch spilled fluid, then loosen the clip and pull the adaptor from the top of the master cylinder.
27   Unscrew the union nut and disconnect the outlet pipe.
28   Unscrew the mounting nuts and withdraw the master cylinder from the bulkhead.
29   Clean the exterior of the master cylinder.
30   Prise of the rubber dust cover, then extract the spring clip from the mouth of the master cylinder and withdraw the pushrod complete with stopper.
31   Unscrew the stop pin from the bottom of the master cylinder and recover the seal.
32   Withdraw the piston assembly and return spring, if necessary tapping the master cylinder on a wooden block.
33   Prise the rubber seals from the piston noting the position of the sealing lips.
34   Clean the master cylinder and components using a suitable solvent such as methylated spirit. Alternatively clean hydraulic fluid may be used.
35   Wipe dry the components then examine them for excessive wear and damage. Check the cylinder bore and piston for scoring and corrosion, and if excessive, renew the complete cylinder. If the compo-

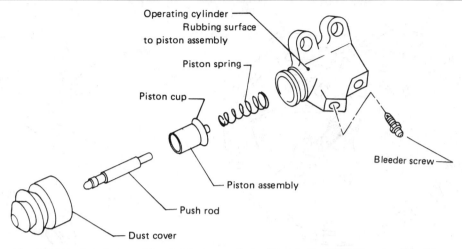

Fig. 13.98 Exploded view of the clutch slave cylinder fitted to the CA18DE engine (Sec 10)

nents are still serviceable obtain a kit of rubber seals.

36   Commence reassembly by dipping the rubber seals in clean hydraulic fluid, then fit them to the piston using the fingers only to manipulate them into position. Make sure that the seal lips face the correct way round (ie into the cylinder).

37   Remove the clevis from the pushrod, fit the new rubber dust cover, then refit the clevis in the same position.

38   Locate the return spring on the piston, then insert both items in the master cylinder bore, making sure that the stop pin slot in the piston is aligned with the hole in the cylinder. As the seals enter the bore make

sure that the lips are not damaged or deformed.

39   Hold the piston depressed, then refit the stop pin and seal.

40   Fit the pushrod to the mouth of the cylinder then insert the stopper ring to its groove.

41   Refitting is a reversal of removal but top up the fluid reservoir, bleed the hydraulic system and adjust the clutch pedal as described previously.

Clutch pedal (CA18DE engine) – removal and refitting

42   The procedure is similar to that described in Chapter 5 except that

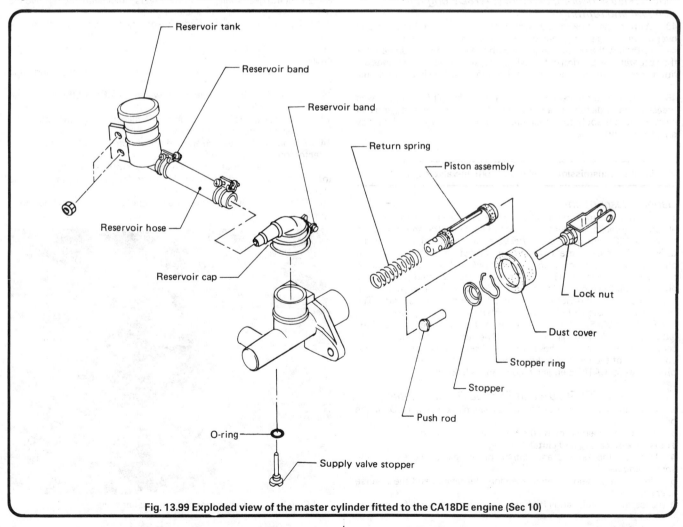

Fig. 13.99 Exploded view of the master cylinder fitted to the CA18DE engine (Sec 10)

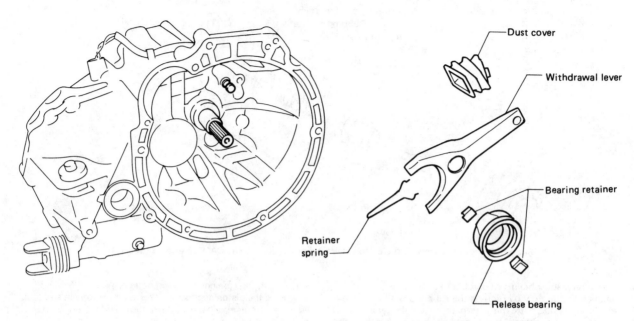

Fig. 13.100 Clutch release bearing and fork components fitted to the CA18DE engine (Sec 10)

the master cylinder pushrod must be disconnected by extracting the spring clip and withdrawing the clevis pin. After refitting, adjust the pedal as previously described.

Clutch release bearing and fork (CA18DE engine) – removal and refitting

43   With the gearbox removed insert the fingers behind the fork and over the retaining spring, then pull the fork from the ball-stud.

44   Withdraw the bearing together with the fork from the guide tube, then separate the bearing noting which way round the small springs are fitted. Remove the rubber grommet from the aperture in the bellhousing.

45   Refitting is a reversal of removal but apply a little lithium-based grease to the guide tube, bearing front face, ball-stud, fork ends, and fork indents. Do not apply too much grease otherwise it may find its way onto the clutch linings.

---

11   Manual transmission (twelve and sixteen-valve engines)

General description

1   The manual transmissions fitted to GA14S engine models are already covered in Chapter 6. The RS5F31A manual transmission fitted to the CA16DE engine is already covered in Chapter 6, however the differential side gears are shouldered and must therefore be removed after removing the pinion gears instead of before. The RS5F31A manual transmission fitted to the GA16S engine is already covered in Chapter 6, and the RN4F231A manual transmission fitted to the same engine is of similar design to the RS5F31A except that it has four speeds. The manual transmission fitted to models with the CA18DE engine is of type RS5F50A or RS5F50V, the former having a standard differential and the latter having a limited slip differential. The removal and refitting procedures are the same as those given in Chapter 6 except for the disconnection of the hydraulic clutch line (photo), however the overhaul procedures for CA18DE engine models are as follows.

Transmission (RS5F50A and RS5F50V) – dismantling

2   Clean away all external dirt from the transmission exterior. Drain the oil.

3   Stand the transmission on the flange of the clutch housing.

Transmission casing and clutch housing

4   Unscrew the 1st/2nd and 3rd/4th detent plugs and extract the springs and balls.

5   Unbolt the position switch, speedometer pinion, and the reverse idler shaft bolt.

6   Unscrew the bolts and lift off the transmission casing. If necessary

break the joint by tapping the casing with a mallet. Recover the shims for the input shaft rear bearing.

7   If necessary drive out the position switch from the inside of the transmission casing.

8   Select 4th gear, then pull out the reverse idler shaft and remove the reverse idler gear from the selector assembly.

9   Pull out the retaining pin and drive out the reverse arm shaft using a suitable drift. Recover the O-ring.

10   Unbolt and remove the reverse lever assembly and recover the check ball.

11   Unscrew the 5th/reverse detent plug and extract the spring and ball.

12   Extract the circlips from the lower ends of the 5th/reverse and 3rd/4th selector forks.

13   Drive out the roll pins securing the selector dog brackets to the 5th/reverse and 3rd/4th selector rods.

14   Pull out the 5th/reverse and 3rd/4th selector rods, then remove the selector forks and dog brackets.

15   Grip the input shaft and mainshaft assemblies and lift them from the clutch housing, together with the 1st/2nd selector fork and rod. Also lift out the final drive/differential assembly.

16   Recover the interlock balls and plunger from the clutch housing.

11.1 Clutch hydraulic line mounting bracket and slip

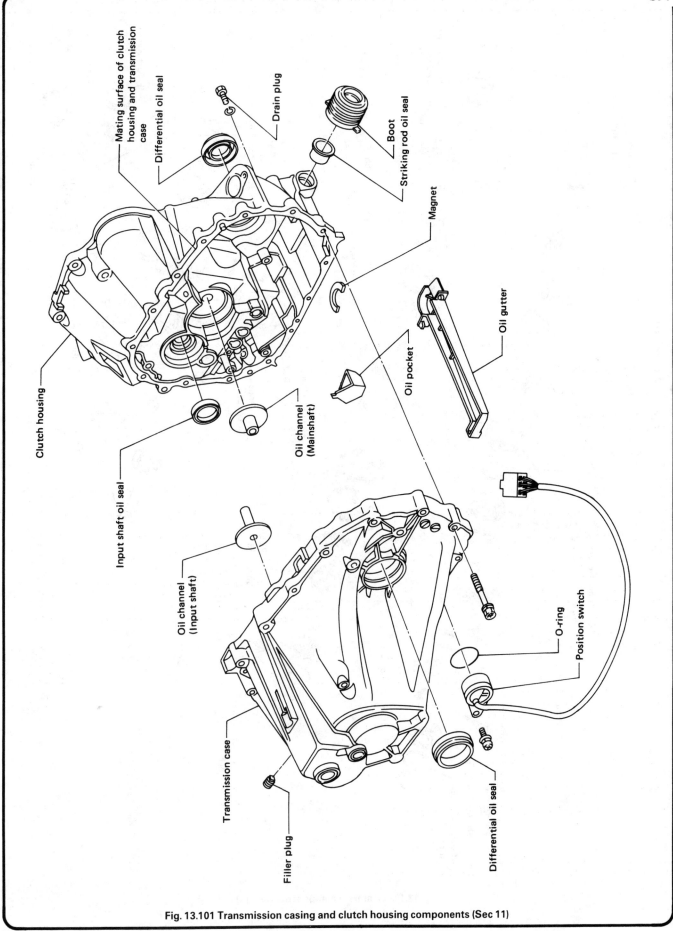

Fig. 13.101 Transmission casing and clutch housing components (Sec 11)

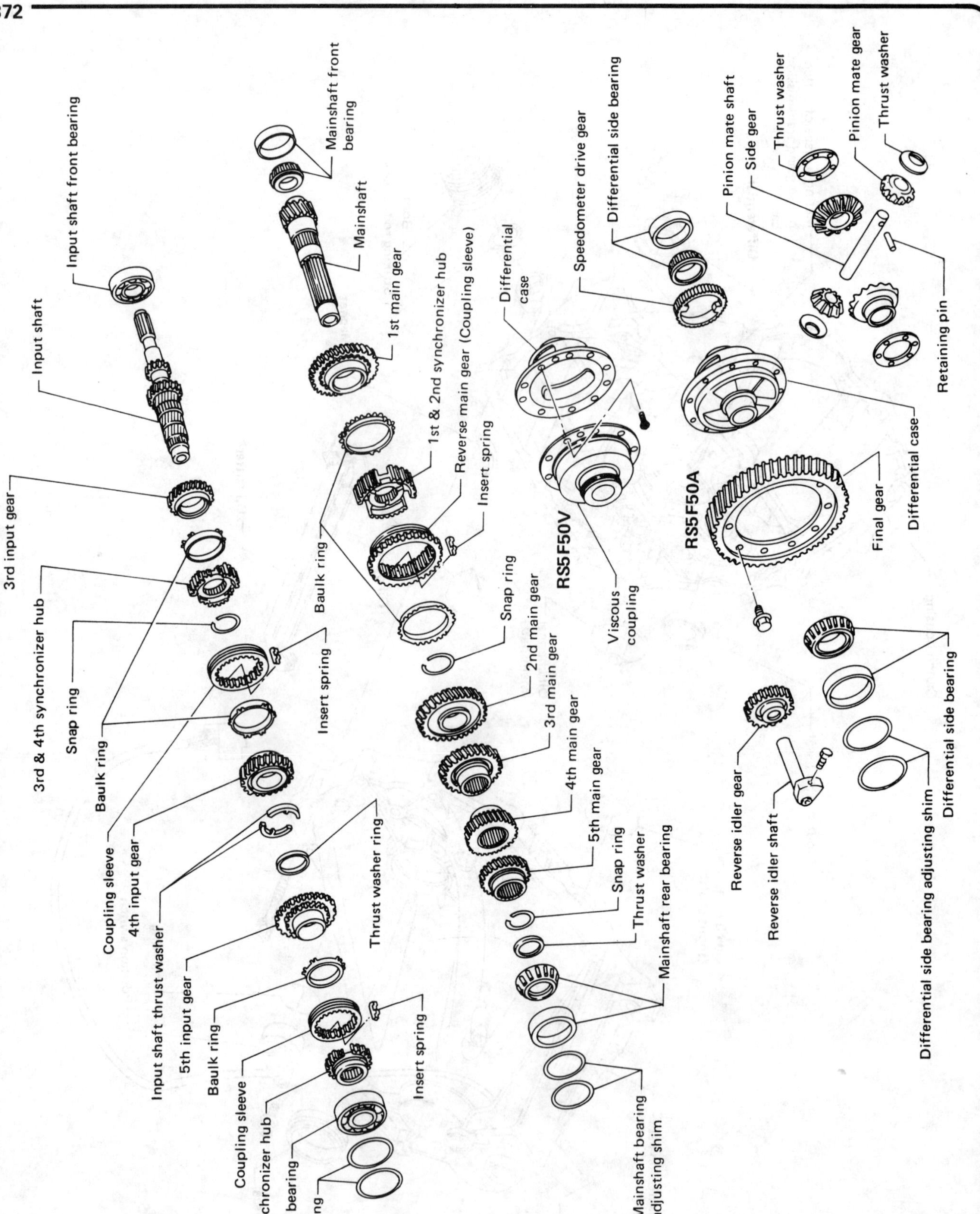

Input shaft front bearing

Input shaft

3rd input gear

3rd & 4th synchronizer hub

Snap ring

Baulk ring

Coupling sleeve

4th input gear

Input shaft thrust washer

5th input gear

Thrust washer ring

Baulk ring

Coupling sleeve

5th synchronizer hub

Insert spring

Input shaft rear bearing

Input shaft bearing adjusting shim

Mainshaft front bearing

Mainshaft

1st main gear

1st & 2nd synchronizer hub

Reverse main gear (Coupling sleeve)

Insert spring

Baulk ring

Insert spring

Snap ring

2nd main gear

3rd main gear

4th main gear

5th main gear

Snap ring

Thrust washer

Mainshaft rear bearing

Mainshaft bearing adjusting shim

Differential case

RS5F50V

Viscous coupling

Speedometer drive gear

Differential side bearing

RS5F50A

Final gear

Differential case

Pinion mate shaft

Side gear

Thrust washer

Pinion mate gear

Thrust washer

Retaining pin

Reverse idler gear

Reverse idler shaft

Differential side bearing adjusting shim

Differential side bearing

Fig. 13.102 Gear train components (Sec 11)

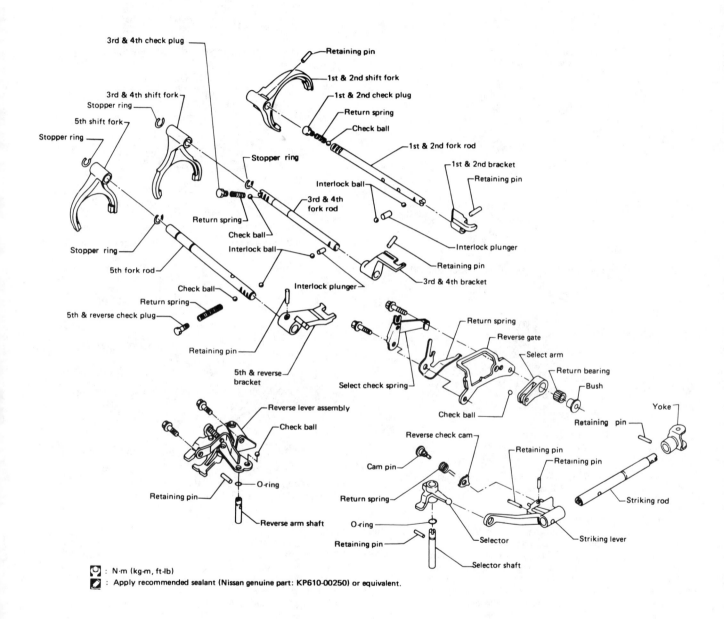

Fig. 13.103 Selector components (Sec 11)

17 Unbolt the reverse check assembly.

18 Drive out the selector shaft retaining pin, then drive out the shaft using a narrow drift and remove the selector.

19 Unscrew the drain plug if still in position, then, from the opposite side of the housing, drive out the striking lever retaining pin.

20 Withdraw the striking rod and remove the lever.

21 Remove the clutch release fork and bearing as described in Section 10.

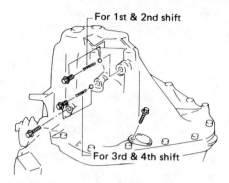

Fig. 13.104 Detent plugs, position switch bolt, and reverse idler shaft bolt (Sec 11)

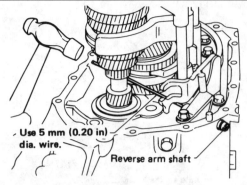

Fig. 13.105 Reverse arm shaft removal (Sec 11)

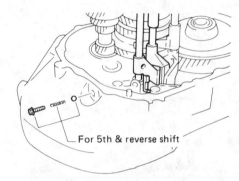

Fig. 13.106 5th/reverse detent components (Sec 11)

Fig. 13.107 5th/reverse and 3rd/4th selector rod removal (Sec 11)

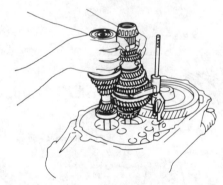

Fig. 13.108 Removing the input shaft and mainshaft assemblies together with the 1st/2nd selector fork and rod (Sec 11)

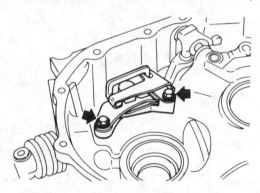

Fig. 13.109 Reverse check assembly removal (Sec 11)

22   Prise out the input shaft oil seal.
23   Remove the oil channel from the clutch housing, then extract the mainshaft bearing outer track using a suitable extractor.
24   Remove the differential side bearing outer tracks from the clutch housing and transmission casing using a suitable extractor. Remove the shims.
25   Remove the mainshaft bearing outer track from the transmission casing using a suitable extractor. Remove the shims.
26   Before dismantling the input shaft and mainshaft, measure and record the endfloat of each gear using feeler blades. Compare the results with the tolerances given in paragraphs 71 and 82. If the endfloat is not within these tolerances, any worn components should be renewed.
Input shaft
27   Remove the rear bearing from the input shaft by supporting the bearing on a vice and driving the shaft through.
28   Similarly support the 5th gear and drive the shaft through the 5th synchro unit and gear.
29   Remove the thrust washer ring and the split thrust washers.
30   Remove 4th gear.
31   Extract the circlip, then support the 3rd gear and drive the shaft through the 3rd/4th synchro unit and 3rd gear.

32   Remove the bearing from the front of the shaft by supporting the bearing on a vice and driving the shaft through.
Mainshaft
33   Support the rear bearing inner race on a vice, then drive the mainshaft through.
34   Remove the thrust washer and extract the circlip.
35   Support the 4th gear on a vice, then drive the mainshaft through to remove 5th and 4th gears together.
36   Similarly support the 2nd gear to remove 3rd and 2nd gears together.
37   Extract the circlip, then support the 1st gear and drive the mainshaft through to remove the 1st/2nd synchro unit and 1st gear.
38   Remove the bearing inner race from the front of the mainshaft by supporting it on a vice and driving the shaft through.
Differential/final drive
39   Unbolt the crownwheel from the differential case.
40   On models fitted with a limited slip differential (ie RS5F50V) remove the viscous coupling.
41   Cut free the speedometer drive gear.
42   Using a suitable puller pull off the side bearing inner races keeping them identified side for side.
43   Using a punch, drive out the pinion shaft lock pin and withdraw the shaft.
44   Remove the pinion and side gears together with the thrust washers.

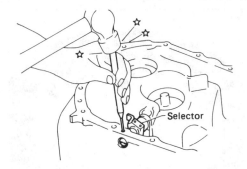

Fig. 13.110 Driving out the selector shaft retaining pin (Sec 11)

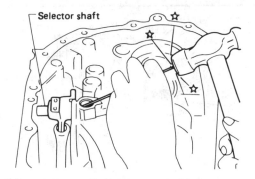

Fig. 13.111 Selector shaft removal (Sec 11)

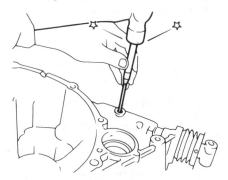

Fig. 13.112 Striking lever retaining pin removal (Sec 11)

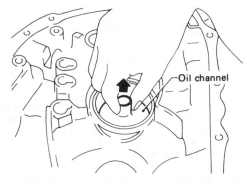

Fig. 13.113 Removing the oil channel from the clutch housing (Sec 11)

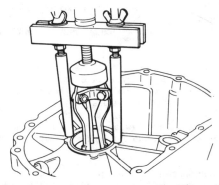

Fig. 13.114 Using an extractor to remove the differential side bearing outer track from the transmission casing (Sec 11)

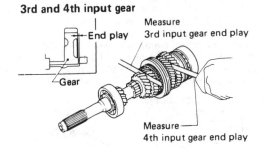

Fig. 13.115 Checking the input shaft gear endfloat (Sec 11)

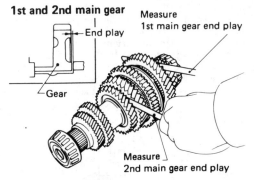

Fig. 13.116 Checking the mainshaft gear endfloat (Sec 11)

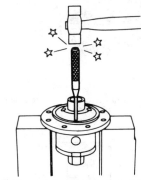

Fig. 13.117 Differential pinion shaft lock pin removal (Sec 11)

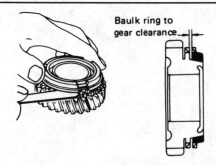

Fig. 13.118 Checking baulk ring wear with a feeler blade (Sec 11)

Transmission components (RS5F50A and RS5F50V) – inspection

45 With the transmission completely dismantled, clean all components and inspect them for wear and damage.

46 Check the gears for chipped teeth and their bushes for wear.

47 Check the shafts for scoring or grooving.

48 Check the bearings for wear by spinning them with the fingers. If they are worn excessively then they must be renewed.

49 Wear in the synchro units will normally be evident before dismantling the gearbox, however even if the units are operating well it is worth checking them in the following manner. First check the play between the splines on the sliding sleeve and the hub. Mark the sleeve and hub then separate them and remove the insert springs. Check the insert springs for wear. Check the baulk rings for wear by locating them on their respective gears and using a feeler blade as shown in Fig. 13.118. If the clearance is less than the specified minimum, renew them. Reassemble the synchro units in reverse order to dismantling but note that the 5th synchro sliding sleeve is marked in the vicinity of the insert spring groove as shown in Fig. 13.119.

50 It is recommended that all oil seals are renewed during a major overhaul. These include those for the differential side bearings, gearchange remote control rod and the input shaft.

51 The oil seals for the differential side bearings and the gearchange remote control rod can be renewed without having to remove the transmission from the vehicle, should anything more than the slightest seepage of oil be observed during normal operation of the vehicle.

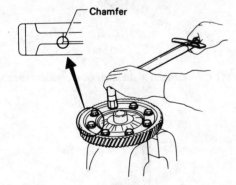

Fig. 13.120 Correct positioning of the differential crownwheel (Sec 11)

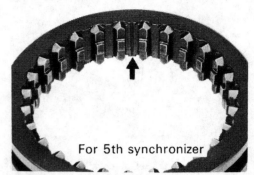

Fig. 13.119 Identification mark on the 5th synchro sliding sleeve (Sec 11)

52 On models with a limited slip differential check the viscous coupling case for cracking and for leakage.

Transmission (RS5F50A and RS5F50V) – reassembly

Differential/final drive

53 Locate the side gears and thrust washers in the differential case, followed by the pinion gears and thrust washers.

54 Carefully insert the pinion shaft taking care not to damage the thrust washers.

55 Where applicable assemble the viscous coupling and temporarily hold with three bolts.

56 Using a dial gauge check the end play of the side gears. If this is not as given in the Specifications it will be necessary to select and fit new side gear thrust washers.

57 Drive in a new pinion shaft roll pin until flush with the differential case.

58 Remove the viscous coupling bolts where applicable.

59 Fit the crownwheel, insert the bolts and tighten them progressively to the specified torque. Make sure that the crownwheel is fitted with the inner chamfer located correctly as shown in Fig. 13.120.

60 Fit a new speedometer drive gear.

61 Drive the side bearing inner races onto the differential/final drive unit using a suitable metal tube on the inner races only. Where the original races are being refitted make sure that they are on the correct sides.

Mainshaft

62 Oil all components liberally as they are reassembled.

63 Press the bearing inner race onto the front of the mainshaft.

64 Fit the 1st gear and locate the baulk ring on it.

65 Press on the 1st/2nd synchro unit, making sure it is the correct way round. For the 2nd baulk ring.

66 Fit the circlip. If the clearance in the groove exceeds 0.10 mm (0.0039 in) obtain a thicker circlip.

67 Locate 2nd gear on the mainshaft.

68 Press on the 3rd gear followed by the 4th and 5th gears.

69 Fit the circlip. If the clearance in the groove exceeds 0.15 mm (0.0059 in) obtain a thicker circlip.

70 Fit the thrust washer, then press on the rear bearing inner race.

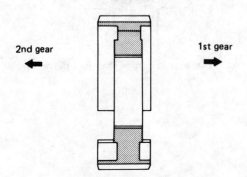

Fig. 13.121 Correct installation of 1st/2nd synchro unit (Sec 11)

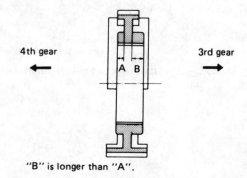

"B" is longer than "A".

Fig. 13.122 Correct installation of 3rd/4th synchro unit (Sec 11)

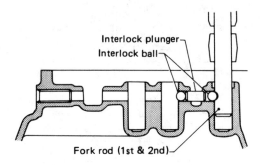

Fig. 13.123 Interlock balls and plunger with 1st/2nd selector rod in place (Sec 11)

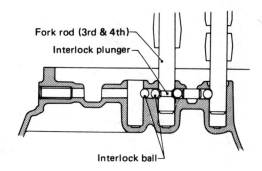

Fig. 13.124 Interlock balls with 3rd/4th selector rod in place (Sec 11)

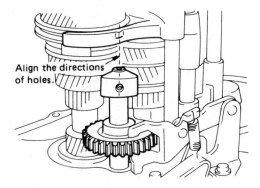

Fig. 13.125 Correct alignment of the reverse idler shaft (Sec 11)

71   Using a feeler blade, check that the gear endfloat is within the following tolerances:

    1st gear .... 0.23 to 0.43 mm (0.0091 to 0.0169 in)
    2nd gear .... 0.23 to 0.58 mm (0.0091 to 0.0228 in)

Input shaft
72   Oil all components liberally as they are reassembled.
73   Press on the front bearing using a metal tube on the inner track.
74   Locate the 3rd gear on the shaft together with the 3rd bulk ring.
75   Press on the 3rd/4th synchro unit making sure it is the correct way round.
76   Fit the circlip. If the clearance in the groove exceeds 0.10 mm (0.0039 in) obtain a thicker circlip.
77   Fit the 4th baulk ring and 4th gear.
78   Fit the split thrust washers and ring. The thrust washers are obtainable in different thicknesses to adjust the gear endfloat to between 0 and 0.06 mm (0 and 0.0024 in).
79   Locate the 5th gear on the shaft together with the 5th baulk ring.
80   Press on the 5th synchro unit.
81   Press on the rear bearing using a metal tube on the inner track.
82   Using a feeler blade (or a dial test indicator), check that the gear endfloat is within the following tolerances:

    3rd gear .... 0.23 to 0.43 mm (0.0091 to 0.0169 in)
    4th gear .... 0.25 to 0.55 mm (0.0098 to 0.0217 in)
    5th gear .... 0.23 to 0.48 mm (0.0091 to 0.0189 in)

Transmission casing and clutch housing
83   Refer to paragraphs 113 to 132 and if necessary carry out the bearing preload procedure in order to determine the correct shims to fit during reassembly.
84   Locate the shims in the transmission casing and drive in the mainshaft bearing outer track.
85   Drive the mainshaft bearing outer track into the clutch housing and refit the oil channel.
86   Similarly fit the differential side bearing outer tracks into the clutch housing and transmission casing.
87   Press a new input shaft oil seal into the clutch housing.
88   Refit the clutch release fork and bearing as described in Section 10.
89   Locate the lever in the clutch housing, then insert the striking rod. Secure the lever by driving in the retaining pin. Refit the drain plug.
90   Engage the selector with the striking lever, then insert the selector

shaft and secure by driving in the retaining pin.
91   Fit the reverse check assembly and tighten the bolts.
92   Stand the clutch housing on the bench and fit the final drive/differential assembly.
93   Insert the 1st/2nd selector rod in the 1st/2nd selector fork and locate the fork on the mainshaft 1st/2nd synchro sleeve.
94   Mesh the input shaft assembly with the mainshaft and lower them into the clutch housing, while guiding the 1st/2nd selector rod into its hole. Take care not to damage the input shaft oil seal.
95   Insert the interlock ball, plunger, and further ball to lock the 1st/2nd selector rod.
96   Locate the 3rd/4th selector fork on the input shaft 3rd/4th synchro sleeve.
97   Locate the selector dog bracket and insert the 3rd/4th selector rod. Align the holes and drive in the roll pin. Fit the circlip to the lower end of the selector fork.
98   Insert the two interlock balls to lock the 3rd/4th selector rod.
99   Locate the 5th selector fork on the input shaft 5th synchro sleeve.
100   Locate the selector dog bracket and insert the 5th selector rod. Align the holes and drive in the roll pin. Fit the circlip to the lower end of the selector fork.
101   Insert the 5th/reverse detent ball and spring and tighten the detent plug.
102   Grease the check ball, locate it in position then fit the reverse lever assembly and tighten the bolts.
103   Insert the reverse arm shaft together with a new O-ring and fit the retaining pin.
104   Select 4th gear. Locate the reverse idler gear, then insert the shaft. Position the shaft end fitting as shown in Fig. 13.125 so that the casing bolt will enter the threaded hole.
105   Check that the swarf magnet is located correctly in the clutch housing.
106   Grease the input shaft rear bearing shims and locate them in the transmission casing.
107   Position the shift selector in the 1st/2nd selector dog bracket or between the 1st/2nd and 3rd/4th selector dog brackets.
108   Apply jointing compound to the mating faces of the transmission casing and clutch housing.
109   Lower the transmission casing onto the clutch housing, then fit and tighten the bolts.

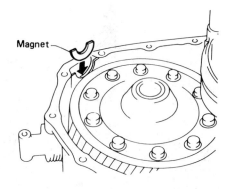

Fig. 13.126 Swarf magnet location on the clutch housing (Sec 11)

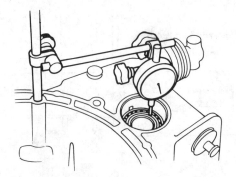

Fig. 13.127 Dial gauge location for checking the final drive/differential bearing endplay (Sec 11)

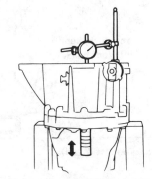

Fig. 13.128 Use a wooden dowel to move the final drive/differential (Sec 11)

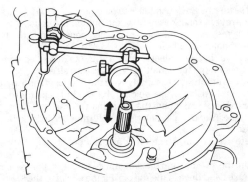

Fig. 13.129 Dial gauge location for checking the input shaft endplay (Sec 11)

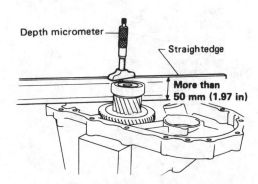

Fig. 13.130 Checking the mainshaft bearing clearance dimension (A) on the transmission casing (Sec 11)

110   Insert the 1st/2nd and 3rd/4th detent balls and springs. Apply sealing compound to the plug threads, then tighten the plugs.
111   Refit the reverse idler shaft bolt, the speedometer pinion, and the position switch (together with a new O-ring) and tighten the bolts to the specified torque.
112   Check that all gears can be selected.

Input shaft endplay and differential side bearing preload

113   If any of the following components have been renewed during overhaul, then the input shaft endplay must be adjusted:

Input shaft
Input shaft bearing
Clutch housing
Transmission case

114   If any of the following components have been renewed during overhaul, then the differential side bearing preload must be adjusted:

Differential case
Differential side bearing
Clutch housing
Transmission case

115   Drive the differential side bearing outer track into the transmission casing without any shims.
116   Locate the input shaft and the final drive/differential assembly in the clutch housing.
117   Fit the transmission casing without the input shaft bearing shims and tighten the bolts.
118   Stand the unit on blocks of wood with the open end of the clutch housing upwards.
119   Attach a dial gauge to measure the movement of the final drive/differential unit, then record the endplay, using a wooden dowel in the lower side gear to move the unit up and down.
120   The thickness of the shims to fit behind the differential side bearing outer track is the amount recorded in paragraph 119 plus a further 0.40 to 0.46 mm (0.0157 to 0.0181 in).
121   Attach the dial gauge to measure the movement of the input shaft, then move the shaft up and down and record the end play.
122   The thickness of the shims to fit in the transmission casing is the amount recorded in paragraph 121 less 0 to 0.06 mm (0 to 0.0024 in).
123   Remove the transmission casing and lift out the input shaft and final drive/differential assembly.

Mainshaft bearing preload

124   If any of the following components have been renewed during overhaul, then the mainshaft bearing preload must be adjusted:

Mainshaft
Mainshaft bearings
Clutch housing
Transmission case

125   Drive the mainshaft rear bearing outer track into the transmission casing without any shims.
126   Invert the transmission casing and locate the mainshaft assembly in the rear bearing outer track.
127   Clean the contact faces of the clutch housing and transmission casing.
128   Locate the front bearing outer track on the mainshaft and rotate it while pressing down on it.
129   Measure the distance (A) from the joint face to the top of the outer track, using a straight-edge and a depth micrometer. Measure the distance in three places to find an average.

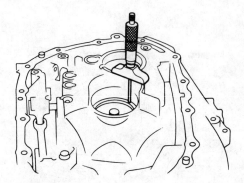

Fig. 13.131 Checking the mainshaft bearing clearance dimension (B) on the clutch housing (Sec 11)

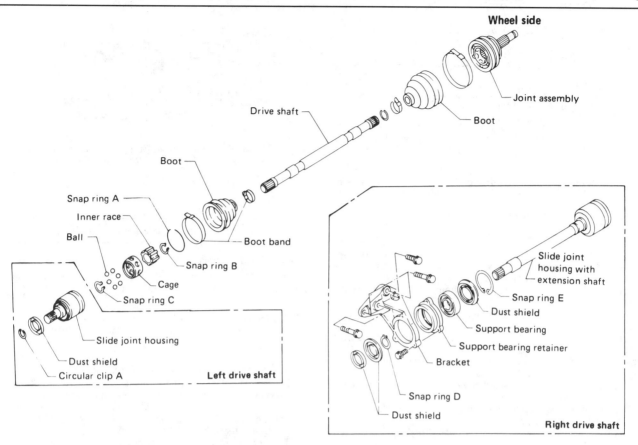

Fig. 13.132 Exploded view of the driveshaft fitted to models with the CA16DE or CA18DE engine (Sec 12)

130   Working on the clutch housing, measure the distance (B) from the joint face to the outer track seating, using a depth micrometer. Measure the distance in three places to find an average.
131   Determine the mainshaft bearing clearance (C) using the following formula:

$$C = B - A$$

132   The thickness of the shims to fit behind the mainshaft rear bearing outer track is dimension (C) plus 0.25 to 0.31 mm (0.0098 to 0.0122 in).

12 Driveshafts

General description
1   The diameter of the inner end of the driveshaft varies according to model, and it is therefore important to give accurate model and chassis numbers when ordering a new unit.
2   On CA16DE and CA18DE engine models the driveshaft incorporates Birfield ball type CV joints, and the driveshaft fitted to the right-hand side is supported by a bearing attached to the rear of the engine cylinder block.

Driveshaft (sixteen-valve engine models) – removal and refitting
3   The procedure is similar to that described in Chapter 8, except that when removing the right-hand driveshaft it is necessary to unbolt the support bearing retainer from the bracket on the rear of the engine

cylinder block (photo) and drive it from the bracket using a long metal rod. The driveshaft is not retained with an expanding circlip so it is not necessary to lever it from the differential side gears. When refitting the driveshaft, tighten the bolts to the specified torque wrench setting.

Driveshaft joints and bellows (sixteen-valve engine models) – removal, inspection and refitting
4   Although the joints are different, the procedure is basically the same as described in Chapter 8. Note however that the grease capacity for the outboard joint is 110 to 130 grams (3.88 to 4.59 oz) and 140 to 160 grams (4.94 to 5.64 oz) for the inboard joint. Set the rubber bellows to the

12.3 Right-hand driveshaft support bearing (sixteen-valve engine models)

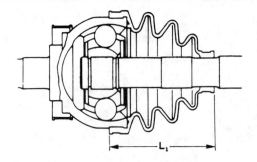

Fig. 13.133 Outer rubber bellows fitting dimension for models with the CA16DE or CA18DE engine (Sec 12)

L1 = 99.5 to 101.5 mm (3.917 to 3.996 in)

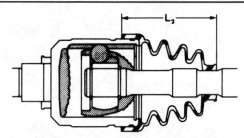

Fig. 13.134 Inner rubber bellows fitting dimension for models with the CA16DE or CA18DE engine (Sec 12)

L2 = 97.0 to 99.0 mm (3.82 to 3.90 in)

dimensions shown in Figs. 13.133 and 13.134. To remove the support bearing from the right-hand driveshaft first prise off the two inner dust shields and remove from the driveshaft.
5   Using circlip pliers extract the circlip from the inner end of the bearing.
6   Support the bearing retainer in a vice then drive the driveshaft down through it.
7   Invert the retainer and drive out the bearing. Recover the dust shield.
8   Clean the retainer. Examine the large circlip for damage and if necessary renew it. Fit a new dust shield.
9   Support the retainer in a vice and drive in the new bearing using a metal tube on the outer track only.
10   Locate the bearing on the driveshaft then use a metal tube on the inner track to drive it into position.
11   Fit a new circlip to the inner end of the bearing making sure that it is located correctly in its groove.
12   Fit two new inner dust shields.

13   Braking system (sixteen-valve engine models)

General description
1   Models fitted with the CA16DE and CA18DE sixteen-valve engines are equipped with disc brakes all round.

Front disc pads – inspection and renewal
2   The procedure is the same as that described in Chapter 9 Section 3 but with reference also to Figs. 13.135 and 13.136.

Rear disc pads – inspection and renewal
3   Chock the front wheels then raise the rear of the vehicle and support on axle stands. Remove the rear roadwheels and release the handbrake.
4   Looking through the aperture in the calipers check that the thickness of the pad linings is not less than the amount given in Specifications. Use a steel rule to make the check.
5   If any pad lining is less than the specified amount then all four rear pads must be renewed.

13.7A Unscrew the slide pins ...

13.7B ... remove them ...

13.7C ... and withdraw the caliper from the disc pads

13.8A Removing the outer disc pad ...

13.8B ... and inner disc pad

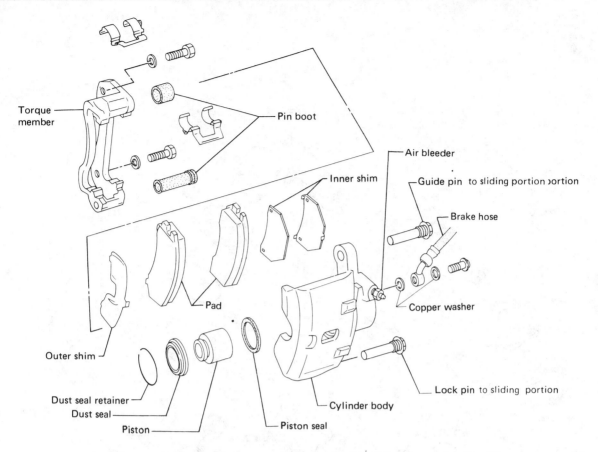

Fig. 13.135 AD18V front brake components fitted to CA16DE engine models (Sec 13)

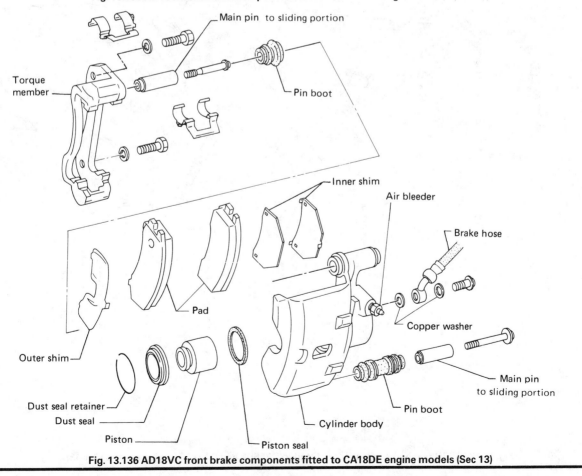

Fig. 13.136 AD18VC front brake components fitted to CA18DE engine models (Sec 13)

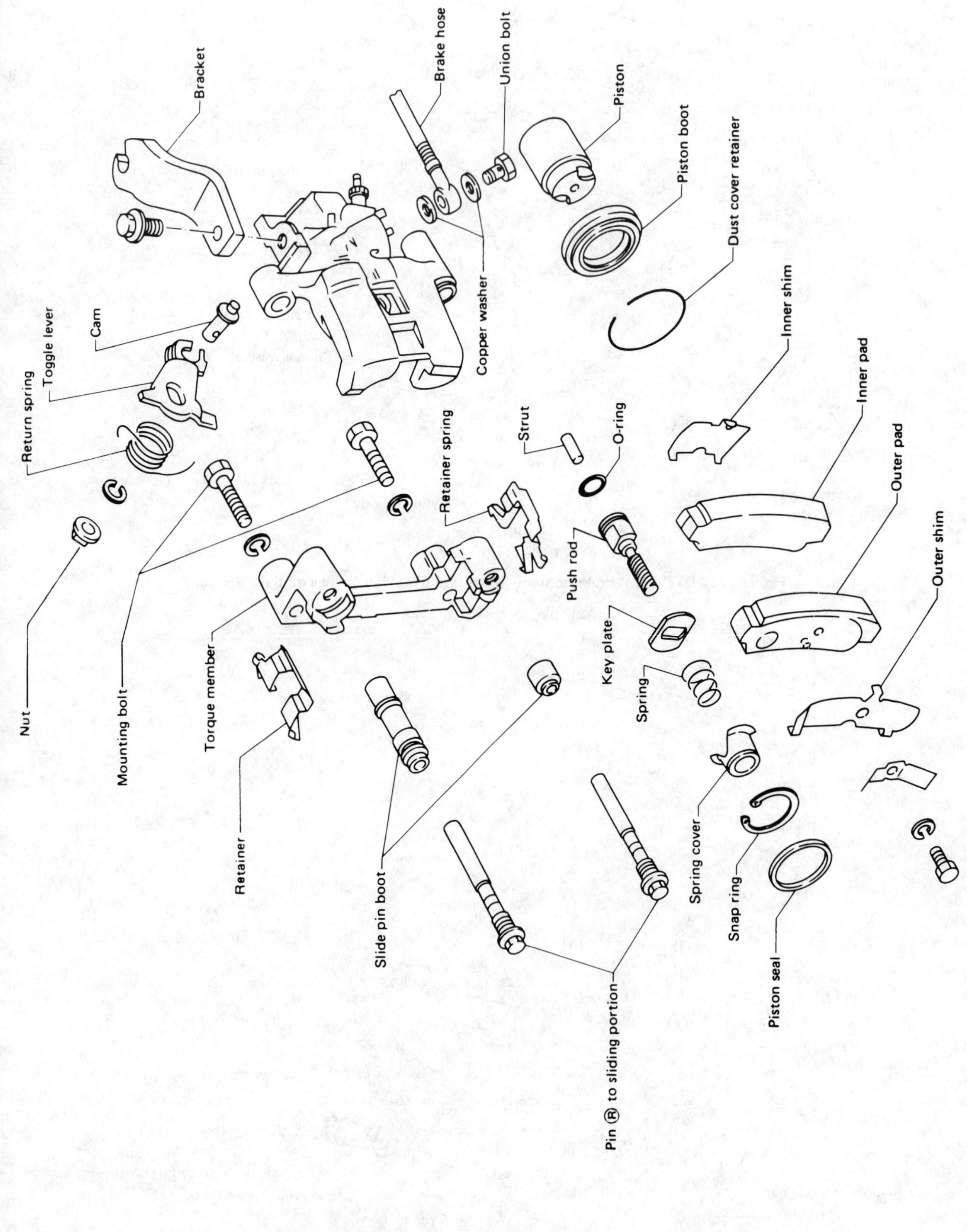

Fig. 13.137 AD7H rear brake components fitted to CA16DE and CA18DE engine models (Sec 13)

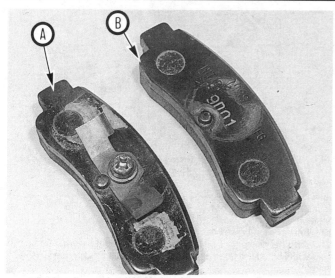

13.9 Outer (A) and inner (B) disc pads

13.12 Retracting the piston into the rear caliper

6   If necessary unscrew the bolt securing the handbrake cable bracket to the rear caliper.
7   Unscrew and remove both slide pins from the caliper mounting bracket, then withdraw the caliper from the disc pads and support it in a raised position (photos). Recover the slide pin boots.
8   Prise off the retaining springs and remove the pads from the torque member (photos).
9   Remove the shims from the pads. The outer shim is bolted to the pad (photo).
10   Brush the dust from the caliper recesses, taking care not to inhale it as it is dangerous to health.
11   Do not touch the brake pedal or handbrake while the pads are out of the caliper.
12   Before fitting the new pads, retract the piston into the cylinder by turning it clockwise using long nose pliers in the piston cut-outs (photo). Take care not to damage the piston boot.
13   Apply just a smear of high melting point brake grease to the backing plates of the new disc pads, then fit them using a reversal of the removal procedure. Apply rubber grease to the sliding portion of each slide pin before inserting and tightening them.
14   Repeat the operations on the opposite side, then refit the road-wheels and lower the car to the ground.
15   Apply the footbrake hard several times to set the pads in their normal position, and finally check the handbrake adjustment with reference to Chapter 9.

Rear brake caliper – removal, overhaul and refitting

16   Remove the disc pads as described previously.
17   Disconnect the handbrake inner cable from the caliper by extracting the spring clip and removing the clevis.
18   Fit a brake hose clamp to the flexible brake hose.
19   Disconnect the brake hose at the caliper by unscrewing the banjo union hollow bolt. Note the sealing washer on each side of the union.
20   Withdraw the caliper from the vehicle.

21   If necessary unbolt the torque member from the rear suspension strut.
22   Clean the caliper and torque member.
23   Prise out the spring clip, and pull the piston boot from the caliper.
24   Using long-nosed pliers in the cut-outs provided, unscrew the piston in an anti-clockwise direction and remove it from the cylinder.
25   From inside the piston extract the circlip using circlip pliers, then remove the spacers, wave washer, bearing and adjusting nut, noting the order of removal. Prise the cup seal from the adjusting nut.
26   Working on the caliper, extract the circlip with circlip pliers, then remove the spring cover, spring, and seat.
27   Extract the circlip with circlip pliers, then remove the key plate, pushrod and plunger. Prise the O-ring from the pushrod.
28   Prise the piston seal from the cylinder using a blunt instrument to prevent damage to the cylinder bore.
29   Unhook the return spring from the handbrake control lever and remove the adjusting cam from the caliper body.
30   Grip the adjusting cam in a soft-jawed vice, then unscrew the nut and remove the spring washer lever and cam boot.
31   Unbolt and remove the cable support bracket.
32   Wash the components in clean brake fluid or methylated spirit, then examine them for wear and damage. If the surfaces of the piston or cylinder bore are scored or corroded, then the complete caliper should be renewed, however if they are in good condition, obtain a repair kit of seals and discard the old ones. Check the handbrake control components for wear and renew as necessary.
33   Fit the cable support bracket and tighten the bolt.
34   Locate the new cam boot on the adjusting cam, then fit the lever, spring washer and nut. Tighten the nuts with the adjusting cam mounted in a vice.
35   Apply brake grease to the adjusting cam, then insert it in the cylinder body and fit the return spring.
36   Fit the new piston seal into the cylinder groove using the fingers only manipulate it into position. Make sure that it is the correct way round, as shown in Fig. 9.13 Chapter 9.

Fig. 13.138 Removing the circlip from the rear brake caliper piston (Sec 13)

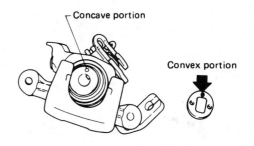

Concave portion

Convex portion

Fig. 13.139 Correct location of the keyplate in the rear caliper (Sec 13)

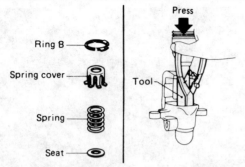

Fig. 13.140 Reassembly of ring B (Sec 13)

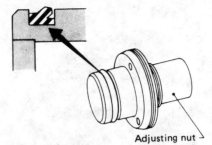

Fig. 13.141 Showing correct fitting of cup seal on the adjusting nut (Sec 13)

37   Ease the O-ring into the pushrod groove.
38   Apply brake fluid to the plunger, pushrod and O-ring.
39   Locate the key plate on the pushrod, so that the dot indicating the convex side will face out of the cylinder. This will ensure correct assembly of the key plate in the concave portion of the cylinder body.
40   Fit the plunger, pushrod and key plate in the cylinder body, and retain with the circlip.
41   Fit the spring seat, spring and cover in the cylinder body and retain with the circlip. It will be necessary to compress the spring in order to engage the circlip in its groove.
42   Fit the cup seal to the adjusting nut as shown in Fig. 13.141, using the fingers only to manipulate it into position.
43   Apply brake fluid to the cup seal, piston and piston seal. Apply rubber grease to the small diameter of the piston boot.
44   Locate in the piston the adjusting nut, bearing, spacer, wave washer and retain with the circlip.
45   Locate the boot on the piston, then insert the piston in the cylinder bore and turn it clockwise until fully entered. Fit the boot to the cylinder body and retain with the spring clip.
46   If removed, refit the torque member to the rear suspension strut and tighten the bolts to the specified torque.
47   Reconnect the handbrake inner cable to the caliper with the clevis and refit the spring clip.
48   Reconnect the brake hose with the banjo union bolt and two new

sealing washers. Tighten the bolt with the banjo union correctly located so that the hose will not be twisted with the caliper in its normal position.
49   Remove the brake hose clamp.
50   Refit the disc pads as described previously, but before refitting the roadwheel bleed the appropriate hydraulic circuit as described in Chapter 9.
51   Apply the handbrake several times to operate the self-adjusting mechanism for the handbrake cable. If necessary, adjust the cable end play as described in Chapter 9.

14   Suspension and steering (sixteen-valve engines)

General description

1   As sixteen-valve engine models are fitted with rear disc brakes, the rear hub is different and therefore the following procedures are different than those given in Chapter 10.

Rear hub bearings – renewal

2   Jack up the rear of the vehicle and support on axle stands. Remove the roadwheel and release the handbrake.
3   Remove the rear brake caliper as described in Section 13, however

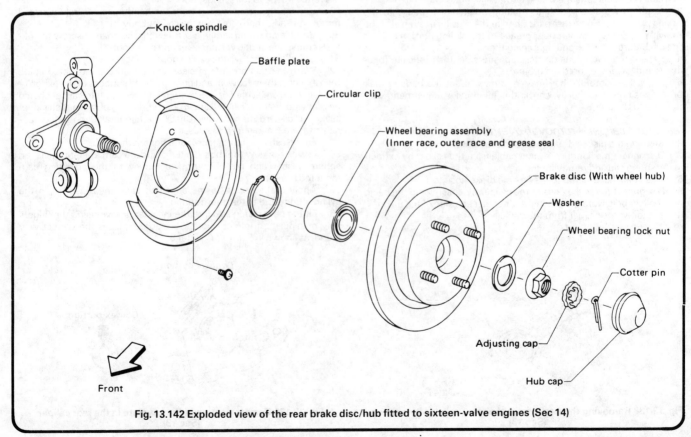

Fig. 13.142 Exploded view of the rear brake disc/hub fitted to sixteen-valve engines (Sec 14)

14.31A Power steering fluid reservoir

14.31B Checking the fluid level

14.31C Power steering fluid pressure switch location

do not disconnect the flexible brake hose. Tie the caliper to one side making sure that the hose is not twisted.

4   Using a suitable tool prise free the hub cap, then clean away the grease from the hub.

5   Extract the split pin and withdraw the adjuster cap from the hub nut.

6   Loosen the hub nut using a socket and extension bar. The nut is tightened to a high torque.

7   Remove the hub nut and special washer.

8   Withdraw the brake disc and hub from the knuckle spindle.

9   If necessary the inner oil seal may be renewed separate to the bearing by prising it out with a screwdriver, then driving the new seal into position using a block of wood. Make sure that the oil seal lip is facing the correct way round.

10   To remove the bearing, first use a suitable tool to extract the special circular clip from the inner end of the hub.

11   Support the hub in a vice with the wheel studs uppermost, then use a metal tube on the bearing inner track to drive the bearing down through the hub. Note that the bearing will be rendered unserviceable by removing it.

12   Clean the brake disc and hub, in particular the bearing seating inside the hub. Check the brake disc for excessive wear and damage, and if necessary renew the disc and hub assembly.

13   Wipe dry the bearing seating inside the hub, then support the hub on a vice with the steel studs facing downwards. Locate the bearing on the hub with the oil seal uppermost, then drive it into the hub using a metal tube on the outer track only. Make sure that the outer edge of the tube is thin enough to rest on the bearing outer track without touching the oil seal otherwise the oil seal may be damaged. Do not attempt to drive on the inner track as the bearing will be damaged.

14   Fit the special circular clip in the groove inside the hub.

15   Apply a little multi-purpose grease to the sealing lip of the oil seal.

16   Wipe clean the knuckle spindle then refit the brake disc and hub.

17   Fit the special washer and screw on the hub nut. Tighten the nut to the specified torque using a socket and extension bar.

18   Rotate the hub and check for smooth running. Check that the bearing endplay is as given in the Specifications using a dial gauge.

19   Fit the adjuster cap so that the serrations are aligned with the split pin hole in the spindle. Insert a new split pin and bend over the ends to secure.

20   Tap the hub cap into position.

21   Refit the rear brake caliper with reference to Section 13.

22   Refit the roadwheel and lower the vehicle to the ground.

Rear suspension knuckle – removal and refitting

23   Chock the front wheels then jack up the rear of the vehicle and support on axle stands.

24   Remove the rear hub/brake disc as previously described.

25   Unbolt the baffle plate.

26   Unscrew and remove the radius rod end nut and also the radius rod front mounting clamp bolts.

27   Unscrew the nut and extract the bolt securing the parallel links to the knuckle.

28   Unbolt the brake hose bracket from the strut.

29   Unscrew the two bolts securing the knuckle spindle to the strut noting their fitted position. Withdraw the knuckle.

30   Refitting is a reversal of removal but tighten all nuts and bolts to the specified torque wrench settings. In the case of the parallel link bolt and radius rod front mounting clamp bolts, delay tightening them until the weight of the vehicle is on the ground.

Power steering system – modifications

31   On later models the power steering fluid reservoir is located on the right-hand side of the engine compartment. In addition a pressure switch is incorporated in the fluid lines (photos).

---

15   Bodywork and fittings

General description

1   Except for the following, the procedures for later models is basically the same as given in Chapter 11. The facelift changes in March 1989 are mainly cosmetic and therefore most procedures are the same as given for earlier models.

Bonnet lock (March 1989-on) – removal, refitting and adjustment

2   The procedure is as given in Chapter 11, however check that the latch engages the bonnet bar by at least the amount shown in Fig. 13.144. To do this, the radiator grille must first be removed.

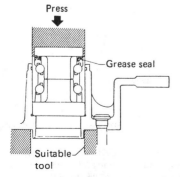
Fig. 13.143 Pressing the bearing into the rear brake disc/hub assembly (Sec 14)

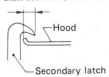

More than 5.0 mm (0.197 in)

Fig. 13.144 Bonnet safety latch engagement dimension for models from March 1989 onwards (Sec 15)

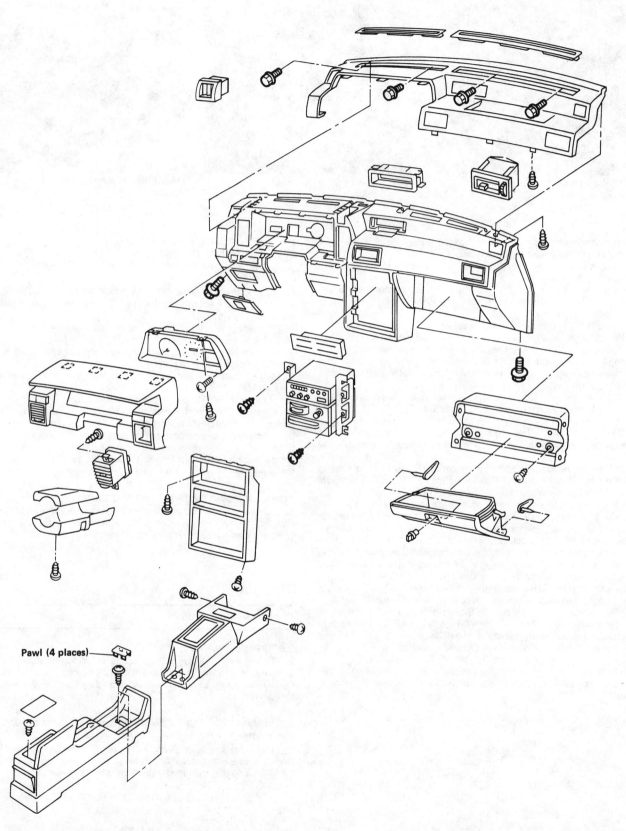

Fig. 13.145 Facia and associated panels and fixings on March 1989-on Saloon and Hatchback models (left-hand drive version shown) (Sec 15)

Pawl (4 places)

Door trim panel (March 1989-on) – removal and refitting

3   Later models may be fitted with a door trim panel which differs slightly from that shown in Chapter 11, however the procedure is basically the same as given for earlier models.

Facia panel (March 1989-on) – description

4   The facia panel fitted to Saloon and Hatchback models from March 1989 onwards is shown in Fig. 13.145 and differs only in the area of the centre panel.

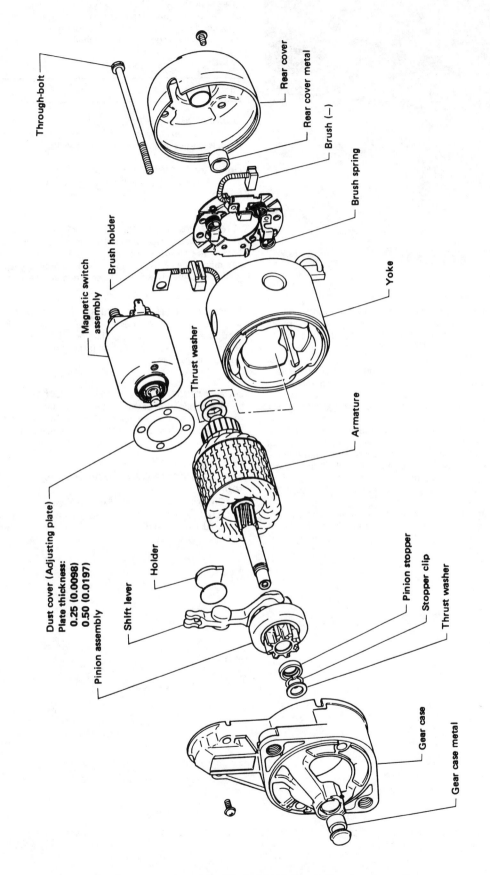

Fig. 13.146 Exploded view of the Mitsubishi M3T27781D starter motor (Sec 16)

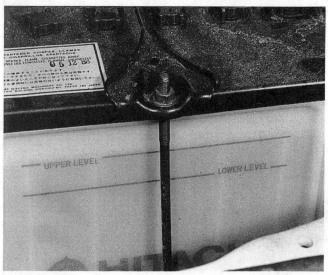

16.2 Battery electrolyte levels

glass adhesive stips, then insert the glass under the retaining lip at one end. Work the glass into place until its edges are evenly covered by the retaining lip all round. Take care during this operation, as it is easy to damage the new glass or the retaining lip.

16 Electrical system

General description
1   With the exception of the following, the electrical system on later models is the same as given in Chapter 12.

Battery maintenance – general
2   The electrolyte level marks on later models are more explicit (photo).

Alternators (later models) – description
3   Later models are fitted with both Hitachi and Mitsubishi alternators which are similar to those described in Chapter 12. The type numbers and differences are given in the Specifications. The exploded diagrams given in Chapter 12 apply to later versions except for minor differences.

Starter motor (later models) – description
4   Three additional types of starter motor have been added to later models as given in the specifications. With the exception of the Mitsubishi type M3T27781D, the later starters have epicyclic-type reduction gears.

Starter motor (later models) – overhaul
5   The procedure for the starter motors fitted to later models is similar to that for earlier models described in Chapter 12, but with reference also to Figs. 13.146 to 13.148 and the Specifications. Types other than those shown are similar in construction.

Starter motor (sixteen-valve engine) – removal and refitting
6   On sixteen-valve engines the area around the starter motor is very restricted, and it may therefore be necessary to remove the inlet manifold in order to gain access to the mounting bolts.

Door mirror glass – renewal
5   Replacement glasses are now available for the door mirrors. Note that they are handed, and that (where electrically-heated mirrors are fitted) a heating element may be incorporated in the glass, so be sure to obtain the correct part.
6   When removing a broken glass, take adequate precautions against cuts by wearing suitable gloves, and it is recommended that safety goggles be worn, to protect the eyes from the danger of flying glass.
7   Using a heat gun (rated between 700 and 1500 W), warm up the retaining lip of the glass mounting base all around the edge of the glass, until the lip is softened.
8   Prise the glass out of the mounting base, using a wide-bladed screwdriver, or a stiff scraper, inserted under the retaining lip. Start at the vertical edge furthest from the car, and take care not to damage the wires to the heating element (where applicable). To reduce the danger of flying glass, **do not** use excessive force.
9   Clean thoroughly the mirror base surfaces which will accept the adhesive strips on the replacement glass.
10   Warm up the retaining lip again, and also the edge of the replacement glass. Remove the protective covering from the replacement

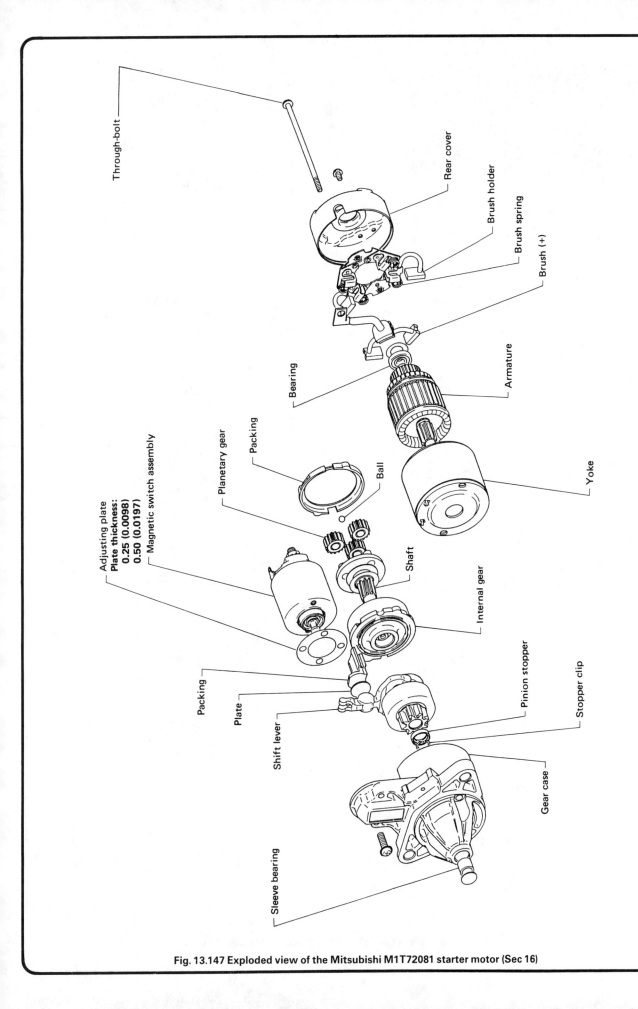

Through-bolt

Rear cover

Brush holder

Brush spring

Brush (+)

Bearing

Armature

Planetary gear

Packing

Ball

Yoke

Adjusting plate
Plate thickness:
0.25 (0.0098)
0.50 (0.0197)

Magnetic switch assembly

Shaft

Internal gear

Packing

Plate

Shift lever

Pinion stopper

Stopper clip

Gear case

Sleeve bearing

Fig. 13.147 Exploded view of the Mitsubishi M1T72081 starter motor (Sec 16)

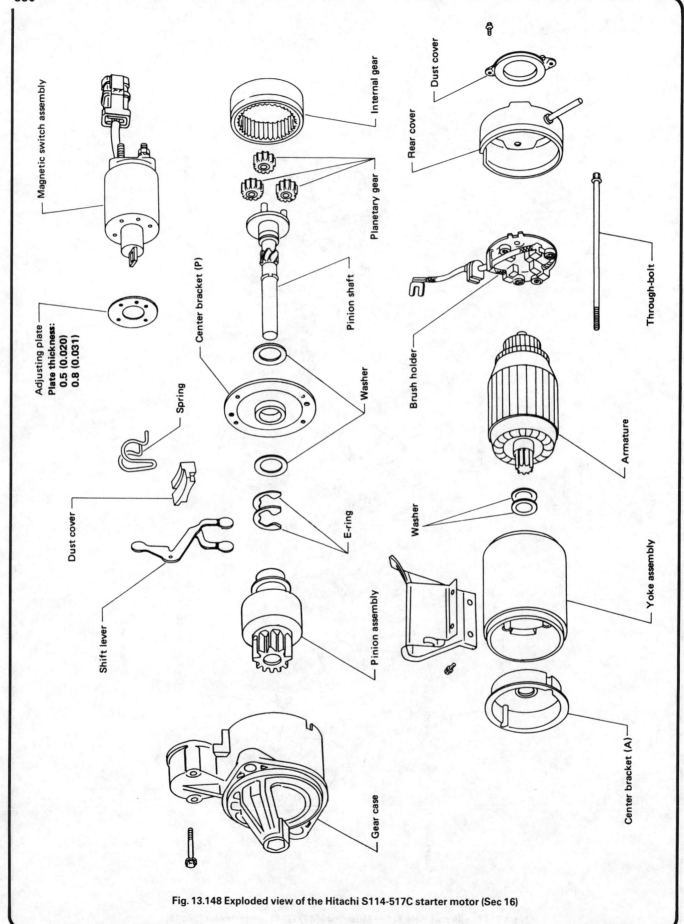

Magnetic switch assembly

Adjusting plate
Plate thickness:
0.5 (0.020)
0.8 (0.031)

Spring

Dust cover

Shift lever

Center bracket (P)

Internal gear

Planetary gear

Pinion shaft

Washer

E-ring

Pinion assembly

Gear case

Dust cover

Rear cover

Brush holder

Washer

Armature

Through-bolt

Yoke assembly

Center bracket (A)

Fig. 13.148 Exploded view of the Hitachi S114-517C starter motor (Sec 16)

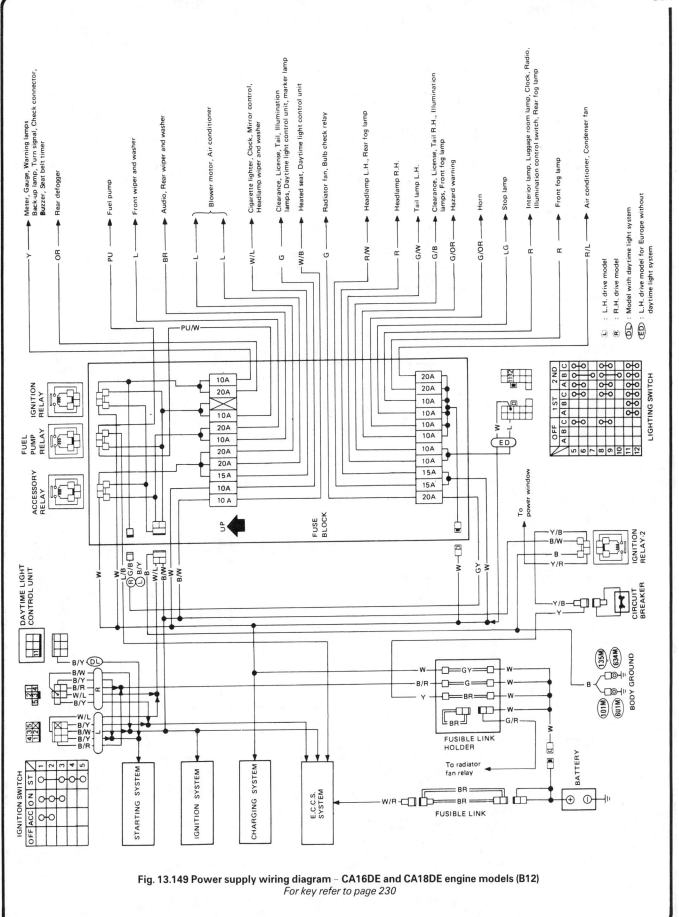

Fig. 13.149 Power supply wiring diagram – CA16DE and CA18DE engine models (B12)
For key refer to page 230

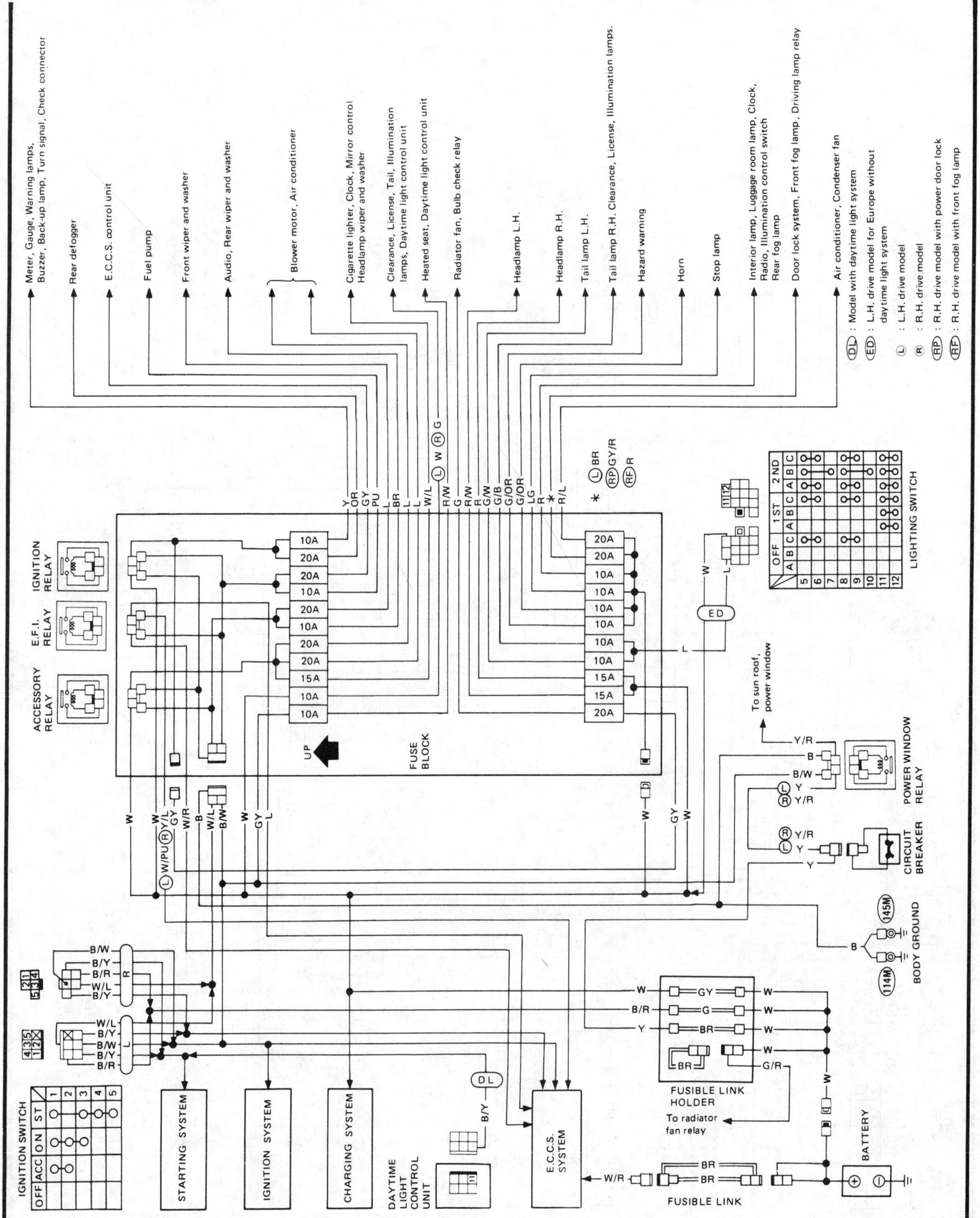

Meter, Gauge, Warning lamps, Buzzer, Back-up lamp, Turn signal, Check connector
Rear defogger
E.C.C.S. control unit
Fuel pump
Front wiper and washer
Audio, Rear wiper and washer
Blower motor, Air conditioner
Cigarette lighter, Clock, Mirror control
Headlamp wiper and washer
Clearance, License, Tail, Illumination lamps, Daytime light control unit
Heated seat, Daytime light control unit
Radiator fan, Bulb check relay
Headlamp L.H.
Headlamp R.H.
Tail lamp L.H.
Tail lamp R.H. Clearance, License, Illumination lamps.
Hazard warning
Horn
Stop lamp
Interior lamp, Luggage room lamp, Clock, Radio, Illumination control switch, Rear fog lamp
Door lock system, Front fog lamp, Driving lamp relay
Air conditioner, Condenser fan

DL Model with daytime light system
ED L.H. drive model for Europe without daytime light system
L L.H. drive model
R R.H. drive model
RP R.H. drive model with power door lock
RF R.H. drive model with front fog lamp

IGNITION RELAY
E.F.I. RELAY
ACCESSORY RELAY

10A
20A
20A
10A
20A
10A
20A
20A
15A
10A

20A
20A
10A
10A
10A
10A
10A
15A
15A
20A

UP
FUSE BLOCK

LIGHTING SWITCH

POWER WINDOW RELAY

To sun roof, power window

CIRCUIT BREAKER

BODY GROUND
145M
114M

IGNITION SWITCH
| | OFF | ACC | ON | ST | 1 | 2 | 3 | 4 | 5 |

STARTING SYSTEM
IGNITION SYSTEM
CHARGING SYSTEM
DAYTIME LIGHT CONTROL UNIT
E.C.C.S. SYSTEM

FUSIBLE LINK HOLDER
To radiator fan relay

FUSIBLE LINK
BATTERY

Fig. 13.150 Power supply wiring diagram – CA16DE and CA18DE engine models (N13)
For key refer to page 230

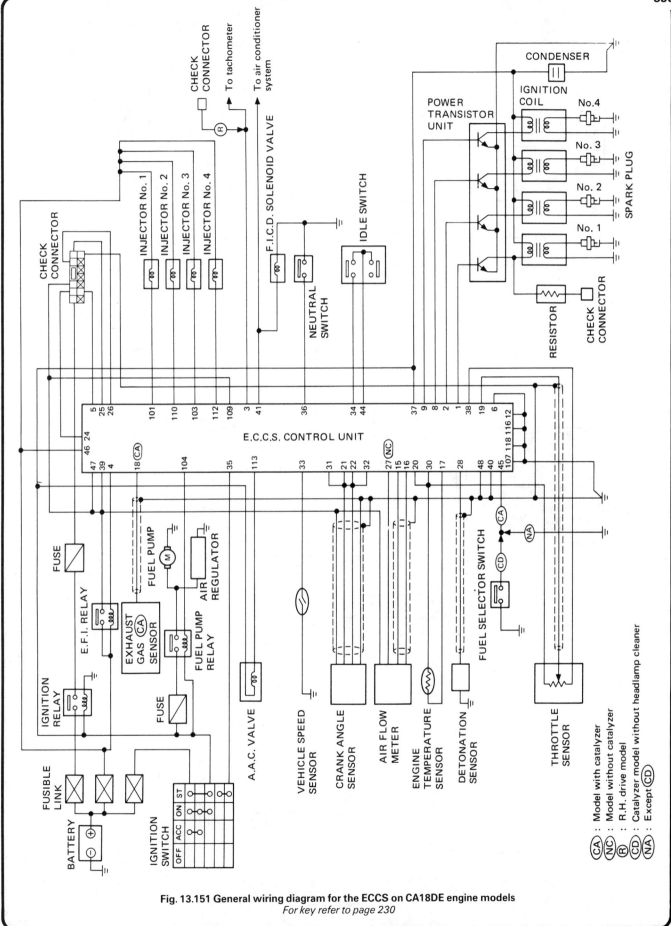

Fig. 13.151 General wiring diagram for the ECCS on CA18DE engine models
For key refer to page 230

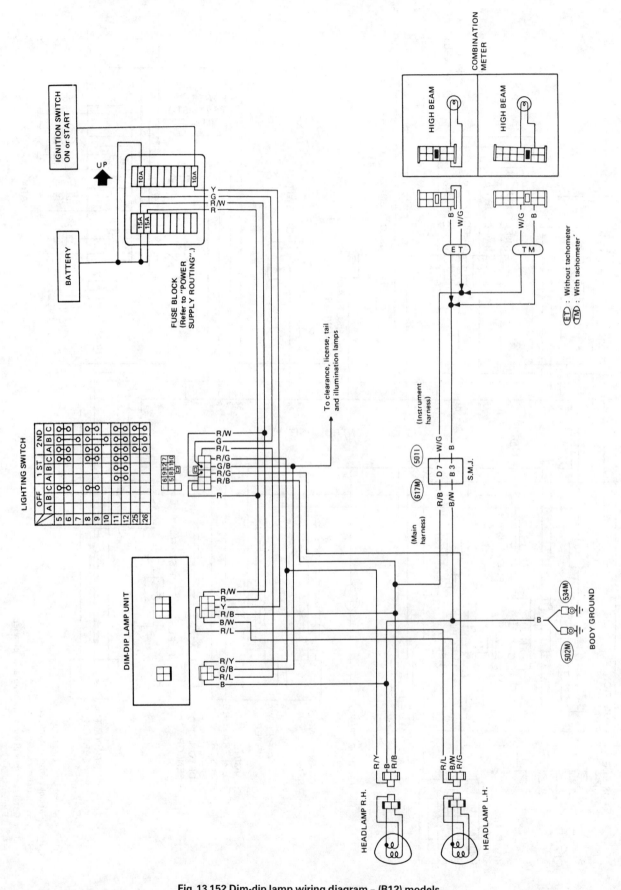

Fig. 13.152 Dim-dip lamp wiring diagram – (B12) models

For key refer to page 230

Index

A

About this manual – 5
Accelerator pedal and cable
  removal, refitting and adjustment – 80
Aerial – 227
Air cleaner
  removal and refitting – 70, 352
  servicing – 70
Air conditioning drivebelt – 63, 342
Air temperature control (ATC) system checking – 71
Alternator
  description – 204, 388
  drivebelt – 63, 342
  maintenance – 18, 204
  overhaul – 205
  precautions – 204
  removal and refitting – 204
Antifreeze – 59
Anti-roll bar removal and refitting – 153
Automatic choke – 73, 76, 343
Automatic transmission – 121 *et seq*
Automatic transmission
  adjustment – 123, 124
  brake band – 124
  description – 121
  differential bearing oil seals – 126
  driveplate – 48
  fault diagnosis – 127
  fluid level – 123
  governor shaft – 125
  inhibitor switch – 124
  kickdown cable – 124
  maintenance – 18, 123
  oil seals – 126
  overhaul – 123
  removal and refitting – 41, 55, 126
  selector cable – 124
  specifications – 121, 290

B

Battery
  charging – 204
  maintenance – 18, 202, 388
  removal and refitting – 204
Bellows removal and refitting
  driveshaft – 130, 379
  steering rack – 163
Big-end bearing shells renewal – 36

Bearings
  big-end – 36
  clutch release – 98
  hub – 156, 158, 384
  main – 47
  mainshaft – 120, 378
Bleeding
  braking system – 142, 143
  clutch hydraulic system – 366
  power-assisted steering – 170
Bodywork and fittings – 174 *et seq*, 385
Bodywork and fittings
  bonnet – 177
  bonnet lock – 180, 385
  boot lid – 187, 190
  bumpers – 180
  damage repair
    major – 177
    minor – 175 to 177
  description – 174, 385
  doors – 184, 185, 186
  door trim panel – 184, 386
  facia – 194, 386
  grille – 184
  locks – 167, 180, 185, 190, 385
  mirrors – 194
  radiator grille – 184
  maintenance – 18, 174, 175
  seat belts – 193
  seats – 193
  sunroof – 198, 199
  tailgate – 187, 190
  trim – 184, 191, 192, 194, 386
  windows – 186, 191
Bonnet
  cable – 177
  lock – 180, 385
  removal and refitting – 177
Boot lid
  lock – 190
  removal and refitting – 187
Brake band adjustment – 124
Brake warning light switches – 226
Braking system – 133 *et seq*, 380
Braking system
  bleeding – 142
  caliper – 139, 383
  description – 134, 380
  disc – 139
  drum – 140
  fault diagnosis – 147
  handbrake – 145
  hydraulic pipes and hoses – 142
  maintenance – 18, 134, 292

master cylinder – 140
pads – 135, 380
pedal – 146
pressure regulating valve – 140
servo – 143, 144
shoes – 137
specifications – 133, 291
vacuum servo unit – 143, 144
wheel cylinder (rear) – 140
Bulb renewal
cigar lighter – 215
front indicator – 219, 220
front/side clearance lamp – 219
headlamp – 219
heater control panel lamp – 221
instrument panel – 221
interior lamp – 221
luggage compartment – 220
number plate lamp – 220
rear combination light – 220
side clearance lamp – 219
sidelamp – 219
side marker/indicator lamp – 219
Bumpers removal and refitting – 180

C

Cables
accelerator – 80
bonnet release – 177
clutch – 96
handbrake – 145
heater – 65
kickdown – 124
selector – 124
speedometer – 225
Caliper
overhaul – 139
removal and refitting – 139, 383
Camshaft examination and renovation – 48
Capacities – 7
Carburettor
accelerator pump – 77, 346
automatic choke – 73, 76, 343
checks and adjustments – 76, 343
choke unloader – 76
dashpot – 76, 348
description – 73, 343
float level – 76, 79, 343
fuel cut-off solenoid valve – 76, 77, 348
idle speed adjustment – 78, 348
idle-up control solenoid – 347
overhaul – 78
mixture adjustment – 78, 348
removal and refitting – 78
secondary throttle vacuum diaphragm – 76
specifications – 68, 288
vacuum break diaphragm – 76
Cigar lighter illumination bulb and unit
removal and refitting – 215
Clock removal and refitting – 222
Clutch – 95 *et seq*, 366
Clutch
adjustment – 96
bleeding hydraulic system – 366
cable – 96
description – 95, 366
fault diagnosis – 100
housing – 106, 115
inspection – 97
master cylinder – 368

pedal – 97, 366, 369
refitting – 99
release bearing – 98, 370
removal – 97
slave cylinder – 368
specifications – 95, 289
Coil (ignition) description and testing – 94
Connecting rods examination and renovation – 48
Conversion factors – 19
Cooling and heating systems – 57 *et seq*, 337
Cooling and heating systems
coolant mixture – 59
cooling fan thermoswitch – 342
description – 58, 337
draining – 59, 337
drivebelts – 63, 342
expansion tank – 64
fan – 62
fault diagnosis – 67
filling – 59, 337
flushing – 59, 337
heater – 64, 65
maintenance – 18, 58, 292
radiator – 60, 62, 338
specifications – 57, 287
temperature switch and gauge – 64
thermostat – 60, 338
water pump – 62, 338, 340
Courtesy lamp switch removal and refitting – 214
Crankcase examination and renovation – 47
Crankshaft and bearings examination and renovation – 47
Cylinder block
eight-valve engine
examination and renovation – 47
core plugs – 49
sixteen-valve engine
dismantling and reassembly – 332
twelve-valve engine
dismantling and reassembly – 308
Cylinder head
eight-valve engine
dismantling and reassembly – 43, 49
overhaul – 43, 49
removal and refitting – 33
sixteen-valve engine
removal and refitting – 320
dismantling and reassembly – 324
twelve-valve engine
removal and refitting – 298
dismantling and reassembly – 305

D

Differential/final drive
bearing oil seal – 126
dismantling – 110, 374
reassembly – 112, 376
Dim-dip lamp system – 215
Dimensions – 7
Disc (brake)
inspection and renovation – 139
pads – 135, 380
Distributor
cap – 93
overhaul – 90, 364
removal and refitting – 89
Doors
lock fittings – 185
removal and refitting – 184
trim panel – 184, 386
window and regulator – 186
Draining (coolant) – 58, 337

Drivebelts
    air conditioning compressor – 63, 342
    alternator – 63, 342
    power steering pump – 63, 342
Driveplate examination and renovation – 48
Driveshafts – 128 *et seq*, 379
Driveshafts
    bellows – 130, 379
    checking – 129
    description – 128, 379
    fault diagnosis – 132
    joints – 130, 379
    maintenance – 18, 128
    removal and refitting – 129, 379
    specifications – 128, 290
Drum (brake)
    inspection and renovation – 140
    shoes – 137

E

Electrical system – 201 *et seq*, 388
Electrical system
    aerial – 227
    alternator – 63, 204, 205, 388
    battery – 202, 204, 388
    bulbs – 217
    cigar lighter – 215
    clock – 222
    courtesy lamp – 214
    description – 202, 388
    dim-dip lamp system – 215
    drivebelt – 63, 342
    fault diagnosis – 228
    fuses – 213
    headlamp – 216, 217, 219
    heated rear window – 226
    horn – 225
    instrument panel – 222
    loudspeakers – 227
    radio/cassette unit – 226
    relays – 213
    removal and refitting – 202
    speakers – 227
    specifications – 201, 292
    speedometer cable – 225
    starter motor – 209, 388
    switches – 62, 64, 124, 167, 214, 226, 342
    wiper arms, blades and motor – 222, 224, 225
    wiring diagrams – 230 to 275, 391 to 394
Emission control system – 80
Engine – 26 *et seq*
Engine (eight-valve)
    big-end bearing shells – 36
    camshaft – 48
    connecting rods – 48
    core plugs – 49
    crankcase – 47
    crankshaft – 47
    cylinder block – 47, 49
    cylinder head – 33, 43, 49
    description – 28
    dismantling – 41
    driveplate – 48
    fault diagnosis – 55
    flywheel – 48
    gaskets – 49
    jackshaft – 48
    lubrication system – 41
    main bearings – 47
    maintenance – 18, 30, 292
    oil pump – 35, 49
    oil seals – 49
    operations possible without removing engine – 30
    pistons and piston rings – 36, 48
    positive crankcase ventilation system (PCV) – 43
    reassembly – 50
    refitting – 54, 55
    removal – 39, 41
    specifications – 26
    start-up after overhaul – 55
    sump pan – 35
    timing belt – 31, 48
    valves – 30
Engine (sixteen-valve)
    cylinder block – 332
    cylinder head – 320, 324
    description – 317
    oil pump – 330
    pistons – 33
    removal and refitting – 335
    specifications – 281
    sump – 328
    timing belt – 319
Engine (twelve-valve)
    cylinder block – 308
    cylinder head – 298, 305
    description – 293
    oil pump – 307
    pistons – 310
    removal and refitting – 310
    specifications – 278
    sump – 306
    timing chain – 293
    valves – 293
Exhaust system – 81, 82
Expansion tank removal and refitting – 64

F

Facia panel
    removal and refitting – 194, 386
    switches – 214
Fault diagnosis
    automatic transmission – 127
    braking system – 147
    clutch – 100
    cooling system – 67
    driveshafts – 132
    electrical system – 228
    engine – 55
    fuel, exhaust and emission control systems – 85
    general – 22
    ignition system – 94
    manual transmisssion – 120
    suspension and steering – 172
Filling (cooling system) – 58, 337
Final drive
    adjustment – 120
    dismantling and reassembly – 110, 112
Fluid level
    automatic transmission – 123
    power-assisted steering – 170
Flushing (cooling system) – 58, 337
Flywheel examination and renovation – 48
Fuel, exhaust and emission control systems – 68 *et seq*, 343, 350
Fuel, exhaust and emission control systems (carburettor models)
    accelerator pedal and cable – 80
    air cleaner – 70
    air temperature control (ATC) – 71
    automatic choke – 73, 76
    carburettor – 73, 76, 78, 343, 348
    description – 69, 343
    emission control system – 80
    exhaust system – 81, 350

fault diagnosis – 85
filler lid – 190
fuel filter – 71
fuel level transmitter and gauge – 73
fuel pump – 73, 343
fuel tank – 73
maintenance – 18, 70
manifolds – 81, 350
specifications – 68, 288
unleaded fuel – 69
Fuel, exhaust and emission control systems (fuel injection models)
air cleaner – 352
checking fuel pressure – 355
description – 350
ECU voltage – 358
fuel filter – 356
fuel injectors – 355, 358
fuel pump – 355
idle speed adjustment – 355
manifolds – 359
mixture adjustment – 355
precautions – 350
releasing fuel pressure – 355
self-diagnostic system – 356
specifications – 288
Fuses – 202, 213

G

Gaskets examination and renovation – 49
Gauges
coolant temperature – 64
fuel level – 73
Gearbox *see* **Manual transmission**
Gear lever and rods (manual transmission)
removal and refitting – 103
Governor shaft (automatic transmission)
removal and refitting – 125

H

Handbrake
adjustment – 145
cables – 145
Headlamps
beam alignment – 216
removal and refitting – 217
Heated rear window – 226
Heater
adjustment – 65
bulb renewal – 221
removal and refitting – 64
Horn removal and refitting – 225
HT leads – 93
Hubs removal and refitting
front – 156
rear – 158, 384

I

Idle speed adjustment – 76, 78, 348, 355
Ignition system – 87 *et seq*, 363
Ignition system
coil – 94
description – 87, 363
distributor – 89, 90, 93, 364
fault diagnosis – 94
HT leads – 93
maintenance – 18, 89, 292
spark plugs – 93, 364
specifications – 87, 289
timing – 92, 364

Input shaft (manual transmission) – 109, 114, 374, 377, 378
Instrument panel
bulb renewal – 221
removal and refitting – 222
Introduction to the Nissan Sunny – 5

J

Jacking – 8
Jackshaft examination and renovation – 48

K

Kickdown cable adjustment and renewal – 124
Knuckle removal and refitting
front suspension – 156
rear suspension – 160, 385

L

Locks
bonnet – 180, 385
boot – 190
door – 185
steering column – 167
tailgate – 190
Lubricants and fluids – 21
Lubrication system – 41

M

Mainshaft (manual transmission)
bearing preload adjustment – 120, 378
dismantling and reassembly – 110, 112, 374, 376
Maintenance *see* **Routine maintenance**
Manifolds and exhaust system – 81, 350, 359
Manual transmission – 101 *et seq*, 370
Manual transmission
casing – 106, 115, 370, 377
description – 102, 370
differential – 110, 112, 374, 376, 378
dismantling – 106, 370
fault diagnosis – 120
final drive – 110, 112, 120, 374, 376
gear lever and rods – 103
input shaft – 109, 112, 374, 377, 378
inspection – 110, 376
mainshaft – 110, 112, 120, 374, 376, 378
maintenance – 18, 102
reassembly – 112, 376
removal and refitting – 39, 54, 104
specifications – 101, 289
Master cylinder (brakes)
overhaul – 140
removal and refitting – 140
Master cylinder (clutch)
removal and refitting – 368
Mirrors removal and refitting
door – 194
interior – 194
Mixture adjustment – 78, 348, 355

O

Oil pump
examination and renovation – 49
removal and refitting – 35, 307, 330

Oil seals
differential – 126
engine – 49

P

Pads (front brakes)
inspection – 135, 380
renewal – 135, 380
Pads (rear brakes)
inspection – 380
renewal – 380
Parallel links (rear suspension) removal and refitting – 160
Pedal adjustment
clutch – 366
Pedals removal and refitting
accelerator – 80
brake – 146
clutch – 97, 369
Pistons and piston rings
disconnecting from con-rods – 310, 335
examination and renovation – 48
renewal – 36
Positive crankcase ventilation system (PCV) – 43
Power-assisted steering
bleeding – 170
drivebelt – 63, 342
fluid level – 170
modifications – 385
pump – 63, 170
Pressure regulating valve (brakes) – 141

R

Radiator
fan and switch – 62, 342
grille – 184
removal and refitting – 60, 338
repair – 60
Radio/cassette
aerial – 227
removal and refitting – 226
Radius rods (rear suspension) removal and refitting – 162
Relays – 213
Repair procedures
body damage – 175, 177
general – 12
Routine maintenance
automatic transmission – 18, 123
bodywork and fittings – 18, 174
braking system – 18, 134, 292
clutch – 18, 96
cooling system – 18, 58, 292
driveshafts – 18, 128
electrical system – 202
engine – 18, 30, 292
fuel, exhaust and emission control systems – 18, 70
general – 15
ignition system – 18, 89, 292
manual transmission – 18, 102
suspension and steering – 18, 152

S

Safety first!
alternator – 204
general – 20
Seat belts
general – 193
warning system – 226
Seats removal and refitting – 193

Selector (automatic transmission)
cable adjustment – 124
Servo *see* **Vacuum servo**
Shoes (rear brakes)
inspection – 137
renewal – 137
Slave cylinder removal and refitting – 368
Spare parts – 10
Spark plugs – 93, 364
Speaker units removal and refitting – 227
Speedometer cable removal and refitting – 225
Stabilizer (anti-roll) bar removal and refitting – 153
Starter motor
description – 209, 388
overhaul – 209, 388
removal and refitting – 209, 388
testing in situ – 209
Steering *see* **Suspension and steering**
Strut removal, overhaul and refitting
front suspension – 153
rear suspension – 163
Sump pan removal and refitting – 35, 306, 328
Sunroof removal and refitting
electric – 199
manual – 198
Suspension and steering – 148 *et seq*, 384
Suspension and steering
anti-roll bar – 153
description – 150, 384
fault diagnosis – 172
front suspension
hub bearings – 156
hub/knuckle unit – 156
strut – 153
transverse link arm – 155
wheel alignment – 170
maintenance – 18, 152
rear suspension
hub bearings – 158, 384
knuckle – 160, 385
parallel links – 169
radius rod – 162
strut – 163
wheel alignment – 170
specifications – 148, 291
stabilizer bar – 153
steering
angles – 170
column – 164, 166, 167
lock – 167
overhaul – 169
power-assisted – 63, 170, 385
rack bellows – 163
removal and refitting – 168
tie-rod end balljoint – 164
wheel – 164
wheel alignment – 170
wheels and tyres – 172
Switches removal and refitting
brake warning light – 226
coolant temperature – 64
cooling fan – 62, 342
courtesy lamp – 214
facia panel mounted – 214
ignition – 167
inhibitor – 124
steering column mounted – 167, 214

T

Tailgate
lock – 190
removal and refitting – 187
strut – 187
wiper motor – 224

Thermostat removal, testing and refitting – 60, 338
Tie-rod end balljoint renewal – 164
Timing belt
    eight-valve engine
        removal and refitting – 31
        tensioner – 48
    sixteen-valve engine
        removal and refitting – 319
Timing chain (twelve-valve engine)
    removal and refitting – 293
Timing (ignition) – 92, 364
Tools and working facilities – 13
Towing – 8
Transverse link arm (front suspension)
    removal and refitting – 155
Trim and mouldings
    exterior – 192
    interior – 184, 191, 194
Tyres – 152, 172

U

Unleaded fuel – 69

V

Vacuum servo unit
    description – 143

    maintenance – 18, 143
    removal and refitting – 144
Valve clearances checking and adjustment – 30, 293
Vehicle identification numbers – 10

W

Washer system – 225
Water pump
    eight-valve engine
        removal and refitting – 62
    twelve-valve engine
        removal and refitting – 338
    sixteen-valve engine
        removal and refitting – 340
Weights – 7
Wheel alignment
    front – 170, 171
    rear – 171
Wheel changing – 8
Wheel cylinder (brakes)
    overhaul – 140
    removal and refitting – 140
Wheels and tyres general care and maintenance – 172
Windows
    rear – 191, 226
    windscreen – 191
Wipers
    arms and blades – 222
    windscreen motor and linkage – 224
Wiring diagrams – 230 to 275, 391 to 394